NEW DIRECTIONS IN CHILDHOOD PSYCHOPATHOLOGY

Volume 1
Developmental Considerations

NEW DIRECTIONS IN CHILDHOOD PSYCHOPATHOLOGY

Volume 1
Developmental Considerations

Edited by

SAUL I. HARRISON, M.D.
AND
JOHN F. McDERMOTT, JR., M.D.

INTERNATIONAL UNIVERSITIES PRESS, INC.
New York

Library of Congress Cataloging in Publication Data

Main entry under title:

New directions in childhood psychopathology.

CONTENTS: v. 1. Developmental considerations.
Bibliography: v. 1, p.
Includes index.
1. Child psychopathology—Addresses, essays, lectures. 2. Child psychology—Addresses, essays, lectures. I. Harrison, Saul I. II. McDermott, John F., 1929-
RJ499.N44   616.9'28'9008   78-70232
ISBN 0-8236-3570-8

Manufactured in the United States of America

Contents

Volume 1: Developmental Considerations

Contents

Volume 2: Deviations in Development

Preface

Since the publication of *Childhood Psychopathology*, we have heard and read many thoughtful assessments of that anthology indicating that we achieved our goal of providing a sourcebook of classic readings central to the education of students in diverse fields. As time passes, however, our colleagues add that they would appreciate a bringing together of the past decade's key publications to serve as a vital supplement to the earlier collection. We sense that this stems from a combination of two factors. One is the sheer quantity of publications in developmental psychopathology in the past decade. The second relates to the growing diversity of foci in recent contributions. These multifaceted approaches enhance the psychodynamic emphasis that characterized so much of the classic clinical literature.

It was on these bases that we undertook an extensive screening of the literature. We requested advice from colleagues regarding which publications in the decade or so since the mid-1960s they thought should be included in an anthology devoted to *New Directions in Childhood Psychopathology*. For their generosity in responding to this request with helpful suggestions, we are deeply indebted to Bettie Arthur, E. H. Auerswald, R. D. C. Becker, Helen Beiser, Elissa Benedek, Irving Berlin, Norman Bernstein, Gaston Blom, Willard Boaz, Martin Buxton, Magda Campbell, Stella Chess, Morton Chethik, Hunter Comly, Henry Coppolillo, Frederick Ehrlich, Aaron Esman, Barbara Fish, Steven Frankel, George Gardner, Wells Goodrich, Fady Hajal, Werner Halpern, Eileen Higham, Richard Jenkins, Lottie Kearney, Clarice Kestenbaum, James Kleeman, Selma Kramer, Edwin Levy, Irwin Marcus, John Meeks, John Money, Tarleton Morrow, Peter Neubauer, Leonard Piggott, James Proctor, John Reinhart, Elinor Rosenberg, Eric Schopler, Marvin Shapiro, Theodore Shapiro, John Showalter, Albert Solnit, Jaime Vazquez, Andrew Watson, Mary Whiteside, and L. David Zinn. All of them were liberal with their advice, and it was much valued. The difficult final selection of what to include and what to exclude, however, was ours alone.

When our choices were winnowed down, the final sifting left 41 selections—14 fewer than had been reprinted in *Childhood Psychopathology*. But, to our amazement, these totaled up to almost twice as many words, probably reflecting the growing complexities of issues in the field. This posed a practical problem in bringing these readings together in a single collection—that is, one that a reader could reasonably hold on his or her lap. Therefore, with the reader's physical comfort in mind, we decided to bind this anthology in two separate volumes. They follow the pattern established in *Childhood Psychopathology* in which developmental factors comprised a substantial initial portion of the book, followed by what were considered to be the major psychopathological diagnostic categories. Thus, this first volume of *New Directions in Childhood Psychopathology* is devoted to developmental considerations, highlighting those biopsychosocial variables that have received increasing attention in recent years. It begins by focusing on a wide range of issues in infancy and moves through childhood and adolescence to a consideration of adult developmental stages. Various family factors are then examined with an emphasis on disruptions in the parent-child bond. Following this, several articles explore significant influences on development such as nutrition. The volume closes with a multifaceted integrative effort highlighting recent biological findings. The second volume explores psychopathological deviations in development. Together, the two volumes represent our sense of the most important contributions to developmental psychopathology within the past decade.

Critical assessments of *Childhood Psychopathology* usually included flattering references to the editors' introductions to the readings. These introductory commentaries had the several aims of sharpening the reader's perspective by placing the chapter in context, bringing the paper up to date, clarifying ambiguities, focusing on significant related issues, raising additional questions, and serving as a guide to the reader who wished to pursue the subject beyond the confines of the volume. This ambitious effort to enrich the selections reprinted in that earlier anthology, so many of which had already withstood the test of time and had achieved classic status within our field, assumes even greater importance in this new collection. The readings reprinted in *New Directions in Childhood Psychopathology* all come from the past few years and thus have had limited opportunity to be tested by endurance. Because of this, our introductory commentaries are more detailed. For each selection in this new anthology, dozens of other articles relating to the issue were reviewed. In innumerable instances it was difficult to decide whether to reprint an article or whether to excerpt it in our prefatory expositions. We hope these introductions will provide the reader with an enriching review, critique, overview, and synthesis of the issue. Indeed, in some cases, readers may find our extensive commentary most useful after they have read· the reprinted article. In an effort to minimize the potential for confusion, however, all of our remarks precede the chapters. Some colleagues have indicated that they found our discussion helpful both *before* and *after* they read the reprinted selection itself.

The process of formulating the introductions was enhanced and their substance enriched through invigorating discussions with colleagues and residents at the University of Michigan and the University of Hawaii. We are particularly grateful to Drs. Bettie Arthur, Bruce Axclrod, Walter Char, John Gordon, Danilo Ponce, Terence Rogers, A. Joseph Sayed, Wen-Shing Tseng, and L. David Zinn for unselfishly sharing their stimulating thoughts with us. Responsibility for the final form of the introductory commentaries, however, rests with the editors.

Of course, we are most indebted to those authors and publishers who granted us permission to reprint their work and to our secretaries, Martha Fisch and Debbie Steinaway, without whom this work would not exist.

Lastly, we want to note the likelihood that over the course of the next several years, and perhaps even in the time interval between the preparation of this manuscript and its appearance in print, enough seminal child developmental and psychopathological literature will appear in journals and books to justify a supplement to this anthology. We welcome hearing from readers with suggestions of articles to include in an anticipated future collection.

Saul I. Harrison
John F. McDermott, Jr.

Contributors

ANNETTE BARAN, M.S.W., L.C.S.W.
Private practice in psychotherapy, West Los Angeles, Cal.

HERBERT G. BIRCH, M.D.
Late Professor of Pediatrics, Albert Einstein College of Medicine, Bronx, N.Y.

MURRAY BOWEN, M.D.
Director, Georgetown University Family Center, Washington, D.C.

T. BERRY BRAZELTON, M.D.
Associate Professor of Pediatrics, Harvard Medical School, Cambridge, Mass.; Chief, Child Development Unit, Children's Hospital Medical Center, Boston, Mass.

DONALD J. COHEN, M.D.
Professor of Pediatrics, Psychiatry, and Psychology, Yale University School of Medicine and the Child Study Center, New Haven, Conn.

KATRINA DE HIRSCH, F.C.S.T.
Consultant in Psychiatry, Columbia University, New York, N.Y.

ROBERT N. EMDE, M.D.
Professor of Psychiatry, University of Colorado School of Medicine, Denver, Col.; Adjunct Professor of Psychology, University of Denver, Denver, Col.

SUE L. EVANS (HUGHES), M.S.W.
Associate Director, Department of Clinical Social Work, Division of Behavioral Science, Children's Hospital of Pittsburgh, Pittsburgh, Pa.

SELMA H. FRAIBERG
Professor of Child Psychoanalysis, Professor of Psychiatry, and Director of Infant-Parent Program, University of California, San Francisco Medical Center, San Francisco, Cal.

CAROL GILLIGAN, PH.D.
Associate Professor of Human Development, Harvard Graduate School of Education, Cambridge, Mass.

ROGER L. GOULD, M.D.
Assistant Professor of Psychiatry, UCLA, Los Angeles, Cal.

RICHARD GREEN, M.D.
Professor, Department of Psychiatry and Psychology, State University of New York, Stony Brook, N.Y.

ROBERT J. HARMON, M.D.
Assistant Professor of Psychiatry (Child), University of Colorado Health Sciences Center, Denver, Col.; Coordinator, Pediatric-Psychiatric Liaison Section, Division of Psychiatry, University of Colorado, Denver, Col.

JOAN B. KELLY, PH.D.
Co-Principal Investigator, Children of Divorce Project, Marin County, Cal.

JOHN H. KENNELL, M.D.
Professor of Pediatrics, Case Western Reserve University School of Medicine and Rainbow Babies' and Children's Hospital, Cleveland, Ohio

STANLEY H. KING, PH.D.
Psychologist and Director of Research, University Health Services, Harvard University, Cambridge, Mass.

MARSHALL H. KLAUS, M.D.
Professor of Pediatrics, Case Western Reserve University School of Medicine and Rainbow Babies' and Children's Hospital, Cleveland, Ohio

LAWRENCE KOHLBERG, PH.D.
Professor of Education and Social Psychiatry, Harvard Graduate School of Education, Cambridge, Mass.

BARBARA KOSLOWSKI, ED.D.
Associate Professor, Department of Human Development and Family Studies, Cornell University, Ithaca, N.Y.

MARY MAIN, PH.D.
Assistant Professor of Psychiatry, University of California, Berkeley, Cal.

MARGARET S. MAHLER, M.D., SC.D. (MED.)
Clinical Professor of Psychiatry Emeritus, Albert Einstein College of Medicine, Bronx, N.Y.

JOHN MONEY, PH.D.
Professor of Medical Psychology and Associate Professor of Pediatrics, Johns Hopkins University School of Medicine, Baltimore, Md.

REUBEN PANNOR, M.S.W., L.C.S.W.
Director, Community Services, Vista del Mar Childcare Center, Los Angeles, Cal.

RICHARD PERRY, M.D.
Clinical Assistant Professor of Psychiatry and Research Child Psychiatrist, Children's Psychopharmacology Unit, New York University, New York, N.Y.

CARL B. POLLOCK, M.D.
Late Assistant Professor of Psychiatry, University of Colorado Medical Center, Denver, Col.

JOHN B. REINHART, M.D.
Director, Division of Behavioral Sciences, Children's Hospital of Pittsburgh, Pittsburgh, Pa.; Professor of Pediatrics and Psychiatry (Child), University of Pittsburgh School of Medicine, Pittsburgh, Pa.

MICHAEL RUTTER, M.D., F.R.C.P., F.R.C.PSYCH.
Professor of Child Psychiatry, Institute of Psychiatry, London, England

THEODORE SHAPIRO, M.D.
Professor of Psychiatry and Professor of Psychiatry in Pediatrics, Cornell University Medical College, New York, N.Y.; Director, Child and Adolescent Psychiatry, Payne Whitney Clinic, New York, N.Y.

ARTHUR D. SOROSKY, M.D.
Associate Clinical Professor of Child Psychiatry, UCLA Medical School, Los Angeles, Cal.; Co-Director, Adoption Research Project, Los Angeles, Cal.

BRANDT F. STEELE, A.B., M.D.
Professor of Psychiatry, University of Colorado Medical Center, Denver, Col.; Acting Director and Psychiatrist, National Center for Prevention and Treatment of Child Abuse and Neglect, Denver, Col.

RUTH A. SUCCOP, M.S.W.
Director, Department of Clinical Social Work, Division of Behavioral Sciences, Children's Hospital of Pittsburgh, Pittsburgh, Pa.

J. M. TANNER, M.D., D.SC., F.R.C.P., F.R.C.PSYCH.
Professor of Child Health and Growth, University of London, England; Honorary Consultant Physician, The Hospital for Sick Children, London, England

MARY ANNE TRAUSE, PH.D.
Clinical Assistant Professor of Psychology, Department of Pediatrics, Georgetown University School of Medicine, Washington, D.C.

JUDITH S. WALLERSTEIN, PH.D.
Principal Investigator, Children of Divorce Project, Marin County, Cal.; Fellow, Center for Advanced Study of Behavioral Sciences, Stanford, Cal.; Lecturer, School of Social Welfare, University of California, Berkeley, Cal.

MARTHA WOLFENSTEIN, PH.D.
Late Associate Clinical Professor of Psychiatry, Albert Einstein College of Medicine, Bronx, N.Y.

1

INTRODUCTION

Evidence for a Sensitive Period in the Human Mother, by John H. Kennell, Mary Anne Trause, and Marshall H. Klaus

In the 1930s ethologists borrowed the embryological concept of critical periods and applied it to psychosocial behavior. Lorenz (1937) related the concept to the phenomenon of imprinting; he claimed that this rapid neonatal "learning" must occur within a delimited time period following birth. Since then, the critical period concept has become well established in the study of animal behavior (see J. P. Scott, 1958; Thorpe and Zangwill, 1961; Vince, 1958, 1959).

The applicability of the critical period concept to human behavior has, however, stimulated lively controversy. Clearly, children learn certain things at an early age more easily than they do later (see Hebb, 1949; Kohlberg, 1968; Lenneberg, 1967). But the extent to which this observation justifies extending the concept of critical periods to human cognitive development remains debatable. Connolly (1972) de-emphasizes the drama of the word *critical* by suggesting that, based on our present knowledge, it would be more prudent to use the term *sensitive* (a choice the authors of the following selection also make). In speaking of human development, Connolly argues that we should concentrate less on critical *periods* and more on critical *events* in trying to understand the mechanisms involved in "sensitive periods." From a different perspective, Peter H. Wolff (1969) points out that the proposition that children must learn at critical periods or else fail to reach their full intellectual potential is often put forth as proven fact although no persuasive evidence supports it. He condemns the wholesale acceptance of this theory, along with what he calls the "infant development industry's" advocacy of enrichment programs for *all* preschool children on the basis of hypothesized critical periods in human cognitive development. In addition, Wolff notes that, when inappropriately applied, such enrichment may even interfere with the mutually nurturing interaction of mother and child. That parental expectation, as well as a variety of other variables, play a major role in developmental variations has been demonstrated by cross-cultural studies (J. W. M. Whiting and Child, 1953).

The major aspect of child development to which these ethological concepts have been applied is the primary mother-infant bond. Attention has been focused largely on the baby's attachment to the mother (e.g., Bowlby, 1969, 1973). Klaus and Kennell (1970) observe that a high proportion of major parenting difficulties include a background of prolonged early parent-infant separation (see also Chapter 21 by Evans, Reinhart, and Succop). This finding has led to speculation about the possibility of a sensitive period for attachment within the mother, as is discussed in the following selection.

In the chapter reprinted below Kennell, Trause, and Klaus present their comparison of infants who enjoyed early and extended contact with their mothers and those who experienced the usual hospital routine. A later follow-up study (Kennell et al., 1974) has shown that at five years of age the extended contact children had significantly higher IQs and were more advanced on two language tests (Ringler et al., 1976).

If such a sensitive period does exist in the mother, its basis deserves continuing study. For instance, in addition to the quantity of early mother-infant contact, is the quality of interaction a factor? (See Chapter 3 by Brazelton, Koslowski, and Main.) What is the effect of maternal medication on the baby (Brazelton, 1961)? From another perspective, what happens if the newborn possesses certain traits that stimulate anxiety or aversive reactions in the mother? Such a situation may arise with premature or handicapped infants by vitue of the discrepancy between the mother's fantasy of the baby *in utero* and the actual infant. Retrospective studies have found mothers of prematures to be more emotionally immature and to express more negative attitudes toward their pregnancies than did controls (A. Blau et al., 1963). They also show greater feelings of inadequacy and more anxiety than do controls (Gunter, 1963). The significance of these findings is difficult to assess in the absence of prospective studies. Elsewhere Klaus and Kennell (1970) have suggested that the mother deprived of contact with a premature baby may undergo anticipatory mourning accompanied by emotional detachment, which is difficult to overcome. It should be noted that we have no data on whether mothers of prematures experience the same postpartum hormonal changes that mothers of full-term babies do (R. Jaffe, 1978, personal communication).

Some variation of the notion of a maternal sensitive period shortly after delivery probably has contributed to the increase of "natural" methods of childbirth (e.g., the techniques of La Maze, Bradley, and LeBoyer). The concept may also have far-reaching implications for adoption procedures, especially in the light of the current controversy about an adoptee's innate need to reunite with the biological parent (see Chapter 16 by Sorosky, Baran, and Pannor). These are but a few of the possible ramifications of this modern interpretation of "maternal instinct." In any case, the evidence would seem to suggest that, regardless of the reason, it is wise to facilitate early parent-infant contact in the hopes of preventing certain future parenting difficulties.

1

Evidence for a Sensitive Period in the Human Mother

JOHN H. KENNELL, MARY ANNE TRAUSE, and MARSHALL H. KLAUS

> How long does the fire of love endure
> If the eyes and touch are not there to kindle it.
> —Dante, *The Divine Comedy*

Is there a unique period in the human mother, soon after delivery, when she is especially sensitive to her baby and most ready to become attached to him? Nursery practices in the modern hospital in the United States do not generally acknowledge this possibility and mother and infant are routinely separated immediately after birth—the mother to be monitored in an adult recovery area and the baby in a transitional care nursery. If there were convincing evidence of an early sensitive period in the human, major changes in hospital care practices would be necessary to ensure that mother and baby remain together.

There are many difficulties in systematically studying whether or not there is a sensitive period in the human. Human maternal behavior is determined by a multitude of factors, including the woman's past experiences with her own mother, the patterns of her culture, whether or not the baby was planned, and the quality of her relationship with the baby's father. In some cases, a mother's intellectual abilities may enable her to bridge potential difficulties such as an early separation from her infant. Because of these many influences, it is difficult to isolate and demonstrate the effects of the sensitive period on

First published in *Parent-Infant Interaction* (Ciba Foundation Symposium 33). New York: Scientific Publishers, 1975, pp. 87–95. Reprinted by permission of Excerpta Medica.

The work reported in the paper would never have have been accomplished without the help of the many medical students who have been associated with us in our studies and the generous support of the Grant Foundation, The Educational Corporation of America, and The Research Corporation. The work in Guatemala has been done in collaboration with Drs. L. Mata, R. Sosa, and J. Urrutia.

maternal attachment. Nonetheless, we believe that a number of observations fit together in such a way as to suggest that this period does have special importance for the development of the mother's bond to her child. This report presents these observations, speculates on their meaning, and suggests questions needing further study.

Valuable insights may be gained by examining animal behavior, even though human behavior is much more complex. The goat, for instance, provides an extreme example of a time-limited maternal sensitive period. If a goat mother and her kid are not kept together during the first five minutes after delivery, she does not develop a specific discriminant attachment to her kid. Without this bond, she treats the kid as an alien and in most cases refuses to care for it, butting or kicking it away as it approaches her (Klopfer, 1971).

We use this example because we believe that there is a similar, although less fixed, period of heightened sensitivity in the human mother during which she interacts with her newborn infant and begins to form a special attachment to him. An attachment can be defined as a unique emotional relationship between two people that is specific and endures through time. Although it is difficult to define this enduring relationship operationally, we have taken as indicators of attachment those behaviors such as fondling, kissing, cuddling, and prolonged gazing which serve to maintain contact with and show affection to a particular individual. "Maternal sensitive period" refers to that time after delivery when the mother forms, or begins to form, a special attachment to her infant. Increased contact, or especially separation, during this period is likely to alter later maternal attachment. We hypothesize that during this early sensitive period a cascade of reciprocal interactions begins between the mother and baby which locks them together and mediates the further development of attachment.

The process that takes place during the maternal sensitive period differs from imprinting in that there is not a point beyond which the formation of an attachment is precluded. This period is the optimal, but not the only one during which an attachment can develop. The process can occur at a later time, although it will be more difficult and take longer to achieve. This is similar to the finding of Hersher, Richmond, and Moore (1963) that if drastic measures were taken to keep a mother goat in a small enclosure with her kid, starting within the first 12 hours after delivery, maternal attachment could still be achieved after the period of her heightened sensitivity. However, a process which took but a few minutes immediately after delivery took an average of ten days once the sensitive period had passed.

Experimental studies that might yield well-defined answers are restricted by the inappropriateness of manipulating the human mother in the same way as the animal. For example, one could never justify presenting a woman with an alien infant immediately after birth to test whether specific attachments are best formed during that time. Thus, conclusions about the existence of specific attachments can be only tentatively drawn.

Clinical observations, however, have suggested that specific attachments are made during this early period. In a remarkable accident in an Israeli hospital, two mothers were inadvertently given the wrong babies, whom they took home and cared for. At the time of the two-week checkup, the error was discovered and efforts to return the babies to their own families were begun. Surprisingly, each mother had become so attached to the baby she had cared for during the first 14 days that she did not wish to give it up. Their husbands, on the other hand, strongly supported correcting the error because of facial and other characteristics that were unique to the individual families (L. Lothstein, personal communication). In other nursery accidents, when the wrong baby has been presented to a mother for the first feeding or to hold for a brief period, we have been greatly impressed by the mother's lingering thoughts about that baby. Often months later, when her own child seems completely satisfactory in every respect, she will refer to that first infant and say, "Oh, that was such a lovely baby."

These observations of the behavior of mothers who had the wrong baby presented to them in the first minutes lead to the question of what happens when a baby is separated from his mother during the newborn period. In our clinical experience, we have noted that a number of mothers who have been separated from their infants are hesitant and clumsy when they begin to care for their full-term or premature infants, taking several visits to learn the simple mothering tasks of feeding and changing that most women pick up rapidly. When the separation is prolonged, mothers report that they sometimes forget momentarily that they even have a baby. After a premature baby has gone home, it is striking to hear how often the mother reports that although she is fond of her baby, she still thinks of it as belonging to someone else—the head nurse in the nursery or the physician—rather than to her.

Even grosser distortions of mother-infant attachment are apparent in the mother of a battered child or the mother of an infant with no organic disease who has failed to thrive, but who gains weight easily when his needs are more adequately met by another caretaker. Prematurity and low birthweight often lead to prolonged mother-infant separation. Significantly, according to a number of studies, prematures constitute a disproportionately high number of both battered children (23–31%) and those with the "failure-to-thrive" syndrome for which no organic cause is found (Fanaroff, Kennell, and Klaus, 1972). Even with the shorter separation associated with delivery by Caesarean section, the incidence of child abuse is ten times greater than with vaginal deliveries (R. E. Helfer, personal communication).

The clinical observations of J. Rose, Boggs, and Alderstein (1960) and Kennell and Rolnick (1960) suggest that affectional ties can be disturbed easily and may be altered permanently during the immediate postpartum period. Relatively mild illness in the newborn appeared to affect the relationship between mother and infant. Among these minor problems were mild jaundice, slow feeding, and the need for incubator care in the first 24 hours for mild respiratory distress. The mother's behavior was often disturbed during the first year of the baby's life or longer, even though the infant's problems had been completely resolved before discharge, and often within a few hours.

Here we give results from eight studies in which the time of first contact between a mother and her neonate was varied and the outcome measured. For example, in a carefully controlled investigation of 28 primiparous mothers and their normal full-term infants, 14 mothers were given their nude babies in bed for one hour in the first two hours after delivery and for five extra hours on each of the next three days of life. The other 14 mothers received the care that is routine in most hospitals in the United States: a glimpse of the baby at birth, a brief contact for identification at six to eight hours, and then visits of 20 to 30 minutes for feedings every four hours. The two groups were matched as to the mothers' age and marital and socioeconomic status and were not significantly different in the infants' sex and weight. The women were randomly assigned to a group, were all given the same explanation of the study, and, to the best of our knowledge, were not aware that there were differences in mother-infant contact in the first three days. Those making the observations in this and the follow-up studies did not know to which group the subjects belonged.

When the mothers and babies returned to the hospital at one month, there were significant differences between the two groups (Klaus et al., 1972). The "early contact" mothers usually stood near their infants and watched during the physical examination, showed significantly more soothing behavior, engaged in more eye to-eye contact and fondling during feeding, and were more reluctant to leave their infants with someone else than were mothers not given the early extended experience of contact. At one year, the two groups were again significantly different (Kennell et al., 1974). "Extended contact" mothers spent a greater percentage of time assisting the physician while he examined their babies and soothing the infants when they cried.

We wondered if just a few mothers in one or both groups had accounted for the persistence and consistency of the differences over the span of 11 months. However, the ranking of the mothers within each of the two groups showed no significant correlation for the measures at the one-month and one-year examinations.

At two years, five mothers were selected at random from each group, and the linguistic behavior of the two groups in speaking to their children was compared. The extended contact mothers used twice as many questions, more words per proposition, fewer content words, more adjectives, and fewer commands than did the controls (Ringler et al., 1975). This study will have to be repeated because, with so few subjects, the differences may have been due to chance selection. However, these findings suggest that 16 extra hours of contact in the first three days of life appear to affect maternal behavior for one year and possibly longer, thus offering support for the hypothesis that there is a maternal sensitive period soon after delivery.

Notice that this study does not test for the specificity of attachment. Also, even the mothers in the experimental group were actually separated from their infants at delivery. The baby was not placed with the mother until 30 minutes to two hours after birth and did not remain with her constantly from birth, as he would in a natural home delivery. Although the amount of anesthesia and drugs given to the mothers in this study would be considered the minimum for primiparous mothers in a university hospital in the United States, the medication received by mothers and infants in both groups may have influenced the effects of this early contact. Thus, differences emerged in spite of a number of factors which could be expected to reduce differences between the groups.

During the past few years, five other studies of mothers and their full-term infants have either been completed or are under way.

In a carefully controlled study, N. Winters (unpublished) gave six mothers in one group their babies to suckle shortly after birth and contrasted these with six mothers who did not have contact with their babies until approximately 16 hours later. All had originally intended to breast-feed, and none stopped because of physical problems. When checked two months later, all six mothers who had suckled their babies on the delivery table were still breast-feeding, whereas only one of the other six was still nursing her baby.

Recently, with Drs. Mata, Sosa, and Urrutia, we started a long-term study in Guatemala using an experimental design similar to that presented earlier. In the IGSS Hospital in Guatemala City 19 mothers in one group were given their babies on the delivery table during the episiotomy repair period, then allowed to stay with them in privacy for 45 minutes. Each mother-infant pair was nude, skin-to-skin, under a heat panel. The 19 mothers in the other group were separated from their babies shortly after delivery, which is the usual routine in this hospital. Except for this difference in initial contact, the care of the two groups was identical. The infants were discharged with free milk at two days, which is the practice of the hospital. When the babies were checked 35 days after birth, the mean weight gain of the infants in the early contact group was 1208 grams, or 203 grams more than that of the control group (1005 grams). The mothers in the two groups did not differ significantly in socioeconomic, marital, housing, or income status.

In a similar study at Roosevelt Hospital, Guatemala City, we found no significant differences in weight gain at 35 days. Information that might help to account for these discrepant findings is not yet available.

In Pelotis, Brazil, P. L. Sousa (unpublished) recently compared the success of breast-feeding during the first two months of life in two groups of 100 women who delivered normal full-term babies in a 20-bed maternity ward. In the study group, the newborn baby was put to the breast immediately after birth and permanent contact between the mother and baby was sustained during the lying-in period, when the baby lay in a cot beside his mother's bed. The control group mothers had the traditional contact with their infants—a glimpse shortly after birth and then visits for approximately 30 minutes every three hours, seven times a day, starting 12 to 14 hours after birth. The babies were kept in a separate nursery. Successful breast-feeding was defined as no complementary feedings other than tea, water, or small amounts of fruit juice until two months after birth. When the babies had reached two months of age, 77% of the early contact mothers were successfully breast-feeding, in contrast to only 27% of the controls. A weakness in this design, which limits the strength of the findings, is that during the experimental period a special nurse was working in the unit to stimulate and encourage breast-feeding. Although not definitive in itself, this study adds weight to our hypothesis.

In another recent study at the Roosevelt Hospital in Guatemala with different subjects, nine mothers in one group were given their babies nude, skin-to-skin, under a heat panel, after they had left the delivery room. In a second group, ten mothers were separated from their infants, according to the usual routine. The babies in both groups were sent to the newborn nursery for the next 12 hours, after which they went to the mother in a seven-bed room for the first breast-feeding. At 12 hours, each mother's interactions with her infant were observed by D. Hales, who did not know to which group they belonged. Observations of the mother's fondling, kissing, looking *en face* at, gazing at, and holding her baby close were made for 15 seconds in every minute for 15 minutes (Figure 1). The group with early contact showed significantly increased attachment behavior.

Two studies, one at Stanford and one at Case Western Reserve, of mothers of premature infants also have designs similar to those already described. In these investigations, half the mothers were permitted to come into the nursery as soon as they were able and the other half after three weeks. In the study at Stanford (Leiderman et al., 1973; Leifer et al., 1972), there were seven

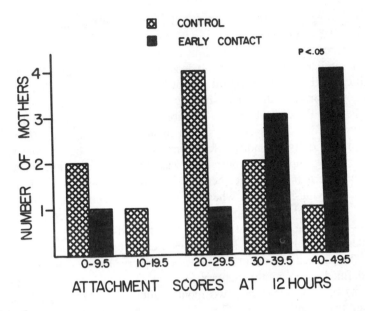

FIGURE 1

Attachment scores at 12 hours in nine mothers who had early contact with their babies and in ten mothers who were separated from their babies after delivery in Roosevelt Hospital, Guatemala City.

interviews with the parents while their babies were in the premature nursery. Thus, the mothers in both groups at Stanford received some attention, whereas in our study at Case Western Reserve statements to the parents were limited.

In our study, significant differences between the early and late contact groups were found at the time of discharge on one measure of attachment behavior: mothers given early contact looked at their infants more during a feeding which was filmed at that time. Also at discharge, mothers of girls in the early contact group held their infants close to their bodies for a greater percentage of time than did mothers of girls in the late contact group. Strikingly, preliminary data on the Standford-Binet IQ scores of these two groups of children at 42 months indicated that those in the early contact group scored significantly higher than those in the late contact group (mean IQ 99 versus 85). Furthermore, a significant correlation ($r = 0.71$) was found between the IQ at 42 months and the amount of time women spent looking at their babies during the filmed feeding at one month of age. This supports our hypothesis that early contact affects aspects of the mother's behavior which may have significance for the child's later development.

At Stanford, the mothers who were separated from their premature babies for three to 12 weeks showed no significant differences in attachment behavior at one month from those permitted early contact. However, there were more divorces (five versus one) in the group of mothers with prolonged separation, and more infants were relinquished by them (two versus zero) (Leiderman et al., 1973, Leifer et al., 1972).

Studies of fathers by J. Lind (personal communication) and of mothers rooming-in by Greenberg, Rosenberg, and Lind (1973) lend further support to the hypothesis that there is an early sensitive period.

Further research is needed to determine exactly when this period begins, how long it lasts, and what events modify it. Also, it is important to study how attachment is affected by the type of contact the mother has with the infant during this period.

In summary, we hypothesize that there is a sensitive period in the human mother which is the optimal time for an affectional bond to develop between the mother and her infant. The suggestion that mother-infant contact and interaction in the early minutes and hours after delivery influence subsequent mothering behavior is supported by the results in six of these eight controlled studies of mothers of premature infants and parents of full-term infants. The effects may persist in the mother of a full-term infant for as long as two years, affect the weight gain of the infants in the first month (in Guatemala), and be manifest in the performance of premature infants 42 months later. These observations have obvious clinical implications for those caring for normal, premature, or sick infants.

2

INTRODUCTION

Endogenous and Exogenous Smiling Systems in Early Infancy, by Robert N. Emde and Robert J. Harmon

The seminal role of the social smile in human development has long been recognized. Spitz (1965) borrowed the embryological concept of "organizer" to highlight the visible signs of a convergence of several different developmental currents within the infant's psychic apparatus. He designated the social smile the first organizer and focused on eight-month stranger anxiety as the second organizer because it indicated a capacity for perceptual differentiation between the familiar and the strange. The third nodal organizer specified was the infant's capacity to master negation in gesture and word, representing the developing capacity for judgment.

The article that follows by Emde and Harmon, coupled with their previous studies, demonstrates the correlation of endogenous smiling with rapid-eye-movement (REM) states, putting to rest the folklore linking these reflex smiles to "gas." (See Chapter 31 by Anders and Weinstein for a further discussion of REM states.) Some of the groundwork for their report has been provided by Peter H. Wolff's (1963) naturalistic investigation of the earliest steps in the ontogeny of smiling. Observing the behavior of eight neonates, he noted spontaneous grimaces within the first 12 hours of birth that were suggestive of smiling despite their incompleteness and apparent lack of function. He traced the development of smiling movements into a phase of unselective social smiling elicited by a human stimulus, beginning about the fourteenth day of life. During the fifth week the voice is replaced by the human face as the most effective stimulus, followed by a phase of intent searching of the face, fixing especially on the eyes. The mother then experiences her baby in a new way. Although by the fourth week the baby smiles more consistently in response to the mother's voice than to other voices, he or she remains less discriminating with visual stimuli and smiles as freely at strangers as at mother until the end of the third month.

The intriguing notion of a built-in bias to prefer a human face to other objects has been opposed by Piaget (1936), who concludes, "The smile is primarily a reaction to familiar images, to what has already been seen" (p. 72). Some support for Piaget's contention is offered by Brackbill (1958), who presented her face to eight three-month-old babies. Each time a baby smiled, she smiled back, cooed, picked the baby, up, and cuddled him or her. As a result of this, the babies all responded with more smiling behavior. Conversely, when Brackbill ceased to respond, the rate of smiling gradually declined until eventually it disappeared.

By connecting the infant's innate reflex smile to the subsequent evolution of the social smile, Emde and his colleagues document a hypothesized link between our biological heritage and our psychosocial development. Their findings may even address certain ideas about phylogenetic development, in particular P. MacLean's (1969) proposal of a "triune" brain, which combines into one what are essentially three chemically and structurally different cerebrotypes derived from discrepant evolutionary levels. The degree of coordination, dysordination, and even antagonism between the reptilian brainstem, the paleomammalian limbic system, and the neomammalian cortex might explain the paradox of the persistence of primitive social behavior in the face of highly advanced scientific and technological development.   ·

Emde and Harmon, however, do not speculate about such extensions of their findings. What they question is the cognitive-learning explanation of the social smile. They note that maturation seems to be the principal determinant of the onset of smiling in response to stimuli, whether the initial stimulus is social or not. Emde and Harmon assert that a cognitive-learning explanation may account for the subsequent shaping or inhibition of the smile response and employ Heinz Werner's (1940, 1957; Werner and Kaplan, 1963) holistic organismic-developmental theory as an explanatory framework. Werner's belief that organisms are naturally directed toward a series of transformations from a state of global undifferentiation to levels of increasing differentiation, followed by a hierarchical integration of the independent parts, may be linked to the contributions of Piaget (see 1962b [Chapter 10 in *Childhood Psychopathology*]). Both Werner's and Piaget's conceptions exist within a developmental-descriptive rather than an antecedent-consequent context (Flavell, 1963), which perhaps explains in part why their work has been so slow to gain acceptance in American child psychiatry, psychology, and education.

2

Endogenous and Exogenous Smiling Systems in Early Infancy

ROBERT N. EMDE and
ROBERT J. HARMON

The infant's social smile has attracted a large amount of practical and theoretical attention from recent developmental research. The regular or predictable "smiling response," which has its onset around two and a half
months, was described by Spitz and Wolf (1946) as a predictable response
to a stimulus pattern consisting of hairline, eyes, nose, and motion—a pattern
ordinarily presented to the infant in a social situation. Since this early description, other studies have systematically quantified this response and documented its characteristics during the first half year of life in a variety of
environmental settings (Ambrose, 1961; Gewirtz, 1965; Polak, Emde, and
Spitz, 1964).

From an ethological perspective, social smiling has been given crucial
theoretical importance in the formation of the mother-infant attachment bond
(Ainsworth, 1969; Bowlby, 1958a). From the viewpoint of psychoanalysis,
Spitz (1959) has labeled it an indicator of the first organizer of the psyche
in his genetic field theory of ego formation. The fact that its frequency can
be brought under experimental control by operant-conditioning techniques
at three to four months of age (Brackbill, 1958) has given impetus to the
learning theory viewpoint that its emergence in development represents a new
learned response. Recently, Kagan (1970), following Piaget (1936), has proposed that the infant's smiling indicates his emerging cognitive capacity to
assimilate an initially discrepant perceptual event. It is noteworthy that these

First published in *Journal of the American Academy of Child Psychiatry,* 11:177–200, 1972.
Reprinted by permission.

This research was conducted at the University of Colorado Medical Center and supported by
U.S. Public Health Service Grant MH-HD 15753 and National Institute of Mental Health Research
Scientist Development Award K3-MH-36808.

discussions often rest on the tacit assumption that social smiling appears suddenly and without precursors. While the appearance of the regular smiling response is often dramatic in terms of its social significance, our research has provided data that contradict this assumption. This paper will present evidence for the origin and unfolding of two systems of smiling that arise in development before the predictable smiling response. One system of smiling arises from the inside as a correlate of an observed behavioral and physiological state pattern, and we refer to it as *endogenous;* the other is stimulated from the outside, and we refer to it as *exogenous.*

ENDOGENOUS SMILING

Unlike the "smiling response," there is a form of smiling that is not the result of external stimulation (Köhler, 1954; P. H. Wolff, 1959). In our previous studies (Emde and Koenig, 1969a, 1969b), we have documented the fact that this form of smiling occurs "spontaneously" as a manifestation of endogenously determined physiological rhythms during the rapid-eye-movement (REM) state in the newborn. As such, it is one of many well-circumscribed, state-related behaviors which occur shortly after birth. We concluded that endogenous smiling is a consistent correlate of the REM state. In the newborn this state sometimes occurred when the eyes were closed (sleep REM) and sometimes when the eyes were open and glassy (drowsy REM). There was no evidence that smiling was related to "gas," as suggested by the folklore of our grandmothers. This form of smiling was found to occur during the REM state with an average density of 11 smiles per 100 minutes of observed state, no matter where it was observed in the feeding cycle or the 24-hour cycle. There was also a tendency for it to occur in bursts, since more than one-third of the smiles in full-term newborns were observed during the same minute as another smile. A subsequent EEG-polygraph study (Emde and Metcalf, 1970) documented a tendency for endogenous smiling to be correlated with an expectable electrophysiological pattern within the REM state.

As a consequence of these initial studies, we formulated a hypothesis about neurophysiological mechanisms of endogenous REM smiling. In this hypothesis we stated that this form of smiling was mediated by limbic structures, since there was evidence for limbic activation in adult REM sleep, and since the limbic system was thought of as the highest level of integration for emotional expression. However, as a result of more recent studies, we have modified this view.

In a study of smiling in premature infants, we compared 20 prematures with 20 full-term newborns and found four to five times the amount of endogenous smiling in the premature group (Emde, McCartney, and Harmon, 1971). The difference between smiling in prematures and full-term controls was significant at the .01 level. There was also more of a burst effect, with two-thirds of the smiles occurring in bursts in prematures, compared with one-third in full-terms. Figure 1 illustrates the rather smooth, negative curve of decreased smiling density when it is plotted against postconceptional age, with data grouped at three-week intervals. The correlation of smiling with postconceptional age was -0.71; $p < .01$. A recent neuroanatomical study of Rabinowicz (1964) has shown that the limbic area, as well as the frontal cortex, is significantly less mature in the eight-month fetus than in the full-term baby. It therefore seemed unlikely that increased premature smiling could be accounted for by a limbic system predominance at the earlier age. Instead, it seemed likely that some other, more mature neural organizing center might be responsible for the greater endogenous smiling in prematures; a center that is later overcome by the maturation of the inhibitory cortex, resulting in a lesser amount of smiling in the full-term.

A second study which has led us to discard the limbic mediation hypothesis

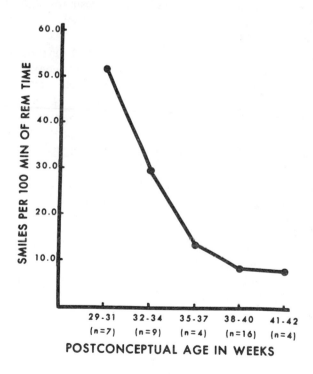

FIGURE 1

concerned clinical-anatomical observations of a microcephalic newborn infant. This infant, who was clinically diagnosed as having congenital toxoplasmosis, was intermittently observed from 22 to 44 days of postuterine life (postconceptional age 38 to 41 weeks.). The infant died at 53 days of age with complications subsequent to an acute paralytic ileus. Detailed pathological examination[1] supported the inference that the infant had severe impairment of function of both the cerebral cortex and limbic system during postnatal life with a relatively intact brainstem. Grossly, the brain was symmetrical but small, weighing 53 grams as compared with an expectable weight of 489 grams for an eight-week-old infant (Coppoletta and Wolbach, 1933). Massive degeneration of neural tissue was evident in all microscopic sections taken from many areas throughout the brain and consisted of marked neuronal loss, reactive gliosis, and deposition of calcium. Sections of basal ganglia and cerebral cortex showed that fewer than 15% (approximately) of the neurons had a normal appearance. On the other hand, midbrain sections showed that more than 85% of the neurons appeared normal but with some architectural malformations throughout the sections. The anatomical findings were consistent with those usually described for toxoplasmosis. More extensive details of the clinical and anatomical findings are presented in another report (Harmon and Emde, 1972).

Detailed behavioral observations were made at 24 days of life by two independent observers. To our surprise, the rate of endogenous smiling was 17/100 minutes of REM state. This was within one standard deviation of the mean for smiling in a normal, full-term comparison group of equivalent postconceptional age. The findings of this case support the more specific conclusion that endogenous smiling and other spontaneous REM behaviors are mediated through the *brainstem,* and that cerebral structures, including those of the limbic system, are not necessary for this mediation.

Our current view is that endogenous smiling is organized and mediated within the brainstem, along with frowning, mouth movements, and other REM-related spontaneous behaviors, which also occurred at characteristic "normal" rates in our microcephalic case. As a result of increasing neurological inhibition, probably related to maturation of the cerebral cortex, endogenous smiling diminishes during the early months of infancy. Ongoing longitudinal research observations indicate that this form of smiling usually continues into the fifth or sixth postuterine months and then disappears or becomes a rarity.

---

[1] The authors gratefully acknowledge the assistance of Dr. Stuart Schneck for his neuropathological analysis. A brief 16-mm motion picture, illustrating smiling and other spontaneous behaviors in this infant, is available by special arrangement with the authors.

LONGITUDINAL STUDY OF EARLY EXOGENOUS SMILING

Unlike endogenous smiling, the other system, the exogenous smiling system, is not present at birth. It begins in an irregular fashion during the end of the first month and increases in specificity and importance throughout the first year, and indeed throughout the life span. Data concerning the emergence of this form of smiling have been provided by our longitudinal study of individual infants. As part of a larger study of normal behavioral and EEG development, infants were observed and tested at weekly intervals from birth through 14 weeks.[2] All of the 16 infants, except two, met strict criteria for normality following birth. One of the exceptions was born one week prematurely (37 weeks gestational age at birth), but was normal otherwise. The other exception was an infant who was healthy except for developing an alternating strabismus, which was detected only when he was three weeks of age. During biweekly home visits, which lasted from one to one and a half hours, maternal reports were obtained according to a prearranged interview schedule, which was designed to elicit information about smiling and other affect expressions, as well as sleep-wakefulness, feeding, and the infant's overall "behavioral day."

Scheduled infant testing included responsivity to a variety of perceptual and neurological tests, which were administered as the state of the infant permitted. Among the perceptual tests were: (1) response to the experimenter's nodding face, which was presented both silently and with the voice; (2) response to a visual 9-inch black and white bull's-eye target held motionless for three minutes at a distance of 18 inches from the infant's eyes; (3) response to a toy horn blown six times at five-second intervals; (4) response to the ringing of a small, high-pitched dinner bell; (5) response to vertical rocking at a rate of one full excursion per second; and (6) response to a gentle tactile stroking of the forehead. Since the overall purpose of the study was to collect a wide variety of behavioral data for correlation with polygraphic recordings, there was no attempt to counterbalance for order effects of stimulus presentation and, except for the nodding face, each stimulus was presented only once or twice. Only those responses which occurred when the infant was judged by two of the observers as being in an initial alert state are included in the discussion below.

THE EMERGENCE OF SOCIAL SMILING

Table 1 presents criteria for our rating of social smiling. In a reliability

---

[2] These data were collected with the collaboration of Mrs. K. Tennes and Drs. A. Kisley and D. Metcalf. The primary goal of the research was to explore hypotheses of John Benjamin concerning the stimulus barrier in early infancy (Tennes et al., 1972).

TABLE 1
SOCIAL SMILING SCALE

Rating	Criteria
1	*None.* No social smiling.
2	*Minimal.* Minimal evidence for social smiling; fleeting or minimal smiles seen on one or two occasions only during alert states. (Might be seen by one observer only.)
3	*Irregular.* Clear and full social smiles (bilateral upturning of the corners of the mouth for more than one second). These occur in response to the human face. However, usually the voice is necessary to elicit a smile and the tester has some difficulty in eliciting it and has the impression that he "has to work at it." The smile occurs relatively infrequently.
4	*Predictable.* Smiling is a predictable social response to the human face. It is a full smile which occurs with high frequency. Sometimes this rating includes a ready smiling to the face in which the voice is also necessary for its predictable elicitation.

study, two independent observers reached 94% perfect agreement for all ratings.

Figure 2 displays the number of cases that had achieved social smiling at various ages. It will be noted that the curves for the ratings of irregular social smiling and the ratings for predictable social smiling have a similar configuration, with one curve lagging behind the other by about two weeks. Fourteen of the 16 cases had a 4 rating of a predictable social smile by 12 weeks. The two exceptions were the same two noted above as being exceptions to our normal health criteria. The infant who was one week premature developed a predictable smiling rating by 14 weeks. The other infant was extremely strabismic by 12 weeks and showed other evidence of abnormal visual-motor development. The strabismic infant did not develop predictable smiling to the nodding face, and it was not until four months that he smiled with regularity in response to his mother's voice. Fourteen of the 16 infants were irregular smilers by eight weeks; again, the only two exceptions were the ones noted above.

SMILING TO MULTIPLE STIMULI

A somewhat surprising finding of our longitudinal research was that most infants evidenced smiling to a wide variety of stimuli during the age period

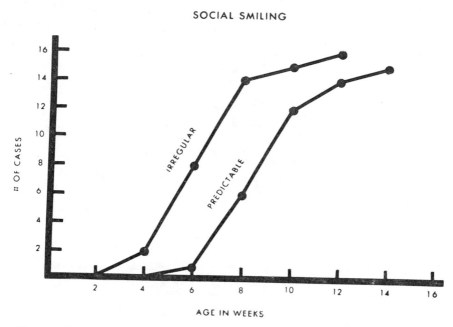

FIGURE 2

of one and a half to three months. Figure 3 illustrates the percentage of cases that smiled at various ages to four categories of "nonsocial" stimuli that were regularly presented during our visits. A total of 52 instances of smiling was recorded in response to these stimuli, and many other instances were seen in response to other stimuli which were not routinely presented. When all instances of such smiles are considered, 86% of them occurred between the ages of six and 12 weeks.

We were struck with a progression of phases in the development of smiling to these multiple stimuli. During the age period of one and a half to two and a half months, such smiling occurred in response to the side of the head as well as to the face, and to the printed page as well as to the bull's-eye target. It was seen to occur as a response to voices, bells, touching, or rocking. The response was, however, unpredictable in contrast to the later predictable social smiling response. During the period from two and a half to three months, it tended to increase in frequency, but it did not become a regular or predictable response, as did the specific visual smiling to the face. It was only during a final phase beginning around three months that this smiling to a wide variety of nonsocial stimuli became a rarity. Table 2 attempts a schematic representation of these phases in the development of exogenous

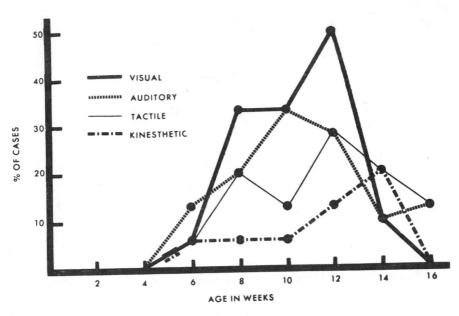

FIGURE 3

Smiling to nonsocial stimuli. The four categories of nonsocial stimuli included: visual response to bull's-eye target, auditory response to high-pitched bell, tactile response to stroking of forehead, kinesthetic response to rocking.

smiling. As this table illustrates, the final phase for smiling to multiple stimuli occurs during a time when the adequate stimulus for social smiling becomes increasingly more specific and complex.

These considerations have led us to the following inference: in the early phases of smiling elicitation, there is a degree of functional equivalence of different sensory modalities, *a sensory equivalence for smiling*. For a period of one and a half months stimuli in any of these modalities may elicit smiling, but the equivalence disappears when the smiling becomes specifically social and endowed with meaning.

The phenomenon of smiling to multiple nonsocial stimuli would seem to provide a challenge to cognitive and learning explanations of the origin of social smiling. If these nonsocial smiles are to be regarded as undifferentiated "mistakes" in recognitive assimilation, or as manifestations of a lack of perceptual discrimination, then one would expect to see evidence of a perceptual gradient of smiling. Such a gradient would be manifested by maximal smiling to stimuli most similar to the human face in its social context, and

TABLE 2
EXOGENOUS SMILING DURING WAKEFULNESS

	Phase			
	I Absent or Rare	*II* Irregular Smiling Response	*III* Regular Smiling Response	*IV* Early Differential Smiling
Approximate Age	Birth to 1½ mo.	1½ to 2½ mo.	2½ to 3 mo.	3 mo.
Social Smiling	—	Not specific	Specific visual: "essential gestalt"	More specific visual: 3-D, familiar faces
Smiling to Multiple Stimuli	—	Nonspecific visual	Increased but not regular to nonspecific visual	Rare or absent
	—	Auditory, tactile, kinesthetic	Increased but not regular to auditory, tactile, kinesthetic	Rare or absent
	—	With frown or fuss	With frown or fuss	Rare or absent with frown or fuss

minimal or no smiling to stimuli least like the face. The current study, while not designed to test systematically for such a gradient, uncovered no evidence of any trends in that direction. Quite to the contrary, we were impressed by the vast differences in the psychophysical qualities of the different stimuli that shared the capacity to elicit smiling during the period of one to three months of age.

As we examined our data, a further challenge to cognitive and learning explanations became apparent. It seemed to us that these would predict non-specific smiling to be limited to the early phases of smiling, when there is maximal uncertainty of action schemata or of rewards, and when the specific social response is therefore unstable; surely, they would not predict it to be characteristic of the later phase when smiling to the face is a regular stable response. Our data are not consistent with this prediction. First, about two-thirds of the observations of smiling to nonsocial stimuli occurred when social smiling was judged to be "predictable" with a rating of 4 on the same visit. Only about one-third of the observations corresponded to an "irregular" social smiling rating of 3. Second, a review of individual infants revealed a tendency for early social smilers to have early smiling to multiple stimuli and late social smilers to have a later onset of smiling to multiple stimuli (two-tailed $p < .10$, Fisher Exact Probability Test [Siegel, 1956]). A contingency table which includes the 14 infants who evidenced smiling to multiple stimuli is presented below (Table 3).

These data would seem to be more consistent with a viewpoint that there is a maturational "push," a time in development when there is an emerging propensity to smile to everything. For a brief period of time, a wide variety of stimuli of moderate intensity will elicit smiling. After three months of age, nonspecific smiling does not survive, presumably because, unlike social smiling, it is not normally reinforced within the social context of the developing infant. Thus, maturation would seem to be the major determinant of the onset of smiling to multiple stimuli, while learning would account for its subsequent shaping and inhibition. This view is consistent with certain theoretical speculations about early smiling presented by Ambrose (1963).

SMILING AND FROWNING TO THE SAME STIMULUS PRESENTATION

Another unexpected finding from our longitudinal study was that sometimes during a stimulus presentation an infant would frown (and occasionally fuss)

TABLE 3
CONTINGENCY TABLE[a]

	Early Social Smiling	Late Social Smiling
Early Smiling to Multiple Stimuli	3	0
Late Smiling to Multiple Stimuli	3	8

[a]Early social smilers were defined as those who had reached ratings of 3 or 4 by six weeks ($N = 6$); late social smilers were those who reached these ratings after that time ($N = 8$). Early smilers to multiple stimuli were defined as those who had evidenced this phenomenon before eight weeks.

before or after a period of smiling. Smiling and frowning appeared close together in time and seemed to alternate in all possible sequences. Fourteen of our 16 longitudinal cases exhibited this at least once during the same age period when there was nonspecific smiling to multiple stimuli. Table 4 tallies all instances in which an infant demonstrated smiling and frowning (or fussing) in the course of the presentation of the nodding face and the bull's-eye target. This phenomenon was occasionally seen in response to nonvisual stimuli; but, in general, auditory, tactile, and kinesthetic stimuli were not presented long enough to provide an opportunity for comparison. As illustrated in Table 4, there seemed to be five categories of smiling and frowning (or fussing) in response to the same visual stimulus.

In considering data concerning alternate smiling and frowning, we were struck by evidence for another kind of functional equivalence in the early phases of smiling elicitation. This equivalence seemed to be one of different responses to the same stimulus. In other words, we inferred evidence for a *response equivalence for smiling and frowning during the same developmental phase as a sensory equivalence for smiling.*

TABLE 4

SMILING AND FROWNING (OR FUSSING) TO THE
SAME STIMULUS PRESENTATION

Category	*Instances in Each Category*
A. Stimulus presented in alert active or alert inactive state results in: smiling, then frowning or fussing. A b-type includes this sequence plus smiling again afterward, while the stimulus is still being presented.	9 (1 of b-type)
B. Stimulus presented in alert active or alert inactive state results in: frowning or fussing, then smiling. A b-type has this sequence and fussing or frowning again afterward, with stimulus still presented.	9 (3 of b-type)
C. Stimulus presented in fussy state results in: smiling, then fussing.	4
D. Stimulus presented in fussy state results in: smiling and definite soothing.	6
E. Stimulus presented in alert active or alert inactive state results in: smiling with crying beginning "almost instantaneously."	2

EXPLANATORY VALUE OF HEINZ WERNER'S THEORY

We now faced the challenge of explaining these two equivalencies. The developmental theory of Heinz Werner (1940) suggested a promising avenue of approach. This theory points out that undifferentiated phases of development are characterized by a tendency for systems to function in a global manner. There is a basic primitive tendency for sensory modalities to be experienced and reacted to as a unity; every sensation is perceived and processed like any other. In addition, undifferentiated structure is characterized by "diffusion," by an equalness of parts, by a homogeneity, instead of integrated hierarchies. Werner's neural model for this structure is the "nerve net" of Colenterates with a "diffuse, undifferentiated, and uncentralized series of nerve cells with branching fibrils running indiscriminately throughout all or part of the body" (p. 42). Thus, undifferentiated activity has a·tendency to be less discrete and compartmentalized; as a consequence, one might expect *overflow* of activation between undifferentiated response systems.

The development of exogenous smiling should provide excellent grounds to test the usefulness of Werner's concepts. Smiling is a response system that is *not* present at birth, but can be observed as it appears and differentiates. The most undifferentiated phases of this response are characterized by a tendency for a wide variety of sensory experiences to be reacted to in a common manner. This is what we have described above as the *sensory equivalence for smiling*. In addition, during the same period of development, one could postulate that a stimulus produces an activation of what is not yet a discrete smiling response system—a diffuse activation resulting in occasional overflow to the frowning and distress response system. These occasions would result in the phenomenon described above as the *response equivalence for smiling and frowning*. It would also imply a structural connection between the two affect-expression systems.

EARLY STRANGER DISTRESS REACTIONS

Werner's theory seems to provide an explanation for several very early stranger distress reactions seen in our longitudinal study during the same age period. Such distress reactions to strangers in the first half-year of life have been noted previously (Tennes and Lampl, 1964) and have been characterized by their irregularity and lack of persistence, in contrast to later stranger reactions which begin at seven to nine months of age. The early distress reactions have been described by John D. Benjamin (1963) as manifestations of a "fear of the strange as such," and as possibly representing the emergence of an innate fear response. Could not Werner's theory provide an alternative view? These negative reactions may also be a result of overflow phenomena during the time when the undifferentiated exogenous smiling system is emerging, an overflow to the distress system in general. In other words, this could be a more intense manifestation of the same phenomenon which we described as the response equivalence for smiling and frowning.

In seven cases we saw a total of eight instances in which the infant, who was in an initial alert and seemingly contented state, developed a pre-cry facies and/or fussed in response to looking at the approaching tester's face. Figure 4 shows the age distribution of instances of these observed distress reactions. The figure also illustrates the similar age distribution for the phenomenon of smiling and frowning to the same stimulus presentation.

SMILING IN CONGENITALLY BLIND INFANTS

We would hope that any conceptual scheme for early smiling would help explain the remarkable phenomenon of exogenous smiling in congenitally blind infants. Selma Fraiberg has been engaged in the longitudinal study of a group of blind-born infants at the University of Michigan. In recent consultations with her, we have had an opportunity to apply our scheme to her

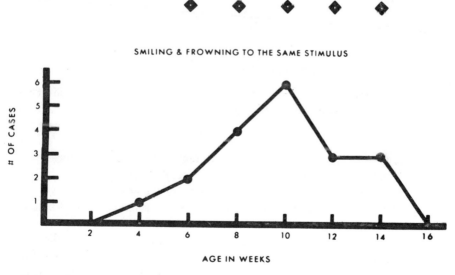

FIGURE 4

data. These infants begin to smile in response to environmental stimuli at the same age as sighted infants (Fraiberg, 1968, 1971b). During the second phase of our schematic smiling development (see Table 2), blind infants exhibit the same irregular smiling response characteristics as do sighted infants, except, of course, there is no visual responsivity. In phase III, however, it would appear that differentiation takes place in the direction of increasing specificity and frequency of smiling to the auditory-tactile modality. In phase IV, smiling tends to be specific to mother, just as it is in sighted infants, only here in the blind it is mother's touch and voice that elicit discriminated smiling. An important difference in the blind, however, is that although smiling becomes more frequent and selective in favor of the mother, even the mother's voice and touch will not *regularly* elicit smiling. As Fraiberg states, "There is no stimulus in the third month, or later, that has true equivalence for the human face Gestalt in the experience of the sighted child" (1971b, p. 115).

The data from Fraiberg's carefully observed cases would seem to illustrate that the central nervous system exhibits a degree of *plasticity* during the undifferentiated phases of exogenous smiling. During these phases there is a certain degree of equipotentiality. Under normal circumstances, vision predominates, and visual smiling will become increasingly differentiated while smiling to other modalities becomes inhibited; if the visual modality is blocked or unavailable as in the blind-born, there will be increasing differentiation of smiling to auditory and tactile modalities instead of inhibition. In other words, the blind-born can achieve what might be considered an adaptive modification of smiling as it is normally observed in sighted children between the ages of three weeks and three months.

RELATIONSHIP BETWEEN ENDOGENOUS AND EXOGENOUS SMILING SYSTEMS

Are the two systems of endogenous and exogenous smiling related? One type of smiling occurs during sleep and drowsy REM states, one type occurs during wakefulness. One is endogenous, and one occurs in response to external stimulation.

We assumed that these were two different maturational systems using elements of the same motor pathway, one system instigated from the inside, and one from the outside. Since these two systems overlap in time, we felt they should interact. We reasoned that Heinz Werner's theory would predict an overflow of activation between systems with summation effects, while a maturational theory of increasing neurological inhibition might predict the opposite—namely, interference with less smiling during this time. Our longitudinal study gave no clear indication of less endogenous smiling during the time when exogenous smiling began. We therefore tried experimental manipulations to explore the possibility of summation effects.

We awakened one- to three-month-old babies from sleep by gentle maneuvers in order to achieve varying degrees of drowsiness so that we could stimulate them. Although we have not yet adequately characterized our resultant experimental drowsy states, we believe we have discovered an intermediary phenomenon between the two systems of smiling. By providing a mild amount of nonspecific stimulation (turning the infant over, rocking him, ringing a bell, etc.), we arouse the infant to a drowsy state and elicit a continual, *repetitive* smiling of a sustained frequency which is greater than that ordinarily seen in either endogenous or exogenous smiling. Sometimes an initial stimulus is sufficient to set off repetitive smiling for ten minutes or more. On other occasions, intermittent low-level stimulation such as rocking or jiggling is necessary to keep the infant in this drowsy state with repetitive smiling. Eventually infants either drift back into REM sleep and stop smiling, or they awaken and stop smiling. Thus far, we have seen the phenomenon last for over five minutes in 15 instances involving 13 separate infants. The "average" case had 11 minutes of this "special drowsy state" with 1.5 smiles per minute, or over 16 smiles for the duration (figures are arithmetic means). Unlike smiling bursts in our newborns, these smiles tended to be evenly distributed across the drowsy state; they were not "clustered" around a few "burst minutes." The mean smile density of these cases during this state was over 18 times that of spontaneous smiling in full-terms during sleep and drowsy REM.

Table 5 presents a schematic view of the development of the two systems of smiling in early infancy as we have conceptualized them. The phenomenon

TABLE 5

DEVELOPMENT OF ENDOGENOUS AND EXOGENOUS SMILING

	Phase I	*Phase II*	*Phase III*	*Phase IV*
Endogenous Smiling (Sleep & Drowsy REM)	Present @ 11/100′	Present	Present	Diminishing or absent
Repetitive Smiling to Nonspecific Stimuli in Drowsiness				
Exogenous Smiling (Awake)	Absent or rare	Irregular smiling response	Regular smiling response	Early differential smiling

of repetitive smiling is viewed as sharing characteristics which are intermediate between the two systems.

DISCUSSION

Werner's developmental theory provides explanations for two phenomena we found characteristic of early exogenous smiling, namely, a tendency for: (1) a sensory equivalence for smiling and (2) a response equivalence for smiling and frowning. It also is consistent with a prediction of an experimental drowsy state with a high frequency of repetitive smiling. Werner's theory, although general, is an extremely useful one and is consistent with other conceptual models of undifferentiated phases of development. Spitz (1945a) has emphasized that the perceptual system of the newborn is characterized by a predominant tendency for "coenesthetic" or diffuse organization of perception, as contrasted with a later developmental predominance of "diacritic" or precise organization of perception. Bergström (1969) has recently presented a model of ontogeny which, without reference to Werner's theory, seems to provide a restatement of it in terms of contemporary neurophysiology and information theory. Following a review of recent neurophysiological data, he concludes:

> Studies concerned with the gross electrical activity of different parts of the brain during ontogenetic development lead to the conclusion that the functional development of the brain proceeds outwards from the whole reticular core . . . to the periphery. Structurally, the core consists of elements which are mutually connected in a random way. . . . The geometrical organization of the units shows an increase in order towards the periphery. The structural organization corresponds to an information flow which exhibits poor time and space relations (tonic) in the random structures, and far more exact time and space relations (phasic) in the ordered structures. This corresponds to low information-carrying capacity in the former, and high capacity in the latter. . . . A structural and functional model of the brain is developed, consisting of a reticular core with random structure (high entropy and low informational content) and of surrounding shell circuits with structures which are more ordered (lower entropy and higher informational content) the nearer a circuit is to the periphery. In sequence ontogenetic development exhibits the different functional properties of the core and the shell circuits [pp. 34ff.].

The correspondence of our findings with Bergström's independent elaboration of Werner's model is striking. From all indications, the newborn's endogenous REM smile is to be considered a manifestation of spontaneous activity of the reticular core of the immature brain. Although such smiles have the same probability of occurring across successive REM periods of a feeding cycle, they tend to occur tonically, or in bursts, within a given REM period.[3] After about one month of postnatal development, the early exogenous smile makes its appearance. Although it occurs in response to a wide variety of stimuli during wakefulness, it does not show the tonic or repetitive characteristics of REM smiling. One might presume that exogenous smiling involves "higher" or more peripheral CNS structures which have since matured. These structures will play an increasing role in the mediation of exogenous smiling as it becomes more specifically social. From this point of view, the *repetitive smiling* phenomenon represents a unique activation of the tonic reticular core which results from the experimental manipulation of the infant's state of arousal; the requisite stimulus input for its elicitation is nonspecific.

The period from two and a half to three months is a nodal one in exogenous smiling development. It is preceded by a diminution in the number of external stimuli that will automatically elicit smiling, and it is followed by an expansion in the number of complex internal factors that may be predisposing determinants. After this time, the commonly used physiological states of the neonatal period (Anders, Emde, and Parmelee, 1971; Hutt, Lenard, and Prechtl, 1969) will no longer suffice as useful descriptions of organismic readiness to smile. Instead, "mood states" will be of increasing importance in determining such readiness. These states will receive contributions not only from physiological processes, but also from expanding psychological processes of memory, cognition, and need representations.

At this point a strong cautionary note seems warranted. Although we have found it useful to refer to a tendency for a sensory *equivalence* for smiling and for a response *equivalence* for smiling and frowning, the formal characteristics of these imputed equivalences remain to be investigated in the manner outlined by Klüver (1936). For example, our data do not allow us to infer a complete equivalence of stimuli for smiling during any of the ages studied; furthermore, the *degree* of equivalence of different stimuli is unknown. Similarly, the range of stimuli that will elicit smiling requires experimental exploration, as does the range of stimuli that will *not* elicit smiling. As Klüver points out, it is only after these areas have been fully described that one can hope to discover underlying factors in stimulus and organismic conditions. The same criticisms apply to the response equivalence for smiling and frowning. In this instance there may be a narrower range of equivalence within the confines of an overall affect-expressive system, yet a systematic study of nonequivalent responses is required for confirmation.

---

[3] Why these "tonic" characteristics are not manifested by very long smiles is an intriguing question we cannot answer given the present state of our knowledge.

Current cross-sectional studies seek to describe the upper and lower age limits for smiling to multiple stimuli and for repetitive smiling. Contrary to our initial impression, repetitive smiling is found to be elicitable over a wide age range from the first week of postnatal life through at least four months, although there may be a peak during the period from one to three months. Part of our uncertainty must be due to our ignorance of determining conditions. We have been successful in eliciting this phenomenon approximately 10% of the time when we have awakened infants experimentally. Thus far we have been unable to affect this success rate by varying the time of awakenings during 24-hour periods or during intervals between feedings.

Repetitive smiling clearly demands a great deal of further investigation. Why have there been no previous reports of this phenomenon? As observers of our movies attest, it produces an emotional response of being unexpected and "weird." One would suppose that mothers have observed such repetitive smiling on occasions when various stimuli have partially interrupted the sleep of their young infants. Indeed, on one occasion, we saw this phenomenon occurring in a three-month-old infant who was being observed by us without intervention and who clearly looked like he was having "disturbed" sleep. The infant had intermittent belches and a considerable amount of flatus, as well as audible borborygmi. It seemed likely to us that in this case the nonspecific stimulation which had triggered this state of arousal with repetitive smiling had come from the infant himself in the form of intestinal spasms. Perhaps this particular form of smiling, occurring rarely under naturalistic circumstances, is a basis for mothers' attributing all REM smiles to "gas expressions" (Emde and Koenig, 1969a).

SUMMARY AND CONCLUSIONS

Evidence is presented for two systems of smiling that emerge in development before the appearance of the regularly elicited "smiling response."

Endogenous smiling is present at birth. It is a "spontaneous" behavior associated with a specific electrophysiological pattern within the REM state. It tends to occur in bursts and does not decline over successive REM periods of an interfeeding interval. Our studies found it to be increased in prematures where a significant negative correlation with postconceptional age was demonstrable. In addition, a microcephalic newborn with minimal amounts of functioning cerebral tissue smiled at "normal" rates during REM periods. We postulate that this form of smiling is mediated by brainstem structures and becomes inhibited by subsequent maturation of the cerebrum.

Exogenous smiling is not present at birth. It begins as an irregular response to external stimuli during the end of the first postnatal month. A longitudinal study of individual infants reveals that this form of smiling occurs to a wide variety of stimuli of different sensory modalities. The onset of social smiling occurs in the midst of what would appear to be a maturational flowering of a propensity to smile to all types of stimuli—nonsocial as well as social. A further finding is that early exogenous smiling may occur close in time to a frowning or distress response during a single stimulus presentation.

The developmental theory of Heinz Werner is used to conceptualize characteristics of early exogenous smiling. This theory offers an explanation for several early stranger distress reactions we saw in our longitudinal study. It also helps in understanding smiling development in congenitally blind infants.

Finally, speculation is offered as to a possible relationship between endogenous and exogenous smiling systems. An experiment is described which may have yielded an intermediary phenomenon between the two systems of smiling. The phenomenon results from our gently arousing a sleeping infant. The effect is a continual repetitive smiling which has a sustained frequency greater than that ordinarily seen in either endogenous or exogenous smiling.

3

INTRODUCTION

The Origins of Reciprocity: The Early Mother-Infant Interaction, by T. Berry Brazelton, Barbara Koslowski, and Mary Main

The search for a unitary etiological explanation of behavior has had various foci over the ages. Recently, we have witnessed an increasing emphasis on parental and other environmental influences on the developing child. At one extreme, the child is viewed as a tabula rasa on which experience inscribes. From a more judicious perspective, the infant is believed to have innate potentials, which are then affected by experience. Most studies, however, tend to see these influences as stemming unidirectionally from the parents and affecting the child. Occasionally, there have been allusions to the child's influence on the parent. Benedek (1959), for instance, discusses how the child's developmental progress reactivates analogous psychological conflicts in the parent. Similarly, Hilgard and Newman (1959) observe that the child's behavior can evoke anniversary reactions in parents. Chess, Thomas, and Birch (1967) have systematically investigated how the child's individuality affects the parent-child interaction (see also Escalona, 1968; Thomas, Chess, and Birch, 1968 [Chapter 4 in *Childhood Psychopathology*]). Other studies, such as the following selection, have focused on very early interactions, illuminating mutual reciprocity in mother-neonate interaction.

In this chapter Brazelton, Koslowski, and Main observe mutual mother-child interaction at a point far earlier than had previously been thought possible. Their data derive from a stop-frame microanalysis of filmed vocal-kinesic interaction patterns (cf. Sander, 1975). A detailed presentation of their method precedes the discussion of their findings. To summarize: the authors compare the interaction of five normal infants with their white, middle-class mothers and with a toy monkey. Two markedly different patterns of attentional, motoric, and affective behavior are demonstrated as early as two to three weeks of age. With the inanimate object, the infant's reactions are characterized by rapt attention, followed by a quick turning away with jerky movements coming in bursts. With the mother, there tends to be a smooth, rhythmical interaction with repeated cycles of initiation, greeting, and disengagement. The neonate's cognitive faculties appear to be more advanced than has generally been assumed, as evidenced by this ability to differentiate the inanimate from the animate.

A full appreciation of the infant's cognitive capacities requires observers to focus on channels of communication ordinarily not noticed. A. MacFarlane (1975), for instance, has demonstrated that neonates not only employ the sense of smell to locate the source of food, but they can distinguish between their own mother and another mother on the basis of olfaction. By five days of age, significantly more babies spent greater amounts of time turning toward their own mother's nursing pad than toward a clean, unused pad, and by six days of age, the infants manifested a differential response to their own and another mother's breast pad. In addition to indicating early cognitive sophistication, this finding suggests that maternal and hospital use of deodorants and lanolin products may have more than a neutral effect from the baby's perspective. Further evidence of early intelligence is found in Condon and Sander's (1974) demonstration of microsecond synchronization between the movements of the awake neonate and linguistic components of human speech as early as the first 12 hours of life.

While it is becoming increasingly clear that the infant and mother are engaged in the dancelike interaction Middlemore described in 1941, there is less certainty as to who is leading whom in the dance. Indeed, that may not be a pertinent question; it may be that each cues the other to keep in step. In the report that follows it is striking that the mother "allows" the baby to turn away from her. The process seems similar to what Mahler describes in Chapter 7 as the mother's "quasi-altruistic surrender" of the toddler's body to the child in normal separation-individuation.

The mother's active contribution to a stable interaction can be seen in what Stern (1974) calls "infant-elicited variations of maternal behavior." But that the infant's early interaction is impressively self-regulated is not as easily perceived. Infantile self-regulation is suggested in the selection reprinted below and further supported by other studies by Brazelton et al. (1975), in which the feedback given to the infant was experimentally distorted. In one instance, the mother was asked to be unresponsive to the infant for three minutes. The infant's reaction suggested a sensing that the normal interaction would not be forthcoming. When repeated attempts to elicit mother's usual behavior failed after two minutes, the infant withdrew and engaged in self-comforting behavior, reminding the observers of Bowlby's (1973) description of older, hospitalized children separated from their parents. Brazelton et al. (1975) also observed a sighted infant interacting with her blind parents. The mother, who had been blind since birth, had an unexpressive face, whereas the father, who had vision until he was eight years old, was described as "talking" with his face. At four weeks of age, this infant would glance only briefly at the mother's eyes and then avert her gaze. In contrast, she carefully watched her father's and the experimenter's faces under similar circumstances. It was impressive that the sightless mother was aware of this behavior, which she detected from the direction of the sound of the baby's breathing. In this case, the rhythmic communication between mother and infant was heightened in the vocal and auditory areas.

Several investigators have reported various types of neonatal sex differences, including differential responsivity to male and female adults, variations in male and female neonatal sensory thresholds, and measurable distinctions in maternal handling of boys and girls in the early weeks of life. Richards, Bernal, and Brackbill (1976), however, question these neonatal gender differences in pointing out that they are derived primarily from studies in the United States, where circumcision is a widespread practice. They assert that similar gender differences have not been found in comparable studies in England and the Netherlands, where circumcision is rarer.

This is but one example of how much remains to be learned about individual differences in infant-caretaker interactions. It is hoped that continued study will serve to identify diagnostic indicators in terms of mother-infant synchrony of movements, facial expressions, and vocalizations, and thus illuminate the study of the chaotic dyssynchrony of autism (see Chapter 39 by Rutter), failure to thrive (see Chapter 21 by Evans, Reinhart and Succop), and child abuse (see Chapter 20 by Steele and Pollock). Indeed, the potential therapeutic application of Brazelton's findings is best appreciated when one watches him "educate" a mother about her own special importance to her infant. Brazelton first engages the infant in mutual facial responsiveness while the mother watches. He then turns the baby toward the mother who imitates what Brazelton did. The mother's self-esteem is dramatically reinforced by the baby, who in this instance shapes the mother rather than vice versa.

There is a story that has the ring of an apocryphal parable but is true that vividly conveys the vital importance of the baby's active contribution to the interaction with his or her caretaker and may also suggest something about individual differences. A husband and wife decided to collaborate in testing certain hypotheses regarding infant development on infant twins requiring foster placement. They intended to supply all the required physical care with meticulous diligence but without the usual pleasurable social interaction. In other words, while feeding, comforting, washing, dressing the infants, they would express no emotion and engage in no playful communication. Fortunately, the experimenters experienced difficulty maintaining these conditions after the infants greeted them with smiles and vocalizations, which forced them to return the babies' smiles and to speak with them (Dennis and Dennis, 1951).

3

The Origins of Reciprocity:
The Early Mother-Infant Interaction

T. BERRY BRAZELTON, BARBARA
KOSLOWSKI, and MARY MAIN

ETHOLOGICAL DESCRIPTION OF EARLY MOTHER-INFANT INTERACTION

Since the early mother-infant relationship forms the base for the child's future psychological growth, it seems fitting to analyze some of the earliest observable interactions between mothers and infants that make up this relationship. We attempted to analyze the behavior of the members of five "normal" mother-infant pairs from two to 20 weeks in a behavioral analysis of a short period of intense interaction between them.

In pediatric practice I had long been impressed with the rhythmic, cyclic quality of mother-infant interactional behavior. There appeared to be a kind of attention-nonattention behavioral cycle—a rhythmic attention-withdrawal pattern present in differing degrees in each participant. Usually, the mother's pattern was synchronized with that of the baby. Occasionally, however, initial synchrony ended in dyssynchrony after a difficult or tense interaction.

First published in *The Effect of the Infant on Its Caregiver*, edited by M. Lewis and L. A. Rosenblum New York: Wiley-Interscience, 1974, pp. 49–76. Copyright © 1974, John Wiley & Sons, Inc. Reprinted by permission of John Wiley & Sons, Inc.

This research was conducted at the Center for Cognitive Studies, Harvard University, and was supported by NIMH Grant No. 12623-02-03-04-05. The authors wish to express their gratitude to Dr. Jerome S. Bruner for his inspiration, and for the opportunity to work at the Center for Cognitive Studies, Harvard University. In addition, Mrs. Roberta Kelly was of primary importance as a research assistant in her work with the mothers and babies, in analyzing the films, and in providing moral and intellectual support for the project in its earliest years. Drs. Colwyn Trevarthan and Martin Richards were instrumental in helping us differentiate the details of the two modes of interaction with objects and with familiar persons. Most important of all, we are deeply indebted to the faithfulness and patience of the five mothers who were willing to bring their babies to us weekly for five months, and were brave enough to be filmed as they interacted with their babies at such a critical period in their lives. We hope the fruits of this study will be just reward for their dedication.

We hoped, on the basis of detailed film studies, to be able to describe several of the significant behavioral components of mother-infant interaction, the patterns of behavior used by each member of the dyad, and the rhythms and cycles that underlie these patterns. The unit of choice became a cycle of looking and nonlooking, or attention and nonattention.

METHOD

Five white, middle-class mothers and their normal full-term infants from my Cambridge pediatric practice were seen weekly at the Harvard Center for Cognitive Studies. The mothers volunteered for the study just prior to their infants' births, and we ascertained that their pregnancies and deliveries were entirely normal. Apgars of the babies at delivery were all above 8–9–9, and my neonatal behavioral evaluation (Brazelton, 1973) and Prechtl's neurological examination (Prechtl and Beintema, 1964) were optimal in each case.

Before the first session each of the mothers was contacted by one of the experimenters who told her, in as much detail as possible, what we would be doing, what equipment we would be using, and what was expected of her—that is, each mother was told that we wanted to film and analyze the normal development of "interaction behavior" between a mother and her infant during the first four months of life. She was told that we were not judging her or her infant's behavior, but wanted to see the development of his ability to respond to her. The initial contact with the mother was important in answering her questions and in establishing rapport with the subject before our first session. Each week she was given an opportunity to voice her concerns and to be reassured by the same person as to the child's development and her own role in mothering him. These prefilming sessions seemed very important in relieving some of the natural tension a mother feels about having her interaction with a child observed so intensively.

The study began with a home visit to each subject between the first and fourth week of the baby's life. These sessions were less controlled than the laboratory sessions that followed, but were important in becoming acquainted with the family. By the time each baby was four weeks old, his mother brought him to our laboratory once a week, at the same time each week.

One baby was not present for three consecutive weeks (11 to 13) because of a trip out of the country. Each of the other subjects missed from one to three weeks because of illness. None was absent for more than three weeks. For each subject we have a minimum of 13 films in the period of four to 20 weeks. Each session involved a standardized procedure. It began informally in the nursery at the Center, where mother and child took off their outer clothes and relaxed. The mother talked with the researchers before going to the laboratory. The infant was fed and diapers were changed when necessary. In the laboratory the mother placed her baby (with assistance from a researcher) in a custom-built, adjustable, reclining seat with a head rest for support designed by Colwyn Trevarthan. The baby reclined at a 30° angle, and the seat permitted the limbs to move freely and the head to turn. The mother was seated in front of him, her face at a distance of about 18 inches. She was free to lean forward, to touch him, or to hold onto him, as he sat securely strapped in his reclining chair. All efforts were made to relieve any distress the baby might feel, and he could be handled or rocked by his mother when his interest or cooperation lagged. (This experimental situation was likened to that at home when a baby is placed in the commonly used plastic chair for infants, and the mother sits in front of him.)

Two mirrors were located in strategic positions around the mother and child, so that an image of each was registered simultaneously on the film. However, neither mother nor child was able to see either of the mirrors. A camera was concealed behind curtains in a corner of the room, out of sight. The room was white, free of patterns, distracting objects, or people. The actual filming was done in two segments. The first was of the mother and child; the second was of the child with an object, a small 3 1/2-inch fuzzy monkey. Each segment was filmed for at least five minutes, and segments were separated by a five-minute interval.[1]

In the segments of film with the baby and his mother, the camera began shooting after everyone had apparently become settled and was at ease. We filmed sequences when the infant was thought to be intently looking at the person opposite him. The camera then ran continuously for 90 seconds unless the baby became upset or appeared to lose interest in the person opposite him. The filming of the baby with the object began when the object, suspended on a string, was brought toward him, from a distance, along his midline. The camera ran continuously as the object was brought into the baby's "reach space" (12 inches from his face), dangled there for a minute, and then slowly taken away along his midline.

Analysis of the filmed sequences resulted in two kinds of system analyses. (1) The object-infant sequence has been analyzed by Colwyn Trevarthan and Martin Richards. Our grosser observations of the baby's interaction with objects are based on our comments as we became struck by the two very different systems we felt we were observing from the first three weeks of

---

[1] We had attempted to monitor vocalization in mother and infant by microphone attachments which transmitted impulses to flashing lights which were recorded on the film and could be analyzed. This method proved to be unreliable since (1) it recorded all noise from the environment, as well as the baby's movements and rustling of clothes, and (2) the lights and microphone distracted mother and infant.

age. The senior author assumes responsibility for the present interpretations of the object-infant behavior. (2) One minute of intense interaction between mother and infant was selected for analysis of mother-infant interaction behavior. The cameraman was instructed to take the first sequence in which both mother and infant were observed to be relaxed and clearly attending to each other. When the minute was disrupted by an event that necessitated picking the infant up, or feeding him, we discontinued the filming and resumed it again after he was back in his chair. The initial segment of the next interaction was then added to the interrupted portion of the previous film to make a total of 60 seconds of interaction for analysis. In effect, each minute was a sample of their interaction *while it was going well*.

We analyzed our films according to several systems. We coded the occurrence of 18 behaviors for the mother and 19 for the infant (see Table 1). These behaviors were ones that we could define and code with an interscorer reliability of 85%. We prepared a descriptive manual for initial training and for reliability. Coding was done from stop-frame analysis of film by two observers simultaneously, and agreement was reached as we coded. Samples of film were analyzed by a third observer for interscorer reliability from time to time. Each behavior was clear-cut, and its onset and offset were unexpectedly easy to determine. Each frame was analyzed with a stop-frame projector, and behaviors were recorded on a running record sheet which allowed simultaneous recording of all the behaviors for both parties. The record noted onset, continuation, and termination of each behavior. Mother and baby behaviors were recorded side by side on the same running record, which permitted visual comparisons of clusters of behavior.

Although this detailed analysis seemed complicated, we felt that this record of 37 coded variables did not adequately describe the interaction. For example, the quality and tempo of each behavior, the spatial relationships within the dyad, the descriptive form (contact was patting, stroking, or shaking), and the affective significance of the behavior within the incident could not be revisualized by this kind of analysis. Hence, in order to understand individual differences in dyads, as well as to make ethological descriptions of significant findings, it was also necessary to dictate a narrative account of the interactions.

OBSERVATIONS

DESCRIPTION OF BEHAVIOR WITH OBJECT

A furry monkey, 3 1/2 inches high, was suspended by a wire and brought slowly along the midline into the baby's reach space (12 inches away from his face). The object was left there for a minute and then gradually moved

TABLE 1
CODED VARIABLES

Mother		Infant	
I	(1) Vocalizing	I	(1) Vocalizing
II	(2) Smiling	II	(2) Smiling
	(2A) Laughing		(2A) Laughing
III	(3) Intent looking (LI)	III	(3) Intent looking (LI)
	(4) Dull looking (LD)		(4) Dull looking (LD)
	(5) Looking away (LA)		(5) Looking away (LA)
			(6) Eyes closed
IV	(6) Reaching	IV	(7) Reaching
	(7) Touching		(8) Touching
	(8) Holding		
	(9) Adjusting		
V	(10) Moving into line of vision	V	(9) Fussy, squirming
	(11) Bobbing and nodding		(10) Body cycling
	(12) Leaning forward		(11) Jerky, excited movements
	(13) Leaning back		(12) Leaning forward
VI	(14) Facial gestures		(13) Leaning back
	(15) Hand gestures	VI	
	(16) Kiss		(14) Crying
	(17) Wiping face		(15) Yawning
	(18) Miscellaneous		(16) Spitting up
			(17) Bowel movement
			(18) Tonguing
			(19) Miscellaneous

out and away. This procedure was repeated each week while he sat in his infant chair, and was an attempt to contrast his responsive behavior to an object with his behavior when his mother was seated in front of him. Marked differences in attention span, state behavior, buildup of excitement, and disruption of attention were noted as early as three weeks of age (cf. Bower, 1966). We felt that we could look at any segment of the infant's body and detect whether he was watching an object or interacting with his mother—so different were his attention, vocalizing, smiling, and motor behavior with the inanimate stimulus as opposed to the mother.

The infant stared fixedly at the object with wide eyes, fixating on it for as long as two minutes, by six weeks, without disruption of gaze or attention. In this period, his face was fixed, the muscles of his face tense in a serious set, with eyes staring and mouth and lips protruding toward the object. This static, fixed look of attention was interspersed with little jerks of facial muscles. His tongue jerked out toward the object and then withdrew rapidly. Occasional short bursts of vocalizing toward the object occurred. During these long periods of attention, the eyes blinked occasionally in single, isolated blinks. The body was set in a tense, immobilized sitting position, with the object at his midline. When the object was moved to one side or the other, the infant tended to shift his body appropriately, so it was kept at his midline. His shoulders hunched as if he were about to "pounce." (This was observed as early as four weeks of age, long before a reach could be achieved, utilizing this antigravity posturing of the shoulders [Bruner, May, and Koslowski, 1972].) Extremities were fixed, flexed at elbow and knee, and fingers and toes were aimed toward the object. Hands were semiflexed or tightly flexed, but fingers and toes repeatedly jerked out to point at the object. Jerky swipes of an arm or leg in the direction of the object occurred from time to time as the period of intense attention was maintained (B. L. White, Castle, and Held, 1964). In this period, the infant's attention seemed "hooked" on the object, and all his motor behavior alternated between the long, fixed periods of tense absorption and short bursts of jerky, excited movement in the direction of the object. He seemed to hold down any interfering behavior which might break into this prolonged state of attention.

As the object was gradually brought into reach space, his entire state of attention and behavior changed. His eyes softened and lidded briefly but continued to scan it with the same prolonged attention. His mouth opened as if in anticipation of mouthing it. The tongue came out toward it and occasionally remained out for a period before it was withdrawn. His neck arched forward as his head strained toward the object. His shoulders were hunched, and his mouth protruded. Swipes of the arms and extensions of the legs at the knee increased in number. Hands alternately fisted and opened in jerky movements toward the object, as early as six weeks of age. Just before an extension of an arm toward the object, there was a very rapid flexor jerk of the extremity, as if extension were first preceded by an involuntary flexor jerk. This flexor jerk seemed to signify an intentional movement of extension in the four- to 16-week period, at a time when mastery of the balance between flexor and extensor muscles is difficult (Twitchell, 1965, 1971). As he mastered extensor activity, by 16 weeks, this early signature of intention became lost. In an attempt to anchor one hand in order to reinforce the efforts of the other, he often grasped his chair, held onto a piece of his clothing or a part of himself, or put his thumb in his mouth. This seemed to free the other hand to reach unilaterally, at a time when bilateral arm and hand activity is still predominant (10 to 20 weeks), and was comparable to a kind of "place holding." Long before reaches could be completed successfully, these segments of such an intention were part of the prolonged states of attention toward the object.

This state of intense, rapt attention built up gradually to a peak which was disrupted suddenly by the infant's turning away from the object, becoming active, and flailing his extremities. He often cried out, breathed rapidly, and looked around the room as if to find relief by looking at something else. When he found another object, such as a door or a corner of the room, he latched onto it. He often looked down or closed his eyes in this interval, as if he were processing information about the object in this period of withdrawal. This flailing activity of body, arms, and legs was accompanied by facial activity, and he seemed to be "letting off steam." The period of disruption was followed by a turning back to the object and a resumption of the "hooked" state of attention.

Striking in all of this was the intent, prolonged state of attention, during which tension gradually built up in all segments of his body until abrupt disruption seemed the inevitable and necessary relief for him. This behavior was most striking by 12 to 16 weeks. Habituation and more gradual turning away from the object seemed to start by 16 weeks and become an alternative to this "hooked" behavior (Brackbill et al., 1966). But before this, and as late as 20 weeks, each segment of his body reflected the "hooked," intense attention and disruption that seemed to be characteristic of his response to an object. This unit of cycling attention and disruption can be compared as a homeostatic model with the units of attention-withdrawal (A-W) described in the following mother-infant sequences (see Figure 1).

DESCRIPTION OF BEHAVIOR WITH THE MOTHER

The contrast of the infant's behavior and attention span when he interacted

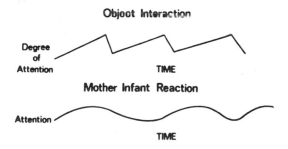

FIGURE 1

Alternating attention and nonattention with object and mother.

with his mother was striking as early as four weeks of age. We felt we could see brief episodes of these two contrasting modes of behavior as early as two to three weeks, but by four weeks we could predict correctly from watching parts of his body and observing his span and degree of attention whether he was responding to the object or to his mother.

Of course, the expectancy engendered in an interaction with a static object, as opposed to a responsive person, must be very different (Piaget, 1936, 1937). But what surprised us was how early this expectancy seemed to be reflected in the infant's behavior and use of attention. When the infant was interacting with his mother, there seemed to be a constant cycle of attention (A), followed by withdrawal of attention (W)—the cycle being used by each partner as he or she approached and then withdrew and waited for a response from the other participant. In the mothers and infants we observed, this model of attention seemed to exist on several levels during an interaction sequence. If she responded one way, their interactional energy built up; if another, the infant might turn away. The same held true for her response to his behavior. In order to predict and understand which behavioral cluster will produce an ongoing sequence of attention, one must understand the affective attention available in each member of the dyad. In other words, the strength of the dyadic interaction dominates the meaning of each member's behavior. The behavior of any one member becomes a part of a cluster of behaviors which interact with a cluster of behaviors from the other member of the dyad. No single behavior can be separated from the cluster for analysis without losing its meaning in the sequence. The effect of clustering and of sequencing takes over in assessing the value of particular behaviors, and in the same way the dyadic nature of interaction supersedes the importance of an individual member's clusters and sequences. The power of the interaction in shaping behavior can be seen at many levels. Using looking and not looking at the mother as measures of attention-nonattention, we found an average of 4.4 cycles of such attention and apparent nonattention in a minute's interaction. Not only were the spans of attention and of looking away of shorter duration than they had been with objects, but they were observably smoother as the attention built up, reached its peak, and then diminished gradually with the mother. Both the buildup as well as the decrease in attention were gradual. A typical period might be described, in segments, as follows.

Initiation. The infant begins to look back at his mother with dull eyes, a relaxed face, and slowly moving extremities and body. The exception to this pattern occurs if the mother has turned away from the infant. He may then turn back abruptly. Although the infant may have been looking away from her, he often has kept her in his peripheral vision, so that when she turns away, he may quickly turn back to re-establish contact.

Orientation. As he looks toward her, his eyes and face brighten, his body orients so that it faces her, and his extremities extend toward her. The same kind of pointing behavior of fingers and toes as is seen with objects may occur briefly at this time as well.

State of Attention. As she responds to his looking at her, the infant assumes a state of attention in which he alternately sends and receives cues. In this state his arms and legs may pedal slowly, his face alerts, and his eyes dull and then brighten, with fleeting smiles, grimaces, and vocalizations. Hands and feet open and close smoothly, and when his fingers or toes move, they move in slower and smoother movements than in the state of interaction with the object. Alternately reaching forward toward her and circling back into positions parallel to his own head, his extremities give him the attitude of alternately reaching out and waiting to receive from her. The constant waxing and waning of degree of tension in all parts of the body seem to parallel the degree of attention and expectancy present in his interaction with his mother.

Acceleration. As the looking sequence builds up, there are fewer oscillations of attention and inattention, and the jerky, lidded quality of the eyes drops out. *Vocalizing* may be preceded by body activity, which builds up in intensity before he can make a vocalization. As he builds up to vocalizing, he seems to need to start with activity of his body. He may whirl his arms, twist his body, and strain forward, with face tense and arms stretched out as he builds up to a vocalization. His mother can cut short this vocal interchange by talking too much. Contingency scores support the observation that an infant vocalizes more when his mother quiets. *Smiling* is reinforced by her contingent smiling. As he begins with a tentative smile, she smiles back. He watches her intently and smiles for longer periods. His smiling may also involve cycling activity of his whole body, but it is smoother and less intense than the buildup in vocalizing. *Tonguing and spitting up* are seen as he accelerates toward the peak of interaction. *Cycling activity* of arms and legs involves wider and wider arcs. Occasional jerky reaches toward his mother are interspersed, but in general the body activity is smooth and rhythmic as he builds up.

Peak of Excitement. At the peak of excitement, his behavior may be very similar to that described with an object—jerky and intense. But there are observable differences. The duration of the tense state is shorter and interspersed with efforts to control the degree of excitement. He may bring his hand to his mouth to suck, suck on his tongue, yawn, or hold onto his hands or another part of his body in what appears to be an effort to decrease the building tension. These efforts provide a more gradual buildup and a smoother plateau of excitement at the peak of their interaction.

On stop-frame analysis of filmed interaction, one can determine the subtle changes in intensity in behavior at this peak which differ from the linear intensity seen in interaction with an object. There is a background rhythm of subtle cyclical changes in attention and inattention, which monitor the degree of investment and provide a smoother appearance. The infant's *eyes* may appear to be intensely fixed on his mother's face. But saccadic movements, brief periods of dulling down of intensity, of lidding, and of blinks, can be noted in a period of what appears to be intense looking. His *face* may be intent in smiling, vocalizing, or reacting to his mother's facial gestures. But there is constant slow movement and change in facial musculature as he reacts. His *vocalizing* may build up to a pitch of output, accompanied by intense activity. *Smiling* can be maintained for long periods at this intense peak, but laughing, spitting up, or even crying may be an end result. As his mother smiles back to him, he alternately dulls down as he watches and then responds with a wide, tense smile. His cycling activity gives way to more excited, high-pitched activity of his arms and legs. His neck may crane forward and then arch backward as he becomes excited, his body twisting from side to side. This intense activity alternates with more cyclic, smooth body behavior. Usually, in contrast to the object behavior, this peak is short-lived and ends in gradual deceleration.

Deceleration. Although this excitement may end in a disruption similar to that seen with objects, the infant usually ends a period of excitement by gradual rather than sudden deceleration of energy. His bright look dims, his eyes dull down and seem to lid over, his face assumes a duller, more relaxed attitude. His smiles fade, decreasing in number and intensity. Vocalizing either ceases or becomes decreased in pitch, intensity, and variability. He may even continue to vocalize, but with a dull, monotonous, "holding" quality. Tonguing and yawning may increase. Blinking increases in frequency and in the duration of each blink. He leans backward into a more relaxed sitting position. Reaching out is replaced by holding onto parts of himself, the chair, or his clothes, thumb sucking, or fingering his hair or ears. His extremities may continue to cycle, but with smoother, more restricted activity. Hands may be loosely clenched or wide and flat. In this state, he seems to be recovering. The outcome of this decelerated state may be toward another period of acceleration or toward a period of turning away from her.

Withdrawal or Turning Away. There are several ways a baby can be observed to withdraw from the looking and interacting situation we have described. Since our major variable is the looking mode, looking away may represent an observed turning away, while the infant may actually continue to be in real contact with the mother. The fact that he turns back quickly when she turns her head, closes her eyes, or leans back in her chair demonstrates the extent to which he keeps her in peripheral vision.

An infant entering this portion of the attention-withdrawal cycle presents various patterns, represented by a glazed or dull expression, reduced activity, and face and eyes not oriented toward the mother. He can look down or away and find another person or object to fix upon. In this partial withdrawal his activity is reduced, and his body moves slightly or not at all. There is none of the fixed, intense attention directed toward a new object, which signals real competing involvement. Instead, the dull attitude toward a peripheral object or person is a signal that he is still basically in touch with the first object of attention—his mother. In fact, in this brief period of withdrawal, he may be processing information which he has received in the previous period of interaction (parallel to that with objects). He may lean back in his chair, suck on his fingers, finger his other hand, or turn his body halfway away from his mother. Other activities tend to reinforce his looking-away behavior; for example, he may vocalize into the room, yawn or whimper halfheartedly and without focus, tongue his lips, suck on his tongue, play with his own clothing, finger his mother's hand absent-mindedly, or smile into the distance. All these activities are without real investment, and seem to be in the service of maintaining his decrease in attention to his mother.

If he builds up to an intense looking-away state, he may begin to fix on an object in the room, orienting toward it, and behave as if he is now really interested in it. As he becomes more excited, he may begin to use real "object" attention and behavior to maintain his involvement with the newly found object. This state of interest is likely to be short-lived and ends in a smooth transition with decelerating interest, until he turns back toward his mother. He then shows he is ready for another period of interaction. This represents the cyclical withdrawal aspect of a synchronous interaction. In this the infant has responded to his own inner timing rather than to any new, noxious, or dyssynchronous aspect of his mother's stimulation.

These withdrawing techniques may be substituted for each other. They serve to initiate the negative part of a cyclical curve with the same smooth, cyclical transition from the positive curve which is represented when the infant is attending to his mother. Thus, it appears that an infant withdraws and even invests energy in the negative part of the cycle—that of turning away and looking away—just as he does when he is attending to his mother. He then adds on behaviors—such as looking at the door, fingering his clothes, and coughing—in order to continue to look away. He can use the period of looking away as if he were attempting to reduce the intensity of the interaction, to recover from the excitement it engenders in him, and to digest what he has taken in during the interaction. These perhaps present a necessary recovery phase in maintaining homeostasis at a time in infancy when constant stimulation without relief could overwhelm the baby's immature systems.

When the interaction is not going well, more intense withdrawal or active rejection of the other actor may occur. This may be the result of a specific, inappropriate stimulus, or occur after a series that overloads his capacity for responsiveness.

We have determined at least four clear strategies for dealing with an unpleasant, inappropriate stimulus:

1. Actively withdrawing from it—that is, increasing the physical distance between the stimulus and oneself by changing one's own position, for example, arching, turning, shrinking.

2. Rejecting it, that is, dealing with it by pushing it away with hands and feet while maintaining one's position.

3. Decreasing its power to disturb by maintaining a presently held position but decreasing sensitivity to the stimulus—looking dull, yawning, or withdrawing into a sleep state.

4. Signaling behavior, for example, fussing or crying, which has the initially unplanned effect of bringing adults or other caregivers to the infant to aid him in dealing with the unpleasant stimulus.

All these were observed in our infants in the first few weeks in responses that appeared to be individually characteristic in tempo and vigor.

CYCLICAL NATURE OF THE INTERACTION

The most important rule for maintaining an interaction seemed to be that a mother develop a sensitivity to her infant's capacity for attention and his need for withdrawal—partial or complete—after a period of attention to her. Short cycles of attention and nonattention seemed to underlie all periods of prolonged interaction. Although we thought we were observing continuous attention to her stimulation, on the part of the infant, stop-frame analysis uncovered the cyclical nature of the infant's looking–not-looking in our laboratory setting. Looking-away behavior reflects the need of each infant to maintain some control over the amount of stimulation he can take in via the visual mode in such an intense period of interaction.

This approach-withdrawal model in infants was first described by Schnierla (1965), and the response was related to the qualities of the stimulus. Habituation and withdrawal from repeated stimulation have also been described (Brackbill et al., 1966; Gerwirtz, 1969; Sharpless and Jasper, 1959). Although the quality and quantity of stimulation must play important roles in determining the timing of the infant's withdrawal, there seems to be a basic regulatory mechanism, which was most evident in the early weeks but which persisted throughout our observations. Just as there is an oscillating regulatory mechanism that maintains homeostasis for physiological parameters such as temperature control or cardiovascular mechanisms, the curve of activation, discharge, and recovery seems to be necessary for attention in an ongoing interaction (Kimberly, 1970). The autonomic system is dominated by this kind of homeostatic mechanism. This homeostatic model, which underlies all the physiological reactions of the neonate, may also represent the immature organism's capacity to attend to messages in a communication system. In the visual system it was apparent that this model was pertinent. Unless the mother responded appropriately to these variations in the infant's behavior, it appeared to us that his span of attention did not increase, and the quality of his attention was less than optimal. For example, in the case of two similarly tense, overreactive infants, the mothers responded very differently. One mother responded with increased activity and stimulation to her baby's turning her off; the other maintained a steady level of activity which gradually modulated her baby's overreactivity. The end result was powerfully in favor of the latter dyad. This latter baby was more responsive, and for longer periods, as our study progressed. Although this effect could have been based on baby variables we were not able to analyze, we felt that the quality of communication changed in this pair; however, the linear tenseness of the first dyad remained throughout the 20 weeks of observation. This baby had learned "rules" about managing his own needs in the face of an insensitive mother. He had learned to turn her off, to decrease his receptivity to information from her. This must have been necessary for him in order to maintain physiological and psychological homeostasis. When this rule was learned, he could then tune in at times when he could tolerate cues from her. These two parallel cases demonstrate that a mother's behavior must not only be reinforcing and contingent upon the infant's behavior, but that it must meet more basic "needs" of the infant in being aware of his capacity to receive and utilize stimuli. This, then, becomes the first rule each must learn from the other. And, as our discussion indicates, we feel that the small infant's needs are greater and must shape the mother first, if she can be sensitive to him. When she is not able to be, communication must assume a different shape.

A striking way of illustrating the behaviors of the mother and the child, as well as the interaction of the two, is to present them in graphic form. To illustrate, Figures 2 to 5 are graphs drawn from interaction periods. Time is measured along the horizontal axis, and the number of behaviors along the vertical axis. Curves drawn above the horizontal line indicate that the person whose behavior the curve represents was looking *at* his or her partner. Curves drawn below the line indicate that he or she was looking *away*. Solid lines represent the mother's behavior; broken lines, the baby's. Thus, a deep, broken line below the horizontal line indicates that the baby was looking away while engaging in several behaviors.

As reflected in Figure 2, the mother looks at the baby after he turns to her. As they look at each other, she adds behavior, smiling, vocalizing, touching his hand, and holding his leg, to accelerate their interaction. He responds by increasing the number of his own behaviors (smiling, vocalizing, and cycling his arms and legs) until the peak at *x*. At this point he begins to decrease his behaviors and gradually cuts down on them toward the end of their interaction.

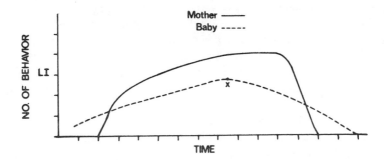

FIGURE 2

Number of behaviors added in a 16-second looking interaction. Baby looking (LI, looking intent).

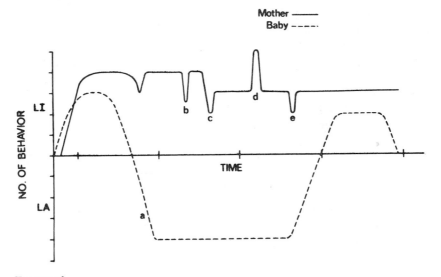

FIGURE 3

Number of behaviors added in a five-second interaction.

She follows his lead by decreasing her behaviors more rapidly and ends her part of the cycle by looking away just before he does. Figure 3 shows a baby starting a cycle by looking at his mother. She follows by looking at him and adding four more behaviors in rapid succession—touching him, smiling, talking, and nodding her head. He watches her, vocalizes, smiles back, cycles briefly, and then begins to decrease his responses and turns away at *a*. She stops smiling as he begins to turn away but rapidly adds facial gestures to try to recapture his interest. She continues to talk, touch him, nod her head, and make facial gestures until *b*. At this point she stops the gestures but begins to pat him. At *c* she stops talking briefly and stops nodding at him. At *d* she makes hand gestures in addition to her facial grimaces but stops them both thereafter. At *e* she stops vocalizing, and he begins to return to look at her. He vocalizes briefly and then looks away again when her activity continues.

In Figure 4 the mother and infant are looking at each other; she is vocalizing, and he is smiling. As she increases her activity by patting him, he turns away. She begins to nod at him at *a,* and he begins to look at the curtain across the room. She tries to quiet at *b* and again at *c*. After a period of less activity from her, he begins to turn to her at *d*. As he returns to look at her, she begins to build up by smiling, vocalizing, and eventually at *e* to pat him. At this he begins to turn away again.

In Figure 5 the mother and baby are looking at each other, smiling and vocalizing together. The baby begins to cycle and reach out to her. At *a* he

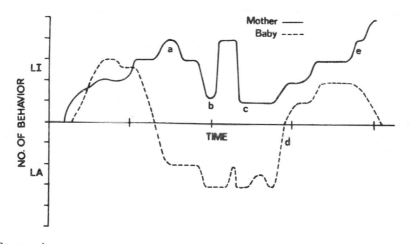

FIGURE 4

Number of behaviors added in a four-second interaction.

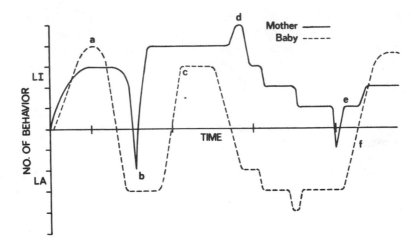

FIGURE 5

Number of behaviors added in a five-second interaction.

begins to turn away from her. She responds by looking down at her hands, and she stops her activity briefly. This brings him back to look at her at *c*. Her smiling, vocalizing, and leaning toward him bring a smiling response from him. In addition, his arms and legs cycle and he coos contentedly as he watches her. As he turns away, she first adds another behavior and gestures. He, however, adds to his activities extraneous to her reminders and turns away from her. She gradually cuts out all her activity, and by *e* she looks away from him. Immediately afterward he begins to look back to her, and the cycle of looking at each other begins again at *f*.

The kind of sensitivity to each other's needs for attention and nonattention that a couple might exhibit is represented by these cycles. Examples *a* and *d* seem to represent real sensitivity. The kind of insensitivity of the mother to the baby's turning away represented by Figure 3 seems to prolong the period of looking away. In Figure 4 reducing her activity acts as a stimulus to bring him back to respond to her after a long period of withdrawal. Figure 5 represents a more cyclical approach on the part of the mother, and an increasing number of cycles of attention from the baby.

MOTHER'S ROLE

A mother's response to her infant's rhythm changes in attention can fit into her infant's needs in one of three ways:

1. By adjusting her rhythm to his, following his cues for attention and

withdrawal, and adding her cues when he demonstrates his receptiveness. This approach serves to increase the amount of time during which the infant looks at her (see Figure 2).

2. By not responding to his rhythm or his withdrawal but continuing her steady bombardment. This serves to reinforce the time the infant spends looking away, and rapidly dulls down the amount of attention he pays to her cues when he looks at her (see Figure 3).

3. By attempting to establish her own rhythm to regulate his—in these instances a mother unconsciously increases and decreases her bombardment of stimuli, but out of phase with her infant, often resulting in short, unsatisfying periods of interaction between them (see Figure 4).

A mother's behavior in a period of interaction might be summarized by five kinds of experience she offers an infant:

1. Reduction of interfering activity.

2. Setting the stage for a period of interaction by bringing him to a more alert, receptive state.

3. Creating an atmosphere of expectancy for further interaction by her behavior.

4. Acceleration of his attention to receive and send messages.

5. Allowing for reciprocity with sensitivity to his signals, giving him time to respond with his own behavior, as well as time to digest and recover from the activation her cues establish.

Each of these segments of her behavior is endowed with an intention on her part. The intention is signified by the quality of her behavior. Variations in each segment can be observed as follows:

1. Reduction of Interfering Activity

The most obvious examples of this are: (a) regulating and satiating needs, such as hunger, being wet or dirty, lack of sleep; (b) containing reflex startle behavior which interferes with the infant's ability to maintain attention; and (c) soothing him when he becomes upset or disintegrated. A mother soon learns the conditions for containing her infant—that she can use restraint by adjusting him in the chair or swaddling his arms or legs with her hands. She finds that she can also hold him with her face, her gestures, or her voice. One mother used smiling to "maintain" her baby's attention and thus reduce his random activity. A mother often interchanges one behavior for another in a particular stage of her infant's becoming upset, expecting the change of mode to maintain his attention a while longer. Thus, a particular mother might initiate her interaction with a simple readjustment, and go on to hold his body or legs which startled as she adjusted him. She continues by stroking or patting his belly as she endeavors to keep him and his startle behavior under control. As this soothing, monotonous activity wears out its usefulness, a mother may begin to talk in a steady, monotonous voice, or to smile continuously. Another may begin to rock and bob her head—all these activities become the individualized background for the rest of their interaction.

When the infant demonstrates unexpected random behavior, such as the jerk of a leg or an arm, the mother responds by stroking or holding that extremity, or by making a directed use of that extremity to jog it gently up and down, thereby turning an interfering activity into one that serves their interaction. In these ways she might be seen to teach the infant how to suppress and channel his own behavior into a communication system.

2. Setting the Stage

As part of containing behavior, she may use a method that orients him toward her. She can adjust his body to the midline so that he faces her, pulling up his sagging torso so that he is in an alert position, reclining at a 30° angle, but alert rather than relaxed. She can move her head so that she is in his direct line of vision, bobbing or making facial gestures to attract his attention. One mother used kissing and another wiped her baby's face in what appeared to be efforts to alert the infants. (Instead, these two behaviors usually caused the baby to turn away.)

When she pats or strokes him, she does so with a rhythm and an intensity designed to alert as well as soothe (e.g., there was a two-per-second rhythm which most mothers used for soothing *and* alerting, and a slower rhythm for simple soothing). When he sags, her intensity and speed increase, or they decrease when he becomes overexcited. The part of his body that she touches also serves a double purpose—of soothing and alerting—for example, as he quiets to her stroking his legs or abdomen, she moves her hands up to his chest and finally to his cheek in order to arouse his attention and focus it on her.

3. Creating an Expectancy for Interaction

As she attempts to elicit a signal from the infant confirming that he is in touch with her, the mother uses any or all of the behaviors at her command. Characteristic of communication, her behaviors have certain features: (a) *Rhythm and intensity*—although they may start off explosively or slowly, they are quickly modulated to respond to the attention of the infant. Vocalizing, nodding, facial gestures, and patting, which start off explosively *or* soothingly, are quickly geared to maintain the interaction. (b) *Amplitude* is meshed in the same way. Large facial or arm gestures may initiate the sequence but are rapidly decreased in amplitude as his attention is caught. (c) *Direction*—since her effort is to orient him to her face as the central focus, all these movements are reduced in amplitude and from the periphery inward in a way that will bring his focus to her face, using her movement to activate and then to siphon his attention into a central focus on her eyes and mouth. (d) *Quality* is especially "appropriate" to an interaction with an infant. Speech is simplified in rhythm and pitched to gain and hold his attention; for example, baby talk is high pitched, vowel-like, and interspersed with alerting consonants such as *b, d, h,* and *tch.*

A mother's eyes and lips widen and close in rhythmic movements designed alternately to alert and soothe her baby. As he quiets, her vocalizations and facial movements become rhythmic and "holding," and then speed up with more staccato and a faster pace. Her eyes alternately narrow and widen, brighten and dull, in a measure appropriate to his state. When he overreacts, her eyes take on a soothing look, becoming wider and brighter, to attract and "hold" his attention.

4. Intensifying His Attention

Within the context of acceleration of attention, 15 of the 18 mother behaviors have the effect of intensifying their interaction. Only three—looking dull, looking away, and leaning back—can be considered decelerative in function. The mother starts with a behavior which seems appropriate to the particular interaction, for example, a smile in response to her baby's smile, or vocalization if she hopes to bring him to vocalizing. Each behavior can be substituted for another in order to accelerate the interaction. Or behaviors can be added in sequence and in clusters, to heighten their information value. For example, one mother held her baby's trunk with both hands. She added smiling to alert the infant further. As she received her alert look back, the mother began to vocalize, stopped smiling, and finally began to emphasize her speech rhythms with head bobbing toward the baby. These behaviors were all designed to heighten the information-giving aspect of this interaction sequence. As long as this mother was sensitive to her infant's increasing interest, these behaviors served their accelerative function. But at a certain point, when her baby seemed to be tiring, she added a touch to her baby's face and the infant turned away from her. (A stimulus that may be accelerative at one point may at another point serve to overload the infant and result in looking away on the part of the baby. Buildup of added behaviors had to be sensitively attuned to the point in the timing cycle of the infant's attention.)

5. Allowing for Reciprocity

When the mother can allow for the cyclic turning away from her, which seems to be necessary for the infant, she can be assured of longer periods of attention when he turns back to her. One of our mothers was particularly striking in her capacity to subside as he decreased his attention to her. She relaxed back in her chair, smiling softly, reducing other activity such as vocalizing and moving, waiting for him to return. When he did look back, she began slowly to add behavior on behavior, as if she were feeling out how much he could master. She also sensed his need to reciprocate. She vocalized, then waited for his response. When she smiled, she waited until he smiled before she began to build up her own smiling agian. Her moving in close to him was paced sensitively to coincide with his body cycling, and if he became excited or jerky in his movement she subsided back into her chair.

We felt she was outstanding in her sensitivity to the importance of reciprocity in this interaction. Whether she felt the danger of overloading him and cutting short their communication, or whether she sensed that pacing her behaviors decreased habituation effects and increased the value to him of each behavior as a signal, she brought out clear evidence of a more intense communication system between them. She provided an atmosphere that led to longer periods of interaction. She seemed to teach him an expectancy of more than just stimuli from her in the guise of her sensitivity to his needs and his cues. As she allowed for these, she seemed to be teaching him how to expand his own ability to attend to stimulation, for "long-term intention" as well as "long-term interaction." Thus, her role took on deeper significance as she established not only the climate for communication but gave him the experience in pacing himself in order to attend to the environment.

COMMUNICATION WITH NEONATAL INFANTS

There seemed to be special characteristics of the behavior of a mother with her new infant. When mothers were asked to communicate with infants of one week, they were essentially being asked to communicate with beings commonly thought "nonintentional." Our mothers were faced with the problem of communicating with infants who, if they were not crying or thrashing, were often hanging limply in the infant seat with closed or semiclosed eyes or, just as frequently, were "frozen" motionless in some strange and uninterpretable posture—staring at nothing. While the infant in the first weeks did seem to look directly into the face of his mother, the communicative aspects of eye-to-eye contact sometimes were dampened when the mother moved her head and found the infant still staring off in the original direction.

The infants' movements contained "startles"—fingers suddenly splayed out, feet and legs shot straight out or up—and seemed purposeless. Most of the time they adopted a peculiarly constricted posture with hands and arms brought up tight against the chest, arms tensely tucked under the neck, legs tense and toes pointing in, while their eyes were either semiclosed or staring into space. In the first week the most definite "interactive" activities we noted on the part of the infants were (1) withdrawal from a "noxious" stimulus such as contact in a sensitive area, (2) efforts to push away the noxious stimulus, (3) slight and quickly fading apparent effort to maintain eye-to-eye contact, (4) lulling to a caress or another stimulus from the mother, (5) brightening of the face and turning of the head to her voice or her face, and (6) responding to holding efforts from her by a gradual quieting and alerting to her.

Perhaps the most interesting response to the challenge of facing an unresponsive infant is this. The mother takes on facial expressions, motions, and postures indicative of emotion, as though the infant were behaving intentionally or as though she and he were communicating. Frequently, in response to a motionless infant, she suddenly acquires an expression of great admiration, moving back and forth in front of him with great enthusiasm; or, again in response to an unmoving infant, she takes on an expression of great surprise, moving backward in mock astonishment; or, in the most exaggerated manner, she greets the infant and, further, carries on an animated extended greeting interchange, bobbing and nodding enthusiastically exactly as though her greeting were currently being reciprocated. It is interesting that surprise, greeting, and admiration seem to share the common elements we have mentioned earlier: raised brows, widely exaggerated eyes, and in two cases even a faintly pursed mouth. Less frequently, mother mock-scolded an infant who was unresponsive.

Most mothers, in sum, are unwilling or unable to deal with neonatal behaviors as though they are meaningless or unintentional. Instead, they endow the smallest movements with highly personal meaning and react to them affectively. They insist on joining in and enlarging on even the least possible interactive behaviors, through imitation. And they perform *as if* highly significant interaction has taken place when there has been no action at all.

DISCUSSION

We had hoped that we would be able to identify synchrony and dyssynchrony in the mother-infant relationship by examining their interaction at a microscopic level. The need for guidelines in diagnosis of mother-infant harmony is great. Failures in mothering—such as are seen in infantile autism, failure to thrive, and child abuse—might be substantiated by such an analysis. We had hoped to identify such a diagnostic and research tool by using a kinesic model suggested by the work of Condon and Ogston (1967) and Birdwhistell (1962). Condon and Ogston have demonstrated that in psychotherapeutic interviews the physical movements of the listener are parallel to transitions in the speech of the speaker. For example, gross bodily movements such as changes in posutre coincide with the speaker's moving from one paragraph to another, whereas small movements of the listener's finger, for example, coincide with transitions between syllables. And to our point, they have demonstrated that this parallel between speaker's speech and listener's body movements is greater when the listener is attracted to the speaker than when this attraction is absent.

Important to our point, Watzlawick, Beavin, and Jackson (1967) speak of the rule of interaction in a setup such as ours—that it is impossible for two persons confronting each other *not* to interact, and that one might speak of positive or negative interaction between two persons, but never of *no* interaction. Our experimental design was constructed in such a way that we could visualize and analyze periods in which the *kind* of interaction could be assessed, in which interaction was obligatory. For analysis of the film sequences, we used Gesell's (1935) stop-frame cinemanalytic techniques of behaviors and combined Kestenberg's (1965a, 1965b, 1967) qualitative assessment of movement patterns. But we quickly became aware of the bimodal quality of interaction behavior. No actor's behavior was *ever* independent of the expectancy of interaction. Each behavior, then, was either positive or negative in its "intent" within this expectancy. It became important to attach an intentional significance to each behavior and cluster of behaviors, based largely on the context within which it occurred and the result it achieved in the sequential shaping of the interaction. We wanted to avoid the classic event recording that had been used to characterize mother-infant interaction behavior in the past. In other kinds of film studies, both event recording and narrative record tended to equate interactions that seem importantly different.

The interaction we described in this study became delineated by the nature of our study. The mothers were "programmed" to seek *attention* from their infants. No amount of reassurance from the observers could counteract the set in each mother's mind that she was expected to bring her infant into a period of constant attention to her and her maneuvers. Hence the laboratory test situation became a period of heightened attention-getting behavior on the mother's part. The anxiety about performance and being observed seemed to be translated into behavior in different ways by each mother. Although we do not presume to think that this filmed behavior is representative of all interactional behavior for each mother, we can assume that it is an example of the behavior she used under certain kinds of stress to produce attention in her infant. In this way it may be a sample of behavior to which the infant must *learn* to react.

We felt that we saw evidence in the infants' responses that demonstrated their awareness of unusual conditions in the laboratory setting. For example, smiling and vocalizing were difficult to produce in the laboratory at a time when they were already responding at home. Our impression was that we were not seeing unusual behavior, but a distortion of each infant's behavior which was characteristic under tension-producing circumstances. A parallel study of filmed interaction at home without the tension-producing qualities of a laboratory would be helpful to establish this.

Our most striking observation was that there were two very different patterns of attentional behavior present early in each infant, which were called upon in response to an object versus a familiar person. These two patterns seemed to be governed by the different kinds of attention and expectancy present as early as we saw these babies. These two modes may be represented in the neonatal period, and their anlage can be seen in the neonate's differential alerting reactions to a human voice versus a similar but nonhuman sound, as well as a human face versus a representative of a human face. Even in a neonate, the intensity and duration of attention seem to be clinically different. Habituation studies, such as studies of attention using cardiac deceleration and other autonomic measures, should establish these differences in time.

At any rate, if there are two differentiated pathways set up in early infancy—with intrauterine preconditioning to human stimuli as fuel for shaping them—we might explain some of the evidence for reactions of the infant to mothering cues, which set off complex reactions in the infant and may fit into a kind of readiness for "imprinting" behavior, as well as reactions to violation of expectancy, which are seen as early as four weeks (Aaronson and Tronick, 1970; E. Tronick, 1972, personal communication). Certainly, the pathways for complex behavior, such as imprintinglike responses, habituation to novel and familiar objects, and expectancy of familiar patterns, may be inborn, and little else in the way of an explanation may be necessary. But if the cue value of a human response is received and treated differently by the infant because of his experience in the uterus, as opposed to the cues of a nonresponsive object, there may be earlier integration and expectancy of interaction cues than we have heretofore credited the infant with.

Evidence for a different degree and duration of attention, as well as disruption of attention, with the mother and with the object was certainly observable in all our infants as early as two to three weeks. The physiological demands of such attention and recovery from the periods of attention appeared to be very different in the two modes of interaction. How they may reinforce each other as the infant "learns" to overcome interfering motor behavior in order to attend to his environment must be the crux of any study that emphasizes the importance of a nurturing environment to an infant's capacity for cognitive acquisitions. They did not appear to be competing patterns in these infants. The mother tends to provide a "holding" framework for her own cues. That is, she holds the infant with her hands, with her eyes, with her voice and smile, and with changes from one modality to another as he habituates to one or another. All these holding experiences are opportunities for the infant to learn how to contain *himself,* how to control motor responses, and how to attend for longer and longer periods. They amount to a kind of learning about organization of behavior in order to attend. With more disruptive mothering or with none at all, one might expect this kind of learning about self-organization to be delayed. In a disturbed environment not only would the experiences that contribute to learning in the sphere of social interaction be sparse, but the crossover to learning the organization necessary for cognitive acquisitions might not be provided. Hence learning would be delayed in an infant who had to acquire this organization by maturation alone, without appropriate environmental experiences. We felt we saw some of the possible variations for such learning in these five infants. In the cases in which mothers were not as sensitive to the attentional organization of their infants, and regularly added more behavior of their own when the infant tried to withdraw his attention, we felt that the periods of attention did not increase over time in the same way they did for the infants of the more sensitive mothers. Our study did not provide evidence for assessing whether this made any real difference in cognitive development among these five babies. We did see evidence for the development of very different interactive styles. Although our focus was not on individual differences but on the regularities in an interaction system between mothers and infants, we were drawn into comparisons of styles and conjectures as to their significance for the infant's future development. A future study should be reserved to follow up the many questions raised in this all-too-brief follow-up.

Some of the questions about mothering styles might be answered by a more detailed analysis of individual differences. Contingency scores did not detect these differences, nor explain the effect on the infant's responsive behavior. The areas in which differences in the mothers' behaviors seemed to produce a difference in outcome of the infants' responses are:

1. *Individual variations in use of specific behaviors.* The choice of behavior may depend on a mother's individual preference for a particular behavior, as well as the specificity in her mind as she uses it. In the first instance, one mother may use a caressing kind of contact in preference to holding, which may be characteristic of another mother. The effect on the infant is likely to differ in quality of response over time, if not in quantity. The specificity of her behavior at any time may be tuned to a learned expectation of the infant's response. For example, some mothers smile at their infants, not intending to evoke a response. No change in their facial expression is noted when their

infant fails to smile, or even cries. In others the intent to evoke a returning smile can be inferred from succeeding behaviors. If a mother smiles, receives no response, and then slowly leans back with a slight frown and a down-turned mouth, we may infer that she smiled with the intention of eliciting a smile in response.

Two mothers whose scores for percentage of time spent smiling, vocalizing, touching, and so on were equal might differ in their individual expectation for the behavior, one using it as a specific response to a specific type of situation, and the other using it nonspecifically. One of our mothers, for example, smiled with pleasure or amusement but not in response to specific infant behaviors; another smiled almost exclusively in response to specific performances, such as a first smile, a first vocalization, a first directed touch. Contingency scores did not differentiate these mothers. Under these conditions a high contingency of smiling with any particular infant behavior was not expected.

2. *The substitution of behaviors to gain a response.* Some mothers tried one thing over and over in order to gain a response, while others substituted one behavior for another. Again, using our example of smiling, some mothers seemed to try smiling over and over to elicit smiling. Others vocalized, or touched in a playful way, or assumed exaggerated expressions. Some engaged in a series of differing behaviors to the end of producing one type of response in the infant.

3. *Qualities of a specific behavior that change its meaning.* (a) *Force.* For example, a series of light pats on the cheek differ radically from a series of heavy, forceful pats. Light pats bring out an alerting response, whereas infants attempt to withdraw from the latter. (b) *Tempo.* Quantitative changes in the tempo of the mother's physical contact seem to occasion qualitative shifts in the "meaning" of the communication to the infant. A slow movement on the part of the mother may fit into the infant's present rhythms. For instance, we have observed the mother move an arm up and down in synchrony with the infant's kicking. As such it became a soothing form of communication. Movement made at the same speed might serve to alert the infant if he were not moving. Accelerated, it might disrupt the infant's ongoing state. In another modality two mothers may spend equal amounts of time vocalizing, but one may speak more slowly than the other, and the effects on the infant cannot be expected to be equal. Infant tempo (activity level) may in turn affect maternal tempo. In our study we found that the two infants whose tempo was most distinctly slow had mothers who communicated at an accelerated tempo, as if they were attempting to change that of their infants. (c) *Distance.* The face-to-face distance kept between mother and infant is not only an important variable in itself, but one that influences the effect of other

variables. Rapid vocalizations from a distance may be less imposing than rapid vocalizations made close to the infant. Certain behaviors can be classified as "close" behaviors—for example, leaning forward, moving into the infant's line of vision, kissing, touching, holding, and adjusting. Others may be more effective at a distance, and are "distance" behaviors—vocalizing, smiling, looking, bobbing, and facial and hand gestures. The characteristics of a mother's distancing may play a role in shaping the interaction behavior in her baby.

4. *Patterns of behaviors*. One of the most interesting questions concerned the patterns of behaviors mothers used to elicit responses from their infants. Some mothers seemed to have a tendency to cluster certain behaviors together in a regular functional unit. The form of the cluster might vary from time to time, and the final behavior that appeared to trigger the infant's response could no longer be considered the stimulus by itself. The importance of the cluster in eliciting his response became more obvious as one analyzed the interaction behaviors.

The context or background for the behavior, the cluster within which it was embedded, as well as its timing in the building up of behaviors, might better explain its trigger effect in producing a contingent response. Certainly, these factors seemed to be more important in understanding our data than were more simplified looks at one modality in the mother and a similar modality in the infant.

Ethological descriptions could encompass the patterns of behavior, as well as the context of their occurrence. We felt and do feel the need for an analytic method that can sort out the patterns we recorded at a descriptive level. Patterns of behavior in a cluster analysis, with some measure of their substitutability for each other, might lead to a better way of documenting individual differences and their outcomes. This kind of analysis will be the goal of future research.

The opportunity to observe the development of these five pairs over 20 weeks impressed us with the need for rule learning in a mother-infant dyad. Each member seemed to need to "learn" the nuances of behavior patterns of the other member of the dyad. Although the psychic energy for learning about the other member must be mobilized during pregnancy and around delivery for the mother, an "imprinting" model, as suggested by Bowlby (1968) and others (Klaus et al., 1972), seems too simple to explain a developing relationship. There seemed to be rules for interaction which were constantly being altered by each member of the dyad, and flexibility and change were necessary for maintaining optimal interaction.

One of the most important rules was concerned with the mother's sensitivity to the baby's capacity for attention and nonattention. In the early weeks this resembled a homeostatic model. We felt that these early weeks provided her with an opportunity for learning the rules about his homeostatic needs in terms of attention and nonattention, as well as purely physiological parameters such as feeding, temperature control, elimination, or restriction of disturbing activity. If her own needs interfere with a sensitivity to his, it might be reflected at this level in their interaction. We hope to develop a system for recording and analyzing mother-infant interactions that will establish her capacity to attend to her infant's needs at this level, which may be of diagnostic value in determining the degree of potential pathology or strength in the relationship. The parallel between the attention-nonattention model and homeostatic functioning of most systems of the infant's body raises the question of how learning in one such mode can be transferred to another mode. If there is an inability to learn reciprocity in this mode, might it not affect the infant's psychological functioning in other modalities?

There are many opportunities for rule learning for the mother. She not only learns the limits for expecting attention and responses from him, but must learn which of her behaviors set up an expectancy of interaction, which "hold" him, which produce his responses, which echo his, and which activate or deactivate him in relation to further goals. The timing of these is important (Chapple, 1970; Kimberly, 1970; C. D. Wilson and Lewis, 1971), but the qualitative aspects of each of her behaviors may be equally important. The type of stimulus, its force, its rhythm, its location, and its duration were powerful qualities in setting the tone of reactions in the infant. Although this may look as if it were "unlearned" behavior in some mothers, the failure to learn it by other mothers may demonstrate the fact that it can be a kind of rule learning. The individuality of each member of the dyad determines the flexibility in the number of rules necessary, and also sets the limits on the variability within each rule that still allows the goal to be achieved.

Another rule is that the mother use her periods of interaction to "model" the baby to become more and more complex. She times the complexity of her models to his stage of development. For example, in the early weeks imitation of his activity is limited and enlarged upon by her. This must serve as a feedback mechanism for him (Bruner, 1971), but one that enlarges upon his awareness of his behavior. He becomes aware of his action, visualizes her imitation of it, and reproduces it for himself again. As he does so, he has the opportunity to add on to it, either by serendipity or by modeling his behavior to match her enlarged version. Either way, he increases its scope. When simple imitation no longer serves her purpose, she provides more than imitative behavior with new goals for him, which leads him into new clusters of behavior and new kinds of learning. The timing of such imitative reinforcement and her sensitivity to his capacity for attention and learning must depend on her having learned this "rule" about him—that concerning his capacity to accept visually her feedback and to use it as a method for further acquisition. The shaping of his curves of attention by sensitive use of behavior on her part might then reflect his ability to "learn" how to attend, and the interdependence of this ability on the sensitivity of his environment.

This interdependence of rhythms seemed to be at the root of "attachment," as well as communication. When the balance was sympathetic to the needs of each member of the dyad, there was a sense of rhythmic interaction, which an observer sensed as "positive." When the balance was not equalized, and one member was out of phase with the other, there seemed to be a "negative" quality to the entire interaction. At the periods of new acquisitions (e.g., at eight and 12 weeks) when the infant was out of phase, the mother reflected the stress she felt in not being able to communicate. As she readjusted or waited for the infant's readjustment, subsequent weeks reflected the re-establishment of a kind of synchrony between them. Sander (1970) says that "each new thrust of activity in the growing infant requires a new period of interactional adjustment with the caretaking environment to reach stable co-ordination on the bases of new changes" (p. 330). The smoothness with which these dyads made such adjustments reflected the depth of their attachment and probably contributed a further opportunity for learning about the other member. Certainly, the strength of the interdependence of the dyad seemed to be more powerful in shaping each member's behavior than did any other force—such as the individual member's style or wish of the moment.

The infant also learns many rules—about his environment and about himself. As he learns how to interact with and master his own physiological needs he frees himself to attend to his external world. In learning how to achieve this kind of control, he learns the rudiments of "ego" function.

We have not answered our questions about the evolution of individuality, or about the relative contribution of each member of the dyad to the interaction. But we have raised questions about how they may be assessed in future studies.

4

INTRODUCTION

Human Behavior Cytogenetics: Review of Psychopathology in Three Syndromes—47,XXY; 47,XYY; and 45,X, by John Money

It is easy to forget that it is barely two decades ago that Tjio and Levan (1956) first demonstrated that humans had 46 chromosomes. A variety of factors divert attention from recalling the relative newness of karyotyping. Among them are the appearance of several scientific journals devoted to behavioral genetics, the headlines in the popular media that have accompanied so many of the findings in the field, and the lively debate stimulated by the ideas of sociobiologists (E. O. Wilson, 1975).

With the notable exception of Down's syndrome (in which karyotyping has demonstrated that marked mental retardation is not invariably a part of the syndrome), the significant chromosomal abnormalities in humans that survive beyond infancy involve the sex chromosomes. This is the subject of the following review by John Money, who has contributed significantly to our knowledge of human development from both the innate and the experiential perspectives. He has pointed to sex of assignment and rearing as potent determinants of sexual orientation in the face of ambiguous or contrary physical indicators (see Chapter 5 by Money and Money, Hampson, and Hampson, 1955; as well as Chapter 6 by Green).

Although the data are scanty and in some respects frustratingly superficial, it is vital to view what is known about behavioral cytogenetics in perspective. This need is highlighted by the tendency to either neglect genetic factors completely or to overemphasize them. For many mental health clinicians, in fact, the major source of information about behavioral genetics has been television and the Sunday magazine section. Indeed, Money illustrates below how a stereotyped myth about the XYY male has grown in such soil. Nevertheless, despite the media inaccuracies, it would be dishonest to ignore the apparent effect of the extra Y chromosome on behavior (L. I. Gardner and Neu, 1972).

It is easy to sense the impetus for developing such a myth. After all, the promise of a genetic test to predict aggressive behavior or antisocial tendencies represents the ultimate in the longstanding search for means to identify potential delinquents and criminals. It is tempting to reason that because females have an XX chromosome pattern and males an XY one, that an additional Y chromosome will increase the likelihood of aggressive behavior. Following such a speculation, Montague (1968) has suggested that it may be desirable to type all infants chromosomally at birth or shortly thereafter in order to implement preventive measures at an early age. The problems inherent in such a proposal are mind-boggling.

Since the XYY abnormality was first reported in the 1960s, such men have been described as tall, mentally dull, and prone to dangerous aggressive behavior. This description reminds one of what Lombroso said a century earlier in his attempt to identify the "criminal man" by atavistic morphological features (see Lombroso, 1876, 1911). But whether the frequency of XYY males is significantly higher in penal or mental institutions and, more important, whether there is any association between this karyotype and aggressive antisocial behavior or lower intelligence remain the subject of widespread public and scientific controversy. As Kopelman (1978) points out, the XYY research was intended to contribute to elucidating the behavioral characteristics of specific genotypes and of preventing or treating abnormal behavior that might be associated with them. She notes that this hope impelled agencies such as the Crime and Delinquency Division of the National Institute of Mental Health and the Law Enforcement Assistance Administration to support the XYY studies. But questions about the worthiness and ethical justifiability of some of the studies persist. The most impassioned arguments have arisen over studies involving infants, who are unable to give their consent to participate; there have even been instances in which infants and children were studied without parental consent. Furthermore, the research is nontherapeutic; uncertain future hopes do not transform research into therapy. What about the risk of stigmatization, loss of self-esteem, invasion of privacy, and prejudicial treatment? Without the benefit of scientific consensus, a child may be placed at risk of uncalled-for reactions from parents, school personnel, physicians, and countless others because of a presumption of future sociopathic behavior. What justification is there for discrimination in parole decisions for men identified as having the XYY karyotype as compared to men with similar behavior, but with an XY karyotype?

Reading Money's recapitulation below of how easy it is for a myth to develop and how difficult it can be to undo should prove sobering. Elsewhere,

Money (1975) decries generalizations that overlook either the individual or the wide variability within a particular syndrome. He describes a study of 38 cases of Turner's syndrome with a normal curve on the Wechsler verbal intelligence scale, but with a lower performance level in conjunction with a specific disability for perception and conceptualization of space-form relations, apparently related to right-left disorientation and dyscalculia. Such delineation of specific neuropsychological deficits points to the need to analyze both cognitive strengths and weaknesses, instead of assuming a global deficiency. (See the introductory comments on right/left hemispheric functional differentiation preceding Chapters 25 by Makita and 26 by Symmes and Rapoport.)

Another thrust in the literature stems from studies of chromosomes in psychiatric disorders. There is reason to suspect a genetic basis for certain childhood psychoses (see Chapters 39 by Rutter and 40 by Fish, as well as Judd and Mandell, 1968) and for hyperactivity in children (Cantwell, 1976; Warren et al., 1971). Some studies have indicated that there are a larger number of chromosomal variants in unselected, hospitalized child psychiatric patients than in control groups of children hospitalized for nonpsychiatric reasons or in large, unselected newborn populations (Say et al., 1977).

The following chapter calls attention to the fact that the cytogenetic disorders of childhood are highly variable in their relationship to intelligence and behavior. Hasty conclusions, based on studies of institutionalized subjects, can produce serious errors which are then taken for granted. Conclusions regarding the significance of behavioral differences in people with chromosomal variations clearly have to remain tentative and should probably be suspected of bias until improved mass-screening methods become available. But here more than mere scientific questions are involved. As noted above, the complex ethical and legal issues inherent in genetic screening, and the handling of information derived from it, often overshadow the substantive findings as subjects of lively debate.

4

Human Behavior Cytogenetics: Review of Psychopathology in Three Syndromes—47,XXY; 47,XYY; and 45,X

JOHN MONEY

INTRODUCTION AND PURPOSE

Since its inception in 1951, the psychohormonal research unit of the pediatric endocrine clinic at the Johns Hopkins Hospital and School of Medicine has been a center for collecting developmental behavioral data on endocrine syndromes, some of which have, since 1951, been discovered to be not only endocrine, but also cytogenetic in origin. Thus, some of the case records originally assembled under only an endocrine diagnosis subsequently proved to constitute, in fact, raw data for behavioral cytogenetics.

Before the technique of actually visualizing and counting chromosomes in man was established in 1959, no syndrome, endocrine or otherwise, could be identified on the basis of its specific cytogenetic anomaly. Anomalies of the sex chromatin or Barr body (K. L. Moore, 1966) had, however, by 1953 established that Klinefelter's syndrome and Turner's syndrome are associated with an anomaly of chromosomal material. Both syndromes had still earlier been among those identifiable on the basis of symptoms of endocrine dysfunction and associated congenital stigmata. By contrast, the 47,XYY syndrome, lacking pathognomonic endocrine or other stigmata, was not recognizable as an entity until after the first XYY karyotype was reported in 1961 by Sandberg and co-workers.

The purpose of the present paper is to present a review of the three syn-

First published in *The Journal of Sex Research*, 11:181–200, 1975. Reprinted by permission. Supported by grant USPHS HD-00325, and by funds from the Grant Foundation.

dromes, Klinefelter's (47,XXY), 47,XYY, and Turner's (45,X), with respect to behavioral disability. The review will draw on published and unpublished material from the psychohormonal research unit at Johns Hopkins, and the published studies of others.

47, XXY (KLINEFELTER'S) SYNDROME

INCIDENCE AND PREVALENCE DATA: 47,XXY AND BEHAVIOR

Incidence studies of the frequency of the 47,XXY karyotype in morphological males at birth show fair agreement in estimating the ratio at 1:500 (Hambert, 1966; N. MacLean et al., 1968; Nielsen, 1969). There have been no long-term developmental behavioral studies of a prospective nature, so that one lacks a definitive answer regarding the occurrence of developmental behavioral disabilities, or their absence, in a random sample or a census of XXY individuals. The likelihood of an increased prevalence of some degree of behavioral disability among XXY individuals has been established, however, on the basis of survey statistics.

It was early recognized that the prevalence of the XXY karyotype is high among institutionalized, mentally retarded males. The pooled result of a number of surveys yields an estimated ratio of 1:50 (Hambert, 1966; Nielsen, 1969). The corresponding estimate among psychiatrically institutionalized males is 1:150 (Nielsen, 1969), the exact proportion in any one survey depending on whether psychiatric disorder combined with mental retardation is included or not. Some psychiatrically disturbed XXY men are placed in maximum security hospitals or institutions for defective delinquents (D. Baker et al., 1970). The prevalence statistic for these institutions is inadequately ascertained but is probably around 1:150 (Hook, 1973). The prevalence of XXY men in regular prisons has not been definitively ascertained. In Maryland it appears to be no greater than 1:500, which is the same proportion as in the population at large (D. S. Borgaonkar, personal communication).

These various prevalence statistics indicate that members of the XXY population of morphological males constitute a population at risk with respect to developmental behavioral disability that may destine them to institutionalization as mental retardates, psychiatric patients, or law breakers with some degree of psychiatric disability. Prevalence statistics of the above type do not indicate the distribution of risk in the XXY population at large, nor the degree or type of disability likely to manifest itself in this population. Here again, for a complete answer, one must await a statistically acceptable, prospective developmental study. In the meantime, it is well documented that many XXY men do not become institutionalized.

COMPARISON WITH CONTRAST GROUP

Some comparative information has been obtained from an investigative design in which an XXY and a matched contrast group were compared. This design has been used by Wakeling (1972) in a study of 11 XXY and 11 XY hypogonadal men admitted to a British psychiatric hospital, and by Nielsen and Thielgaard and their co-workers in a Danish study (Nielsen et al., 1970; Thielgaard et al., 1971).

The Danish investigators obtained a sample of 34 XXY men from an outpatient clinic for hypogonadal men (not a psychiatric clinic) and matched them with a contrast sample of 16 hypogonadal men from the same clinic with the 46,XY karyotype. Statistical comparison between the two groups was made on the basis of behavior checklists and symptom ratings. The two groups were also compared on the basis of psychological test scores. These comparisons were made blindly, without knowledge of each patient's cyto-genetic diagnosis. Both sets of comparisons showed a statistically significant difference between the two groups—a difference that points to the greater vulnerability of the XXY group to some degree of behavioral disability.

Nielsen, Thielgaard, and their co-workers did not find any special likelihood that a given behavioral diagnosis would correlate with the XXY diagnosis. Their outpatient sample, as one would expect, lacked major, incapacitating signs of behavioral disability. The number of minor signs per patient was higher in the 34 XXY than in the 16 XY hypogonadal men, the mean psychiatric weighted scores for the two groups being, respectively, 9.3 ± 5.4 and 1.2 ± 1.3. Fifteen different behavioral criteria were used in arriving at these scores. In order of their statistically differentiating significance they were as follows: immature, school performance below average, weak sexual libido, few or no friends, previously mentally ill, older than 20 and never had sexual intercourse, little energy and initiative, insecure, few or no spare-time interests, word blind, poor relations with parents or siblings, vocationally unskilled laborer, boastful and self-assertive behavior, unexacting work, and present mental illness.

In the absence of a standard taxonomy of human behavior, the Nielsen group developed their own list of 15 traits. Other clinicians before them had reported more anecdotal impressions of the behavior of XXY men. All show fair agreement, despite the lack of a standard system of behavioral classification and nomenclature.

Major symptoms of behavioral disability of the type found in XXY men in psychiatric institutions have shown the same nosological diversity as major symptoms of XY men in the same institutions, with no single diagnosis predominating. As culled from many sources, the disabilities include: schizophrenia, paranoia, pseudologia fantastica, transsexualism, depression, suicidism, obsessional anxiety, phobia, alcoholism, criminal delinquency, sex offenses, epilepsy, gross mental deficiency, and others.

SEXUAL APATHY, FATIGABILITY, AND LOW ASSERTION

All the behavioral traits, except major psychiatric symptoms, that have been attributed to men with the XXY syndrome would appear to be secondary to three basic conditions or characteristics of the syndrome: sexual apathy, easy fatigability, and low dominance assertion. These three characteristics create an impression of what, in the older French literature, was called neurasthenia and, in the U.S. literature today, is often referred to as inadequate personality.

All three characteristics may be seen as stemming from a common origin in insensitivity or hyporesponsiveness of XXY cells to androgen. The basis of this statement lies in the well-known clinical facts of the XXY syndrome at puberty, namely, that the onset of puberty may be relatively tardy and that adult virilization is typically below average, or even inadequate. Moreover, in some cases, as also occurs in the 46,XY syndrome of androgen insensitivity, estrogen in amounts normally produced by the male testis is sufficient to feminize the breasts and hips of XXY adolescents (requiring surgery to flatten the chest). The amount of the ejaculate, per emission, was below par in 40% of XXY cases, according to the study of Sipova and Raboch (1961), and in that 40% sexual apathy was increased. Sterility is standard and is consequent on degeneration of the seminiferous tubules of the testes.

Although the plasma testosterone levels of XXY men are usually measured as being within normal range, in some patients, if not all, it is possible to get a positive response by injecting long-acting testosterone enanthate in an amount (300 mg every four weeks) sufficient to be a complete replacement dosage for a castrate. The positive response is mild and is manifested as an increased frequency of erotic imagery and initiative, improved feeling of well-being, strength and energy, and decreased fatigue and sleepiness.

In response to testosterone therapy, there is no corresponding increase of dominance assertion sufficient to be clearly observed. One may speculate here to the effect that dominance assertion is dependent, initially, on androgenization of certain limbic system pathways in the brain in fetal life. Cellular resistance to androgen during the critical fetal period might well result in a permanent deficit in dominance assertion.

VULNERABILITY TO BEHAVIORAL DISABILITY

Resistance or hyporesponsiveness of the cells of the central nervous system to androgen at the critical phase of fetal life when the fetal testes produce this hormone is, hypothetically, one explanation for the high risk of behavioral disability in the XXY syndrome. Though it sounds far-fetched, this hypothesis is tenable in view of the preliminary evidence (summarized in Money, 1971) that an excess of fetal androgen enhances IQ. The degree to which the XXY fetus is destined to become IQ deficient might be a function of the degree of XXY cellular resistance to androgen.

It is purely speculative as to whether other symptoms of behavioral disability, including epilepsy and related EEG abnormality, might be fetally androgen-related when they occur in the XXY syndrome. The very diversity of these symptoms in association with a supernumerary X chromosome does open for inquiry the interesting possibility that all psychiatric symptoms ultimately share a common mechanism of cellular malfunction in their etiology. Regardless of the role that fetal androgen may or may not play in the etiology of behavioral disability in the XXY syndrome, it seems perfectly obvious that the extra X chromosome in the nucleus of every cell of the brain somehow or other makes the organism more vulnerable to the risk of developmental behavioral disability.

In some XXY cases, it would appear that all the risk lies in the brain cells themselves. In others, it appears that the major risk lies in whether the postnatal environment, including the social environment, will be benign or malignant. It is easy to push an XXY boy over the edge, so to speak, and to multiply behavioral disability, by rearing him in an environment of behavioral pathology. Another XXY boy may become behaviorally disabled, despite a nonpathological environment. In this respect, it is of some relevance that Nielsen (1969) could not find a relationship between psychopathology in the XXY syndrome and what he called disharmony in childhood, or father's or brother's employment, patient's employment, number of siblings, parental age, or incidence of mental illness or mental retardation in parents or siblings.

It is possible that the years of puberty and adolescence are years of special, though not exclusive, risk for the development of behavioral disability, especially for those XXY boys whose bodies virilize poorly or whose sexual apathy makes them feel socially outcast. There is no solid evidence one way or the other on this issue at present, primarily because of an insufficiency of longitudinal studies. It is likely that the decisive factor is not inadequate adolescent development per se, but the way in which other people react to it and the pressure that they may bring to bear on the boy.

47,XYY SYNDROME

INCIDENCE AND PREVALENCE DATA: 47,XYY AND BEHAVIOR

Incidence studies of the frequency of the 47,XYY karyotype in morphological males at birth were laboriously slow and expensive until the discovery in 1970 of the fluorescent staining (quinacrine mustard) technique for rapid screening of Y chromosomes (Pearson and Bobrow, 1970). Today, progress is further hindered in the U.S., in the aftermath of antiscientism from the mass media and the American Civil Liberties Union, both misguidedly claiming that karyotyping of infants will lead to their being branded guilty of criminality by karyotype, before they are even old enough to commit a crime.

At present, therefore, the frequency incidence of XYY in the newborn is uncertain. Different studies have produced incidence ratios varying from 0:2000 to 1:1000 to 1:250. A summation of all studies suggests a provisional figure of 1:975 births (Hook, 1973).

As in the case of the XXY syndrome, there have been no prospective studies of XYY behavioral development. One has, as yet, no definitive answer regarding the occurrence or absence of developmental behavioral disabilities in a random sample or census of XYY individuals.

Behavioral disabilities in the case of both the XXY and the XYY karyotypes became unjustifiably stereotyped because of the types of institutions in which the karyotype first became easy to find. Thus, XXY became the mental retardation karyotype and XYY the aggression karyotype. The XYY behavioral stereotype began with the title of the first report by Jacobs et al. (1965): "Aggressive Behavior, Mental Subnormality and the XYY Male." The purpose of the paper was "to report our findings in a survey of mentally subnormal male patients with dangerous, violent or criminal propensities in an institution where they are treated under conditions of special security." Unfortunately for the history of behavioral genetics, no effort was made to check the actual behavior of the XYY males concerned. It was defined according to the stereotype specified for inmates of the institution, which was later found not to be entirely correct (Jacobs et al., 1968; Price and Whatmore, 1967).

The media took up the stereotype. Almost overnight the supernumerary Y chromosome became, alas, the crime chromosome. Prevalence studies were, for the next few years, directed toward tall males in jails or institutions for delinquents or the criminally insane. Today, in consequence, prevalence statistics are informative only with respect to XYY men who have gotten into trouble with the law. Information about those who do not tangle with the law is either negligible or anecdotal, and not statistically systematic. Nonetheless, it is of significant importance to know that some quiet-living XYY men have been discovered. Noel and Revil (1974), for instance, found no XYY men in a maximum-security military prison in France, but two of them among young recruits who were assigned to guard duty and had no history of behavioral disability.

The most recent statistics regarding XYY prevalence studies are those cited by Hook (1973). He reviewed 36 studies conducted in penal institutions of the maximum-security type, designated as for the criminally insane or for defective delinquents. In 22 of the 36 institutions, frequency of the XYY karyotype was higher than the ratio of 1:975 in the newborn (p = .006), in seven lower, and in seven uncertain. These findings are biased, however, insofar as in many institutional surveys only tall inmates were karyotyped. This bias was avoided in 20 surveys ranging geographically over Europe, the U.S., Canada, and Australia. Pooling the data from these 20 surveys, Hook estimated carriers of the XYY karyotype to be 1:50 or 2% of the men in the institutions surveyed.

This prevalence rate of 1:50 is notably higher than that obtained from surveys conducted in regular (nonpsychiatric) prisons or in nonpenal psychiatric hospitals. Figures for the latter are meager and inconclusive. For regular prisons, Hook's review of 26 studies disclosed that in nine the prevalence of XYY was higher than among the newborn; in twelve, lower; and in five, inconclusive.

As in the case of nonpenal psychiatric hospitals, so also in the case of nonpenal institutions for the mentally retarded: XYY prevalence figures are meager and inconclusive. The frequency of low IQ in the XYY male is an unknown. Nonetheless, it is known that average and high IQs are compatible with the XYY genotype, and it is likely that high IQ occurs more frequently in the XYY syndrome than in the XXY syndrome, in which it may also occur. No final, confirmatory statement is possible, however, until more data are obtained.

Conjectures about behavior made on the basis of the kind of institution in which XYY individuals are segregated are poor substitutes for actual biographical behavioral data. Published XYY behavioral studies are very few. They are still mostly at the phenomenological stage. The observations and recordings of behavior in XYY men are from samples known to be highly biased in favor of behavioral disability, by reason of their institutional location and/or ascertainment procedure (Court Brown, 1968; Court Brown, Price, and Jacobs, 1968; Daly, 1969; Jacobs et al., 1968; Kessler and Moos, 1970; Money, Gaskin, and Hull, 1970; D. R. Owen, 1973; Price and Jacobs, 1970; Price and Whatmore, 1967; Raffaelli, 1972). It has not yet been possible to assemble a random behavioral sample from the XYY population at large, since the latter has not been identified. Also, there has been no contrast group in an XYY behavioral study to correspond to the hypogonadal males used by Nielsen and associates for comparison with XXY patients.

COMPARISON WITH CONTRAST GROUPS

Contrast or comparison groups for behavioral XYY studies, when used, have been of two types: a matched group of XY prisoners from the same institution in which the XYY men were incarcerated (as in the study by Price and Whatmore, 1967) and a matched group of XXY prisoners (D. Baker et al., 1970) or of XXY patients not in prison (Money et al., 1974).

Comparison of matched institutionalized XYY and XY groups has shown, in the final analysis, more behavioral similarity than difference between them. However, some differences have been reported. Price and Whatmore (1967) found the mean age of first arrest was lower for XYY than XY cases—13 versus 18 years, respectively. The records of XYY showed fewer convictions for crimes of violence against persons than those of XY prisoners—9% versus 22% of convictions, respectively. The XYY prisoners had more convictions for stealing and destruction of property. The siblings of XYY were less likely than those of XY prisoners to have criminal records—1:31 (one theft) versus 13:63 (13 siblings in seven families with a total of 139 convictions), respectively. This finding is consistent with the hypothesis that XYY behavioral disability is less dependent on siblings' shared social and family environment than is corresponding disability in matched XY cases. The finding is further consistent with a sociological survey of the census of 15 Johns Hopkins XYY cases (Franzke, 1972), which indicated that family socioeconomic level related to XYY behavioral disability on only one variable, namely, availability of medical (psychiatric) instead of penal treatment. Juvenile case studies, rare as they are (Cowie and Kahn, 1968; Money, 1970; and one unpublished case) would seem to indicate that at least some XYY boys show behavioral disability that makes them not only a great problem in family management, but also quite disparate from other family members in their behavior together.

Comparison of XYY and XXY cases indicates that there may be some behavioral overlap, on the criterion of type of penal institution inhabited. By and large, however, differences are as impressive as similarities. Whereas XYY individuals are more likely to manifest behavioral disabilities that get them into trouble with society and the law because they infringe on the rights of other people, XXY individuals are more likely to be personally disabled or impaired behaviorally, and to need the supportive help of others (Money et al., 1974). For XXY people, society has provided the institutions of medicine and treatment, and for XYY people, the institutions of law and punishment.

BEHAVIORAL THRESHOLDS AND MATURATIONAL DELAY

So many investigators focused so much attention on aggression and criminality in the XYY syndrome that other behavioral traits were overlooked. The most noteworthy oversight, initially, was with respect to sexual behavior (Daly, 1969; D. Baker et al., 1970; Money, Gaskin, and Hull, 1970). In addition to consensual homosexuality or bisexuality, the incidence of socially uncondoned sexual behavior appears to be elevated. Reports of such behavior include bisexual child incest, pedophilia, voyeurism, exhibitionism, transvestism, indecent assault, sadomasochism, and, in one instance, sex murder.

Tabulating behavioral data from 31 published cases, plus four studied in detail at Johns Hopkins, Money, Gaskin, and Hull (1970) listed various forms of behavior that may prove to be pathognomonic, albeit not universally distributed in the XYY syndrome. The list is: difficult child, problems in school, excessive daydreaming, loner, drifter, unrealistic future expectations, impulsiveness, sudden violence and aggression, imprisonment, homosexual versus heterosexual experience, paraphilias.

If one searches for a common denominator of all the traits or disabilities of behavior, it may well be an impairment of the brain's function of inhibition at the threshold where image is translated into action. In more familiar terms, one says that XYY boys and men are highly impulsive, flighty in attention span, and not good at self-regulation of behavior.

Impulsive or poorly self-regulated behavior, as I have observed it in XYY individuals, ranges over a broad spectrum and is by no means confined to fighting, rage attacks, temper tantrums, destructive violence, and the like. It extends to the extreme of self-destructiveness in suicide. It includes also impulsive sexual behavior representing many of the paraphilias, impulsive love affairs, impulsive comradeship, impulsive giving, impulsive spending, impulsive stealing, impulsive mystical or religious experience, impulsive drug use, impulsive getting drunk, impulsive eating, impulsive sleeping, impulsive working spells, impulsive crying spells, and impulsive running away.

In ordinary behavioral development, one expects impulsive, poorly self-regulated behavior to be, in varying degree, characteristic of the years of infancy and immaturity. Such immaturity seems to be greatly prolonged in XYY individuals, so that in the years of young adulthood, for example, they are still behaving as juveniles or young adolescents. There is some evidence to suggest that they do eventually catch up in behavioral maturation, provided they survive the vicissitudes of the years of prolonged lagging behind.

VULNERABILITY TO BEHAVIORAL DISABILITY

By contrast with the XXY syndrome, there is no known endocrine or metabolic correlate of the XYY syndrome on which to build a speculative hypothesis as to the etiology of behavioral disability. After puberty, XYY androgen levels may be elevated, medium, or low (Baghdassarian et al., 1975; Migeon et al., 1975) so that behavioral disability cannot be attributed to excess androgen.

In a rather foolish way, there has been some published speculation to the effect that tall XYY youths may feel that they are awkward misfits because of their height, and may be punitively discriminated against because of it. Comparison of behavior in actual cases of tall and not-tall XYY youths and men rather discredits this speculation, and it is further discredited by the early age of onset of behavioral disability in some XYY infants.

There are some critics of behavioral genetics who would like to say, especially for legal purposes, that XYY people cannot be proved different from XY people, since not all XYY individuals are exactly alike. These critics miss the point that there is no cytogenetic syndrome in which all diagnosed cases are replicas of one another. In Turner's syndrome, for instance, the physical stigmata are variably distributed. Even in Down's syndrome, mental deficiency is not a *sine qua non* of trisomy 21, as was once believed.

Critics of behavioral genetics also point to the fact that XYY behavioral findings are not unique to the syndrome but can be matched in XY individuals, as for example on the issue of impulsiveness. The answer may well be that when the molecular biology of behavioral disability in the XYY syndrome is finally uncovered, it may prove to be the key to similar disability in XY individuals.

My personal disposition, despite the methodological incompleteness of current statistical data, is definitely to favor the hypothesis that XYY individuals constitute a population at risk for behavioral disability, with or without an abnormal EEG, related to impulsiveness in its varying manifestations. Developmentally, their disability can be, to some degree, ameliorated by a benign rearing environment, or aggravated by a socially malignant environment. In a benign environment, the parents and other responsible adults may need to be exceptionally well trained and counseled in child-rearing. Otherwise they themselves may be rendered behaviorally incompetent and disabled by the exceptional and taxing demands of the task of rearing an XYY boy.

45,X (TURNER'S) SYNDROME

INCIDENCE AND PREVALENCE: 45,X AND BEHAVIOR

Turner's syndrome, like the 47,XXY syndrome, can be brought to clinical attention cytogenetically in mass-screening studies of the sex chromatin or Barr body, which is present in 47,XXY and missing in 45,X. Mosaic (e.g., 45,X/46,XX) and related variants also occur. For present purposes, no distinction is made between 45,X and other variants since they appear to be behaviorally indistinguishable.

The incidence of Turner's syndrome is now widely agreed on as being 1:2500 live-born infants who look like morphological females.

Originally, Turner's syndrome was described as an endocrine entity characterized pathognomonically by statural growth failure and congenital absence of ovaries, which, in turn, dictated pubertal failure. Various other congenital defects might or might not be associated. Mental retardation was earlier specified as a likely defect, though in retrospect the occurrence of mental retardation in a sample of patients must be adjudged fortuitous.

Mental retardation hospitals have not proved likely hunting grounds for cases of Turner's syndrome (N. MacLean et al., 1968). However, IQ impairment may be wrongly construed in some Turner patients who have a specific disability for nonverbal or visuoconstructional intelligence, that is, a partial form of so-called space-form blindness akin to visual agnosia and constructional apraxia—a disability first discovered and documented in Turner's syndrome in the psychohormonal research unit at Johns Hopkins (Alexander, Ehrhardt, and Money, 1966; Alexander and Money, 1965, 1966; Alexander, Walker, and Money, 1964; Money, 1963, 1964, 1968, 1973; Money and Alexander, 1966; Money, Alexander, and Ehrhardt, 1966; Money and Granoff, 1965; Shaffer, 1962).

Patients with Turner's syndrome seldom are housed in institutions. They are no more likely to be housed in psychiatric or penal institutions than they are in institutions for the mentally retarded (N. MacLean et al., 1968). They grow up to be rather remarkably free of psychiatric complaints. The special features of their behavioral functioning have therefore been ascertained from sample populations referred to clinics (usually endocrine clinics) for short stature and/or pubertal failure, where they are maintained on follow-up estrogen replacement therapy in adulthood.

COMPARISON WITH CONTRAST GROUP

At the present time, the use of Turner's syndrome as a resource in behavioral cytogenetics is sufficiently new that little has been accomplished by way of comparison with control groups. Many behavioral findings are still largely phenomenological and descriptive. Other findings, namely, those obtained by means of standardized tests, have been evaluated against general population norms. Thus, the documentation of a specific space-form deficit in cognitive functioning (see above) was made possible by the use of tests with standardized norms. Likewise, conformity to the stereotype of the feminine role could be evaluated on standardized femininity scales (Ehrhardt, Greenberg, and Money, 1970; Garron, 1972; Money and Mittenthal, 1970; Shaffer, 1962). However, there are no tests or norms for many aspects of behavior that one wants to evaluate in Turner's syndrome—for example, the differential effect of short stature and delayed puberty, irrespective of cytogenetic anomaly, on selected behavioral variables. To make such evaluations, one must find a matched comparison or contrast group with a different diagnosis and etiology—no mean task in clinical logistics, in many instances.

One such comparison is with other diagnostic groups of short-stature individuals. Drash, Greenberg, and Money (1968) showed that in four syndromes of dwarfism the specific cognitive deficit peculiar to Turner's syndrome is not related to shortness per se, nor is the phlegmatic behavioral disposition. Garron (1972) similarly showed that short stature per se does not account for the same behavioral disposition assessed on the California Personality Inventory.

Another way of confirming behavioral findings as not being fortuitous, or an artifact of local observation, is to have them independently replicated in different clinical populations. The special features of cognitive functioning, namely, those associated with nonverbal intelligence, have not been replicated in Chicago or Stockholm (Garron et al., 1973), Leiden (Bekker and van Gemund, 1968), Copenhagen (Thielgaard, 1972), or Tel Aviv (J. J. Frankel and Z. Laron, personal communication).

There has been a similar replication of observations concerning relative freedom from behavioral disability manifested by Turner patients despite the adversities of appearance and pubertal physique that confront them (Engel and Forbes, 1965; Garron, 1972; Hampson, Hampson, and Money, 1955; Nielsen, 1970; Shaffer, 1962; Wallis, 1960).

Some other earlier reports were written without specifying the likelihood of sampling bias and from divergent ideological viewpoints. Thus, in some reports there has been too narrow a focus on body image and the motivational effects of short stature and pubertal failure, to the exclusion of behavioral genetic considerations.

My own studies (Money and Mittenthal, 1970) have led me to formulate the concept of what, for want of a more operational term, I have called inertia of emotional arousal in Turner's syndrome. This phlegmatic behavioral feature, instead of being negative, as one might have predicted, protects against the blows of adversity. As in the case of many other nonpathognomonic symptoms or features of the syndrome—for example, congenital heart or kidney defect, webbed neck, or space-form disability—inertia of emotional arousal is not a *sine qua non* of Turner's syndrome. There are some patients who develop symptoms of behavioral disability, but they are few in number—and remarkably few in view of the burden of growing up dwarfed in stature, pubertally deficient (until estrogen-treated, which is often late, in order to maximize statural growth), and, in many instances, not very attractive-looking. Their phlegmatic stoicism and stolidity in facing life is not simply a correlate of smallness (see above).

Space-Form Disability and Inertia of Emotional Arousal

There is no hypothesis by which to link space-form disability and inertia of emotional arousal in Turner's syndrome, other than that both may be derived from the cytogenetic error of a missing X chromosome. It is not presently possible to formulate a good hypothesis as to the mechanism whereby the genetic error eventually affects both aspects of behavior. One may conjecture a direct genetic effect on fetal brain development, possibly mediated by way of biogenic amine dysfunction, or an indirect effect mediated by absence of gonadal hormones during the fetal period of brain development.

The hypothesis of a direct genetic effect confronts one with a paradox regarding space-form disability, in that genetic males, with their one X chromosome, are considered, by and large, to be superior in space-form ability to genetic females, with their two X chromosomes. On the criterion of their having only one X chromosome, Turner patients should not manifest space-form disability as they do. The hypothesis of a fetal hormonal effect on the central nervous system circumvents this paradox, for Turner patients are not exposed to fetal testicular hormones as are genetic males, and they are also deprived of any as yet unknown effect from the fetal ovaries on the developing central nervous system of genetic females.

By extreme stretching of the scientific imagination, one might apply the same kind of reasoning to the issue of inertia of emotional arousal—except that there is no good evidence that genetic males are quicker in emotional arousal than are genetic females, especially in relation to the kinds of stress that life hands out to patients with Turner's syndrome, even though the arousal may be sex-stereotypic.

Vulnerability to Behavioral Disability

In their relative lack of symptoms of psychopathology, people with Turner's syndrome differ from, and have an advantage over, their counterparts in both the genetic male and genetic female population. They are not, however, totally invulnerable, in that some few individuals have shown major psychiatric symptoms (Christodorescu et al., 1970; Money, 1963; Money and Mittenthal, 1970; Sabbath et al., 1961), including suicidal depression, schizophrenia, and hysterical dissociation with multiple personality. In Money and Mittenthal's (1970) data, there tended to be a relationship between the incidence of life stress in the family and the incidence of psychopathology in the patient, though not invariably so. In these same data, there was also a relationship between delayed maturation of adolescent behavior in teenagers and delay in onset of pubertal hormonal therapy, both being related to age-inappropriate treatment by others.

EPILOGUE

The future growth and development of human behavioral cytogenetics—indeed, of human behavioral genetics in its entirety—needs a catalogue of human behavioral elements or entities, an agreed-upon nomenclature for them, and a logical system for their classification. There are animal behavioral models as a guide, for example, Frank Beach's catalogue of the elements of rodent copulatory behavior (see Money and Ehrhardt, 1972, pp. 66–67), but these models are themselves only a beginning and grossly incomplete. Another guide is the lexical model, with its catalogue of words and its grammatical nomenclature and classification.

The lexical model applies to vocal language. The analogous model we need will deal with the language of behavior, the proverbial actions that speak louder than words. Some actions are vocalizations, and some vocalizations are sentences, but sentences as behavior don't necessarily mean what they purport to say lexically. They have also a second meaning, carried in the tone of voice and accompanying facial and body gestures—the behavioral language.

The Babel that exists today in human behavioral genetics, as in behavioral science in general, stems from the fact that behavioral scientists and others have few conventions of agreement or consensus about behavioral language, its messages, and their decipherment. We are like explorers lost among a jungle people with a language never before heard, each of us with different lexical ideologies and principles as to how to decipher what the people are saying.

If we set our minds to the task, we will one day have a common tradition for the recording and scientific treatment of behavioral language in animals and men. It will require the sacrifice of some cherished ideologies, beliefs, and principles of ancient lineage, like motivation, drive, instinct, the unconscious, voluntary choice, emotion, feeling, and consciousness, but the achievement will be worth the effort.

SUMMARY

Behavioral stereotypes in the 47,XXY (Klinefelter's), 47,XYY, and 45,X (Turner's) syndromes have become established as a consequence of medical-sociological factors fortuitously associated with early studies of the syndromes. Thus, mental deficiency is the 47,XXY stereotype; aggression, criminality, and violence the 47,XYY stereotype; and delay of adolescent maturity the 45,X stereotype. The stereotypes persist, even when new data require their revision.

Severe mental deficiency may be a concomitant of the 47,XXY syndrome, though the IQ may also be normal or superior, and many other behavioral and psychiatric disabilities may also occur, including epilepsy, gross phobic anxiety, and schizophrenia. The supernumerary X chromosome would appear to unstabilize the central nervous system and make it vulnerable to developmental pathology, which ranges extensively over the psychiatric nosology from mild to severe.

In the 47,XYY syndrome, the stereotype, promulgated by the mass media, of aggressive, violent criminality is not confirmed, even in biased samples obtained by screening tall, institutionalized men. The two most commonly shared features of behavioral pathology in the XYY syndrome are general impulsiveness of reaction (not restricted to aggression) and delayed attainment of behavioral adulthood, with persistence of juvenile and adolescent behavior. There may be a greater than average incidence of bisexualism. The risk of mental retardation is not great. As in the 47,XXY syndrome, there is much variability between individuals, and some do not come to professional or institutional attention except as a result of cytogenetic screening of the general population. The frequency incidence of the 47,XYY syndrome has not yet been ascertained, but has been guessed at 1:750-1000 male births, on the basis of still incomplete studies.

In the 45,X (Turner's) syndrome, there is a high incidence of a specific cognitive disability manifested as partial space-form blindness and failure of direction sense. There may be a corresponding, though lesser disability with numbers. Verbal ability is not affected and may be superior. The frequency of mental retardation (on the criterion of full-scale IQ) is not increased. Despite the stigmatizing handicaps of short stature, agonadism, and the other possible congenital anomalies of the syndrome, there is a high incidence of mental health in girls and women with Turner's syndrome. Lack of psychopathology may be a function in part of the high incidence of a feature of behavior that may be called inertia of emotional arousal. This feature makes for stolidity and stability, even in the face of adversity, and even when proper prognostic counseling has not been available. Whether or not psychosexual maturation is delayed in Turner's syndrome is a function of the timing of estrogenic therapy to induce puberty and maintain hormonal maturity, combined with the effectiveness of counseling and guidance when delay is advised in the interest of increased statural growth. In Turner's syndrome, one has an example of the genetics not of psychopathology, but of psychological health. The incidence of the syndrome is 1:2500 female births.

5 and 6

INTRODUCTION

Nativism versus Culturalism in Gender-Identity Differentiation, by John Money
Sexual Identity: Research Strategies, by Richard Green

The following two chapters, by Money and by Green, are introduced in tandem. Together they present a needed multidimensional approach to the complex issue of gender identity. Our knowledge about human sexuality has been punctuated by the mystique enveloping certain findings and opinions. Some appear to be pure mythology, such as the alleged distinction between the presumably immature clitoral orgasm and the ostensibly more mature vaginal orgasm. Other findings seem valid, but opinion may accord them an inappropriate degree of primacy or even exclusiveness. Contributing to the confounding of sexual epistemology is the fact that ideas once discarded because of lack of evidence may regain prominence with enhanced technological sophistication, as Green discusses under the heading "Sexual Identity and Gonadal Hormones."

The disadvantage in these two selections' broad sweep is that the authors inevitably only touch lightly on most variables. But a detailed clinical or research report, whether by Money, Green, or a contributor of comparable stature like Stoller (1968), would focus on only one or at best a few of the variables, thereby perhaps reinforcing the prevalent tendency to premature closure. The reader who is stimulated to pursue any of the issues in greater depth is referred to the sources cited in Green's overview. If the reader desires a clinically oriented, concise statement of what is known about human sexuality, from prenatal infuences to geriatric manifestations, he or she can turn to the 200-page handbook published by the American Medical Association (1972).

Derived primarily from a series of experiments in nature, Money's contributions to the study of human sexuality are legion, as is noted in Green's subsequent overview (see also Money's Chapter 4 and Money and Ehrhardt, 1972). The selection reprinted here presents a data-based biopsychosocial statement on gender identity that is remarkably coherent. Money focuses on the prototypical development of two genetic and gonadal females with adrenogenital syndrome, one of whom was reared as a female while the other was reared as a male. These two case histories vividly and *accurately* depict the complex, multidimensional determinants of gender identity, despite the deceptively simple anecdotal style of presentation. Money's concise style here precludes his retracing the complex paths that led to his conclusions, but these are not *ex cathedra* pronouncements. They are reliably based on data accumulated over the years. His landmark studies in the 1950s showed that girls in whom fetal hyperadrenalism caused masculinization of the external genitalia developed an average degree of femininity if they were properly diagnosed and reared as females (Money, 1955; Money, Hampson, and Hampson, 1956). This conclusion has since been modified; more sophisticated observations by Ehrhardt, Evers, and Money (1968) have led to describing them as "tomboyish" although heterosexual (Money, 1969). As Green notes below, these studies suggest the possibility of prenatal hormonal effects in humans comparable to those found in animals. For instance, female monkeys who receive a male hormone *before* birth are considerably more "masculine" in their behavior than controls, while the same hormone *after* birth does not effect behavior, even though it masculinizes the body (W. Young, Goy, and Phoenix, 1964).

Green began investigating feminine behavior in boys while he was a medical student under Money's tutelage. During his residency in psychiatry he had the opportunity to collaborate with Stoller, and he now edits *Archives of Sexual Behavior,* from which his paper is reprinted. In it, Green points to several directions vital for future research, but it should be noted that clinical practice may also shed light on these issues (e.g., Harrison, 1970). In the case of one young adult transsexual, who related the usual story of always having felt trapped in the wrong-sexed body, detailed child psychiatric documentation was, by chance, discovered for several years of inpatient hospitalization during childhood. Review of these reams of material suggested that this young adult transsexual had an ulterior motive for falsifying his childhood history in his quest for sex-change treatment (Harrison, Cain, and Benedek, 1968).

At present it is difficult to specify the interaction of nature and nurture in determining gender roles. There is no consensus among clinicians, biologists, anthropologists, and sociologists (not to mention special interest groups, such as feminist or gay organizations). Two recent experiments in nature highlight this difficulty. Money and Ehrhardt (1972) describe a set of male twins circumcised by cautery, where an accident caused one to have his penis irreparably burned off. Backed by the assumption that sex is primarily a social phenomenon and identity is learned, the decision was made to raise the penectomized boy as a girl. The other twin was raised as a boy. The stage was set to assess if rearing as a female would overcome the biology of the male. Several years later, at about age six, the twin reared as a girl was assessed by Money and Ehrhardt to identify as and generally behave like a girl, aside from some tomboyish behavior, and to accept the role of a girl. According to them, "she" dressed, played, and fantasized her future like a girl. The twin brother identified as and behaved like a normal boy. This observation has been seen as support for the power of socializing forces over biology. Nevertheless, to overcome male biological influences and enhance female biological maturation, the penectomized twin was subsequently castrated to remove the endocrine source, underwent surgical reconstruction to enhance appearance as a female, and was placed on a schedule for female hormones.

The contrasting experiment in nature took place in a small isolated community in the Dominican Republic, where due to a genetic-endocrine problem, a large number of males were born who appeared at birth to be females (Imperato-McGinley et al., 1974). They had a blind vaginal pouch instead of a scrotum and a clitorislike phallus instead of a penis. The uneducated parents were not aware of anything unusual, so these gonadal males were raised as typical females. Only much later did the disorder became obvious to the community. Prior to this awareness, however, these 18 unsuspecting "girls" experienced typical masculinizing puberty characterized by the development of a functional penis, descent of the testicles with complete spermatogenesis and ejaculation, a substantial increase in muscle mass, etc. These youngsters then abandoned their female rearing in favor of a male identity. The biochemically oriented researchers conclude: "sex of rearing as female appears to have a lesser role role in the presence of two masculinizing events—testosterone exposure in utero and again at puberty with development of male phenotype."

Prior to either of these experiments in nature, Stoller (1968) summarized the issue well: "A sex-linked genetic biological tendency towards masculinity in males and femininity in females works silently but effectively from fetal existence on, being overlaid after birth by the effects of environment, the biological and environmental influences working more or less in harmony to produce a preponderance of masculinity in men and of femininity in women. In some, the biological is stronger and in others weaker" (p. 74).

Although information about the basis for gender identity is constantly being expanded, there is still validity to Freud's closing commentary in his "Three

Essays on the Theory of Sexuality" (1905): "we know far too little of the biological processes constituting the essence of sexuality to be able to construct from our fragmentary information a theory adequate to the understanding alike of normal and of pathological conditions" (p. 243).

5

Nativism versus Culturalism in Gender-Identity Differentiation

JOHN MONEY

INTRODUCTION

From our Platonic and Biblical forebears, you and I have the heritage of dichotomizing. Dichotomies are dangerous, for they may be wrong. It is wrong to dichotomize the learned and the biological—learning is a biological function, for all acts of learning are also activities of the central nervous system.

In order not to separate learning from biology, I have set up a 2 x 2 x 2 scheme (Table 1) in which nativism versus culturalism is cross-classified with that which is species-shared (phyletic) versus that which is individually unique (biographic), and subclassified as imperative versus optional. Imperatives, which may be decreed phyletically or may be unique to a single biography, represent inevitable sequelae or conditions that follow given prior events or conditions. Options, which also may be decreed either phyletically or individually, represent sequelae or conditions for which there is at least one degree of freedom in that there may have been an alternative or substitute event or condition.

The entries in Table 1 are illustrative examples only, with no pretense at enumerative completeness.

SEQUENTIAL VARIABLES

There are imperative and optional, nativistic and cultural, and phyletic and individual components to the differentiation of sex role (variously represented in chronological sequence in Figure 1).

First published in *Sexuality and Psychoanalysis*, edited by E. Adelson. New York: Brunner/Mazel, 1975, pp. 48–62. Reprinted by permission.

Supported by grant USPHS HD-00325, and by funds from the Grant Foundation and the Erikson Educational Foundation.

TABLE 1
EXAMPLES OF GENDER-ROLE DETERMINANTS
ACCORDING TO A 2 × 2 × 2 SCHEME

		Nativistic	*Cultural*
Phyletic (Species-Shared)	Imperative	Menstruation, gestation, lactation (woman) vs. impregnation (men).	Social models for identification and complementation in gender-identity differentiation.
	Optional	Population size, fertility rate, and sex ratio.	Population birth-death ratio. Diminishing age of puberty.
Biographic (Individually Unique)	Imperative	Chromosome anomalies, e.g., 45,XO; 47,XXY; 47,XYY. Vestigial penis. Vestigial uterus. Vaginal atresia.	Sex announcement and rearing as male, female, or ambiguous.
	Optional	Getting pregnant. Breast-feeding. Anorexic amenorrhea. Castration.	Gender-divergent work. Gender-divergent cosmetics and grooming. Gender-divergent childcare.

Instead of sex role, I prefer the term *gender role*. It is more comprehensive than sex role, which is too readily confounded with copulatory role. Moreover, the reciprocal of gender role is gender identity, which is one's own experience of one's gender role, which itself is the public manifestation of one's gender identity.

You can see in Figure 1 that the early variables of gender-identity differentiation variously lend themselves to being identified as biological or innate. The more comprehensive term is *nativistic*. It encompasses everything that is native to the organism, regardless of its etiology, including those factors which will subsequently facilitate or impede postnatal learning, or selective aspects thereof.

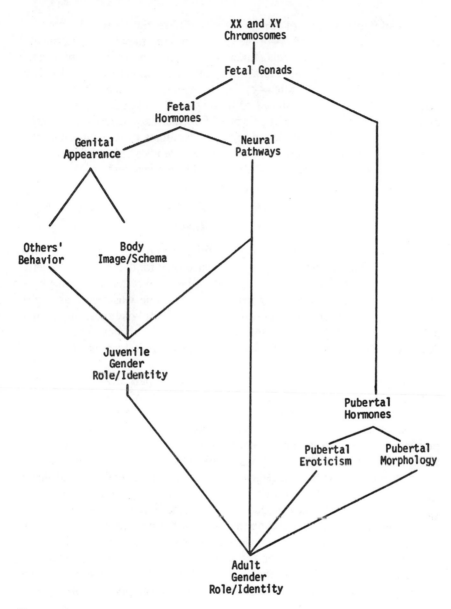

FIGURE 1

Variables in the differentiation of gender role and gender identity.

Nativistic determinants of gender-identity differentiation may be phyletically shared by other members of the species, or they may be biographically unique to a particular individual. Likewise, though contrary to the way most people take for granted, cultural determinants, transmitted to the individual by other members of the species—or even by members of other species—also may be either phyletically shared or biographically unique. Cultural determinants are heavily weighted in favor of information and learning, though not exclusively so. Among the Aboriginal Australians of Arnhem Land, the anatomical circumcision ceremony at age nine or ten is a cultural determinant of a boy's masculine anatomy as well as of his gender identity.

MATCHED PAIR OF CASES, CONCORDANT FOR DIAGNOSIS, DISCORDANT FOR REARING

Let me now bring Figure 1 to life by reference to the development of two children. They constitute a matched pair, concordant for diagnosis, as genetic and gonadal females with the adrenogenital syndrome of female hermaphroditism, but discordant for sex or rearing—that is, one was reared as a girl and one as a boy. There are other similar matched pairs I have studied, though extra cases of boys by rearing are hard to find in the modern era of early, accurate diagnosis. By contrast there are many parallel cases of girls by rearing.

At the moment of conception, each possessed the pair of X chromosomes (46,XX) characteristic of the female. The genetic code of these chromosomes soon instructed the indifferent tissue that would become the sex glands to differentiate as ovaries, not testes. With no testes present, the mullerian ducts, precursors of the internal female organs, were instructed to differentiate into a uterus and its two fallopian tubes. In the absence of androgen from the testes, the undifferentiated anlagen of the external genitalia should have differentiated as female. But they did not. Instead, they were instructed by an excess of fetal androgen produced by abnormally functioning cortices of the two adrenal glands (their abnormality itself the product of a genetically dictated error) to differentiate as male. The genital tubercle (Figure 2) became a penis with a foreskin plus, on the underside, a midline fusion of skin to form the urethal tube, instead of a clitoris with a hood and two unfused labia minora. The labioscrotal swellings fused to become an empty scrotum, instead of two unfused labia majora.

At around the same time in fetal life when the external genital tissues were responding to the excess of adrenocortical androgens, certain pathways in the central nervous system of this pair of patients also were making their own response. At least one infers this to have been so on the basis of direct brain-

EXTERNAL GENITAL DIFFERENTIATION IN THE HUMAN FETUS

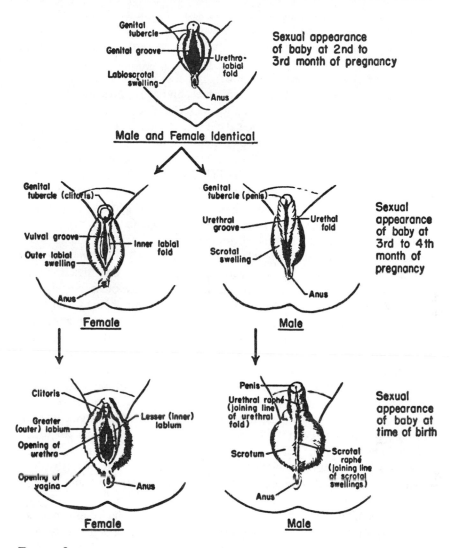

FIGURE 2

Male and female progression of sex organ differentiation.

hormone experiments in laboratory animals, and on the basis of behavioral parallels in genetic female rhesus monkeys, experimentally androgenized *in utero,* and in human genetic females affected by prenatal androgenization.

The one word that succinctly describes the behavioral effect of this prenatal androgenization is *tomboyism*.

Before the central nervous system has sufficient time, developmentally, to instruct behavior to be tomboyish, however, the external genitalia, on the day of birth, instruct other people how to behave toward the new child, then and subsequently. In each of the pair presently under consideration, the external genitalia informed the world, ''It's a boy.'' In one case the announcement remained unchanged, and the child was, thenceforth, reared consistently as a boy, with presumedly undescended testes. In the other case the complicating symptoms of neonatal dehydration and salt loss led to further diagnostic workup. In consequence, the child's sex was soon reannounced as female, to agree with the genetic sex, the ovaries, and the internal reproductive organs. Shortly thereafter the first stage of surgical feminization of the external organs was carried out, so that their appearance thenceforth instructed others to treat her as a girl. As her comprehension grew, the child absorbed the same instruction from her genital appearance.

Both children, as they advanced through the stage of understanding language and, in particular, the gender differences embodied in language, had antithetical experiences. These experiences signified to one that he was a boy, and to the other that she was a girl. The language of the vocal cords was paralleled by body language—the language of gesture, haircut, and clothing, assisted by toys and other artifacts. For each child, vocal language and body language both were subject to positive and negative reinforcement, that is, to reward and punishment training. Day by day, this dimorphism of exogenous training and expectancy was reiterated and expanded. At the same time the endogenous or self-perceived image or schema of the body directly reinforced the exogenous or socially prescribed schema of sexual dimorphism. The morphological, visual, and haptic instructions of body image coalesced with the historical and cultural instructions of how to behave as a boy versus how to behave as a girl. Between the ages of approximately 18 months and four years, this coalition of instructions completed its function of establishing in each individual an irrefutable conviction of gender identity—the juvenile gender identity of Figure 1.

What about the prenatal, androgenic instruction of the central nervous system to program postnatal tomboyish behavior? The effect of this instruction was, analogically speaking, to add a special tint or flavor to the differentiation of the girl's feminine gender identity, though not to defeminize it. The same addition, in the case of the boy, was perfectly compatible with the differentiation of a masculine gender identity.

The girl's tomboyism was marked especially by outdoor vigor of energy expenditure, competitiveness, and dominance assertion. She liked to join boys in their competitive group games. The boy did likewise. Other boys permitted him the license of assertive dominance, though he seldom bothered with jockeying for position in the boyhood power hierarchy. By contrast, the girl was more or less kept in her place from becoming too dominantly assertive among the boys, whose acceptance of her in their play activities was provisional. Belligerent aggressiveness and fighting were not noteworthy manifestations in either child.

The counterpart of energetic competitiveness and dominance assertion in tomboyism might well be a high barrier or threshold for the rehearsal of maternal caretaking in childhood play and other mothering opportunities. When the girl played house with her girlfriends and their dolls, she played the role of father. In preference to stereotypical girls' toys, she preferred boys' toys and the activity generated in using them.

Both children preferred utilitarian styles in clothing and personal grooming. For the boy, this preference was in accord with cultural dictates in boyhood. For the girl it meant indifference toward the idealized feminine stereotypes of ruffles and lace, embroidery and jewelry, though not a phobic avoidance of them, such as one might see in a child with a diagnosis of transvestism. She preferred overalls for school and play, but did not balk at wearing a dress for Sunday school and other dressy occasions.

In the childhood years, boys and girls both are able to evaluate the relative merits of membership in either sex. The boy of the present pair had no second thoughts about having been born a boy. The girl, like other tomboy girls with her diagnosis, saw many merits to being a boy, could she have chosen the sex in which to have been born. Yet there was no overt or expressed inclination toward a reassignment of sex.

She anticipated the eventual probability of reaching the boyfriend stage, marriage, and motherhood. Like many girls in childhood, she already had a companionship with a boy whom she considered her special boyfriend. Nonetheless, she shared with other, older girls of the same diagnosis the ideal of priority for a nondomestic career in addition to marriage and domesticity.

The boy, who was already adolescent in development, had a special companionship, elaborated into true romance in his imagery, the companion being a girlfriend. He fitted easily into the stereotype of the male role in marriage, irrespective of the fact that he and his partner would both have 46,XX chromosomes.

Prenatally androgenized tomboyish girls, like those among their genetically male brothers who were also exposed to an excess of prenatal androgen, tend as a group to be elevated in IQ. The girls tend also to be high achievers scholastically and vocationally—the brothers perhaps somewhat less so. The girl, in the pair under consideration, was a good scholar. The boy's scholastic achievement was adequate, but secondary to his outdoor, athletic, and sporting interests.

The girl in this matched pair was too young to manifest evidence of adolescent lesbian eroticism. Twenty-odd older girls of the same diagnosis and similar medical history, but born with less masculinized genitalia, have, however, when mature, shown no lesbian erotic traits. Thus, one may infer that prenatal androgenism does not predestine the differentiation of a lesbian gender identity. The latter requires additional social input during the postnatal, primarily social stage of gender-identity differentiation.

The child reared as a boy did, in fact, encounter a full complement of this additional, masculinizing social input. His case, therefore, raises the tendentious question of whether or not it is one of contrived or iatrogenic lesbianism. In physique and appearance, and by rearing, he is a boy with a penis whose romantic attraction is toward a girl. According to the record of his chromosome count and gonadal sex, he is, by birth, female. Common sense dictates that the chromosomal and gonadal sex are here subordinate to the sex of physique, external genital anatomy, behavior, and to the gender identity, all of which declare the boy to be a heterosexual male. In coitus he can function as a man, not as a woman.

Differentiation of the juvenile gender identity in these two cases, as in the case of all normal children, included erotic functioning, if at all, only as play. Erotic and sexual play in childhood is a rehearsal, so to speak, in anticipation of instructions that will be added by the hormones of puberty. The pubertal hormones instruct the body in somatic dimorphism of maturation. They also lower the threshold for the arousal of erotic response and the release of erotic behavior, androgen being requisite to this effect in both sexes. In the girl of the present pair, masculinizing early puberty would have occurred as a sequel to adrenocortical malfunction had it not been therapeutically regulated by treatment with cortisone. Early adrenal masculinizing puberty had appeared in the boy and then, by reason of therapeutic confusion and poor management, had been changed to ovarian feminization under the influence of late-instituted cortisone therapy. This turn of events is especially noteworthy, for the growth of breasts and approaching onset of menstrual bleeding (through the penile urethra) did not change or negate the boy's masculine gender identity. He viewed feminization as a disease or deformity and urgently wanted to be relieved of it. His treatment, surgical and hormonal, thenceforth was masculinizing.

The discrepancy between the discordant gender identity and the concordant genetic and gonadal sex of this boy and his matched partner, the girl, is indeed remarkable. This pair is not unique. I have already indicated that I have studied several other pairs and there are more, in other clinics around the country, who exhibit the same discrepancy. There are also parallel pairs of individuals who are genetic males. In two instances, one of the pair began life as a normal male and was reassigned as a female after total loss of the penis in an accident of circumcision by cautery. One child, now age seven, clearly shows female gender-identity differentiation. The other child is still a baby.

POSTNATAL DIFFERENTIATION: COMPLEMENTATION AND IDENTIFICATION

All of these matched pairs demonstrate the extensive proportion of gender-identity differentiation that, by nature's decree, is destined to take place after birth. One finds here an analogy with native language: whereas full linguistic communication is exclusively dependent on a human central nervous system prenatally differentiated in preparation for language use, without linguistic stimulation from others the human central nervous system does not differentiate the function of linguistic communication. Gender-identity differentiation also needs a central nervous system prenatally differentiated in preparation for the postnatal establishment of full gender identity under the influence of social stimulation and response.

The social stimuli of gender-identity differentiation fall into two great classes, those for identification and those for complementation. The principle of identification has long been recognized in sex-role learning, but the principle of complementation is newly recognized. Identification means that a girl copies her mother, or other female models, whereas a boy copies his father, or other male models. Ideally, both parents and all other subsidiary models agree in reinforcing and approving a child's behavioral manifestations of gender identification.

Complementation means that a girl reciprocates her behavior as a complement to that of her father or other males. A boy reciprocates his behavior as a complement to that of his mother or other females. Ideally, as in the case of identification, each parent and other members of each sex agree in reinforcing and approving a child's behavioral manifestations of gender complementation. Inconsistency and contradiction on the part of parents and/or other leading identification and complementation models in a child's life induce inconsistency and contradiction into the child's own gender identity as it differentiates.

Identification and complementation learning entail that every child, girl or boy, establishes and stores in the brain two gender schemata. One is masculine, the other feminine. One is coded as positive and as belonging personally to oneself. The other is coded as negative and not belonging personally, except as a schema of what to expect to have to respond to, or complement, in relations with the other sex. In most children, these two schemata differentiate with clear boundaries. When they do not, the result is an error of gender-identity differentiation, of which there are many variants.

ERRORS OF GENDER-IDENTITY DIFFERENTIATION

The errors of gender-identity differentiation may be classified along two dimensions: total versus partial transposition and episodic versus chronic transposition. To illustrate: a total episodic transposition appears clinically as transvestism with dual personality, each personality having its own name and wardrobe. By contrast, a total chronic transposition appears clinically as transsexualism, the condition in which the individual has the chronic and pervasive conviction of belonging to the sex opposite to that of the genital anatomy, and becomes rehabilitated as a member of that sex or yearns to do so, with appropriate hormonal and surgical sex reassignment. Partial transposition on an episodic basis appears clinically as bisexuality (or facultative homosexuality), and on a chronic basis as essential or obligatory homosexuality. Obligatory homosexuality may manifest itself as effeminate or virile, dependent on the extent or degree of partial gender-identity transposition.

By nosological convention, the diagnoses of transvestism, transsexualism, bisexuality, and homosexuality (and of transitions between them) imply a variable degree of gender-identity transposition, which itself implies involvement of the sex organs and their erotic functioning. In the majority of instances, these diagnoses also imply transposition of gender role in the affected person's imagery, if not in actual erotic practice, vis-à-vis the sex of the erotic partner as man or woman.

These four diagnoses also involve, in varying degrees, transposition of nonerotic aspects of gender role—for example, work and avocational activities conventionally dichotomized as masculine or feminine. Transposition of these nonerotic aspects or attributes of gender role also may be manifested, either episodically or chronically, in the absence of erotic transposition—that is, in people who are not bisexual, homosexual, transvestic, or transsexual. The relationships of the six types of transposition to one another are shown in the 3 x 2 arrangement of Table 2. In the table it can be seen that, apart from tomboyism, there are no nouns in our language with which to identify gender-role transpositions that apply to nonerotic sex stereotypes in avocations and careers. For example, there is no antonym for tomboy. The nearest approximations are dandy or dude, which carry too strong a connotation of ridicule, and sissy or effeminate, which carry too strong a connotation of homosexuality. There is no name for men and women whose avocations depart from sex-stereotypic conventions. The deficiency of our language in not providing

TABLE 2
GENDER-ROLE TRANSPOSITIONS

	Total	*Partial*	*Optional*
Episodic	Transvestism	Bisexualism	Recreational role transposition
Chronic	Transsexualism	Homosexualism	Occupational role transposition (e.g., tomboyism)

names for optional, nonerotic types of sex-stereotypic nonconformity undoubtedly indicates how strong is the taboo in our society against nonconformity to the stereotypes. Especially in the case of males, nonconformity to the stereotype is likely to be construed as carrying homosexual overtones. There is an important implication here for liberated women of the Women's Lib generation; until their number is matched by a new generation of men liberated from the masculine sex stereotype, there will be a shortage of liberated males to be the partners of liberated females.

OPTIONAL VERSUS IMPERATIVE SEX DIFFERENCES

As compared with the multiplicity and range of conventional, stereotyped, and optional gender-role differences, the imperatives of sex difference can be reduced to four: women menstruate, gestate, and lactate whereas men impregnate. These four are the basic nativistic and phyletically decreed sex differences. Other, secondary differences derive from these four, notably the hormonal and somatic secondary sexual characteristics of puberty. However, none of these derivative sex differences is absolute or imperative, nor is associated sexually dimorphic behavior. Variations in the quality, intensity, or frequency of their manifestations among the members of one sex cover so wide a range that, at the extremes, individuals of one sex may be more disparate from one another than from representatives of the other sex. In statistical parlance, male and female within-group differences are as extensive as between-group differences.

The range of male or female within-group variation in morphological and behavioral sex has its basis in variable thresholds of response.

Among genetic males, to give but one example, there are different thresholds of growth response in breast tissue, so that the range of breast development in adolescent males is from zero to female size (adolescent gynecomastia). The same range applies to genetic females, but in reverse order, and with an extension at the positive extreme of excessive, ever-expanding breast growth (virginal hyperplasia of the breasts).

Variable response thresholds in the differentiation of sexual dimorphism of both bodily and behavioral traits constitute the basis on which cultural definitions of idealized masculinity and idealized femininity have differentiated, historically, and become fixed in social custom, religion, and law. Parentalism, or caretaking of the young, is a good example. Whereas care of the young is not a sexually dimorphic but an ambisexual trait among mammals, the threshold of its elicitation is distinctly sexually dimorphic. The threshold is typically lower in females than males, and is especially low in lactating females. In the human species, the ideal of paternal caretaking, once defined in our culture as clearly unmasculine, is now, as everyone knows, undergoing a redefinition as ambisexual.

Parentalism in child care constitutes an example of behavior that can be either gender-shared or gender-divergent. It represents a cultural and personal biographic option, the opposite of a nativistic and phyletic imperative (Table 1).

The majority of gender-divergent roles belong in the optional category. Historically, however, there has been extensive stereotyping of roles as masculine or feminine. In consequence, they are transmitted to each new generation of children as male-female absolutes, and not as optional and ambisexual or gender-shared. Masculine-feminine divergence tends to have prevailed over gender-sharing, much to the disadvantage of those individuals, not only women, but men also, who do not neatly fit the dichotomies dictated by cultural custom.

Those men and women who did obey the cultural dictates of gender divergence as they grew up do not, and cannot, automatically change themselves by edict. Therefore, they tend to perpetuate their own conventional, gender-divergent roles by transmitting them to their children. The children of parents with less divergent roles, by contrast, more easily learn gender roles that are more sex-shared. The disparity between the sharing and the divergent types is now strong enough itself to be a cultural force in our midst.

6

Sexual Identity: Research Strategies

RICHARD GREEN

INTRODUCTION

Children from the first two years of life show an awareness that they are either male or female. Later they usually behave in ways culturally appropriate to this awareness. Still later they exhibit a preference for sexual partners of one or the other sex. These three developmental phases—(1) core morphological identity, (2) gender-role behavior, and (3) sexual-partner orientation—constitute *sexual identity*, a basic personality feature. My concern is with how sexual identity develops. Many strategies exist for answering this question; some will be reviewed here.

PRENATAL HORMONAL INFLUENCES

Do sex hormone levels before birth affect postnatal sex-typed behavior? Female rhesus monkeys exposed to large amounts of testosterone *in utero* behave more like young male monkeys than female rhesus monkeys whose prenatal hormonal environment has not been altered; they become "tomboy" monkeys (W. Young, Goy, and Phoenix, 1964). Postnatal exposure to this same androgen does not have a comparable behavioral effect.

Is this phenomenon also true of humans? While the hormonal exposure of the human fetus cannot be altered experimentally, a genetic defect has performed this "experiment" for us. In the adrenogenital syndrome, the female fetus produces excessive adrenal androgen. Girls with this syndrome, like female rhesus monkeys also exposed to high androgen levels *in utero*, appear more tomboyish than typical girls. When compared with their hormone-normal sisters, they are *less* interested in doll play and wearing dresses and are *more* interested in rough-and-tumble play (Ehrhardt, 1973; Ehrhardt, Epstein,

First published in *Archives of Sexual Behavior*, 4:337–349 (and appropriate bibliographic references from pp. 485–492), 1975. Reprinted by permission of Plenum Publishing Corporation.

and Money, 1968). However, the effect of these hormones on adult sexual identity is not as dramatic; studies of adult women with the adrenogenital syndrome do not reveal an excess likelihood of transsexual or homosexual behavior (Ehrhardt, Evers, and Money, 1968).

There is an analogous phenomenon in human males. For about 20 years, it was the practice in one clinic to give pregnant diabetic women large doses of estrogen and lesser amounts of progesterone to compensate for a suspected hormone deficiency complicating the pregnancy of diabetics. Comparing two groups of sons, aged six and 16, born to these women with the sons of non-hormone-treated women, we found that boys exposed prenatally to exogenous female hormones were *less* rough-and-tumble, *less* aggressive, and *less* athletic. The possibility remains, of course, that the behavioral differences were related to the mother's chronic illness rather than to altered hormonal levels *in utero* (Yalom, Green, and Fisk, 1973).

In a section below, boys who are behaviorally very feminine and who also do not engage in rough-and-tumble play are discussed. It should be noted here, however, that the boys born to the diabetic mothers, although less rough-and-tumble than the contrast groups, were not overtly "feminine." Thus, while it may be that an innate low level of aggressivity contributes to feminine behavior in boys, a particular style of parenting (R. Green, 1974; Stoller, 1968), perhaps one which positively reinforces feminine behavior, may *also* be required for this innate contribution to permit the full picture of boyhood femininity to develop.

Research must distinguish direct from indirect effects of prenatal hormone exposure. In a culture that does not label some forms of childhood behavior (such as rough-and-tumble play) as masculine and others as feminine, subtle effects of prenatal hormone exposure might pass unnoticed in the welter of other individual differences. In our culture, however, the same variations may have far-reaching consequences. A boy with less than the usual boyhood aggressivity may be labeled "sissy"—with profound effects on peer group socialization and father-son interaction. A low level of aggressivity may result in a boy's accommodating more easily to the company of women and girls. "Boys play too rough" is an explanation given by the feminine boys described later who prefer female companionship and have an alienated relationship with father.

How can we study the effects of prenatal sex-steroid levels in the normal human? While we cannot experimentally alter the prenatal hormonal milieu, we may be able to measure it—perhaps by periodically sampling amniotic fluid or by periodically assaying maternal plasma or urine. If a reliable index of the hormonal exposure of the human fetus could thus be found, we might begin to trace correlations between prenatal hormones and neonatal and childhood behaviors. We might also be able to determine the stages of fetal development—critical periods—during which the hormone exerts its later behavioral effect. Studies such as this, despite their science-fiction flavor today, should not be excluded from an agenda for future research.

EARLY-LIFE SEX DIFFERENCES IN BEHAVIOR

Neonatal and infant studies designed to assess sex differences have been described by M. Lewis (1972); therefore, only brief attention will be paid to this research strategy. I endorse the premise that studies of the human neonate hold considerable potential for isolating the early roots of male-female dimorphism. These reported sex differences, which group into displays of greater muscle strength, sensory differences, degree of affiliative behavior to adults, and patterns of maternal care, have been reviewed elsewhere (R. Green, 1974; Maccoby and Jacklin, 1974).

I shall here underscore a strategy in utilizing these differences—that of studying atypical children of both sexes. Many measures have a bell-shaped distribution. Males and females who fall at the ends of the distribution could be longitudinally studied to determine correlations between neonatal behavior and later developmental attributes. Of interest would be those infants whose patterns fall within the zone typically found for the other sex. For example, will males with a female pattern of taste preference (greater appeal of sweet) or within the female range for elevating the prone head (less ability) show later childhood behaviors which are culturally feminine, e.g., preferring doll play to rough-and-tumble play? Will infants handled by mothers in a manner more typical for other-sex infants show later atypical sex-typed behavior?

ANATOMICALLY AMBIGUOUS CHILDREN

Next consider infants with anatomically ambiguous external genitals (pseudohermaphrodites). Among infants in whom the ambiguity is great, some have been labeled male at birth and raised as boys; others with the same genital ambiguity have been labeled female at birth and raised as girls. Both groups generally develop a sexual identity consonant with the sex to which they have been assigned and as which they have been consistently reared (Money and Ehrhardt, 1972; Money, Hampson, and Hampson, 1955; Stoller, 1968).

An infant with the virilizing adrenogenital syndrome who is designated male at birth and raised male, despite a female chromosome array (44 plus XX), and despite the presence of ovaries and a uterus, will typically identify as a male, show masculine behavior in childhood, and be erotically attracted to females in adulthood. If designated female and raised as female, the child will identify as female, show primarily feminine behavior, and later be erotically attracted to males. Such "experiments of nature versus nurture" indicate that environmental factors can outweigh whatever innate biological influences may be present in such cases.

From these patients we learn more. They teach us when the earliest components of sexual identity are "set." If such an infant is unambiguously raised as a male for the first few years (up to approximately the fourth birthday), subsequent reassignment as a female is generally not successful (Money, Hampson, and Hampson, 1955; Stoller, 1968).

These classical studies and concepts, first announced nearly 20 years ago, have been challenged (Diamond, 1965; Zuger, 1970). More recently, they have also been confirmed—even in cases where sex of assignment is in dramatic conflict with genital appearance. Thus, an adult female with the adrenogenital syndrome, raised as a girl, is described as feminine and heterosexual despite the presence of a 7-cm clitoris, her major obstacle to heterosexual coitus (Lev-Ran, 1974).

Some investigators have challenged the model of the anatomically intersexed child as appropriate for the study of "typical" sexual-identity development. However, a study of monozygotic male twins currently under way may answer some of these objections. As a result of a circumcision accident early in life, one twin suffered a sloughing of the penis and is being raised as a female. That child appears to be developing a female identity (Money and Ehrhardt, 1972).

Studies of monozygotic twins offer additional promise. Our research has identified two sets of twins, one set male and one female, with discordant sexual identities. One male twin at the age of ten is very feminine and wishes to become a girl; the other is typically masculine. The 25-year-old female pair consists of one person who urgently seeks sex-change surgery and a feminine sister. Differential early socialization experiences are described for both twin pairs (R. Green and Stoller, 1971). In such twin studies, prenatal hormonal and genetic differences can be given less consideration as an explanation for behavioral differences.

Do adults with "intersexed" sex-chromosome abnormalities—such as the XXY configuration—also show "intersexed" behavioral differences? Some studies indicate that they do (H. J. Baker and Stoller, 1968; Money and Pollitt, 1964). Our difficulty is that we know only those cases which are reported. We do not know what proportion of XXY or XYY children and adults are leading lives *without* conspicuous behavioral sequelae such as transsexualism or transvestism. Here is another research opportunity. One male infant in 700 is born with the XXY chromosomal pattern. These infants look normal at birth but can be identified by karyotyping. Thus, if we karyotype an extensive series of newborn male infants, we can expect to identify about 14 infants with this syndrome out of 10,000. Follow-ups on these 14 would provide a study of the effects of this atypical karyotype on subsequent behavior in a random sample. Large-scale karyotyping studies are in fact currently under way.

Study of neonatal sex differences could also find applicability with samples of the anatomically intersexed. If one or another sex difference is replicated on normal infants (e.g., taste preference), would anatomically intersexed babies (e.g., adrenogenital females or XXY males) also be behaviorally intersexed?

Neonatal karyotyping studies, however, raise ethical questions. If an infant is identified as XXY, should this information be withheld from or provided to parents? If parents receive input, how will this affect the child's rearing? Would any possible adverse effects outweigh potential benefits? One civil suit in Maryland recently blocked the identification of XXY male children on the grounds that such identification may stigmatize.

CHILDREN OF THE ATYPICAL

Increasing numbers of children are being brought up by homosexual couples or in a home where one parent has undergone sex-change surgery. Transsexual couples are adopting children neonatally; others are rearing children born to the prior marriage of one partner. Females married to men who were formerly women are giving birth to and raising children conceived through donor insemination. In a recent court case, a chromosomal female now living as a man was awarded custody of a child of an earlier marriage; "he" is thus now in the role of father of the child of whom he was formerly the mother.

Lesbian mothers and couples are receiving considerable attention in the press and in courts of law, where they are fighting for child custody. What effect does being raised by one or two homosexual adults have on children? What is the effect on a child of recognizing that a parent is homosexual, or of peer group reactions to a child's atypical household?

Role models of the other sex and the model of heterosexuality are not omitted from the lives of children who live in homosexual-parent households. Children are repeatedly exposed to hetereosexual adults of both sexes in the person of relatives, parents of peers, and adults at school. Then there is the additional exposure to the conventional nuclear-family constellation on television and in books.

The effect on a child's later sexual preferences of knowing that at least one parent is homosexual is questionable. This will partly depend on the degree to which partner preference is a result of role modeling. The Role modeling cannot account for the *entire* process of sexual-identity development, however, in that the vast majority of homosexuals were raised by *heterosexual* parents. The view held by the homosexual parent, or couple, of individuals of the other sex may be significant. The image, positive or negative, painted of these absentee figures may shape later affectional elements.

Yet another issue is a possible biological predisposition to homosexuality, perhaps inherited, such as atypical gonadal hormone levels. Should such a developmental basis be demonstrated, would raising a child so predisposed in either a homosexual or a heterosexual household significantly affect future sexuality?

These "social experiments" will teach us much about the development of sexual identity and are yet to be harnessed (R. Green, 1975).

THE CHILDHOOD OF ATYPICAL ADULTS

The first strategy to be adopted in the effort to unravel the etiology of adult sexual atypicality was that of Freud, who asked atypical adults about their childhood. This has been the traditional approach to understanding the parents of the atypical adult and his or her early socialization experiences. This technique, although limited, has research value.

Case histories given by transsexuals reveal that there are anatomically normal adults with an intense, irreversible conviction of belonging to the other sex, who recall the onset of this cross-sex identity during early childhood (H. Benjamin, 1966; R. Green and Money, 1969; Stoller, 1968). Invariably, these persons report having role-played as persons of the other sex, having dressed as children of the other sex, having preferred opposite-sex children as playmates, and having avoided the toys and games typical for their sex.

Retrospective histories of transvestites (heterosexual males who cross-dress with accompanying sexual arousal but do not desire sex change) also demonstrate the early onset of atypical sexuality. Approximately half of 500 transvestites in one series reported commencing cross-dressing prior to adolescence (Prince and Bentler, 1972).

Retrospective reports by homosexuals again point to the enduring significance of atypical childhood gender-role behavior. One study reported that about a third of 100 homosexual adult male patients recalled playing predominantly with girls during boyhood (compared with 10% of the heterosexual control group) and 83% displayed an aversion to competitive group games (compared with 37% of the heterosexuals) (Bieber et al., 1962). Another study of a nonpatient homosexual sample reported that two-thirds of

89 males recalled "girl-like" behavior during childhood (compared with only 3% of the heterosexual controls). For female homosexuals, over two-thirds of a group of 57 were tomboyish during childhood (compared with 16% of the heterosexuals), with half persisting with tomboyism into adolescence (compared with none of the heterosexuals) (Saghir and Robins, 1973).

But retrospective approaches have shortcomings. First, we cannot be sure how much the reports are contaminated by knowledge of the outcome. They are certainly not made up out of whole cloth, however; family picture albums, for example, sometimes show a male transsexual or transvestite already dressing in women's clothes and struggling with high-heel shoes at the age of two or three (R. Green, 1974; Stoller, 1968). But the detailed sequence of events in the early years is not documentable in this way. Prospective studies, beginning at an early age, are needed to circumvent these shortcomings. Further, retrospective studies cannot tell us how many children who display atypical sex-role behavior later "outgrow" it and become adults without an atypical identity.

Prospective studies are not without *their* problems, however. A percentage of subjects are always lost at follow-up. And (unless a large control group is included) they may cast little light on the large number of behaviorally typical boys who accept themselves as male, who display masculine behavior, but who in adulthood display a preference for male sexual partners.

ATYPICAL BEHAVIOR IN ANATOMICALLY NORMAL CHILDREN

My principal research strategy consists of identifying, at an early age, a population of anatomically normal children who display atypical sex-role behavior. These children are matched with a control group of children displaying typical sex-role behavior. Both groups are then followed longitudinally.

We have generated a sample of 65 boys, under the age of 11, who show a strong preference for the activities, toys, dress, and companionship of females, state that they want to be girls, and role-play typically as females in "house" or "mother-father" games. These children are being compared with typical boys of the same age, sibling order, socioeconomic level, and family constellation. So far we have matched 50 boys. While we are necessarily dependent on retrospective inquiry in reconstructing the sequence of events before a child enters the study, recollections when a child is six or seven should be less subject to error than after another two decades.

Parents and siblings of both groups are studied via a variety of procedures (R. Green, 1974). The boys referred because of "feminine" behavior test similarly to same-aged girls (another control group) on a variety of psychological procedures and differently from control boys. When constructing fantasies, they typically utilize female family figures and an infant (as do girls, whereas boys utilize male figures and pay much less attention to an infant). When requested to draw a person, the figure drawn is usually female (girls do the same; most boys draw a male). Left alone in a playroom stocked with sex-typed toys, they play mostly with a "Barbie" doll (as do girls, while other boys play with a truck). On the It-Scale for Children (in which a "neuter" figure "It" selects a variety of sex-typed preferences illustrated on cards [D. Brown, 1956]), their selection for sex-typed toys, playmates, and accessories is the same as that of girls but differs from that of most boys. When they complete picturecard sequences in which a child of their own sex joins a parent engaged in an adult sex-typed activity, they join the female parent in a feminine activity (as do girls, but not most boys) (R. Green, 1974). In addition, preliminary spectral analyses of electroencephalographic recordings on a subsample of boys from both groups provide patterns which correctly discriminate the feminine from masculine boys with 90% accuracy (Hanley and Green, unpublished).

In every family with one behaviorally feminine boy there is not a *second* behaviorally feminine boy. Why? Our attention must also focus on within-family differences, not merely on ways in which feminine-boy families differ from control families. Features that distinguished the feminine boy from siblings during the first years and styles in which parents differentially responded to the femininely behaving boy receive close scrutiny.

A tentative review of findings suggests that this feminine behavior evolves as an interactional, sequential effect engaging innate features of the child and early postnatal socialization experiences (R. Green, 1974). These children may indeed be innately less rough-and-tumble and aggressive. This translates into differential mother-child and father-child interaction patterns, and further affects the child's early peer socialization. These boys typically complain that "boys play too rough." Their early socialization experiences are usually with girls, and greater competence in feminine socialization patterns develops during the preschool years. Feminine interests help promote a closer affective relation with the mother but contribute to alienation from the father. Not getting the affirmative feedback that he expects or that he gets from his other son(s), the father labels the boy a "mama's boy." During early school years, male peer group alienation evolves. The boy is labeled "sissy." Ostracism escalates as the rejected boy gravitates more toward the female group and begins to show feminine gestures which "tag" his uniqueness and isolate him further from male peers.

The effect of same-aged group relations during grade school years deserves more study. Boys with girl "friends" during boyhood are more likely to have male "lovers" during adulthood. The relationship between early peer group interaction and later genital sexuality is enigmatic. One possibility is that the feminine boy's lack of positive affective responses from males during earlier years (peer group and father) yields "male affect starvation," compensated for in adulthood by male-male romantic relationships. Alternatively, the young male whose peer group is female may be so completely socialized within that group that he evolves similar later romantic attachments (males). The manner in which preadolescent *homosocial* peer group relationships typically evolve into adolescent and adult *heterosexual* relationships and *heterosocial* peer group relationships into *homosexual* ones is a little understood facet of sexual-identity development. These very active "latency" years deserve more study.

TREATMENT OF THE CHILD WITH ATYPICAL SEXUAL IDENTITY

Intervention into the behavior of the very feminine boy engages both research and ethical issues. First: research questions.

What do we know about the natural course of boyhood femininity? What might intervention do? Follow-up studies tell us something of the natural course. Twenty-seven adult males previously seen for boyhood femininity have been re-evaluated in three studies. Fifteen are currently transsexual, transvestic, or homosexual (R. Green and Money, cited in R. Green, 1974; Lebovitz, 1972; Zuger, 1966). The manner (if any) of treatment intervention with most of these patients is not clear. By contrast, the adult transsexuals, transvestites, and homosexuals in the series noted earlier were rarely *evaluated* during childhood, let alone treated.

Consider again the three components of sexual identity: at first, self-awareness of being male or female (core morphological identity); later, culturally defined masculine and feminine (gender-role) behavior; still later, preferred sex of partner for genital sexuality. All three components are atypical for male-to-female transsexuals (they consider themselves female, behave like women, and are attracted to anatomically same-sexed partners). Transsexuals report that their parents felt their atypical behavior was insignificant and would pass, and so they were not treated. For them, sexual identity remained fully atypical. Although a few boys seen by Money and myself over a decade ago were initially behaving in a manner similar to that recalled by transsexuals, they underwent evaluation and are not now transsexual. Most are homosexual. Why did the first two components of sexual identity undergo change and the third component remain atypical?

We can speculate. Core morphological identity appears to be set to a substantial degree during the first two to three years of life. Thus, a considerable portion of sexual identity has evolved by the time the atypical child is initially evaluated. Gender-role behavior, a later identity component, may still be modifiable, however. Therefore, one outcome of early intervention may be that a young male who feels he is or wants to be a female might be convinced that the change is not possible and, with a change in his milieu (pleasurable nonfeminine activities and non-rough-and-tumble male play-mates), may experience adequate comfort with anatomical maleness and male peer group socialization. If so, the later request for sex change may be averted. However, no attention is being specifically addressed to the third component, genital sexuality, since such behavior is not manifested during these years.

The critical factor at issue in whether the behavior of an atypical boy changes may be whether the parents seek evaluation. Those parents who request evaluation are initiating a new milieu for their son, one which dis-courages feminine behavior and encourages masculinity. Because of this, the second component of sexual identity, and perhaps indirectly the first com-ponent, may be modified. If such is the case, the pre-transsexual male may then mature into a homosexual male. (The degree to which change in the first two components might influence the third component is even less clear.)

Should clinicians attempt to modify the behavior of the child whose sexual identity is significantly atypical? The very feminine male child experiences considerable social conflict as a consequence of his behavior. He is teased, ostracized, and bullied. Parents who bring their very feminine boy for profes-sional consultation are concerned about his behavior and want something done. What then is the professional's responsibility toward the parents and their child?

It can be argued that the conflict experienced by the feminine boy derives mainly from the culture in which he lives, a culture that dictates, for irrational reasons, that boys and girls behave in specified dimorphic ways. While some societal change is taking place, most children continue to label feminine boys "sissy." Unless the entire society undergoes dramatic, ultrarapid change, the distress experienced by today's very feminine boy will augment during the teens. While the clinician may prefer that the pediatric and adult culture immediately change, there is more basis for optimism in helping a single individual to change.

But what kind of change? Treatment need not forge the feminine boy into an unduly aggressive, insensitive male. However, it can impart greater bal-ance to a child's interests and behavior where previously skewed patterns have precluded comfortable social integration. For example, consider the exclusively female peer group of the feminine boy. Intervention may help the feminine boy find unstigmatized boys who prefer "sex-role-neutral" activities, thus widening his range of social interactions.

Clearly, "to treat or not to treat" is a dilemma. The standard of many clinicians is to be nonjudgmental, with the patient dictating goals. In the event that (1) the parents want their child to be happier, (2) the child is in serious conflict, and (3) the likelihood of reducing that conflict is greatest by promoting behavioral change, is it ethical to refuse intervention? A more extended discussion of this ethical quicksand is found in R. Green (1974, 1975).

TOMBOYISM AND ADULT SEXUAL IDENTITY

Tomboyism is much more common than its counterpart, boyhood femininity. However, adult females who request sex-change surgery and who typically recall tomboyish behavior during childhood are outnumbered 3:1 by males requesting sex change. Although two-thirds of a recent sample of adult female homosexuals also recall having been tomboys (Saghir and Robins, 1973), the incidence of female homosexuality appears to be about half that of male homosexuality (Kinsey, Pomeroy, and Martin, 1948; Kinsey et al., 1953). Thus, tomboyism can, in more cases than boyhood femininity, be validly considered a "passing phase" with no adult counterpart in atypical sexual identity.

Yet there do exist some tomboys for whom this cross-gender *behavior* reflects a fundamental feature of *identity*, a feature that will continue beyond childhood and express itself in transsexualism or homosexuality. But, in contrast to very feminine behavior in boys, masculine behavior in girls causes less concern on the part of parents and less conflict for the child. Thus, clinical facilities are less likely to have tomboys referred for evaluation. Consequently, we have insufficient data to determine which few tomboys are those whose sexual identity will be atypical during subsequent years, although some pilot data have been reported (R. Green, 1974).

SEXUAL IDENTITY AND GONADAL HORMONES

Following decades during which a hormonal basis for atypical human sexual behavior fell into disrepute, a revival of interest now exists. Exquisitely sensitive hormonal assays have opened a new era of investigation. Where previous studies utilizing gross, nonspecific measures failed to show differences between homosexuals and heterosexuals, some recent studies have found differences. These several studies have been compiled elsewhere (R. Green, 1975).

More important than reciting the provocative, although conflicting findings are the questions of specificity regarding the reported differences. Rigorous attention has not been paid to possibly confounding variables, especially stress, drug intake, and recency of sexual activity. Heterosexual males under military stress have testosterone levels lowered to the same degree as those reported for some homosexuals (Kruez, Rose, and Jennings, 1971; R. Rose, Bowne, and Poe, 1969). (Homosexuals, because of their stigmatized life style, may be under greater stress than heterosexuals.) Data on marijuana ingestion may be given for one group of subjects (homosexuals), but not for the other. Tetrahydrocannabinol appears to reduce plasma testosterone (Kolodny et al., 1974). Whereas one study (in contrast to the remainder) found homosexuals to have higher androgen levels (Brodie et al., 1974), data are not given for sexual activity prior to plasma sampling. (Sexual activity can raise plasma testosterone: Fox et al., 1972; Pirke, Kockott, and Dittmar, 1974.)

Individual variations in both levels of plasma testosterone and sexual activity range widely for the human. Also, the correlation between the two is not very high; indeed, some castrated males retain sexual activity for years. Thus, individual or group differences may have little behavioral meaning. In addition, the range of individual tissue responsivity to the same level of hormone may vary widely, making control for tissue response possibly even more significant than controlling for the other confounding factors noted above.

An alternative strategy is collecting longitudinal assays on children with atypical behavior from childhood through adolescence and into adulthood. Correlating developmental behavioral attributes with hormonal maturation could constitute a significant integration of the neuroendocrine and developmental psychology disciplines and promote a new research dimension.

Typical Children with Atypical Backgrounds

In the event that certain variables appear to predispose a child to a later same-sex sexual-partner preference (for example, father-absence in the male, to cite a common theory), then children without fathers who do *not* become feminine or homosexual could be studied to determine the roots of their heterosexuality. A too infrequently used strategy is study of the "high-risk" child who develops normally to ascertain "what went right."

Bisexuality

The term *bisexuality* (or *ambisexuality*) has many usages. Here it is narrowly restricted to those persons who rate "3" on the 7-point Kinsey scale, with 0 designating exclusive heterosexuality and 6 exclusive homosexuality.

Individuals equally disposed in fantasy and overt behavior to males and females are not common.

True bisexuality raises theoretical and research questions. Explaining homosexuality as an anxiety or phobic reaction to one genital configuration (typically the male rendered anxious by the "castrated" female) is problematic in understanding the individual capable of sexual satisfaction with both sexes. Further, if future research documents that specific developmental routes, social or biological, promote either an exclusive male or an exclusive female sexual-partner preference, would bisexuals fall in the middle range for these attributes? Finally, will the current changes in early childhood socialization that less clearly demarcate sex roles promote more bisexuality during adulthood?

CROSS-CULTURAL STUDIES

Studies of atypical children need to be conducted in cultures with different patterns of child-rearing and different definitions of "masculinity" and "femininity." The anthropological literature is replete with examples of adults and children who have adopted the sex role opposite to that expected by virtue of their anatomy (R. Green, 1974). Missing from these accounts, however, is *why* these atypical individuals adopted their unique life style.

CONCLUSION

These strategies are varied. They are ambitious. Pieced together, addressed by scholars from developmental psychology, neuroendocrinology, human ethology, anthropology, and sociology, the puzzle will reveal a most fundamental behavioral attribute. The designs are available. The tools are forged. The researchers are trained. The populations wait. Will the support be forthcoming?

7

INTRODUCTION

Symbiosis and Individuation:
The Psychological Birth of the Human Infant,
by Margaret S. Mahler

Our volume on *Childhood Psychopathology* began with the assertion of "our conviction that a knowledge of the concepts and data of normal development is vital to an understanding of the emotionally disturbed child" (Harrison and McDermott, 1972, p. 1). Striking testimony to the fruitfulness of integrating studies on development and pathology is evident in retracing Margaret Mahler's scientific contributions (Prall, 1971; Ritvo, 1971). The chapter reprinted here is an outgrowth of Mahler's contributions beginning more than 50 years ago in pediatrics and evolving into her landmark explorations of infantile psychosis (see Mahler, 1952, 1968). It capsulizes the ideas richly documented in *The Psychological Birth of the Human Infant* (Mahler, Pine, and Bergman, 1975).

Mahler conceives of life beginning with three or four weeks of a *normal autistic* phase, followed by four or five months of *symbiotic fusion* with the mother, from which the infant emerges in the *separation-individuation phase*. (The reader may be surprised that Mahler did not originate this term—it was suggested to her by Annemarie Weil [Mahler, 1972]). This major period is subdivided into four subphases. The *differentiation* subphase, characterized by exploration of the mother's body, continues until about 10 months when the infant's further exploration of his or her universe evolves into the *practicing* subphase (between approximately 10 and 15 months). This subphase is characterized by moving away from mother and finally by free, upright locomotion. With neurophysiological maturation and increased representational intelligence, the "little conqueror" assesses his or her autonomy more realistically. At this point, the child traverses the highly vulnerable *rapprochement* subphase, commonly referred to as the toddler stage. During this period there is greater awareness of physical separateness from the mother and a consequent return to interaction with her as the child realizes that the world is *not* his or her "oyster." The fourth subphase, starting in the child's third year, is marked by the enhancement of *beginning emotional object constancy* and the consolidation of individuality. The sense of separateness evolves with the development of psychic structure from a diffuse, global symbiosis through a differentiation of discrete elements, eventuating in the integration of these elements in a smoothly functioning whole.

Many consider Mahler's work to be the most comprehensive modification of psychoanalytic developmental theory since Freud (1905) formulated his psychosexual stages, which were primarily derived reconstructively from treatment of adult patients. On the other hand, Tanguay (1977) criticizes Mahler's methodology as lacking a clear-cut objective view of what in fact does happen between mother and child. He notes that the pilot phase of the project was successful in that it did allow the investigators to detail a number of hypotheses concerning development; however, these were not adequately tested and thus Tanguay considers the project's results of questionable scientific validity. He insists that although the clinician may find Mahler's ideas useful as a framework, empirical validation is of crucial importance from a scientific perspective.

Unquestionably, Mahler's data and formulations have implications for innumerable pertinent issues. From the point of view of mother-infant interaction, for instance, it is of interest that Mahler correlates the early "cracking of the 'autistic' shell" with John D. Benjamin's (1961a) observation of a neuromaturational crisis at around three or four weeks of age. Both Benjamin and Mahler relate this to Freud's (1920, 1925b) stimulus barrier concept. That is, they see the mature central nervous system as equipped with a "protective shield," which serves as an inhibitory barrier to stimulation—a hypothesis that Benjamin's collaborators have continued to investigate (Tennes et al., 1972). Benedek (1949) has addressed the same phenomenon from the maternal side of the interaction. Based on her investigations of the interrelationship between female hormonal cycles and psychodynamic processes (Benedek and Rubenstein, 1942), she perceived Gesell and Ilg's (1943) observation of increased infantile crying at three or four weeks of age as consequent to the mother's starting to turn away from the baby and becoming more active in other areas of her life. This shift on the mother's part evokes a demand from the baby for the re-establishment of what Benedek designated symbiosis. Does this interaction relate to the sensitive period for maternal bonding postulated by Kennell, Trause, and Klaus in Chapter 1?

Mahler marks the infant's psychological birth at the point the endogenous smiling response evolves into the specific social smile, indicating a specific bond between infant and mother (see Chapter 2 by Emde and Harmon). This step represents the principal psychological achievement of the symbiotic phase. An absolute requirement for normal separation-individuation is the mother's "quasi-altruistic surrender" of the infant's body to the child. One surprising observation here is that free, upright locomotion is primarily in a direction away from, not toward the mother—even in the absence of the mother. This reminds one of Brazelton, Koslowski, and Main's observation (see Chapter 3) that for smooth mother-infant synchrony to be maintained, it is essential that the mother sensitively "allow" the baby to look away. At another juncture in development, Blos (1967) has used Mahler's ideas to describe adolescence as a "second individuation process." (Chapter 36 by Wieder and Kaplan on drug abuse also employs these formulations.)

Mahler (1971) has discussed how fixation at the rapprochement subphase of development may be applied to borderline psychopathology. Her patient's determined splitting of the object world was fueled by a search for the good symbiotic mother, as opposed to the forbidding "bad" mother of separation, so that he saw the world as "bad" and women as "engulfing." In the book by Mahler, Pine, and Bergman (1975), there are implicit links to Chapters 5 and 6 by Money and Green in terms of the vicissitudes of the rapprochement subphase effecting subsequent development of gender identity.

Finally, it should be noted that the concept of individuation has been developing along similar lines in areas as nominally disparate as family systems theory (see Chapter 15 by Bowen). The concept now seems to have emerged as a field of inquiry in its own right. This convergence of interest suggests its potential for integrating phenomenological, transactional, and intrapsychic concepts and for achieving a rapprochement between psychoanalytic and family systems orientations, between individual and interrelational dynamic theories.

7

Symbiosis and Individuation: The Psychological Birth of the Human Infant

MARGARET S. MAHLER

I would like to start on a somewhat personal note, to indicate how, amidst my reconstructive studies in the psychoanalytic situation, this observational, normative work, one of whose yields is the present paper, came about.

During my own formative years, when I was still a trainee at the Psychoanalytic Institute in Vienna, my experiences as head of a well-baby clinic in the late 1920s brought the (albeit preconscious) impression again and again to my mind that the human infant's *biological, actual birth experience* did not coincide with his "psychological birth." The sensorium of the newborn and very young infant did not seem to be "tuned in" to the outside world; he appeared to be in a twilight state of existence.

Then, in the 1930s, when I had a number of neurotic child and adult psychoanalytic patients, there happened to be among them two latency-age patients whom I found myself unable to treat with the traditional psychoanalytic method. One of them, a highly intelligent eight-year-old boy, was referred by his parents and school because he did not seem to comprehend the necessary requirements of the reality situation in the classroom, nor was he able to listen to and act upon the reality requirements of family life.

He needed his mother's almost continual attendance. She had to—and sometimes did—guess his primary-process thoughts and wishes; otherwise, the patient—with or without an initial temper tantrum—retreated into a bizarre dream-world of his own. The contents of this dream-world were discernible

First published in *The Psychoanalytic Study of the Child*, 29:89–106. New Haven: Yale University Press, 1974. Reprinted by permission.

This paper draws on material that is presented in greater detail in Mahler, Pine, and Bergman (1975).

in those instances in which he acted out his delusional fantasies; for example, he donned his father's derby hat and walking stick, fully believing that appropriating these paraphernalia of his father actually made him the father and, in addition, made him the absolute ruler of the universe.

The analyst was permitted, I soon discovered, to play one of two roles only: either I had to act as an inanimate extension of the patient's ego, a quasi-tool of the patient's delusionary aggrandized self, or else I had to be completely passive—quasi-deanimated, another (albeit somewhat more significant) piece of furniture in the room.

The animate and individuated existence of the human objects—father, brother, analyst, classmates, and even mother—was blotted out as far as possible. If these deanimation and dedifferentiation mechanisms (Mahler, 1960) did not work, every so often the patient fell into a panic-stricken rage attack, and then slumped into the twilight state of the psychotic.

In spite of the immense difference between these two groups of human beings—the very young infant and the psychotic child—one basic similarity between the two groups made a great impression on me: neither seemed to have been *psychologically* born, that is to say, "tuned in" to the world of reality. What the youngest babies have *not yet* achieved, the psychotics have *failed* to achieve—psychological birth: that is to say, becoming a separate, individual entity; acquiring an, albeit primitive, first level of self-identity.

This common feature of a perceptual twilight state of the two groups of human beings slowly percolated in my mind, with the result that I asked myself two questions: (1) How do the vast majority of infants manage to achieve the obligatory second: the psychic birth experience? How do they emerge from what is obviously a twilight state of symbiotic oneness with the mother—an innate given—that gradually allows them to become intrapsychically separated from her and to perceive the world on their own? (2) What are the genetic and structural concomitants that prevent the psychotic individual from achieving this second birth experience, this hatching from the symbiotic "common boundary with the mothering one"?

After another decade of experience with psychotic children, I embarked in the late 1950s on a systematic study of "The Natural History of Symbiotic Child Psychosis,"[1] which used a tripartite design.

We attempted to establish what Augusta Alpert would have called a "corrective symbiotic relationship" between mother and child, with the therapist acting as a bridge between them. We became more and more convinced that the "basic fault" in the psychotic was his inability to perceive the self and

[1] This study was conducted at the Masters Children's Center with Dr. M. Furer. It was funded by Grant No. 3363 of the NIMH, 1959-1963, Bethesda, Maryland.

the mother as separate entities, and thus to use the mother as a "beacon of orientation in the world of reality," as his "external ego." This is in contrast to normal children or to children whose disturbances belong to other categories of pathology.

Soon after initiating the psychosis project (and almost parallel with it), we started a pilot study, in which we endeavored to find out how *differentiation* and *self-boundary formation* do develop in most human beings. (Practically no specific data were available about this at that time.) This pilot study was a bifocal observational study of randomly selected mother-infant pairs, who were compared with each other and with themselves over time. The pilot study of the average mother-infant pairs was undertaken with the hypothesis that "there exists a normal and universal intrapsychic separation-individuation process in the average child, which is preceded by a normal symbiotic phase."

It is my conviction that, in the *normal individual*, the sociobiological utilization of the mother, of the "outer half of the self" (Spitz, 1965), and later on, the emotional availability of the love object—the postsymbiotic partner—are the necessary conditions for an *intrapsychic* separation-individuation process. This is, in fact, synonymous with the *second*, the psychological birth experience: a rather slow and very gradual *hatching-out process*, as it were.

As a result of my clinical work in the psychoanalytic situation, and my observational studies of the first years of life, I am now able to state with a fair degree of accuracy what many of my colleagues have found in their mainly reconstructive work: namely, that milder than outrightly psychotic clinical pictures are derived from disturbances in the orderly progression of the subphases of the separation-individuation process. Hence, I shall briefly review that orderly developmental process.

I

The biological unpreparedness of the human infant to maintain his life separately is the source of that species-specific, prolonged, absolute dependence on the mother (Parens and Saul, 1971), which has been designated by Benedek (1949) and myself as "the mother-infant symbiosis." I believe that it is from this symbiotic state of the mother-infant dual unity that those experiential precursors of individual beginnings are derived which, together with inborn constitutional factors, determine every human individual's unique somatic and psychological makeup.

The symbiotic patterning, such as the molding or stiffening of the body when it is held, as well as the specific and characteristic nursing situations and countless other variables within the symbiotic dyad, give us some clues as to what is going on in the infant, but translation of the observable phenomena of early pre-ego states—in our terms, the autistic and early symbiotic periods—into psychological terms is exceedingly difficult. Extrapolations drawn from preverbal behavioral data are even more precarious than the use of hypotheses deduced from observational data of later periods of life To understand *preverbal* phenomena, as Augusta Bonnard (1958) succinctly stated, "We are   compelled to seek out their connotations, either through their pathological or normal continuance in somewhat older individuals than an infant, or else through their regressive manifestations" (p. 583).

As I have described in many of my publications, we have learned a great deal about the symbiotic nature of human existence by intensively studying the preverbal phenomena of symbiosis in their pathological and regressive manifestations

In our normative study, however, we have tried not only to validate our hypothesis of the *symbiotic origin of human existence,* but to follow development into that period of early life that I named the separation-individuation phase We studied randomly selected mother-infant pairs, and observed their interaction *beyond* the normal symbiotic phase

As soon as signs of differentiation appear, the data are considerably easier to read—and constructions appear to be more reliable. This is because the infant's behavior has been polarized and rendered more meaningful through the presence and availability or lack of availability of the mother The mother's presence and her interaction with the child furnish a circular yet bipolar frame of reference baby and mother, transacting with each other in a more readable way

This has enabled us to study the psychological birth of the human infant, the main dynamics of which are. the major shifts of libidinal and aggressive cathexis in the bodily self, and the changing nature and level of the approach and distancing behaviors between infant and mother during the course of the developmental process, from biological birth till the open-ended phase of libidinal object constancy

In the weeks preceding the evolution to symbiosis, the newborn's and very young infant's sleeplike states far outweigh the states of arousal. They are reminiscent of that primal state of libido distribution that prevailed in intrauterine life, which resembles the model of a closed monadic system, self-sufficient in its hallucinatory wish fulfillment

Ribble (1943) has pointed out that it is by way of mothering that the young infant is gradually brought out of an inborn tendency toward vegetative-splanchnic regression and into increased sensory awareness of and contact with the environment. In terms of energy or libidinal cathexis, this means that a progressive displacement of drive energy has to take place from the inside of the body (particularly from the abdominal organs) toward its periphery. *The shift from predominantly proprioenteroceptive toward sensory perceptive cathexis of the periphery*—the rind of the body ego (as Freud called it)—*is a major step in development.*

The well-known peripheral pain insensitivity as well as the panic-creating hypersensitivity to enteroceptive ("gut") sensations, which are equated with bad introjects in psychosis, bear witness to the fact that this important and massive cathectic shift has failed to occur.

I believe that this major cathectic shift marks the progression from the normal autistic to the normal symbiotic phase.

The main task of the autistic phase is that, with predominantly physiological mechanisms, the homeostatic equilibrium of the organism be maintained, under the changed postpartum conditions.

Through the inborn and autonomous perceptive faculty of the primitive ego (Hartmann, 1939), deposits of memory traces of the two primordial qualities of stimuli, of "good"—that is, pleasurable—and "bad"—that is, painful—occur We may further hypothesize that these are cathected with primordial undifferentiated drive energy.

John D. Benjamin (1961a) found that an interesting physiological maturational crisis occurs at around three to four weeks. This is borne out in electroencephalographic studies, and by the observation that there is a marked increase in overall sensitivity to external stimuli. "Without intervention of a mother figure for help in tension reduction," Benjamin says, "the infant tends to become overwhelmed by stimuli, with increased crying and other motor manifestations of undifferentiated negative affect" (p. 9).

I believe that this crisis—from our developmental point of view—marks the cracking of the "autistic" shell, the beginning dissolution of the negative, that is to say, uncathected, stimulus barrier. It marks the beginning of its replacement—through the aforementioned cathectic shift—by a positively cathected *protective* and *selective* stimulus barrier which creates a common "shield," as it were, a quasi-semipermeable membrane enveloping both parts of the mother-infant dyad.

The symbiotic phase is marked by the infant's increased attention to and perceptual-affective investment in stimuli that *we* (the adult observers) recognize as coming from the world outside, but which (we postulate) the infant does not recognize as having a clearly outside origin. Here begins the establishment of "memory islands" (Mahler and Gosliner, 1955), but not as yet a differentiation between inner and outer, self and other. The principal psychological achievement of the symbiotic phase is that the specific bond between infant and mother is created, as is indicated by the specific smiling response (Spitz and Wolf, 1946).

The period of five to seven months is the peak of manual, tactile, and near-visual exploration of the mother's mouth, nose, and face, as well as the "feel" of the mother's skin. With these behaviors, the infant seems to begin to distinguish between contact-perceptual experiences and those originating in his own body and to single out experiences of the hitherto completely coenaesthetic global sensory experiences of mother's and his own bodies. Furthermore, these are the weeks during which the infant discovers with fascination inanimate objects worn by the mother—a brooch, eyeglasses, or a pendant. He begins looking around within the symbiotic dual unity by straining away from the mother's body as if to have a better look at her, and also to look beyond the symbiotic orbit—for example, in the pursuit of toys. There may be engagement in peek-a-boo games, in which the infant still plays a passive role (Kleeman, 1967). These exploratory patterns later develop into the cognitive function of checking the unfamiliar against the already familiar.

It is during the first, the differentiation subphase (four or five to ten months of age), that all normal infants achieve their initial tentative steps of breaking away, in a bodily sense, from their hitherto completely passive, lap babyhood—the stage of dual unity with the mother One can observe individually different inclinations and patterns, as well as the general characteristics of the *stage of differentiation itself.* All infants like to venture and stay just a bit of a distance away from the enveloping arms of the mother, and, as soon as they are motorically able to, they like to slide down from the mother's lap. But they tend to remain or crawl back, as near as possible, to play at the mother's feet.

The baby now begins "comparative scanning," "checking back to mother." He becomes interested in and seems to compare "mother" with "other," the familiar with the unfamiliar, feature by feature, it would seem. He appears to familiarize himself more thoroughly, as it were, with what *is* mother; what feels, tastes, smells, looks like, and has the "clang" of mother. *Pari passu,* as he learns the "mother *qua* mother," he also finds out what belongs and what does not belong to mother's body (such as a brooch, the eyeglasses). He starts to discriminate between mother and whatever it is—he or she or *it*—that looks, feels, moves differently from or similarly to mother.

In children for whom the symbiotic phase has been optimal and "confident expectation" has prevailed, curiosity and wonderment—discernible through the "checking-back" pattern—are the predominant elements of the inspection of strangers. By contrast, among children whose basic trust has been less than optimal, an abrupt change to acute stranger anxiety may make its appearance; or there may be a prolonged period of mild stranger reaction, which transiently interferes with pleasurable inspective behavior. This phenomenon and the factors underlying its variations constitute, we believe, an important aspect of and a clue to our evaluation of the libidinal object, socialization, and the first step toward emotional object constancy. This inverse relation between basic confidence and stranger anxiety deserves to be emphasized and further verified (Mahler and McDevitt, 1968).

In cases in which the mother showed ambivalence or parasitism, intrusiveness, or "smothering," differentiation in the child was disturbed to various degrees and in different forms. The seeking of distance from the symbiotic partner appeared in some of our babies surprisingly early—at the peak of the symbiotic phase. During the differentiation subphase, this distance-seeking seemed to be accompanied by greater awareness of mother as a special person (full establishment of the libidinal object [Spitz, 1965]), even though in very rare cases this awareness may already have been suffused at that stage with negative aggressive affect. This we were able to deduce from primitive, but sometimes quite unmistakable avoidance behaviors.

The differentiation subphase overlaps with the practicing period, which is the second subphase of the separation-individuation process. In the course of processing our data, we found it useful to think of the practicing period in two parts: the *early* practicing phase, overlapping differentiation and ushered in by the infant's earliest ability to move away from the mother (by crawling, paddling, climbing, and righting himself—yet still holding on) and the practicing period proper, phenomenologically characterized by free, upright locomotion. At least three interrelated, yet discriminable developments contribute to and, in circular fashion, interact with the child's first steps into awareness of separateness and into individuation. They are: the rapid *body differentiation* from the mother, the establishment of a *specific bond with her,* and the *growth and functioning of the autonomous ego apparatuses in close proximity to the mother*

It seems that the new autonomous achievements, plus the new pattern of relationship to mother, together pave the way for the infant to spill over his interest in the mother onto inanimate objects—at first those provided by her, such as a blanket, a diaper, a toy that she offers, or the bottle with which she parts from him at night. The infant explores these objects near-visually with his eyes, and "tests" their taste, texture, and smell with his contact-perceptual organs, particularly the mouth and hands (Hoffer, 1949) One or the other of these objects may become a transitional object (Winnicott, 1953) Moreover, whatever the sequence in which the infant's functions develop during the differentiation subphase, the characteristic of this early stage of practicing is that, while there is interest and absorption in these activities, interest in the mother definitely seems to take precedence

Through the maturation of his locomotor apparatus, the child begins to venture farther away from the mother's feet He is often so absorbed in his own activities that for long periods of time he appears to be oblivious to the mother's presence—yet he returns periodically to the mother, seeming to need her physical proximity

The optimal distance in the *early practicing subphase* would seem to be one that allows the moving, exploring quadruped infant freedom and opportunity to exercise his autonomous functions at some physical distance from mother At the same time, however, mother continues to be needed as the "home base," for what Manuel Furer has termed *emotional refueling*

It is worth noting, however, that despite the children's apparent obliviousness to their mother during the early practicing period, most of them seemed to go through a brief period of increased separation anxiety. The fact that they were able to move away independently, yet remain connected with their mother—not physically, but by way of their seeing and hearing her—made the successful use of these distance modalities extraordinarily important The children did not like to lose sight of mother; they might stare sadly at her empty chair, or at the door through which she had left

We had not expected and were surprised by the finding that the advent of the capacity for free, upright locomotion seems to take place in a direction not *toward* but *away from* mother, or even in the absence of mother This is, we feel, an indicator that the normal infant is endowed with an innate given that prompts him at a certain point of his autonomous maturation to separate from mother—to further his own individuation. Walking makes possible for the toddler an enormous increase in reality discovery and the testing of his world through his own control, as a quasi-magic master It coincides with the upsurge of goal-directed, active aggressiveness

The mother's renunciation of possession of the body of the infant boy or girl, at this point of the toddler's development, is a *sine qua non* for normal separation-individuation Most mothers recognize—empathically or even verbally—that this quasi-altruistic surrender of the infant's body to himself is a deplorable but necessary step in promoting the infant's autonomous growth This, I feel, is also the first prerequisite for the development of the child's self-esteem The practicing toddler's self-love and love of the object world, both his narcissism and his potential object love, are at their acme

The child is exhilarated by his own capacities—he wants to share and show He is continually delighted with the discoveries he makes in the expanding world; he acts as though he were enamored of the world and with his own grandeur and omnipotence

The obligatory exhilaration of the practicing period seems to hinge upon the ascendancy of the infant's upright, free locomotor capacity In those children in whom locomotion is delayed, this obligatory exhilaration is also delayed, seems to be of shorter duration, and is much less in evidence. Besides being the function by which the child can physically distance himself from mother or approach her at will, locomotor capacity provides him with a variety of other experiences. His body is more exposed, but his plane of vision and the relation of his upright body in space enable him to see the world from a different—and relatively grown-up—angle. We know from Piaget that sensorimotor intelligence at this point is supplemented by a beginning representational intelligence; thus, symbolic thinking and upright, free locomotion herald attainment of the first level of self-identity, of being a separate individual entity.

Even though some children were further advanced in their perceptual, cognitive, and other autonomous functions of the ego; more advanced in their reality-testing function—that is to say, in their autonomous individuation—locomotion was the behavioral sign that indicated most visibly to the observer the end of the "hatching process," that is to say, *psychological birth*.

II

Success in goal-directed activity seemed in inverse relation to the manifestations of hostile aggression, which was also involved in this, the second great shift of cathexis in the growing-up process.

Not only was the child in love with himself (narcissism), but substitute familiar adults in the familiar setup of our nursery were easily accepted and even engaged. This was in contrast to what occurred during the next subphase, the subphase of rapprochement.

During the entire practicing subphase, the child has evoked the delighted and automatic admiration of the adult world, specifically of his average "ordinary devoted mother" (Winnicott, 1960). Her admiration, when it is forthcoming, augments the practicing toddler's sound narcissism, his love of himself Every new achievement, every new feat of the fledgling elicits admiration, at first unsolicited, later more or less exhibitionistically provoked by him from the entire adult object world around him. This kind of admiration, which does not even need to be expressed in words or gestures, may be one of the feeding lines that, on the one hand, promotes progression of the ego's autonomous functioning and, on the other, furnishes a great accretion to the practicing toddler's feeling of grandeur—often exalted self-esteem.

In a circular fashion, the mirroring admiration also seems to augment the budding ego's readiness for mirroring the love object. Along with the rapid growth of cognition, it gradually leads to internalization processes of the *new, fully born* (structured) *ego* Eventually, these result in true ego identifications, in Jacobson's (1954) sense.

Now, however, the price of this precious progress in development of autonomy has to be paid! As the 16- to 18-month-old's cognitive development progresses, he becomes more and more aware of his loss of the "ideal sense of self"—of well-being—when he notices his mother's absence from the room. At such times, we observed what we came to call *low-keyedness:* the toddler's gestural and performance motility slowed down, his interest in his surroundings diminished, and he appeared to be preoccupied with an inwardly concentrated attention. It was as if he wished to "image" another state of self—the state that he had felt at the time when the symbiotically experienced partner had been "one" with him.

As the toddler's awareness of separateness grows—an awareness stimulated by his maturationally acquired ability physically to move away from his mother and by his *cognitive growth*—he seems to experience an increased need and wish for his mother to *share* with him his every new acquisition of skill and experience. These are the reasons for which I called this subphase of separation-individuation the period of *rapprochement*.

At the very height of mastery, toward the end of the practicing period, it begins to dawn on the junior toddler that the world is *not* his oyster; that he must cope with it more or less "on his own," very often as a relatively helpless, small, and *separate* individual, unable to command relief or assistance merely by feeling the need for them or even by giving voice to that need. The quality and measure of the *wooing* behavior of the toddler toward his mother during this subphase provide important clues to the assessment of the normality of the individuation process.

The junior toddler gradually realizes that his love objects are separate individuals with their own individual interests. He must gradually and painfully give up his delusion of his own grandeur and participation in the still delusionally believed-in omnipotence of mother and father. Dramatic fights may ensue with mother, and temper tantrums may be the order of the day. (Many years ago, I recognized the significance of temper tantrums as a behavioral indication by which outward directed aggression is turned back onto the "self." Therefore, this mechanism may be looked upon as a precursor of internalization of aggression, and also as a precursor of superego formation.)

Be that as it may, as far as our observational research indicated, this phase of development is a *crossroads*, which my co-workers and I have termed the *rapprochement crisis*.

From around 18 months on, we observed that our toddlers were quite eager to exercise their rapidly growing autonomy Increasingly, they chose not to be reminded of the times when they could not manage on their own. On the other hand, the desire to be separate, grand, and omnipotent often conflicted with the desire to have mother magically fulfill all one's wishes—without the need to recognize that help was *actually coming from the outside*. Thus, in a majority of cases, the prevalent mood swung to that of general dissatisfaction and insatiability, and a proneness to rapid swings of mood and to temper tantrums developed. The period of rapprochement was thus characterized by a sometimes rapid alternation of the desire to reject mother, on the one hand, and to cling to her with coercive, determined tenacity in words and acts, on the other hand—a behavioral sequence that the word *ambitendency* describes most accurately But often at that age there already was a *simultaneous* desire in both directions—i.e., the characteristic *ambivalence* of the 18- to 22-month-olds.

In the rapprochement period, which follows the earlier-described psychological birth, the source of the child's greatest pleasure shifts from independent locomotion and exploration of the expanding inanimate world to *social interaction*. Peek-a-boo games, as well as games of imitation, become favorite pastimes. Recognition of mother as a separate person in the large world goes parallel with awareness of other children's separate existence, their being different from the own self. This was evidenced by the fact that children now showed a greater desire to *have* or to *do* what another child had or did—that is, a desire for mirroring, imitating, and coveting what the other child had For example, the desire to acquire a "second bellybutton" (a penis) was sometimes quite openly expressed by girls. Along with this important development, there appeared the "no" and definitely goal-directed anger, aggressiveness, if the desired aim could not be obtained. We are not, of course, losing sight of the fact that these developments take place in the midst of the anal phase, with its characteristics of anal acquisitiveness, jealousy, envy, and negativism, but also with a much earlier detection than we had previously believed of the anatomical sexual difference.

Depending upon her own adjustment, the mother may react either by continued emotional availability and playful participation in the toddler's world, or by a gamut of less desirable attitudes. If the mother is "quietly available" with a ready supply of object libido, if she shares the toddling adventurer's exploits, playfully reciprocates and thus helps his attempts at imitation, externalization, and internalization—then the relationship between mother and toddler is able to progress to the point at which verbal communication takes over, even though vivid gestural behavior (that is, affectomotility) still predominates. By the end of the second or the beginning of the third year, the predictable emotional participation of the mother seems to facilitate the rich unfolding that is taking place in the toddler's thought processes, reality testing, and coping behavior. In most favorable cases, the toddler is, at this point, on the way to emotional object constancy in our and (I believe) in Hoffer's sense

III

I should like to conclude my paper with some general statements, which go beyond the topic that the title implied

It is a generally accepted hypothesis among psychoanalysts that unless the child successfully traverses the symbiotic phase, and that first subphase of separation-individuation termed *differentiation,* psychosis will ensue (Mahler, 1968)

Milder than psychotic disturbances, I believe, occur in children who, though they have passed through a separation-individuation process, have shown ominous deviations from the orderly progression of the subphases If there is too much overlapping, or other serious disturbance in the differentiation and practicing subphases, and if the rapprochement crises are extreme and do not give way to any degree of object constancy, which is the open-ended fourth subphase of the separation-individuation process, fixation points are created What may thus ensue is: narcissistic character formation and/or borderline pathology (with splitting mechanisms of the self and of the object world) (See Kernberg, 1967, 1970; Kohut, 1971)

We are still underestimating the pathogenicity, but also the character-building, the personality-integrative role of preverbal levels of development, and we are underestimating in particular the importance of ego and superego precursors—and especially their capacity for creating hard-to-decipher proclivities to intrapsychic conflicts!

8

INTRODUCTION

Insights from the Blind: Comparative Studies of Blind and Sighted Infants, by Selma H. Fraiberg

The following chapter by Fraiberg eloquently attests to the wisdom of Weiss's (1961) plea for the integration of pathological and developmental biology: "Deformities become valuable clues to the inner workings of formative processes . . . so that our understanding of the 'abnormal' will become but an extension of our insight into the 'normal,' while *pari passu*, the study of the 'abnormal' will contribute to the deepening of that very insight" (pp. 134, 150). Fraiberg also offers an elegant model for blending parental guidance designed to prevent psychopathology (in congenitally blind infants) with a sophisticated investigation of ego development. In her use of naturalistic observational data collected in the home (instead of by questionnaires and checklists), Fraiberg demonstrates the shortsightedness of considering controlled studies conducted by "blind" investigators the *only* valid research methodology. At the same time she provides a vital service to her subjects and their families as advocate for the baby and teacher to the parents.

Although Fraiberg's findings point to the rich potential of nonvisual experience in the development of the congenitally blind, they also illustrate the central importance of vision as an "organizer of experience." Fraiberg (1968) documents that vision is a vital ingredient of what Heinz Werner (1940) called the "synesthesia" of sensations in constructing a stable mental representation of the object. The chapter reprinted here depicts the contribution of vision to the expressive use of the face and hands, which serves as a bridge between the self and the external world. Fraiberg outlines the role of vision in taking the initiative in affection, finding motor pathways for the expression of aggression, facilitating gross motor achievement, and acquiring language. The blind toddler's helplessness points to his or her special need for human protectors during the separation-individuation phase (see Mahler's Chapter 7).

Elsewhere, Fraiberg (1971a, 1977) has described the shock and rejection provoked by the birth of a blind baby The hazards facing that baby in the first 18 months of life call for a sustained crisis intervention by teams of professionals who, in essence, teach parents to relate to their babies. As an outgrowth of their clinical-investigative program, Fraiberg and her colleagues have developed an innovative infant mental health program that is a model of service delivery, investigation, and professional education (Fraiberg, Adelson, and Shapiro, 1975). The deceptively simple finding, for instance, that blind infants do not bring their hands to the midline spontaneously, thereby derailing further cognitive and motor development, not only informs the traditional association between congenital blindness, autism, and mental retardation, but has led to easily instituted compensatory interventions, such as parent-child patty-cake games.

The following chapter also points in the direction of some of Fraiberg's other contributions. Among these is her blending of psychoanalytic and Piagetian concepts in suggesting that distinguishing between "recognition memory" and "evocative memory" can clarify the literature on "object constancy" (1969).

A fascinating corollary of this type of naturalistic observation has been described by Fraiberg's original collaborator in the New Orleans phase of the blind-infant investigation. D. A. Freedman et al. (1976) studied a boy with immune deficiency disease who was confined in one of the most unnatural child-rearing environments ever conceived: a space-age, germ-free isolation bubble. In contrast to the only other observations under similar conditions (C. Simons, Kohle, and Genscher, 1973), Freedman's findings suggest that cognitive as well as affective development "can proceed along normal lines despite the fact that the infant or toddler has had no single constant maternal object, and is denied such otherwise ubiquitous infantile experiences as being able to mold, to engage in ventral/ventral clinging, and to experience those cutaneous and olfactory sensations which are inevitable components of normal child rearing" (p 602)

8

Insights from the Blind:
Comparative Studies of Blind
and Sighted Infants

SELMA H. FRAIBERG

In the 15 years since a group of blind young children in a New Orleans social agency brought our attention to the extraordinary adaptive problems presented by blindness in the sensorimotor period of development, we have been able to translate our findings into a guidance program on behalf of blind young infants. The research, which began with unsolved clinical problems, found solutions, and the gift from science was returned, as it should be, to the clinic.

In this chapter we shall summarize the major findings and their implications for developmental theory in the sensorimotor period and for the evaluation of blind infants.

CENTRAL FINDINGS

Our findings cannot be generalized to the larger population known as "blind," for several reasons. In the general population designated as blind, there are children who have varying amounts of useful vision and there is a high incidence of brain damage and multiple handicaps. Many children in the larger population lost their vision *after* the crucial period of sensorimotor organization and were advantaged in early personality development through the establishment of primary visual-motor schemas.

Total blindness from birth is, fortunately, a rare occurrence. Our criteria for the primary research group—blind from birth (minimal light perception

Chapter 12 from *Insights from the Blind Comparative Studies of Blind and Sighted Infants,* by Selma Fraiberg, with the collaboration of Louis Fraiberg, © 1977 by Selma Fraiberg, Basic Books, Inc , Publishers, New York Reprinted by permission admissible), neurologically intact, no other sensory or motor handicaps—were met by only a small number of the children referred to us, despite the fact that during the decade of the University of Michigan study we had all the resources of a major medical center in case finding.

Our criteria, then, provided optimal conditions for the study of the effects of a single sensory deficit, blindness, upon the organization of personality in the sensorimotor period. Our concurrent intervention program maximized the potentials for adaptation in the areas of human attachments, prehension, locomotion, and language development.

We are, then, able to say, "Our findings are derived from longitudinal studies of ten children blind from birth but intact in all other systems, whose development was facilitated by a home-based education and guidance program." Under these optimal conditions for study, the effects of blindness per se could be examined, and inferences regarding the function of vision in sensorimotor organization could be made through the study of the effects of the deficit. Blindness as an impediment to adaptation was clearly discerned in each of the areas of development in this study, even when we employed our knowledge to facilitate development and helped the child and his parents find adaptive solutions.

In relation to the larger population designated as "blind," our babies, then, were *advantaged* through intactness of other systems and *disadvantaged* by their total blindness from birth.

Our central findings are summarized below.

HUMAN ATTACHMENTS

At the point that each child entered the study (ages one to eleven months) and without prior intervention, we were able to identify the extraordinary problems for the blind baby and his parents in making the vital human connections. Blindness had robbed the baby of a large part of the vocabulary of signs and signals which are read by his partners as "recognition," "knowing," and "preference and valuation." We noted the unique course of smiling, the absence of differentiated and modulated facial expressions, and the reactions of the baby's parents to a child who "spoke an alien language."

Our educational work entailed becoming the interpreters to the parents of the blind baby's language of preference and valuation (often read through motor signs and vocalizations). It succeeded in bringing about the conditions under which the baby achieved focused human partnerships and the parents found rewards in their babies. Even grief and depression at the birth of a blind baby could be overcome to some measure when the baby brought his own gifts of love and valuation to his parents.

Our findings reflect our interventions on behalf of the baby and speak for the potential of blind infants in attaining qualitatively good human attachments. For comparison with sighted children, we employed specific indicators of human attachment and age of onset which were emerging from a large number of studies of sighted children during the sixties.

In our blind group we saw that discrimination of mother and stranger and negative reactions to the stranger appeared within the ranges for sighted children. When mobility emerged in the second year, there were patterns of following the mother, returning to the mother as a secure base, and distress when mother could not be located. The onset of separation distress was delayed by sighted-child norms, and the delay was linked in our thinking to the blind child's concomitant delay in achieving the concept of the mother as object (stage 4 on a Piagetian scale). Thus, with the "mother not present," the affective sense of "loss" appears to be linked, as it is in the sighted child, with the emergence of the concept of mother as "object," external to the self. Without an elementary sense of mother as object, there can be no sense of "loss."

Qualitative differences between the attachment behaviors of our blind children and sighted children were seen chiefly in the high level of distress when the mother left the child's perceptual field and could not be found, or when the child was separated from the mother for a few hours or longer. This speaks for the helplessness of the blind child when his mother is not present, and it also relates to a conceptual problem in the second year for the blind child, who does not yet have a mental representation of the mother which can sustain him in her absence.

In short, where the capacity for focused affectionate attachment could be assessed and compared with that of sighted children, our blind babies compared favorably with sighted babies. (This tells us, of course, that the tactile-auditory vocabulary of discrimination and love available to the blind child could serve him well in human attachments; vision is not indispensable for the formation of human bonds.) Differences between our blind babies and sighted babies appear only in the delay in the constitution of mother as object, and here the visual deficit is reflected in the unique problems of the blind child in conferring objectivity upon persons and things in the second half of the first year.

PREHENSION

Seven of our ten babies entered the study between the ages of four and eleven months, or, with correction for prematurity, four and eight months. These children, who had received no prior intervention, gave eloquent testimony at the point of initial observation for the impediment of blindness in the area of prehension. During the period in development when the sighted child is achieving, or has achieved, proficiency in the coordination of reaching and attaining an object within his reach (three to seven months), these blind babies made not a gesture of reach for persons or toys at tactile remove, even when voice or sound provided cues Sound did not yet connote substantiality for the blind baby.

The characteristic posture of these babies seen in initial observation was one in which the hands were maintained at shoulder height with inutile fingering. A biological sequence, normally facilitated by vision, had been derailed by blindness. Where vision would have brought the hands together at midline, for mutual fingering, transfer, and coordinate use, the hands of the blind baby remained at their station at the shoulders, a posture seen typically in sighted children only during the neonatal period. When toys were offered and placed within the blind baby's grasp, we did not observe interest or investment in exploring the toy in our first observations. We did, however, see interest in and exploration of the faces of parents and familiar persons during the same period.

The blind baby's hands, which must serve as primary sensory organs (not "intended" in the biological program), were mainly inutile hands as we saw them in these initial observations

We could now understand why a very large number of children blind from birth have "blind hands," too. A very large number of blind children of school age, among them children who have no neurological impairment, have hands that do not make sensitive discriminations, do not seek or explore objects, and are, of course, incapable of Braille reading. It is impossible to estimate how many of the uneducable blind children in special classes today are children who reached an impasse in adaptive hand behavior during the sensorimotor period. Those of us who have seen blind infants without intervention, as well as blind school-age children who could not find the adaptive solution in infancy, can recognize, with pain, the hand stereotypies of the school-age blind child and those of blind infants who have not yet found the adaptive solutions. The stereotyped fingering and the stereotyped posture at shoulder height speak for the failure of those hands to find meaning in experience. What we see in these hands are simple reflex movements, exercised in the near void of personal experience—empty, inutile, vestigial patterns.

In our intervention program we employed game strategies to bring about midline organization of the hands and reciprocity between the hands, the essential conditions for all later stages in adaptive hand behavior. With the collaboration of our parents we provided both interpersonal exchanges and experiences with toys to create a maximally engaging and interesting surround in which the hands, now organized at midline, could reach out and make contact with persons and things within range and obtain rich, polysensory experience in exploring the qualities of persons and things Where vision normally lures the child to discoveries of his surround, we created the con ditions under which persons and things could provide tactile-auditory lures There is reason to believe that our interventions facilitated the coordination of ear and hand in reaching for and attaining objects in the last trimester of the first year (median age 8 27, ranges 6 5 to 11 months)

It is of special interest, then, that even with intervention our blind infants did not achieve the coordination of ear and hand within age ranges that correspond to the coordination of eye and hand in sighted children The coordination of ear and hand for the blind child is a conceptual problem In the absence of vision, the blind infant must infer the substantiality of persons and things "out there" when only one of the attributes (voice or sound) is given him Thus, the tactile-auditory unity of a person or thing experienced manually, for example, is broken up when the same person or thing manifests itself through "sound only" at tactile remove The blind baby must recon stitute that unity in space before he will reach for a person or toy with the "expectation" that sound connotes substantiality In support of the evidence from our blind studies, we cited the observations of Piaget (1937) and the study of D A Freedman et al (1970), which show that a sighted child will not uncover a screened toy that is experimentally sounded under the screen until the last trimester of the first year

GROSS MOTOR DEVELOPMENT

As early as the period of the New Orleans studies our observations of Toni and the larger group of blind children in the Family Service Society program had provided us with both a picture of typical delays in the achieve ment of locomotor milestones and a useful hypothesis for the examination of these delays Typically, we saw that the *postural* attainments of these blind children appeared within the ranges for sighted children but that the *mobility* items which normally followed each postural attainment were de layed markedly and fell outside of sighted ranges We reasoned that if the postural attainments spoke for neuromuscular adequacy the locomotor delays were related to the impediments of blindness Our hypothesis was that mo bility for the sighted child was initiated through visual lures out there and that the blind child was impeded in his locomotor development through the absence of a lure that substituted for the visual incentive We had already seen that sound for Toni did not constitute a lure for either reaching or locomotor progression until ten months of age

The clues to the blind baby's locomotor delays came from the prehension study. Until the blind baby could demonstrate "reach on sound cue only," he had no incentive, no stimulus "out there" to lure him to creeping, cruising, or walking. In fact, no child in our group learned to creep or to find any mode of forward progression until he had first demonstrated "reach on sound cue only." We saw, then, that mobility in sit, in bridging, and in stand was, in fact, a form of reach, the extended "reach" of the torso toward a lure in space. We also saw—but only for a brief interval with most of our babies—motor stereotypes in the blind baby during these periods of "postural readiness" and "no mobility." Thus, a child with good control of his trunk in a bridging posture, with "readiness," we would say, for creeping, might be observed on all fours, rocking steadily, "ready to go" with "no place to go." The motor impetus, which normally leads to mobility, was exercised in a vacuum. Again typically, when mobility was achieved, the stereotyped rocking was extinguished. This becomes an important clue to the origins of motor stereotypies commonly seen in the blind population. If there is a long delay in the achievement of mobility—and this is characteristic of the general blind population—the patterns become stereotyped and later employed as an all-purpose, undifferentiated form of discharge.

Our intervention (as described by Fraiberg [1977]) demonstrably facilitated the locomotor development of the children in our group. We were able to compare their locomotor achievements with those of sighted children and with a comparable blind infant population (Norris, Spaulding, and Brodie, 1957). Our blind group came closer to sighted-child norms than to blind-child norms. Thus, free walking was achieved by our blind group within the ranges 12 to 20 months. The ranges for sighted children are 11 to 14 months. In the study by Norris, Spaulding, and Brodie (1957), 50% of their sample had achieved free walking at two years of age.

Yet it is important to note that we did not employ "mobility training" in our intervention program. These good achievements in our blind group actually reflect our educational work in the areas of human attachments and prehension. Through the enhancement of the blind baby's surround, through providing the lures of persons and things "out there," the child who had postural (maturational) readiness for mobility and an elementary concept of the object in space had the incentives for creeping and for walking. Under these circumstances, sound could not substitute for sight in providing a distant lure for initiation of the mobility pattern.

We could test this experimentally. If a blind child had attained "midline reach for the person or toy on sound cue only" and had also attained a stable bridging posture (maturational readiness for creeping), he typically began to creep within a few days after the demonstration of "reach on sound." If he did not find mobility spontaneously, we could lure him into creeping by choosing a propitious moment when he was up on all fours and sounding a toy within a few inches of his hands. He would then attempt a reach which propelled him forward a few inches. We might need to sound the toy again. The baby, predictably, advanced a few inches more and finally attained the toy. Within a few days this mobility pattern—which is characterized in its practice phase as a reach and a collapse, a reach and a collapse—became a fluid and coordinated pattern of creeping. The practice phase and the attainment will strike the reader as identical to that which is seen in sighted babies lured by the distant object.

This, then, is not "training," a method commonly employed by educators of the blind, but a form of guidance which derives from the developmental principles we had uncovered in our research. If the developmental principles are not available to the parents or the educator, there is great peril for the baby in finding the route toward mobility. Clearly, if a baby has not yet demonstrated "reach on sound," all efforts to entice him to creep with a distant voice or sound will fail. Many blind babies have been wrongly labeled as "retarded" or "neurologically impaired" on the basis of motor performance alone. Many parents and educators may attempt to "teach" a blind baby to creep by putting him through the exercise of creeping, manipulating his legs and arms. It is a method doomed to failure and typically results in a resistant and outraged baby, who flips over on his back and has a monumental tantrum.

An educational program that is attuned to developmental principles needs to take into account the impediment of blindness to "reach on sound" and to provide the blind infant with the incentives for initiating mobility. Then it can confidently wait for the baby to "invent" mobility for himself. Except in the cases of severe brain damage (seen in our consultation group), the blind child will then become mobile without a protracted delay. In the case of the brain-damaged blind child, it is, of course, not blindness alone that is the impediment to mobility but the second damaged system which affects maturational processes and is further caught up in the constrictions of blindness. In our consultation-education program group we have helped many blind children with neurological impairment to achieve free mobility following the same principles we have described. For these children, of course, the delays in the achievement of mobility are marked. (They would also occur, of course, if the child was brain-damaged and sighted.) In working with these children, we watch for signs of maturational readiness in the attainment of trunk control, and we facilitate, when possible, the conditions for achieving control of the trunk. The brain-damaged blind child, in contrast to our otherwise intact blind babies, will show the effects of neurological impairment in marked delays in achieving *postural* milestones. Even here, however, we must be cautious in the interpretation of retardation in postural attainments, since if there are no positive indications of neurological impairments, it is important to ascertain through home visits whether or not the blind child is being deprived experientially of the conditions that lead to adequate control of the trunk.

LANGUAGE

Our findings show that the majority of our advantaged group of blind babies attained language milestones during the first two years within ranges for sighted children. The typical delays in language acquisition reported in the general blind population need careful analysis. Our own findings suggest that for those blind children who are neurologically intact, and intact in other systems, the delays in language acquisition may reflect experiential poverty

Our education and guidance in the area of language learning during the first two years of life was very largely based on the developmental principles underlying language acquisition for intact infants. There was no formal "speech training," even as there was no formal "training" in any area of our intervention program. We reasoned that everything we did to promote human attachments, manual tactile, aural experience, and locomotion would affect the investment of persons and things, and the representation of persons and things would, in turn, lead to naming wants, naming things, and combining words. In those cases where the home language environment was poor and would have affected language learning even in a sighted child, we provided much help to the parents in understanding how vocal discourse with even a young baby leads him to produce his own sounds, later to imitate sounds and words, and finally to acquire words Through our own discourse with babies during our home visits, we demonstrated to some puzzled, amused, and initially unbelieving parents who never "talked to" babies, that their babies responded to these speeches in very specific ways. Parents who had never done so with their sighted babies began to play the game and were, predictably, rewarded. A ranking of our babies according to "maximally stimulating language environment" and "minimally stimulating language environment" shows a pattern that reflects exactly the quality and quantity of the language environment. The highest-ranking babies on each item of the Bayley scales were the children of the highest-ranking language environments. The two children who appear outside the Bayley ranges for the higher-language items are children who reflect the limitations of their language environment, even with our guidance

Yet the distribution of scores on two of the advanced language items shows a clustering below the Bayley median We suggested that here the scores may reflect the impediment of blindness in concept development.

Blindness demonstrably impedes representational intelligence in the period two and a half to four years for five children who were available to us for study beyond the age limits of our original investigation. The acquisition of the nonsyncretic "I" is a late achievement even for our two highest-ranking children. The capacities to represent the self as "I" and to represent the self in play are both delayed as compared with estimated sighted norms. Our highest-ranking girl in overall development illustrated the extraordinary problem for a blind child in representing the self as "I" in a universe of "I's." Her language profile shows a detour for a two-and-a-half-year period, then comes back on the main pathways between the ages of four and five. By age five her discourse can barely be distinguished from that of sighted children.

When we consider that these delays in the acquisition of stable "I–you" concepts appeared in a group of blind children who had no neurological impairment and were educationally advantaged through our program, the implications for the larger population of blind preschool children are sobering.

We can now understand that among the large numbers of blind children who show undifferentiated personalities at school entrance, there must be an unknown number who are neurologically intact but impeded in their development by the extraordinary problem for the blind child in constituting an "I" and a "you."

For some of these children, there may still be hope that an "I" will be constituted in the further course of development. This is not, of course, a prescription for speech training. The concept of "I" will not be attained through lessons in "I" and "you." Through our own work, we are convinced that this conceptual education must concern itself with the strengthening of human attachments, in the home and the school, and with the provision of a home and school environment that lures the child into discoveries of himself and the external world.

A CONCISE SUMMARY

As we have examined each sector of development in our group of blind children, we find that we have come full circle to the central finding: We were able to facilitate the blind infant's development in every sphere of development, but the impediment of blindness could be discerned at every point in development at which *representational intelligence* would lead the sighted child into the organization of an object world. We could facilitate the affective ties to human partners, but the constitution of those partners as objects was delayed by comparison with sighted-child norms. We could facilitate the coordination of hand and ear, but this coordination was still dependent upon the blind child's ability to attribute substantiality to persons and things when only one of their attributes, sound, was given. We facilitated locomotion, but we could still discern the impediment to locomotion, the absence of the distant lure usually provided by vision, the reach for "something out there." We saw that blindness was not a major impediment to the acquisition of language in the first two years of life when we were able to maximize the experience of the blind child and his language environment. But the impediment of blindness revealed itself most cruelly in the protracted delay in the constitution of a stable concept of "I."

Finally, the effects of intervention can be summarized: In those areas of development where comparative data are available, our educationally advantaged blind infants came closer to sighted-child ranges than blind-child ranges.

9

INTRODUCTION

Early Language Development,
by Katrina de Hirsch

Theories explaining language acquisition tend to evolve hand in hand with changing perspectives on the nature of humanity. Without bluntly asserting, as John D. Benjamin (1961a) did, that "the only appropriate answer to the question: 'nature *or* nurture?' is—nuts!," de Hirsch, in the following chapter, adopts a comparable position. She occupies a middle ground between the behavioralist view that language acquisition is a special instance of learning in general and therefore can be explained by operant conditioning (Skinner, 1957) and the generative grammarian view that humans possess an innate knowledge of a universal grammar so that despite their superficial differences, all languages arise from a similar internal structure (Chomsky, 1968). Indeed, the author asked the editors to underscore that this chapter, which is oriented primarily to the needs of the clinician, was written before major theoretical contributions to developmental linguistics.

Unlike most linguists, who are interested in the formal properties of language, de Hirsch emphasizes the reciprocal relationship of language development and ego structuralization. She raises questions as to what linguistic deficits mean in terms of the child's overall psychic structure. As Mahler (1971) points out, the symbolic use of words is a crucial step in the process of individuation. Since individuation itself seems to be a prerequisite for the development of language, it is clear that a disturbance in one process will be reflected in the other.

The complicated issue of interrelationships of language and cognition (which often resembles the chicken-and-egg debate) is also addressed in the following chapter from a pluralistic perspective. With her focus on language development, de Hirsch quite naturally does not dwell on cognitive development in children who are language-deprived like the deaf. This area has been explored by Furth (1966), who discusses cognition without language in the framework of Piaget's developmental theory. But he has been challenged by Blank (1965) that the special language training given many deaf children makes it inappropriate to consider deafness a linguistic deficiency Furth (1971), in turn, has replied that this criticism is inconsistent with the markedly retarded reading development found in the hearing-impaired (Wrightstone, Aronow, and Moskowitz, 1963) and the fact that the conventional sign language for the deaf is available at an early age only to that small percentage of deaf children whose parents are deaf. In consequence, most deaf children spend their formative years without a systematized language. It is impressive, however, that they construct their own symbols for early representational thinking. Furth concludes that up to and including Piaget's concrete-operational stage of intelligence, linguistic support is not required The relationship of language to formal-operational thinking is less clear

In normally developing children, we find both universal stages and individual variations in language acquisition. For instance, with maturation, the child's concept of the purpose of language evolves from communicating needs and feelings and establishing contact, to classifying objects and occurrences, and then to informing others of these systems as a means of communication and validation. Kagan, Moss, and Sigel (1960) point out that certain children fail to acquire the set of symbols that would allow them to conceptualize important aspects of their experience. The acquisition of these symbols, however, depends on adequate interpretation of this experience. In order to conceptualize experience, the child must understand the grammatical structures that provide him or her with linguistic options. It is widely accepted that language stabilizes perception and also serves as a mediator for nonverbal performance (Luria, 1961). Verbal children talk themselves through a puzzle; this is how people with good linguistic endowment compensate for perceptual deficits. Language makes possible operations such as categorization and serialization. It allows the individual to determine the common property of things and to group them into larger entities, thereby facilitating the shift from associative to cognitive levels of operation (de Hirsch, 1975; Luria, 1961).

Menyuk (1971) notes that children progress differently through various developmental language stages, independent of diagnostic classification Some infants display difficulty in moving from vocalization to babbling, while others may falter in the transition from babbling to single-word utterances. Still others may experience difficulty in progressing from the expression of fundamental relations to the development of transformational rules Although these individual differences are not yet well defined, they do not correlate with currently employed nosological systems.

What influence does the nature of the mother-infant synchrony, discussed in Chapter 3 by Brazelton, Koslowski, and Main, exert on language acquisition? G Wyatt (1969) describes the early verbal interaction between the mother and infant as a mutual feedback system based on unconscious iden tification. Piaget (1923) calls it *contagion verbale* M C Bateson (1971) has described "conversational" patterns between mother and infant in the second month of life, while Condon and Sander (1974) have demonstrated an inter action between the human voice and the infant's movements as early as 12 hours following birth What effect do these observations have on the critical period for language acquisition that Lenneberg (1967) estimates spans a decade? Noting the great difference in propensity for acquiring foreign lan guages from the pre-teen to the post-teen years, Lenneberg postulates a second "critical period" for language acquisition, which coincides with the time during which the human brain attains full maturity in terms of structure function, and biochemistry (electroencephalographic pattern stability lags behind slightly)

In Chapter 5 Money comments on the relationship between linguistic and gender-identity development Beit-Hallahmi et al (1974), in a fascinating report, assess the extent to which a person's native language forces him or her to make grammatical gender distinctions These investigators note that the English language, in which sex affects only third-person pronouns, oc cupies a middle ground of "gender-loading" between the extremes of the Hungarian and Finnish languages, in which sex exerts absolutely no influence on grammar, and Semitic languages, like Arabic and Hebrew, in which almost every word uttered requires the speaker to consider simultaneously both his or her own sex and the sex of the person addressed in order to be grammatically correct. In consequence, children learning to speak Hebrew or Arabic are constantly being educated about their own gender as well as everyone else s via modeling, approval, and /or correction of every communication In con trast, children learning to speak Hungarian and Finnish have neither the benefit nor the annoying intrusion of this sort of input The results of this ambitious cross-cultural comparative study are as yet inconclusive Further observations are awaited

These are but some of the multitude of possible questions regarding lan guage development The acquisition of language provides a striking example of the remarkable capacity of infants and children to process and integrate new information and develop new skills without the benefit of previous knowledge to which the new can be related—a capacity that seems to atrophy with age, except perhaps in the instance of rare geniuses

9

Early Language Development

KATRINA DE HIRSCH

Language pathology can be understood only in the framework of normal language development. This article discusses some of the milestones in the process of language acquisition, a process which is part of the child's organismic growth within a given social matrix. To quote from M. M. Lewis (1963): "The linguistic growth of the child moves forward as a result of the interaction of two factors, those that spring from within the child himself and those that impinge upon him from the community. Children are richly endowed with the potentialities for symbolisation, the most potent of which is language."

From his earliest days the baby vocalizes. These vocalizations utilize the expiratory phase of the respiratory cycle. The air flow is modified by the vocal cords and by the various parts of the peripheral speech mechanism. This permits the resulting sound waves to be detected auditorily. The same process holds for all vocal productions: the baby's cry, his cooing, and, at a later time, his speech. Lieberman (1967) has shown that the wave forms of the baby's cry have the same characteristics as adult sentences. Alterations in breathing produce the intonations which are instrumental in carrying messages long before the child uses words.

Hunger, pain, and discomfort will make the neonate cry. These discomfort cries approximate narrow-front vowels and are usually nasalized. A few weeks later the baby will produce relaxed, open-back vowels in the range *a–ae* during states of well-being. For the baby's mother, each characterisitic vocal pattern has a distinct meaning. Very early, then, the child uses the physiological mechanisms of respiration and phonation effectively for expressive purposes.

During the first months of life, the baby learns to associate his mother's

First published in *Developmental Medicine and Child Neurology*, 12:87–97, 1970. Reprinted by permission.

voice with pleasant situations such as feeding. Her voice is probably at first experienced as part of a total constellation: a smiling face, the presence of caresses, the satisfaction of bodily needs. At three months the baby reacts positively to friendly tones and negatively to angry tones (Bühler and Hetzer, 1935). Two or three months later he responds differentially to tones, to music, and to male and female voices. And long before he responds to the phonetic pattern of words, he responds to the prosodic features of language, to variations in intonation and pitch which carry the emotional load of communication.

The vocalizations the mother uses in her communication with the baby are tailored to his affective needs. They differ from those she uses in other situations in a number of features: dynamic accent, melody and rate, and a marked tendency to rhythmic iterations (Grewel, 1959). Di Carlo (1964) has made the pertinent observation that the mother caresses the child with her voice. G. Wyatt (1957) calls the dialogue between the mother and her baby a process of mutual feedback. The learning of the "mother language," she says, is achieved through unconscious identification. Infants are continually talked to in situations that are essential to their well-being. The vocal communication between mother and child during bathing, feeding, and dressing must, of necessity, play an important part in the shaping of the child's communicative behavior, of which language is but one aspect. The mother's voice, specifically, is bound to be heavily invested with affect for the baby, and one might assume that such an investment would have a bearing on his subsequent listening attitudes.

We know that with children brought up in institutions, maturational processes are delayed or interfered with. This is shown beautifully by Provence and Lipton in a study of such infants (1962), who were late in smiling, handling toys, and responding differentially to people, and whose vocal and verbal development was usually severely delayed. Well-mothered babies have a repertoire of most of the vowels and half of the consonants by the end of the first year. Brodbeck and Irwin (1946) have compared the frequency and variety of such children's vocalizations with those of children cared for in orphanages and found significant differences between the two groups as early as the first two months of life. The discrepancies became more marked by the fourth and sixth months. Similar findings are reported by Fisichelli (1950).

Between the fifth and tenth month of life, usually around the time the baby attempts to sit up, he begins to babble. The transition from expressive sounds to babbling is not well marked; the various stages of language development overlap. Babbling differs from expressive sounds in that it is not tied to specific situations such as hunger. Now the baby lies in his crib, plays with his fingers and toes, and plays with sounds he produces spontaneously, for

the sheer pleasure of making them. There is no mistaking the intense gratification the baby derives from the mouthing of sounds, and it is thus not
surprising that analysts are impressed by the role this oral activity plays in
early psychosexual development.

Every mother knows that she can stimulate long babbling exchanges between herself and her baby. It has been shown that nonsocial stimuli such
as the sound of chimes do not increase infants' vocalizations. Nor does the
mere presence of the human being result in more copious babbling (Todd
and Palmer, 1968). The human voice stimulates babbling and its effect is
reinforced by the presence of the adult.

During babbling the baby "discovers" how to mold the outgoing breath
stream so as to produce a whole repertoire of sounds. At the same time an
auditory feedback loop is being established. As sound-producing movements
are repeated over and over again, a strong link is forged between tactual and
kinesthetic impressions, on the one hand, and auditory sensations, on the
other. A pattern of alternate hearing and uttering is set up. Sounds heard
evoke more vocalizations, which are no longer entirely random, but tend to
resemble the phonemic and intonational configurations of the original model.
One of the main functions of babbling is thus an intensive kinesthetic-pro-
prioceptive-auditory learning experience resulting in primitive sound-move-
ment schemata being established during babbling. The baby not only produces
a whole range of different sounds, but he derives pleasure from imitating
those he himself produces. This achievement reflects his growing capacity
to store—if only for a limited time—and to retrieve the auditory-motor configurations that serve him as models for repetition. Recent research seems
to show (Yeni-Komshian, Chase, and Mobley, 1968) that the auditory feedback monitoring system is already operative at the age of eight months and
that the capacity to monitor one's own speech grows until the age of nine.

Intactness of the central nervous system is a prerequisite for the auditory-
motor feedback loop. This loop does not become functional in babies who
are deaf or hard of hearing. Deaf babies babble, but they discontinue after
a while because they lack the feedback of hearing their own sounds, as well
as those of the environment. Recent investigations (Fry, 1966) have demonstrated that with amplification at the babbling stage, that is to say, with
the very early establishment of the auditory feedback loop, the language
development of severely hard-of-hearing children approximates that of normal
ones.

In the more advanced babbling stage, certain sounds which were produced
during early babbling activities tend to drop out. Menyuk (1968) has found
that during the first few months the sound repertoire of Japanese and American
babies is very similar, but that by the ninth month the sounds used during

babbling are similar to those produced by the child's particular language environment.

Around the tenth month and with the developing control over volume, pitch, and intonation, the baby enters the echolalic stage, when he attempts to imitate not only his own sounds but also the more patterned utterances he hears spoken around him. He begins to repeat words heard but not necessarily understood. Echolalia is a normal phase in language development, and echolalic responses comprise a significant portion of children's speech up to 29 months. Some toddlers repeat new words or new combinations of words for purposes of clarification. Echolalia is pathognomonic for mental retardation, autism, or aphasia only if it is the only response available to the child or if it occurs in older children.

Comprehension and production of language facilitate each other. However, comprehension, which places a lesser load on the immature organism, usually precedes production; passive control precedes active control. Before the baby uses words, he begins to interpret first the intonational and later the phonemic patterns of those around him. What happens when we say a child "understands"? He must be ready to make a modicum of sense out of the world that surrounds him; he must use some objects appropriately; he must have a rudimentary sense of self, of being separate. Probably he will then respond at first simply to the intonational configuration as part of a specific situation. Slowly, the phonemic pattern becomes intertwined with intonational and situational features until very gradually, as further differentiation takes place, the phonemic pattern takes dominance, irrespective of the situation.

We do know that in order to produce meaningful speech, the child must comprehend verbalizations directed to him. We do not, however, know which factors determine the ability to process linguistic information. Nor do we know exactly what happens when the child uses his first meaningful utterances. McCarthy (1954) says there is a tremendous psychological gap to be bridged between the mere production of the phonemic form of a word and the symbolic representational use of that word in an appropriate situation.

During the past 10 to 15 years a good deal of disagreement has arisen between psychologists and linguists as to the relationship between babbling, that is to say, nonsymbolic vocalization, and the first meaningful words. Psychologists say that language is slowly shaped out of the multitude of babbling sounds by means of selective reinforcement on the part of the parents, who show their delight when the child produces sound combinations that resemble actual words. As a result of such reinforcement, the child gradually assembles a sound repertoire approximating that of the language he is reared in and begins to associate these sound combinations with specific situations, people, or objects. Linguists such as Jakobson and Halle (1956), on the other hand, draw a sharp dividing line between babbling and representational speech, while R. Brown (1958), in an intermediate position, suggests a "babbling drift" in describing the transition from babbling to language. We know that at the age of 12 months the child is able to imitate the intonational contours of his mother's speech. Many preverbal babies utter long strings of sounds which resemble those of adults in terms of melody and pitch. Mothers respond to these vocalizations as if they were definite messages, statements, commands, or questions. (That intonation plays a vital role in communication is testified to by the fact that autistic children's speech, which is devoid of communicative intent, is so often monotonous and poorly inflected.) A degree of meaning, a message, is thus associated with the modulated strings of sounds the baby produces before the emergence of single words. Advanced babbling *is* a kind of language and we cannot, therefore, talk of the emergence of symbolic utterances as a sudden event, but we must look on this development as an ongoing process. This process, the behaviorists say, is solely the result of continuous and selective reinforcement, while linguists maintain that it is a process reminiscent of embryonic development, in the sense that it constitutes the unfolding of an inherent potential.

The baby's first words appear between the ages of 12 and 20 months and are usually strongly affectively colored. They are by no means stabilized in terms of meaning, however. In the beginning, words are often simply by-products of action. The child frees himself only slowly from the constraint of specific situations and—as time goes on—learns to use words as substitutes for action. The growth of the child's vocabulary reflects a continuing process of modification which involves both the acquisition of new words and the expanding and refining of word meanings previously learned. *Goggie* is at first only the child's small, fluffy toy dog; a little later the word is used to describe the real dog he sees at a neighbor's; and in the end it stands for all members of the species *dog*. The meaning of the word has been expanded. The opposite process takes place when the child says, for instance, "Me write a picture" (Cazden, 1966). In this case the child will find out that the word *write* refers only to those graphic activities which involve letters and numbers—the meaning of the word *write* has been contracted and refined.

By the age of two years, the average child has 200 to 300 words in his usage vocabulary; his understanding vocabulary is much larger. After the age of two, he makes giant strides in the comprehension and production of meaningful words. However, we do not know whether the child's growing ability to use words symbolically depends on general organismic capacities which reach a critical minimum level around the age of 18 months, or whether there are factors *specific* to language which mature around that time, which are more or less independent of general processes. Lenneberg (1966) maintains that the ability to acquire language is a biological phenomenon relatively independent of that elusive property called intelligence. He suggests the possibility that intelligence is the *result* of the ability to comprehend and use language, rather than the other way around.

The enlargement of vocabulary, the growth of meaning which belongs to the semantic aspect of language, continues throughout the individual's entire life. This growth depends on the child's cultural background (the best single predictor of his recognition vocabulary is his mother's vocabulary score on the WISC), and on his inherent linguistic endowment. Above all, it depends on the affect tie between mother and child, the give and take between the two and the constant and responsive guidance by the significant people who share his life experiences.

Around the time the child makes large strides in the acquisition of new words, he forges ahead toward mastery of the phonological system of his language. Phonology describes the matrix of features that differentiate one speech sound from another by virtue of certain characteristics—for instance, presence or absence of voice in the sounds *b* and *p*. Jakobson (1962) maintains that language development is characterized by the learning of successive contrasts in a more or less fixed sequence—the vowel-consonant contrast probably being the first to be learned.

We assume that children perceive linguistically significant contrasts and distinctions before they can produce them (the production of sounds is usually discussed under the heading of articulation). A four-year-old may say "dwess," but he may shake his head when the adult uses the wrong form. According to Menyuk (1967a), there is little research on the perceptual distinctions children are able to make between the ages of one and three. Sounds for the young child are probably at first indistinguishable from one another. Menyuk found that Japanese and American children acquire phonemic distinctions in approximately the same order, indicating that this hierarchy of distinctions depends primarily on the inherent developing perceptual and productive capacity of the child.

Children have to learn to distinguish not only between *single* features of sounds, but often between bundles of them. The child who says "dar" instead of "car" misses out both on place of articulation and on the voiced-unvoiced contrast. Young children whose articulation develops normally tend to substitute only one feature at a time, but older children with articulatory problems usually fail to distinguish several simultaneously, which raises questions as to possible gaps in memory and storage (Menyuk, 1968). Articulatory errors may be due to a variety of factors: they may result from perceptual confusion, such as failure to recognize the diacritic feature that distinguishes a *t* from a *k*, or from inability to execute complex motor patterns such as the consonant cluster *str* in the word *string*. That there is a strong link between auditory-perceptual and motor aspects of speech is stressed by Winitz (1967), who suggests that the road from perception to output is not a one-way street. Winitz, who adheres to the motor theory of perception, maintains that discrimination errors are frequently the result rather than the cause of misarticulation. Some articulatory errors, finally, are on a linguistic basis. A child may perceive the difference between sounds such as *f* and *v*, he may be able to produce both, but he may use the plural *leafs* because he has failed to incorporate the linguistic rule requiring a change from *f* to *v* in the pluralization of certain nouns.

Articulatory competence varies from child to child, at least within certain limits. Obviously not all 40-odd sounds of the phonological system of the English language crystallize at the same time. Development proceeds from crude and primitive to more complex and more differentiated forms. The child's earliest utterances contain only two or three phonemes. At 18 months he may have mastered from eight to 12 of them, including diphthongs. From then on his production of the sounds of his language increases by leaps and bounds as a result of further differentiation. Sudden spurts are followed by phases of consolidation, but, according to Templin (1966), the five-year-old child should produce 88% of all sounds correctly.

The order in which phonemic units are being mastered depends on several factors. One is degree of difficulty. The phoneme *s*, for instance, which requires intricate adjustments of the peripheral speech mechanism, may not be adequately produced until the age of seven. Frequency is another factor. The child will use those phonemes first which occur most often in the vocabulary he hears and uses.

As a rule children produce only those sound sequences which are part of their native language. An English child will not, for instance, produce the cluster *pf*, which is a common one in German (as in the word *pferd*), but he will use the cluster *pl*, which is acceptable in English. The sequence *ng*, which occurs frequently during babbling in all positions, becomes restricted to the middle and the final position of words. Children do not usually need formal training to incorporate these rules which they acquire fairly early. It is obvious that the mastery of the phonological system of the language requires a degree of central nervous system maturation. Beyond it we know that the child needs, if not systematic teaching, at any rate, a model. Without such a model he may falter on the road to mastery. It is the mother who serves as the primary language model, who literally feeds back to the child those sound sequences which are acceptable in his particular language environment. It is only later that the child learns to monitor his own speech. We assume that there are certain critical stages in language development when the model is of decisive importance, and we believe that imitation of and identification with a mother figure play an important role not only in the growth of vocabulary, but also in the mastery of the phonological system.

In the acquisition of syntax and grammar, on the other hand, imitation, according to linguistic theory, is by no means of primary importance. The transition from nonrelational—one-word utterances—to relational speech, consisting of two or more words, represents a tremendous step in development. If one considers the enormous complexity of syntax and grammar, one can only marvel at the fact that this process develops so rapidly; by the age of five, children use virtually all the structures they will ever use. They operate at first with stored fragments of speech heard. These imitations preserve word order, which is an important linguistic signal in English. Because of limitation in auditory memory span and because, according to R. Brown and Bellugi (1964), this is as far as the child can "program," the early imitations are usually limited to a range from two to four units. More important, such imitations are not "progressive" in the sense that they are not applied to different contexts, they are not generalized.

The first nonimitative two-and three-word combinations, which appear between 12 and 24 months, are by no means random. They consist of content words—nouns, labels, verbs—open-class words which carry the information, coupled with functors—"pivot words"—such as *off, more.* "More car" is an example. Such telegraphic speech, which is characterized by omission of most unstressed words, conforms, nevertheless, to a regular pattern. The subsequent form, the noun phrase ("my big car") described by R. Brown and Bellugi (1964), is a cohesive grammatical unit that can be expanded through the use of modifiers. These early grammatical constructions reflect the child's discovery of basic phrase structure which leads to the formation of "kernel sentences." On this level one finds designative sentences ("This is a big car"), predicative sentences ("The car is broken"), actor-action sentences ("Mummy give milk"). From such "kernel sentences," new forms evolve through the use of "transformations" by means of additions, deletions, and rearrangements. Pronouns are substituted for noun phrases, serialization is affected through the use of the word *and*, questions are formulated by prefacing sentences with *wh* words. Thus, beginning with the simplest two-word combinations, one can trace the gradual emergence of phrases to the formulation of kernel sentences from which transformations can be derived. Three-and-a-half-year-olds use complete sentences of at least four words, including relational ones.

By means of a series of ingenious experiments, Berko (1960) investigated children's ability to make transformations. These experiments illustrate what is meant by "generating new forms." The experimenter, for instance, points

to a doll and says: "Here is a man who knows how to wug, today he is . . ."
and the child fills in *wugging* although he has never heard the present participle
of *wug*. Children's very mistakes indicate that they do not simply imitate
longer and longer bits of speech they hear. The limited linguistic corpus they
are exposed to serves them as a source for grammatical generalizations and
permits them to generate forms they have never heard. The child who says,
"I have seen two mouses," proves that he has incorporated the rule that asks
for the ending *es* in the pluralization of words such as house. The two-and-
a-half-year-old who says, "Mommy, I want a chee" assumes that a "chee"
is the singular of "cheese." Both children have overgeneralized, but their
mistakes show, nevertheless, that they have derived a set of abstract rules
from a relatively small sample of linguistic input. These rules are basic to
the decoding and encoding of language (Chomsky, 1965). Mastery of these
rules is a gradual process; the three-year-old, for instance, understands the
contrast between subject and object in the active but not in the passive voice.
The understanding and use of the passive voice belongs to an older age.

The impressive fact about normal language development is its universality
and consistency. While children vary in the rate with which they incorporate
the linguistic code—at least within certain limits—early speech milestones
appear at roughly the same time. The large majority of children babble, use
stress and intonation, utter two-to-three-word combinations, and acquire the
basic rules of their language at about the same age. Without formal training,
children incorporate a set of assumptions and rules regarding their language
which allows them to understand and generate new forms. According to
McNeill (1966), this proves that children are born with a set of "linguistic
universals" as part of their innate endowment. Children, he says, are neurologically so "pre-programmed" with a language acquisition device that a
minimum of stimulation is required for the realization of this potential. A
less radical view assumes that children are born not so much with linguistic
universals, but with propensities, *anlagen,* which enable them to extract from
the linguistic input the relevant data needed to organize language into a
consistent system.

Children whose language development deviates pass through the normal
grammatical stages later than do others. Menyuk (1967b) gives as an example
the phrase "he no big boy." This is a normal construction at age three, but
may be used at age six by children with difficulties in the language area.
Furthermore, speech-defective children often fail to make the generalizations
expected in normal language development. In fact, they may even perform
linguistic operations that do not form part of their own language system.
Their hypotheses as to the rules of grammar and phonology differ from those
of children whose linguistic development runs smoothly. It may be of interest

to mention in this context that grammar is relatively resistant to remedial help. Some very intelligent children need long-term assistance to achieve acceptable grammar.

While it is true that normal language development goes forward without formal training, *expansion* is an effective device in language learning (R. Brown, 1964). Most mothers respond to children's telegraphic speech by presenting them with the nearest correct sentence, that is to say, they modify children's utterances by means of functor words, inflectional affixes, etc. Thus, a child may say, "Mummy lunch" and the mother may counter by saying, "Yes, Mummy is having her lunch." Such a response is far from being a correction. Cazden (1968) has rightly pointed out that correction extinguishes communication altogether. Expansion, on the other hand, "supplies a model of more explicit encoding of intended meaning . . . at a time when the child's attention is directed to the significant clues of the message." It is, however, by no means easy to determine what is effective: *amounts* or *kinds* of stimulation.

There is a teaching device that supplies richer stimulation than does expansion. *Expatiation* consists of enlargement of the child's utterances. Thus, when a child says, "Dog bark," the adult does not limit himself to the closest correct sentence but adds, "He barks at the kitty, but he won't bite it." This kind of response provides a richer linguistic corpus to draw from than does expansion.

Mothers instinctively present to the children different language models at different stages in the language-learning task. However, we know relatively little about what happens when a child is exposed precociously to advanced language models, nor are we entirely sure about what occurs when he is presented with such models at a late stage.

There is, of course, no doubt that there is far less expansion and expatiation in deprived environments than there is in middle-class ones. Lenneberg (1967) maintains, nevertheless, that not only is the sequence of language milestones relatively independent of environmental conditions, but also the timing. Time of speech onset, appearance of the first two-word combinations, and mastery of the grammatical system all occur more or less at the same time regardless of milieu; even children suffering from gross neglect learn to talk with relatively little delay. Lenneberg's position is open to question since there are so many neglected children whose speech is deficient in the absence of a demonstrable neurological deficit. It would be foolish, furthermore, to deny that language dimensions, such as richness and complexity of verbal output, ability to express feelings and ideas, and level of abstraction, are heavily dependent on environmental support.

Bernstein (1961) has found that the speech of lower-class individuals is characterized by rigidity of syntax and restricted structural possibilities for sentence organization. He states that middle-class speech, in contrast, facilitates verbal elaboration and provides a complex conceptual framework for the organization of experience. This position is shared by Hess and Shipman (1966), who found that the flow of language between mother and child varies according to social grouping. They view the mother as a teacher, a programmer of experience during the preschool years, and they have shown in a series of ingenious experiments that mothers from different social levels use different styles of processing information. This information processing is mediated through language. Hess and Shipman's findings clearly demonstrate that the "teaching style" of lower-class mothers is far less explicit and less effective than that of middle-class mothers, and that teaching style is related to the cognitive functioning of the child.

The problem of language acquisition in disadvantaged children is even more complex for groups whose dialect differs from standard English. Differences in phonology and, above all, in grammatical structure in Negro children's speech are often wrongly viewed as language deficits. Cazden (1966) in an excellent paper discusses the difference-deficiency issue. Disadvantaged children, she says, tend to be deficient in many measures of verbal skills. One must be sure, however, that developmental language scales do not distort the assessment of children who speak a nonstandard dialect. Povich and Baratz's study (1967) has shown that the proportion of linguistic transformations is the same in Negro children as in middle-class ones of comparable age. However, those transformations differ in kind. The form "he brother" for "his brother," for instance, or the use of the double negative is a typical transformation in the language code for adult Negroes. Thus, these forms cannot be regarded as grammatically defective in the case of Negro children.

It is of interest that in all social groups, girls are more advanced in language development than boys, probably as a result of the relatively slower neurophysiological maturation of boys compared with that of girls. First-born do better than younger children. Twins and triplets who have to share the mother's lap are worse off than are single babies, as elaborated on by McCarthy (1958).

It is impossible to overrate the importance of language in children's development. Language is our main tool in the construction of an organized universe. The preverbal child probably has some schemata, some ways of structuring the world, but these schemata can be assumed to be amorphous. The ability to use symbols permits the child to impose order on his experience and to arrive at some clarification of his outer and inner cosmos.

Language, Edelheit (1968) states, is an obligatory component of human biological organization and plays a crucial role in the formation of the ego, which is the special human organism of adaptation. He adds that it is by no means clear to what extent ego organization is reflected in the language system and to what extent the internalized language system constitutes the regulatory organ of the ego. There is, however, no doubt as to the fact that ego development depends largely on an optimal level of verbal expression and that, conversely, ego defects of whatever origin are reflected in disturbances of language. As far back as 1936 Anna Freud had this to say: ". . . the attempt to master drive processes . . . by linking them to verbal signs which can be dealt with in consciousness was one of the . . . earliest and most necessary accomplishments of the ego, not one of its activities."

Things acquire stability and permanence by being named. Verbal signs anchor the significant people in the child's environment, they reassure him that the mothering person will return even if she is gone for a while, and they thus contribute to what is called "object constancy."

Language helps the child to a clearer concept of self and nonself. The child probably has an emerging sense of self even before he begins to verbalize. But, as Peller (1966) points out, the distinction between self and nonself becomes much more differentiated when categories such as "I," "mine," and "self" emerge.

Language permits the child to express feelings, to externalize magical fantasies, and thus to render them less dangerous. It makes possible the distinction between fantasies, on the one hand, and reality, on the other, thus assisting reality testing, which is one of the essential functions of the ego (Katan, 1961).

Words are needed for the direction of behavior and for impulse control. Planning ahead and postponing gratification are infinitely more difficult without the use of words. The formation of conscience is immensely facilitated when the child learns to internalize rules, and internalization remains precarious without the use of verbal concepts.

It has often been pointed out that language is an indispensable tool for cognition. By freeing the child from the "here and now," by making possible operations such as classifying, serializing, and formulizing, words allow him to discover the common properties of separate perceptions and events, which in turn permits the grouping of these single entities into new wholes. Language helps in the shift from associative to cognitive levels of functioning; it mediates—as pointed out by Luria (1961)—even during nonverbal tasks.

It should be emphasized, however, that the potentialities of language are fully realized only during the later phase of ontogenesis. Ombredane (1951) distinguishes the affective, the ludic (playful), the practical, the representational, and the dialectic functions of language. In the young child, speech is as yet mainly a means of expressing feelings and demands, a thing with which to play, a device which substitutes for action, or an attempt to control and regulate the behavior of others. B. Kaplan (1959) describes young children's speech as governed by affective, playful, and practical needs, and as highly charged and infused with personal meanings.

Freud (1915) said that language brings into being a higher psychical organization—one way to trace this road is to study the acquisition of language in the small child.

10

INTRODUCTION

Latency Revisited: The Age Seven, Plus or Minus One, by Theodore Shapiro and Richard Perry

Throughout the eight decades of its conceptual existence, the idea of a latency period has been characterized by ambiguity, misunderstanding, and controversy. The years between five or six and puberty were once thought to be a sexually latent period as a consequence of a repression of sexual interest and little psychosexual development (Fries, 1959). It is now clear that this is not a universal truth; during middle childhood, heterosexual interests frequently continue to develop (Rutter, 1971b). Anthropologists first pointed out that whatever happens in Western societies, in sexually permissive cultures, sex play and lovemaking are common during middle childhood (Malinowski, 1929). (It may be that in Vienna at the beginning of the century, social pressures led to repression of sexual interests in middle childhood.) These issues, accompanied by a comprehensive discussion of the value of the concept of latency, are the focus of a recent book by Sarnoff (1976).

Over the years various observers have recommended labeling children between ages six and twelve by any one of a number of other designations. Thomas and Chess (1972), for instance, assert that latency is a "confusing and inappropriate" label. They note that the developmental shift in psychological organization from action to ideation is particularly evident in both normal development and symptom formation in this age range, which they prefer to call "middle childhood." In the vast majority of children of this age, sexual interest and activity are evident without pathological significance. In any case, while the term *latency* is probably a misnomer from the perspective of current knowledge, the designation has become part of our language and will not easily disappear from use.

In their New York longitudinal study, Thomas and Chess (1972) confirm observations made in Buffalo by Lapouse and Monk (1964) and in California by J. W. MacFarlane, Allen, and Honzik (1962) that increasing age is correlated with a decreasing prevalence of behavior disorders in elementary school children. Despite their focus on the early identification of temperamental variables, Thomas and Chess assume this diminution in frequency of behavior disorders is related to the decreasing number of new environmental demands and expectations placed on middle-class children during this age period. But, as Shapiro and Perry note in the article reprinted below, there may be a substantial biological basis for this change.

While supporting Freud's assumption that latency has a biological foundation, Shapiro and Perry de-emphasize the notion of a biological lessening of drive activities, which is integral to the concept of a biphasic sexual drive. Instead, they focus on the complex reorganization of ego functioning related to discontinuities in central nervous system development and concomitant nonlinear progression in perceptual and cognitive development around age seven. This maturation is considered prerequisite for the resolution of the Oedipus complex; it is the stability of the mental processes and the new cognitive structure that *permits* the inhibition and control of drives, a key distinction from earlier theories of causation. In postulating that neurophysiological processes provide the maturational substratum for development in the latency period, Shapiro and Perry are not only reformulating psychoanalytic theory, but also building a bridge linking psychoanalytic concepts of repression and secondary-process thinking in elementary school children to neurobiological findings. By blending early theory with new knowledge, these authors have leapfrogged over the many prominent psychoanalytic and developmental commentators who have expressed disillusionment with how little psychoanalytic psychology has to offer concerning the critical aspects of the latency period (e.g., Jersild, 1968; Lidz, 1968). For years the concept of latency has been mired in apparent contradictions, which Shapiro and Perry have contributed much to resolving and synthesizing. (A clinical application of Shapiro and Perry's formulations to enuresis is given in Chapter 33 by Esman.)

10

Latency Revisited: The Age Seven, Plus or Minus One

THEODORE SHAPIRO and RICHARD PERRY

Scientific investigation generally proceeds within disciplinary lines. Chemists do chemistry and biologists do biology. However, there is also an interpenetration of individual scientific approaches when data derived from one method seem relevant to the theories and constructs of another. Psychoanalysis is not exempt from this interpenetration or the revisions in theory made necessary by advances in other sciences. Indeed, awareness of such changes is sometimes salutary in that they elaborate or better define ideas derived from the psychoanalytic method alone. While Freud (1895, 1919) sought to keep analysis methodologically free of encroachment by other therapeutic modalities, he frequently borrowed from data of biologists of his time and often modified his theory to bring it into relation with current clinical practice and data from other sciences. Among Freud's more controversial concepts was the idea of a biological basis for the latency period, an idea which was both supported and criticized during his lifetime and since his death. He seemed ever expectant that biological and chemical studies would provide the evidence that clinical science could not provide regarding the source of drives and their postulated quantitative alterations during development. His hope revealed a tacit belief in the complementarity of all science.

This paper will examine the concept of latency in the light of recent research gathered from methods outside of psychoanalysis. We shall argue that these new data tend to support Freud's initial surmise that latency has a biological

First published in *The Psychoanalytic Study of the Child*, 31:79–105. New Haven: Yale University Press, 1976. Reprinted by permission.

The title of this paper is offered with considered respect to George A. Miller (1956), who wrote of a "Magical Number Seven, Plus or Minus Two," which concerns limits in the capacity for processing information.

Partial support for this project derives from NIMH Training Grant #MH07331.

basis, but not for the reasons he proposed. We shall suggest that (1) the functional changes in the child's neurobiological, perceptual, and cognitive development that cluster about the seventh year of life are probably functionally associated with the dissolution of the Oedipus complex; (2) these functional changes in the organization of mental life and their dynamic concomitants provide latency with the behaviors that characterize this stage; (3) these assertions are supported by correlative evidence gleaned from other sciences which, while discontinuous in their method and vantage point, provide a remarkable concordance of new information useful to clinical psychoanalysts.

Among the data we present, we place special emphasis on the remarkable fact that the chronological age of seven, plus or minus one, is referred to so frequently as to suggest a milestone marking discontinuous development. Had Freud never alerted us to latency in the first instance, we would have been compelled to discover it anew. Indeed, the longer view of history and sociology of childhood antedating Freud's work indicates that empirically many cultures had already discovered the unique competence of seven-year-olds that permitted them to assume new roles not available when they were younger.

Society seemed to know empirically when to begin its push on the child toward greater autonomy. During the Middle Ages, children were sent away from home to become pages at court at age seven (Pinchbeck and Hewitt, 1969), and later, at the time of the guilds, children were apprenticed at seven. In modern society children are considered to be ready for learning in school at age seven, plus or minus: grade school begins at six in the U.S., at seven in the USSR.[1] Kohlberg and Gilligan (1971) state that there is an implicit recognition by almost all cultures of "two great stages, or transformations of development" (p. 1056). These are the years of five to seven and adolescence, which respectively usher in and end the period of compulsory education. The Roman Church considers age seven "the age of reason" in that only then can the child differentiate between the bread of everyday life and the "host." Therefore, first communion also coincides with latency. Moreover, in English common law, children under seven are deemed incapable of criminal intent.

Among the post-Freudian authors, Erikson (1950) refers to latency as an "era of industry," accentuating the positive step in ego formation rather than the suppression of sexuality. Prior to Erikson, Sullivan (1940) focused on

---

[1] Nursery school and kindergarten do of course also prepare for learning; some continuous educational aim is exploited at these earlier stages, *but* these remain *pre*-first-grade groups and have appeared somewhat late on the historical scene.

the interpersonal shift to peer relations and talked of a "juvenile era" which has lasting portent for future human interactions. Longitudinal observations of urban children led Thomas and Chess (1972) to opt for abandoning the term as misleading because they found that not much was "latent" during this period of childhood. Even their "interactionist" point of view, which places great stress on the temperamental continuities evolving within a social milieu, suggests to them, however, that during what they prefer to call "middle childhood" a number of different patterns are available which need to be distinguished from earlier periods. Any view of development that is "simply biological" necessarily omits the crucial influence of culture, but the converse is also true. In this essay we are attempting to tease out just which, if any, biological alterations underlie the observable behaviors that Freud designated as latency. When Freud wrote about the concept of latency, he could not yet draw on the broad array of facts that recent scientific advances have provided. These facts constitute the basis of our argument for biological maturation as a most important variable in determining the changes we call latency.

PSYCHOANALYTIC LITERATURE

In 1905, Freud states that development is in part "organically determined and fixed by heredity" and indicates that there are mental forces such as shame, disgust, and moral ideas that "impede the course of the sexual instinct and, like dams, restrict its flow" (p. 177). He further stresses that education "will not be trespassing beyond its appropriate domain if it limits itself to following the lines which have already been laid down organically" (p. 178). With these statements, Freud laid the groundwork for our view that latency is biological in origin and relatively immutable in the march of development.

While continuing his testimony to its biological basis, Freud later assigned more importance to the environmental contributions to latency, as well as to the effects of castration anxiety. In a footnote added to his autobiography (1925a) in 1935, he states, "The period of latency is a physiological phenomenon. It can, however, only give rise to a complete interruption of sexual life in cultural organizations which have made the suppression of infantile sexuality a part of their system. This is not the case with the majority of primitive peoples" (p. 37). Thus, throughout his life, Freud maintained the assertion of biological determinism.

Among the factors associated with the psychological manifestations of latency were the vicissitudes of the incestuous object choice, the resolution of the Oedipus complex, and superego formation. In 1919 Freud wrote, "Most probably [incestuous loves] pass away because their time is over, because the children have entered upon a new phase of development in which they are compelled to recapitulate from the history of mankind the repression of an incestuous object-choice, just as at an earlier stage they were obliged to effect an object-choice of that very sort'' (p. 188). Then in 1924, while noting the necessary disappointments associated with the dissolution of the Oedipus complex, Freud reaffirmed his deterministic biological stance: ''the Oedipus complex must collapse because the time has come for its disintegration, just as the milk-teeth fall out when the permanent ones begin to grow'' (1924a, p. 173).

The post-Freudian writers on latency may be divided into theoretical speculators, who reason by analogy to other scientific observations, and a second group of authors, who base their conclusions on direct child observation. Another group derives from Kardiner's early opposition to Freud's strict biological maturational scheme. The so-called culturalists, who took up this banner, denied latency as nothing more than a cultural imposition of certain Western societies and an artifact of rearing practices.

We shall review here only those analytic investigators who observed children directly and did not rely on reconstructions or re-experiences in the analyses of adults. The speculative theories of Ferenczi (1913), Lampl (1953), and Yazmajian (1967) are summarized in the original version of this chapter (T. Shapiro and Perry, 1976).

On the basis of observations of ''thousands of children over a ten-year period,'' Alpert (1941) states that ''the seven-year-olds represent the closest approximation of the sexual quiescence supposedly characteristic of the period from five to puberty.'' Even though the seven-year-old's impulses and conflicts are held to be only disguised, there is a relative calm compared with the six-year-old, who shows an ''active frank sexual curiosity,'' and the eight- to eleven-year-old, who shows an ''active, homosexual and heterosexual curiosity and interest, often of an aggressive and sadistic sort'' (p. 127). Berta Bornstein (1951) divides latency into two periods, the first extending from five and a half to eight years, the second from eight until ten. In the first, ''The ego, still buffeted by the surging impulses, is threatened by the new superego which is not only harsh and rigid but still a foreign body'' (p. 280). Moreover, in this first phase, defenses are directed against both genital and pregenital impulses. In the second phase, the ego is exposed to fewer conflicts because of lesser sexual demands as well as a less rigid superego.

Two more recent investigators have arrived at similar conclusions on the basis of neurological and physiological findings, as well as the personalities of latency children. E. B. Kaplan (1965), following Bornstein, also divides latency into two periods, while Williams (1972) prefers a triphasic division into early latency (five to seven), latency proper (seven to nine), and late latency (nine to eleven). The children in latency proper, compared with those in the early phase, "pursue their activities with greater concentration. Their elaboration of a theme, while playing or drawing, shows more cohesion and permits easier access to their defenses, functioning, and interests" (p. 601). Late latency children are more balanced in functioning, but prepubertal phenomena begin to encroach on the earlier quiescence.

The papers summarized in the original version of this chapter (T. Shapiro and Perry, 1976) suggest that the views concerning the biological origins of the latency period are based on evolutionary speculation, anatomic-psychological analogy, and reconstructions derived from the analyses of adult patients, most of whom belonged to the middle class. Moreover, those authors who work essentially within the psychoanalytic framework and who observe children directly agree on the subdivisions of the latency period. Kaplan goes beyond clinical observation to cite recent neurological and physiological data that she feels support her subdivision. Similarly, our own review of the recent literature from disciplines which lie adjacent to analysis suggests that we may have arrived at a point of scientific convergence where we can outline the biological and/or cognitive substrate for the preservation of latency. In our discussion we maintain the "levels concept" and suggest that there may not be a one-to-one parallel between behavior and mind and body data, and that any linkage implied should be seen as supportive, converging, and compatible rather than confirming. Each discipline proceeds within its methodological confines, applying its skills at specific levels of biological organization. We do not yet have the tools or the theory to make clean linkages. We therefore state consistencies and convergences.

In accord with Hartmann, Kris, and Loewenstein's (1951) distinction, we shall first look at maturational growth processes which "are relatively independent of environmental conditions" and then at developmental growth processes that are "more dependent on environmental conditions" (p. 90). While keeping to this plan, we shall highlight the compelling concatenation of discontinuities in development at age seven within the data of each scientific discipline.

BRAIN-BEHAVIOR CORRELATIONS AND MATURATION

Brain-behavior correlations may not hold any more hope than sexual-tissue-hormone-behavior correlations if one is concerned only with one-to-one intercorrelation between substrate and function. However, at this point in scientific knowledge, the brain is clearly the material basis of significant higher integrative functions, and there does seem to be a striking correspondence of timetables in brain anatomy, physiology, and chemistry with changes at perceptual and cognitive levels. This section should not be taken as a plea for reductionism any more than we accept the earlier analogizing to changes in sexual-tissue substrate. However, it is another sector of work to notice where the age of seven intrudes on awareness. Moreover, the changes described may be enabling for the cognitive shift of latency. At the same time we have no adequate understanding of the mechanism of interaction between levels of organization. We do, however, note simultaneity.

The anatomical growth of the brain follows what Scammon (1930) calls the "neural type of growth." The "growth pattern" that typifies height and weight and most of the other organ systems is more linear. By contrast, at the age of seven the brain has attained about 90% of the total weight gain from birth to 20 years. Microscopic structure and differentiation also change in the frontal lobes at six and seven, according to Blinkov and Glezer (1964). The rate of growth of pyramidal cells throughout the frontal lobe decreases with age, with intermittent critical stages of pyramidal cell growth at about three months, two to three years, and about six to seven years. The dimensions of pyramidal cells also vary and "the maximal values of the coefficients of variation are observed synchronously in all areas and they coincide with the above-mentioned critical growth of the dimensions of the cells" (p. 190). Blinkov and Glezer (1964) have verified this proposition by cross-sectional study.

Data concerning longitudinal and cross-sectional changes in material substrate are but one source of information regarding neurological development. Neural scientists have traditionally learned much of brain-function relations from the study of lesions and ablations as well. Loss of function late in life also may point to a critical age for the establishment of functions that may not be developed adequately if lesions occur early in life.

The frontal lobe comprises about one-third of the hemispheric surface; it includes the primary motor areas, premotor areas, and frontal eye fields, and "represents a relatively late phylogenetic acquisition which is well developed only in primates, especially in Man" (Truex and Carpenter, 1969, p. 587). Russell (1948) stresses the importance of the frontal lobes in maturation, stating that in children with frontal lesions, behavior is disinhibited and they are consequently less educable. However, following frontal lobotomy, adults sometimes show little change in behavior. Russell feels that "the frontal mechanism during mental development impresses the pattern of behavior" (p. 359) in such a way that its influence may persist after the prefrontal lobes have been severed from the lower centers, thus suggesting that experience "writes" on a maturing brain at levels lower than the cortex itself.

The frontal lobe also plays a role in the verbal regulation of behavior.

Teuber (1962) describes patients who had undergone *frontal* lobectomies, which included the superior frontal regions, for relief of focal seizures. They were given a card-sorting task by Milner (1962), who found that they would perseverate in sorting the cards following a certain criterion, e.g., color, even after that ceased to be appropriate. "They thus show a curious *disassociation* between the ability to verbalize the requirements of the test and the ability to *use this verbalization* (and other verbal cues) as a guide to action" (p. 322f.; italics added). In maze learning she found the patients with frontal lobectomies disregarded the maze that was outlined on the floor, and they went directly from start to finish without regard for the one permissible route.

In their experience with patients with massive frontal lobe tumors, Luria and Homskaya (1962) found that behaviors formerly controlled by verbal instruction were no longer amenable to this mode of regulation. These authors also state that whereas the behavior of a small child can be initiated by a verbal instruction, it cannot be arrested or reprogrammed by instructions until after five. They further cite workers in the Soviet Union who document the efficacy of verbal regulation only after five years, which seems to parallel frontal lobe maturation.

Such a relationship of the frontal lobes to self-regulation, particularly verbal self-regulation, is of central importance to psychoanalytic concepts of superego and ego controls, which are expected following the resolution of the Oedipus complex.

Among those authors who seek brain-behavior correlations in their work, E. B. Kaplan (1965) alone bases her subdivision of latency on neurological and physiological data as well as behavioral observation. She supports her argument for this division with the following maturational data: "By eight years myelinization of the tracts from the cortex to the thalamus is completed. Around the same age, the alpha wave pattern on the EEG stabilizes" (p. 227). These data are attributed to the unpublished work of Madow and Silverman (1956). However, Dustman and Beck (1969), studying the visually evoked respondes of 215 normal subjects, found that there was a rapid increase in responses recorded from the occiput, reaching a maximum level in the five- to six-year-old, followed by a decline in amplitude. At 13 to 14 an abrupt increase in amplitude appeared and stabilized at about age 16. They suggest that it is reasonable to infer that behavioral changes seen during latency may be related to these neurophysiological alterations.

At yet another level of observation of substrate changes, Bogoch (1957) found that children of six or below had low values of CSF neuraminic acid, whereas the children age seven to 16 had higher levels. He hypothesizes a "barrier antibody system" designed to isolate the brain from substances that pass readily from the blood to other tissues and notes that the low level of

CSF neuraminic acid in children under seven may reflect a chemical immaturity. No other significant data on biochemical alterations have been discovered, but many recent studies of severely disturbed children are seeking disturbances at this level of organization.

Biochemical and histological discontinuity in development is far removed from psychological and behavioral processes, but we include data from such disparate methods to indicate the significant convergence on the age seven landmark.

The changes in brain substrate occurring at seven do not stand alone. A number of measures of perceptual and neurological development and cognitive organization also show significant discontinuities. To facilitate our presentation, we divide these advances into several groups. The first deals with perception and integration of external stimuli; the second with temporospatial orientation; and the third covers cognitive processes.

1. *Perceptual-postural maturation,* which is said to underlie the development of body image (Schilder, 1935), has been studied by simple tests that rest on general laws of development such as *cephalocaudal maturation* and *intersensory integration.* Each of these processes provides the neural and perceptual base for sensory input and screening. The data derived from the senses are ultimately integrated centrally. Such integrations must perforce influence mental organization and, strikingly, can be shown to reveal discontinuities at seven years. M. Bender (1952), studying two-point, face-hand discrimination in the maturing child, showed that only about one-sixth of a group of three- to six-year-olds reported two stimuli, whereas in a group of seven to twelve-year-olds, half made both responses and thus approximated the performance of the adults studied.

Pollack and Goldfarb (1957a) and Pollack and Gordon (1959–1960) showed that children having a mental age of seven years or more on a standard IQ test made very few errors on the face-hand test. In a normal six-year-old group, 41% made errors, whereas only 6% of the seven-year-olds did so. In a longitudinal study of 59 children of ages five to seven, Kraft (1968) similarly found that 78% of the seven-year-old group made mature responses, whereas 54% of the six-year-olds and only 14% of the five-year-olds did so. These findings represent nonlinear progressions in maturation and are dramatic discontinuities in neuroperceptual appreciation.

Studying intersensory integration, Birch and Lefford (1964) and Birch and Belmont (1965) likewise demonstrate that children between the ages of five and seven change rapidly. Birch and Belmont (1965) state that "it is of interest that the rapid period of integrative growth in auditory-visual functioning coincided with those ages . . . [of] the most rapid emergence of visual-haptic, visual-kinesthetic and haptic-kinesthetic integrative competence'' (p. 303). While these integrations are proceeding, the authors stress, the child is moving from a stage where visceral and skin sensations appear to be predominant in directing behavior to a stage where vision and audition are paramount. Such work echoes Sherrington's proposition that organisms move from proximal to distal receptor preference, as well as Freud's and Mahler's notion of splanchnic to peripheral cathexis.

L. Bender (1938) borrowed Wertheimer's figures, which were used to demonstrate the basic laws of Gestalt perception, and adapted them to the study of the maturing visual-motor functions of children and brain-damaged adults. The age of seven again receives special notice in that 70% of the figures are drawn correctly at this point. Moreover, Fabian (1955) has noted a peculiar tendency in children at seven to verticalize angled figures and then to return to the slanted position. Koppitz (1964) elaborates that ''for children 7 years and younger the Bender test is useful for the identification of both immature and bright youngsters; for children 8 years or older, the Bender test can only screen out those with immature or malfunctioning visual motor perception'' (p. 35). In her studies of figure drawings Koppitz (1968) found poor integration of parts of a figure in both brain-injured and non-brain-injured boys at age six. However, while 44% of the drawings of the brain-injured boys aged seven to twelve were poorly integrated, only 5% of the human figure drawings of the healthy control subjects showed poor integration. These investigations again assign special significance to age seven.

2. *Temporospatial orientation* also matures at approximately the same time. The child can discriminate his own right from left at about the age of six. Then, after one or two years, he can also make these discriminations in an examiner sitting across from him.

Ames (1946) studied time concepts in a group aged two and a half to eight years and found that ''as to general divisions of time, the child first knows whether it is morning or afternoon (4 years), then what day it is (5 years), then what time it is (7 years), . . . what year (8 years), and what day of the month (8 years). Days of the week are named correctly by 5 years, months of the year not until 8 years'' (p. 123).

Pollack and Goldfarb (1957b) demonstrated that in normal children between the ages five and eight, ''it was not until seven years that a majority of the children attained correct knowledge of time of day and calendar organization'' (p. 540). Furthermore, they found that responses of the majority of seven-year-olds were in terms of specific measurements, whereas those of five- and six-year-olds were relativistic or approximate. They suggest that this reflects a "conspicuous improvement in orientation between the fifth and seventh years" (p. 549).

Piaget (1947) found that by the age of about seven or eight, the child is capable of temporospatial operations. At the age of about seven or eight there are constituted "the qualitative operations that structure space: the spatial order of succession and the joining together of intervals or distances; conservation of lengths, areas, etc." (p. 145). At about the age of eight the relations of *temporal order* (before and after) are coordinated with *duration* (longer or shorter length of time).

While this presentation will not accentuate Piaget's contributions, recent work by Laurendeau and Pinard (1970) must be mentioned. These authors studied five tests of spatial representation (stereognostic recognition, construction of projected straight line, topographic localization, left-right distinctions, and appreciation of perspectives) in order to assess whether there is a topological level that precedes a later period when projective and Euclidian relations become possible in spatial orientation. They found that the use of the configuration of the object and its environs that characterizes topological organizations had an upper limit of seven; two years. They also offer evidence of the relationship of their findings to concepts of egocentrism, which tends to drop off during the same period, as a correlative organizer of the spatio-temporal world.

Elkind, Koegler, and Go (1964) also have shown that there is rapid advance in children's abilities to perceive both parts and wholes in drawings at seven and eight. They state that their work, in general agreement with Piaget's study of the decentering of perception, has also shown "that the seven- to eight-year level is the point of abrupt perceptual improvement" (p. 86). Other studies by Elkind and Scott (1962) and Elkind and Weiss (1967) appear to support this finding.

3. *Cognitive changes at seven.* We do not argue here that neuromaturational and integrative advances underlie cognitive progression and new skills; rather, we continue to present data from cognitive studies that also suggest a discontinuity of function at seven.

T. S. Kendler and H. H. Kendler (1962) examined problem solving by using a simple learning task that involved presentation of two abstract forms that differed in one of two qualities—color and size (a white and a colored square of two sizes). The child was asked to discover or explicate a rule of organization that unifies the forms. Significant differences were found in the responses of children younger than six or seven from those of older ones (12% of six- to seven-year-olds gave direct integrative responses versus 67% of the eight- to ten-year-olds). The authors suggest that the direct integrative response reflects reasoning, insight, and inferential behavior, whereas the indirect, nonintegrated response that predominates in the younger children is based on trial-and-error learning. Studying children performing a task that again permitted two ways of responding, H. H. Kendler and T. S. Kendler (1962) found that with age children develop a tendency to respond in a mediational manner.

In an experiment examining a similar problem, Kuenne (1946) found that 100% of children with a mental age of six were capable of far transposition, compared with 50% of children with a mental age of three. This is attributed to the older child's ability to use verbal cues in making discriminations. Kuenne suggests that younger children tend to transpose in the manner similar to infra-human primates.

In more recent work concerning the importance of verbal mediators in transposition tasks, H. R. Marshall (1966) showed that children aged four and a half to five and a half who had verbal knowledge of the concept of middle-sizedness did better on a middle-size transposition task than children of the same age who had either a nonverbal knowledge of the concept or no knowledge of it at all. Among the older children studied, including some up to six and a half years, there were more children with verbal knowledge of the concept than those in the other two groups.

Whereas the above procedures report on specific aspects of the child's cognitive development, S. H. White (1965) and the work of Piaget bring such work into a broader scope for generalized application.

White reviews current developmental research extensively to support his thesis of a "hierarchical arrangement of learning processes." Focusing on the behavioral changes in children of age five to seven, he argues that they reflect a transition between two levels of mental functioning. The first level, which he calls *associative* functioning, is present before the age of five and is inhibited by a new "higher" cognitive level of function after the age of seven. The transitions in cognitive strategies are geared toward (1) the change in use of language representation as a "pure stimulus act," to second-order cues evoking behavior that the stimuli themselves would not call forth; (2) the ability to maintain orientation toward invariant dimensions in a surround of variance; (3) the ability to string together internal representations of stimulus-response-consequence into sequences which can be projected into the future to allow planning and projected into the past to allow inference; (4) increased sensitivity to distance receptors of vision and audition and decreased sensitivity to near receptors.

Corsini and Berg (1973) followed White's suggestion and explored the performance of children aged four, six, and eight on three tasks that White had said required the subject to maintain "orientation (toward invariant dimensions) in a surround of variance." They support his observation that the "5–7 year age period is one of great transition" (p. 473).

Piaget also found the child of five to eight years to be capable of temporal and spatial operations, which undergo transition in strategy. The ability to carry out certain tasks differentially at this stage reflects the passage from the preoperational level of cognitive functioning to the level of concrete operations. Piaget (1947) describes the thought of the preoperational child as intuitive, egocentric, subjective; children at this stage are incapable of social cooperation. "Oscillating between distorting egocentricity and passive acceptance of intellectual suggestion, the child is, therefore, not yet subject to a socialization of intelligence which could profoundly modify its mechanism" (p. 162). The "essential characteristic of logical thought is that it is operational" (p. 36) and it succeeds preoperational thought at about the ages of seven and eight. Operationality, whether at the concrete or abstract level, demands a stability of mental structure, a frame to apply to experience, rendering events less heterologous.

The relevance of Piaget's work to the views proposed in this paper is best exemplified in research involving the development of moral thinking and socialization by theorists heavily influenced by his cognitive theories.

Kohlberg (1964) indicates that the development of moral thinking is a stepped process in which he discerned six sequential stages. His data support the fact that moral character is dependent on ego strength and the ability to make decisions. In 1971, Kohlberg and Gilligan clearly point to the relation between cognition and morality, stating that cognitive maturity is a necessary, but not a sufficient condition for moral judgment maturity (p. 1071).

Damon (1975) also investigated the relation between cognitive development and the development of the concept of positive justice and found that "logical and moral reasoning inform and support each other in the course of ontogenesis" (p. 312). The children who had arrived at the last two of six substages of positive justice were eight years old and had also passed from the cognitive preoperational stage to that of concrete operation. Rubin and Schneider (1973), also following Piaget, contend that egocentric thought and immature moral judgment in the preoperational child are determined by the inability to decenter. Fifty-five seven-year-old children were tested and their results "provide clear support for the hypothesis that among 7-year-olds there is a positive relationship between decentration skills, as indicated by scores on measures of communicative egocentrism, and moral judgment and the incidence of altruism" (p. 664).

Zigler (1971) highlights the importance of cognitive development for socialization and offers an explanation for differences in social-class behavior as an alternative to the simply sociogenic explanations. He posits an ontogenetic "developmentally changing hierarchy of reinforcers" that serve to regulate social behavior. Self-cuing, the possibility of "turning against the self," and guilt accompany increasing cognitive development; i.e., these phenomena represent a movement away from action and toward thought and therefore increased mediation. Studies of lower- and middle-class seven-year-olds showed that the former were more responsive to verbal reinforcers such as "good and fine," while the latter did better with "right and correct" (Zigler and Kanzer, 1962). Zigler uses these and other data to suggest that cognitive capacity alone does not make manifest behavior, but capacity in interaction with social milieu helps to ensconce preferred reinforcers.

To conclude this section we again must return to the practical implications of the capacity for cognitive strategies in the carrying out of life tasks. Moreover, one might wonder if there is a minimal neural maturation that is required to achieve new cognitive levels. While we have kept data from investigations of substrate separate from data of higher-level functions in this review, some authors study two or more levels simultaneously and confound our intention, but stimulate our integrative interest. Cohn (1961) studied children with reading and writing disabilities. Both of these skills are practical in our world and require the integrity of a number of functions. He examined the neurological competence of both impaired and normal children by "all tests that potentially could be correlated with structural lesions of the brain" (p. 153). Four categories of test were used—language, somatic receiving and expressive systems, personal spatial organization, and social adaptation. A composite of test results served as an index of neurological deficit. In the group of 130 control children, those of ages seven to ten had the lowest index of neurological deficit and the change approached its limit at the age of eight. Thus, again the phenomenon is repeated that curves of functional development in many sectors level off at seven, plus or minus one.

DISCUSSION

What light does the research on maturation and development gathered from diverse scientific investigations shed on the psychoanalytic concept of the latency period? Although Freud assumes that the emergence of the latency period follows some biological timetable, it appears that a biphasic growth of the sexual drive is not the significant substratum on which this timetable is based. We would argue that processes within the central nervous system and cognitive strategies derived from maturation may provide latency with its biological clock.

The normal child of seven, plus or minus one, has reached a level of maturation and development that permits autonomy. He is emotionally less dependent on his family, has at his disposal a neuromuscular apparatus that is ready for the challenge of environmental mastery, and has a new set of cognitive strategies to outwit and control his environment. This we view as a discontinuity in behavioral development.

The greater stability and invariance of mental processes and the new cognitive structure at seven also permit the *inhibition and control of drives* and the postponement of action. The intrusive animism of the preoedipal child, which is based on associative thinking, is no longer as intrusive. Stable structures have replaced earlier instabilities and can now be used in the service of new cognitive skills while keeping sexual drive components in greater isolation. What we call repression may rest upon the splitting and reorganization of archaic and more integrated forms of thinking which complement each other and are simultaneously present in different organizational frames within the same psychic apparatus. Lipin (1969) suggests that maturation provides the possibility of two such organizations and elaborates the conditions under which the archaic levels may irrupt into consciousness as sensory elements rather than thoughts within and outside of the analytic situation.

Psychoanalytic theory has defined a number of factors that facilitate the socialization characteristic of the latency child's functioning. Among these are the transition from primary- to secondary-process modes of discharge; the cognitive basis for the structuralization of the mental apparatus, which includes the possibility of resolving the Oedipus complex; infantile amnesia; and the establishment of an invariant, internalized superego to direct and modulate behavior without the constant need for external controls. We recognize that man in conflict is the essential datum of the psychoanalytic clinical practice, *but* man in conflict depends upon opposing internalized structures, which in turn are a feature of the new abilities of the seven-year-old.

We note that although our researches have led us to conclusions that differ from Freud's as to just what the biological basis of latency is, it is a tribute to Freud that several of his ideas regarding the cognitive basis of latency were prescient.

In 1911, Freud dealt with the transition from the pleasure principle to the reality principle. The latter is established as a result of the inevitable inadequacies of drive satisfaction. This transition implies that secondary processes evolved because drive satisfaction was not achieved by rapid discharge. Because hallucinatory wish fulfillment does not suffice, ''the psychical apparatus had to decide to form a conception of the real circumstances in the external world and to endeavour to make a real alteration in them . . . the new demands [of the reality principle] made a succession of adaptations necessary in the psychical apparatus'' (p. 219f.). The adaptations Freud discussed are: the greater importance and *consciousness* of sense organs; the function of attention necessary to search the external world when a need arises; a system of notation, which is a part of memory; an impartial passing of judgment, which has to decide the truth or falseness of ideas; and the process of thinking, which allows for the restraint of motor discharge and its conversion into action.

These "adaptations," by and large, would now fall under the category of autonomous ego functions (Hartmann, 1939). Their relevance to the concept of latency is evident because they are a feature of the maturational and developmental changes that are documented in this review. It therefore appears that the seven-year-old has made the greatest step in his utilization of secondary-process modes of discharge to achieve the gratifications dictated by the pleasure principle under the adaptive guidance of what is possible in reality.

The last "adaptation" referred to above, that of thinking, deserves more attention, particularly in its relationship to motor discharge and Freud's ideas concerning the "binding of energy," which remains the central factor in distinguishing primary and secondary processes. First elaborated in 1895, this idea was next taken up in 1900 when Freud spoke of two *psi* systems in which the activity of the first *psi* system is directed toward securing the free discharge of the quantities of excitation, while the second system succeeds in inhibiting the discharge and in transforming the cathexis into a quiescent one, with a simultaneous elevation of its excitation level. When the second system has concluded its exploratory thought activity, it releases the inhibition and allows discharge as movement. This inhibitory mechanism—its relationship to thought and its importance in Freud's explanation of the transition from primary to secondary process—is again emphasized in the 1911 paper where Freud states that under the direction of the secondary process:

> Motor discharge was not employed in the appropriate alteration of reality; it was converted into *action*. Restraint upon motor discharge (upon action), which then becomes necessary, was provided by means of the process of *thinking*, which was developed from the presentation of ideas. Thinking . . . is essentially an experimental kind of acting, accompanied by displacement of relatively small quantities of cathexis together with less expenditure (discharge) of them. For this purpose the conversion of freely displaceable cathexis into 'bound' cathexes was necessary [p. 221].

The relationship of "the binding of energies," thought, and the alteration of reality can perhaps be reconciled with the work cited by the Kendlers, White, and Piaget. According to these investigators, children of seven to eight respond more frequently in "a mediational manner" and are capable of operational thought. One might say that the thought processes at this stage are more structured inasmuch as the energies underlying them are relatively bound, whereas at earlier stages they are closer to the primary process inasmuch as there is a freer discharge of energies. The *pars pro toto* nature of associational thinking is one datum to suggest this, and the academic psychologists' claim that the original associational thinking is replaced by the mediated processes is another way of stating the same proposition. Indeed, recent work suggests that prior to seven, children tested on word-association tasks use attributive *has* and syntagmatic connections, and after seven they use copula *is* connections for their associations. For example, prior to seven, the word *table* is more likely to elicit "eat" or "legs," while after seven "furniture" might be the response.

One could further argue that memory traces organized according to the associational form of thinking become less available to consciousness once the second mode is established; when ideas organized in the first mode are raised to consciousness, they may appear in more archaic forms as percepts (Lipin, 1969), or according to categorical lines more appropriate to early childhood. The concepts of repression and infantile amnesia might find their organizational base in this two-system arrangement, which is conveniently ordered in a developmental hierarchy.

Significantly, the resolution of the Oedipus complex and the structuralization of the mental apparatus into its three functional agencies also depend on the newly established mediational thinking which brings about a new organization of thought and invariant cuing from within. The superego in its function as a guiding pilot seems to utilize internalized verbal prohibitions. The development of such capacities has also been noted in the work of the Soviet neurodevelopmentalists. Nass (1966) argues that Piaget's findings on moral development, which are based on levels of cognitive organization, correspond with the psychoanalytic timetable, which is derived from the stages of libidinal development, object relations, levels of ego functioning, and the formation of psychic structures. The replacement of outer control by inner control and organization and the consequent propensity toward conflict may then have a material base in the establishment of neurodevelopmental structure. *We would argue that these confluences in development are not fortuitous but are part of the design feature of the human organism, and this design feature permits higher-level organization and therefore latency.*

By now it must be clear we believe that what separate the data from the varied sectors examined are method and vantage point. One would hardly expect a neurophysiologist to arrive at conclusions regarding cognitive organization. Similarly, the psychoanalytic method is an exquisite tool for investigating the meaning of experience and internalized conflict, but it cannot say much about the growth limits of neurons. The limits of each method require complementarity of findings to round out our knowledge. However, these limitations also require that the data from one scientific method not be contradicted by data from another. This excursion through many disciplines converged on a crucial age in the child's development, no matter which sector of behavior or level of organization was studied, and this coincidence, we believe, is worth noting.

In the course of this review, one problem had to be put aside and now will be reconsidered. The central tenets of psychoanalysis rest upon the concept of a "dynamic" unconscious, which in turn is based on data derived from the couch. These data attest to the pressure of wishes and the countercathectic powers of the ego and its defensive operations. The explorations of cognitive psychologists and neural developmentalists say little about such dynamic matters and their affective components. Yet, these dynamic features are the motivational core of man and constitute the raison d'être of psychoanalysis as a separate branch of investigation.

We believe that the dynamic core of psychoanalytic theory can utilize the mass of data accumulated as corroborative information rather than as an antagonistic system. Freud's dynamic principles did not falter, though he argued for and surmised biological timetables. He went so far as to suggest that latency was as inevitable as the loss of deciduous teeth. Hartmann's demands that ego psychology be expanded to include academic psychological findings did not relinquish a dynamic point of view. In short, the dynamic reasons for the resolution of the Oedipus complex and repression, as well as the specific genetic reasons for a specific variety of superego organization, depend on the meaning of experience, which is what the psychoanalyst studies. To refer to the fact that the organization of meaning rests on species-specific neuronal substrates which mature according to biological timetables and provide specific cognitive propensities is merely to restate the "levels" principle. We study what we study with the tools we have, and each tool excludes the possibility of other kinds of knowledge. On the other hand, the psychoanalyst's grasp of the whys of behavior must include the limits and tendencies of the substrate lest he ascribe dynamic significance to behaviors that are not determined by conflict. Moreover, knowledge about latency arose from psychoanalytic speculations and postulations about the maturation of libidinal energic organization and the ontogenetic sequence in the ebb and flow of fantasies which are part of being human. Latency was postulated as universal because it seemed to transcend particular fantasy constellations and was less idiosyncratic in its essential form than other mental events.

The data presented here represent an attempt to look at the concept of latency in the light of new data from other disciplines. We assert the clinical utility of this concept. However, finding one's way through the evidence presented requires that psychoanalysis burn some old foundations based on older biological analogy and accept some supports from newer findings by the other sciences.

11

INTRODUCTION

Sequence, Tempo, and Individual Variation in the Growth and Development of Boys and Girls Aged 12 to 16, by J. M. Tanner

Puberty and early adolescence pose the monumental challenge of adjusting to major body changes and to a new social role which is constantly increasing in complexity. Another adaptational hurdle is set up by the abrupt transition from elementary to junior high school, a change many youngsters appear to experience as more stressful than initial school entry. The junior high school student no longer has the support of a small peer group and the consistent teacher. In addition, the minimal capacities for cognitive generalization, symbolization, and objective processing of information at this age (Elkind, 1967), combined with the priority typically assigned to egocentric concerns about body image, social role, and status, rarely fail to distract the youngster from increasing academic demands.

The foregoing statement is predicated on the assumption of the interrelationship of biological and psychosocial factors. But our inability to refer the reader to demonstrable bases for this assumption only serves to highlight the tendency for one set of observers to investigate hormonal and other biological changes while another set studies the psychosocial and behavioral changes independently. There has been too little correlation between the two types of study. At best, we can cite studies of adult females that relate the hormonal changes of the menstrual cycle to normal mood states as well as to suicidal and violent behavior and psychiatric admissions (Bolton, 1964; A. Coppen and Kessell, 1963; Mandell and Mandell, 1967). The affective and behavioral effects of the hormonal changes of puberty have yet to be demonstrated.

The lively controversy sparked by psychosocial studies is discussed in Chapter 12 by King. The chapter by Tanner, reprinted below, summarizes vital physical developmental data with which too few mental health workers are conversant, including psychiatrists who have had an extensive education in biology. The clinician's focus on pathology often results in what A. Kaplan (1967) has aptly labeled a "trained incapacity" to recognize, conceptualize, and appreciate normative data. This relative inattention to physical development is not shared by adolescents; typically, they are tremendously preoccupied by either the presence or absence of physical changes. They could make excellent use of the information presented in the following chapter if only parents, teachers, counselors, and clinicians conveyed it to them sensitively.

Tanner focuses on developmental age, as opposed to chronological age, in describing the at least five-year span of puberty and the two-year differential between girls and boys (which does not suddenly begin at adolescence). He authoritatively documents the great variation between the sexes and between individuals in onset, tempo, duration, and even sequence of pubertal body changes. However, the psychosocial effects of extreme variations in the timing of pubertal onset are not as clear-cut as Tanner suggests by his comment that early maturers generally have things their way and his brief reference to Mussen and Jones's (1957) study of subsequent personality. It is generally accepted that youngsters with incongruous pubertal development experience difficulty in reconciling self-concept or body image with actual physique (see, for instance, Money and Clopper, 1974; Rutter, 1971b). Delayed puberty in males appears to affect them more adversely at the time than precocious puberty does, whereas girls seem more self-conscious with early puberty. Teenagers with delayed puberty face the problem of keeping social age congruent with chronological age as there is a marked tendency for both peers and adults to treat them according to physical age instead of chronological age. The consequent infantilization may foster delay in social development as evidenced by the youngster's preferring to play with younger children or becoming a loner. On the other hand, precocious children may have difficulty in forming friendships. Although they may choose to play with children who resemble them in size and strength, they lack the cognitive and social expertise of the older children and thus may not be accepted. Concurrently, in their own age group, they may be rejected because of their larger physique and greater strength and energy. As a result, the physically precocious child may view himself or herself as a freak, a misfit, rather than feeling superior because of greater size.

Peskin (1967) notes that many of the studies emphasizing the psychosocial disadvantages of late puberty in boys rely heavily on the late maturer's feelings of inferiority *at the time*. Peskin has observed, however, that *several years later* these late maturers tend to outdistance their peers, who matured earlier, in terms of activity level, intellectual curiosity, exploratory behavior, and lack of social submission. The late maturers are reported *eventually* to place a premium on inner life, whereas earlier maturers prize the outer social life. The late maturer seems to perceive his drives as positive and constructive, in contrast to the early maturer, who focuses more on the potential danger of uncontrollable impulses. Theoretically, Peskin postulates that the late maturer's longer childhood preparation allows for a greater enrichment of ego functioning in anticipation of the sudden intensification of drives in adolescence. This point of view fits the truism that it is far easier to achieve biological manhood than to reach psychosocial manhood (Adams, 1972a).

Comparable observations have been reported in Shipman's (1964) study of adult women's recollections of menarche timing (obviously not the most reliable measure). Again, the age of onset was recalled as being subjectively meaningful at the time, but with the passage of the years, it assumed less importance. Those who recalled a late menarche tended to be self-directed, independent, and aggressive, with a readiness to experiment and to question ideas. In comparison, those women who recalled an early menarche were described as more conservative, less critical in their thinking, more inexact, more trusting of others, and more group-dependent. The middle menarche group was reported to be the most "feminine" and tended also to have the most children.

Although research is obviously needed in these areas, enough information is at hand to address the clinician's need to deal intelligently and sensitively with the youngster's current concerns. Pubertal delay must be appropriately assessed (Adams, 1972a, 1972b), with a realization that the clinician's concepts may differ markedly from those of the individual boy or girl, the parents, and peers regarding what is "delayed," "different," "defective," "wrong," "bad," "queer," etc.

11

Sequence, Tempo, and Individual Variation in the Growth and Development of Boys and Girls Aged 12 to 16

J. M. TANNER

For the majority of young persons, the years from 12 to 16 are the most eventful ones of their lives so far as their growth and development is concerned. Admittedly, during fetal life and the first year or two after birth, developments occurred still faster and a sympathetic environment was probably even more crucial, but the subject himself was not the fascinated, charmed, or horrified spectator who watches the developments, or lack of developments, of adolescence. Growth is a very regular and highly regulated process, and from birth onward the growth rate of most bodily tissues decreases steadily, the fall being swift at first and slower from about three years. Body shape changes gradually since the rate of growth of some parts, such as the arms and legs, is greater than the rate of growth of others, such as the trunk. But the change is a steady one, a smoothly continuous development rather than a passage through a series of separate stages.

Then, at puberty, a very considerable alteration in growth rate occurs. There is a swift increase in body size, a change in the shape and body composition, and a rapid development of the gonads, the reproductive organs, and the characteristics signaling sexual maturity. Some of these changes are common to both sexes, but most are sex-specific. Boys have a great increase in muscle size and strength, together with a series of physiological changes, making them more capable than girls of doing heavy physical work and running faster and longer. The changes specifically adapt the male to his

First published in *Daedalus*, 100:907–930, 1971. Reprinted by permission.

primitive primate role of dominating, fighting, and foraging. Such adolescent changes occur generally in primates, but are more marked in some species than in others. Male, female, and prepubescent gibbons are hard to distinguish when they are together, let alone apart. No such problem arises with gorillas or rhesus monkeys. Man lies at about the middle of the primate range, both in adolescent size increase and degree of sexual differentiation.

The adolescent changes are brought about by hormones, either secreted for the first time, or secreted in much greater amounts than previously. Each hormone acts on a set of targets or receptors, but these are often not concentrated in a single organ, nor in a single type of issue. Testosterone, for example, acts on receptors in the cells of the penis, the skin of the face, the cartilages of the shoulder joints, and certain parts of the brain. Whether all these cells respond by virtue of having the same enzyme system, or whether different enzymes are involved at different sites is not yet clear. The systems have developed through natural selection, producing a functional response of obvious biological usefulness in societies of hunter-gatherers, but of less certain benefit in the culture of invoice clerk and shop assistant. Evolutionary adaptations of bodily structure usually carry with them an increased proclivity for using those structures in behavior, and there is no reason to suppose this principle suddenly stops short at twentieth-century man. There is no need to take sides in the current debate on the origins of aggression to realize that a major task of any culture is the channeling of this less specifically sexual adolescent energy into creative and playful activity.

The adolescent changes have not altered in the last 15 years, or the last 50, or probably the last 5,000. Girls still develop two years earlier than boys; some boys still have completed their whole bodily adolescent development before other boys of the same chronological age have begun theirs. These are perhaps the two major biological facts to be borne in mind when thinking of the adolescent's view of himself in relation to his society. The sequence of the biological events remains the same. But there has been one considerable change; the events occur now at an earlier age than formerly. Forty years ago the average British girl had her first menstrual period (menarche) at about her fifteenth birthday; nowadays it is shortly before her thirteenth. Fifty years ago in Britain social-class differences played a considerable part in causing the variation of age of menarche in the population, the less well-off growing up more slowly. Nowadays, age at menarche is almost the same in different classes and most of the variation is due to genetic factors.

In this essay, I shall discuss (1) the growth of the body at adolescence and its changes in size, shape, and tissue composition, (2) sex dimorphism and the development of the reproductive system, (3) the concept of developmental age and the interaction of physical and behavioral advancement, (4) the interaction of genetic and environmental influences on the age of occurrence of puberty and the secular trend toward earlier maturation.

GROWTH OF THE BODY AT ADOLESCENCE

The extent of the adolescent spurt in height is shown in Figure 1. For a year or more the velocity of growth approximately doubles; a boy is likely to be growing again at the rate he last experienced at about age two. The peak velocity of height (PHV, a point much used in growth studies) averages about 10.5 centimeters a year (cm/yr) in boys and 9.0 cm/yr in girls (with a standard deviation of about 1.0 cm/yr), but this is the "instantaneous" peak given by a smooth curve drawn through the observations. The velocity over the whole year, encompassing the six months before and after the peak, is naturally somewhat less. During this year a boy usually grows between 7 and 12 cm and a girl between 6 and 11 cm. Children who have their peak early reach a somewhat higher peak than those who have it late.

The average age at which the peak is reached depends on the nature and circumstances of the group studied more, probably, than does the height of the peak. In moderately well-off British or North American children at present the peak occurs on average at about 14.0 years in boys and 12.0 years in girls. The standard deviations are about 0.9 years in each instance. Though the absolute average ages differ from series to series the two-year sex difference is invariant.

The adolescent spurt is at least partly under different hormonal control from growth in the period before. Probably as a consequence of this, the amount of height added during the spurt is to a considerable degree independent of the amount attained prior to it. Most children who have grown steadily up at, say, the 30th centile line on a height chart till adolescence end up at the 30th centile as adults, it is true; but a number end as high as the 50th or as low as the 10th, and a very few at the 55th or 5th. The correlation between adult height and height just before the spurt starts is about 0.8. This leaves some 30% of the variability in adult height as due to differences in the magnitude of the adolescent spurt. So some adolescents get a nasty and unavoidable shock; though probably the effects of early and late maturing (see below) almost totally confuse the issue of final height during the years we are considering.

Practically all skeletal and muscular dimensions take part in the spurt, though not to an equal degree. Most of the spurt in height is due to acceleration of trunk length rather than length of legs. There is a fairly regular order in which the dimensions accelerate; leg length as a rule reaches its peak first, followed by the body breadths, with shoulder width last. Thus, a boy stops growing out of his trousers (at least in length) a year before he stops growing out of his jackets. The earlier structures to reach their adult status are the head, hands, and feet. At adolescence, children, particularly girls, sometimes complain of having large hands and feet. They can be reassured that by the time they are fully grown their hands and feet will be a little smaller in

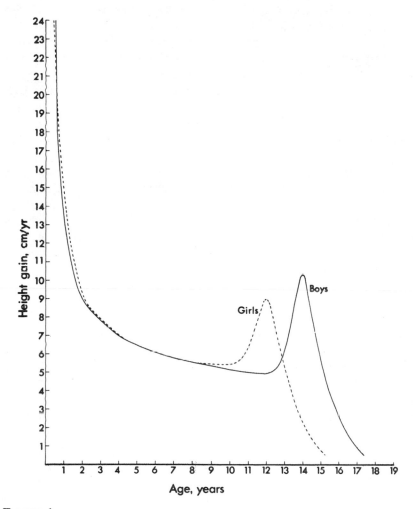

FIGURE 1

Typical individual velocity curves for supine length or height in boys and girls. These curves represent the velocity of the typical boy and girl at any given instant. (Tanner, Whitehouse, and Takaishi, 1966).

proportion to their arms and legs, and considerably smaller in proportion to their trunk.

The spurt in muscle, both of limbs and heart, coincides with the spurt in skeletal growth, for both are caused by the same hormones. Boys' muscle widths reach a peak velocity of growth considerably greater than that reached by girls. But since girls have their spurt earlier, there is actually a period, from about 12 1/2 to 13 1/2, when girls on the average have larger muscles than boys of the same age.

Simultaneously with the spurt in muscle there is a loss of fat in boys, particularly on the limbs. Girls have a velocity curve of fat identical in shape to that of boys; that is to say, their fat accumulation (going on in both sexes from about age six) decelerates. But the decrease in velocity in girls is not sufficiently great to carry the average velocity below zero, that is, to give an absolute loss. Most girls have to content themselves with a temporary go-slow in fat accumulation. As the adolescent growth spurt draws to an end, fat tends to accumulate again in both sexes.

The marked increase in muscle size in boys at adolescence leads to an increase in strength, illustrated in Figure 2. Before adolescence, boys and girls are similar in strength for a given body size and shape; after, boys are much stronger, probably due to developing more force per gram of muscle as well as absolutely larger muscles. They also develop larger hearts and lungs relative to their size, a higher systolic blood pressure, a lower resting heart rate, a greater capacity for carrying oxygen in the blood, and a greater power for neutralizing the chemical products of muscular exercise such as lactic acid (Tanner, 1962). In short, the male becomes at adolescence more adapted for the tasks of hunting, fighting, and manipulating all sorts of heavy objects, as is necessary in some forms of food-gathering.

The increase in hemoglobin, associated with a parallel increase in the number of red blood cells, is illustrated in Figure 3 (H. B. Young, 1963). The hemoglobin concentration is plotted in relation to the development of secondary sex characteristics instead of chronological age, to obviate the spread due to early and late maturing (see below). Girls lack the rise in red cells and hemoglobin, which is brought about by the action of testosterone.

It is as a direct result of these anatomical and physiological changes that athletic ability increases so much in boys at adolescence. The popular notion of a boy "outgrowing his strength" at this time has little scientific support. It is true that the peak velocity of strength is reached a year or so later than that of height, so that a short period may exist when the adolescent, having completed his skeletal and probably also muscular growth, still does not have the strength of a young adult of the same body size and shape. But this is a temporary phase; considered absolutely, power, athletic skill, and physical

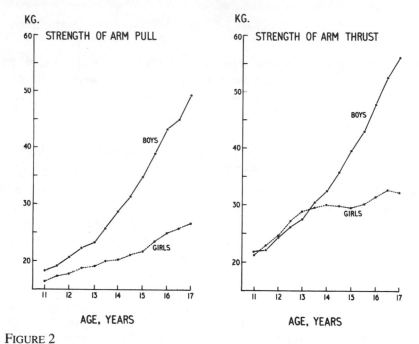

FIGURE 2

Strength of arm pull and arm thrust from age 11 to 17. Mixed longitudinal data: 65 to 95 boys and 66 to 93 girls in each age group (Jones, 1949; Tanner, 1962).

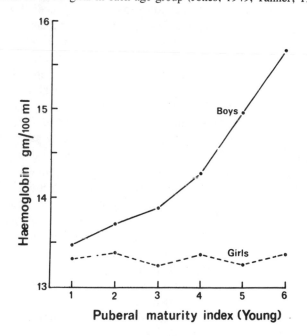

FIGURE 3

Blood hemoglobin level in girls and boys according to stage of puberty—cross-sectional data. (Tanner, 1969; H. B. Young, 1963).

endurance all increase progressively and rapidly throughout adolescence. It is certainly not true that the changes accompanying adolescence enfeeble, even temporarily. If the adolescent becomes weak and easily exhausted, it is for psychological reasons and not physiological ones.

SEX DIMORPHISM AND THE DEVELOPMENT OF THE REPRODUCTIVE SYSTEM

The adolescent spurt in skeletal and muscular dimensions is closely related to the rapid development of the reproductive system which takes place at this time. The course of this development is outlined diagrammatically in Figure 4. The solid areas marked "breast" in the girls and "penis" and "testis" in the boys represent the period of accelerated growth of these organs, and the horizontal lines and the rating numbers marked "pubic hair" stand for its advent and development (Tanner, 1962). The sequences and timings given represent, in each case, average values for British boys and girls; the North American average is within two or three months of this. To give an idea of the individual departures from the average, figures for the range of age at which the various events begin and end are inserted under the first and last point of the bars. The acceleration of penis growth, for example, begins on the average at about age 12 1/2, but sometimes as early as 10 1/2 and sometimes as late as 14 1/2. The completion of penis development usually occurs at about age 14 1/2 but in some boys is at 12 1/2 and in others at 16 1/2. There are a few boys, it will be noticed, who do not begin their spurts in height or penis development until the earliest maturers have entirely completed theirs. At ages 13, 14, and 15 there is an enormous variability among any group of boys, who range all the way from practically complete maturity to absolute preadolescence. The same is true of girls aged 11, 12, and 13.

In Figure 5 three boys are illustrated, all aged exactly 14.75 years, and three girls, all aged exactly 12.75. All are entirely normal and healthy, yet the first boy could be mistaken easily for a 12-year-old and the third for a young man of 17 or 18. It is manifestly ridiculous to consider all three boys or all three girls equally grown up either physically or, since much behavior at this age is conditioned by physical status, in their social relations. The statement that a boy is 14 is in most contexts hopelessly vague; all depends, morphologically, physiologically, and to a considerable extent sociologically too, on whether he is preadolescent, midadolescent, or postadolescent.

The psychological and social importance of this difference in the tempo of development, as it has been called, is very great, particularly in boys. Boys who are advanced in development are likely to dominate their contemporaries in athletic achievement and sexual interest alike. Conversely, the late developer is the one who all too often loses out in the rough-and-tumble

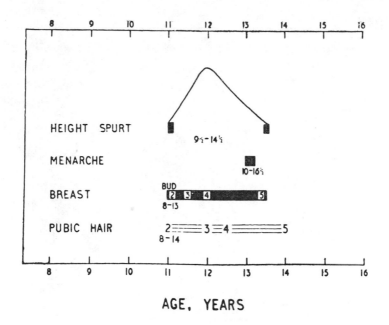

AGE, YEARS

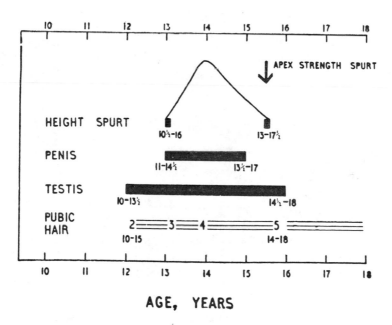

AGE, YEARS

FIGURE 4

Diagram of sequence of events at adolescence in boys and girls. The average boy and girl are represented. The range of ages within which each event charted may begin and end is given by the figures placed directly below its start and finish (W. A. Marshall and Tanner, 1970).

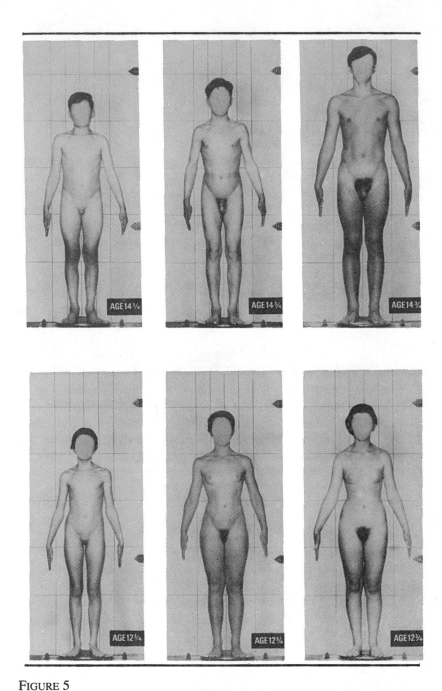

FIGURE 5

Differing degrees of pubertal development at the same chronological age. Upper row: three boys, all aged 14.75 years. Lower row: three girls, all aged 12.75 years (Tanner, 1969).

of the adolescent world; and he may begin to wonder whether he will ever develop his body properly or be as well endowed sexually as those others he has seen developing around him. A very important part of the educator's and the doctor's task at this time is to provide information about growth and its variability to preadolescents and adolescents and to give sympathetic support and reassurance to those who need it.

The *sequence* of events, though not exactly the same for each boy or girl, is much less variable than the age at which the events occur. The first sign of puberty in the boy is usually an acceleration of the growth of the testes and scrotum with reddening and wrinkling of the scrotal skin. Slight growth of pubic hair may begin about the same time, but is usually a trifle later. The spurts in height and penis growth begin on average about a year after the first testicular acceleration. Concomitant with the growth of the penis, and under the same stimulus, the seminal vesicles and the prostate and bulbo-urethral glands enlarge and develop. The time of the first ejaculation of seminal fluid is to some extent culturally as well as biologically determined, but as a rule it is during adolescence, about a year after the beginning of accelerated penis growth.

Axillary hair appears on the average some two years after the beginning of pubic hair growth—that is, when pubic hair is reaching stage 4. However, there is enough variability and dissociation in these events that a very few children's axillary hair actually appears first. In boys, facial hair begins to grow at about the time the axillary hair appears. There is a definite order in which the hairs of mustache and beard appear: first at the corners of the upper lip, then over all the upper lip, then at the upper part of the cheeks in the midline below the lower lip, and finally along the sides and lower border of the chin. The remainder of the body hair appears from about the time of first axillary hair development until a considerable time after puberty. The ultimate amount of body hair an individual develops seems to depend largely on heredity, though whether because of the kinds and amounts of hormones secreted or because of the reactivity of the end-organs is not known.

Breaking of the voice occurs relatively late in adolescence; it is often a gradual process and so not suitable as a criterion of puberty. The change in pitch accompanies enlargement of the larynx and lengthening of the vocal cords, caused by the action of testosterone on the laryngeal cartilages. During the period of breaking, the pitch is variable, and the true adult pitch associated with full growth of the larynx may not be established until late adolescence. In addition to change in pitch, there is also a change in quality or timbre, which distinguishes the voice (more particularly the vowel sounds) of both male and female adults from that of children. This is dependent on the enlargement of the resonating spaces above the larynx, due to the rapid growth of the mouth, nose, and maxilla which occurs during adolescence.

In the skin the sebaceous and apocrine sweat glands, particularly of the axillae and genital and anal regions, develop rapidly during puberty and give rise to a characteristic odor; the changes occur in both sexes but are more marked in the male. Enlargement of the pores at the root of the nose and the appearance of comedones and acne, though liable to occur in either sex, are considerably more common in adolescent boys than girls, since the underlying skin changes are the result of androgenic activity. A roughening of the skin, particularly over the outer aspects of the thighs and upper arms, may be seen in both sexes during adolescence, but again is more common in boys than girls.

During adolescence the male breast undergoes changes, some temporary and some permanent. The diameter of the areola, which is equal in both sexes before puberty, increases considerably, though less than it does in girls. Representative figures are 12.5 mm before puberty, 21.5 mm in mature men, and 35.5 mm in mature women. In some boys (between a fifth and a third of most groups studied) there is a distinct enlargement of the breast (sometimes unilaterally) about midway through adolescence. This usually regresses again after about one year.

In the girls the appearance of the "breast bud" is as a rule the first sign of puberty, though the appearance of pubic hair precedes it in about one in three. The uterus and vagina develop simultaneously with the breast. The labia and clitoris also enlarge. Menarche, the first menstrual period, is a later event in the sequence. It occurs almost invariably after the peak of the height spurt has been passed. Though it marks a definitive and probably mature stage of uterine development, it does not usually signify the attainment of full reproductive function. The early cycles may be more irregular than later ones and are in some girls, but by no means all, accompanied by dysmenorrhea. They are often anovulatory, that is, unaccompanied by the shedding of an egg. Thus, there is frequently a period of adolescent sterility lasting a year to 18 months after menarche, but it cannot be relied on in the individual case. Similar considerations may apply to the male, but there is no reliable information about this. On the average, girls grow about 6 cm more after menarche, though gains of up to twice this amount may occur. The gain is practically independent of whether menarche occurs early or late.

NORMAL VARIATIONS IN PUBERTAL DEVELOPMENT

The diagram of Figure 4 must not be allowed to obscure the fact that children vary a great deal both in the rapidity with which they pass through the various stages of puberty and in the closeness with which the various events are linked together. At one extreme, one may find a perfectly healthy girl who has not yet menstruated though she has reached adult breast and pubic hair ratings and is already two years past her peak height velocity; at the other, a girl who has passed all the stages of puberty within the space of two years. Details of the limits of what may be considered normal can be found in the reports of W. A. Marshall and Tanner (1969, 1970).

In girls the interval from the first sign of puberty to complete maturity varies from one and a half years to six years. From the moment when the breast bud first appears to menarche averages two and a half years but may be as little as six months or as much as five and a half years. The rapidity with which a child passes through puberty seems to be independent of whether puberty is occurring early or late. There is some independence between breast and pubic hair developments, as one might expect on endocrinological grounds. A few girls reach pubic hair stage 3 (see Figure 4) before any breast development starts; conversely, breast stage 3 may be reached before any pubic hair appears. At breast stage 5, however, pubic hair is always present in girls. Menarche usually occurs in breast stage 4 and pubic hair stage 4, but in about 10% of girls it occurs in stage 5 for both, and occasionally may occur in stage 2 or even stage 1 of pubic hair. Menarche invariably occurs after peak height velocity is passed, so the tall girl can be reassured about future growth if her periods have begun.

In boys a similar variability occurs. The genitalia may take any time between two and five years to pass from G2 to G5, and some boys complete the whole process while others have still not gone from G2 to G3. Pubic hair growth in the absence of genital development is very unusual in normal boys, but in a small percentage of boys the genitalia develop as far as stage 4 before the pubic hair starts to grow.

The height spurt occurs relatively later in boys than in girls. Thus, there is a difference between the average boy and girl of two years in age of peak height velocity, but of only one year in the first appearance of pubic hair. The PHV occurs in very few boys before genital stage 4, whereas 75% of girls reach PHV before breast stage 4. Indeed, in some girls the acceleration in height is the first sign of puberty; this is never so in boys. A small boy whose genitalia are just beginning to develop can be unequivocally reassured that an acceleration in height is soon to take place, but a girl in the corresponding situation may already have had her height spurt.

The basis for some children having loose and some tight linkages between pubertal events is not known. Probably the linkage reflects the degree of integration of various processes in the hypothalamus and the pituitary gland, for breast growth is controlled by one group of hormones, pubic hair growth by another, and the height spurt probably by a third. In rare pathological instances the events may become widely divorced.

The Development of Sex Dimorphism

The differential effects on the growth of bone, muscle, and fat at puberty increase considerably the difference in body composition between the sexes. Boys have a greater increase not only in the length of bones but in the thickness of cortex, and girls have a smaller loss of fat. The most striking dimorphisms, however, are the man's greater stature and breadth of shoulders and the woman's wider hips. These are produced chiefly by the changes and timing of puberty, but it is important to remember that sex dimorphisms do not arise only at that time. Many appear much earlier. Some, like the external genital difference itself, develop during fetal life. Others develop continuously throughout the whole growth period by a sustained differential growth rate. An example of this is the greater relative length and breadth of the forearm in the male when compared with whole arm length or whole body length.

Part of the sex difference in pelvic shape antedates puberty. Girls at birth already have a wider pelvic outlet. Thus, the adaptation for childbearing is present from a very early age. The changes at puberty are concerned more with widening the pelvic inlet and broadening the much more noticeable hips. It seems likely that these changes are more important in attracting the male's attention than in dealing with its ultimate product.

These sex-differentiated morphological characteristics arising at puberty—to which we can add the corresponding physiological and perhaps psychological ones as well—are secondary sex characteristics in the straightforward sense that they are caused by sex hormone or sex-differential hormone secretion and serve reproductive activity. The penis is directly concerned in copulation, the mammary gland in lactation. The wide shoulders and muscular power of the male, together with the canine teeth and brow ridges in man's ancestors, developed probably to drive away other males and ensure peace, an adaptation which soon becomes social.

A number of traits persist, perhaps through another mechanism known to ethologists as ritualization. In the course of evolution a morphological characteristic or a piece of behavior may lose its original function and, becoming further elaborated, complicated, or simplified, may serve as a sign stimulus to other members of the same species, releasing behavior that is in some ways advantageous to the spread or survival of the species. It requires little insight into human erotics to suppose that the shoulders, the hips and buttocks, and the breasts (at least in a number of widespread cultures) serve as releasers of mating behavior. The pubic hair (about whose function the textbooks have always preserved a cautious silence) probably survives as a ritualized stimulus for sexual activity, developed by simplification from the hair remaining in the inguinal and axillary regions for the infant to cling to when still transported, as in present apes and monkeys, under the mother's body. Similar considerations may apply to axillary hair, which is associated with special apocrine glands, which themselves only develop at puberty and are related histologically to scent glands in other mammals. The beard, on the other hand, may still be more frightening to other males than enticing to females. At least ritual use in past communities suggests this is the case; but perhaps there are two sorts of beards.

THE INITIATION OF PUBERTY

The manner in which puberty is initiated has a general importance for the clarification of developmental mechanisms. Certain children develop all the changes of puberty, up to and including spermatogenesis and ovulation, at a very early age, either as the result of a brain lesion or as an isolated developmental, sometimes genetic defect. The youngest mother on record was such a case; she gave birth to a full-term healthy infant by Caesarian section at the age of five years, eight months. The existence of precocious puberty and the results of accidental ingestion by small children of male or female sex hormones indicate that breasts, uterus, and penis will respond to hormonal stimulation long before puberty. Evidently an increased end-organ sensitivity plays at most a minor part in pubertal events.

The signal to start the sequence of events is given by the brain, not the pituitary. Just as the brain holds the information on sex, so it holds information on maturity. The pituitary of a newborn rat successfully grafted in place of an adult pituitary begins at once to function in an adult fashion, and does not have to wait till its normal age of maturation has been reached. It is the hypothalamus, not the pituitary, that has to mature before puberty begins.

Maturation, however, does not come out of the blue, and at least in rats a little more is known about this mechanism. In these animals small amounts of sex hormones circulate from the time of birth and these appear to inhibit the prepubertal hypothalamus from producing gonadotrophin releasers. At puberty it is supposed that the hypothalamic cells become less sensitive to sex hormones. The small amount of sex hormones circulating then fails to inhibit the hypothalamus and gonadotrophins are released; these stimulate the production of testosterone by the testis or estrogen by the ovary. The level of the sex hormone rises until the same feedback circuit is re-established, but now at a higher level of gonadotrophins and sex hormones. The sex hormones are now high enough to stimulate the growth of secondary sex characteristics and support mating behavior.

Developmental Age and the Interaction of Physical and Behavioral Advancement

Children vary greatly in their tempo of growth. The effects are most dramatically seen at adolescence, as illustrated in Figure 5, but they are present at all ages from birth and even before. Girls, for example, do not suddenly become two years ahead of boys at adolescence; on the contrary, they are born with a slightly more mature skeleton and nervous system, and gradually increase their developmental lead (in absolute terms) throughout childhood.

Clearly, the concept of *developmental* age, as opposed to *chronological* age, is a very important one. To measure developmental age we need some way of determining the percentage of the child's growth process that has been attained at any time. In retrospective research studies, the percentage of final adult height may be very effectively used, but in the clinic we need something that is immediate in its application. The difficulty about using height, for example, is that different children end up at different heights, so that a tall-for-his-age 12-year-old may either be a tall adult in the making with an average maturational tempo, or an average adult in the making with an accelerated tempo. Precisely the same applies to the child who scores above average on most tests of mental ability.

To measure developmental age we need something that ends up the same for everyone and is applicable throughout the whole period of growth. Many physiological measures meet these criteria, in whole or in part. They range from the number of erupted teeth to the percentage of water in muscle cells. The various developmental ''age'' scales do not necessarily coincide, and each has its particular use. By far the most generally useful, however, is skeletal maturity or *bone* age. A less important one is dental maturity.

Skeletal maturity is usually measured by taking a radiograph of the hand and wrist (using the same radiation exposure that a child inevitably gets, and to more sensitive areas, by spending a week on vacation in the mountains). The appearance of the developing bones can be rated and formed into a scale; the scale is applicable to boys and girls of all genetic backgrounds, though girls on the average reach any given score at a younger age than do boys, and blacks on the average, at least in the first few years after birth, reach a given score at a younger age than do whites. Other areas of the body may be used if required. Skeletal maturity is closely related to the age at which adolescence occurs, that is, to maturity measured by secondary sex characteristic development. Thus, the range of *chronological* age within which menarche may normally fall is about 10 to 16 1/2, but the corresponding range of *skeletal* age for menarche is only 12 to 14 1/2. Evidently the physiological processes controlling progression of skeletal development are in most instances closely linked with those which initiate the events of adolescence. Furthermore, children tend to be consistently advanced or retarded during their whole growth period, or at any rate after about age three.

Dental maturity partly shares in this general skeletal and bodily maturation. At all ages from six to 13, children who are advanced skeletally have on the average more erupted teeth than those who are skeletally retarded. Likewise, those who have an early adolescence on the average erupt their teeth early. Girls usually have more erupted teeth than boys. But this relationship is not a very close one, and quantitatively speaking, it is the relative independence of teeth and general skeletal development that should be emphasized. There is some general factor of bodily maturity creating a tendency for a child to be advanced or retarded as a whole: in his skeletal ossification, in the percentage attained of his eventual size, in his permanent dentition, doubtless in his physiological reactions, and possibly in the results of his tests of ability. But not too much should be made of this general factor; and, especially, it should be noted how very limited is the loading, so to speak, of brain growth in it. There is little justification in the facts of physical growth and development for the concept of "organismic age" in which almost wholly disparate measures of developmental maturity are lumped together.

PHYSICAL MATURATION, MENTAL ABILITY, AND EMOTIONAL DEVELOPMENT

Clearly the occurrence of tempo differences in human growth has profound implications for educational theory and practice. This would especially be so if advancement in physical growth were linked to any significant degree with advancement in intellectual ability and in emotional maturity.

There is good evidence that in the European and North American school systems children who are physically advanced toward maturity score on the average slightly higher on most tests of mental ability than children of the same age who are physically less mature. The difference is not great, but it is consistent and it occurs at all ages that have been studied—that is, back as far as six and a half years. Similarly, the intelligence test score of postmenarche girls is higher than the score of premenarche girls of the same age (Tanner, 1962, 1966). Thus, in age-linked examinations physically fast-maturing children have a significantly better chance than slow-maturing ones.

It is also true that physically large children score higher than small ones, at all ages from six onward. In a random sample of all Scottish 11-year-old children, for example, comprising 6,440 pupils, the correlation between height and score in the Moray House group test was 0.25 ± 0.01, which leads to an average increase of one and a half points Terman-Merrill IQ per inch in stature. A similar correlation was found in London children. The effects can be very significant for individual children. In 10-year-old girls there was nine points difference in IQ between those whose height was above the 75th percentile and those whose height was below the 15th. This is two-thirds of the standard deviation of the test score.

It was usually thought that both the relationships between test score and height and between test score and early maturing would disappear in adulthood. If the correlations represented only the effects of co-advancement both of mental ability and physical growth, this might be expected to happen. There is no difference in height between early- and later-maturing boys when both have finished growing. But it is now clear that, curiously, at least part of the height-IQ correlation persists in adults (Tanner, 1966). It is not clear in what proportion genetic and environmental factors are responsible for this.

There is little doubt that being an early or a late maturer may have repercussions on behavior, and that in some children these repercussions may be considerable. There is little enough solid information on the relation between emotional and physiological development, but what there is supports the common-sense notion that emotional attitudes are clearly related to physiological events.

The boy's world is one where physical powers bring prestige as well as success, where the body is very much an instrument of the person. Boys who are advanced in development, not only at puberty, but before as well, are more likely than others to be leaders. Indeed, this is reinforced by the fact that muscular, powerful boys on the average mature earlier than others and have an early adolescent growth spurt. The athletically built boy not only tends to dominate his fellows before puberty, but also, by getting an early start, he is in a good position to continue that domination. The unathletic, lanky boy, unable, perhaps, to hold his own in the preadolescent rough and tumble, gets still further pushed to the wall at adolescence, as he sees others shoot up while he remains nearly stationary in growth. Even boys several years younger now suddenly surpass him in size, athletic skill, and perhaps, too, in social graces. Figure 6 shows the height curves of two boys, the first an early-maturing muscular boy, the other a late-maturing lanky one. Though both boys are of average height at age 11, and together again at average height at 17, the early maturer is four inches taller during the peak of adolescence.

At a much deeper level the late developer at adolescence may sometimes have doubts about whether he will ever develop his body properly and whether he will be as well endowed sexually as those others he has seen developing around him. The lack of events of adolescence may act as a trigger to reverberate fears accumulated deep in the mind during the early years of life.

It may seem as though the early maturers have things all their own way.

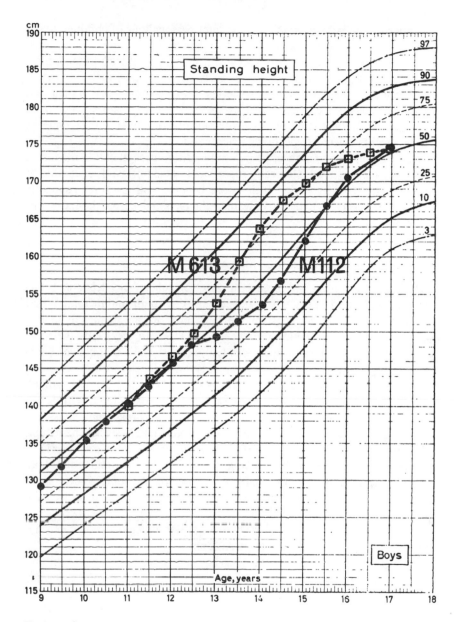

FIGURE 6

Height attained of two boys, one with an early and the other with a late adolescent spurt. Note how at age 11 and again at age 17 the boys are the same height (Tanner, 1961).

It is indeed true that most studies of the later personalities of children whose growth history is known do show early maturers to be more stable, more sociable, less neurotic, and more successful in society, at least in the United States (Mussen and Jones, 1957). But early maturers have their difficulties also, particularly the girls in some societies. Though some glory in their new possessions, others are embarrassed by them. The early maturer, too, has a longer period of frustration of sex drive and of drive toward independence and the establishment of vocational orientation.

Little can be done to reduce the individual differences in children's tempo of growth, for they are biologically rooted and not significantly reducible by any social steps we may take. It therefore behooves all teachers, psychologists, and pediatricians to be fully aware of the facts and alert to the individual problems they raise.

TREND TOWARD LARGE SIZE AND EARLIER MATURATION

The rate of maturing and the age at onset of puberty are dependent, naturally, on a complex interaction of genetic and environmental factors. Where the environment is good, most of the variability in age at menarche in a population is due to genetic differences. In France in the 1950s the mean difference between identical twins was two months, while that between nonidentical twin sisters was eight months (Tisserand-Perrier, 1953). In many societies puberty occurs later in the poorly-off, and in most societies investigated children with many siblings grow less fast than children with few.

Recent investigations in Northeast England showed that social-class differences are now only those associated with different family sizes. The median age at menarche for only girls was 13.0 years, for girls with one sibling 13.2, two siblings 13.4, three siblings and over 13.7. For a given number of siblings the social class, as indicated by father's occupation, was unrelated to age at menarche (Roberts, Rozner, and Swan, 1971). Environment is still clearly a factor in control of age at menarche, but in England, at least, occupation is a less effective indicator of poor housing, poor expenditure on food, and poor childcare than is the number of children in the family.

During the last hundred years there has been a striking tendency for children to become progressively larger at all ages (Tanner, 1968). This is known as the "secular trend." The magnitude of the trend in Europe and America is such that it dwarfs the differences between socioeconomic classes.

The data from Europe and America agree well: from about 1900, or a little earlier, to the present, children in average economic circumstances have increased in height at age five to seven by about 1 to 2 cm each decade, and at 10 to 14 by 2 to 3 cm each decade. Preschool data show that the trend starts directly after birth and may, indeed, be relatively greater from age two to five than subsequently. The trend started, at least in Britain, a considerable time ago, because Roberts, a factory physician, writing in 1876, said that "a factory child of the present day at the age of nine years weighs as much as one of 10 years did in 1833 . . . each age has gained one year in 40 years" (Tanner, 1962). The trend in Europe is still continuing at the time of this writing, but there is some evidence to show that in the United States the best-off sections of the population are now growing up at something approaching the fastest possible speed.

During the same period there has been an upward trend in adult height, but to a considerably lesser degree. In earlier times final height was not reached till 25 years or later, whereas now it is reached in men at 18 or 19. Data exist, however, that enable us to compare fully grown men at different periods. They lead to the conclusion that in Western Europe men increased in adult height little, if at all, from 1760 to 1830, about 0.3 cm per decade from 1830 to 1880, and about 0.6 cm per decade from 1880 to 1960. The trend is apparently still continuing in Europe, though not in the best-off section of American society.

Most of the trend toward greater size in children reflects a more rapid maturation; only a minor part reflects a greater ultimate size. The trend toward earlier maturing is best shown in the statistics on age at menarche. A selection of the best data is illustrated in Figure 7. The trend is between three and four months per decade since 1850 in average sections of Western European populations. Well-off persons show a trend of about half this magnitude, having never been so retarded in menarche as the worse-off (Tanner, 1966).

Most, though not all, of the differences between populations are probably due to nutritional factors, operating during the whole of the growth period, from conception onward. The well-nourished Western populations have median menarche ages of about 12.8 to 13.2 years; the latest recorded ages, by contrast, are 18 years in the Highlands of New Guinea, 17 years in Central Africa, and 15.5 years in the poorly-off Bantu in the South African Transkei. Well-nourished Africans have a median age of 13.4 (Kampala upper classes) or less, comparable to Europeans. Asians at the same nutritional level as Europeans probably have an earlier menarche, the figure for well-off Chinese in Hong Kong being 12.5 years.

The causes of the secular trend are probably multiple. Certainly better nutrition is a major one and perhaps, in particular, more protein and calories in early infancy. A lessening of disease may also have contributed. Hot climates used to be cited as a potent cause of early menarche, but it seems now that their effect, if any, is considerably less than that of nutrition. The annual mean world temperature rose from 1850 to about 1940 (when it began

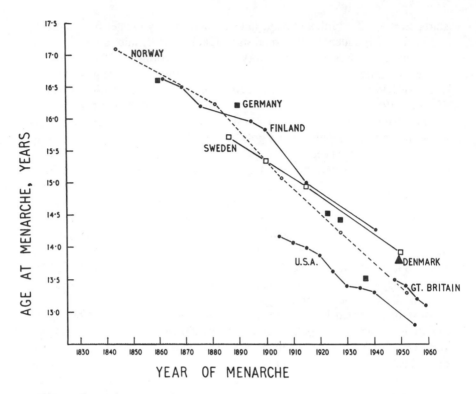

Figure 7

Secular trend in age at menarche, 1830–1960. (Sources of data and method of plotting are detailed in Tanner, 1962).

to fall again); the polar ice caps have been melting and the glaciers retreating, but on present evidence it seems unlikely that this general warming up has contributed significantly to the earlier menarche of girls.

Some authors have supposed that the increased psychosexual stimulation consequent on modern urban living has contributed, but there is no positive evidence for this. Girls in single-sex schools have menarche at exactly the same age as girls in coeducational schools, but whether this is a fair test of difference in psychosexual stimulation is hard to say.

12

INTRODUCTION

Coping and Growth in Adolescence, by Stanley H. King

In *Centuries of Childhood*, Ariès (1962) describes how only centuries after differentiating children from miniature adults did adolescence become recognized as a separate stage of development. Not until the nineteenth century did the concept receive attention. Since then, adolescence as a distinct phase has become increasingly visible, and its duration has even been extended at both ends. The earlier and earlier biological onset of puberty (see Tanner's Chapter 11) has advanced the beginning of adolescence, while sociocultural and economic factors have postponed its end. The latter prolongation stems from the greater skills required for adulthood in our postindustrial society and may well be a consequence of active efforts to keep young people out of the job market as long as possible.

Although in 1904 G. Stanley Hall published a two-volume study of adolescence, the developmental stage was relatively neglected for quite some time thereafter; in clinical work, it was often characterized as a stepchild. Hall's focus on the inevitability of turbulence during adolescence was eventually elaborated by a psychoanalytic theory of adolescence (see Blos [1962b; Chapter 16 in *Childhood Psychopathology*] and Wolfenstein's poetic analogy of adolescence and the mourning process in Chapter 18).

Nevertheless, based on a longitudinal study of adolescent psychiatric patients and controls, Masterson (1967) asserts that the tendency to attribute all adolescent symptomatology to developmentally appropriate, transient "turmoil" can result in a dangerous delay of the intensive treatment necessary to prevent severe psychopathology. He advises the clinician to lower substantially his or her index of concern as to how much of the clinical picture stems from turmoil and to assume the burden of proof that the adolescent's situation is not indicative of a serious psychiatric illness—a point of view supported by Weiner and Del Gaudio's (1976) longitudinal study of the diagnostic patterns and stability of 1,334 adolescent patients. Similarly,

Masterson (1968) claims that in his patients "adolescence was but a way station in a long history of psychiatric illness that began in childhood and followed its own inexorable course—a course only temporarily colored by the developmental stage of adolescence" (p. 1550). Masterson attributes the discrepancy between his findings and widely held notions about the inevitability of adolescent turmoil to a common feature in the psychoanalytic and psychiatric literature. He notes an imperceptible (and unacknowledged) drift from discussing a specific clinical problem in a patient to generalizing about normal adolescent growth and development.

The essay that follows combines King's observations of Harvard undergraduates with several other studies of adolescents in nonclinical contexts, as well as some comparing patient and control groups. These several reports speak for themselves in refuting the inevitability of adolescent turmoil; however, a variety of factors deserve consideration in evaluating them. Most significant is their tendency to focus on late adolescence, which, as B. A. Hamburg (1974) points out, does not represent a suitable model for understanding puberty and early adolescence, when a variety of hormonal, cognitive, and sociocultural factors may impoverish coping skills and increase vulnerability. To Hamburg, these changes bespeak a heightened need for parental stability and guidance on the part of the early adolescent. This need is in contrast to the appropriateness of the older adolescent's desire for independent decision making and autonomy. Indeed, in one of the cited studies of older modal adolescents, Baittle and Offer (1971) indicate that both the parents and the adolescents agreed that the greatest difficulties in everyday relationships had occurred in their pre-high-school years between ages 12 and 14.

Another consideration is that the observations highlighted in King's chapter, as well as in other large surveys, reflect an increased representation of middle-class adolescents. In studies involving more selective patient groups, it is likely that the lowest and the highest social classes may have been disproportionately represented.

Thought should also be given to the extent to which the investigator's mode of observation may have influenced the data observed. The psychoanalyst tends to focus on internal processes in individuals, whereas the investigator of larger groups focuses more on external adaptation. Of course, it is difficult to imagine the action-oriented "homoclite" (Grinker, Grinker, and Timberlake, 1962) in a psychoanalyst's office, except perhaps during puberty or early adolescence.

In the chapter below King delineates four major patterns of personality change in Harvard undergraduates: progressive maturation, delayed maturation, crisis and reintegration, and deterioration. On the surface, the categories appear comparable to Offer's (1969) three psychological routes from childhood to adulthood: continuous growth, surgent growth, and tumultuous growth. (Offer did not find any adolescents who fit King's deterioration group, which may be a result of the differences in their initial selection processes.) King then proposes what amount to four different groups of adolescents (he actually designates only three as he combines the middle two): the seriously impaired, the modal, the highly competent, and the sensitive/vulnerable. The first and the last groups probably have contributed most of the biographical detail found in both the clinical literature and in creative writing.

Despite their disagreement with the *inevitability* of turmoil, the studies discussed below do not suggest the absence of turmoil. They propose that notions of adolescent competence, coping, and relating be added to ideas about adolescent crisis, turmoil, and rebelliousness. The finding of only minimal evidence of a generation gap (accompanied by speculation about parental "permissiveness") in the normative studies has been attributed by some to the time in history when the observations were made. It may also be that adults tend to perceive the "generation gap" as stemming entirely from the younger generation. Here we need to consider the reactivation of internal conflicts in the parents themselves provoked by their child's adolescence (Benedek, 1959), as well as the older generation's reaction to the fact that the young are preparing to replace them when they, the adults, have no desire yet to relinquish their positions (Anthony, 1969).

King, whose study started just prior to the upheaval of the 1960s, did observe early evidence of the social unrest and alienation to come. Elsewhere, from a social perspective, King (1971) has addressed the conditions under which adolescent turmoil intensifies, especially among upper-middle-class youth. Among these conditions are shifts in social value systems, loss of transition points to adulthood, and confusion about adult role expectations. When society's cohesiveness is disrupted, rebellion and alienation increase. It is for the reader to ponder over the effects on today's youth of the political and social ferment of the sixties. The sit ins and be ins, draft card and bra burning, the Altamonts and Woodstocks, all seem to have passed into history. But many aspects of the sixties continue—the use of drugs, freedom in sexual relationships, legal adulthood at 18, the civil rights and women's movements, religious cults, vegetarianism, etc.

12

Coping and Growth in Adolescence

STANLEY H. KING

Recent years have witnessed subtle and important shifts in the study and understanding of adolescents, marked primarily by less emphasis on data obtained from the consulting room and by more emphasis on studies of nonclinical groups. The effect of the change is still minimal because of limitations in the studies of normals, as well as the recency of the research, yet because of the potential impact on theory, it is an appropriate time to review current positions.

The most prominent view of personality development during adolescence and young adulthood might be characterized as the crisis or psychiatric orientation. In simple terms, conflict, turmoil, and rebellion are expected to some degree in adolescence as part of the process of growing up. Some writers imply that, without turmoil, development is in some way impaired and the achievement of maturity is delayed. This view finds support from various writers through the centuries, as Kiell (1964) has demonstrated; and certainly within this century the crisis theme has been expounded by novelists and other observers of contemporary life. The strongest support in recent years, however, has come from the clinical literature, especially that written by psychoanalysts.

One respected theorist, Anna Freud, has described the adolescent years as a ''developmental disturbance'' (1969). The task of the adolescent is to learn how to handle increased sexual and aggressive drives and to find new ways of relating to parents and peers. She does not feel these can be accomplished without upheaval because the ego is not strong enough at that time to handle the increased drives in an integrated, harmonious way.

Another writer, Erik Erikson (1950), has described the major task of the adolescent years as the establishment of a stable identity. As the individual

First published in *Seminars in Psychiatry*, 4:355–366, 1972. Reprinted by permission of Grune & Stratton, Inc. and the author.

questions his values and ponders what kind of person he is, there may be conflict with parents and other authority figures. There may be rebellion and anger, lack of communication with adults, and even apathy and depression. The identity crisis may extend into the young adult years. Although Erikson does not state that an identity crisis is part of normal development, his term has become part of the common parlance of the day.

Although the crisis model is useful in understanding the behavior of many adolescents, it does have a serious bias if used as a general explanation of adolescent development. The data on which it is based are drawn primarily from the consulting room, with the assumption that an accurate picture of healthy functioning can be obtained from a study of disturbed functioning. There is another assumption that health is the absence of disease, and that health does not involve any new conceptions of functioning that are absent in illness. Both these assumptions are questionable. By so questioning, I would not deny that adolescence is a time of substantial physical and emotional change, nor that the adolescent is particularly vulnerable to stress. Rather, I would suggest that a review of recent studies suggests that turmoil and conflict are not necessarily the hallmark of adolescent development.

One of the more interesting studies of recent years is that by Offer (1969) of a group of high school boys who were the "modal" group of a range between psychopathology and superior adjustment, as determined by psychological tests. The subjects were interviewed at intervals from their freshman through senior years.

In the *handling of drives and affects,* few of the subjects had difficulty controlling impulses; as a group they were poised, well-mannered, and did not show any strongly deviant behavior. Mood swings were not dramatic, nor depression prolonged. When the latter occurred, the cause was usually exogenous and the boys worked out of it by turning attention to other activities. As for anger, they had adequate controls and outlets. They never had chronic rage reactions toward their parents and usually were able to sublimate anger in physical activity.

There was some conflict about the sexual drive, especially in the early years, and the boys did not feel they could communicate openly with parents or teachers about sex. However, their curiosity about girls enabled them to overcome their unease and by their senior year most of them were enjoying relationships with girls.

Anxiety and fear were present at times, but the effect was facilitative, a prelude to action, rather than inhibiting or disabling.

The major reason for effective handling of drives was the use of good *coping mechanisms,* particularly the recourse to physical action. Sports offered the opportunity for controlled and socially approved aggression but other kinds of social activities offered outlets for energy and achievement motivation. Offer's subjects were primarily "doers" rather than introspective or brooding teenagers, and appeared to have a limited fantasy life.

At the same time, the subjects were able to deal openly with painful affect, confronting conflict or trauma and talking with others about the feelings involved. They also searched for interpretation of their behavior, and Offer commented that they were good amateur psychologists. Thus, they sought reassurance about themselves and often found it.

They could also be appropriately critical of themselves, but when they evaluated their faults they did not dwell on guilt or lose self-esteem. Their self-criticism was, therefore, constructive rather than denigrating, and led to changes in behavior. This was one other way of being open and direct.

One coping mechanism that they used was humor, not often seen in clinical patients. This helped self-criticism because they could laugh at themselves and thus reduce guilt and anxiety to manageable proportions. But humor also provided a release of negative affect and provided a feeling of enjoyment of life, and a way of sharing pleasurable experiences with others.

The idea of sharing leads us to a third area of results: *interpersonal relations* with parents, teachers, and peers. Although the boys were often critical of their parents, the communication was generally good, and most of them felt that the ideal parent was very much like the one of their own parents to whom they felt closer. Basically, they shared their parents' values, and the vast majority said that their parents were fair and reasonable in discipline. There was rebellion, most often in the early adolescent years, and it appeared in the form of chronic disagreements with parents and teachers. Rules of the home or school were broken, which produced annoyance, but this rebellion almost never involved major differences in values or life style and was not flagrantly antisocial or illegal. The rebelliousness led to individuation from parents without losing love and respect for parents, and without loss of the ego ideal that had been drawn from parents. The rebelliousness and negative behavior decreased in the later years of high school when the subjects became more involved in activities outside the home.

Much of the professional literature stresses a breakdown in family communication and a generation gap, but in Offer's study family life for most subjects was well integrated. There was a division of family roles that closely followed the traditional middle-class pattern, with mother as warm and understanding, while father was more likely to be viewed with respect and distant admiration.

Offer concluded that the adolescent years do present a challenge on many fronts, but that his subjects were able to cope successfully with these growth tasks. They did not show the turmoil that we might expect from the crisis model of growth, because their egos were strong enough to withstand the pressures.

Additional data come from a study by Masterson (1967), in which he compared a group of adolescent patients with a group of matched controls, with a focus on the diagnostic category of adolescent turmoil. Although both groups had painful affect and limited functioning, these were more severe in the patient group. Fewer controls had severe depression or patterns of acting-out behavior. When Masterson compared the "healthiest" of the control group with the patients, he found some striking differences in family relationships. In the healthy group, parents accepted their offspring and felt and acted toward them in constructive ways, and, in turn, the adolescents were accepting of parents and siblings. But within the patient group, family members were more often engaged in chronic conflict, and father was absent more often from the home. The healthy subjects were action-oriented, much like Offer's subjects, while the patients more often had restricted interests and much more limited interaction with the environment. Masterson concluded by urging modification of current pathology-based theories.

MIDDLE THROUGH LATE ADOLESCENCE

The bulk of data on the functioning of healthy adolescents comes from this later age span and information in these studies about the early adolescent years depends on retrospective accounts by the subjects. This is a limitation on the conclusions that can be drawn, but it is a limitation that applies equally well to data based on studies from the consulting room, where reconstruction of events also depends on retrospective accounts.

The first study to be cited was conducted by an interdisciplinary group at the National Institute of Mental Health (Coelho, Hamburg, and Murphey, 1963; Coelho, Silber, and Hamburg, 1962; D. A. Hamburg and Adams, 1967; Silber et al., 1961a, 1961b), who followed a group of high school seniors into college. Although the group was small (15 subjects), the findings are provocative.

The subjects were "competent adolescents." By this term, the researchers meant that their subjects had demonstrated the ability to carry out academic work, and form close relationships with a peer(s) and have active participation in social groups.

In their behavior these subjects sought out and dealt with manageable levels of challenge in the environment. They regarded the new as exciting and desirable, a problem to be solved and something to be mastered. Thus, they demonstrated R. W. White's (1959) concept of *competence* or *effectance striving*. As one illustration, they assumed much of the responsibility in making preparations for college and went about this task with a sense of purpose and autonomy. The reader should note that the crisis model of adolescence stresses self-doubt and conflict more than competence and pleasurable engagement with the environment, yet for many adolescents this latter emphasis may be more accurate.

The coping strategies that these competent adolescents used were numerous. In planning for college, they referred to analogous past experiences, especially ones they had mastered, and thus could transfer to the new situation a sense of familiarity and probable success. They carried out an anticipatory socialization before leaving home by thinking through separation from parents and contemplating the kinds of behavior that would be expected of them as young adults. They learned as much as they could about the college they were to attend and in a sense went through a role rehearsal, or "dry run," of what was to come. Even though they made mistakes, they built a framework within which new experiences could be fitted. They lowered their level of aspiration as a cushion against disappointment, but not to the point of an adverse effect on self-image. They focused on the encouraging aspects of the new situation rather than on dangers or unpleasant aspects. They were aware of discouraging elements but elected not to dwell on them. Like subjects in other studies, they were anxious at times but used this feeling as a facilitator of action, and also reduced the anxiety by sharing their feelings with others.

When they moved into college their anticipatory or planning mechanisms enabled them to look ahead and see clearly what was expected in terms of academic and other requirements. They could distinguish short-term and long-term goals and distinguish between primary and secondary demands on their time, yet find activities that provided some sense of immediate satisfaction.

From a cognitive point of view, they had good power of concentration, for long stretches or under difficult conditions. When they started a task, they could sort out extraneous material and quickly come to the central issue. Another aspect of this was a sensitivity to environmental demands, what I have referred to elsewhere as "polling the environment" (King, 1973).

They reached out for new friends, sought information from upperclassmen, and were ready and open in sharing feelings and experiences with peers.

The competent adolescents were also compared with a matched group of patients by using a college-oriented Thematic Apperception Test. Of interest is the finding that the competent group projected a view of college where problems were manageable and peers were viewed optimistically, whereas the patients saw problems as yielding few solutions, people were seen as passive in the face of obstacles, and peers were seen as malevolent.

Subjects in a similar situation, that is, moving from high school to college, were studied by Westley and Epstein (1969) in Montreal. The writers drew subjects from white, Anglo-Saxon, Protestant families, and by interviews and tests they selected ten healthy and ten disturbed students and their families. The disturbed were defined by presence of structured psychiatric symptoms, social and occupational maladaptation, and moderate or severe psychopathology with moderate or severe anxiety.

The two groups were distinguished from each other in a variety of ways. The healthy students and families were more willing to cooperate in the study, welcoming new experience as a way of deepening and enriching their lives. They also responded with a full range of human emotions. The disturbed students, correspondingly, felt threatened and attempted to withdraw, and had problems in the expression of rage. All subjects had some anxieties in the sexual area, but the problem was greater for those who were disturbed. The healthy subjects were more aware of the demands of the future, while the less healthy were more confused and vague about goals and occupational future. Much of the difference could be summarized by saying that the healthy students had developed a sense of inner self that was congruent with their social group and the world around them, while the disturbed students had not.

Differences were also observable among the families of the two groups, particularly in the area of problem solving and communication. Families with emotionally healthy children recognized and talked about things that were emotionally important, while those with disturbed offspring seemed largely unaware of emotional problems. In other ways also, the families of healthy students showed positive coping. They dealt with threats to the family's physical and emotional well-being directly and in ways that did not damage family equilibrium. They felt they could meet and solve problems, yet were sensitive to the needs of individual family members. Families with disturbed children more often showed negative coping and had difficulty in identifying and dealing with problems, or did so at the expense of a family member.

Families were most effective when the parents seemed to satisfy each other's needs and were secure with each other. This was the "emotional thermostat" of family life. Westley and Epstein noted that psychopathology in the parents was not necessarily associated with disturbed children if parents did not project their difficulties onto the children or use the children as objects of anxiety or contained rage. They also noted that the balance of power between parents had important effects and that the healthiest children were found in families that were "father led" and had a balanced division of labor, in contrast to egalitarian families or those where one parent was dominant.

There are limitations to the conclusions that can be drawn from the Westley and Epstein data, due to the small size of the sample, its social and ethnic narrowness, and the difficulty in getting families of disturbed children to cooperate with the study. However, the data suggest hypotheses to be tested under more rigorously controlled conditions; to wit, that active engagement with the environment is associated with effective coping, that openness of communication within the family and identification of problems aid in the development of healthy children, and that a balance of power between parents is more often associated with satisfaction in the family and healthy offspring.

LATE ADOLESCENCE INTO YOUNG ADULTHOOD

The most vigorous research has come in this age span, and within the last two decades. Of the many studies there are four that are particularly relevant to the argument presented in this paper.

In looking for subjects for psychosomatic research, Grinker, Grinker, and Timberlake (1962) "discovered fortuitously" a group of healthy young men at George Williams College. As in many other studies, the subjects came primarily from white, middle- and lower-middle-class, Protestant backgrounds. In this particular group there was also the factor of a rather strict and rigorous religious training.

On the basis of responses to psychological tests, 65 of the students were classified as healthy. As a group they were not given much to introspection and were not bothered by internal anxiety. They were action-oriented, like the subjects in studies previously cited here, and used physical activity as a way of dissipating tension or anger. Although they felt anxiety or depression at times, the sources were usually exogenous, and the feelings were not generally severe or prolonged.

The typical home environment of these students was stable, with love from both parents and consistency in discipline. The division of labor in the family seemed much like the balanced power in the Westley and Epstein (1969) study; responsibilities and interests between parents were shared. In general, mother was viewed by the students as warmer, and father more as the disciplinarian, though not a harsh one.

Grinker and his colleagues found no evidence of identity crises as the young men went through adolescence. There was some rebelliousness and conflict in early adolescence, but like Offer's subjects, it seemed to be in the service of individuation. The students were conventional in social outlook, not especially creative in fantasy, nor did they show much use of abstraction, but they were solid in personality functioning and integration.

Further insight into development comes from a comparison Grinker and his colleagues made of a group of very well adjusted (VWA) students and a group of marginally adjusted (MA) students. In the VWA group, parental relationships were more positive in terms of agreement about child-rearing and in expressed affection. In the MA group, father was more often dominant. There was more conflict between children and parents in early adolescence for this group and the subjects more often felt that their parents did not understand them. They were less socially involved during adolescence than the VWA group, less focused, and less able to specify goals. They more often used fantasy in their attempts to solve problems. They often became bored and depressed; they inhibited anger rather than using it in some kind of constructive engagement with the environment.

Haverford College was the setting for the next study to be cited, where Heath (1965, 1968) has conducted some extended research on the topic of maturity. Although his subjects might be classified as intellectually elite, his conclusions can also provide the basis for hypotheses to be tested in further research. Subjects were divided into groups of more mature and less mature. The mature person was defined as stably organized in both a cognitive and emotional sense, as consistent and integrated, as allocentric and adjusted to reality (but without repressing autocentric trends when they were appropriate), and as less burdened by more primitive and unsocialized material in thought and fantasy. Yet the mature person could regress in the service of the ego.

Test batteries and observer ratings were used to form the study groups. Students in the more mature group had higher academic achievement and were less depressed and less impaired by self-centered trends. They described their siblings as effective and stable people, while every student in the immature group subtly derogated at least one sibling in some manner. Also, among the immature, achievements were more sporadic and often directed toward some capricious part of themselves, rather than toward some aspect of the external world.

From a set of adjectival statements by the two groups, Heath concluded that the less mature group showed less stability and control, was more labile in emotions, was more introspective, and evidenced more painful affect. Although individuals like these could not be characterized as showing structured psychiatric symptoms, they might be subject to a more stormy adolescence.

A final point of interest: the immature group used the medical clinic more frequently and reported more headaches, fatigue, localized pain, and accidental injuries. This finding is comparable to King's (1968) finding that students who visited a psychologist or psychiatrist also used the medical and surgical clinics more frequently than did other students.

The last two studies to be cited are longitudinal, following large samples of subjects through the four years of college.

Our study at Harvard (Finnie, 1970; King, 1973) utilized a 25% random sample of students who matriculated in the fall terms of 1960 and 1961. The subjects were given an extensive battery of tests and questionnaires and were retested each year. In addition, a subsample of 50 students was also interviewed regularly.

We observed four major patterns of personality change: *progressive maturation, delayed maturation, crisis and reintegration,* and *deterioration.* The majority of students were characterized by the first of these patterns and showed a strong feeling of continuity between past and present. Like students in the NIMH study, our students found experiences in the past in which they had coped and could transfer aspects of these experiences to present problems. They also brought forward the satisfying aspects of interpersonal relationships with parents, other adults, siblings, or peers and used these experiences in forming new relationships. These students were successful at adapting.

Change over four years of college occurred mainly in six areas for students in the progressive maturation pattern. In *object relations,* students worked out their feelings about parents and by graduation had formed reciprocal and rewarding relationships with peers. They learned to accept ways in which they were like father, and to be free of guilt in their uniqueness from him, which seemed to release emotional energy that could be invested in relationships with others. Many students described the most important part of their Harvard experience in terms of interpersonal rewards, rather than academic gains.

There was an increase in *self-esteem* and in a sense of competence, and by graduation students knew better where their strengths lay. They knew they could have an effect on people and events, and thereby had an increase in their sense of power.

Stabilization of mood also occurred, and when shifts in mood did take place, they were more likely to result from changes in the environment than from changes in internal states. Students became more adept at recognizing reasons for depressive shifts and found ways of modifying the depressed feelings. As in the other studies cited previously, the healthy adolescent and young adult is not necessarily at the mercy of his moods but can alter them by turning to other activities.

Interests did not often change in direction, but there was a deepening of them, a process of discrimination and synthesis, and greater recognition of the way in which interests fitted in with needs and values.

We noted a rise in the level of aspiration and in *goal-directed activity*. By the senior year, students more often selected careers on the basis of status and prestige. Students also were moving away from absolute value positions, and by the senior year they were emphasizing a life style that allowed personal freedom in moral decisions. We may have seen in our data an underlying shift in value positions that preceded many of the striking life style changes of recent years.

Under changes in *ego control* there was both a freeing of impulse expression and greater impulse control. Though a seeming paradox, in reality students became easier with their impulse life and brought more rationality and selectivity into it. In the directing of energy, students learned to handle the environment more effectively, to take account of contingencies, and to plan ahead with ease and comfort. There was also an increased tolerance for painful feelings by the senior year. In some cases there appeared to be more anxiety, but we saw it not as a sign of disturbance but as a growing ease in allowing anxiety to surface.

These changes were less evident among students in the pattern of delayed maturation, where there was a discontinuity with past experience that was heightened by being in college. Such students sensed a disjunction between their personality characteristics and those of their parents, and between themselves and their background. Most often it took place in students who lacked solid identification with individuals or with a racial or ethnic group. Few of our black students were in this group, because their sense of racial identification was strong, and they felt a keen sense of continuity with their cultural background.

Students in the delayed maturation group were sometimes unhappy and depressed and seemed to be more at the mercy of the environment than engaging and transforming it. They seemed to be searching and waiting.

A more classic picture of late adolescent disturbance came in the crisis and reintegration pattern. Often there was anxiety of sufficient severity to interfere with sleep or study, or depression that at times included suicidal ideation, psychosomatic disorders, and confusion. Some of these students dropped out of college while others remained in a state of reduced effectiveness. Although these crises were severe, most students moved into a reintegration phase by the senior year and showed some of the changes characteristic of students in the progressive maturation pattern, but the changes were less consistent. Looking back, these students had not learned how to deal with people effectively, often had problems with anger, and could not share their feelings easily. They were often hostile to key identification figures in childhood. There were negative feelings about the self, and, as a result, these students felt overwhelmed by the pressures in college. Resolution of the crisis involved coming to terms with their feelings of guilt, anger, and helplessness.

A few students showed a deterioration pattern, with an impairment in reality testing that led to unrealistic fantasies about their ability and their future achievement. With an increase in environmental stresses, they relied more on fantasies and retreated to primitive defenses rather than using coping mechanisms.

The final study to be cited was conducted by Katz et al. (1968) at Stanford and Berkeley. They, too, did not find turmoil and identity crisis among as many students as they had expected; for most students adaptation to the role demands of college and to the expectations of their future roles in society took place without conscious conflict. Students changed toward more adequate self-conceptions and improved in their ability to relate to others in mutually gratifying ways. The data from this study and the Harvard study emphasize the developmental tasks of achieving intimacy and its overriding importance in cognitive and social concerns.

Although there was little evidence of crisis, many students showed an incompleteness of identity by graduation and deferred an occupational life commitment till later years. Yet the students continued to move within the life space of their families. They showed a strong sense of continuity with their families in values, occupational preferences, and social expectations. Once again, evidence supports the existence of close ties rather than a gap between parents and offspring.

We might wonder from these studies if the changes that occur are due to the college experience or are universal and would be found in a cross-section of the 18- to 22-year-old group. Data are sparse, but there is a study by Trent and Medsker (1968) of nearly 5,000 high school graduates, who were studied over a four-year period. Subjects who persisted in college were more likely than the others to move toward an open-minded, flexible, and autonomous disposition, whereas those who went to work or into full-time homemaking were more constricted, had less intellectual curiosity, less interest in new experiences, and a lower tolerance for ambiguity. The authors concluded that those who go to college can learn more about themselves, their potential, and their desires. College students seemed to have more awareness of their environment and to be more open to it.

We must be careful not to conclude that those who went to college were healthier than those who went to work or married immediately after high school. Psychologists and psychiatrists have a bias that open-mindedness, autonomy, and creativity are necessary for successful coping and emotional health, but we cannot confirm that conclusion without obtaining much more systematic data than are currently available.

COMMON FINDINGS

In one way or another, the following findings appear in most or all of the studies that have been cited: (1) Turmoil and conflict are limited in adolescence and the identity crisis is not common. A developmental disturbance is not necessary for successful progress through adolescence. (2) There is little evidence for a generation gap, and although there is rebellion in adolescence, the relations between parents and offspring are generally good. (3)

Healthy adolescents have good relations with peers, are able to share feelings, and are not generally shy and withdrawn. (4) Although adolescents at times have doubts about themselves, self-esteem and a sense of competence are high; depression is limited; and most adolescents have ways of working out of depressed states. (5) Adolescents cope by dealing directly with painful affect and sharing such feelings with others. They also cope by turning away from painful feelings to other topics and activities, often of a physical nature. They can sublimate sexual and aggressive energy in social activities and sports, and find thereby a sense of satisfaction as well as a release of tension. They also use humor in coping, to blunt feelings of anxiety, limit guilt, and provide a sense of perspective on their problems. They use role rehearsal and cognitive planning for new situations and utilize anxiety as a facilitator in action rather than an inhibitor. Finally, they are able to integrate new experiences with past ones where they have felt satisfaction and success.

These common findings are not typical of all adolescents, nor of any adolescent all the time, but they do suggest that the capacity to cope is greater than we would be led to expect from theories based primarily on data from the consulting room. These findings also suggest the possibility that alternate models to the crisis model of adolescence are in order.

TYPES OF DEVELOPMENT IN ADOLESCENCE

Most of the readers of this article, at least those in clinical practice, will be familiar with adolescents who are *seriously impaired,* who show antisocial behavior, who cannot control their impulses, who are overcome by anxiety or depression, and who show abundant evidence of crisis and turmoil. This is one kind of adolescent development, and there is good reason to believe that the waning of adolescence still leaves these individuals vulnerable and subject to adjustment problems throughout their lives.

A second group has been described in this article—the *normal and competent.* Although numbers are not available, this group may constitute a majority of adolescents. These individuals are successful in coping, begin to develop a sense of identity, and show strong continuity with past experiences.

There is reason to believe that this second group is actually two subgroups: the modal or average and the highly competent. The former cope successfully but are not dreamers or exciting innovators, and their fantasy is limited. The highly competent are more likely to be innovators, leaders, and generally more exciting people. Both subgroups are well integrated in personality functioning but different in a creative sense.

A third group is composed of the *sensitive and vulnerable,* for whom adolescence may be a time of some distress. They may show some combination of an active fantasy life, sudden and extensive swings of mood, painful questioning about self-esteem, difficulty in sharing feelings with others, periods of strong depression, unrealistically high idealism, and active rebellion. They can be characterized by identity concerns and will often say that they are desperately trying to find out who they are. Often they tend to be loners and cannot talk easily with adults. They may be sent to counselors, or psychologists, or psychiatrists for help, or they may seek it out themselves.

Adolescents in this group are different from the emotionally disturbed in that they have a basic capacity to form meaningful relationships with others and can share feelings if they are helped to do so. They do need support and advice, but they are able to utilize that help. Most important, the upheaval these people experience is limited in time, and in most cases they become well integrated and mature as adults.

The third group may well be the source of many of our ideas about adolescent development. They are often the ones who are described in novels or autobiographical accounts, or who are seen in the consulting room. They are puzzling and frustrating to adults, and their very actions draw our attention, as if to demand the need for explanation. We can't help but notice them, but it is questionable if they are in the majority and if their lives provide the most reliable conceptual model for understanding adolescence and young adulthood.

Adolescent Development in Historical Perspective

Many people feel that the third type of development just described occurs with greater frequency today than in other generations, and indeed some historical perspective is useful in understanding adolescence. The key is the interrelationship between psychological development and social processes (King, 1969).

Passage through adolescence is relatively smoother under certain social conditions. One of these is the presence of *meaningful adult roles,* with appropriate rewards for their fulfillment, which are accepted by all members of the society. Another is the utilization of *clearly defined transition points* from child to adult status, which are important in the formation of firm identity. Also, there must be *stability and consensus in the value system* of the society so that daily activities make sense in terms of those values. These conditions are most often met when a society is stable, cohesive, and has a well-defined set of traditions and life style.

When there is instability and social change, or upheaval in the social order, there is more likely to be upheaval in adolescent development. When there is confusion about adult roles, and when transition points between statuses become fuzzy, and when value systems are changing, then the adolescent may feel pulled in two directions at once. These social conditions are characteristic of most industrialized countries today, and, as a consequence, we might expect more adolescents to fall into the sensitive and vulnerable category of development outlined above.

The situation is further complicated by two other factors that are particular to the United States. In the past few decades we have seen a change in child-rearing practices in this country. This change has been brought about by the admonitions of educators, psychologists, and psychoanalysts, who felt that development could be hampered by overrigid control. Many parents have responded by rearing their children in a more permissive manner, but in the process some have lost a sense of direction in child-rearing. In these families, children have often grown up with a vague uneasiness that their parents did not really care for them.

The other factor comes from the "American Dream," which leads us to believe that the manner in which we were born does not prevent us from attaining social prestige or from making some kind of significant contribution to our society. The "Dream" has been a significant factor in the history of the United States, but in the present situation of rapid technological advances, an adolescent or young adult may feel that infinite potentialities are open to him. As a consequence, there may be a reluctance to limit options on the future, but such reluctance can make more difficult the attainment of goals and direction in life.

Not all adolescents will be affected adversely by these social conditions, but the potential for a sense of crisis and turmoil will be increased. The effect will probably be felt most acutely by children of the professionals, the intellectuals, and the managers in the social system, because they are very aware of the social changes taking place but can do little to change their own lives. It is no surprise that many of our contemporary alienated youth come from such upper-middle-class families, and fewer from middle- and lower-middle-class groups were social change comes more slowly.

It is easy in the present day to feel that the majority of adolescents are in crisis, or turmoil, or active rebellion, or withdrawal, and to feel that what we see around us confirms the crisis model of adolescent development. Yet, that view may be misleading. The studies that have been reviewed here certainly suggest that a significant proportion of the younger generation are able to come to grips with the problems that arise in a changing society and to cope successfully with problems in their own lives. They can do this because they have had successful experiences in the past with coping, because they feel secure, and because they can share their feelings of anxiety and of confidence with others. If this is true, some revision of our views of adolescent and young adult development is in order.

13

INTRODUCTION

The Adolescent as a Philosopher:
The Discovery of the Self
in a Postconventional World,
by Lawrence Kohlberg and Carol Gilligan

The following chapter focuses on two interrelated themes. The first is adolescence, whose core phenomenon the authors perceive as the discovery of the subjective self with parallel questioning of adult reality. Kohlberg and Gilligan assert that this emphasis on subjective experience sets the adolescent apart from the younger child, who focuses on the event itself as important. Both, however, share an egocentric, hedonistic orientation. In a sense, Kohlberg and Gilligan bridge the differences between the findings about adolescent adaptation reported by King in Chapter 12 and the psychoanalytic theory of the adolescent's inner turbulence presented by Blos (1962b [Chapter 16 in *Childhood Psychopathology*]) with their assertion that "theoretical understanding of adolescence as a stage must stress its ideal type potential, not its 'average' manifestations."

The second focus stems from Kohlberg's extensive investigations of the development of moral thinking, which began with his doctoral dissertation in 1958 (see Kohlberg, 1963). Based on data from numerous interviews with youngsters, in which hypothetical moral dilemmas were posed, Kohlberg has formulated a universal, invariant sequence of moral orientation. He sees the child's morality developing from a preconventional level to conventional role conformity to a postconventional level of self-accepted moral principles. The chapter reprinted below expands on these levels and interweaves them with Piaget's (1932) cognitive developmental stages.

Kohlberg's contribution has substantially enriched the generative legacy of Durkheim's (1906) sociological concepts and of Freud's psychoanalytic contributions (1914, 1921, 1923a, 1927, 1930). Both frameworks tended to perceive moral development as a consequence of internalizing culturally dictated standards through processes of identification and reinforcement of rewards and punishments. The resulting, much-heralded superego–ego ideal concept has long been a source of controversy and productive ferment, even though therapists tended to avoid this concept in indexing clinical material (Sandler, 1960). Although developmental considerations have been paramount in theoretical formulations, clearly delineated levels of superego development have remained implicit, rather than explicit.

Adolescence and morality are brought together in the chapter below by an exploration of the changes in adolescent relativism over the course of recent history, an issue that has attracted considerable clinical attention (e.g., Settlage, 1972; Settlage et al., 1970; Solnit, 1972). Kohlberg and Gilligan reason that an important contributory factor to some of the current adolescent dilemmas is that some adolescents possess formal logical capacities without having developed correspondingly mature moral judgment. All adolescents, however, are increasingly exposed to a neatly packaged, postconventional questioning culture that provides partial answers. As the "moral dilemma" has, to some extent, been manufactured for them, rather than arising spontaneously, identity crises and questioning of adult cultural values occur earlier and earlier and no longer depend on individual cognitive and moral development. Such questioning is no longer the prerogative of an adolescent elite.

As Kohlberg and Gilligan point out, the dramatic cognitive changes in adolescence are changes in content, but not necessarily in structure. In considering the educational implications of adolescent cognitive development, the authors first examine the other end of compulsory schooling—the transformation from five to seven years (see also Chapter 10 by T. Shapiro and Perry). They then note that the curriculum reform of the late fifties and early sixties in our nation's schools *assumed* formal-operational thought rather than attempted to develop it. Proponents of the "new math" or the "new science" became discouraged as only a subgroup of the school population was engaged by these programs. This finding suggests the need for rethinking and reformulating society's role (via the school) in developing logical and moral thought rather than presupposing its existence. Kohlberg and Gilligan thus extend the thesis developed in Chapter 24 by E. Shapiro and Biber, as they urge high schools to take these considerations into account in program planning.

13

The Adolescent as a Philosopher: The Discovery of the Self in a Postconventional World

LAWRENCE KOHLBERG and CAROL GILLIGAN

> Those whose exterior semblance doth belie
> Thy Soul's immensity;
> Thou best Philosopher . . .
>
> Thou little child, yet glorious in the might
> Of heaven-born freedom on thy Being's height,
> Why with such earnest pains dost thou provoke,
> The years to bring the inevitable yoke?
> Thus blindly with thy blessedness at strife?
> Full soon thy Soul shall have her earthly freight,
> And customs lie upon thee with a weight
> Heavy as frost, and deep almost as life!
>
> The thought of our past years in me doth breed
> Perpetual benediction; not indeed
> For that which is most worthy to be blest;
> Delight and liberty, the simple creed of childhood . . .
> But for those obstinate questionings
> Of sense and outward things,
> Fallings from us, vanishings,
> Blank misgivings of a creature
> Moving about in worlds not realized,
> High instincts before which our mortal Nature
> Did tremble like a guilty thing surprised:
>
> —Wordsworth, *Intimations of Immortality*

The central themes of this essay are: first, the definition of adolescence as a universal stage of development; second, the way in which the universal

First published in *Daedalus*, 100:1051–1086, 1971. Reprinted by permission.

features of adolescence seem to be acquiring unique colorings in the present era in America; and third, the implications of these changes for education.

ADOLESCENCE AS A ROLE TRANSITION AND AS A STAGE OF DEVELOPMENT

In turn-of-the-century America, G. Stanley Hall (1904) launched developmental psychology with his discussion of adolescence as a stage of development. For the next 50 years, however, most American educators and psychologists tended to think about adolescence not as a stage but as a period in life, "the teens." The teenager was viewed as half-child, half-grownup, with a half-serious peer "culture" or "youth culture" of his own. Textbook after textbook on adolescence was written telling in statistical detail the sort of information which could be gathered from reading *Seventeen* or Harold Teen.

Even with the textbook description of the teenager, one could surmise that the central phenomenon of adolescence is the discovery of the self as something unique, uncertain, and questioning in its position in life. The discovery of the body and its sexual drive, and self-conscious uncertainty about that body, is one stock theme of adolescent psychology. The romantic concerns and hopes for the self's future have always been another element of the stock description of the adolescent. The third stock theme implied by the discovery of the self is the need for independence, for self-determination and choice, as opposed to acceptance of adult direction and control. The fourth stock theme implied by the adolescent discovery of self is adolescent egocentrism and hedonism, the adolescent's focus on events as they bear upon his self-image and as they lead to immediate experiences. (While the child is egocentric and hedonistic, he is not subjective; he focuses on events, not on his subjective experience of the events, as what is important.)

While the discovery of the self in the senses just listed has been a stock theme in American discussion of adolescence, it has been subordinated to another theme, the theme of adolescence as a marginal role between being a child and being grown-up. The adolescent sense of self, with its multiple possibilities, its uncertainties, and its self-consciousness has been viewed as the result of a social position in which one is seen and sees oneself, sometimes as adult, sometimes as child. In the marginal role view, the adolescent's need for independence and fantasies of the future are seen as the desire to "be grown-up," his conflicts and instabilities are seen as the conflict between the desire to be grown-up and a role and personality not yet consistent with being grown-up.

This social-role view of adolescence, the adolescent as teenager, placed the instability of the adolescent self against the background of a stable society.

Against the background of the moods and tantrums and dreams of the American teenager lay an unquestioned acknowledgment of the stability and reality of the social order the adolescent was to enter. Underneath the hedonism and rebellion of the teenager lay the conformist. Harold Teen's and Andy Hardy's first law was conformity to the norms of the peer group. Beneath this conformity to the peer group, however, was the teenager's recognition that when the chips were down about your future you listened to dear old Dad. An extreme example in reality of the American image of the teenager as cutting up while basically conforming is a group of California suburban high school seniors of the late 1950s. This group celebrated graduation by a summer of well-planned robberies. Their one concern while they engaged in their delinquent activities was that if they were detected, they would not get into the college of their choice.

Conformity to the peer culture, then, was the first theme of the American treatment of the adolescent in the fifties, of August Hollingshead's (1949) *Elmtown's Youth*, James Coleman's (1961) *Adolescent Society*, Albert K. Cohen's (1955) *Delinquent Boys*. The second theme was that this peer culture was itself determined by the realities of adult social class and mobility in which the peer culture was embedded. Whether grind, jock, or hood, glamour girl, sex kitten, or Plain Jane, the teenager's discovery of self led to the enactment of the stock roles of the adolescent culture. At a different level from the sociology of the teenager, American literature also presented adolescence as accepting unquestioningly the reality of adult society. Adolescence was presented as an imaginative expansion of the innocence of childhood facing the sordid but unquestionable reality of adult life. From *Huckleberry Finn* to *Catcher in the Rye*, the true American adolescent brought the child's innocence to a new awareness of adult reality, leading to a vision of the phoniness and corruption of the adult world, which was, however, unquestioned in its reality. Sherwood Anderson's story of the 14-year-old finding his father figure with a prostitute is titled "I Want to Know Why." While the American adolescent might be shocked by the sordid elements of adult life and might "want to know why," there was no question that he would eventually enter and accept "adult reality." Even when he wanted to know why, the American adolescent seldom questioned the American assumptions of progress and upward mobility, the assumption that society was moving ahead. Rather, he questioned the wisdom of his parents because they were old-fashioned. This questioning was itself an expression of faith in the adult society of the future. The adolescent's sense of the superiority of his values to those of his parents was an expression of the adolescent's belief in a greater closeness to the adult society of the future than his parents had; it was a faith in progress.

Today, we are aware of the possibility of a deeper questioning by the adolescent than was true at earlier times. Our image of the adolescent must accommodate to the phenomena of the counterculture, of the hippie and the revolutionary who do not believe in progress and upward mobility. Both hippies and the New Left reject not only the *content* of adult society but its *forms*. The new radical refuses to organize as his revolutionary predecessors of the thirties did. Unlike the revolutionary of the thirties, he does not want to be a grownup, to really transform and govern the adult society of the future. And beneath a questioning of social *forms* is a questioning of social *functions*. The current radical rejection of adult society seems to be the rejection of any adult society whatsoever, if an adult society means one including institutions of work, family, law, and government. Radicals have always questioned the social *forms* of authority, of competitive achievement, and of the nuclear privatistic family, and have dreamed of a more egalitarian and communal society. The essential realities of the social *functions* of work, child-rearing, and of an organized social order were never questioned, however. Since Paul Goodman's (1960) *Growing Up Absurd,* we have been aware that the reality of work and making a living has come into question. Now the new ethics of population control and the Women's Liberation Movement lead to the questioning of the supreme reality of adulthood, being a parent and having children. Finally, the reality of social order is in question. When current adolescents talk of revolution, they do not seem to mean merely that adult society is evil and is resistant to rational change. More deeply, they seem to be saying that there is no real social order to destroy anyway. Social order is a myth or illusion in the adult's mind and revolution is not the destruction of an order, whether good or bad. On the optimistic side, this is the message of Charles Reich's (1970) "revolution on consciousness," the idea that the young can transform society without entering or dealing with it. On the pessimistic side, the popular versions of the counterculture reiterate the theme of *Easy Rider,* the theme that the adult culture is hostile and absurd, that it does not want you to join it but that it envies you and will destroy you in the end no matter what you do.

To summarize, all accounts of adolescence stress both the sense of questioning and the parallel discovery or search for a new self of the adolescent. Usually this questioning and search for self have been seen as the product of the adolescent's marginal role between childhood and adulthood. Usually, too, it has been assumed that there are underlying givens beneath the questioning, that whatever uncertainties the adolescent has, he wants to be a grownup. Recent experience makes real for Americans that much deeper form of questioning which may characterize adolescence, one which is not merely a matter of roles. The potential for a deeper questioning by the adolescent is implied by the identity conflict central to Erik Erikson's psychohistorical stage theory of adolescence. It is the philosophic doubting about truth, goodness, and reality implied by Jean Piaget's epistemological stage theory of adolescence. It is the doubting represented by Dostoevsky's adolescents, not Mark Twain's. Deeper doubting is still a rare phenomenon for adolescents. Beneath most hippie exteriors is an interior more like Harold Teen than Hamlet or Raskolnikov. But theoretical understanding of adolescence as a stage must stress its ideal-type potential, not its "average" manifestations.

Taking adolescent questioning seriously is not only important for psychological theory, it is also central to a successful resolution of the current problems of the American high school. For education, the problem of meaning just raised is the problem of whether the high school has meaning to the adolescent. We said that American psychology placed the adolescent discovery of the self against a stable but progressive social order. It saw the discovery of self within a desire to be "grown-up," however confused or vague this image of the grownup was. The high school had a double meaning to the adolescent from this point of view. First, it was the locus of the peer culture in which he found his immediate identity, whether as grind, jock, or hood. Second, on the academic side, it was a point of connection to a place in the adult world. In most high schools these meanings still remain and the questioning of the reality of adulthood is not that deep. In others, however, it is a serious problem and high school is essentially a meaningless place. Before we can solve the problem of the felt meaninglessness of high school, a clearer view of adolescent questioning is required. For this, we must turn to stage theory of the Erikson and Piaget variety.

THE MEANING OF THE STAGE CONCEPT—ILLUSTRATED FROM THE PRESCHOOL YEARS

To understand the universal meanings of adolescence as a stage and its implications for education, it will help to examine briefly an earlier stage and its implications for education, one more thoroughly understood than the stage of adolescence. Almost all cultures implicitly recognize two great stages or transformations in development. Adolescence, the second transformation, traditionally terminated compulsory schooling. The first transformation, occurring from five to seven years of age, initiated compulsory schooling (S. H. White, 1970). This five-to-seven shift is termed the "onset of the latency period" by Freudian theory, the onset of concrete logical thought by Piaget. As embodied in educational thought, the Freudian interpretation of the five-to-seven shift implied letting the child grow, letting him work through his fantasies until he had repressed his sexual instincts and was ready to turn his energies to formal learning. This Freudian interpretation of the preschool stage suffered both from lack of confirmation by empirical research and from irrelevance to the intellectual development and everyday behavior with which the schools were concerned. When the Great Society decided to do something for the disadvantaged child, the Freudian "let him work through his Oedipus complex" implications of the five-to-seven shift were dismissed as a luxury for the wealthy. Programs of preschool intellectual stimulation and academic schooling were initiated, with the expectation of long-range effects on intelligence and achievement. These programs failed to fulfill their initial promise of changing general intellectual maturity or long-range achievement (Jensen, 1969; Kohlberg, 1968).

One reason they failed was because they confused specific teaching and learning with the development of new levels of thinking truly indicative of cognitive maturity. The evidence of limitations of these early education programs, together with growing positive research evidence of the existence of cognitive stages, convinced early educators of the reality of the stage transformation at age five to seven. The stage transformation of the period five to seven is now conceived in quite a different way from that in the vogue of Freudian education. In the Freudian view, the preschooler was in a stage of domination of thought by sexual and aggressive fantasies. The new stage, which succeeded this, was defined negatively as latency, rather than positively. Under the influence of Piaget, more recent thinking sees the preschool child's fantasy as only one aspect of the preschooler's pattern of prelogical thought. In the prelogical stage, subjective appearance is not fully distinguished from "reality"; the permanent identities of things are not differentiated from their momentary transformations. In the prelogical stage view, the preschool child's special fantasy is the expression not of an instinct later repressed, but of a cognitive level of thought. The decline of fantasy in the years five to seven, longitudinally documented by Scheffler (1971), is not a repression; it is closely related to the positive development of concrete logical patterns of thought.

The child's changed orientation to reality in the five-to-seven period is part of the development of concrete logical operations then. During this period the child develops the operations of categorical classification, serial ordering, addition, subtraction, and inversion of classes and relations. This development occurs in the absence of schooling in African and Taiwanese villagers in much the same way that it occurs in the American suburban child (Kohlberg, 1966, 1968).

As a concrete example, Piaget and the authors have asked children if they had a bad dream and if they were frightened when they woke up from their bad dream (Kohlberg, 1966). Susie, age four, said she dreamed about a giant and answered, "Yes, I was scared, my tummy was shaking and I cried and told my mommy about the giant." Asked, "Was it a real giant or was it just pretend? Did the giant just seem to be there, or was it really there?" she answered, "It was really there, but it left when I woke up. I saw its footprint on the floor."

According to Piaget, Susie's response is not to be dismissed as the product of a wild imagination, but represents the young child's general failure to differentiate subjective from objective components of his or her experience. Children go through a regular series of steps in their understanding of dreams as subjective phenomena. The first step, achieved before five by most American middle-class children, is the recognition that dreams are not real events. The next step, achieved soon thereafter, is the realization that dreams cannot be seen by others. The third step is the notion that dreams are internal (but still material) events.

By age six to eight children are clearly aware that dreams are thoughts caused by themselves. To say such cognitive changes define stages implies the following things.

1. It implies that young children's responses represent not mere ignorance or error, but rather a spontaneous manner of thinking about the world that is qualitatively different from the way we adults think and yet has a structure of its own.

2. The notion of different developmental structures of thought implies consistency of level of response from task to task. If a child's response represents a general structure rather than a specific learning, then the child should demonstrate the same relative structural levels in a variety of tasks.

3. The concept of stage implies an invariance of sequence in development, a regularity of stepped progression regardless of cultural teaching or circumstance. Cultural teaching and experience can speed up or slow down development, but they cannot change its order or sequence.

The concept of stage, then, implies that both the youngest children's conceptions of the dream as real and the school-age children's view of the dream as subjective are their own; they are products of the general state of the children's cognitive development, rather than the learning of adult teachings.

Cross-cultural studies indicate the universality of the basic sequence of development of thinking about the dream, even where adult beliefs about the meaning and significance of dreams are somewhat different from our own (Kohlberg, 1966). While the stage of concrete operations is culturally universal and in a sense natural, this does not mean it is either innate or that it is inevitable and will develop regardless of environmental stimulation. In the United States, the doctrine of stages was assumed for some time to mean that children's behavior unfolded through a series of age-specific patterns, and that these patterns and their order were wired into the organism. This indeed was the view of Gesell and Freud, and Americans misunderstood Piaget as maintaining the same thing. The implications of the Gesellian and Freudian theory for early education were clear; early teaching and stimulation would do no good since we must wait for the unfolding of the behavior, or at least the unfolding of the readiness to learn it.

In contrast, Piaget used the existence of stages to argue that basic cognitive structures are not wired in, but are general forms of equilibrium resulting from the interaction between organism and environment. If children have their own logic, adult logic or mental structure cannot be derived from innate neurological patterning because such patterning should hold also in childhood. (It is hardly plausible to view a succession of logics as an evolutionary and functional program of innate wiring.) At the same time, however, Piaget argued that stages indicate that mental structure is not merely a reflection of external physical realities or of cultural concepts of different complexities. The structure of the child's concepts in Piaget's view is not only less complex than the adult's, it is also different. The child's thought is not just a simplified version of the adult's.

Stages, or mental structures, then, are not wired into the organism though they depend upon inborn organizing tendencies. Stages are not direct reflections of the child's culture and external world, though they depend upon experience for their formation. Stages are, rather, the products of interactional experience between the child and the world, experience which leads to a restructuring of the child's own organization rather than to the direct imposition of the culture's pattern upon the child. While hereditary components of IQ, of the child's rate of information processing, have some influence on the rate at which the child moves through invariant cognitive sequences, experiential factors heavily influence the rate of cognitive-structural development.[1] The kind of experience that stimulates cognitive stage development is, however, very different from the direct academic teaching of information and skills, which is the focus of ordinary schooling. Programs of early education that take account of cognitive stages, then, look neither like the permissive "let them grow" nursery school pattern nor like the early teaching programs popular in the sixties. They are a new form now coming into being (Kohlberg, 1968).

---

[1]Cognitive stage maturity is different from IQ, a separate factor, though the two are correlated (Kohlberg and DeVries, 1971). General impoverishment of organized physical and social stimulation leads to retardation in stage development. Culturally disadvantaged children tend to be somewhat retarded compared with middle-class children with the same IQs in concrete-operational logic. Experimental intervention can to some extent accelerate cognitive development if it is based on providing experiences of cognitive conflict which stimulate the child to reorganize or rethink his patterns of cognitive ordering.

COGNITIVE STAGES IN ADOLESCENCE

The older children get, the more difficult it is to distinguish universal stage changes from sociocultural transitions in development. We said that the core phenomenon of adolescence as a stage was the discovery of the subjective self and subjective experience and a parallel questioning of adult cultural reality. The manifestations of this discovery, however, are heavily colored not only by historical and cultural variations, but also by previous patterns of life history of the child.

In our first section, we discussed one manifestation of the discovery of the self, the discovery of the body and its sexual drives. In part this is, of course, a biological universal, the physical growth spurt marking adolescent puberty and an accompanying, qualitatively new sexual drive. If there is anything that can be safely said about what is new in the minds of adolescents, it is that they, like their elders, have sex on their minds. These changes, of course, have been the focus of Freudian thinking about adolescence as a stage. If anything, however, Freudian thinking has underestimated the novel elements of sexual experience in adolescence. For the Freudian, early adolescent sexuality is the reawakening of early childhood sexuality previously latent, with a consequent resurrection of oedipal feeling. Although it is true that adolescent sexuality bears the stamp of earlier experience, it is not the resurrection of earlier sexual feelings. Adolescent sexual drive is a qualitatively new phenomenon (Kohlberg, 1966).

While sexual drives are awakened at puberty, there are vast individual and cultural variations in the extent to which they determine the adolescent's behavior and experience. Sexuality is a central concern for the self of some 14-year-olds; it is something deferred to the future for others. What is common for all, however, is an intensified emotionality, whether experienced as sexual or not. This emotionality, too, is now experienced as a part of the self, rather than as a correlate of objective events in the world. Ellinwood (1969) studied the age development of the verbal experiencing and expression of emotion on projective tests and free self-descriptions. She found that prior to adolescence (age 12 or so), emotions were experienced as objective concomitants of activities and objects. The child experienced anger because events or persons were bad; he experienced affection because persons were good or giving; he felt excitement because activities were exciting or fun. At adolescence, however, emotions are experienced as the result of states of the self rather than as the direct correlate of external events.

The difference may perhaps be clarified by reference to middle-class drug experiences. Occasionally, psychologically, a preadolescent may take drugs, as he may drink beer or sneak cigarettes. When he does this, he does this as an activity of an exciting, forbidden, and grown-up variety. For the adolescent drug-taker, drugs represent, rather, a vehicle to certain subjective moods, feelings, and sensations. In many cases, the drug experience is a vehicle for overcoming depression, felt as an inner subjective mood. In any case, drug-taking is not an activity with an objective quality; it is a mode of activating subjective inner feelings and states. The same is true of such activities as intensive listening to music, an activity characteristically first engaged in at early adolescence (age 11 to 14). The rock, folk-rock, and blues music so popular with adolescents is explicitly a presentation of subjective mood and is listened to in that spirit.

Associated with the discovery of subjective feelings and moods is the discovery of ambivalence and conflicts of feeling. If feelings are objective correlates of external good and bad events, there can be little tolerance and acceptance of feeling hate and love for the same person, of enjoying sadness and feeling sad about pleasure. Ellinwood's (1969) study documents that adolescents are consciously expressing such ambivalence, which is of course the stock-in-trade of the blues and folk-rock music beamed to them.

We have spoken of the adolescent discovery of subjective moods and feelings as linked to puberty. More basically, it is linked to the universal cognitive stages of Piaget. We have said that the five-to-seven transition is defined by Piaget as the transition to *abstract, reflective* thought. More exactly, it is the transition from logical inference as a set of *concrete operations* to logical inference as a set of *formal operations* or "operations upon operations." "Operations upon operations" imply that the adolescent can classify classifications, that he can combine combinations, that he can relate relationships. It implies that he can think about thought, and create thought systems or "hypothetico-deductive" theories. This involves the logical construction of all possibilities—that is, the awareness of the observed as only a subset of what may be logically possible. In related fashion, it implies the hypothetico-deductive attitude, the notion that a belief or proposition is not an immediate truth, but a hypothesis whose truth value consists in the truth of the concrete propositions derivable from it.

An example of the shift from concrete to formal operations may be taken from the work of Peel (1967). Peel asked children what they thought about the following event: "Only brave pilots are allowed to fly over high mountains. A fighter pilot flying over the Alps collided with an aeriel cable-way, and cut a main cable causing some cars to fall to the glacier below. Several people were killed." A child at the concrete-operational level answered: "I think that the pilot was not very good at flying. He would have been better off if he went on fighting." A formal-operational child responded: "He was either not informed of the mountain railway on his route or he was flying too low; also his flying compass may have been affected by something before or after take-off, thus setting him off course, causing collision with the cable.''

The concrete-operational child assumes that if there was a collision, the pilot was a bad pilot; the formal-operational child considers all the possibilities that might have caused the collision. The concrete-operational child adopts the hypothesis that seems most probable or likely to him. The formal-operational child constructs all possibilities and checks them out one by one.

As a second example, we may cite one of Piaget's tasks, systematically replicated by Kuhn, Langer, and Kohlberg (1971). The child is shown a pendulum whose length may vary as well as the number of weights attached. The child is asked to discover or explain what determines the speed of movement (or ''period'') of the pendulum. Only the formal-operational child will ''isolate variables,'' that is, vary length while holding weight constant, and so forth, and arrive at the correct solution (for example, that period is determined by length). Success at the task is unrelated to relevant verbal knowledge about science or physics, but is a function of logical level.

In fact, the passage from concrete to formal operations is not an all-or-none phenomenon. There are one or two substages of formal operations prior to the full awareness of all possibilities just described. These substages are described in Table 1, which presents an overview of Piaget's cognitive stages. For simplifying purposes, we may say that for middle-class Americans, one stage of formal operations is reached at age 10 to 13, while the consideration of all possibilities is reached around 15 to 16. At the first formal-operational stage, children became capable of reversing relationships and ordering relationships one at a time or in chains, but not of abstract consideration of all possibilities. (They are capable of ''forming the inverse of the reciprocal,'' in Piaget's terminology, but not of combining all relationships.) A social-thinking example of failure to reverse relationships is shown in concrete-operational children's responses to the question: ''What does the Golden Rule tell you to do if someone comes up on the street and hits you?'' The typical answer is: ''Hit him back, do unto others as they do unto you.'' The painful process of the transitional formal-operational child in responding to the question is given in the following response: ''Well, for the Golden Rule you have to like dream that your mind leaves your body and goes into the other person, then it comes back into you and you see it like he does and you act like the way you saw it from there.''[2]

We have described Piaget's stage of formal operations as a logical stage. What is of special importance for understanding adolescents, however, is not

[2]Another example of a transitional stage response is success on the question: ''Joe is shorter than Bob, Joe is taller than Alex, who is the tallest?'' The transitional child can solve this by the required reversing of relations and serial ordering of them, but will fail the pendulum task.

TABLE 1

PIAGET'S ERAS AND STAGES OF LOGICAL AND COGNITIVE DEVELOPMENT

Era I (age 0–2): Sensorimotor Intelligence

Stage 1: Reflex action.

Stage 2: Coordination of reflexes and sensorimotor repetition (primary circular reaction).

Stage 3: Activities to make interesting events in the environment reappear (secondary circular reaction).

Stage 4: Means-ends behavior and search for absent objects.

Stage 5: Experimental search for new means (tertiary circular reaction).

Stage 6: Use of imagery in insightful invention of new means and in recall of absent objects and events.

Era II (age 2–5): Symbolic, Intuitive, or Prelogical Thought

Inference is carried on through images and symbols which do not maintain logical relations or invariances with one another. "Magical thinking" in the sense of (a) confusion of apparent or imagined events with real events and objects and (b) confusion of perceptual appearances of qualitative and quantitative change with actual change.

Era III (age 6–10): Concrete-Operational Thought

Inferences carried on through system of classes, relations, and quantities maintaining logically invariant properties and which *refer to concrete objects*. These include such logical processes as (a) inclusion of lower-order classes in higher-order classes; (b) transitive seriation (recognition that if $a > b$ and $b > c$, then $a > c$); (c) logical addition and multiplication of classes and quantities; (d) conservation of number, class membership, length, and mass under apparent change.

Substage 1: Formation of stable categorical classes.

Substage 2: Formation of quantitative and numerical relations of invariance.

Era IV (age 11 to adulthood): Formal-Operational Thought

Inferences through logical operations upon propositions or "operations upon operations." Reasoning about reasoning. Construction of systems of all possible relations or implications. Hypothetico-deductive isolation of variables and testing of hypotheses.

Substage 1: Formation of the inverse of the reciprocal. Capacity to form negative classes (for example, the class of all not-crows) and to see relations as simultaneously reciprocal (for example, to understand that liquid in a U-shaped tube holds an equal level because of counterbalanced pressures).

Substage 2: Capacity to order triads of propositions or relations (for example, to understand that if Bob is taller than Joe and Joe is shorter than Dick, then Joe is the shortest of the three).

Substage 3: True formal thought. Construction of all possible combinations of relations, systematic isolation of variables, and deductive hypothesis-testing.

the logic of formal operations, but its epistemology, its conception of truth and reality. In the previous section we said that the child's attainment of concrete operations at age six to seven led to the differentiation of subjective and objective, appearance and reality. The differentiation at this level was one in which reality was equated with the physical and the external. We cited the child's concept of the dream, in which the unreality of the dream was equivalent to its definition as an inner mental event with no physical external correlate. The subjective and the mental are to the concrete-operational child equated with fantasies, with unrealistic replicas of external physical events. The development of formal operations leads, however, to a new view of the external and the physical. The external and the physical are only one set of many possibilities of a subjective experience. The external is no longer the "real," the "objective," and the internal, the "unreal." The internal may be real and the external unreal. At its extreme, adolescent thought entertains solipsism or at least the Cartesian *cogito*, the notion that the only thing real is the self. I asked a 15-year-old girl: "What is the most real thing to you?" Her unhesitating reply was "myself."

The lines from Wordsworth introducing this essay represent his own adolescent experience described by him as follows: "I was often unable to think of external things as having external existence, and I communed with all that I saw as something not apart from, but inherent in, my own material nature. Many times while going to school have I grasped at a wall or tree to recall myself from this abyss of idealism to the reality. At this time I was afraid of such processes" (Trilling, 1941).

Wordsworth's adolescent solipsism was linked to his awakened poetic sense, to his experience of nature, and to his transcendental religiosity. It seems that for all adolescents the discovery of the subjective is a condition for aesthetic feeling in the adult sense, for the experience of nature as a contemplative experience, and for religiosity of a mystical variety. It is probably the condition for adolescent romantic love as well. This whole constellation of experiences is called romantic because it is centered on a celebration of the self's experience as the self enters into union with the self's counterpart outside. The common view of romanticism as adolescent, then, is correct in defining the origins of romanticism in the birth of the subjective self in adolescence.

If the discovery of subjective experience and the transcendental self is one side of the new differentiation of subjective and objective made by the adolescent, the clouding and questioning of the validity of society's truths and its rightness is the other. To consider this side of adolescence we must turn from cognitive to moral stages.

Before we turn to adolescent moral thought we need to note a real difference between the development of concrete operations and the development of formal operations. There are two facts that distinguish the adolescent revolution in logical and epistemological thinking from the five-to-seven revolution in thinking. The first is that the adolescent revolution is extremely variable as to time. The second is that for many people it never occurs at all. With regard to concrete operations, some children attain clear capacity for logical reasoning at five, some at eight or nine. But all children ultimately display some clear capacity for concrete logical reasoning (Kohlberg, 1966). This is not true for formal-operational reasoning. As an example, Kuhn, Langer, and Kohlberg (1971) found the percentage of 265 persons at various ages showing clear formal-operational reasoning at the pendulum task to be as follows:

Age 10 to 15: 45%
Age 16 to 20: 53%
Age 21 to 30: 65%
Age 45 to 50: 57%

The subjects studied were lower-middle and upper-middle-class California parents (age 45 to 50) and their children (age 10 to 30). The figures indicate that it is not until 21 to 30 that a clear majority (65%) attain formal reasoning by this criteria. They suggest that there is no further development of formal reasoning after age 30. This means that almost 50% of American adults never reach adolescence in the cognitive sense. The figures should not be taken with too great seriousness, since the various tasks requiring formal operations are of somewhat varying difficulty. In the study cited, another problem, a "correlation problem," was used and was passed by even fewer members of the adult population. It is possible that easier tasks could be devised which would lead to more people displaying formal reasoning. The point, however, is that a large proportion of Americans never develop the capacity for abstract thought. Most who do, develop it in earlier adolescence (age 11 to 15), but some do not reach full formal reasoning until their twenties. We should note, too, that rate of attainment of formal operations is not simply a function of IQ: the correlations between Piagetian and IQ measures are in the fifties. Finally, in simpler cultures—for example, villages in Turkey—full formal operations never seem to be reached at all (though this level is researched by urbanized, educated Turks).

The high variability in age of attainment of formal operations, then, indicates that we cannot equate a cognitive stage with a definite age period. Puberty, the attainment of formal operations, and the transition from childhood to adult status are all components of adolescence variable in time and in their relations to one another.

MORAL STAGES IN ADOLESCENCE
AND THEIR RELATION TO COGNITIVE STAGES

Joseph Adelson (1971) documents the way in which the adolescent's thinking about political society is transformed by the advent of formal-operational thought. To understand the adolescent's social thinking, however, we need to be aware not only of logical stages but also of stages of moral judgment. In our research, we have found six definite and universal stages of development in moral thought. In our longitudinal study of 76 American boys from preadolescence, youths were presented with hypothetical moral dilemmas, all deliberately philosophical, some of them found in medieval works of casuistry.

On the basis of their reasoning about these dilemmas at a given age, each boy's stage of moral thought could be determined for each of 12 basic moral concepts, values, or issues. The six stages of moral thought are divided into three major levels: the *preconventional*, the *conventional*, and the *postconventional* or autonomous.

While the preconventional child is often "well behaved" and is responsive to cultural labels of good and bad, he interprets these labels in terms of their physical consequences (punishment, reward, exchange of favors) or in terms of the physical power of those who enunciate the rules and labels of good and bad. This level is usually occupied in the middle class by children aged four to ten.

The second or conventional level usually becomes dominant in preadolescence. Maintaining the expectation and rules of the individual's family, group, or nation is perceived as valuable in its own right. There is concern not only with conforming to the individual's social order, but also in maintaining, supporting, and justifying this order.

The postconventional level is first evident in adolescence and is characterized by a major thrust toward autonomous moral principles which have validity and application apart from the authority of the groups or persons who hold them and apart from the individual's identification with those persons or groups.

Within each of these three levels there are two discernible stages. At the preconventional level we have: *Stage 1*: Orientation toward punishment and unquestioning deference to superior power. The physical consequences of an action regardless of their human meaning or value determine its goodness or badness. *Stage 2*: Right action consists of that which instrumentally satisfies one's own needs and occasionally the needs of others. Human relations are viewed in terms like those of the marketplace. Elements of fairness, reciprocity, and equal sharing are present, but they are always interpreted in a physical, pragmatic way. Reciprocity is a matter of "you scratch my back and I'll scratch yours," not of loyalty, gratitude, or justice.

At the conventional level we have: *Stage 3*: Good-boy–good-girl orientation. Good behavior is that which pleases or helps others and is approved by them. There is much conformity to stereotypical images of what is majority or "natural" behavior. Behavior is often judged by intention—"he means well" becomes important for the first time and is overused. One seeks approval by being "nice." *Stage 4*: Orientation toward authority, fixed rules, and the maintenance of the social order. Right behavior consists of doing one's duty, showing respect for authority, and maintaining the given social order for its own sake. One earns respect by performing dutifully.

At the postconventional level we have: *Stage 5A*: A social-contract orientation, generally with legalistic and utilitarian overtones. Right action tends to be defined in terms of general rights and in terms of standards which have been critically examined and agreed upon by the whole society. There is a clear awareness of the relativism of personal values and opinions and a corresponding emphasis upon procedural rules for reaching consensus. Aside from what is constitutionally agreed upon, right or wrong is a matter of personal values and opinion. The result is an emphasis upon the legal point of view, but with an emphasis upon the possibility of changing the law in terms of rational considerations of social utility, rather than freezing it in the terms of stage 4 law-and-order. Outside the legal realm, free agreement and contract are the binding elements of obligation. This is the official morality of American government, and finds its ground in the thought of the writers of the Constitution. *Stage 5B*: Orientation to internal decisions of conscience, but without clear rational or universal principles. *Stage 6*: Orientation toward ethical principles appealing to logical comprehensiveness, universality, and consistency. These principles are abstract and ethical (the Golden Rule, the categorical imperative); they are not concrete moral rules like the Ten Commandments. Instead, they are universal principles of justice, of the reciprocity and equality of human rights, and of respect for the dignity of human beings as individual persons.

These stages are defined by 12 basic issues of moral judgment. On one such issue—Conscience, Motive Given for Rule Obedience or Moral Action—the six stages look like this:

1. Obey rules to avoid punishment.
2. Conform to obtain rewards, have favors returned, and so on.
3. Conform to avoid disapproval, dislike by others.
4. Conform to avoid censure by legitimate authorities and resultant guilt.
5A. Conform to maintain the respect of the impartial spectator judging in terms of community welfare.
5B. Conform to avoid self-condemnation.

In another of these moral issues—the value of human life—the six stages can be defined thus:

1. The value of a human life is confused with the value of physical objects and is based on the social status or physical attributes of its possessor.
2. The value of a human life is seen as instrumental to the satisfaction of the needs of its possessor or of other persons.
3. The value of a human life is based on the empathy and affection of family members and others toward its possessor.
4. Life is conceived as sacred in terms of its place in a categorical moral or religious order of rights and duties.
5. Life is valued both in terms of its relation to community welfare and in terms of being a universal human right.
6. Belief in the sacredness of human life as representing a universal human value of respect for the individual.

We call our types "stages" because they seem to represent an invariant developmental sequence. True stages come one at a time and always in the same order.

All movement is forward in sequence and does not skip steps. Children may move through these stages at varying speeds, of course, and may be found half in and half out of a particular stage. An individual may stop at any given stage and at any age, but if he continues to move, he must move in accord with these steps. Moral reasoning of the conventional or stage 3–4 kind never occurs before the preconventional stage 1 and stage 2 thought has taken place. No adult in stage 4 has gone through stage 6, but all stage 6 adults have gone at least through 4.

While the evidence is not complete, our study strongly suggests that moral change fits the stage pattern just described. Figures 1 and 2 indicate the cultural universality of the sequence of stages which we found. Figure 1 presents the age trends for middle-class urban boys in the United States, Taiwan, and Mexico. At age 10 in each country, the order of use of each stage is the same as the order of its difficulty or maturity. In the United States, by age 16 the order is the reverse, from the highest to the lowest, except that stage 6 is still little used. The results in Mexico and Taiwan are the same, except that development is a little slower. The most conspicuous feature is that at the age of 16, stage 5 thinking is much more salient in the United States than in Mexico or Taiwan. Nevertheless, it is present in the other countries, so we know that this is not purely an American democratic construct.

Why should there be such a universal invariant sequence of development? In answering this question, we need first to analyze these developing social concepts in terms of their internal logical structure. At each stage, the same

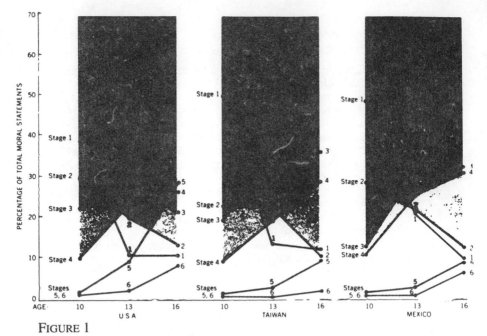

FIGURE 1

Middle-class urban boys in the U.S.A., Taiwan, and Mexico. At age 10, the stages are used according to difficulty. At age 13, stage 3 is most used by all three groups. At age 16, U.S. boys have reversed the order of age 10 stages (with the exception of stage 6). In Taiwan and Mexico, conventional (3–4) stages prevail at age 16, with stage 5 also little used.

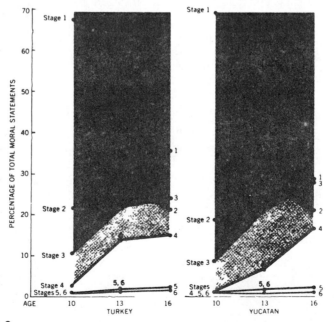

FIGURE 2

Two isolated villages, one in Turkey, the other in the Yucatan, show similar patterns in moral thinking. There is no reversal of order, and preconventional (1–2) thought does not gain a clear ascendancy over conventional stages at age 16.

basic moral concept or aspect is defined, but at each higher stage this definition is more differentiated, more integrated, and more general or universal. When one's concept of human life moves from stage 1 to stage 2, the value of life becomes more differentiated from the value of property, more integrated (the value of life enters an organizational hierarchy where it is "higher" than property so that one steals property in order to save life), and more universalized (the life of any sentient being is valuable regardless of status or property). The same advance is true at each stage in the hierarchy. Each step of development, then, is a better cognitive organization than the one before it, one which takes account of everything present in the previous stage, but makes new distinctions and organizes them into a more comprehensive or more equilibrated structure.

What is the relation of moral stage development in adolescence to cognitive stage development? In Piaget's and our view, both types of thought and types of valuing (or of feeling) are schemata which develop a set of general structural characteristics representing successive forms of psychological equilibrium. The equilibrium of affective and interpersonal schemata, justice or fairness, involves many of the same basic structural features as the equilibrium of cognitive schemata logicality. Justice (portrayed as balancing the scales) is a form of equilibrium between conflicting interpersonal claims, so that "in contrast to a given rule imposed upon the child from outside, the rule of justice is an imminent condition of social relationships or a law governing their equilibrium" (Piaget, 1932).

What is being asserted, then, is not that moral judgment stages are cognitive—they are not the mere application of logic to moral problems—but that existence of moral stages implies that normal development has a basic cognitive-structural component.

The Piagetian rationale just advanced suggests that cognitive maturity is a necessary, but not a sufficient condition for moral judgment maturity. While formal operations may be necessary for principled morality, one may be a theoretical physicist and yet not make moral judgments at the principled level.

As noted in the previous section, Kuhn, Langer, and Kohlberg (1971) found that 60% of persons over 16 had attained formal-operational thinking (by their particular measures). Only 10% of subjects over 16 showed clear principled (stages 5 and 6) thinking, but all these 10% were capable of formal-operational logical thought. More generally, there is a point-to-point correspondence between Piagetian logical and moral judgment stages, as indicated in Table 2. The relation is that attainment of the logical stage is a necessary, but not sufficient condition for attainment of the moral stage. As we shall note in the next section, the fact that many adolescents have formal logical capacities without yet having developed the corresponding degree of moral

TABLE 2
RELATIONS BETWEEN PIAGET'S LOGICAL STAGES
AND KOHLBERG'S MORAL STAGES[a]

Logical Stage	Moral Stage
Symbolic, intuitive thought	Stage 0: The good is what I want and like.
Concrete operations, Substage 1: Categorical classification	Stage 1: Punishment-obedience orientation.
Concrete operations, Substage 2: Reversible concrete thought	Stage 2: Instrumental hedonism and concrete reciprocity.
Formal operations, Substage 1: Relations involving the inverse of the reciprocal	Stage 3: Orientation to interpersonal relations of mutuality.
Formal operations, Substage 2	Stage 4: Maintenance of social order, fixed rules, and authority.
Formal operations, Substage 3	Stage 5A: Social contract, utilitarian law-making perspective.
	Stage 5B: Higher law and conscience orientation.
	Stage 6: Universal ethical principle orientation.

[a]All relations are that attainment of the logical stages is necessary, but not sufficient, for attainment of the moral stage.

judgment maturity is a particularly important background factor in some of the current dilemmas of adolescents.

ADOLESCENT QUESTIONING AND THE PROBLEM OF
RELATIVITY OF TRUTH AND VALUE

The cornerstone of a Piagetian interpretation of adolescence is the dramatic shift in cognition from concrete to formal operations by which old conceptions of the world are restructured in terms of a new philosophy. Piaget defined the preschool child as a philosopher, revolutionizing child psychology by demonstrating that the child at each stage of development actively organizes his experience and makes sense of the physical and social world with which he interacts in terms of the classical categories and questions of philosophers concerning space, time, causality, reality, and so on. It is, however, only in adolescence that the child becomes a philosopher in the formal or traditional sense. This emergence of philosophic questioning has been studied most carefully in the moral realm.

The transition from preconventional to conventional morality generally occurs during the late elementary school years. The shift in adolescence from concrete to formal operations, the ability now to see the given as only a subset of the possible and to spin out the alternatives, constitutes the necessary precondition for the transition from conventional to principled moral reasoning. It is in adolescence, then, that the child has the cognitive capability to move from a conventional to a postconventional, reflective, or philosophic view of values and society.

The rejection of conventional moral reasoning begins with the perception of relativism, the awareness that any given society's definition of right and wrong, however legitimate, is only one among many, both in fact and theory. To clarify the issue of moral relativism as perceived by an adolescent we will consider some adolescent responses to the following dilemma:

> In Europe, a woman was near death from a very bad disease, a special kind of cancer. There was one drug that the doctors thought might save her. It was a form of radium that a druggist in the same town had recently discovered. The drug was expensive to make, but the druggist was charging 10 times what the drug cost him to make. He paid $200 for the radium and charged $2,000 for a small dose of the drug. The sick woman's husband, Heinz, went to everyone he knew to borrow the money, but he could only get together about $1,000, which was half of what it cost. He told the druggist that his wife was dying, and asked him to sell it cheaper or let him pay later. But the druggist said, "No, I discovered the drug and I'm going to make money from it." Heinz got desperate and broke into the man's store to steal the drug for his wife.

Should the husband have done that? Was it right or wrong? Bob, a junior in a liberal private high school, said:

> There's a million ways to look at it. Heinz had a moral decision to make. Was it worse to steal or let his wife die? In my mind I can either condemn him or condone him. In this case I think it was fine. But possibly the druggist was working on a capitalist morality of supply and demand.

I went on to ask Bob, "Would it be wrong if he did not steal it?"

> It depends on how he is oriented morally. If he thinks it's worse to steal than to let his wife die, then it would be wrong what he did. It's all relative; what I would do is steal the drug. I can't say that's right or wrong or that it's what everyone should do.

Bob started the interview by wondering if he could answer because he ''questioned the whole terminology, the whole moral bag.'' He went on:

> But then I'm also an incredible moralist, a real puritan in some sense and moods. My moral judgment and the way I perceive things morally changes very much when my mood changes. When I'm in a cynical mood, I take a cynical view of morals, but still whether I like it or not, I'm terribly moral in the way I look at things. But I'm not too comfortable with it.

Here are some other juniors from an upper-middle-class public high school:

> *Dan*: Immoral is strictly a relative term which can be applied to almost any thought on a particular subject . . . if you have a man and a woman in bed, that is immoral as opposed to if you were a Roman a few thousand years ago and you were used to orgies all the time, that would not be immoral. Things vary so when you call something immoral, it's relative to that society at that time and it varies frequently. [Are there any circumstances in which wrong in some abstract moral sense would be applicable?] Well, in that sense, the only thing I could find wrong would be when you were hurting somebody against their will.

> *Elliot*: I think one individual's set of moral values is as good as the next individual's . . . I think you have a right to believe in what you believe in, but I don't think you have a right to enforce it on other people.

> *John*: I don't think anybody should be swayed by the dictates of society. It's probably very much up to the individual all the time and there's no general principle except when the views of society seem to conflict with your views and your opportunities at the moment and it seems that the views of society don't really have any basis as being right and in that case, most people, I think, would tend to say forget it and I'll do what I want.

The high school students just quoted are, from the point of view of moral stage theory, in a transitional zone. They understand and can use conventional moral thinking, but view it as arbitrary and relative. They do not yet have any clear understanding of, or commitment to, moral principles that are universal, that have a claim to some nonrelative validity. Insofar as they see any ''principles'' as nonrelative, it is the principle of ''do your own thing, and let others do theirs.'' This ''principle'' has a close resemblance to the ''principles'' characteristic of younger children's stage 2, instrumental egoistic thinking. The following examples of a 10-year-old's naïve egoistic and a college student's transitional relativistic responses are more clearly of this instrumental egoistic form.

> *Jimmy* [American city, age 10]: It depends on how much he loved his wife. He should if he does. [If he doesn't love her much?] If he wanted her to die, I don't think he should. [Would it be right to steal?] In a way it's right because he knew his wife would die if he didn't and it would be right to save her. [Does the druggist have the right to charge that much if there's no law?] Yes, it's his drug, look at all he's got invested in it. [Should the judge punish?] He should put him in jail

for stealing and he should put the druggist in because he charged so much and the drug didn't work.

Roger [Berkeley Free Speech Movement student, age 20]: He was a victim of circumstances and can only be judged by other men whose varying value and interest frameworks produce subjective decisions which are neither permanent nor absolute. The same is true of the druggist. I'd do it. As far as duty, a husband's duty is up to the husband to decide, and anybody can judge him, and he can judge anybody's judgment. If he values her life over the consequences of theft, he should do it. [Did the druggist have a right?] One can talk about rights until doomsday and never say anything. Does the lion have a right to the zebra's life when he starves? When he wants sport? Or when he will take it at will? Does he consider rights? Is man so different? [Should he be punished by the judge?] All this could be avoided if the people would organize a planned economy. I think the judge should let him go, but if he does, it will provide less incentive for the poorer people to organize.

Relativity, Moral Stages, and Ego Identity

We first came across extreme relativist responses in some of our longitudinal subjects shortly after college entrance in the early sixties (Kohlberg and Kramer, 1969). At that time, we interpreted their responses as a regression to stage 2 thinking. Fifteen percent of our college-bound male students, who were a mixture of conventional (stage 4) and social-compact–legalist (stage 5) thought at the end of high school, "retrogressed" to an apparent stage 2, instrumentalist pattern in college.

In terms of behavior, every one of our retrogressed subjects had high moral character ratings in high school, as defined by both teachers and peers. In college at least half had engaged in anticonventional acts of a more or less delinquent sort. As an example, a stage 2 Nietzschean had been the most respected high school student council president in years. In his college sophomore interview, however, he told how two days before he had stolen a gold watch from a friend at work. He had done so, he said, because his friend was just too good, too Christ-like, too trusting, and he wanted to teach him what the world was like. He felt no guilt about the stealing, he said, but he did feel frustrated. His act had failed, he said, because his trusting friend insisted he lost or mislaid the watch and simply refused to believe it had been stolen.

The forces of development which led our 20% from upstanding conventional morality to Raskolnikov moral defiance eventually set them all to right. Every single one of our "retrogressors" had returned to a stage 5 morality by age 25, with more stage 5, social-contract principle and less stage 4 or convention than in high school. All, too, were conventionally moral in behavior, at least as far as we could observe them. In sum, this 20% was among the highest group at high school, was the lowest in college, and again among the highest at 25.

In other words, moral relativism and nihilism, no matter how extensive, seemed to be a transitional attitude in the movement from conventional to principled morality.

COGNITIVE MORAL STAGES AND EGO IDENTITY

In considering further the meaning of relativism in adolescence, it is helpful to relate logical and moral stages to Erikson's stages of ego identity. Logical and moral stages are structures of thought through which the child moves sequentially. Erikson's stages are rather segments of the life histories of individuals; they define the central concerns of persons in a developmental period. An adolescent does not know or care that he is moving from concrete to formal thought; he knows and cares that he is having an Erikson "identity crisis."

Cognitive developmental stages are stages of structure, not of content. The stages tell us *how* the child thinks concerning good and bad, truth, love, sex, and so forth. They do not tell us *what* he thinks about, whether he is preoccupied with morality or sex or achievement. They do not tell us what is on the adolescent's mind, but only how he thinks about what is on his mind. The dramatic changes in adolescence are not changes in structure, but changes in content. The adolescent need not know or care that he is going from conventional to principled moral thinking, but he does know and care that sex is on his mind. In this sense, cognitive-structural stages may be contrasted with both psychosexual and Eriksonian stages (Loevinger, 1966).

When we turn to Erikson's ego stages, we are partly dealing with a logical sequence, as in logical and moral stages. Within Erikson's stages is the logical necessity that every later disposition presupposes each prior disposition, that each is a differentiation of prior dispositions. Erikson's ego stage centers around a series of forms of self-esteem (or their inverse, negative self-esteem). The first polarity trust-mistrust is one in which self and other are not differentiated. Trust is a positive feeling about self-and-other; mistrust is a negative feeling. The next polarity, autonomy versus shame, involves the self-other differentiation. Autonomy is a trust in the self (as opposed to the other); shame is a depreciation of self in the eyes of another whose status remains intact. Shame, however, is itself a failure to differentiate what one is from what one is in the eyes of the other, a differentiation implied in the sense of guilt. Similarly, initiative (I can be like him; it's all right to be or do it) is a differentiation from autonomy (I can do it). Such sequential progressive differentiations in self-esteem are involved throughout the Erikson stages. While there is an inherent logical (as opposed to biological) sequence to the Erikson ego stages, they are not hierarchical in the way cognitive stages are. Resolutions of identity problems are not also resolutions of trust or initiative problems, that is, each of the earlier problems and dispositions persists rather than being integrated into or being hierarchically dominated by the next. As a result, when we turn to Erikson's stages as defining focal concerns, we have a stage scheme which is so multidimensional as to resist empirical proof in the sense in which Piagetian stages may be proved. Ultimately, Erikson's stages are "ideal-typical" in Weber's sense. They are not universal abstractions from data, but purifications and exaggerations of typical life histories. They do not predict regularities in the data; they aid in establishing historical connections in case histories. As Erikson uses his stage schema, it helps to suggest historical connections in a particular life, like Luther's. The truth of the stage schema is not in question; the truth of particular historical connections is. The stage schema helps select and illuminate these historical connections. In this sense, the stage of identity formation is not a step in an abstract but observable universal sequence, but is an ideal-typical characterization for a concrete historical period of adolescence.

As such, it need not have any exact logical relation to logical and moral stages, as they must to one another. While Erikson's stages cannot be defined, measured, or logically handled in the same sense as cognitive developmental stages, suggestive empirical relations between ego-identity terms and moral stages are found.

Podd (1969) gave an ego-identity interview to 134 male college juniors and seniors, as well as the moral judgment interview. Following Marcia (1966), the identity interview covered occupational choice, religious beliefs, and political ideology. "Crisis" and "commitment" are assessed in each of these areas and serve to define each identity status. When an individual undergoes active consideration of alternative goals and values, he is said to have experienced a "crisis." "Commitment" is the extent to which an individual has invested himself in his choices. The identity statuses operationally defined are: (1) identity achievement—has gone through a crisis and is committed; (2) moratorium—is in crisis with vague commitments; (3) foreclosure—has experienced no crisis but is committed to goals and values of parents or significant others; (4) identity diffusion—has no commitment regardless of crisis.

Subjects in the Podd study could be grouped into three major groups, the conventional (stages 3 and 4), the principled (stages 5 and 6), and the transitional. The transitional subjects could in turn be divided into two groups, those who were a combination of conventional and principled thinking and the extreme relativists who rejected conventional thought and used more instrumental egoistic ("stage 2") modes. Two-thirds of the principled subjects had an "identity-achievement" status. So, too, did about 40% of the conventional subjects, the remainder being mainly in "identity foreclosure" (a status missing among the principled). None of the morally transitional subjects had an identity-achievement status, and very few had foreclosed identity questioning.

Essentially, then, morally transitional subjects were in transition with regard to identity issues as well as moral issues. Stated slightly differently, to have questioned conventional morality you must have questioned your identity as well, though you may continue to hold a conventional moral position after having done so.

The impact of the Podd study is that the relativistic questioning of conventional morality and conventional reality associated with logical and moral stage development is also central to the adolescent's identity concerns. As a corollary, morally conventional subjects have a considerable likelihood of never having an identity crisis or an identity questioning at all. Erikson's picture of an adolescent stage of identity crisis and its resolutions, then, is a picture dependent upon attainment of formal logical thought and of questioning of conventional morality. It fits best, then, the picture of adolescence in the developmentally elite and needs further elaboration for other adolescents.

HISTORICAL CHANGE IN ADOLESCENT RELATIVISIM

We have linked adolescent relativism to a transition from conventional to principled morality, associated with identity crisis. This picture emerged most clearly from our longitudinal data from the late fifties and early sixties, reported by Kohlberg and Kramer (1969). In this study only a small minority of college students entered a phase of moral nihilism and relativism in the transition from conventional to principled morality. Typically they attempted to construct or select an ideology of their own in this transitional phase, ideologies which ranged from Nietzschean racism to Ayn Rand objectivism to early SDS New Left formulations. In these college subjects of the early sixties, it was possible to see an intense identity crisis, in Erikson's terms. These college relativist-egoists were rare, and they all seemed to have been moralistic and guilt-prone in high school. As part of their identity crisis, they seemed to have had strong problems in freeing themselves from childhood moral expectations and guilt.

There were two universal developmental challenges to conventional morality to which these "regressors" were also responding: first, the relativity of moral expectations and opinion; second, the gap between conventional moral expectations and actual moral behavior. It is clear that these developmental challenges are universal challenges; the integration of one's moral ideology with the facts of moral diversity and inconsistency is a general "developmental task" of youth in an open society; its solution is the formation of a universal principled morality.

For our extreme relativists or amoralists, there seemed to be an additional task in the need to free themselves from their own early "rigid" morality. In Erikson's terms our retrogressors were living in a late adolescent psychosocial moratorium, in which new and nonconforming patterns of thought and behavior are tried out. Their return to morality or moral thought is the eventual confirmation of an earlier identification as one's own identity. To find a sociomoral identity requires a rebellious moratorium, because it requires liberations of initiative from the guilt from which our retrogressors suffer. At the "stage" of identity, the adult conforms to his standards because he wants to, not because he anticipates crippling guilt if he does not.

By the 1970s the extreme doubt and relativism, which earlier characterized only a minority of college students, appear both earlier and much more pervasively. They are now sometimes found toward the end of high school (Gilligan, Kohlberg, and Lerner, 1972). In our own Harvard undergraduate course for freshmen and sophomores, about two-thirds of the students assert that there are no such things as valid moral rules or principles, no objective sense in which one thing is morally better than another. It appears that a majority rather than a minority of adolescents are now aware of relativism and of postconventional questioning, though it is still a minority who really attempt postconventional or principled solutions to these questions.

Parallel historical changes seem to have occurred in the relationship of extreme moral relativism to identity issues. Podd's (1969) findings from the *late* sixties differ from those of Kohlberg and Kramer (1969) in the *early* sixties in one important way. Kohlberg and Kramer found their extreme relativists, the stage 2 or regressed subjects, in a condition of moratorium, in a state of "crisis" with vague and uncertain commitments. In contrast, Podd found them in a condition of identity diffusion with no sense of commitment and not necessarily a sense of crisis. In other words, extreme relativism no longer appeared to be a temporary, ego developmental maneuver of a small group of subjects in crisis, but rather to represent a more stable, less crisislike pattern of low commitment. It seems likely to us that the psychological meaning of extreme relativism has changed in the five to ten years since the data reported by Kohlberg and Kramer (1969). Extreme relativism is no longer the struggle for independence from a strongly internal conventional morality in a period of moratorium and crisis in one's identity.

The relativisitic rejection of convention, once individually and spontaneously developed by adolescents in the course of reflecting on their own experience, is now manufactured as a cultural industry called the "counterculture." Further, the adult culture itself offers a very unsteady counter to the counterculture, particularly from the viewpoint of the adolescent to whom it offers a dwindling number of jobs and a world already overcrowded and crying out for less rather than more. It is clearly seen that one result of affluence, technology, and increased longevity has been to decrease the need of the adult community for its adolescents. Instead, it has some stake in keeping them in the youth culture since, in one sense, they only further threaten an already-defensive adult world with fewer jobs and still more people. Thus, the adults at once produce and market a counterculture and present themselves as a less-than-appealing alternative to it.

From the point of view of the adolescent, the counterculture has other meanings. The rejection of the conventional culture can be seen as a rebellion which can either turn into submission spelled backwards, or into the formation of principles. In our terms, the former remains conventional in form with only the content changed by being stood on its head. Although the impetus for the counterculture may have been once either principled or the expression of young people in identity crisis, the manufacture of the counterculture transforms it into yet another conventional system, although one lacking the solidity of the traditional conventional society.

While only a minority of adolescents actually have a postconventional view of morality and society, many more live in a postconventional culture or society. As a specific example, the majority of a sample of Haight-Ashbury hippies (N. Haan and C. Holstein, unpublished data, 1971) emerge as mixtures of preconventional stage 2 and conventional stage 3 thinking. While hippie culture appears to be postconventional, it is almost entirely a mixture of stage 2 "do your own thing" and stage 3 "be nice, be loving" themes. The hippie culture continually questions conventional morality but on stage 3 grounds of its being harsh and mean, or stage 2 grounds of "Why shouldn't I have fun?" rather than in terms of its irrationality. Many hippies, then, belong to a counterculture which is largely conventional in its appeal, but which lacks the solidity of traditional conventional society and is not embedded in it. As moral counterculture, the hippie culture differs primarily from the conventional culture in its extreme relativism and consequent fluidity, not in any positive forms of moral thought different from the conventional.

In most eras of the past, the adolescent went through questioning of value, meaning, and truth in a world of adults apparently oblivious to these doubts. Reflective adolescents have always considered adults as benighted for accepting conventional norms and imposing them on youth, for never doubting the truth and goodness of their world. The questioning adolescent has always seen the adult acceptance of the conventional social world as reflecting the hypocrisy, insensitivity, and dreariness of the adult. Equally, the questioning adolescent has always expected to remake the adult world nearer to his heart's desire, and at given moments in history has succeeded. What is new is the creation of a questioning culture providing half-answers to which adolescents are exposed prior to their own spontaneous questioning.

The adolescent is faced then with not one but two cultures offering alternative ideologies and ways to live. Both present resolutions to the postconventional doubt which now appears to be so pervasive. Both may be embraced in our sense conventionally for the set of answers they provide, or they may be seen in principled terms, their validity as social systems resting on the principles of justice they more or less successfully embody.

IMPLICATIONS FOR EDUCATION

The extreme relativism of a considerable portion of high school adolescents provides both a threat to current educational practice and a potentiality for a new focus in education.

We said earlier that the five-to-seven shift has been traditionally represented in education by the beginning of formal schooling. The traditional educational embodiment of the adolescent shift has been a different one, that of a two-track educational system dividing adolescents into two groups, an elite capable of abstract thought and hence of profiting from a liberal education and the masses who are not. At first, this division was made between the wealthy and those who went to work. As public high schools developed, the tracking system instead became that of an academic school or lycée, leading to the university, and a vocational school. The clearest formulation of this two-track system as based on the dawn of abstract thought was found in the British 11 + system. Based on his score on an intelligence test given at the dawn of adolescence, a child was assigned to either a grammar (academic) or a modern (vocational-commercial) high school.

The aristocratic tracking system just described rested on the assumption that the capacity for abstract thought is all or none, that it appears at a fixed age, and that it is hereditarily limited to an elite group in the population. The evidence on formal-operational thought does not support these assumptions. However, when democratic secondary education ignored the existence of the adolescent cognitive shift and individual differences in their attainment, real difficulties emerged. Most recently this ignoring occurred in the wave of the high school curriculum reform of the late fifties and early sixties in America—the "new math," the "new science," and the "new social studies."

These curriculum reforms were guided by the notion that more intellectual content could be put into high school and that this content should not be factual content and rote skills, but the basic pattern of thinking of the academic disciplines of mathematics, physics, or social science. The focus was to be on understanding the basic logical assumptions in reflective or critical thinking and problem solving. Clearly the new curricula assumed formal-operational thought, rather than attempting to develop it. Partly as a result of ignoring this, some of the most enlightened proponents of the new curricula became discouraged as they saw only a subgroup of the high school population engaging with it. The solution we have proposed is that the new curricula be reformulated as tools for developing principled logical and moral thought rather than presupposing it (Kohlberg and Lockwood, 1970; Kohlberg and Turiel, 1971).

Experimental work by our colleagues and ourselves (Kohlberg and Blatt, 1972) has shown that even crude efforts based on such objectives are challenging and are successful in inducing considerable upward stage movement in thought. We hope our efforts are the beginning of reformulating the "new" high school science, mathematics, social studies, and literature as approaches using "disciplines" as vehicles for the stimulation of the development of thought, rather than making young Ph.D.'s.

The difficulties and failure of the new curricula and of the general movement to democratize higher learning or liberal education, then, are not due to hereditary differences in capacity, used to justify the two-track system. They represent, instead, the failure of secondary education to take developmental psychology seriously. When stage development is taken seriously by educators as an aim, real developmental change can occur through education.

In saying this, we return to the thought of John Dewey, which is at the heart of a democratic educational philosophy. According to Dewey, education was the stimulation of development through stages by providing opportunities for active thought and active organization of experience.

> The only solid ground of assurance that the educator is not setting up impossible artificial aims, that he is not using ineffective and perverting methods, is a clear and definite knowledge of the normal end and focus of mental action. Only knowledge of the order and connection of the stages in the development of the psychical functions can, negatively, guard against those evils, or positively, insure the full maturation and free, yet, orderly, exercises of the physical powers. Education is precisely the work of supplying the conditions which will enable the psychical functions, as they successively arise, to mature and pass into higher functions in the freest and fullest manner. This result can be secured only by a knowledge of the process of development, that is only by a knowledge of "psychology" [Dewey, 1964].

Besides a clear focus on development, an aspect of Dewey's educational thought which needs revival is that school experience must be and represent real life experience in stimulating development. American education in the twentieth century was shaped by the victory of Thorndike over Dewey. Achievement rather than development has been its aim. But now the achieving society, the achieving individual, and even the achievement tests are seriously questioned, by adults and adolescents alike. If development rather than achievement is to be the aim of education, such development must be meaningful or real to the adolescent himself. In this sense, education must be sensed by the adolescent as aiding him in his search for identity, and it must deal with life. Neither a concern with self nor one with life is a concern opposed to intellectuality or intellectual development. The opposition of "intellect" and "life" is itself a reflection of the two-track system in which a long period of academic education provided a moratorium for leisurely self-crystallization of an adult role identity by the elite while the masses were to acquire an early adult vocational identity, either through going to work or through commitment to a vocation in a vocational high school.

Our discussion of adolescent relativism and identity diffusion suggests that the two tracks are both breaking down and fusing. Vocational goals are evaded by relativism and counterculture questioning, as are deferred goals of intellectual development. An identity crisis and questioning are no longer the prerogative of the elite, and they now occur earlier and without the background of logical and moral development they previously entailed. If the high school is to have meaning it must take account of this, which means it must take account of the adolescent's current notion of himself and his identity. Like most psychologists, most adolescents think the self has little to do with intellectual or moral development. The relativistic adolescent is content to answer "myself" to questions about the source and basis of value and meaning. Like most psychologists, he tends to equate the content of self-development with the ego, with self-awareness, with identity. The other pole of ego or self-development, however, is that of new awareness of the world and values; it is the awareness of new meanings in life.

We discussed the moral strand of ego development, which is clearly philosophical. We have also noted aesthetic, religious, metaphysical, and epistemological concepts and values born in adolescence. One side of ego development is the structure of the self-concept and the other side is the individual's concept of the true, the good, the beautiful, and the real. If education is to promote self-development, ego development must be seen as one side of an education whose other side consists of the arts and sciences as philosophically conceived. We have pointed to the need for defining the aims of teaching the arts and sciences in developmental terms. In this sense, one basic aim of teaching high school science and mathematics is to stimulate the stage of principled or formal-operational logical thought, and of teaching high school social studies, to stimulate principled moral judgment. A basic aim of teaching literature is the development of a stage or level of aesthetic comprehension, expression, judgment. Behind all of these developmental goals lie moral and philosophic dimensions of the meaning of life, which the adolescent currently questions and the school needs to confront. The adolescent is a philosopher by nature, and if not by nature, by countercultural pressure. The high school must have, and represent, a philosophy if it is to be meaningful to the adolescent. If the high school is to offer some purposes and meanings which can stand up to relativistic questioning, it must learn philosophy.

14

INTRODUCTION

The Phases of Adult Life:
A Study in Developmental
Psychology, by Roger L. Gould

Pediatrics is well established and geriatrics is developing, but there is no specialty of mediatrics, to borrow an anonymous neologism. A paradoxical corollary is that while practically no one has addressed the normative development of the adult, almost all physicians and mental health clinicians are considered capable of helping with the problems of "middlescence." Developmental-stage theorists have focused entirely on childhood (see Freud, 1923b; Gesell, 1940; Piaget, 1962a, 1962b [Chapters 6, 5, 11, and 10 respectively in *Childhood Psychopathology*]). As noted in Chapter 8 of *Childhood Psychopathology*, Erikson (1963) did extend his psychosocial theory of sequential developmental stages beyond adolescence to the entire life cycle and integrated it with the concept of crises, representing critical transition points marked by different developmental tasks. But the aspect of Erikson's work that has received the greatest attention concerns adolescents and younger children; his less complete work on postadolescent development, like Frenkel-Brunswick's (1936) earlier delineation of adult developmental stages, is rarely noted.

This situation changed suddenly in 1976 with the publication of Gail Sheehy's best-selling *Passages*. She presents, in breezy prose, biographical composites derived from a series of interviews. Her account is based on the work of Levinson et al. (1974), Vaillant and McArthur (1972), Neugarten and Datan (1974), and Roger Gould, the author of the article reprinted below. Sources like these, reinforced by the reader's sense of their validity, suggest that the much-discussed "passages" from the "trying twenties" to the "throbbing thirties" into the "forlorn forties" represent more than a passing phase of an empty pop-psychology. Some of these alliterations may join the "terrible twos" as a permanent part of our colloquial language.

Even if these predictions are true, why reprint information about adult stages of development in a book about childhood? There are several disparate reasons. Any examination of child development should look at a future as well as a past and a present, if one is to be faithful to the idea of developmental tasks. Also, the interactive perspective on parent-child relationships underscores the mutual influencing of infant and adult in the early years of life (see Chapter 3 by Brazelton, Koslowki, and Main). Nor does the generation gap stem solely from the adolescent (see Chapter 12 by King). In addition, clinical intervention with children, which cannot proceed without consideration of the parents, is markedly different if the parent of the seven-year-old is 28 or 45 years old. Lastly, the dynamics of the family system, discussed in Chapter 15 by Bowen, are influenced by adult development. The life cycle of the family from marriage, through childbearing, children leaving the home, the "empty nest" period, and final dissolution through death has witnessed marked changes with the later age of marriage, the decreased size of the family, and increased life expectancy (Glick and Parke, 1965). In her consideration of parenthood as a developmental stage, Benedek (1959, 1970) addressed the intersection of individual adult and family cycles. She notes that the family, as a system, and the personality of each spouse, as a subsystem, should provide for each partner's becoming part of the self-system of the other in an exchange of ego ideals, common ambitions, desires, and children that strengthens the identification between marital couples. Her concern about the future is succinctly stated: modern marriage requires each partner to negotiate the conflict between yesterday's patriarchal and today's individualistic values; the children of this marriage, already leaning away from the patriarchal toward the individualistic, may lack the convictions necessary to convey a well-integrated value system to their own children!

The following chapter by Gould advances preliminary but rich, generative hypotheses about developmental changes in adulthood. His ideas have a ring of truth despite the methodological shortcoming he notes of using cross-sectional data to formulate a longitudinal developmental perspective. Drawing lines connecting the top of bar graphs never constructs a reliable longitudinal picture. Consider, for example, the differences between being 20 during World War II after an adolescence during the great depression and traversing the third decade of life in the 1970s, after experiencing adolescence in the 1960s. It is difficult to anticipate the developmental tasks of the sixth decade in life awaiting today's 20-year-old on the basis of data derived from his or her parents' generation. Other methodological shortcomings in Gould's work are the limitations inherent in relying on medical students' social networks for selection of the nonpatient population studied and the failure to distinguish between the sexes. Sheehy (1976) comments vividly on the latter: "Especially if Dick and Jane are the same age, they are much of the time out of sync. During the twenties, when a man gains confidence by leaps and bounds, a married woman is usually losing the superior assurance she once had as an adolescent. When a man passes 30 and wants to settle down, a woman is often becoming restless. And just at the point around 40, when a man feels himself to be standing on a precipice, his strength, power, dreams, and illusions slipping away beneath him, his wife is likely to be brimming with ambition to climb her own mountain'' (p. 15). Lest the reader be tempted to dismiss this as nothing more than overstated generalization, Sheehy quotes Glick and Norton (1972), who found that census data indicated "The median duration of marriage before divorce has been about seven years for the last half century.'' This figure is consistent with a computer review of 200 consecutive intakes at the Marriage Council of Philadelphia (Berman, 1976). The peak number of intakes occurred with couples who had been married for an average of seven years where at least one partner was in the 27- to 32-year-old age group. The rate of intake for this age group was almost two times that for 22- to 27-year-olds and 32- to 37-year-olds.

Although Gould presents a range of thought-provoking graphs indicating the transitional periods in adult life, the only Q-sort questions detailed are those relating to the perplexing issue of the significance of time. The responses illustrate the difference in children's and adults' perspectives on this vital existential issue. With increasing age the adult's sense of time quickly running out provides the organizing framework for subjective and objective events central to the person's existence. Children, in contrast, typically experience time as moving too slowly as they, impatiently, cannot wait to grow older. Clearly, for the clinician to function effectively he or she has to appreciate both points of view, particularly when they seem to be lightyears apart.

14

The Phases of Adult Life: A Study in Developmental Psychology

ROGER L. GOULD

In the work that is to be reported in this paper, the assumptions have been made that people continue to change over the period of time considered to be adulthood and that developmental phases may be found during the adult span of life if they are looked for properly. The focus of this work is on the sequential change that takes place with time rather than on a full description of any one stage. The work is intended to be descriptive and the hypotheses to be generating. The results of direct observations of patients and a questionnaire given to nonpatients will be presented.

When Freud (1893–1895) began his exploration of the depths of the mind, he first found the submerged child in the supposed-to-be adult. He later carried out, against the resistance of the civilized world, the bold rescue of the sentient child from the sterile and static adultomorphism preferred by his culture (Freud, 1905). This twofold discovery forced the world to abandon in part the preferred view that adults populate the world and act rationally as adults should. It is interesting to note that the preferred view that adults are rational is a strongly held prejudice of mankind and has fit well the needs

First published in *The American Journal of Psychiatry*, 129:521–531, 1972. Copyright © 1972, the American Psychiatric Association. Reprinted by permission.

This work was conducted with the generous support of the UCLA Department of Psychiatry outpatient staff. Special efforts and consultation were contributed by Peter Gelker, M.S., Allan Warner, M.D., and William Beckwith, Ph.D. Other contributing members of the "phase of life" study group were: Herbert Eveloff, M.D., Jerome Karasic, M.D., Louise Epps, Ph.D., Andrew Comrey, Ph.D., John Kennedy, Ph.D., Roberta Crutcher, M.D., and Craig MacAndrews, Ph.D.; and medical students: Alan Arnold, Richard Cicinelli, Bruce Merl, Edward Rose, William Schleiter, Peter Tamulevich, and Mikel Weinberg.

of a Christian theology and a structure of civilization built on the law. It is against this ingrained view of man as a fully formed, static, rational adult that the observations and insights of dynamic psychiatry and psychoanalysis struggle.

Though adolescence has been shown, since the time of Freud, to be a period of dynamic and vital growth, we have not made any significant changes in our conceptualization of the periods of adulthood following the identity struggle of youth. We have not proposed any coherent view of the procession through time of the adult or of psychological growth and change as a function of time in the adult years. Adults are conceived of as being in dynamic conflict, but without direction. The resolution of conflict is thought to lead to higher levels of integration and adaptiveness, but not into a new personality era. Adulthood is still seen as a period of marking time and is not seen as a progression of stages, much like the phases of rapid and slow growth of childhood and adolescence.

We have learned to understand the intrapsychic struggles of individuation in childhood and adolescence as struggles keyed by the imposed role task of progressive separation from objects and pushed from within by a complemental evolution of internally programmed biological changes. Both separation from objects and changes in our biological equipment are mediated by time. Why, in our conceptualizations, do we seem to assume that time no longer functions systematically after 21 years of age and to rely henceforth on thematic and adventitious factors to anchor our understanding of change? After all, both object and biological changes continue throughout life. In fact, object changes are even more dramatic in the period after 21 than before 21.

If we could take ego autonomy as our ideal state of individuation, we would have to consider under what conditions ego autonomy prevails. To be autonomous while living alone is entirely different from that in daily living with a spouse. To maintain autonomy while sorting out the pressing demands of spouse and children and employer is a task of greater magnitude than previous tasks and requires a more highly developed psychic apparatus if an optimal level of individuation is to be maintained. There is a difference between living in the world with live, healthy, and powerful parents in the background ready to support you and living with enfeebled, dependent parents in the background. If anything, the changes that take place in one's parents and in one's children would suggest that time-mediated object changes are of the utmost importance during the adult years and that the necessity for change is as imperative as in the period before age 21. From a commonsense point of view, then, there would be no justification for our conceptualizations to imply that time no longer functions systematically after 21 years of age and no justification for our theories of change to rely on thematic and adventitious factors as the essential elements.

SURVEY OF THE LITERATURE

Although adulthood as a topic for developmental psychology has largely been ignored, several contributions have been made to the topic. Erikson's (1959) work on the stages of man is probably the best known of these efforts. He considers his last three stages to be the stages of adulthood: the first adult stage is that of "Intimacy and Distantiation versus Self-Absorption." It represents the success or failure in one's ability to be truly open and capable of a "trusting fellowship" rather than formal separateness or pseudo-intimacy. This is the task of young adults before they work on the next task, "Generativity versus Stagnation." In this phase of adulthood, roughly spanning the mid-twenties on, the individual must create for himself a continuing giving of himself to his world in a creative, caretaking, participatory way that is progressive, in order to avoid the pit of stagnation. The final stage, "Integrity versus Despair," includes the span from later adulthood to death; in this stage the individual comes to grips with his own life as "one's one and only life cycle." Erikson's description of these life phases is very brief. He encourages others to flesh them out with detailed investigations and descriptions. When we compare these skeletal sections on adulthood with his fuller previous sections on childhood, we find vivid evidence that adulthood as a topic has been neglected. Erikson has broadly stroked the thematic dilemmas of being an adult while directing our attention to adulthood as a part of the series of phases extending throughout the life span.

Benedek (1959) has added an in-depth view of the psychology of being a parent in her work "Parenthood as a Developmental Phase." She notes that there is an emotional normative symbiosis between parent and child that is based on the parent's prior experience of childhood and that operates through the mental principle that "the introjected object is merged with the introjected self in the drive experience and thereby object representations and self-representations are established in inseparable connection with each other." That is, the parent is capable of structural change because in the deep part of his mind the experiences he has with his child are opportunities to rework intimately tied, structure-determining memories of his own childhood. This is all made possible by a kind of limited regression and emotional symbiosis on the part of the adult parent to the level of the developing child. This normative regression and blurring of self-definition is a detailed look at what Erikson called mutuality during the stage of generativity.

Rangell (1955), in his paper "The Role of the Parent in the Oedipus

Complex," points out that the Oedipus complex is a structure that continues into later life and organizes much of adult emotional behavior. His case examples illustrate particularly well the reversal of themes after the adult has passed his prime. The parent finds himself envious of his child, who is seen as being at the acme of instinctual potency.

Jaques (1965) has offered a penetrating appraisal of the mid-life crisis occurring in the mid-thirties and resolving itself in the early and mid-forties. He adds to his clinical observation and case example the weight of the words and lives of famous artists and writers. He discusses this crisis period as a painful confrontation with the inevitability of death and the finitude of time. He sees it as a period requiring that the depressive position be worked through again. The outcome depends on the balance of life-and-death forces that were structuralized in the style of living before the crisis, and its success or failure is judged in terms identical with those of Erikson's stage of integrity versus despair.

All these analytic contributions bring important clinical insights to bear on the subject of adult changes over time and suggest areas for more rigorous investigation. They lack, however, the base of detailed comprehensive data on the entire adult life span for a large number of people who can be compared on the same axis of measurement.

Other investigators have attempted to gather this base of data through three fundamentally different approaches. Bühler has spent a lifetime collecting individual biographies of creative and everyday people and has conceptualized her material predominantly from the view of value changes over the life span. This is the longitudinal approach. She finds that the phasic phenomena of the life cycle, as reflected in her biographical studies (Bühler and Massarik, 1968), can best be described as a three-phasic process: "1) a growth period from birth until the organism is fully developed; 2) a stationary growth period during which the organism's power to maintain itself and develop is equal to the forces of decline; and 3) a last period of decline" (p. 13). Each phase can be broken into subphases and given rough time zones that prescribe the orientation of the self and organize the goals of living for that time period.

Neugarten and associates (1964), in a large field study in Kansas City, studied 710 people in the mid-1950s, both by interview and by projective test schedules. They concentrated on middle life and their sample was from 40 to 90 years old:

> When all of the studies in this book are considered together, it appears that they form two groups. Those in which chronological age provides order in the data are those when the focus was on the intrapsychic, the processes of the personality that are not readily available to awareness or conscious control and which do not have direct expression in overt patterns of social behavior. The second group, those in

which individual differences are relatively independent of age, are those where the focus was on more purposive processes in the personality, processes in which attempted control of the self and of the life situation are conspicuous elements [p. 192].

Another conclusion from these studies is that there is an increase of interiority as aging advances that is clearly demonstrable by the mid-forties and that there is a decrease in personality complexity with "an increasing dedication to a central core of values and to a set of habit patterns and a sloughing off of earlier cathexes which lose saliency for the individual" (p. 198).

In a study concerning the changing time perspective in middle age, Neugarten (1968) reports:

Both sexes, although men more than women, talked of the new difference in the way time is perceived. Life is restructured in terms of time-left-to-live rather than time-since-birth. Not only the reversal in directionality but the awareness that time is finite is a particularly conspicuous feature of middle age. Thus, "you hear so much about deaths that seem premature. That's one of the changes that comes over you over the years. Young fellows never give it a thought. . . ." The recognition that there is "only so much time left" was a frequent theme in the interviews. In referring to the death of a contemporary, one man said, "there is now the realization that death is very real. Those things don't quite penetrate when you're in your twenties and you think that life is all ahead of you. Now you know that death will come to you, too" [p. 97].

Another interviewee added: "It is as if there are two mirrors before me, each held at a partial angle. I see part of myself in my mother who is growing old, and part of her in me. In the other mirror, I see part of myself in my daughter. I have had some dramatic insights, just from looking in those mirrors. . . . It is a set of revelations that I suppose can only come when you are in the middle of three generations" (p. 98).

Neugarten notes that her studies have relevance for a theory of the life cycle in two ways:

First, in indicating that the age structure of a society, the internalization of age-norms, and age-group identifications are important dimensions of the social and cultural *context* in which the course of the individual life line must be viewed; Second, because these concepts point to at least one additional way of structuring the passage of time in the life span of the individual, *providing a time clock* that can be superimposed over the biological clock, together they help us to comprehend the life cycle. The major punctuation marks in the adult life line tend (those, that is, which are orderly and sequential) to be more often social than biological—or, if biologically based, they are often biological events that occur to significant others rather than to oneself, like grandparenthood or widowhood [p. 146].

The third method adopted by psychologists has been to study specific questions over time—the ages of greatest happiness, most mental problems, most hospitalizations, greatest change in specific functions, most divorces, greatest contentment with age, etc. The composite of all these studies could shed light on the life cycle as a whole. The number of such studies is great and they comprise a large percentage of the psychological and sociological literature. Several authors have contributed studies that are pertinent to the issues in this paper (Dykman, Heimann, and Ken, 1952; Lehman, 1953; Lewin, 1939; Pressey and Kuhlen, 1957; Slotkin, 1952; Strong, 1931; Terman, 1938).

STUDY I

Only Bühler and Erikson have looked at the whole life span, but neither of them supplies us with exactly the kind of information we are looking for. Erikson becomes quite sweeping and thematic in his approach to adulthood after the identity crisis and Bühler applies a rational overview of the life span in terms of physiological stages, but neither bears down on the chronological change in the subjective "sense of the world." By "subjective sense of the world" I mean the out-of-focus, interior, gut-level organizing percepts of self and nonself, safety, time, size, etc., that make up the background tone of daily living and shape the attitudes and value base from which decisions and action emanate. Such a vague but central phenomenon requires a careful and thorough investigation (as well as a more precise definition) of individuals, with some optimal combination of the methods of psychoanalytic investigation and Neugarten's methods. Before considering such an effort, we decided to inspect the terrain of the whole adult life span to see whether we could catalog the obvious and construct a platform from which to begin. This section of the paper presents the results of this attempt.

METHOD

We started with a simple descriptive effort. During 1968, all of the patients who were in group therapy at the UCLA Psychiatric Outpatient Clinic were assigned to homogeneous age groups. There were seven groups, composed of the following age ranges: 16–18, 18–22, 22–28, 29–34, 35–43, 43–50, and 50–60 or more. At the end of six months a second set of seven groups was constituted and observed. These 14 groups were treated by 14 third-year residents as part of their psychiatric training. Each of the 14 groups was observed continuously by one of the study group staff, either as cotherapists or as supervisors via tape-recordings. The 10 study group members (psychiatrists, psychologists, and an anthropologist) met every two weeks to report their observations and to make simple first-order comparisons.

Although many detailed observations were made, in order to begin our study on solid and safe ground we asked each member to characterize the age group he was studying on the simplest, most self-evident level. We asked for a level of psychological sophistication so low that any naïve, honest observer watching the group would have to agree with the description. We were apparently successful in achieving this goal of simplicity and replicability by two simple measures. With the composition of a second set of groups after six months, the staff members rotated age groups and were able to confirm the observations of their colleagues on new groups. The following summer eight first-year medical students, psychologically naïve but bright, listened to the tapes of the group sessions and picked out the same central and salient characteristics.

RESULTS

The observations made about each phase of life are familiar, often anticipated by common sense; many can easily be corroborated by everyday experience and anecdotal accounts. It is the interrelationship of each age phase with the others that is unique and that gives us an empirically based portrayal of the changes in the subjective "sense of the world" or "posturing of the self" over time.

In the group aged 16 to 18, we are unavoidably struck with the theme that is like a motto: "We have to get away from our parents." The theme is loud and repetitively verbalized, but not connected with any implementary action. They are all safely part of their families and consider themselves more as family members than as true individuals. They see the future as some vague time "out there" when they will be liberated and mainly have a fantasy conception of what their own adulthood will be like. Their autonomy is precarious, often fortified by negativism, and subject to erosion from moment to moment. Although they long for deep, close relationships with peers, the closeness most often found is instantaneous and unstable and is followed by a temporary rebound back to parents.

In the next age group, 18 to 22, we find a continuation of the theme, "We have to get away from our parents," but from a different position. They feel themselves to be halfway out of the family and are worried that they will be reclaimed by the family pull and not make it out completely. They are involved in many kinds of implementing actions—living away from home at school, working, paying rent, owning their own cars—but are not quite totally committed to their current time base since it is not quite adult yet. The real living is just around the corner. They are especially supportive of each other in the group and talk of re-creating with their peers the family they are leaving. The peer group becomes the ally that will help them out of the family, but in itself it becomes a new threat that endangers the pureness of their own authentic emerging beliefs by imposing the group belief as an essential for membership and alliance. They see their intimates as betrayers if the intimate person's way of thinking is not identical to their own or if the intimate cannot perform all of the soothing functions that the family had performed. Their own autonomy is felt to be established, but in jeopardy. They perceive a vague feeling that they have to keep a lid on themselves lest anger, fear, or depression escape.

There is a considerable shift in the next group, 22 to 28. They feel quite established and autonomous and separate from their families and feel they are engaged in the work of being adults. They particularly feel that what they are doing is the true course in life and there is very little energy wasted in considering whether their general commitments are the right ones or not. Most of their energy is spent mastering what they are supposed to be. They feel their "self" to be well defined, even if they are not fully satisfied with it. They see their parents as people with whom they want to establish a modus vivendi, but to whom they still have to prove their competence as adults. The peers are still important but not to be relied on as much as self-reliance and, although they can still be hurt by a peer's response to them, it is not seen as potentially devastating. The spouse is seen as a person who may not be mature enough now, but with whom there is a commitment to make a marriage work. There is a definite feeling that "now" is the time for living, as well as growing and building for the future. Extreme emotions are still guarded against, but now not so much to prevent a leak as to prevent disappointment. It is not sensible to get too high and excited because it may be followed by a low. The emphasis is on modulating the emotional tone in an experimental effort to learn the proper tone for adult life.

The following group, 29 to 34, seems to have quite a different experience of their world. Whereas those aged 22 to 28 feel they are on the relatively unquestioned true course of life and can devote themselves to the mastery of what they are supposed to be, the 29 to 34 age group is beginning to question: "What is this life all about now that I am doing what I am supposed to?" and "Is what I am the only way for me to be?" Marriage and career lines have been established and young children are growing, but some inner aspect is striving to be accounted for. They feel weary of devoting themselves to the task of being what they are supposed to (although they continue on), and just want to be what they are. In particular, there is a dawning awareness that their will alone is not all of them, and that inner forces reproduce patterns of behavior and relationships that they don't particularly want to exist, but can no longer ignore or will away. They no longer see the necessity to prove themselves to their parents or highlight their differences, and in such a situation feel free to acknowledge and accept parts of themselves as being like and coming from their parents. They often see their spouses as preventing this new emergence by acting as witness to their supposed-to-be former self and not being willing enough to see the new self. A most poignant desire is to be accepted by the spouse "for what I am." Their children are becoming companions and love objects.

Just as they want to be accepted for "what I am," they want to accept their own children for "what they are becoming" and not impose roles on them. This conscious attempt to let their children grow freely is interfered with by a series of confusing temporary identifications with their growing children. Often the anecdotes of their children's behavior described in the group sessions were so commingled with similar memories from their own pasts that it was unclear who felt what.

In the subsequent age group, 35 to 43, there is a continued look within and an existential questioning of self, values, and life itself, but with a change of tone toward quiet desperation and an increasing awareness of a time squeeze. This tone applies to themselves, their parents, and their children. Instead of "I just want to be" with a sense of timelessness, there is "Have I done the right thing?"; "Is there time to change?" The children are seen as emerging end-products of their parenting and reflections of their worth. There is a sense that not only is there little time left to shape the behavior of their adolescent children, but there is uncertainty about which value lines to follow in the shaping and how fast their control over the children is waning. Their own parents at this stage turn more toward them, and there is a muffled renewal of old conflict lines that is kept suppressed by the thought that, since the parents are getting older and time is running out for them, direct criticism would be guilt-provoking. The sense of time during this stage emphasizes the finitude of time, and there is an eye toward the past, present, and future equally. Under this time pressure of conflict and questioning, the person looks to the spouse, who is often in a similar life position and is looking for the same support. Work is often looked to as offering the hope of compensation for all of this, but in a fantasy way—"one last chance to make it big."

In the 43- to 50-year-old group, we see some definite changes from the 35- to 43-year-old group and in some ways it is as though the issues anticipated are now being lived with. That is, in the earlier age group the emerging sense that time is finite is hedged by the compensating feeling that there is still time if you hurry to make some dreams come true, but in the forties it is not hedged. Finite time is resigned to as reality and as not so malleable by self-illusions. The "die is cast" feeling is present and is seen as a relief from the internal tearing apart of the immediately previous years, even though it is a bitter pill to swallow. They feel as if their personalities are pretty well set and on occasion are vocally critical of their parents and tend to blame them for their life problems. They are eager to have social activities and friends, but more on a superficial basis and more tinged with negative, competitive casts. They are still actively involved with their young adult children, but now not as ones emerging but as ones who have emerged and are separate. They tend to be watchful of their children's adult progress in a specific style, i.e., with a readiness to find the error in their ways. They very actively look for sympathy and affection from their spouses, who in many ways they seem to be dependent on, in a mode similar to that of their former dependency on parents.

In the fifties there is a mellowing and warming up. The negative cast of the forties diminishes in their relationships to themselves, their parents, their children, and their friends. Their parents are no longer the cause of their problems, but are affectionately called "Mom" and "Dad." The children's lives are now seen as potential sources of warm comfort and satisfaction, and they are concerned not so much with their children's achievements as with their happiness in personal terms. They value their own spouses more and look within themselves at their own feelings and emotions, although not with the critical "time pressure" eye of the late thirties or with the infinite omnipotentiality of the early thirties, but with a more self-accepting attitude of continued learning from a position of general stability. The spouse is seen now as a valuable source of companionship in life and less like a parent or source of supplies. Criticisms of the previous years are realigned to take into account this central change. However, all is not as comfortable as it might appear from the description of the fifties so far. There is a narrow time span, with little concern for the past or future, which seems to be related to the unmentioned but imminent presence of mortality. With this there is a renewed questioning about the meaningfulness of life, as well as a review of one's own work contributions to the world. In addition, there is a hunger for personal relationships from a position of indelible uniqueness, but a necessity to stay away from emotion laden topics and a concentration on petty annoyances, health topics, and an unexpected guilty shadow about personal sexual views.

STUDY II

The results of Study I are given descriptively and stand for themselves. We were impressed by the facts that differences among age groups could be found by the use of simple observation and that the differences seemed quite substantial. We were not at all confident about the specificity of our age groupings, nor about the generalizability of our observations to a non-help-seeking population. We have no socioeconomic data for disaggregating our sample into subgroups. This second study adds more information on age specificity and generalizability, but does not contribute to our knowledge of possible subgroup variability based on such factors as sex, income, race, religion, or occupation.

METHOD

We constructed a questionnaire that could be administered simply to a nonpatient population. The items that composed the questionnaire were salient statements heard in the "phase of life" groups. To avoid overweighting the questionnaire with the clinical bias we developed during the group observations, we enlisted the aid of eight first-year medical students. These students were presented with all of the tape-recordings of the two sets of "phase of life" groups. The students broke up into small groups and listened to the tapes after receiving one simple instruction from me: "List the statements describing personal feelings that stood out during the tape-recorded sessions." A compilation of these statements from all the age groups was then organized into topical sections. The topical section titles were inductively arrived at from the content of the statements. We decided to include only 16 statements in each topical section since we had decided on a forced-choice ranking format.

The titles were not printed on the questionnaire, but the eight titled sections were: (1) sense of time; relationships to (2) parents, (3) friends, (4) children, (5) spouses; and feelings about (6) own personality, (7) job, and (8) sex. We added two additional sections that were not empirically determined, sections 9 and 10. In section 9 we asked the subjects to rank-order a list of major concerns in life. In section 10 we asked them to rank-order the importance of the major people in their everyday life—children, parents, spouse, self, and boss—in regard to each of the following: companionship, approval, decision making, and general influence. Section 1 of the questionnaire is included here as an example of the wording and type of statements in the questionnaire:

1. I feel that some exciting things are going to happen to me.
2. I never plan on what tomorrow may bring.
3. It hurts me to realize that I will not get some things in life I want.
4. I live for today; forget the past.
5. I think things aren't as good as they used to be.
6. I believe I will some day have everything I want in life.
7. My life doesn't change much from year to year.

8. There is little hope for the future.
9. I try to be satisfied with what I have and not to think so much about the things I probably won't be able to get.
10. I wish I could change the past.
11. I dream about life ten years from now.
12. I spend more time now thinking about the past then about the future.
13. There's still plenty of time to do most of the things I want to do.
14. I would be quite content to remain as old as I am now.
15. I find myself daydreaming about good experiences in the past.
16. I will have to settle for less than I expected, but I still think I will get most things I want.

The questionnaire was then given to a white, middle-class, educated population of 524 who were selected by two criteria; they were not psychiatric patients and they were available through a network of acquaintances emanating from a core of eight medical students and several hospital volunteers. Monitoring of the age of the respondent as the questionnaires were returned allowed us to purposively sample ages not represented in the early returns. Our final sample included approximately 20 subjects for each year between 16 and 33 and 20 subjects for each three-year span between 33 and 60. The male-female ratio was approximately 1:1 for the total sample, but was unevenly distributed, with women being disproportionately represented over age 45.

RESULTS

Each subject supplied each of the 16 statements in each section with a rank order from 1 to 16. Curves for each statement were plotted on the basis of the average rank-ordering for the 20 subjects at each age. Since there were 142 separate statements composing the questionnaire, there were 142 scores for each age between 16 and 60 and 142 curves were developed from these scores. Each age-point on each curve therefore represents the *average* rank order of 20 same-aged subjects for that statement relative to the other 15 statements in its section.

By putting all of the curves on a single type of graph (using ages 16–60 as the abscissa), we were able to see clearly the unstable periods when response scores changed, i.e., when the greatest number of statements changed rank order (see Figure 1). These change periods were interpreted as transitional periods or time-zone boundaries. The bulk of the responses stabilized in the period between ages 22 and 29 and remained stable throughout the life span. The stable response curves of this period provide us with a well-established baseline. The responses of the 16- to 17-year-olds were almost identical, except in age-inappropriate areas (children, job security,

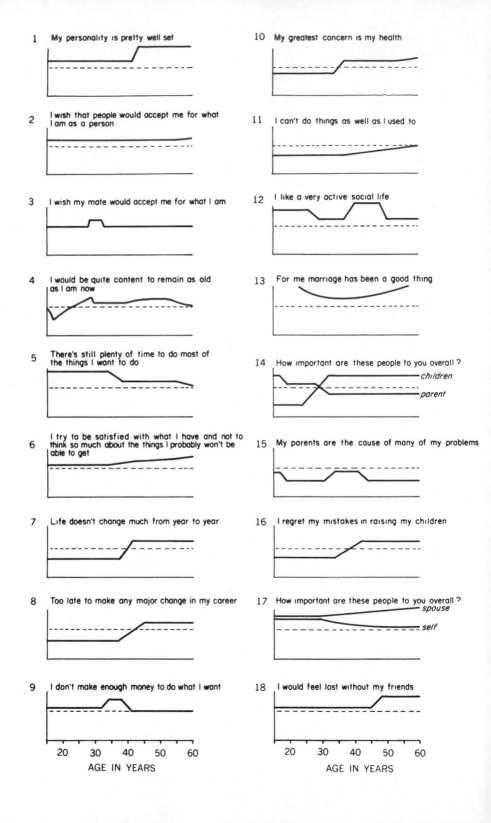

1 My personality is pretty well set

2 I wish that people would accept me for what I am as a person

3 I wish my mate would accept me for what I am

4 I would be quite content to remain as old as I am now

5 There's still plenty of time to do most of the things I want to do

6 I try to be satisfied with what I have and not to think so much about the things I probably won't be able to get

7 Life doesn't change much from year to year

8 Too late to make any major change in my career

9 I don't make enough money to do what I want

10 My greatest concern is my health

11 I can't do things as well as I used to

12 I like a very active social life

13 For me marriage has been a good thing

14 How important are these people to you overall?
children
parent

15 My parents are the cause of many of my problems

16 I regret my mistakes in raising my children

17 How important are these people to you overall?
spouse
self

18 I would feel lost without my friends

20   30   40   50   60
AGE IN YEARS

20   30   40   50   60
AGE IN YEARS

etc.), to the stable patterns of those aged 22 to 29. In contrast, the 18- to 22-year-olds responded discontinuously. After 29, the rank order of selected statements began to change from the age baselines at two ages, 30 and 37. Most of these late-changing curves stabilized at around age 43. A less impressive, but definite series of response fluctuations occurred at the end of the fourth decade. Thus, there are suggestions of seven distinct age periods: 16–17, 18–21, 22–28, 29–36, 37–43, 44–50, and 51–60.

In the previous step, we were not interested in which statements changed rank order, only the number of changes in rank order at a certain time. To begin to look at the content of the statements with changing scores between 16 and 60, we graphed each topical section individually. Since the statements are empirically determined, there is no correct answer and no logical connection that can be applied in rank-ordering the section. Therefore, the change in rank for each statement from one year to the next becomes the measure of a type of collective subjective accounting, representing the average "hunches" of 20 subjects at each age. A statement that rings a bell or connects with a feeling of immediacy will rise in rank for that age group and will have to compete with other such statements or consistently popular stereotyped statements.

For the purposes of establishing the time boundaries of the adult life span, those curves with the most rapid and stable changes (and face validity when compared with the bulk of unchanging curves) interest us the most and are presented in Figure 1. Several of the curves lend weight to our clinical observation of the groups and add a knowledge of age specificity that we did not have. As can be seen in graph 1, the ranking of the statement "My personality is pretty well set" takes a dramatic jump to a new level between 41 and 43.

In another group observation, we noted that the strong desire to be "accepted for what I am by my spouse" is present in the 28- to 34-year-old group. That statement was present in two forms in the questionnaire under two separate sections: "I wish that people would accept me for what I am as a person" under the friend section, and the more specific "I want to be accepted for what I am by my spouse" under the marital section. The two curves are shown in graphs 2 and 3, and it can be seen that the excursion from the baseline is quite specifically related to spouse and takes place between ages 28 and 32.

In the statement "I am content to remain as old as I am," there is a gradual continuous rise during the twenties starting from a low at 18 to 19 until a peak is reached at 29 with a sharp descent in the thirties. This adds weight

←――――――

FIGURE 1

Sample curves associated with the time boundaries of the adult life span.

to our observation that there is a marked subjective experience in the early thirties, that life is much more difficult and painful than it appeared in the twenties.

By comparing them with the twenties, we can use these three curves (graphs 2–4) to bracket the thirties with some evidence that a change or opening-up process begins in the thirties and a stabilization and closing-off process begins in the early forties—around 43 as experienced and reported by our sample. Now let us look more closely at our curves for the thirties, which add weight to the observation that this age period is a time of active psychological change.

We can categorize the curves of the thirties as demonstrative of two major shifts. There is a gradual peeling away of the magical illusions of omnipotence and omnipotentiality and there is an identification of the self with the family.

Under the first category are the curves of graphs 5 through 11. As can be seen, there are significant changes beginning in the thirties as the sense of time becomes finite while a reconciliation with the limitations of being merely mortal involves work choice, the sense of well-being, money resources, and the deterioration of some general abilities. It is well to note that most of these processes start in the mid-thirties and leave the early thirties free of the constricting sense of time that characterizes the late thirties and early forties in our group observation.

The curves interpreted as part of the process of turning inward toward the family and a blurring of self-definition with the family are shown in graphs 12 through 17. There is direct evidence in this series of curves that the preference schedule for involvement switches in the early thirties from the stable patterns of the twenties. There is a turning away from an active social life outside the family to a focus on their own children and a reconsideration of their parents' mistakes with them while they are considering their mistakes with their own children. In addition, there is a drifting downward in the sense of satisfaction in the marriage as compared with the highly valued marriage of the twenties. There is also increased difficulty in making the marriage work and complaints of not being able to communicate with the spouse (graph not shown). Parent, child, self, and spouse are all intimately interrelated and interchangeable by the substitution processes that seem to appear in these graphs.

In the forties, two things happen to the curves of the questionnaire answers. Between 40 and 43 there is a series of temporary excursions from well-established lifelong baselines on statements dealing with personal comfort, indicating an acutely unstable period with a great deal of personal discomfort. In addition to the return to baseline on these statements at 43, there is a general stabilization and leveling off of the changes started in the early and mid-thirties. This coincides with the dramatic affirmation of the feelings that one's personality is pretty well set (graph 1) and that life does not change from year to year (graph 7).

Marital happiness and contentment with the spouse continue to increase, along with a renewed interest in friends and social activities, as seen in graph 18. Friends and social activities are not substitutes for concern with one's own children, which continues at a very high level.

In the fifties, the curves indicate that one begins to feel less responsible for one's children and begins to look for the children's approval as a meaningful concern to be ranked as coequal with self-approval and the spouse's approval. The concern with health increases during the fifties. The certainty that time is running out is reflected in several curves, especially graphs 5 and 6.

DISCUSSION AND CONCLUSIONS

There is a great danger in trying to use cross-sectional data as an aid to our understanding of a continuous process. The difference in responses by age may reflect the sequence of cultural values learned during formative years by different groups, rather than a response determined primarily by the age of the responder. The questions with moral implications are most likely to fall in the former category. Most of the changing curves presented in this paper do not fall into the moral, learned response category, but are questions related to time sense that are most likely to be age-determined. With these limitations in mind, I think we are on safe ground in considering that the longitudinal process is represented in this sequential series of cross-sectional samples.

Some of the results of our questionnaire study, fortunately, are supported by the few independent studies already in the psychological literature that deal with this subject. In particular, our curves on marital happiness (Terman, 1938), contentment to remain the same age (Pressey and Kuhlen, 1957, p. 373), anxiety in the forties in relation to performance (Welford, 1969), a sense of the finiteness of time in the mid-thirties (Lewin, 1939), reconciliation in the forties (Slotkin, 1952), health concerns (Dykman, Heimann, and Ken, 1952), decreased interest in social activities in the thirties, and increased interest in friends and organizations in the forties (Strong, 1931) all conform to the results of previous studies using different methodologies and different populations. The correlation of the questionnaire results with these independent studies, and the similarity of the findings of our direct observation of patients to those of the questionnaire study of nonpatients, certainly provide evidence that the adult period is a time of active and systematic change. In addition, there is strong evidence that a series of distinct stages can be demarcated.

The studies reported in this paper have been designed to cancel out individual differences in order to highlight whatever sameness inheres in a group of age-peers. Patients and nonpatients are not discriminable in these studies, but this in no way implies there is no difference between the groups. We looked only at the contents of the subjective experience relative to age, not the intensity of the degree to which this reality of time interacts with other powerful factors in people's lives. Although the results may be considered factual inasmuch as they can be confirmed or negated by other observers, they are not observations pertinent to any one individual, but constructs derived from specific groups that may be applicable to other groups.

The results are best thought of as a description of a sequence of process fluctuations that define the posturing of the self to its inner and outer world over time. The fluctuations are time-dominated, but not necessarily age-specific for any one individual. In addition, the fluctuations take place within the context of a total personality, life style, and subculture and each man can be compared only with his own self at a former time. How these shifts are expressed and coped with is a matter of individual psychology beyond the scope of this paper. The subject of this paper has been the manner in which the passage of time influences the actuality of experiences during the adult life span.

15

INTRODUCTION

Family Systems Theory,
by Murray Bowen

The previous chapters in this volume have focused on isolated parts of the family system. But no matter how thoroughly the observer understands each separate subsystem within the family, it is not the same as understanding the family as a unit. Families are more complicated than the simple sum of their parts. Consequently, observers have begun to organize their data within a systems theory framework, to which the following chapter is dedicated. This approach reflects a major conceptual reorientation over the past few decades in many sectors of the scientific community. Linear, deterministic notions of causality have been enriched by concepts such as reciprocal feedback chains, which look at the multiple reverberating factors that result in the whole being different from the aggregate of its parts.

In this light, the family is perceived as functioning as a self-regulating, open system with its own unique history and structure. Its structure is constantly evolving through the dynamic interaction between the family's mutually interdependent individuals and larger subsystems with a complementarity of needs. Efforts to describe the emotional fabric of family life can thus be compared to trying to capture a series of moving lights and shadows (Westley and Epstein, 1969).

Attempting to apply the terminology of traditional cause-and-effect psychodynamic thinking to the apparently unlimited complexity of the family—with all its possible combinations of individuals, pairs, triangles, foursomes, and what have you—has not proved as generative as using a systems perspective. The spatial and temporal concepts emphasized by this approach may have a strange-sounding ring for clinicians. In the chapter that follows, however, Bowen conveys these ideas in everyday language.

It is not hyperbole to designate Bowen as a true clinical pioneer in family therapy. His foresight and courage can be seen in his hospitalization of families for the treatment of a schizophrenic patient almost three decades ago at a time when many therapists considered it to be a clinical error, to phrase it euphemistically, to have *any* contact with a member of the patient's family. Guerin (1976) has identified two major roots from which the family therapy movement developed. One is the child guidance wing exemplified by Ackerman and Minuchin. The other comprises family investigations of schizophrenia in which Bowen in Topeka and then in Washington was at the forefront, along with Bateson, Jackson, Weakland, and Haley in California; Lidz in Baltimore and New Haven; Whitaker and Malone in Atlanta; and Scheflen and Birdwhistell in Philadelphia.

With regard to another, different pioneering undertaking, Bowen has been described as the "family therapist's family therapist" (Framo, 1972). This designation stems from Bowen's suggestion that as a family therapist one should first extricate oneself from the complexities of one's own family before attempting to assist others in their differentiation from familial embeddedness. His advice is analogous in many respects to the personal analysis required of the prospective psychoanalyst. A vivid, moving account of such an undertaking is given by Anonymous in the volume edited by Framo (1972).

Beels and Ferber (1972) have categorized family therapy styles in terms of the therapist's relation to the family group. They characterize Bowen, along with Ackerman, Minuchin, and Satir, as "conductors." In contrast, there are the "reactors," a category that is further subdivided into "analysts" (e.g., Whitaker, Wynne, Boszormenyi-Nagy, Framo) and "systems purists" (e.g., Zuk, Haley, Jackson).

Guerin (1976) has proposed two basic theoretical orientations of family therapists: a family systems orientation and a psychoanalytic one. Guerin then offers four subcategories for each of these two perspectives. He subdivides the family systems theory orientation into general systems (which has not been translated into clinical relevance), Minuchin's structural family therapy, strategic therapy, and what he designates as the "Bowenian family systems theory and therapy." His psychoanalytic classification also has four subcategories. First there are the innumerable therapists with some degree of family orientation who practice primarily with individuals. Then, there are those who base their practice on a group model, defining the family as a natural group as opposed to an artificial group, such as one formed by the therapist. Guerin asserts that therapists like Bell, Wynne, Beels, as well as most other family therapists, approach the family in therapy in a manner comparable to the approach to a T-group: family interaction is encouraged and the therapist observes and intervenes in order to direct or clarify process. Guerin's third psychoanalytic subcategory encompasses the experiential family therapist (e.g., Whitaker and Ferber), who defines the operating clinical territory as the time and space of the therapy session itself, de-emphasizing what transpires between sessions. The fourth subdivision is what Guerin labels the "Ackermanian" approach, exemplified by Zwerling and Minuchin, although Guerin points out that Minuchin has increasingly moved from a psychoanalytic theoretical base to a systems one, as indeed the entire family therapy field has been doing in the past decade.

That these introductory comments should focus so much on pragmatic clinical strategies and styles reflects certain important aspects of the family therapy field. On the one hand, it is often asserted that family therapy is not just another treatment modality to be added to the clinician's roster of therapeutic options. Instead, it represents an entirely distinct perspective on the human condition and thus is not conceptually interchangeable with other treatment methods. At the same time, it is possible to characterize family therapy as a method in search of a theory (McDermott and Harrison, 1977). It is not that the field suffers from any shortage of fruitful theoretical constructs, but that, to a large extent, these generative concepts defy concise systematization.

Initially, these creative ideas came primarily from psychoanalytic sources such as Benedek's (1959) suggestion that the child's development reactivated the parents' unresolved childhood conflicts and Sperling's (1950) and A. M. Johnson and Szurek's (1952) observations of the effects of parents' unconscious mental functioning on childhood psychopathology (see also A. M. Johnson, 1949 [Chapter 35 in *Childhood Psychopathology*]). The subsequent outpouring of reports from authors identified with family therapy has led to today's rich conglomerate of ideas. In particular, the delineation of certain pathologically significant intrafamilial modes of relating has attracted enduring clinical attention. G. Bateson et al. (1956), for example, have pinpointed the "double-bind" mode of communication, in which the parent simultaneously or alternatively accepts and rejects the child, rendering it virtually impossible for the child to discriminate between or satisfy the congruent parental expectations. This pattern was originally outlined in the context of schizophrenia, but has since been applied to a wider range of psychopathological syndromes. Another clinically highlighted mode of interaction is "scapegoating" (Ackerman, 1958). Here the family maintains a stable equilibrium at the expense of a particular member's growth, by focusing on that individual's psychopathology. This family environment may explain why in certain cases otherwise appropriate therapeutic work with the identified patient produces only minimal evidence of change. Still another family mechanism is what Wynne et al. (1958) call "pseudo-mutuality." Differences within the family are excluded from recognition, if not delusionally reinterpreted, so as to eliminate divergences of opinions or roles that might enable an individual family member to differentiate his or her identity.

Maintaining the priority of the family's fitting together over individual needs may be aided by "mystification" (Laing, 1965) and the "transmission of irrationality" (Lidz, 1973).

Two other major approaches to family study have complemented the delineation of communication processes. One centers on the *content* and significance of roles within the family, e.g., the nurturer, spokesperson, controller, rescuer, persecutor, victim, scapegoat, saboteur, arbitrator, distractor, baby, pet, peacemaker (Rollins et al., 1973). Currently, however, much attention is devoted to the *structure* of these roles within the family. This focus stems in large measure from Minuchin's (1974) tightly reasoned conceptual model of family structure, development, and adaptation, which appears to be based on his style of clinical orchestration. Minuchin employs a lucid spatial metaphor of intrafamilial boundaries to describe a spectrum of family functioning. At one pole of the continuum are disengaged families, characterized by inappropriately rigid boundaries, while at the opposite end are enmeshed families with diffuse, amorphous boundaries. In the healthy middle range are families with functionally flexible, but clear boundaries. These concepts concerning transactional style have been applied to the various constellations of subsystems within a family, whether these subsystems are individuals or groupings defined by generation, sex, interests, or function. Combined with the functional demands placed on the family and its subsystems, these structural concepts constitute an exceedingly useful framework for clinicians in assessing the alliances, coalitions, and splits within a family and in designing therapeutic interventions to modify those that are dysfunctional.

The systems framework outlined by Bowen in the chapter that follows attempts a comprehensive formulation. In that respect it differs from Minuchin's compact configurational model, although it, too, emphasizes a systems-based theory of emotional dysfunction, along with the communication theory formulations and the related symptom-focused, brief strategic therapy derived from Bateson's project (e.g., Fisch, Haley, Jackson, Satir, Watzlawick, and Weakland).

The integration of family systems theory with developmental and psychopathological theory remains a vital challenge, both operationally and conceptually. The added dimension of the child's role in the family and the function that social role serves within the family dynamics enhance the clinical assessment of an individual child and can have vital implications for treatment efforts. Similarly, the youngster's individual psychobiological system merits meticulous attention in family assessment. The systems theory truism that knowledge of the individual parts does not explain the whole should not cancel out the converse truism that knowledge of the whole does not guarantee an understanding of all of the parts, particularly those individual parts that are developing and changing most rapidly (McDermott and Char, 1974).

It would be a pity if child-oriented clinicians allowed their reaction to what often impresses them as neglect of individual child development and psychopathology to interfere with their benefiting from and contributing to the productive ferment emanating from the field of family therapy and study. To that end, Bowen's clearly written chapter can be read with profit not only by clinicians and investigators, but also by anyone who is a member of a family.

15

Family Systems Theory

MURRAY BOWEN

All organisms are reasonably adaptable to acute anxiety. The organism has built-in mechanisms to deal with short bursts of anxiety. It is sustained or chronic anxiety that is most useful in determining the differentiation of self. If anxiety is sufficiently low, almost any organism can appear normal in the sense that it is symptom-free. When anxiety increases and remains chronic for a certain period, the organism develops tension, either within itself or in the relationship system, and the tension results in symptoms or dysfunction or sickness. The tension may result in physiological symptoms or physical illness, in emotional dysfunction, in social illness characterized by impulsiveness or withdrawal, or by social misbehavior. There is also the phenomenon of the infectiousness of anxiety, through which anxiety can spread rapidly through the family, or through society. There is a kind of average level of differentiation for the family, which has certain minor levels of difference in individuals within the family. I shall leave it to the reader to keep in mind that there is always the variable of the degree of chronic anxiety which can result in anyone appearing normal at one level of anxiety, and abnormal at another higher level.

DIFFERENTIATION OF SELF

This concept is a cornerstone of my theory, and if my discussion becomes repetitive, I beg the reader's indulgence. The concept defines people according to the degree of *fusion*, or *differentiation*, between emotional and intellectual functioning. This characteristic is so universal it can be used as a way of categorizing all people on a single continuum. At the low extreme

First published in *Family Therapy: Theory and Practice*, edited by Philip J. Guerin, Jr. New York: Gardner Press, 1976, pp. 65–90. Also published in *Family Therapy in Clinical Practice*, by Murray Bowen. New York: Aronson, 1978, pp. 426–432. Excerpts reprinted by permission.

are those whose emotions and intellect are so fused that their lives are dominated by the automatic emotional system. Whatever intellect they have is dominated by the emotional system. These are the people who are less flexible, less adaptable, and more emotionally dependent on those about them. They are easily stressed into dysfunction, and it is difficult for them to recover from dysfunction. They inherit a high percentage of all human problems. At the other extreme are those who are more differentiated. It is impossible for there to be more than relative separation between emotional and intellectual functioning, but those whose intellectual functioning can retain relative autonomy in periods of stress are more flexible, more adaptable, and more independent of the emotionality about them. They cope better with life stresses, their life courses are more orderly and successful, and they are remarkably free of human problems. In between the two extremes is an infinite number of mixes between emotional and intellectual functioning.

The concept eliminates the concept of *normal,* which psychiatry has never successfully defined. It is not possible to define *normal* when the thing to be measured is constantly changing. Operationally, psychiatry has called people normal when they are free of emotional symptoms and behavior is within average range. The concept of differentiation has no direct connection with the presence or absence of symptoms. People with the most fusion have the most problems, and those with the most differentiation, the fewest; but there can be people with intense fusion who manage to keep their relationships in balance, who are never subjected to severe stress, who never develop symptoms, and who appear normal. However, their life adjustments are tenuous, and, if they are stressed into dysfunction, the impairment can be chronic or permanent. There are also fairly well-differentiated people who can be stressed into dysfunction, but they recover rapidly.

At the fusion end of the spectrum, the intellect is so flooded by emotionality that the total life course is determined by the emotional process and by what "feels right," rather than by beliefs or opinions. The intellect exists as an appendage of the feeling system. It may function reasonably well in mathematics or physics, or in impersonal areas, but on personal subjects its functioning is controlled by the emotions. The emotional system is hypothesized to be part of the instinctual forces that govern automatic functions. The human is adept at explanations to emphasize that he is different from lower forms of life, and at denying his relation with nature. The emotional system operates with predictable, knowable stimuli that govern instinctual behavior in all forms of life. The more a life is governed by the emotional system, the more it follows the course of all instinctual behavior, in spite of intellectualized explanations to the contrary. At higher levels of differentiation, the functions of the emotional and intellectual systems are more clearly distinguishable.

There are the same automatic emotional forces that govern instinctual behavior, but intellect is sufficiently autonomous for logical reasoning and
decisions based on thinking. When I first began to present this concept, I
used the term *undifferentiated family ego mass* to describe the emotional
stuck-togetherness in families. Although this phrase was an assemblage of
words from conventional theory, and thus did not conform to the plan to use
concepts consistent with biology, it fairly accurately described emotional
fusion. I used it for a few years because more people were able to hear the
concept when it was put into words they understood.

As I began to present the concept of a well-differentiated person as one
whose intellect could function separately from the emotional system, it was
common for mental health professionals to hear the intellectual system as
equivalent to intellectuality, which is used as a defense against emotionality
in psychiatric patients. The most common criticism was that a differentiated
person appeared to be cold, distant, rigid, and nonfeeling. It is difficult for
professional people to grasp the notion of differentiation when they have
spent their working lives believing that the free expression of feelings represents a high level of functioning and intellectualization represents an un-
healthy defense against it. A poorly differentiated person is trapped within
a feeling world. His effort to gain the comfort of emotional closeness can
increase the fusion, which can increase his alienation from others. There is
a lifelong effort to get the emotional life into a livable equilibrium. A segment
of these emotionally trapped people use random, inconsistent, intellectual-
sounding verbalizations to explain away their plight. A more differentiated
person can participate freely in the emotional sphere without the fear of
becoming too fused with others. He is also free to shift to calm, logical
reasoning for decisions that govern his life. The logical intellectual process
is quite different from the inconsistent, intellectualized verbalizations of the
emotionally fused person.

In earlier papers I presented this as the Differentiation of Self Scale. I did
that to convey the idea that people have all gradations of differentiation of
self, and that people at one level have remarkably different life styles from
those at other levels. Schematically, I presented a scale from 0 to 100, with
0 representing the lowest possible level of human functioning and 100 representing a hypothetical notion of perfection to which man might evolve if
his evolutionary change goes in that direction. I wanted a spectrum broad
enough to cover all possible degrees of human functioning. To clarify the
fact that people are different from each other in terms of emotional-intellectual
functioning, I did profiles of people in the 0 to 25, the 25 to 50, the 50 to
75, and the 75 to 100 ranges. Those profiles are still amazingly accurate
some 10 years later. In that first paper, I also presented the notion of functional

levels of differentiation that can shift from moment to moment, or remain fairly constant for most of a life (Bowen, 1966). Some of the major variables that govern the shifting were presented as a way of clarifying the concept and categorizing the apparent complexity of human functioning into a more knowable framework. The schematic framework and the use of the term *scale* resulted in hundreds of letters requesting copies of "the scale." Most who wrote had not grasped the concept or the variables that govern the functional levels of differentiation. The letters slowed down my effort to develop a more definite scale that could be used clinically. The theoretical concept is most important. It eliminates the barriers between schizophrenia, neurosis, and normal; it also transcends categories such as genius, social class, and cultural-ethnic differences. It applies to all human forms of life. It might even apply to subhuman forms if we only knew enough. Knowledge of the concept permits the easy development of all kinds of research instruments, but to attempt to use this scale without knowledge of the concept can result in chaos.

Another important part of the differentiation of self has to do with the levels of *solid self* and *pseudo-self* in a person. In periods of emotional intimacy, two pseudo-selfs will fuse into each other, one losing self to the other, who gains self. The solid self does not participate in the fusion phenomenon. The solid self says, "This is who I am, what I believe, what I stand for, and what I will do or will not do," in a given situation. The solid self is made up of clearly defined beliefs, opinions, convictions, and life principles. These are incorporated into the self from one's own life experiences, by a process of intellectual reasoning and the careful consideration of the alternatives involved in the choice. In making the choice, one becomes responsible for self and for the consequences. Each belief, each life principle is consistent with all the others, and the self will take action on the principles even in situations of high anxiety and duress.

The pseudo-self is created by emotional pressure, and it can be modified by emotional pressure. Every emotional unit, whether it be the family or the total of society, exerts pressure on group members to conform to the ideals and principles of the group. The pseudo-self is composed of a vast assortment of principles, beliefs, philosophies, and knowledge acquired because it is required or considered right by the group. Since the principles are acquired under pressure, they are random and inconsistent with one another, without the individual's being aware of the discrepancy. Pseudo-self is appended onto self, in contrast to solid self which is incorporated into self after careful, logical reasoning. The pseudo-self is a "pretend" self. It was acquired to conform to the environment, and it contains discrepant and assorted principles that pretend to be in emotional harmony with a variety of social groups, institutions, businesses, political parties, and religious groups, without the self's being aware that the groups are inconsistent with each other. The joining of groups is motivated more by the relationship system than the principle involved. The person may "feel" there is something wrong with some of the groups, but he is not intellectually aware. The solid self is intellectually aware of the inconsistency between the groups, and the decision to join or reject membership is an intellectual process based on careful weighing of the advantages and disadvantages.

The pseudo-self is an actor and can be many different selfs. The list of pretends is extensive. He can pretend to be more important or less important, stronger or weaker, or more attractive or less attractive than is realistic. It is easy for most people to detect gross examples of pretense, but there is enough of the impostor in all of us so that it is difficult to detect lesser degrees of the impostor in others. On the other hand, a good actor can appear so much for real that it can be difficult for the actor or for others without detailed knowledge of how emotional systems function to know the dividing line between solid self and pseudo-self. This also applies to therapists, mental health professionals, and researchers who may attempt to estimate the level of differentiation in themselves or in others. The level of solid self is stable. The pseudo-self is unstable, and it responds to a variety of social pressures and stimuli. The pseudo-self was acquired at the behest of the relationship system, and it is negotiable in the relationship system.

Based on my experience with this concept, I believe that the level of solid self is lower, and that of pseudo-self much higher, in all of us than most realize. It is the pseudo-self that is involved in fusion and the many ways of giving, receiving, lending, borrowing, trading, and exchanging self. In any exchange, one gives up a little self to the other, who gains an equal amount. The best example is a love relationship where each is trying to be the way the other wants self to be, and each in turn makes demands on the other to be different. This is pretending and trading in pseudo-self. In a marriage, two pseudo-selfs fuse into a we-ness in which one becomes the dominant decision-maker or the most active in taking initiative for the we-ness. The dominant one gains self at the expense of the other, who loses it. The adaptive one may volunteer to give up self to the dominant one, who accepts it; or the exchange may be worked out after bargaining. The more that the spouses can alternate these roles, the healthier the marriage. The exchanging of selfs may be on a short- or long-term basis. The borrowing and trading of selfs may take place automatically in a work group in which the emotional process ends up with one employee in the one-down or deselfed position, while the others gain self. This exchanging of pseudo-self is an automatic emotional process, which occurs as people manipulate each other in subtle life postures. The exchange can be brief—for instance, criticism that makes one feel bad for a few days—or it can be a long-term process in which the adaptive spouse becomes so deselfed, he or she is no longer able to make decisions and collapses in selfless dysfunction (psychosis or chronic physical illness). These mechanisms are much less intense at better levels of differentiation or when anxiety is low, but the process of people losing and gaining self in an emotional network is so complex and the degree of shifts so great that it is impossible to estimate functional levels of differentiation except from following a life pattern over long periods.

CLINICAL PROFILE OF A FAMILY

This clinical example is presented to help illustrate the value of the Differentiation of Self Scale in estimating present problems and predicting future problems in a family. It is impossible to do scale values for any month or year, but it is possible to estimate the general levels of differentiation over a period of years, and from this one can make fairly accurate predictions of things to come. I shall start with a mother with two young children, one that grows up with a poor level of differentiation and the other with a good level of differentiation. The same mother can have two children who are quite different. The differences will be exaggerated here to illustrate the point.

The mother's first child was conceived when her life was unsettled and anxious. Anxiety and marital disharmony decreased during the pregnancy. (This is good evidence that a family projection process is already in progress.) The child, a girl, was tense and fretful and required more than average mothering attention. A second child was born 18 months later. The pregnancy was uneventful, except for the mother's worry about the older child's reaction to a sibling. She wondered if she could provide adequate care for the baby without "hurting" the older one. (This is more evidence of a projection process.) The mother was aware of something different. She mentioned it to her pediatrician and friends, who assured her this was not unusual for first babies. She concluded the problem would disappear if she could be a calm, patient, "giving" mother. (Projection of the mother's anxiety onto the child and treating it as a problem in the child help perpetuate the problem in the child. A better approach would be to work on her relationship with her husband, or with her own mother.) The second child, a son, was an easy baby. (This is an indication that most of the basic problem was being "absorbed" by the oldest.) The mother kept trying to resolve the clinging attachment of the first child.

An example from the preschool years will illustrate critical qualities of the mother's relationship with each child. In dressing the children to play outside, the younger one was eager to dress and get started, while the older one was a dawdling problem. Outside, the younger one ran ahead to explore and play alone. The older child was too preoccupied with the mother to have energy for play. The mother tried to help the girl get started in play. It worked well as long as the mother was there. When the mother tried to sneak away, the girl stopped her play and ran to the mother. The older child, with as much investment of self in the mother as the mother had in the child, was able to "read" the mother's facial expressions, tone of voice, body posture, and footsteps. (These are examples of a goal-directed child and a relationship-oriented child.)

The first nodal point came when the children started school. The older child had a moderate "school phobia." She was fearful about school, with many questions about what would happen in school. The mother tried to prepare her by walking her to school to show her the building and grounds. When school started, the tearful, anxious parting was finally accomplished by the teacher, who permitted the mother to sit in the room a few days while the teacher devoted extra attention to the child. The mother was pleased when the mission was accomplished. At home, the mother's thoughts still went to the child. She was encouraged by her frequent telephone conversations and conferences with the teacher, and overjoyed at the good reports. The younger child had no anxiety as he reached school age. He was interested in when he would finally be able to go and when he could learn to read and write. He had the same "understanding" teacher that his older sister had had. The teacher and the mother had a good relationship from conferences about the daughter. The mother credited the teacher's counseling for help in solving the older child's problem. The teacher reported the younger child was "no problem"—"He is more interested in learning than in me."

For the older child, this was a smooth transition from home to school. The child developed the same relationship pattern with the teacher that she had with her mother. The teacher was a shy woman with a poor level of differentiation, who was relationship-oriented in her own life. She was said to have "a way" with shy children. Of the older child she said, "I do well with children like this. I can bring them out. I *give something to them,* and *they give me something in return,* and we do well." The child was attached to the teacher, and the teacher helped place the child with other "understanding" teachers as the child progressed through the six years in that school. In their meetings at PTA and school functions, the teacher always inquired about the older child, but never about the younger child, who was self-motivated and who did well academically and socially. He had numerous friends among the other boys and was an achiever in the Boy Scouts. The older child also did well academically, but she was less consistent. When she was with a teacher she "liked," she worked hard at pleasing the teacher and was at the top of the class. With teachers who gave her less attention (less of the relationship-oriented "giving and receiving" to and from each other), she did less well in school, she was often absent from school because of illness, she complained about the teacher, she was more dependent on her mother, and her school performance fell. The mother blamed the bad years on time lost because of illness and teachers who were too "hard on her." This child found it easier to relate to adults than to other children in the grade school years (a common characteristic of children overattached to parents). The mother was concerned and became a Girl Scout leader to help her cultivate friends among the other girls. She compliantly participated when her mother was present for Girl Scout activities, but found reasons not to participate when her mother was not there.

The first major change in the girl's life came rather suddenly in the seventh grade, the first year of junior high school. The problem surfaced at midyear, about the time of her thirteenth birthday. Two developments appeared about the same time. Since childhood, the mother had had an "open" and honest relationship with the girl, who told the mother "everything" in a "giving-and-receiving" relationship that both enjoyed. Early in the seventh grade, the girl began to confide less and less. The mother missed these heart-to-heart talks, and in addition, she wondered what was going on in the girl. The mother's anxiety increased, and the more she pushed for information, the more the child gave brief answers and withdrew to her room. The mother tried to be calm, telling herself the girl had never told her a lie, that this was a phase and it would pass. The second development came with a poor report card. The mother resumed her push to know what was happening, and for the first time they had an angry exchange of words. The girl withdrew more and more and began long telephone talks with friends. This was the beginning of overt conflict between mother and daughter. The mother was afraid to ask too many questions lest she start a fight. The mother contained her anxiety as much as possible, but she was also good at reading the daughter's facial expressions, tones of voice, and actions, and when she "felt" the daughter was upset or anxious, she would again press for explanations. The daughter learned to be evasive and distant, and that "white lies" would settle her mother's immediate anxiety. The girl's school record was erratic, but with little effort before exams, she could manage to get average grades in most subjects. Socially, the girl became part of a group of "fast" girls, whom the mother blamed for the daughter's behavior, which became increasingly more extreme and antifamily. Periodically, at the time of an anxiety episode, the mother would seek information and counsel from the school, but there was no longer a single teacher and the school counselor, who had little direct contact with the girl, first reassured the mother that this was normal and then later suggested psychiatric help. When the mother mentioned this to the girl, it elicited the angriest response of all. The mother herself saw a psychiatrist, who explained the adolescent rebellion and adolescent sexual conflict, and who suggested an evaluation and possible psychotherapy for the mother to help her find answers in herself. The girl's refusal to have anything to do with a "shrink" terminated that effort.

The adolescent period is fast-moving and difficult for such a relationship-oriented child. The girl started life with a moderately intense fusion of self with the mother. Much of the mother's psychic energy, which included worry, concern, "love," and anger, was invested in the girl, and the girl invested an equal amount of herself in the mother. This investment of self, or fusion, exists in all levels of intensity, which parallel the levels of differentiation of self on the scale. Once a child is "programmed" for a certain level of "giving and receiving" with mother, this level remains relatively fixed throughout life. The child can have an "open and loving" relationship only when conditions for that level of investment of self in each other are met. There are certain variables that govern these "conditions," which are discussed elsewhere [see Bowen, 1978]. The degree of the mother's undifferentiation that fuses with the child is determined by her total amount of undifferentiation and by the amount absorbed elsewhere. If the mother's undifferentiation is absorbed in one child, her relationships with her other children will be more normal. This mother had no excessive worry or concern about the other child. There is a spectrum of families in which the other children "grow up" outside the parental fusion with the involved child and they are free to grow toward goal-directed lives.

This mother was "successful" in managing a fairly calm relationship with the girl throughout childhood. She found a school situation that was extremely favorable for keeping the child free of symptoms. The teacher had a similar low level of differentiation herself and she fitted well as a relationship figure for the next six years. A less favorable "fit" would have resulted in more symptoms early in school, and probably more symptoms as the child moved through the elementary school years. The child managed to do better than average schoolwork. A better school adjustment would have been one in which the child was an overachiever who put in sufficient work to excel academically in order to "receive" approval from teachers and parents. Another child of about the same level of differentiation and with a little less free intellect to apply to school could become an underachiever to relieve the pressure of academic success, and still receive an acceptable amount of psychic energy, directed toward the poor school record. The problems with poorly differentiated youngsters who are academically brilliant are discussed elsewhere [see Bowen, 1978]. The difficulty that such a child has in relating to other children is familiar. The average small child is not capable of relating to other children, and an impaired child has little energy outside the adult "giving-and-receiving" sources. The breakdown in the successful school adjustment period came at the beginning of junior high school, which is a common breakdown point for impaired children. There is no longer a single room and single teacher. The children move from room to room with a different teacher for each subject. The system works well for better-integrated children, but chances are not too good for an impaired child's finding an efficient "giving-and-receiving" relationship with a teacher. Children are also maturing physically, which moves them away from parents.

The combination of age and circumstance brings the students into the first "natural selection" process for the choosing of personal friends. Here is a large group, and a high percentage have a significant dependent attachment to their parents, which they handle by turning away from the parents. They form themselves into groups determined by the life style of "giving and receiving" into which they were programmed by their mothers. Those with the lowest level of functional self do the greatest rejection of the parents, and therefore have the most emotional "needs" to be met in the group. There are other groups made up of successive better levels of integration. Groups are organized around "leaders" and "best friend" principles. The group quickly becomes an active network of triangles. All the students have been well schooled in relationship-oriented experience, and seeking and giving "love" and approval. They put as much energy into the relationship in the group as they formerly devoted to their mothers, with primary energy into the current "best friend," with whom there is frequent contact, as well as endless telephone conversations. In general, the groups are "anti-parent" and "secret" and each has its own specified type of activity determined by the intensity of the negative "cutoff" with parents. The group prescribes language, dress, and behavior. A minimal amount of excessive behavior is necessary to be accepted, but the most approved member is the one who shows the most "cool" in taking chances at getting caught. There is a premium on "standing up" to parents and authorities, and standing up to someone means doing or saying something that will "get a reaction" from the parent. There is satisfaction in shocking and getting reactions from parents, not because they enjoy hurting (as is commonly assumed), but from the satisfaction of "being a grown-up self." This is the level of thinking for someone with this level of undifferentiation.

There is one important aspect of teenage groups which has to do with relationships with parents at home. They are still *financially dependent on parents* and the parents are *emotionally dependent* on the youngsters, who still have the ability to dissolve the selfs of the parents. It is easy for parents to yield to meeting excessive demands for money and privileges, in the hope the youngster has finally changed.

The daughter in this clinical profile belonged to one of the middle-range "groups" in her school. There were antiestablishment things her group would not do that were commonplace for lower-level groups. There were activities in her group that better-integrated groups would not do. In the junior high years her activities included staying out late, staying overnight with her "best friend" without telling the parents, "cool" parties, shoplifting, and the use of four-letter words that would shock others. The group placed high approval on those who reported escapades on beer, wine, and marijuana, and who were most successful in "making out" with boys. In high school her dress became more extreme, and involvement with sex, drug use, and the use of obscene language was routine. She had run away to live with her boyfriend so many times, after fights with her mother, that the family hardly reacted to it. She was moderately addicted to hard drugs, supplied by her boyfriend. She had hepatitis from drug injections, and she was in two serious car wrecks. She and the boyfriend were living together when she managed to graduate from high school. She tried college, but dropped out, and then moved across the country with her boyfriend, where they now have a car, an apartment, and they manage to live without working except for part-time jobs in antiestablishment activity.

In the meantime, the goal-directed younger son has led an orderly life. He was an honor graduate in high school and he was not functionally affected by his sister's erratic course. He maintained close contact with his parents without being affected by their emotional involvement with his sister. He is now nearing the end of college, which will be followed by graduate school. He has a long-time girlfriend from high school days, who went to another college, and they plan to marry when the realities of education and finances permit.

One last item is important in this clinical profile. The daughter's boyfriend, also a refugee from his parental family, has the exact pattern of investment of self in the other as the daughter had originally with her mother, and as she has had in subsequent relationships. They can "read" each other's feelings from facial expressions, voice, and movement; each feels pity for the other at any sign of inner pain, and they somehow are able to keep the intense "giving to each other" in equilibrium as long as neither works and they devote self fully to the other. From observing their relationship in the past, neither is able to cope with serious illness, injury, or other serious reality needs, and either will run away from the disabled one. Their emotional cocoon can continue to be fairly stable as long as they can keep the total investment in each other, and as long as neither works and the cocoon is not threatened by inner or outer forces. This girl might have been a periodically hospitalized, marginally adjusted mental patient if she had been born a generation earlier.

The therapy based on differentiation is no longer thearpy in the usual sense. This therapy is as different from the conventional therapy as the theory is different from conventional theory. The overall goal is to help individual family members to rise up out of the emotional togetherness that binds us all. The instinctual force toward differentiation is built into the organism, just as are the emotional forces that oppose it. The goal is to help the motivated family member to take a microscopic step toward a better level of differentiation, in spite of the togetherness forces that oppose. When one family member can finally master this, then other family members automatically take similar steps. The togetherness forces are so strong in maintaining the status quo that any small step toward differentiation is met with vigorous disapproval of the group. This is the point at which a therapist or guide can be most helpful. Without help, the differentiating one will fall back into the togetherness to get emotional harmony for the moment. Conventional therapy is designed to resolve, or talk out, conflict. This does accomplish the goal of reducing the conflict of that moment, but it can also rob the individual of his budding effort to achieve a bit more differentiation from the family togetherness. There are many pitfalls in the effort toward differentiation. If the individual attempts it without some conviction of his own, he is blindly following the advice of his therapist and is caught in a self-defeating togetherness with the therapist. I believe that the level of differentiation of a person is largely determined by the time he leaves the parental family and attempts a life of his own. Thereafter, he tends to replicate the life style from the parental family in all future relationships. It is not possible ever to make more than minor changes in one's basic level of self; but from clinical experience I can say it is possible to make slow changes, and each small change results in the new world of a different life style. As I see it now, the critical stage is passed when the individual can begin to know the difference between emotional functioning and intellectual functioning, and when he has developed ways for using the knowledge for solving future problems in a lifelong effort on his own. It is difficult to assess differentiation during calm periods in a life. Clinically, I make estimates from the average functional level of self as it operates through periods of stress and calm. The real test of the stability of differentiation comes when the person is again subjected to chronic severe stress.

TRIANGLES

The triangle, a three-person emotional configuration, is the molecule or the basic building block of any emotional system, whether it is in the family or any other group. The triangle is the smallest stable relationship system. A two-person system may be stable as long as it is calm, but when anxiety increases, it immediately involves the most vulnerable other person to become a triangle. When tension in the triangle is too great for the threesome, it involves others to become a series of interlocking triangles.

In periods of calm, the triangle is made up of a comfortably close twosome and a less comfortable outsider. The twosome works to preserve the togetherness, lest one become uncomfortable and form a better togetherness elsewhere. The outsider seeks to form a togetherness with one of the twosome, and there are numerous well-known moves to accomplish this. The emotional forces within the triangle are constantly in motion from moment to moment, even in periods of calm. Moderate tension states in the twosome are characteristically felt by one, while the other is oblivious. It is the uncomfortable one who initiates a new equilibrium toward more comfortable togetherness for self.

In periods of stress, the outside position is the most comfortable and most desired position. In such periods of stress, each works to get the outside position to escape tension in the twosome. When it is not possible to shift forces in the triangle, one of the involved twosome triangles in a fourth person, leaving the former third person aside for reinvolvement later. The emotional forces duplicate the exact patterns in the new triangle. Over time, the emotional forces continue to move from one active triangle to another, finally remaining mostly in one triangle as long as the total system is fairly calm.

When tensions are very high in families and available family triangles are exhausted, the family system triangles in people from outside the family, such as police and social agencies. A successful externalization of the tension occurs when outside workers are in conflict about the family while the family is calmer. In emotional systems such as an office staff, the tensions between the two highest administrators can be triangled and retriangled until conflict is acted out between two who are low in the administrative hierarchy. Administrators often settle this conflict by firing or removing one of the conflictual twosome, after which the conflict erupts in another twosome.

A triangle in moderate tension characteristically has two comfortable sides and one side in conflict. Since patterns repeat and repeat in a triangle, the people come to have fixed roles in relation to each other. The best example of this is the father-mother-child triangle. Patterns vary, but one of the most common is basic tension between the parents, with the father gaining the outside position—often being called passive, weak, and distant—leaving the conflict between mother and child. The mother—often called aggressive, dominating, and castrating—wins over the child, who moves another step toward chronic functional impairment. This pattern is described as the family projection process. Families replay the same triangular game over and over for years, as though the winner were in doubt, but the final result is always the same. Over the years the child accepts the always-lose outcome more easily, even to volunteering for this position. A variation is the pattern in which the father finally attacks the mother, leaving the child in the outside position. This child then learns the techniques of gaining the outside position by playing the parents off against each other.

Each of the structured patterns in triangles is available for predictable moves and predictable outcomes in families and social systems. A knowledge of triangles provides a far more exact way of understanding the father-mother-child triangle than do the traditional Oedipus complex explanations. Triangles provide several times more flexibility in dealing with such problems therapeutically.

Knowledge of triangles helps provide the theoretical perspective between individual therapy and this method of family therapy. An emotionally involved relationship is unavoidable in the average two-person, patient-therapist relationship. Theoretically, family therapy provides a situation in which intense relationships can remain within the family and the therapist can be relatively outside the emotional complex. This is a good theoretical premise which is hard to achieve in practice. Without some special effort, it is easy for the family to wrap itself around the therapist emotionally, install the therapist in an all-important position, hold the therapist responsible for success or failure, and passively wait for the therapist to change the family. I have elsewhere discussed ways other therapists have dealt with the therapeutic relationship, as well as my continuing effort to operate from outside the family emotional system [see Bowen, 1978]. Initially that included making the family members responsible for each other, avoiding the family tendency to assign importance to me, and promising no benefits except those from the family's own effort to learn about itself and change itself. Most important was a long-term effort to attain and maintain emotional neutrality with individual family members. There are many subtleties to this. Beyond this effort, it was knowledge of triangles that provided the important breakthrough in the effort to stay outside the emotional complex.

One experience, above all others, was important in learning about triangles. That was a period in which much of my family therapy was with both parents and the behavior-problem adolescent child. It was possible to see the workings of the triangle between parents and child in microscopic detail. The more I could stay outside the triangle, the more clearly it was possible to see the family emotional system as it operated on well-defined emotional circuits between father, mother, and child. Therapeutically, the family did not change its original patterns. The passive father would become less passive; the aggressive mother, less aggressive; and the symptomatic child would become asymptomatic. The average, motivated family would continue for 30 to 40 weekly appointments and terminate with great praise for the "good result." In my opinion, the family had not changed, but I had learned a lot about triangles. It was possible to observe a family and know the next move in the family before it occurred.

From this knowledge of triangles, I hypothesized that the situation would be different by excluding the child and limiting the therapy to the two parents and the therapist. Rather than dealing in generalities about staying out of the family emotional system, I was then armed with specific knowledge about the parents' triangling moves to involve the therapist. Therapeutically, the results were far superior to anything before that time. This has remained the one basic therapeutic method since the early 1960s. On a broad theoretical-therapeutic level, if the therapist can stay in viable emotional contact with the two most significant family members, usually the two parents or two spouses, and he can be relatively outside the emotional activity in this central triangle, the age-old fusion between the family members will slowly begin to resolve, and all other family members will automatically change in relation to the two parents in the home setting. This is basic theory and basic method. The process can proceed regardless of content or subject matter discussed. The critical issue is the emotional reactiveness between the spouses, and the ability of the therapist to keep self relatively detriangled from the emotionality. The process can proceed with any third person who can keep self detriangled, but it would be difficult to find such an outside relationship. The method is as successful as other methods in short-term crisis situations. In the early years I was active in engaging the family emotionally in consultations and short-term crisis situations. A calm, low-keyed, detriangling approach is more effective with a single appointment, or with many.

NUCLEAR FAMILY EMOTIONAL SYSTEM

This concept describes the patterns of emotional functioning in a family in a single generation. Certain basic patterns between the father, mother, and children are replicas of those in past generations and will be repeated in the generations to follow. There are several rather clear variables that determine the way the family functions in the present generation, which can be measured and validated by direct observation. From a careful history, in connection with knowledge of the details in the present generation, it is possible to do a rather remarkable reconstruction of the way the process operated in past generations. From knowledge about the transmission of family patterns over multiple generations, it is possible to project the same process into future generations, and, within limits, make some reasonably accurate predictions about future generations. No one person lives long enough to check the accuracy of predictions into the future, but there is enough detailed knowledge about some families in history to do a reasonable check on the predictive process. Based on experience in family research, the predictions of 10 to 20 years ago have been rather accurate.

The beginning of a nuclear family, in the average situation, is a marriage. There are exceptions to this, just as there have always been exceptions, which is all part of the total theory. The basic process in exceptional situations is similar to the more chaotic pattern in poorly differentiated people. The two spouses begin a marriage with life-style patterns and levels of differentiation developed in their families of origin. Mating, marriage, and reproduction are governed to a significant degree by emotional-instinctual forces. The way the spouses handle them in dating and courtship and in timing and planning the marriage provides one of the best views of the level of differentiation of the spouses. The lower the level of differentiation, the greater the potential problems for the future. People pick spouses who have the same levels of differentiation. Most spouses can have the closest and most open relationships in their adult lives during courtship. The fusion of the two pseudo-selfs into a common self occurs at the time they commit themselves to each other permanently, whether it be the time of engagement, the wedding itself, or the time they establish their first home together. It is common for living-together relationships to be harmonious, and for fusion symptoms to develop when they finally get married. It is as if the fusion does not develop as long as they still have an option to terminate the relationship.

The lower the level of differentiation, the more intense the emotional fusion of marriage. One spouse becomes more the dominant decision-maker for the common self, while the other adapts to the situation. This is one of the best examples of the borrowing and trading of self in a close relationship. One may assume the dominant role and force the other to be adaptive, or one may assume the adaptive role and force the other to be dominant. Both may try for the dominant role, which results in conflict; or both may try for the adaptive role, which results in decision paralysis. The dominant one gains self at the expense of the more adaptive one, who loses self. More differentiated spouses have lesser degrees of fusion, and fewer of the complications. The dominant and adaptive positions are *not* directly related to the sex of the spouse. They are determined by the position that each had in their families of origin. From my experience, there are as many dominant females as males, and as many adaptive males as females. These characteristics play a major role in their original choice of each other as partners. The fusion results in anxiety for one or both of the spouses. There is a spectrum of ways spouses deal with fusion symptoms. The most universal mechanism is emotional distance from each other. It is present in all marriages to some degree, and in a high percentage of marriages to a major degree.

Other than the emotional distance, there are three major areas in which the amount of undifferentiation in the marriage comes to be manifested in symptoms. The three areas are marital conflict, sickness or dysfunction in one spouse, and projection of the problems onto children. It is as if there were a quantitative amount of undifferentiation to be absorbed in the nuclear family, which might be focused largely in one area or distributed in varying amounts to all three areas. The various patterns for handling the undifferentiation come from patterns in their families of origin, and the variables involved in the mix in the common self. The following are general characteristics of each of the three areas.

MARITAL CONFLICT

The basic pattern in conflictual marriages is one in which neither gives in to the other or in which neither is capable of an adaptive role. These marriages are intense in the amount of emotional energy each invests in the other. The energy may be thinking or action energy, either positive or negative, but the self of each is focused mostly on the other. The relationship cycles through periods of intense closeness, conflict that provides a period of emotional distance, and making up, which starts another cycle of intense closeness. Conflictual spouses probably have the most overtly intense of all relationships. The intensity of the anger and negative feeling in the conflict is as intense as the positive feeling. They are thinking of each other even when they are distant. Marital conflict does not in itself harm children. There are marriages in which most of the undifferentiation goes into marital conflict. The spouses are so invested in each other that the children are largely outside the emotional process. When marital conflict and projection of the problem onto the children are both present, it is the projection process that is hurtful to the children. The quantitative amount of marital conflict that is present reduces the amount of undifferentiation that is focused elsewhere.

DYSFUNCTION IN ONE SPOUSE

This is the result when a significant amount of undifferentiation is absorbed in the adaptive posture of one spouse. The pseudo-self of the adaptive one merges into the pseudo-self of the dominant one, who assumes more and more responsibility for the twosome. The degree of adaptiveness in one spouse is determined from the long-term functioning posture of each to the other, rather than from verbal reports. Each does some adapting to the other, and it is usual for each to believe that he or she gives in more than the other. The one who functions for long periods in the adaptive position gradually loses the ability to function and make decisions for self. At that point, it requires no more than a moderate increase in stress to trigger the adaptive one into dysfunction, which may be physical illness, emotional illness, or social illness, such as drinking, acting out, and irresponsible behavior. These illnesses tend to become chronic, and they are hard to reverse.

The pattern of the overfunctioning spouse in relation to the underfunctioning spouse exists in all degrees of intensity. It can exist as an episodic phenomenon in families that use a mixture of all three mechanisms. When used as the principal means of controlling undifferentiation, the illnesses can be chronic and most difficult to reverse. The sick or invalided one is too impaired to begin to regain functions with an overfunctioning spouse on whom he or she is dependent. This mechanism is amazingly effective in absorbing the undifferentiation. The only disadvantage is the dysfunction in one, which is compensated for by the other spouse. The children can be almost unaffected by having one dysfunctional parent as long as there is someone else to function instead. The main problem in the children is inheriting a life pattern as caretaker of the sick parent, which will project into the future. These marriages are enduring. Chronic illness and invalidism, whether physical or emotional, may be the only manifestations of the intensity of the undifferentiation. The underfunctioning one is grateful for the care and attention, and the overfunctioning one does not complain. Divorce is almost impossible in these marriages unless the dysfunction is also mixed with marital conflict. There have been families in which the overfunctioning one has died unexpectedly and the disabled one has miraculously regained functioning. If there is a subsequent marriage, it follows the pattern of the previous one.

IMPAIRMENT OF ONE OR MORE CHILDREN

This is the pattern in which parents operate as a we-ness to project the undifferentiation onto one or more children. This mechanism is so important in the total human problem it has been described as a separate concept—the family projection process.

There are two main variables that govern the intensity of this process in the nuclear family. The first is the degree of the emotional isolation, or cutoff, from the extended family, or from others important in the relationship system. I shall discuss this below. The second important variable has to do with the level of anxiety. Any symptom in the nuclear family, whether marital conflict, dysfunction in a spouse, or a symptom in a child, is less intense when anxiety is low and more intense when anxiety is high. Some of the most important family therapy efforts are directed at decreasing anxiety and opening the relationship cutoff.

FAMILY PROJECTION PROCESS

The process through which parental undifferentiation impairs one or more children operates within the father-mother-child triangle. It revolves around the mother, who is the key figure in reproduction and who is usually the principal caretaker for the infant. It results in primary emotional impairment of the child; or, it can superimpose itself on some defect or on some chronic physical illness or disability. It exists in all gradations of intensity, from those in which impairment is minimal to those in which the child is seriously impaired for life. The process is so universal it is present to some degree in all families.

A composite of families with moderately severe versions of the projection process will provide the best view of the way the process works. It is as if there were a definite amount of undifferentiation to be absorbed by marital conflict, sickness in a spouse, and projection onto the children. The amount absorbed in conflict or sickness in a spouse reduces the amount that will be directed to the children. There are a few families in which most of the undifferentiation goes into marital conflict, essentially none into sickness in a spouse, and relatively small amounts into the children. The most striking examples of this have been in families with autistic, or severely impaired, children in which there is little marital conflict, both spouses are healthy, and the full weight of the undifferentiation is directed toward a single, maximally impaired child. I have never seen a family in which there was not some projection onto a child. Most families use a combination of all three mechanisms. The more the problem shifts from one area to another, the less chance the process will be crippling in any single area.

There are definite patterns in the way the undifferentiation is distributed to children. It focuses first on one child. If the amount is too great for that child, the process will select others for lesser degrees of involvement. There are families in which the amount of undifferentiation is so great it can seriously impair most of the children, and leave one or two relatively out of the emotional process. There is so much disorder and chaos in these families, it is difficult to see the orderly steps in the process. I have never seen a family in which children were equally involved in the family emotional process. There may be some exceptions to the process described here, but the overall patterns are clear, and the theory accounts for the exceptions. There are suggestions about the way children become the objects of the projection process. On a simplistic level, it is related to the degree of emotional turn-on or turn-off (both equal in emotional systems terms) the mother feels for the child. This is an automatic emotional process that is not changed by acting the opposite. On a more specific level, it is related to the level of undifferentiation in the parents, the amount of anxiety at the time of conception and birth, and the orientation of the parents toward marriage and children.

The early thoughts about marriage and children are more prominent in the female than the male. They begin to take an orderly form before adolescence. A female who thinks primarily of the husband she will marry tends to have marriages in which she focuses most of her emotional energy on the husband, and he focuses on her, and symptoms tend to focus more on marital conflict and sickness in a spouse. Those females whose early thoughts and fantasies go more to the children they will have than the man they will marry, tend to become the mothers of impaired children. The process can be so intense in some women that the husband is incidental to the process. Spouses from lower levels of differentiation are less specific about marriage and children. The children selected for the family projection process are those conceived and born during stress in the mother's life; the first child, the oldest son or oldest daughter, an only child of either sex, one who is emotionally special to the mother, or one the mother believes to be special to the father. Among common special children are only children, an oldest child, a single child of one sex among several of the opposite sex, or a child with some defect. Also important are the special children who were fretful, colicky, rigid, and non-responsive to the mother from the beginning. The amount of initial special emotional investment in such children is great. A good percentage of mothers have a basic preference for boys or girls, depending upon their orientation in the family of origin. It is impossible for mothers to have equal emotional investment in any two children, no matter how much they try to protest equality for all.

On a more detailed level, the projection process revolves around maternal instinct, and the way anxiety permits it to function during reproduction and the infancy of the child. The father usually plays a support role to the projection process. He is sensitive to the mother's anxiety, and he tends to support her view and help her implement her anxious efforts at mothering. The process begins with anxiety in the mother. The child responds anxiously to the mother, which she misperceives as a problem in the child. The anxious parental effort goes into sympathetic, solicitous, overprotective energy, which is directed more by the mother's anxiety than the reality needs of the child. It establishes a pattern of infantilizing the child, who gradually becomes more impaired and more demanding. Once the process has started, it can be motivated either by anxiety in the mother, or anxiety in the child. In the average

situation there may be symptomatic episodes at stressful periods during childhood, which gradually increase to major symptoms during or after adolescence; intense emotional fusion between mother and child may exist, in which
the mother-child relationship remains in positive, symptom-free equilibrium
until the adolescent period, when the child attempts to function on his own.
At that point, the child's relationship with the mother, or with both parents,
can become negative and the child can develop severe symptoms. The more
intense forms of the mother-child fusion may remain relatively asymptomatic
until young adulthood, but the child can collapse in psychosis when he
attempts to function away from the parents.

The basic pattern of the family projection is the same, except for minor
variations in form and intensity, whether the eventual impairment in the child
is one that leads to serious lifelong dysfunction, or one that never develops
serious symptoms and is never diagnosed. The greatest number of people
impaired by the projection process are those who do less well with life and
who have lower levels of differentiation than their siblings, and who may go
for a few generations before producing a child who becomes seriously impaired symptomatically. This theory considers schizophrenia to be the product
of several generations of increasing symptomatic impairment, with lower and
lower levels of differentiation, until there is a generation that produces schizophrenia. In clinical work we have come to use the term *the triangled child*
to refer to the one who was the main focus of the family projection process.
Almost every family has one child who was more triangled than the others,
and whose life adjustment is less good than that of the others. In doing
multigenerational family histories, it is relatively easy to estimate the family
projection process and identify the triangled child by securing historical data
about the life adjustments of each sibling.

EMOTIONAL CUTOFF

This concept was added to the theory in 1975 after having been a poorly
defined extension of other concepts for several years. It was accorded the
status of a separate concept to include details not stated elsewhere, and to
have a separate concept for the emotional process between the generations.
The life pattern of cutoffs is determined by the way people handle their
unresolved emotional attachments to their parents. All people have some
degree of unresolved emotional attachment to their parents. The lower the
level of differentiation, the more intense the unresolved attachment. The
concept deals with the way people separate themselves from the past in order
to start their lives in the present generation. Much thought went into the
selection of a term to best describe this process of separation, isolation,

withdrawal, running away, or denying the importance of the parental family. However much *cutoff* may sound like informal slang, I could find no other term as accurate for describing the process. The therapeutic effort is to convert the cutoff into an orderly differentiation of a self from the extended family.

The degree of unresolved emotional attachment to the parents is equivalent to the degree of undifferentiation that must somehow be handled in the person's own life and in future generations. The unresolved attachment is handled by the intrapsychic process of denial and isolation of self while living close to the parents, or by physically running away, or by a combination of emotional isolation and physical distance. The more intense the cutoff with the past, the more likely the individual is to have an exaggerated version of his parental family problem in his own marriage, and the more likely his own children are to do a more intense cutoff with him in the next generation. There are many variations in the intensity of this basic process and in the way the cutoff is handled.

The person who runs away from his family of origin is as emotionally dependent as the one who never leaves home. They both need emotional closeness, but they are allergic to it. The one who remains on the scene and handles the attachment by intrapsychic mechanisms tends to have some degree of supportive contact with the parents, to have a less intense overall process, and to develop more internalized symptoms under stress, such as physical illness and depression. An exaggerated version of this is the severely impaired person who can collapse into psychosis, isolating himself intrapsychically while living with the parents. The one who runs away geographically is more inclined to impulsive behavior. He tends to see the problem as being in the parents and running away as a method of gaining independence from the parents. The more intense the cutoff, the more he is vulnerable to duplicating the pattern with the parents with the first available other person. He can get into an impulsive marriage. When problems develop in the marriage, he tends also to run away from that. He can continue through multiple marriages, and finally resort to more temporary living-together relationships. Exaggerated versions of this occur in relationship nomads, vagabonds, and hermits, who either have superficial relationships or give up and live alone.

In recent years, as the age-old cutoff process has become more pronounced as a result of societal anxiety, the emotional cutoff has been called "the generation gap." The higher the level of anxiety, the greater the degree of generation gap in poorly differentiated people. There has been an increase in the percentage of those who run away, and who become involved in living-together arrangements and communal living situations. These substitute families are very unstable. They are made up of people who ran away from their own families; when tension builds up in the substitute family, they cut off from that and move on to another. Under the best conditions, the substitute family and outside relationships are poor substitutes for the original family.

There are all gradations of emotional cutoff. An average family situation in our society today is one in which people maintain a distant and formal relationship with the families of origin, returning home for duty visits at infrequent intervals. The more a nuclear family maintains some kind of viable emotional contact with the past generations, the more orderly and asymptomatic the life process in both generations. Compare two families with identical levels of differentiation. One family remains in contact with the parental family and remains relatively free of symptoms for life, and the level of differentiation does not change much in the next generation. The other family cuts off with the past, develops symptoms and dysfunction, and a lower level of differentiation in the succeeding generation. The symptomatic nuclear family that is emotionally cut off from the family of origin can get into cyclical, long-term family therapy without improvement. If one or both parents can re-establish emotional contact with their families of origin, the anxiety level subsides, the symptoms become softer and more manageable, and family therapy can become productive. Merely telling a family to go back to the family of origin is of little help. Some people are very anxious about returning to their families. Without systems coaching, they can make the problem worse. Others can return, continue the same emotional isolation they used when they were in the family, and accomplish nothing. Techniques for helping families to re-establish contact have been sufficiently developed so that it is now a family therapy method in its own right. This differentiation of a self in one's own family has been presented in another paper (Bowen, 1974b). It is based on the experience that a spouse who can do a reasonable job at differentiating self in his or her parental family will have accomplished more than he or she would if involved in regular family therapy with the other spouse.

MULTIGENERATIONAL TRANSMISSION PROCESS

The family projection process continues through multiple generations. In any nuclear family there is one child who is the primary object of the family projection process. This child emerges with a lower level of differentiation than the parents and does less well in life. Other children, who are minimally involved with the parents, emerge with about the same levels of differentiation as the parents. Those who grow up relatively outside the family emotional process develop better levels of differentiation than their parents. If we follow the most impaired child through successive generations, we will see one line of descent producing individuals with lower and lower levels of differentiation. The process may go rapidly for a few generations, remain static for a generation or so, and then speed up again. Once I said it required at least three generations to produce a child so impaired he would collapse into schizophrenia. That was based on the notion of a starting point with fairly good surface functioning and a process that proceeded at maximum speed through the generations. However, since I now know the process can slow down or stay static for a generation or two, I would now say that it would require perhaps eight to ten generations to produce the level of impairment that goes with schizophrenia. This is the process that produces the poorly functioning people who make up most of the lower social classes. If a family encounters severe stress in perhaps the fifth or sixth generation of a ten-generation process, it may produce a social failure who is less impaired than the schizophrenic person. The degree of impairment in schizophrenia comes from those poorly differentiated people who are able to keep the relationship system in relatively symptom-free equilibrium for several more generations.

If we follow the line through the children who emerge with about the same levels of differentiation, we see a remarkable consistency of family functioning through the generations. History speaks of family traditions, family ideals, and so on. If we follow the multigenerational lineage of those who emerge with higher levels of differentiation, we will see a line of highly functioning and very successful people. A family at the highest level of differentiation can have one child who starts down the scale. A family at the lowest level can have a child who starts up the scale. Many years ago I described schizophrenia from a phenomenological standpoint as a natural process that helps to keep the race strong. The weakness from the family is fixed in one person who is less likely to marry and reproduce and more likely to die young.

SIBLING POSITION

This concept is an adaptation of Toman's work on the personality profiles of each sibling position. His first book in 1961 was remarkably close to the direction of some of my research. He had worked from an individual frame of reference and only with normal families, but he had ordered his data in a way no one else had done, and it was easy to incorporate them into the differentiation of self and the family projection process. Toman's basic thesis is that important personality characteristics fit with the sibling position in which a person grew up. His 10 basic sibling profiles automatically permit one to know the profile of any sibling position, and, *all things being equal,* to have a whole body of presumptive knowledge about anyone. His ideas provide a new dimension toward understanding how a particular child is chosen as the object of the family projection process. The degree to which a personality profile fits with normal provides a way to understand the level of differentiation and the direction of the projection process from generation to generation. For instance, if an oldest turns out to be more like a youngest, that is strong evidence that he was the most triangled child. If an oldest is an autocrat, that is strong evidence of a moderate level of impaired functioning. An oldest who functions calmly and responsibly is good evidence of a better level of differentiation. The use of Toman's profiles, together with differentiation and projection, makes it possible to assemble reliable presumptive personality profiles on people in past generations on whom verifiable facts are missing. Knowing the degree to which people fit the profiles provides predictive data about how spouses will handle the mix in a marriage, and how they will handle their effort in family therapy. Based on my research and therapy, I believe that no single piece of data is more important than knowing the sibling position of people in the present and past generations.

SOCIETAL REGRESSION

I have always been interested in understanding societal problems, but the tendency of psychiatrists and social scientists to make sweeping generalizations from a minimal number of specific facts resulted in my interest's remaining peripheral except for a personal reading. Family research added a new order of facts about human functioning, but I avoided the seductive urge to generalize from them. In the 1960s, there was growing evidence that the emotional problem in society was similar to the emotional problem in the family. The triangle exists in all relationships, and that was a small clue. In 1972, the Environmental Protection Agency invited me to do a paper on human reaction to environmental problems. I anticipated doing a paper on assorted facts acquired from years of experience with people relating to larger societal issues. That paper led to a year of research, and a return to old files for confirmation of data. Finally, I identified a link between the family and society that was sufficiently trustworthy for me to extend the basic theory about the family into the larger societal arena. The link had to do, first, with the delinquent teenaged youngster, who is a responsibility for both the parents and society, and second, with changes in the way the parents and the agents of society deal with the same problem.

It has not yet been possible to write this up in detail, but the overall structure of the concept was presented in outline form (1974a). The concept states that when a family is subjected to chronic, sustained anxiety, the family begins to lose contact with its intellectually determined principles, and to resort more and more to emotionally determined decisions to allay the anxiety of the moment. The results of the process are symptoms and eventually regression to a lower level of functioning. The societal concept postulates that the same process is evolving in society; that we are in a period of increasing chronic societal anxiety; that society responds to this with emotionally determined decisions to allay the anxiety of the moment; that this results in symptoms of dysfunction; that the efforts to relieve the symptoms result in more emotional band-aid legislation, which increases the problem; and that the cycle keeps repeating, just as the family goes through similar cycles to the states we call emotional illness. In the early years of my interest in societal problems, I thought that all societies go through good periods and bad, that they always go through a rise and fall, and that the cyclical phenomenon of the 1950s was part of another cycle. As societal unrest appeared to move toward intensification of the problems through the 1960s, I began to look for ways to explain the chronic anxiety. I was looking for concepts consistent with man as an instinctual being, rather than man as a social being. My current postulation considers the chronic anxiety as the product of the population explosion, decreasing supplies of food and raw materials necessary to maintain man's way of life on earth, and the pollution of the environment, which is slowly threatening the balance of life necessary for human survival.

This concept proceeds in logical steps from the family to larger and larger social groups, to the total of society [see Bowen, 1978].

SUMMARY

Most members of the mental health professions have little interest in, or awareness of, theory about the nature of emotional illness. I have developed a family systems theory of emotional functioning. For some 10 years I have been trying to present the theory as clearly as it is possible for me to define it. Only a small percentage of people are really able to hear it. In the early years I considered most of the problem to be my difficulty in communicating the ideas in ways others could hear. As the years have passed, I have come to consider that the major difficulty is the inability of people to detach themselves sufficiently from conventional theory to be able to hear systems concepts. In each presentation I learn a little more about which points people fail to hear. I have devoted much of this presentation to some broad background issues which I hoped would set the stage for people to hear more than they had heard before, and to clarify some of the issues between my family systems theory and general systems theory.

I believe that some systems theory will provide a bright new promise for comprehending emotional illness. Whether the ultimate systems theory is this one or another remains to be seen. After some 20 years of experience with this theory, I have great confidence in it. It does mean that the therapist must keep the whole spectrum of variables in his head at once; but, after some experience, knowing the variables well enough to know when one is out of balance becomes automatic.

16

INTRODUCTION

Identity Conflicts in Adoptees,
by Arthur D. Sorosky, Annette Baran,
and Reuben Pannor

Although the frequency seems to vary considerably, it is generally accepted that adopted children are overrepresented in the caseloads of child psychiatric clinics (Offord, Apointe, and Cross, 1969). According to Kirk (1964), approximately 2.5% of the children in the United States are adopted (this statistic includes those instances in which kinship ties exist, which are estimated to constitute approximately half of all adoptions). But simply counting the number of adopted children in the child psychiatric clinic population may be misleading. Consideration must be given to variables such as the adoptive parents' prior contacts with social and other helping agencies, race, social status, and the frequency of adoption in the immediately surrounding community. When this is done, it is estimated that the proportion of adopted children in child psychiatric clinics is somewhere between one and one-half and five and one-half times that of adopted children in the community (J. D. Goodman, Silberstein, and Mandell, 1963; Simon and Senturia, 1966). This figure represents a much lower estimate than Schechter's (1960) 100:1 ratio (Legg, 1977).

As Bohman (1972) notes, adoption affords society a potent instrument for social therapy in which the responsibility of placing children calls for the highest level of knowledge and decision making. Too few representative studies have been undertaken, however, to shed light on the various aspects of adoption. Most studies of adoption focus on small clinical populations in which the basis for selection is not specified. Nevertheless, there appears to be some consensus on a few points.

1. Placement of the child should be undertaken as early as possible, although there is still disagreement as to whether this means placement prior to the third or fourth weeks of life rather than merely during the first or even the second year (Kellner, 1967).

2. Environmental factors appear to be more important than genetic factors in the development of adopted children's general character, whereas the greater part of the variation in intelligence is attributable to genetic factors (Leahy, 1935).

3. The personalities of the adoptive parents and their mutual relationship have the greatest bearing on the outcome of an adoption, while their ages, income, socioeconomic status, and education appear to be of secondary importance (Wetner et al., 1963). But little research has been done regarding the influence of genetic, prenatal, and perinatal factors on the outcome of adoption, and not much is known about how society's attitudes toward adoption affect the adoptive family.

One aspect of societal attitudes is now exploding into prominence via the controversy over the sealed adoption record. Courts, social agencies, and psychiatric clinics for adolescents and adults have long been approached by adoptees, independent of their adoptive parents, who feel haunted by a compelling need to find out about their biological heritage. Professionals have often ascribed these strong feelings to neurotic conflicts, acting out, rebelliousness, and the like. To some extent, these descriptive phrases may represent a valid assessment, but it is sobering to realize that such judgments were made without coherent integrating concepts of the identity conflict of adoptees. The article reprinted below attempts such a formulation. It is based on a synthetic review of the literature in the light of the authors' experience with adopted adolescents and young adults trying to cope with "identity lacunae" by finding out more about their genealogy. The authors then suggest guidelines for future social policy.

Although individual considerations are paramount, assessment of the adopted person's need to open the adoption record will inevitably be influenced by the professional's perception of social policy. The sealed adoption record was instituted to protect all sides of the adoptive triangle: to guard the biological parents' privacy, to keep the adoptive parents free from intrusion by the biological parents, and to shield the adopted child from interference in his or her attachment to the adoptive parents and allegedly to protect the child from the "awful truth."

The adoptive status of Moses and Esther in the Bible and Oedipus and Hercules in mythology indicate that adoption has probably been universally practiced throughout history. Current practices, however, tend to mute the actual history of adoption policy. English common law never recognized adoption. Not until 1958 were British adoptees accorded legal status in the family equivalent to that of a natural-born child. Although these safeguards appeared in American statutes a century earlier, influenced by French and Spanish civil law (Legg, 1977), only within the past three decades has confidentiality of the original birth certificate been written into law in most states. This is not to say that adopted children have not always been exposed to all sorts of fabrications, whether about their adopted status or the "death" of their biological parents. Indeed, not long ago adoption agencies advised adoptive parents not to disclose to the child that he or she was not their biological offspring. This policy was modified during the 1940s, but the practice of matching for race, religion, physical features, personality, and intelligence continued until the past decade. At that point, because of improved contraception, greater access to abortion, and the increased tendency of unwed mothers to raise their own children, fewer healthy newborns were available for adoption. As a result, couples motivated to adopt are increasingly accepting the difficult-to-place children, those who are older, handicapped, and of different racial backgrounds.

As indicated above, the sealed adoption record is not a well-established tradition, as so many of us assume. In fact, in Finland, Israel, Scotland, and Sweden adult adoptees have ready access to this information. The extent to which current policy protects all three sides of the triangle should be the subject of careful investigation. To shed light on this question, Sorosky, Baran, and Pannor (1976) placed requests in the lay press for volunteers to share their reactions to reunions with their birth parents. Forty-five of the 50 adult adoptees who responded experienced the reunion as satisfying; they felt it effected a sense of closure, resolved genealogical concerns, and decreased identity conflicts. Forty-one of the birth parents reacted positively, but five experienced the reunion adversely. In contrast, the third side of the adoptive triangle experienced much more difficulty. Eighteen of the adoptive parents were understanding and cooperative, ten were described as mildly upset, and five were quite hurt. (The remaining adoptive parents were either dead or had not been informed of the reunion in order to spare them anticipated hurt.) Although 50% of the adoptees developed meaningful relationships with their biological parents following reunion, it should be emphasized that poor relationship with the adoptive parents was not a motivation for seeking the contact. It was of interest, though, that 30 of the 50 had been raised as only children. In addition, disclosure of adoption was often reported as "disruptive" or "late": 16 of the volunteers learned of their adoption from sources other than their parents and the median age of disclosure for the entire group was seven.

This study has evoked considerable controversy. Jerome D. Goodman (1977) and Stephen Blau (1977) point out that not only were the conclusions based on biased sampling (i.e., volunteers who responded to advertisements), but that no attempts were made to control for psychopathology. Goodman contends that in his own work a significantly higher incidence of running away was correlated with the child's being given information about his or biological origins. He even suggests withholding facts about biological parentage. Although he believes that generally children should be told of their adoption, he argues that too often they are "overtold" and unnecessarily burdened at crucial developmental stages with the fact that they were "abandoned" by biological parents. In response, Sorosky (1977) has pointed out that the Child Welfare League of America originally shared these views, but in May 1976 they issued an interim policy statement instructing member agencies to give adoptees information about their biological parentage ("short of names") and to tell the adoptive parents of this policy change and to assist them in dealing with it. The real issue, Sorosky asserts, is not *whether* a child is told about his or her biological parents but *how*. If the adoptive parents have unresolved feelings of inadequacy secondary to infertility or are uneasy about a child's illlegitimacy, these feelings may affect the manner of disclosure. Although Sorosky opposes providing identifying information to adolescent adoptees because this would complicate the resolution of the typical identity conflicts of that stage, he believes most interested adopted teenagers would be reassured to know that this information will be available to them when they reach adulthood.

Increasingly, these views are shared by adoption workers. Burgess (1977), for instance, highlights the prevailing feeling of rejection experienced by many adoptees, who wonder: "Why did my mother give me away?" Burgess compares the plight of amnesia victims with the "identity confusion" experienced by adoptees in adolescence and young adulthood, in the face of their incomplete sense of genealogical connection. Both are searching for "lost identities," yet society has very different attitudes toward them. Like many other adoption workers, Burgess advocates changing current laws so that mature adoptees can have access to their birth records on request. In advocating this position, she asserts that adoption agencies have confused their priorities by honoring the desires for confidentiality of the adoptive parents and the birth parents over the needs of the adopted person. Burgess makes the telling point that "the principal client"—the adoptee—is the only one who has no voice in the arrangements—past or present.

Sorosky believes that most adoptees who first find out in later life about their adoptive states feel totally shaken. His point is illustrated by the moving story of a child psychiatrist (Livingston, 1977). After conducting a workshop for professionals on the "dual-identity" problems generated by the secrecy surrounding adoption, he was discussing with his cousin the strength of a child's need to search for natural parents. He asserted that someday he would help his own adopted son do so because he was convinced it would not alter their basic loving relationship. At this point, the cousin informed him that he himself had been adopted. The fears, questions, and uncertainties he went through during his own driven search for his biological mother are both unsettling and reassuring.

The appropriate age to inform children of their adoption remains a focus of controversy. The contention that children should be told as soon as they can understand, in order to avoid the potentially devastating effects of their being told by someone other than their adoptive parents, has been challenged by Peller (1963), Schechter et al. (1964), and Wieder (1977). Wieder makes the point that being told of adoption will be upsetting at any age. He urges that "upset" be distinguished from the potentially "traumatizing" effect of disclosure at a very young age, when it may prove disruptive to ego development.

Although there is much ferment and flux, it remains clear that adoption is not a single event, but a lifelong process that requires both continuing support and more study—including data about successful adoptions.

16

Identity Conflicts in Adoptees

ARTHUR D. SOROSKY, ANNETTE BARAN, and REUBEN PANNOR

Adoption as a social phenomenon has always been a center of emotional controversy and subjected to the prejudices of vested interest groups. The theoretical framework has been repeatedly assaulted by contradictory data and research findings. The vulnerability of the adoptee to stress and the subsequent development of psychological problems have been emphasized by some authors and disputed by others. Most of the previous studies on the adoptee have concentrated on the childhood and early adolescent years. In this paper we would like to call attention to the late adolescent and young adult stage of psychosocial development which we feel is a period of special predilection for the development of identity problems in adopted individuals.

Erikson pointed out that the problem of identity is that it must establish a continuity between society's past and future and that adolescence in all its vulnerability and power is the critical transformer of both (Evans, 1967). The American Academy of Pediatrics Committee on Adoptions (1971) concluded that determining identity is a difficult-enough process for someone brought up by his natural parents; it is even more complex for the adopted individual whose ancestry is unknown to him. Both Tec at al. (1967) and Frisk (1964) described examples of specific identity conflicts developing in adolescent adoptees.

In both psychiatric settings and adoption agencies, we have been encountering a number of adopted adolescents and young adults struggling with identity problems and an urgent need to find out more about their genealogical background. An increasing number of adult adoptees have been insisting that they have a constitutionally based civil right to have access to their "sealed" birth records, which would, in effect, reveal the true identity of their birth

First published in *American Journal of Orthopsychiatry*, 45:18–27, 1975. Copyright © American Orthopsychiatric Association, Inc. Reproduced by permission.

parents (Prager and Rothstein, 1973). Two activist organizations—the Orphan Voyage and the Adoptees' Liberty Movement Association (ALMA), under the direction of Jean M. Paton (1954, 1960, 1968, 1971) and Florence L. Fisher (1972, 1973) respectively—have become active in arranging reunions between adoptees and their birth parents, as well as instigating test cases in the courts in the hope of bringing about a change in the present adoption laws.

REVIEW OF THE LITERATURE

As part of an investigation into the outcome of reunions between adoptees and their birth parents, we have undertaken a thorough review of the existing literature pertaining to the occurrence of genealogical concerns and the development of identity conflicts in adopted individuals. In order to facilitate matters, we have organized the material into four categories of psychological difficulties: (1) disturbances in early object relations, (2) complications in the resolution of the Oedipus complex, (3) prolongation of the "family romance" fantasy, and (4) "genealogical bewilderment."

DISTURBANCES IN EARLY OBJECT RELATIONS

Many researchers have been able to demonstrate that the severity of behavioral and emotional problems in adopted children and adolescents can be directly correlated with the age of adoption placement and the extent of early maternal deprivation (Humphrey and Ounsted, 1963; McWhinnie, 1967, 1970; Offord et al., 1969; Pringle, 1967; Witmer et al., 1963). It follows that these same troubled youngsters will continue to have difficulties, including identity problems, in late adolescence and adulthood as a result of the traumatic scars remaining from their disturbed early object relations.

In situations where the adoption occurred at a young age, without any overt deprivation, it is somewhat more difficult to detect the subtle disturbances that might have taken place in the early relationship of the infant adoptee and his adoptive mother. In the light of our awareness, however, of the adoptive mother's susceptibility to feelings of unworthiness and insecurity because of infertility, it would appear that there would be a greater likelihood of problems developing than in the natural mother-child dyad (Humphrey and Ounsted, 1963; Pringle, 1967). Unfortunately, studies based on direct observation of the early adoptive interaction have never been done.

Goldstein, A. Freud, and Solnit (1973) pointed out that the waiting period of adoption is often a period of insecurity and uncertainty for the parents. It is not, as it ought to be, a full opportunity for developing secure and stable attachments. Reeves (1971) suggested that the absence of a prior biological tie between the mother and child during the infant's earliest maturation makes for an inherently labile primary identification, which may break down and lead to an experience, for both the mother and child, of premature disillusionment. Both Schwartz (1970) and Clothier (1942) asserted that the probability of conflicts in identification with the adoptive parents is likely to be increased for these children, because the unknown parental figure may continue to exist as a possible identification model.

COMPLICATIONS IN THE RESOLUTION OF THE OEDIPUS COMPLEX

Easson (1973) postulated that the adopted adolescent has difficulty in three areas of emotional growth which can affect the development of a stable adult sexual identity: (1) the process of emancipation of the adopted adolescent from the adoptive parents, (2) the resolution of incestuous strivings in the adoption relationship, and (3) the final identification with the parent of the same sex and the establishment of a stable growth-productive relationship with the parent of the opposite sex.

Among other authors, Sants (1965) and Tec et al. (1967) viewed the resolution of the Oedipus complex to be particularly difficult for the adoptee. Furthermore, Schechter (1960) and Peller (1961, 1963) advised postponing the revelation of the child's adoptive status until after the resolution of the oedipal conflict to avoid complicating this stage of psychosexual development.

PROLONGATION OF THE FAMILY ROMANCE FANTASY

Freud (1909) proposed that as a part of normal child development there are episodes of doubt for the child that he is, in fact, the natural child of his parents. This fantasy represents a brief state and is abandoned once the child accepts that he can love and hate the same individual. Conklin (1920) verified this theory after interviewing a number of eight- to twelve-year-old natural-born children, many of whom imagined themselves to be adopted. Clothier (1939, 1942, 1943) discussed the unusual dilemma of the adopted child, who in fact has two sets of parents. He cannot use the family romance as a "game," as the natural child can, because for him it is "real." The adopted child can accept as a reality, for example, the idea that he came from highly exalted or lowly debased parents.

Glatzer (1955) showed how the family romance fantasy is reinforced and prolonged in adopted children. Eiduson and Livermore (1952) viewed the family romance fantasy as being activated by a feeling of rejection from the adoptive mother, whereas Kohlsaat and Johnson (1954) saw the fantasy as being prolonged only in those adoptive situations where the parents put the children under a great deal of pressure. In contrast, Schwartz (1970) could find no indication of a fixation or prolongation of the family romance fantasy in adopted children. Furthermore, Lawton and Gross (1964) felt that an adopted child would have a greater tendency to enhance the image of the adoptive parents and not that of the natural parents, of whom he has had no direct experience.

Schechter (1960) pointed out how the adoptive child has a chance of splitting the images of his parents and attributing the good elements to one set and the bad to the other. The anxiety the child manifests often refers to the possibility of returning to his original parents or, having been given up once for undetermined reasons, that he may be given up again at some future time—also for undetermined, fantasied reasons. Simon and Senturia (1966) felt that the adoptee's identification with the "bad" biological parents is quite strong.

GENEALOGICAL BEWILDERMENT

Clothier (1943) stated that the trauma and severing of the individual from his racial antecedents lie at the core of what is peculiar to the psychology of the adopted child. She felt that the ego of the adopted child, in addition to all the normal demands made upon it, is called upon to compensate for the wound left by the loss of the biological mother. Kornitzer (1971) stated that the adolescent's identity formation is impaired because he has the knowledge that an essential part of himself, as it were, has been cut off and remains on the other side of the adoption barrier.

Frisk (1964) conceptualized that the lack of family background knowledge in the adoptee prevents the development of a healthy "genetic ego," which is then replaced by a "hereditary ghost." These issues become intensified during adolescence when heightened interests in sexuality make the adoptee more aware of how man and his characteristics are transmitted from generation to generation. When this "genetic ego" is obscure, one does not know what is passed on to the next generation. Furthermore, the knowledge that his natural parents were unable to look after him is interpreted by the adoptee as proof of his natural parents' inferiority, and gives rise to a fear of being handicapped himself by hereditary psychical abnormalities.

Wellisch (1952) called attention to the fact that a lack of knowledge of their real parents and ancestors can be a cause of maladjustment in children. Under normal circumstances, special attention is not paid to one's genealogy; it is usually accepted as a matter of fact. Sants (1965) elaborated further on these ideas and introduced the term *genealogical bewilderment*. He described a state of confusion and uncertainty developing in a child who either has no knowledge of his natural parents or only uncertain knowledge of them. Very often in adolescence the child will begin searching for clues, and in some cases will develop an obsession about his genealogical past. Sants showed how a state of genealogical bewilderment can lead to the development of poor self-esteem and a confused sense of identity. The adoptee is unable to incorporate known ancestors into the self-image and may develop a fear of unknowingly committing incest with blood relatives.

Schechter (1960) referred to a letter from P. W. Toussieng, which described a number of cases in which adopted children in adolescence started "roaming" around almost aimlessly, though sometimes they claimed to be intentionally seeking the fantasied "good, real parents." Toussieng (1962) later reinterpreted the "roaming" phenomenon as an acted-out search for stable, reliable objects and introjects that were never provided by elusive adoptive parents. He stated that if the parental figures clearly show that they view the presence of the adopted child as a narcissistic injury, as evidence that they themselves are "damaged," the child in trying to identify with such parents may well acquire shaky and defective introjects.

Frisk (1964) also described a restless wandering about by some adoptees, which he interpreted to be a symbolic search for the real parents, with the underlying purpose of discovering what their true character was. Some sought company in fundamentally different social groups, on a lower level than the rest of their family. This pursuit was "instinctive" and seemed to be an effort to find a group identity corresponding to the predestined group the child imagined he belonged to.

There continues to be controversy as to the extent of interest and curiosity that adoptees, in general, have about their genealogical background. Some authors contend that this concern is ubiquitous in all adoptees and is not a sign of emotional disturbance or family conflict (Kirk, 1964; Linde, 1967; McWhinnie, 1967; Pringle, 1967). Schechter et al. (1964) detected overt fantasies regarding natural parents in 45% of adoptees interviewed. Many adoption workers feel that the only reason the curiosity does not surface more readily in most adoptees is the concern about hurting the adoptive parents.

Other authors have shown that the curiosity is greatest in adoptive homes where there has been a strained relationship and difficulty in communicating openly about the adoption situation (Clothier, 1942; Hubbard, 1947; Jaffe and Fanshel, 1970; Lemon, 1959; E. Smith, 1963; Triseliotis, 1973). Kornitzer (1971) stated that the more mysterious the adoptive parents make things for the child, the more he will resort to fantasy. H. Lewis (1965) felt that the reason many adolescent adoptees become so dreamy and inaccessible is that they become preoccupied with fantasies about their forebears. Rogers

(1969) described the turmoil felt by the adopted adolescent whose natural parents have been "hidden" from him. She postulated that this may lead to an intense curiosity and preoccupation about the riddle of life—about its beginning, ending, and, in some, even about its purpose.

Others have suggested that an adoptee's preoccupation with the past may merely be a reflection of his own unique personality makeup. Some persons are basically more curious and inquisitive, and their genealogical concerns may have little to do with their adoptive status (Clothier, 1942). Senn and Solnit (1968), on the other hand, maintained that fantasies about the birth parents are usually built from disguised impressions and wishes about the adoptive parents, and have little to do with the birth parents per se.

From a review of previous studies, and in our own observations, we have noted that there are certain developmental stages or events that intensify the adopted person's curiosity and interest in acquiring further information about his genealogical background. The pubescent young adolescent becomes aware of the biological link of the generations and begins to visualize himself as part of the chain that stretches from the present into the remote past (Rautman, 1959). Late adolescence and young adulthood is the period of intensified identity concerns and a time when the feelings about adoption become more intense and questions about the past increase.

Attaining adult legal status also accelerates the genealogical concerns (Dalsheimer, 1973; Linde, 1967). Pre-engagement or a pending marriage reawakens the desire for information to a surprising intensity (Rautman, 1959; Triseliotis, 1973). Interests can also be heightened by involvement with such experiences as taking out life insurance (E. Smith, 1963), requesting a birth certificate (Lemon, 1959), illness, civil service exams, and property disputes (Triseliotis, 1973).

Pregnancy elicits concerns regarding unknown hereditary weaknesses (Rautman, 1959; Triseliotis, 1973). Death of one or both adoptive parents creates a feeling of loss or relieves the burden of concern and guilt about hurting the adoptive parents (Lemon, 1959; Triseliotis, 1973). Separation or divorce triggers feelings of rejection and abandonment, with an increased interest in past ties (Triseliotis, 1973). The "crisis" of middle age is felt by some adoptees to be a last opportunity to do something for the birth mother, who would now be elderly and perhaps in need of some kind of support (Triseliotis, 1973). Lastly, the approach of old age may bring about a final yearning for knowledge denied previously (Rautman, 1959).

Some adoptees develop a particularly urgent need to find out more about their birth parents, and in some cases develop an obsessive urge to search for them. Paton (1954) reported that half of her sample of 40 adult adoptees had made some attempt to search for their natural parents at some time or another. Lemon (1959) cited a few cases of adult adoptees who were reunited with their birth parents, but she did not report on the outcome. She characterized the adoptees seeking reunion as suffering from intense feelings of separation. Simon and Senturia (1966) saw the fantasy of reunion with the birth parents as an effort to deal with depression that grows out of fantasies about abandonment. Hubbard (1947) warned that when a reunion is agreed upon by both parties, the adoptee must be warned of the possible conflict between his imaginary picture of his unknown parents and the reality.

Triseliotis (1973) pointed out that, because of personality or other special factors, it is very possible that for some adoptees no amount of information or counseling will deter them from their goal of meeting the natural parent. They may see such a meeting as the only solution to their problems. E. Smith (1963) stressed the need for the adoption agency to serve as a protective and supportive mediator, if both parties are determined to have a reunion. It is of interest that, in a recent survey in England, 65% of adoptive parents questioned felt that the adoptee should have access to his birth certificate after age 18. They seemed more concerned about the welfare of the birth mother than their own feelings of rejection by the child (Seglow, Pringle, and Wedge, 1972).

In Scotland, any adopted person over the age of 17 can write or visit the Register House in Edinburgh and, on production of evidence about himself, ask for a copy of his original birth certificate. Triseliotis (1973) studied 70 adult adoptees who made such requests over a two-year period. As might be expected, he found that the greater the dissatisfaction with the adoptive family relationship and with themselves, the greater the possibility that they would now be seeking a reunion with the birth parents; whereas the better the image of themselves and of their adoptive parents, the greater the likelihood that they were merely seeking background information. Eighty percent of the group found the experience personally beneficial. They now had something tangible upon which to base their general outlook and feelings about their genealogical background.

DISCUSSION

In reviewing the literature, we were surprised to find that in spite of multiple references to identity conflicts in adoptees, no one had previously attempted to organize and integrate these ideas. Most of the impressions cited in the articles were theoretical formulations based on clinical observations of a handful of cases. Research in the field of adoption has quite obviously been hampered by the privacy that necessarily surrounds such a highly personal and intimate undertaking.

We have had the opportunity to interview in depth a large number of adoptees who are searching for their birth parents or have already accomplished a reunion. Our findings would tend to validate the impressions garnered from the literature review that adoptees are more vulnerable than the population at large to the development of identity problems in late adolescence and young adulthood because of the greater likelihood of encountering difficulties in the working through of the psychosexual, psychosocial, and psychohistorical aspects of personality development. In certain of these cases, the conflicts manifest themselves as a preoccupation with genealogical concerns and a desire to make contact with the birth parents. It is conceivable that, if it were not for the fear of hurting the adoptive parents or the reluctance to intrude upon the lives of the birth parents, these searches and reunions might be even more prevalent.

Many adoptees are preoccupied with existential concerns and a feeling of isolation and alienation due to the break in the continuity of life-through-the-generations that their adoption represents. For some, the existing block to the past may create a feeling that there is a block to the future as well. The adoptee's identity formation must be viewed within the context of the "life cycle," in which birth and death are closely linked unconsciously. This becomes evident when we observe how frequently marriage, the birth of the adoptee's first child, or the death of his adoptive parent triggers an even greater sense of genealogical bewilderment and a desire to search for the birth relatives.

This is not to say that there aren't adoptees who have an obsessive need to search for their birth parents because of neurotic problems or secondary to an emotionally barren relationship with their adoptive parents. Some of these persons are perpetual searchers, always stopping short of a reunion. It is the search itself, and the associated fantasies, which is the significant process that serves to hold these persons together. It would appear that these individuals would almost prefer to live with their fantasies, a prolongation of the classic family romance theme, rather than face reality with a possibly disillusioning reunion with the birth parent. The obsessive preoccupation serves to repress from consciousness feelings of profound loneliness and depression.

It is also important to distinguish, from these other situations, a special form of quasi-searching, in which the adolescent adoptee goes through a period of threatening his parents with the idea of going off and searching for his birth parents. This is simply a typical example of adolescent acting out, no different from the nonadoptee's threatening to run away or move into his own apartment. However, adoptive parents are especially vulnerable to such threats and often overreact with intense fear or anger, which only serves to reinforce their youngster's manipulative powers.

Adoptive parents are generally very insecure and uncomfortable when it comes to dealing with their child's conception and hereditary background.

Any interest shown by the adoptee in meeting the birth relatives is viewed by the adoptive parents as an indication of their personal failure as parents or as a sign of ingratitude on the part of their children. Their fear of being abandoned by the adopted child seems to relate to old unresolved feelings of separation and loss associated with infertility and their resulting childless state. It is difficult for adoptive parents to dissociate themselves and to view their children's genealogical concerns as stemming from personal identity conflicts associated with the unique psychological experience of adoption.

It has been generally assumed that the birth parents wish to suppress the memories of the pregnancy and make a life anew for themselves. This may not always be the case, however; many birth mothers inquire about their children's welfare, from time to time, at the agencies that handled the original adoption arrangements. We have received a large number of letters from birth mothers who learned about our research efforts and offered to share their feelings with us. In general, they expressed a desire to share current information about themselves with their children and to receive periodic reports on their children's welfare. As a group, they seemed responsive to their children's needs and a majority would be agreeable to a reunion if it would be beneficial to the adoptee. Most of them expressed a reluctance to intrude upon or disrupt the lives of their children or the adoptive parents.

Adoption agencies have contributed to the confusion by assuming the role of protector, in which capacity they have become watchmen and censors of the truth. The results have often been negative, largely because the information given out by adoption agencies has been recognized as shadowy, unreal, and, therefore, unsatisfying to the adoptee. Withheld data does not protect adoptees, but instead gives them the feeling that full information would reveal "awful truths."

The aura of secrecy has also been more of a burden than a protection to adoptive parents. On the one hand, adoption agencies have insisted that adoptees be told early and clearly about their adoption. Yet, on the other hand, little help has been provided to adoptive parents in dealing with the complicated feelings arising out of their adoptee's dual identity, nor have they been educated to understand and to dissociate themselves personally from their child's genealogical concerns and identity.

The time has come for adoption agencies to establish programs and to set up procedures to meet these challenges. The agency should begin by accepting the adult adoptee as a full client, who has the right to complete information and to the cooperation of the agency. The role of the agency as intermediary among adoptee, birth parents, and adoptive parents is a most important one. It should be considered in a new, more creative way.

17

INTRODUCTION

Parent-Child Separation:
Psychological Effects on the Children,
by Michael Rutter

Caldwell (1970) credits the reports by Spitz (1945b, 1946b) with launching what she designates the "maternal deprivation decade." But a year before Spitz's first report, Bowlby (1944) published the landmark paper that led to his book *Forty-Four Juvenile Thieves* (1946). In these publications Bowlby pointed to early maternal deprivation as affecting the delinquent's personality in a way that was indistinguishable from "psychopathy," which referred to an assumed constitutional defect. Bowlby's subsequent World Health Organization monograph (1951) headlined the importance for mental health of the emotional relationship between mother and infant in a persuasive summary of the existing literature. This historical link between maternal deprivation and antisocial behavior is considered in the chapter below by Rutter. Although its title highlights the psychological effects on children of all types of separation from their parents, the paper primarily addresses the relationship of separation to antisocial behavior.

It is reprinted here for several reasons. First, it raises compelling questions about that historical link. These questions stem from the epidemiological method which Rutter and his colleagues have applied to a range of vital issues in child psychiatry. Not only does the thrust of this report differ from Bowlby's pioneering work, it also contrasts markedly with Bowlby's (1961a) Adolf Meyer lecture on the implications for psychiatry of what he then called childhood mourning. (Bowlby's lecture is reprinted in Chapter 19 of *Childhood Psychopathology* and should be reviewed in connection with the following chapter.)

Studies of deprivation, such as those by Ainsworth (1962b), Caldwell (1967, 1970), the World Health Organization (1962), and Yarrow (1961, 1964), have highlighted the inherent methodological difficulties in identifying the truly salient elements of nutriment that are missing. They have also noted that the impact of an impoverished environment varies with the individual and species involved, as well as with the exact timing, degree, and duration of the deprivation and the availability and suitability of compensatory alternatives. The effects of deprivation are amazingly complicated and uneven in their distribution; indeed, the impact may become visible only in later developmental periods. It should also be emphasized that not all the effects of such deprivation are irreversible, nor do they merit being classified as defects or pathology. Although animal studies have not been thoroughly consistent (Griffin and Harlow, 1966), they do allow for an experimental model in which the independent variable can be manipulated and quantified. In contrast, studies involving humans of necessity entail a less rigorous, naturalistic approach. These studies have been accompanied by an appropriate broadening of the "independent variable" from maternal deprivation to the entire biopsychosocial spectrum. Nevertheless, this wider view in no way minimizes the significance of persuasive findings such as those reported by Décarie (1962). She compared the development of 30 institutionally reared infants during the first two years of life with that of 30 infants reared in their biological parents' homes and 30 infants placed in foster homes. The institutionally reared children lagged behind the other two groups. In addition, their developmental progress tended to be deviant and more variable. The children in foster homes, all of whom had experienced at least one separation and relocation, typically scored between the institutionally reared and the home-reared children.

Rutter's purpose is not to minimize the effect of separation and loss (highlighted in Wolfenstein's depth-psychological study in Chapter 18). He is more concerned with affording a perspective on certain aspects of observable data and emphasizing the difficulty in disentangling one type of deprivation from another. He warns that expert assertions regarding child-rearing practices (see Wolfenstein's [1953] review of trends in infant care, reprinted in Chapter 12 of *Childhood Psychopathology*) have been made in good faith, but after widespread application have often proved wrong. He not only makes a plea for demonstrable evidence, but also highlights the need for scientific rigor in research on child development and childhood psychopathology. More attention should be paid to the interaction of a wide range of factors—including those that protect the child from or ameliorate the potential effects of deprivation.

17

Parent-Child Separation: Psychological Effects on the Children

MICHAEL RUTTER

The importance of the family as a formative influence on a child's personality growth needs no arguing. Particularly in early childhood, it is the matrix within which the child develops, the area where his strongest emotional ties are formed, and the background against which his most intense personal life is enacted (A. J. Lewis, 1956). The family is the most intimate, one of the most important and most studied of all human groups and yet our knowledge of it remains rudimentary (Anthony and Koupernik, 1970).

Misconceptions, myths, and false knowledge on the effects of different patterns of child-rearing are rife. Generations of doctors, psychologists, nurses, and educators have pontificated on what parents need to do in order to bring up their children to be healthy and well-adjusted adults. Over the last 50 years we have been exhorted in the name of mental health to suppress masturbation, to feed children by the clock, and then to let them gratify their impulses in whatever way they wish (Stendler, 1950; Wolfenstein, 1953). However, the claims that these policies were necessary for normal emotional development were made in the absence of supporting evidence. Research findings have failed to show any significant effects stemming from patterns of feeding, time of weaning, type of toilet training, and the like (Caldwell, 1964), and the consequences of different patterns of discipline appear surprisingly slight (Becker, 1964).

Uninterrupted mother-child contact has also been the subject of firm claims. Bowlby (1946) suggested that "prolonged separation of a child from his mother (or mother substitute) during the first five years of his life stands

First published in *Journal of Child Psychology and Psychiatry*, 12: 233–260, 1971. Reprinted by permission.

foremost among the causes of delinquent character development and persistent misbehaviour.'' More recently, he reiterated that because of its long-term consequences a child should be separated from his parents only in exceptional circumstances (Bowlby, 1958a, 1958b). These statements are arguable (O'Connor, 1956), but they are cautious compared with those of some other writers. For example, Baers (1954) claimed that the normal growth of children is dependent on the mother's *full-time* occupation in the role of child-rearing and that "anything that hinders women in the fulfilment of this mission must be regarded as contrary to human progress.'' Similarly, a WHO Expert Committee (World Health Organization, 1951) concluded that the use of day nurseries and crèches inevitably caused "permanent damage to the emotional health of a future generation.'' It is perhaps noteworthy that assertions of this kind have mostly been made by men, and from the tenor of their comments we might well agree with Margaret Mead (1954) when she suggests that the campaign on the evils of mother-child separation is just another attempt by men to shackle women to the home. Nevertheless, it would be wrong to dismiss the argument on these grounds. If mother-child separation actually does lead to delinquent character formations and if care by fathers cannot compensate, then, however much the Women's Liberation Movement may protest, it is necessary for women to be tied to their children during the growing years.

But, first, we must know the facts. We are still not sufficiently in the habit of critically examining the facts about a question before arriving at our conclusions about it (Fletcher, 1966). Many of the statements I have quoted imply that we understand exactly what sort of upbringing a child needs and precisely which factors cause psychiatric disorder in children. But we do not, and it is our failure to *recognize* our ignorance that has led to these confident but contradictory claims. It is not the ignorance as such that is harmful, but rather our "knowing" so many things that are not true. Our theories on the importance of the family have multiplied and become increasingly certain long before we know what the facts are that the theories have to explain.

Of course, it would be quite futile to collect facts without a purpose. As Medawar (1967, 1969) has described so well, science consists of both discovery and proof, hypothesis and then careful testing to discriminate between alternative hypotheses.

My purpose in this paper is to illustrate this process with respect to family studies. In order to emphasize that research is the *act* of scientific enquiry, the *search* for truth and not the *statement* of knowledge, I am going to describe how my colleagues and I set out to answer just one simple question on the psychological effects of a child's separation from his mother. This question was chosen as one which has aroused great interest, which carries with it wide-ranging implications for community policies, and which, as my introduction has shown, has been the subject of very strong claims concerning its consequences.

The research method I shall use is that of epidemiology. Epidemiology is simply the study of the distribution of disorders in a community together with an examination of how the distribution varies with particular environmental circumstances. Originally this was a technique used with great success in the study of the cause of infectious diseases and other medical conditions (J. N. Morris, 1957; Terris, 1964). On the other hand, it can also be used to study the social causes of psychiatric disorder (Lin and Standley, 1962; Shepherd and Cooper, 1964) and the psychological effects of family influences (Christensen, 1969). That is the way I shall be using it here.

In order to give some "feel" of the successive steps of research, I shall confine more detailed descriptions to the work carried out over the last 10 years by my collaborators and myself. In doing this, I should emphasize that I am speaking as the representative of a research team, or more accurately several research teams, and many of the ideas I express stem as much from them as from me.

However, the validity of any observation is upheld only when it is repeated in other independent investigations. There are now many family studies using a variety of methods (Anthony and Koupernik, 1970; Christensen, 1964; Handel, 1967) and I shall try to point out which of our findings have been supported by other research.

MEASUREMENT OF FAMILY CHARACTERISTICS

The first task that faced us in our family studies was how to measure the family characteristics in which we were interested and how to assess children's psychological development. We wanted to determine what actually happened in the home with regard to different aspects of family life, and interview methods were developed for this purpose (G. W. Brown and Rutter, 1966; Rutter and Brown, 1966).

The interview served two quite distinct functions: (1) to obtain an accurate account of various events and happenings in the family (who put the children to bed, how often the parents played or talked with the children, how often they quarreled, and so forth), and (2) to provide a standard stimulus for eliciting emotions and attitudes (warmth, criticism, hostility, dissatisfaction, and the like). Different techniques were necessary for these two aspects of the interview.

As our interviewing techniques have been outlined previously (G. W. Brown and Rutter, 1966; Rutter and Brown, 1966), I shall merely state that some three years were spent in devising methods which could differentiate successfully between different aspects of family life. In particular, it was found essential to distinguish between what people did in the home and what they felt about it—between the acts and the emotions accompanying the acts. It was also necessary to measure emotions separately in relation to different members of the family. Quite often parents may be very warm toward one child and yet reject another. Finally, it was important to consider negative and positive feelings separately. Frequently, people have "mixed" feelings, both loving and hating someone at the same time. By making these distinctions, it proved possible to devise reasonably accurate measures of the central features of family life. Systematic investigation showed that the ratings had a satisfactory level of reliability and validity.

MEASUREMENT OF PSYCHIATRIC STATE

Similar care had to be taken in the measurement of the children's emotional and behavioral states. For this purpose, we used both questionnaire and interview measures of behavior in different situations. As with the family measures, the reliability and, as far as possible, the validity of the ratings were tested and found adequate (P. Graham and Rutter, 1968a; Rutter, 1967; Rutter and Graham, 1968; Rutter, Tizard, and Whitmore, 1970).

SAMPLES

The effects of different family influences on children's psychological development have been examined in several populations. For the purpose of this paper, I shall refer to only two—both of which, as it happens, were being studied primarily for other reasons. This has the advantage that we have a lot of information on additional aspects of children's circumstances and development which help to put the family findings into perspective.

The first group studied consisted of the families of nine- to twelve-year-old children living in a community of small towns—namely, the Isle of Wight. This study[1] investigated the educational, physical, and psychiatric handicaps in school-age children (Rutter, Graham, and Yule, 1970; Rutter, Tizard, and Whitmore, 1970). The second sample was a representative group of London families, in which one or both parents had been under psychiatric care (Rutter, 1970b). The study[2] was designed to investigate the difficulties

[1]This study was carried out in collaboration with Professor J. Tizard, Dr. K. Whitmore, Dr. P. Graham, Mr. W. Yule, and Mr. L. Rigley.

[2]This study was undertaken together with Mrs. S. George, Dr. P. Graham, Miss B. Osborn, Mr. D. Quinton, Miss O. Rowlands, Miss C. Tupling, and Mr. P. Ziffo.

faced by families when one parent became sick, with the aim of determining to what extent their needs were being met by the current provision of services. In both cases we have been extremely fortunate in the cooperation we have received and we are most grateful to the many families who have helped us in this work.

PARENT-CHILD SEPARATION

So much for the background. Let me now consider the findings on the effects of parent-child separation. If separation is such a serious hazard to mental health as is claimed, there are vital implications for public health policy and important opportunities for the prevention of psychiatric disorder. But are the claims true?

In order to answer that question, we first have to pose it more precisely. All children must separate from their parents at some time if they are to develop independent personalities. Furthermore, most youngsters experience some form of temporary separation from their parents during childhood. For example, Douglas et al. (1966) found that one in three children were separated from their parents for at least one week before the age of four and a half years. Obviously most of these turn out to be quite normal boys and girls, so the question is not "Should separation be allowed?" but rather "What sort of separation, at what age, for how long, and for what reason leads to psychological disturbance?" Also, we need to specify separation from which parent. Most emphasis has been placed on *mother*-child separation, the father being regarded as a relatively insignificant figure with respect to a child's personality development. Is this so? Finally, it has been suggested that it is necessary for children to have a relationship with a *single* mother-figure and that harm will come if mothering is divided among several people. So the apparently simple question "Is separation from their parents bad for children?" turns out to be quite complicated.

SHORT-TERM EFFECTS

In attempting to provide a solution to the problem, it may be appropriate to begin with the short-term effects of parent-child separation. This has been most studied in children admitted to hospital. Bowlby and his colleagues noted the frequency with which children were upset after admission and described three phases to the disturbance (Bowlby, 1958b, 1968, 1969; James Robertson and Bowlby, 1952). First, the child cries and shows acute distress, the period of *protest*; he then appears miserable and withdrawn, the phase of *despair*; and finally there is a time when he seems to lose interest in his parents, the stage of *detachment*. When the child returns to his parents, he often ignores them at first and then becomes clinging and demanding.

Some investigators have failed to confirm these findings (Davenport and Werry, 1970), but on the whole the observations have received support from other studies (Vernon et al., 1965; Yarrow, 1964). Nevertheless, a number of important qualifications have had to be introduced. The response described is most marked in children aged six months to four years, but even at this age it occurs in only some children (Illingworth and Holt, 1955; Prugh et al., 1953; Schaffer and Callender, 1959). Moreover, it is misleading to regard the separation as only from the mother. While children at this age are often most attached to their mother, they are also attached to their father and to their brothers and sisters (Ainsworth, 1967; Schaffer and Emerson, 1964). In the past the strength of these other attachments has often been underestimated. Their importance is shown by the finding that when children are admitted to hospital with their brothers or sisters, they show less distress (Heinicke and Westheimer, 1965). Although the separation is probably the principal factor even in hospital admission, the care during the separation is also relevant (Faust et al., 1952; Prugh et al., 1953).

Some of the reasons why children differ in their responses to separation can be found in their temperamental characteristics prior to separation (Stacey et al., 1970). Similar findings have been found in subhuman primates (Hinde, 1970). Finally, with regard to the short-term effects of separation, it appears that children used to brief separations of a happy kind are less distressed by *unhappy* separations such as hospital admission (Stacey et al., 1970). This last point suggests that in some circumstances separation experiences may actually be beneficial to the child.

In summary, children are not inevitably distressed by separation from their parents and we are beginning to learn what factors determine whether they are upset, and how we may take steps to diminish the emotional disturbance associated with separation. Even so, despite these qualifications, the main point—that a child's separation from his family is a potential cause of short-term distress and emotional disturbance—has received substantial support from research findings.

LONG-TERM EFFECTS

The next issue is what *long-term* effects follow separation experiences and this, rather than the immediate response to separation, is what my colleagues and I have been concerned to investigate. In order to discuss our findings, it will be necessary to divide separation experiences into several categories. I shall start with children whose mothers go out to work.

Working Mothers

This is a situation that exemplifies both recurrent very brief separations and also maternal care provided by several or even many mother-figures. In the past it has been claimed that the children of working mothers are particularly likely to become delinquent or develop some form of psychiatric disorder. Little time need be spent on this topic as there is abundant evidence from numerous studies, including our own, that this is not so (Douglas, Ross, and Simpson, 1968; Rutter, Tizard, and Whitmore, 1970; Yudkin and Holme, 1963). Indeed, in some circumstances, children of working mothers may even be *less* likely to become delinquent (West, 1969). There is no evidence that children suffer from having several mother-figures so long as stable relationships and good care are provided by each (T. W. Moore, 1963). This is an important proviso, but one which applies equally to mothers who are not working. A situation in which mother-figures keep changing so that the child does not have the opportunity to form a relationship with any of them may well be harmful, but such unstable arrangements usually occur in association with poor-quality maternal care, so that up to now it has not been possible to examine the effects of each independently.

Day nurseries and crèches have come in for particularly heavy criticism and, as already noted, the World Health Organization actually asserted that their use inevitably caused permanent psychological damage. There is *no* evidence in support of this view. Of course, day nurseries vary greatly in quality and some are quite poor. Bad childcare, whether in day nurseries or at home, is to be deplored, but there is no reason to suppose that day nurseries, as such, have a deleterious influence. Indeed, day-care need not interfere with normal mother-child attachment (Caldwell et al., 1970) and to date there is no reason to suppose that the use of day nurseries has any long-term ill effects (Yudkin and Holme, 1963). Although the evidence is still incomplete, the same conclusions probably apply also to communities such as the Israeli kibbutzim where children are, in effect, raised in residential nurseries although they retain strong links with their parents (Irvine, 1966; L. Miller, 1969).

Why, then, have "experts" asserted that working mothers and day nurseries cause delinquency and psychiatric disorder? The claim was made in good faith, but without substantiating evidence, and subsequent research has shown the charge to be wrong. It is important that we listen carefully to the advice and testimony of individuals who have studied a problem, but it is equally important that we demand that they present the evidence relevant to their recommendations. Science does not consist of experts' answers, but rather of the process by which questions may be investigated and the means of determining the relative merits and demerits of different explanations and

Transient Separations

Transient parent-child separation can lead to acute short-term distress, as already discussed. Can it also lead to long-term psychological disturbance? Several independent investigations have shown that children can be separated from their parents for quite long periods in early childhood with surprisingly little in the way of long-term ill effects (Andry, 1960; Bowlby et al., 1956; Douglas, Ross, and Simpson, 1968; Naess, 1959[3]). Yet most studies have shown that children subjected to separation experiences in early childhood do have a slightly increased risk of later psychological disturbance (Ainsworth, 1962a), and it is necessary to explore the possible explanations for this association. To do this, we must examine more closely the nature of the separation experience.

In our study of patients' families, we divided separation experiences into those involving separation from one parent only and those involving separations from both parents at the same time. In each case, separations were counted only if they had lasted at least four consecutive weeks.

It was immediately apparent that children separated from both parents came from more disturbed homes than did children who had never experienced separation. Many of the children were separated because they had been taken into care following some family crisis, and often this occurred against a background of more long-standing difficulties (Schaffer and Schaffer, 1968).

As a measure of family disturbance, we used one of our most reliable summary ratings on the quality of the parental marriage. This is based on a wide range of information concerning such items as affectional relationships between the parents, marital dissatisfaction, shared leisure activities, communication between husband and wife, mutual enjoyment of each other's company, quarreling, tension, and hostility.

Figure 1 (total $N = 151$) shows the association between parent-child separation and antisocial behavior in boys, after controlling for the quality of the parental marriage. In this and in subsequent figures, the measure of children's behavior used is the score on a behavioral questionnaire completed by teachers (Rutter, 1967). This has been shown to be a reliable and valid instrument, and it can be scored to differentiate between neurotic and antisocial disturbance (Rutter, 1967; Rutter, Tizard, and Whitmore, 1970). We

[3]A further study by Naess (1962) confirmed that prolonged separation experiences were no more frequent in delinquents than in controls, but also suggested that separations might be more frequent in a small group of serious delinquents. As this study is sometimes quoted in support of Bowlby's (1946) paper, it may be appropriate to give Naess' conclusions in full: "Our conclusion is that mother-child separation as such is a minor criminogenic factor; it does not stand 'foremost among the causes of a delinquent character development', but may be conceived as part of the picture of an unstable family life."

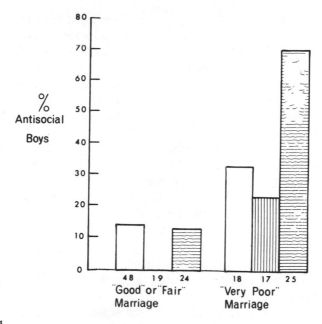

FIGURE 1

Discord or separation as causes of antisocial behavior in boys. *Open bar:* No separation. *Vertically striped bar:* Separation from one parent at a time. *Horizontally striped bar:* Separation from both parents or institutional care. *NOTE:* On this and all subsequent figures, the numbers at the base of the histogram refer to the number of cases for that column.

chose to use this measure because it is the one most independent of our family measures and because it concerns the child's behavior outside the home. However, the comparisons have also been made using more detailed clinical assessments and the findings are closely similar regardless of which behavioral measure is employed.

The largest differences in antisocial behavior are associated with the marriage rating and not with separation experiences. In each type of separation circumstance, the proportion of antisocial boys was higher when there was a "very poor" marriage than when there was a "good" or "fair" marriage.[4] Furthermore, regardless of the parental marriage relationship, separations from one parent only carried *no* increase in the rate of antisocial disorder. Indeed, although the differences are well short of statistical significance,

[4]The marital rating scale has three main subdivisions, each being split into two parts making a six-point scale in all. There are instructions for raters defining each point.

rather *fewer* of the separated children showed antisocial behavior.

This comparison took into account neither *which* parent had been separated from the child nor the *age* of the child at the time of separation. Accordingly, the comparisons were repeated making these differentiations. Again we found *no* difference. Comparisons were repeated for neurotic disorders and still no differences were found. It may be concluded that in the sample studied there was *no* association between separation from one parent only and any type of psychiatric or behavioral disorder in the children.

But there was an association between separation from *both* parents and antisocial disorder in the children. On the face of it, this might seem to indicate that this type of separation experience is a factor leading to psychological disturbance in later childhood. But it can be seen that this difference applied *only* in homes where there was a very poor marriage relationship between the parents ($p < 0.05$). No such difference was found in cases where there was a "fair" or "good" marriage. This difference according to the marriage rating suggests that the association may not be due to the fact of separation from both parents, but rather to the discord and disturbance that surrounded the separation.

To investigate this possibility, we divided separations from both parents into those due to some event *not* associated with discord (namely, the child's admission to hospital for some physical illness or his going on a prolonged, usually convalescent, holiday), and those in which the separation was due to some deviance or discord. In the majority of cases this followed family breakup due to quarrels, but in some instances separation was due to one parent's having a mental disorder and the other parent's being unable to keep the family together, so that the child stayed with relatives or went into care.

As shown in Figure 2 (total $N = 83$), it is the *reason* for the separation that mattered, not the separation itself. When the children were separated from both their parents because of physical illness or a holiday, the rate of antisocial disorder was quite low. When the separation was due to some type of family discord or deviance, on the other hand, nearly half the children exhibited antisocial behavior, a rate over four times as high as in the other children ($p < 0.05$).

It seems that transient parent-child separation as such is unrelated to the development of antisocial behavior. It only appears to be associated with antisocial disorder because separation often occurs as a result of family discord and disturbance. I should add that this conclusion still holds after taking into account the child's age at the time of separation. As other studies have produced contradictory and statistically insignificant associations with age of separation (Douglas, 1970; Gibson, 1969), we may conclude that this is not a crucial variable with respect to long-term effects, although it is with respect to short-term effects.

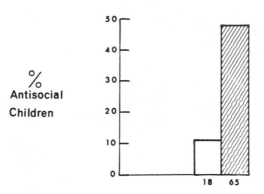

FIGURE 2

Reason for total parent-child separation and antisocial behavior in children. *Open bar:* Separation due to physical illness or vacation. *Diagonally striped bar:* Separation due to family discord or psychiatric illness.

Permanent Separations

If we accept that transient separations are of little long-term importance, can we also conclude that prolonged or permanent separations are equally innocuous? To answer that question, let us examine what happens when there is an irreversible breakup of the family due to parental death, divorce, or separation. In our several family studies, we found that children who were in some type of anomalous family situation showed a higher rate of antisocial disorder than did children living with their two natural parents. This finding agrees with the large literature linking "broken homes" with delinquency (Rutter and Brown, 1966; Rutter, Graham, and Yule, 1970; Rutter, Tizard, and Whitmore, 1970; Yarrow, 1961, 1964; Wootton, 1959), and it may be accepted as a fact that, overall, children from a broken home have an increased risk of delinquency. This association does not apply to neurosis, but it may apply to some types of depression as well as to delinquency (Caplan and Douglas, 1969; Wardle, 1961).

But is this association due to parent-child separation, and if not, how is it to be explained? Bowlby (1951) has laid most emphasis on loss of the maternal figure and has suggested that disorder in the child arises from a disruption of the affectional bond with his mother or other parent substitute (Bowlby, 1968, 1969). Thus, he suggests that it is the separation or loss which is important and that the disorder in the child has some of the elements of grief and mourning (Bowlby and Parkes, 1970). This explanation may well be correct with respect to the short-term effects of mother-child separation (Heinicke and Westheimer, 1965), but there are good reasons for doubting the hypothesis with respect to long-term effects, and it is these with which we are concerned here.

One important issue concerning the mechanisms involved in the association between "broken homes" and delinquency is whether the harm comes from disruption of bonds or distortion of relationships. This question may first be examined by comparing homes broken by death (where relationships are likely to have been fairly normal prior to the break), and homes broken by divorce or separation (where the break is likely to have been preceded by discord and quarreling—or at least by a lack of warmth and affection). Figure 3 shows this comparison as made in three independent investigations.

In all three studies the delinquency rates are nearly *double* for boys whose parents had divorced or separated (Douglas et al., 1966; Douglas, Ross, and Simpson, 1968; Gibson, 1969; Gregory, 1965), but for boys who had lost

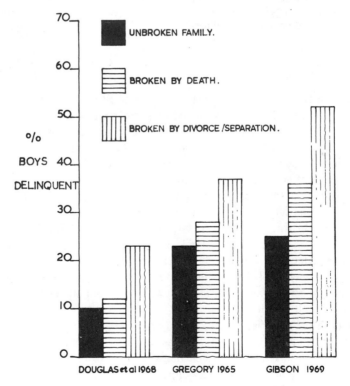

FIGURE 3

Cause of family disruption and delinquency. *Open bar:* Unbroken family. *Horizontally striped bar:* Family broken by death. *Vertically striped bar:* Family broken by divorce or separation.

a parent by death the delinquency rate was only slightly (and nonsignificantly) raised. In other studies, too, delinquency and conduct disorders have been found to be associated with parental divorce or separation, but *not* with parental death (F. Brown, 1966; Glueck and Glueck, 1950).

This suggests that it may be the discord and disharmony, rather than the breakup of the family as such, which lead to antisocial behavior. To test that hypothesis it is first necessary to show directly that parental discord is associated with antisocial disorder in the children even when the home is unbroken. There is good evidence from several studies that this is the case (Craig and Glick, 1965; McCord and McCord, 1959; Tait and Hodges, 1962). Figure 4 (total $N = 124$) shows our own findings in this connection from the study of patients' families.[5]

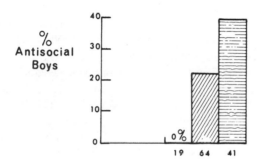

FIGURE 4

Marital relationship and antisocial behavior in boys living with both natural parents. *Open bar:* Good marriage. *Diagonally striped bar:* Fair marriage. *Horizonatally striped bar:* Very poor marriage.

The rate of disorder in boys rises steadily from 0% in homes where there is a "good" marriage to 22% when the marriage is "fair" to 39% when there is a "very poor" marriage (linear trend significant: $p < 0.001$). Parental discord is associated with antisocial disorder in the children. However, we

[5]These findings still apply after controlling for social class. In our sample parental occupation was not related to either the marriage rating or to antisocial behavior. It is frequently assumed that delinquency is more common in the lower social classes (Wootton, 1959), but the evidence is contradictory (Rutter, Tizard, and Whitmore, 1970). Furthermore, even in communities where social class is associated with behavioral disorder or delinquency in the children, this association often disappears once the effects of IQ are partialed out (Rutter, Tizard, and Whitmore, 1970) or family discord and disruption are taken into account (Conger and Miller, 1966; Langner et al., 1969a, 1969b; Robins and Hill, 1966). The association between social class and marital discord or family disorganization is also inconsistent; it applies in some communities, but not in others (W. A. Barry, 1970; Christensen, 1964).

can take the matter one stage further. If parental discord is more important than breakup of the home as a cause of deviant behavior, the rate of antisocial disorder should be higher for children living with their two natural, but unhappily married parents than for children living in harmonious, but broken homes. In our study we had too few cases of the latter variety for the comparison to be meaningful, but information is available from several other investigations which have shown that delinquency tends to be more common in unhappy unbroken homes than in harmonious, but broken ones (Jonsson, 1967; McCord and McCord, 1959). For example, McCord and McCord (1959) in a well-controlled study showed that broken homes resulted in significantly less juvenile delinquency than did unbroken, but quarrelsome and neglecting homes.

The conclusions on "broken homes" are surprisingly straightforward. Although parental death may play a part in the pathogenesis of some disorders (Rutter and Brown, 1966; Schlesinger, 1969), delinquency is mainly associated with breaks which follow parental discord rather than with the loss of a parent as such. Even within the group of homes broken by divorce or separation, it appears that it is the discord prior to separation, rather than the break itself, which was the main adverse influence.

The present findings suggest that separation as such is of negligible importance in the causation of delinquency. It is important not to generalize too readily from the results of one study, and it could be said that the sample studied was one with a rather high rate of family discord. Perhaps in families with happier relationships, separation experiences could be more influential in the causation of antisocial behavior. Perhaps, but our evidence suggests not. In this study separation from both parents had some association with antisocial disorders when there was a "very poor" marriage, but none at all when there was a good marriage. As Gibson's findings (1969) were somewhat different, it would be unwise to be dogmatic. I cannot state that separation experiences have no adverse effects on a child's psychological development. What we can conclude is that, at most, they can only be a minor factor in the development of delinquent behavior.

Could it be, though, that we have been looking at the wrong index of psychological development? Maybe separations lead to neurosis rather than delinquency. The evidence is firmly against this proposition. Separation experiences of any kind have never been shown to be associated with child neurosis (Rutter, Graham, and Yule, 1970; Rutter, Tizard, and Whitmore, 1970). Indeed, we know surprisingly little about the causes of child neurosis. Disturbed family relationships are associated with antisocial behavior, but not neurosis. Family disruption has been associated also with depression (Caplan and Douglas, 1969) and with enuresis (Douglas, 1970), but in neither case has it been shown that the disorders are due to separation as such rather than to the family disturbance surrounding separation.

Lastly, in defense of the proposition that separation per se is an adverse factor, it might be suggested that there is a delayed effect, that the ill effects are to be found in adult life, not in childhood. This remains a possibility. Some studies have suggested that bereavement in childhood is followed by depressive disorders in adult life (F. Brown, 1961; Dennehy, 1966; O. Hill and Price, 1967). However, other studies have found this association only in severe depression (Birtchnell, 1970; Munro, 1966; Munro and Griffiths, 1969) and still others have not found it at all (Abrahams and Whitlock, 1969; Brill and Liston, 1966; Gregory, 1966; Pitts et al., 1965). It remains uncertain whether this is a valid finding. Even if it is, it is probably of little relevance to the present discussion in that most studies indicate that the association is particularly with deaths during *adolescence,* not early childhood. We may still conclude that parent-child separation in early childhood, in itself, is probably of little consequence as a cause of serious long-term psychological disturbance.

This is not to say that separation experiences in early childhood are without long-term effects. Unhappy separations in a *few* children may lead to clinging behavior lasting many months or even a year or so. These experiences may also render the child more likely to be distressed by separations when older. However, many children show *no* such long-term effects and even in those that do the effects are generally relatively minor. Serious sequelae are so rare that taken overall they are of very little pathogenic importance.

Parental Death and Delinquency

Before discussing the effects of parental discord, we should pause for just a moment to consider why parental death is followed by *any* increase in disorder. Although in the delinquency studies cited in an earlier figure, the differences were small and statistically not significant, there was an apparent trend for parental death to be associated with a slight increase in delinquency. If it is, and the evidence is only weakly suggestive, does it mean that, after all, parent-child separation is of some importance in its own right, even if it is a minor influence compared with parental discord? Possibly, but there are other equally plausible explanations (Birtchnell, 1969). In the first place, death often follows a long illness and it has been shown that chronic physical illness (probably by virtue of the accompanying emotional distress and tension) may be associated with an increased risk of disorder in the children (Rutter, 1966). A second factor is the grief of the surviving parent, which often lasts as long as two years (Marris, 1958). Children may well be more affected by the distress and emotional disorder of the bereaved parent than they are by the death of the other. Third, families in which a father dies tend to be characterized by other adverse factors and the death is frequently followed by economic and social deterioration (Douglas, Ross, and Simpson, 1968; Rowntree, 1955). Again, these may be more important than the death itself. At the moment, we do not know which of these influences is the greatest. It is clear that when a parent dies the situation is much more complex than just a disruption of the parent-child relationship. The association between parental death and delinquency is quite weak and even this weak association may not be attributable to parent-child separation.

Parental Discord and Disharmony

We should now return to a more detailed consideration of the effects of parental discord and disharmony. If left at this stage, we are really saying little more than "bad homes lead to bad children," which does not take us very far. In order for the association to have much theoretical or practical value, we have to go on to ask in more detail how long disharmony has to last before the child is affected, how permanent its effects are, what sorts of disharmony are particularly associated with antisocial behavior, what factors in the home may mitigate the effects of discord and tension, and what factors in the child determine why only some children are affected by quarrelsome homes. At the present time we have only partial answers to some of these questions, but let us see how far the analysis of findings from our own study can take us.

We have no direct measure of the duration of discord and tension in the home, but we do have some indirect measures in the study of patients' families, all of which suggest that the longer the tension lasts, the more likely the children are to develop antisocial problems. First, we can look at children going through their second experience of a home with unhappily married parents. When children have experienced parental discord followed by divorce and then, after the parents remarry, a second very poor marriage, the rate of disorder is double that for children going through the first experience of parents who cannot get on together ($p < 0.05$). Second, where children were separated from their parents in early childhood because of family discord and were *still* in a quarrelsome home at the time we interviewed the parents, the rate of antisocial disorder was again unusually high (see Figure 5). Third, within homes with a very poor marriage, the children were more likely to be deviant if one or both parents had shown impaired personal relationships throughout the whole of their adult life (see Figure 11). In each case the differences were large and statistically significant. The evidence is circumstantial, but it strongly suggests that the longer the family disharmony lasts, the greater the risk to the children. However, we have no findings that enable any estimate of how long there must be disharmony before there is any effect on the children.

But we can look at what happens when disharmony *stops,* in order to determine whether the ill effects of bad family relationships in early childhood are transient or permanent. Figure 5 (total $N = 65$) shows the findings on children, all of whom were separated from their parents through family discord or deviance. It compares those whose present family situation is still very poor with those whose present situation is fair or good. In most cases, the family situation remained rather unsatisfactory and there were only a few children living in happy and harmonious homes. Accordingly, the comparison more accurately concerns children with very poor homes and children with less poor homes. Nevertheless, there is a large and significant difference (*p* < 0.05); the rate of antisocial disorder was double in children currently in a very poor family situation. The effects are *not* permanent and, given a change for the better in the family situation, the outlook for the child's psychological development correspondingly improves. How readily, how completely, and how often the adverse effects of disturbed relationships in early childhood may be reversed, we cannot answer. That remains one of the many important questions requiring further research.

The next issue is what *type* of family disharmony leads to antisocial disorder

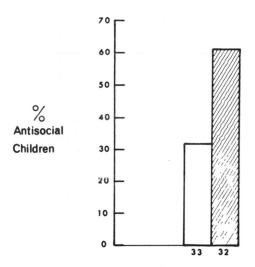

FIGURE 5

Antisocial behavior in children previously separated through family discord or deviance in relation to current family situation. *Open bar:* Current family situation fair or good. *Diagonally striped bar:* Current family situation very poor.

in the children. Broadly speaking, unhappy families can be divided into those where there is active disturbance (quarreling, hostility, fighting, and the like) and those which merely lack positive feelings (where relationships are cold and formal and the home is characterized by emotional uninvolvement and lack of concern).

Figure 6 (total $N = 103$) compares these two situations. As a measure of active disturbance, I have taken "tension," a rating which reflects the extent to which discord leads to a persistent atmosphere in the home so that visitors sense the disharmony and feel ill-at-ease. The "warmth" rating assesses positive feelings. It is based on feelings expressed by the parents at interviews in terms of tone of voice, facial expression, and words used. It has been shown to be a reliable measure which accurately predicts emotional expression in other situations. A rating of "low" warmth means that *both* the parent-child *and* the husband-wife relationship lacked warmth. This is a rather infrequent situation, so the numbers are small. In particular, there needs to be a study of more families where there is low warmth, but also low tension. However, it seems that there is an interaction effect. There is little disorder

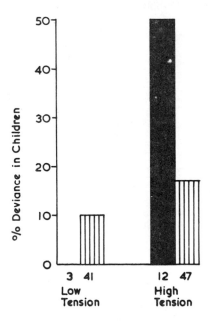

FIGURE 6

Warmth/tension in the home and antisocial behavior in the children. *Open bar:* Low warmth. *Vertically striped bar:* High warmth.

in the children when there is low tension, but when there is high tension, the rate of disorder is significantly higher ($p < 0.05$) if there is also low warmth. In short, both a lack of feeling and active discord are associated with deviant behavior in the children.

This last comparison did not differentiate between the marital relationship and the parent-child relationship. Figure 7 makes this comparison with regard to warmth (total $N = 104$). On the whole, adults who are warm toward their spouses are also warm toward their children so that the number of cases when the two are discrepant is small. Nevertheless (although the differences fall just short of statistical significance), it does seem that the rate of antisocial behavior in the children is raised if *either* relationship lacks warmth; the rate is particularly high if both relationships are cold.

Quite often in clinical practice one is faced with the problem of a very disturbed home situation where one parent behaves in a very deviant fashion and yet the child still has a good relationship with the other parent. The question then is: To what extent can a good relationship with one parent "make up" for a family life which is grossly disturbed in all other respects? Figure 8 (total $N = 60$) shows a comparison which provides some answer to this question. Families were first divided according to the quality of the

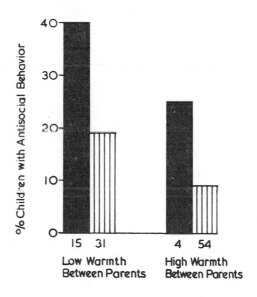

FIGURE 7

Warmth in family relationships and antisocial behavior in the children. *Open bar:* Low warmth to children. *Vertically striped bar:* High warmth to children.

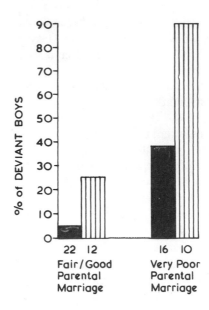

FIGURE 8

Parent-child relationships, parental marriage, and deviant behavior in boys. *Open bar:* Good relationship with one or both parents. *Vertically striped bar:* Poor relationship with both parents.

marriage relationship and then, within each marriage rating, a comparison was made between children who had a good relationship with one parent and children who did not have a good relationship with either parent. For this purpose, a good relationship was defined in terms of the parent's expressing both positive warmth *and* very little negative feeling. No account was taken of the child's behavior toward the parent in making the rating.

There was again an interaction effect. Whatever the parent-child relationship, the rate of disorder in the sons was significantly higher ($p < 0.05$ for good parent-child relationship and $p < 0.01$ for poor parent-child relationship) if the marital relationship was bad. Conversely, whatever the marital relationship, the child was better off if he had a good relationship with at least one parent ($p < 0.05$ for difference within "very poor" marriage). A good relationship with one parent was *not* sufficient to remove the adverse effect of marital discord, but it could go quite a long way in mitigating its effects.

Father-Child and Mother-Child Relationships

So far not much attention has been paid to whether good or bad relationships have been with the father or with the mother. This has been because for the most part in our current studies this has not proved to be a relevant variable. It has not made much difference which parent the child got on well with so long as he got on well with one parent. Yet, it would be wrong to assume that it never matters, as other studies have suggested its importance.

For example, in an earlier study of mine (Rutter, 1966) examining the effects of parental death and parental mental illness on children attending a psychiatric clinic, there was a sex-linked association. Boys were more likely to show psychiatric disorder if it was the father who had died ($p < 0.05$) or who was ill ($p < 0.05$). Figure 9 shows the findings for parental death, but the association for parental mental illness was similar.

Or again in a study of delinquent children (Figure 10), Gregory (1965) found that delinquency rates were higher in boys if the father was absent from the home, but in girls the rate was higher if the mother was missing.

We did not find this association in the present study and it has not always been found in other investigations (Gibson, 1969), so that the matter must remain open for the moment. It may be that the importance of the same-sexed parent is marked only at certain ages, perhaps in adolescence. The issue requires further study.

I have touched on the subject here, in spite of the inconclusive findings, because, however the problem is finally resolved, it is evident that the father-child relationship is an important one, and in some circumstances it may even be more influential than the mother-child relationship (Bronfenbrenner, 1961; Peterson et al., 1959; Robins, 1966). Of course, it is also true that a mother generally has more contact with very young children and her influence on them often predominates (S. Wolff and Acton, 1968). The point, quite simply, is that both parents are important with respect to their children's development

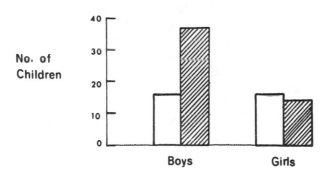

FIGURE 9

Association between sex of dead parent and sex of child attending psychiatric clinic. *Open bar:* Mother dead. *Diagonally striped bar:* Father dead.

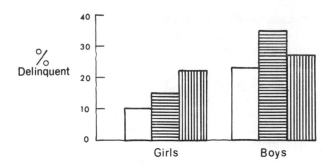

FIGURE 10

Family composition and delinquency. *Open bar:* Child with both parents. *Horizontally striped bar:* Father absent. *Vertically striped bar:* Mother absent.

and which parent is more important varies with the situation and with the child. It should be added that the influence of each parent cannot be regarded as independent factors. The mental health of one parent may influence that of the other (Kreitman et al., 1970) and may also affect the marriage relationship (W. A. Barry, 1970). It is useful to try to separate the effects of different dyads in the family, but it is also important to remember that the family is a social group in its own right (Handel, 1967).

THE DIRECTION OF THE RELATIONSHIP

So far the effects of parental discord have been discussed with the implicit assumption that it was the discord that led to the antisocial behavior, not that the antisocial children caused their parents' marriage to be disturbed. This assumption must be tested for it is important not to forget that children can influence parents just as parents can influence them (Bell, 1968). This has been shown, for example, by studies of foster parents (Yarrow, 1963), of nursing mothers (Bell, 1968; Yarrow, 1963) and of parents of children with congenital handicaps (Bell, 1964; Cummings, Bayley, and Rie, 1966).

Accordingly, we must ask whether the antisocial behavior is a cause or a consequence of family discord (Robins, 1969). Our own study provides only circumstantial evidence on this point. However, we found that when children were separated from their parents in the first few years of life because of family discord, antisocial disorders often developed later. In some of these cases, the marital difficulties must have preceded the child's birth because older children had already been taken into care following some family crisis.

Other investigations have measured parental behavior when the children were young and then have followed the development of the children into early adolescence. These studies have shown that it is possible, on the basis of the early family assessment, to predict the development of later delinquency at a level considerably better than chance (Craig and Glick, 1965; Tait and Hodges, 1962; West, 1969).

The effects are not entirely unidirectional and a circular process is probable (Yarrow, 1968), but we may conclude that parental discord can start off a maladaptive process which leads to antisocial disorder in the children. This may fairly be regarded as a causal relationship.

PARENTAL PERSONALITY

Genuine and spurious relationships have still to be distinguished (Hirschi and Selvin, 1967). Because parental discord leads to later antisocial behavior, it does not necessarily follow that it is the discord itself that is the cause of the antisocial disorder. It could be that the discord is only important because it is associated with some other factor of a more basic kind. One possible factor of this kind is parental personality. In many of the very bad marriages, one or both parents had a gross personality disorder. Was this the more basic factor? Were the children antisocial because their parents were abnormal rather than because the home was unhappy? Figure 11 (total $N = 70$) shows findings relevant to this question.

Families have been subdivided according to the quality of the marriage, as before, and also on the basis of whether either parent showed a handicapping personality disorder. Much the most important factor in relation to antisocial disorder in the sons was the parental marriage rating. Regardless of whether one parent had a personality disorder, antisocial behavior was many times more common when the marriage was "very poor" than when it was "good" or "fair." Furthermore, within the group of families with a satisfactory marriage, there was *no* effect attributable to parental personality disorder. These findings make it most unlikely that the association between parental discord and antisocial disorder is due to the presence of abnormalities of personality in the parent.

Even so, the difference associated with parental personality within the families with a "very poor" marriage requires explanation, although the difference falls just short of statistical significance at the 5% level ($\chi^2 = 3.832$). By definition, the parents with a personality disorder had shown disordered behavior or relationships throughout their adult life and in most cases this was associated with prolonged marital discord (in some cases this had occurred throughout two marriages). We do not have a measure of the duration of marital discord, but it is highly probable that discord was of much

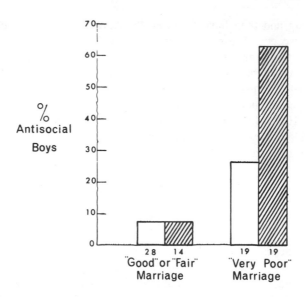

FIGURE 11

Personality of parents, parental marriage, and antisocial behavior in boys. *Open bar:* Neither parent has personality disorder. *Diagonally striped bar:* One or both parents have personality disorder.

longer duration when one parent had a personality disorder. Whether this is so, and if so, whether it accounts for the difference is not known. All that can be said is that regardless of whether or not a parental personality disorder acts as a contributory factor in the causation of antisocial disorder, its influence is not such as to account for the effects of parental discord.

GENETIC INFLUENCES

This result makes it less likely that the association between parental discord and antisocial disorder in the children could be explicable in genetic terms, but this possibility must be examined. The whole association could be accounted for in terms of heredity if a gene led both to delinquent behavior and to personality difficulties giving rise to marital disharmony. Again, this could not be tested directly, but other studies allow an indirect test of the hypothesis. A recent Swedish study by Bohman (1970) examined deviant behavior in *adopted* children in relation to characteristics of the children's biological parents. Information was available on criminality and alcohol abuse in the true father who, of course, had no contact with the children. Bohman (1970) found *no* association between these characteristics of the true fathers and deviant behavior in the adopted children. This negative result stands in sharp contrast to the findings of many studies that criminality and alcoholism *are* associated with deviant behavior in the children when the children are brought up by their criminal or alcoholic parents (Jonsson, 1967; Nylander, 1960; Robins, 1966). This finding and similar findings from studies of foster children (Roe and Burks, 1945) strongly suggest that the passing on of delinquent behavior from parent to child largely involves environmental rather than genetic influences.

Twin studies also suggest that genetic factors play but a small part in the pathogenesis of delinquency (Rosanoff, Handy, and Plesset, 1941; Shields, 1954, 1968). The concordance of monozygotic pairs with regard to antisocial disorders is only slightly greater than that of dizygotic pairs, showing that genetic factors have only a minor influence. That concordance rates are high in both types of twins suggests the importance of familial influences of an environmental type.

In short, the evidence shows that delinquent behavior is not inherited as such and that personality disorders in the parents probably lead to antisocial difficulties in the children through their association with family discord and disturbance, rather than through any direct genetic influence. Of course, that is not to say that genetic factors play no part. They probably are of importance with respect to the temperamental features that render children more susceptible to psychological stress (see below).

FACTORS IN THE CHILD

In concentrating, as I have for the purposes of this paper, on the effects associated with family discord, it should not be thought that I am suggesting that this is the only factor involved in the causation of antisocial behavior. Obviously it is not. Other studies have shown that a variety of social, cultural, psychological, and biological factors all play a part in the genesis of delinquency (West, 1967). The Tower Hamlets studies of Power and his colleagues (1967) suggest that factors in the school as well as in the home may be important. In addition, there are a number of factors in the child himself which may make him more likely to develop some type of behavioral disorder. For example, our own studies on the Isle of Wight showed that children with organic brain disorders were more likely to develop deviant behavior (Rutter, Graham, and Yule, 1970) and that children with severe reading difficulties were especially prone to exhibit antisocial tendencies (Rutter, Tizard, and Whitmore, 1970).

However, at the moment we can only be concerned with the factors which aggravate or ameliorate the adverse influence of family discord. In this connection, there are two factors in the child which have to be discussed.

The first of these is the child's sex. Nearly all the findings mentioned so far have referred to boys. This is not accidental. In our studies the effects of parental discord have been found to be much more marked in boys than in girls. The size of this difference is illustrated in Figures 12 and 13. Figure 12 (total $N = 151$) shows the association between marital disharmony and deviant behavior in boys. As noted previously, the rate of deviant behavior rises steeply the poorer the parental marriage, and there is an association with parental personality disorder.

In girls this association was not found (Figure 13, total $N = 139$). The rate of deviant behavior was much the same in girls regardless of whether a parent had an abnormal personality and regardless of the state of the parental marriage. This implies that boys may be more susceptible to the effects of family discord than are girls. The evidence from other studies is incomplete and rather unsatisfactory, but there does seem to be a tendency for the male

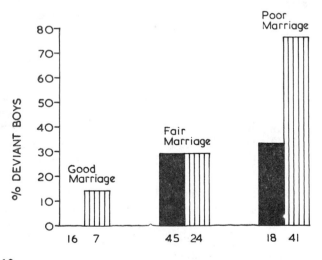

FIGURE 12

Personality of patient, parental marriage, and deviant behavior in boys. *Open bar:* Parent/patient has normal personality. *Vertically striped bar:* Parent/patient has personality disorder. *NOTE:* Unlike Figure 11, Figures 12 and 13 refer to personality disorder in the patient alone (not both parents). This information was available on a larger sample.

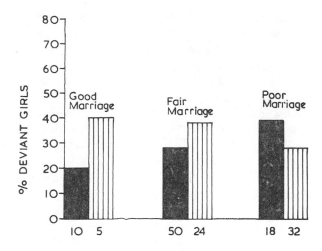

FIGURE 13

Personality of patient, parental marriage, and deviant behavior in girls. *Open bar:* Parent/patient has normal personality. *Vertically striped bar:* Parent/patient has personality disorder.

to succumb more readily to psychological stress (Rutter, 1970a, 1970b), parallel perhaps to the very well documented finding that the male is much more susceptible to biological stress (Rutter, 1970a, 1970b; Tanner, 1968). The evidence on children's responses to acute separation is somewhat contradictory, but in both humans and subhuman primates there is some suggestion that the young male may be more vulnerable (Hinde, 1970; Sackett, 1969; Stacey et al., 1970; Vernon et al., 1965). The matter is far from settled at the moment and further research is required, but on the whole the evidence tends to point to the male being more likely to suffer from the ill effects of parent-child separation and family discord.

TEMPERAMENTAL MAKEUP

The other factor in the child which we have to consider is his temperamental makeup. There is now substantial evidence that, even in the infancy period, children differ sharply one from another (Berger and Passingham, 1971). The young child responds selectively to stimuli in terms of his idiosyncratic and developmental characteristics; to a considerable extent he *elicits* responses from other people (Yarrow, 1968). Thomas and his colleagues in New York have shown that it is possible to measure the temperamental attributes of young children (Thomas et al., 1963). In the course of a longitudinal study, they have followed a group of children from soon after birth up to middle childhood. A proportion of the children have developed emotional and behavioral difficulties, and it has been found that the children's temperamental attributes as measured at the age of one to three years were associated with the development of behavioral difficulties a few years later (Rutter et al., 1963). Children who were irregular in their eating and sleeping habits, who were very intense in their emotional responses, who adapted slowly to new situations, and who showed much negative mood were those most likely to develop behavioral problems. This study showed that a child's own characteristics influenced the development of emotional and behavioral disorders and it seemed that it did so through effects on parent-child interaction (Thomas, Chess, and Birch, 1968).

In our study of patients' families,[6] we investigated children's temperamental attributes in a somewhat similar way. These were assessed when the children were four to eight years old and the influence of temperament was measured against behavioral deviance in school (i.e., in a different situation) one year later. Figure 14 shows the findings.

Children who lacked fastidiousness (that is, they did not mind messiness and disorder) were significantly more likely ($p < 0.05$) to show deviant behavior one year later. The same was true of children who lacked malleability ($p < 0.05$), whose behavior was difficult to change (a measure quite similar to the New York group's category of nonadaptability). As in the New York study, children who were markedly irregular in their eating and sleeping patterns were also more likely to develop behavioral problems ($p < 0.01$). There was a similar, but statistically insignificant ($p < 0.2$), tendency for highly active children to be at greater risk.

The findings demonstrated that children differed in their susceptibility to family stress, and they showed which temperamental attributes were important in this respect. The attributes were not ones concerned with deviance, but rather were features which determined *how* a child interacted with his environment. That we were measuring more than just aspects of deviant behavior is suggested by the finding that the attributes tended to have a stronger association with deviance one year later than with deviance at the time. Furthermore, the association was as strong with respect to the child's deviance at school as at home, in spite of the fact that temperament was assessed only in relation to the child's mode of behavior when with his family.

It is no new observation that children differ in their responses to stress situations, but until recent years surprisingly little attention has been paid to

----

[6]Dr. Philip Graham was responsible for planning this part of the study.

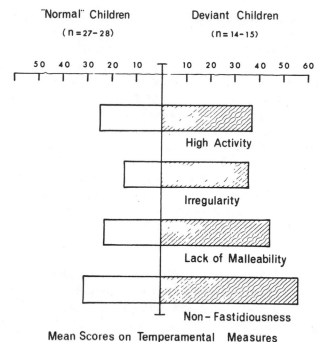

"Normal" Children
(n = 27 – 28)

Deviant Children
(n = 14 – 15)

High Activity

Irregularity

Lack of Malleability

Non – Fastidiousness

Mean Scores on Temperamental Measures

FIGURE 14

Temperamental characteristics and deviant behavior (one year later) in children of mentally ill parents.

this side of parent-child interaction. It warrants further study and the dividends of such study should be great.

THEORETICAL EXPLANATIONS

It has been found that a child's separation from his family constitutes a potential cause of short-term distress, but that separation is of little direct importance as a cause of long-term disorder. Moreover, even the short-term effects cannot be regarded solely as a response to maternal separation. Other family members are also very important in this context. Although separation experiences have an association with the later development of antisocial behavior, this is due not to the fact of separation itself, but rather to the family discord which accompanies the separation. The same applies to the more permanent separations due to family disruption consequent upon parental death or divorce. For the most part, the child is adversely affected by the tension and disharmony; the breakup of the family is only a minor influence. Studies of unbroken families show that boys in homes where there is an unhappy marriage between the parents are much more likely to become deviant than are boys in harmonious homes. Both active discord and lack of affection are associated with the development of antisocial disorders. A good relationship with one parent can go some way toward mitigating the harmful effect of a quarrelsome, unhappy home. The longer the family discord lasts, the greater the effect on the child, but the effects are not necessarily permanent. If the child later lives in a harmonious home, the risk of antisocial problems drops. The association between family discord and antisocial disorders seems to be largely due to environmental influences with hereditary factors of lesser importance. Nevertheless, the family discord cannot be regarded as an independent influence; it acts through the medium of parent-child interaction. This is a dyad in which the child also plays an active role and both the child's sex and his temperamental attributes have been shown to affect the interaction.

While these findings have added to our understanding of the long-term consequences of family disruption, this is far form the end of the problem, although it is where we shall have to leave it now. I should just remind you that we have still to determine the psychological mechanisms involved. *Why* and *how* does family discord interact with a child's temperamental characteristics to produce antisocial behavior?

Let me conclude with three suggestions on possible mechanisms. First, there is evidence from both retrospective and prospective studies that the parents of delinquent boys differ from other parents in their approach to the discipline and supervision of their children (Craig and Glick, 1965; Glueck and Glueck, 1962; Sprott, Jephcott, and Carter, 1955; West, 1969). Could it be that it is the child-rearing practices that are the main factor in the causation of delinquency and the discord is important only insofar as it is associated with erratic and deviant methods of bringing up children? Second, experimental studies have shown how readily children imitate other people's behavior and how a model of aggressive or deviant behavior may influence the children to behave similarly (Bandura, 1969). Perhaps the family discord is important only because it provides the child with a model of aggression, inconsistency, hostility, and antisocial behavior which he copies. The third alternative is that the child learns social behavior through having a warm stable relationship with his parents, that this relationship provides a means of learning how to get on with other people, and that difficulties in interpersonal relationships constitute the basis of antisocial conduct.

It is not difficult to think of situations in which these three hypotheses lead to different predictions, but that is another story. We have come a long way from the simple question with which we started: "Is separation from their parents bad for children?" The conclusions from research suggest a more complex interaction than that implied in the original question, but one which is still susceptible to critical analysis. There is some distance yet to go before we understand the mechanisms and processes by which family life helps shape children's psychological development. However, the problems are soluble and the solutions should be of practical importance in knowing how best to help children and families who are going through a period of psychological difficulties.

SUMMARY

The literature on parent-child separation is reviewed and findings are reported from a detailed and intensive longitudinal study of patients' families. It is concluded that a child's separation from his family constitutes a potential cause of short-term distress, but separation is of little direct importance as a cause of long-term disorder. Separation experiences have some association with the later development of antisocial behavior, but this is due not to the fact of separation itself, but rather to the family discord which precedes and accompanies the separation. Both active discord and lack of affection are associated with antisocial disorder, but a good relationship with one parent can go some way toward mitigating the harmful effect of a quarrelsome, unhappy home. The association between family disharmony and antisocial disorder is probably largely mediated by environmental influences. Children differ in their responses to family discord; these differences are associated with both sex and temperamental factors.

18

INTRODUCTION

How Is Mourning Possible?
by Martha Wolfenstein

The following chapter by Wolfenstein is in many ways related to the preceding one by Rutter, yet it is markedly different. Rutter addresses epidemiological data, while Wolfenstein presents a psychoanalytically oriented investigation focusing on the internal processes in 42 youngsters who experienced parental death. This difference in perspective resembles the contrast between the studies of adolescents reported by King in Chapter 12 in this volume and the psychoanalytic view of adolescence presented by Blos (1962b) in Chapter 16 in *Childhood Psychopathology*. (It is of interest that Wolfenstein offers a poetic comparison of the process of mourning with the process of adolescence, which she considers the developmental precondition for the ability to mourn.)

Another difference between the two chapters is that Rutter examines parent-child separations stemming from a variety of causes, while Wolfenstein focuses on the child's reaction to the permanent separation of parental death. Indeed, it might be said that her report addresses the exact opposite of the processes highlighted in the first three chapters in this volume, which deal with different aspects of the developing bond between parent and child. Wolfenstein examines the mechanisms children employ to dissolve their attachment in an already-formed object relationship. Lastly, Rutter zeroes in on a specific aspect of pathological outcome correlated with parent-child separation. In contrast, Wolfenstein does not address issues of normality or pathology, but explores the psychological processes in depth.

This last difference raises a disconcerting methodological consideration. Wolfenstein's penetrating study primarily entails youngsters who were judged (by unspecified criteria) to be in need of therapeutic intervention either before or after the parent's death. Although this need creates the opportunity for in-depth observations, it may also constitute a major methodological contaminant. The reader is never expressly informed why Ruth, for instance, entered psychoanalytic therapy in the first place. The vivid case report mentions that Ruth was overweight and felt ill-at-ease with her schoolmates, which raises questions as to whether a presumably heightened orality may have fueled her desperate efforts to cling to her lost mother, thereby reinforcing her denial of the finality of the loss. It is not our intent in this speculation to use the case of Ruth as a straw man; rather, it illustrates a methodological concern about the data on which Wolfenstein bases her thesis of children's developmental unreadiness to mourn prior to adolescence. This concern also applies to many of the psychoanalytic studies of children's bereavement processes reviewed by Nagera (1970) and J. B. Miller (1971).

These reviews, as well as the contributions they cover, lend support to Wolfenstein's thesis of adolescence as a developmental precondition for mourning. Children's reactions to major object loss tend to entail a denial of the finality of the loss. This denial is maintained, either overtly or covertly, along with an acknowledgment of the parent's death in what Wolfenstein designates a superficial deference to reality. The acknowledgment remains isolated from a persisting expectation, on another psychic level, of the parent's return. Wolfenstein cites the deeply moving example of Walter, who was not a patient, to illustrate that adaptive reactions to parental death in childhood pursue a course that is markedly different from mourning.

Other psychoanalytic investigators of parent loss agree with Wolfenstein that mourning does not occur in preadolescent children (e.g., Deutsch, 1937; Fleming and Altschul, 1963; Rochlin, 1965). They hold that the process of mourning, involving as it does the tolerance of powerful painful affects and repeated demands for reality testing in opposition to strong wishes, requires ego functions to which the child does not yet have firmly established access. Although there is psychoanalytic disagreement with this notion that children are developmentally incapable of mourning, it is best described as a qualified, partial dissent. Bowlby, for instance, has modified his earlier apparent equivalence of adult and child bereavement processes (Bowlby, 1960) by noting that the child's reactions most closely resemble *pathological* mourning in the adult (Bowlby, 1963). Furman (1964a, 1964b) asserts that therapeutic intervention facilitates and thus allows for the process of mourning in those children mature enough to possess a concept of the meaning of death. Although this perspective tends to be dismissed by Wolfenstein, it is essentially the basis for preventive intervention (Kliman, 1968). The intervention referred to here is not predicated on preventing specific pathological outcomes, about which Rutter in Chapter 17 in this volume and Bowlby (1961a) in Chapter 19 in *Childhood Psychopathology* have written from different perspectives. It aims to minimize developmental interferences (Nagera, 1966, 1970), which do not necessarily lend themselves to clear-cut nosological categorization.

It focuses, for instance, on those aspects of the positive self-image and sense of well-being that are lost with the love object, which may result in lifelong damage to self-esteem (Rochlin, 1965; Sandler and Joffe, 1965).

Elsewhere, Wolfenstein (1969) vividly describes the rage that may be so much a part of a child's or adolescent's reaction to death of a parent—a rage that is usually out of tune with the grief of the surviving parent. She delineates how this can be compounded by the child's subtle, vindictive determination to prove that no one can help, perhaps stemming from an unconscious endeavor to repeat the disappointment and loss in the hope that it might be different this time. Of course, this reaction can lead to great difficulties with the surviving parent and with others. The resultant problems in object relations may not be nosologically categorizable except to say, as Wolfenstein (1969) does, that the vindictive need to prove mistreatment entails turning oneself ''into a living and dying reproach'' (p. 433).

18

How is Mourning Possible?

MARTHA WOLFENSTEIN

I

The ability to form and also, when necessary, to dissolve object relations is essential to the development of every human being. At present we know more about the progress and vicissitudes of developing object relations than we do about reactions to their being broken off in different phases of life. In "Mourning and Melancholia" (1917), Freud described the phenomenon of mourning as it occurs in adults in reaction to the death of a loved person. There is a painful and protracted struggle to acknowledge the reality of the loss, which is opposed by a strong unwillingness to abandon the libidinal attachment to the lost object. "Normally, respect for reality gains the day. Nevertheless its orders cannot be obeyed at once. They are carried out bit by bit, at great expense of time and cathectic energy, and in the meantime the existence of the lost object is psychically prolonged. Each single one of the memories and expectations in which the libido is bound to the object is brought up and hypercathected, and detachment of the libido is accomplished in respect of it" (pp. 244–245). The lost object is thus gradually decathected, by a process of remembering and reality testing, separating memory from hope. The mourner convinces himself of the irrevocable pastness of what he remembers: this will not come again, and this will not come again. That the decathexis of the lost object is accomplished in a piecemeal way serves an important defensive function, protecting the mourner from the too-sudden influx of traumatic quantities of freed libido. Painful as it is to endure, mourning serves an invaluable adaptive function, since by this process the mourner frees major amounts of libido which were bound to the lost object, which he can utilize

First published in *The Psychoanalytic Study of the Child*, 21:93–123, 1966. New York: International Universities Press. Reprinted by permission.

for other relations and sublimated activities in the world of the living (Pollock, 1961).[1]

When in the sequence of development does an individual become capable of responding to a major object loss in this adaptive way? Bowlby, in a series of papers (1960, 1961a, 1961b, 1963), has explored reactions to separation and loss in young children. He has stressed the persistence of the demand, on a more or less conscious level, for the return of the lost object, the inability to renounce it, which he finds also characterizes nonadaptive reactions to loss in adults. Bowlby (1961b) raises the question: "At what stage of development and by means of what processes does the individual arrive at a state which enables him thereafter to respond to loss in a favourable manner?" And he adds his impression that "an early dating of this phase of development . . . is open to much doubt" (p. 323). Investigators who have reported on adult patients who lost a parent in childhood or adolescence have confirmed that expressions of grief, acceptance of the reality of the loss, and decathexis of the lost parent have not occurred. Helene Deutsch (1937) spoke of "absence of grief" in an adult patient whose mother had died when he was five, and whose inhibition of sad feelings had extended to all affects. Fleming and Altschul (1963) have reported cases in which the patients suffered the loss of parents in adolescence, but had never mourned and continued covertly to deny the reality of the loss. Jacobson (1965), speaking of related cases, recounted persistent fantasies of finding the lost parents again.

In contrast to these observations, Robert Furman (1964a) has advanced the view that mourning can occur in quite early childhood. He specifies as its preconditions the acquisition of a concept of death and the attainment of the stage of object constancy, both of which are possible by the age of four. I would suggest that these may well be necessary conditions, but they may be far from sufficient to enable the immature individual to tolerate the work of mourning. We need more empirical observations of how children in various phases of development actually do react to the loss of a major love object.

[1]There has been some confusion in discussions of whether or not children mourn, because the discussants have attached different meanings to the term *mourning*. I shall use the term *mourning* in the sense in which Freud used it in "Mourning and Melancholia," to mean that reaction to loss in which the lost object is gradually decathected by the painful and prolonged work of remembering and reality testing. Bowlby (1960, 1961a, 1961b, 1963) has extended the term *mourning* to include a wider range of reactions to loss. Those reactions in which the demand for the return of the lost object persists then become *pathological mourning*. Bowlby feels that, in order to establish the relations between reactions to loss in early childhood and in later life, it is necessary to bring them under a common rubric. There is no logical necessity for this. All relations, whether of cause or similarity, can be established among distinct phenomena, whether we call them by the same or different names. It seems to be in the interest of clarity to confine the meaning of a term to a distinct phenomenon, rather than extend it to a range of differing phenomena.

Furman (1964b) has reported the case of a six-year-old patient whose mother died while he was in analysis, and whose reactions Furman characterizes as "mourning." However, the main manifestation was that the boy painfully missed his mother in many circumstances where formerly she was with him. The expression of such feelings is no doubt useful in helping the patient to avoid the pathological affectlessness which developed in Helene Deutsch's patient. But the evidence remains inconclusive as to whether a mourning process, in the sense of decathecting the lost object, was under way. We can miss and long for someone we still hope to see again.

In the psychoanalytic literature there have been many contributions on adult reactions to loss, particularly those which take a pathological course, eventuating in one or another form of depressive illness. In recent years there have also appeared an increasing number of observations on reactions of very young children to separation from their mothers (notably Bowlby, 1960, 1961a, 1961b, 1963; A. Freud and Burlingham, 1943, 1944; James Robertson, 1958; Spitz, 1946a). However, relatively little has been reported on reactions to loss of a major love object of children in the age range from the beginning of latency into adolescence.[2]

In this paper I shall draw on research data on children within this age range who have lost a parent by death.[3] Our subjects are children and adolescents in treatment in a child guidance clinic (and some cases from private practice). The clinical material has also been supplemented by observations of non-patient subjects. The age at which our subjects suffered the death of a parent varied from earliest childhood to well into adolescence. The time of their coming under our observation also varied. In some instances, our acquaintance with the child antedated the parent's death; in others, it began only years afterwards. However, as compared with efforts to reconstruct the effects of such a loss in adult analysis, we were in most instances much closer in time

[2] Some observations of children in the beginning latency period who had suffered the loss of a parent may be found in Scharl (1961) and Shambaugh (1961).

[3] The research project, some findings of which I am reporting here, has been conducted in the Division of Child Psychiatry at the Albert Einstein College of Medicine. Forty-two cases of children and adolescents who have lost a parent by death have been observed or are currently under observation. At the time of entering treatment the patients ranged in age from three and a half to 19 years, the majority being in adolescence. We have had one child under six, 11 between the ages of six and 11, 18 between 12 and 15, and 12 between 16 and 19. Sixteen of the patients came under observation within a year of the parent's death; eight within two or three years; 18 from four to 14 years later.

The following have participated in this project: Drs. Raymond Bernick, Peter Bokat, Betty Buchsbaum, Richard Evans, Daniel Feinberg, Karl Fossum, Lester Friedman, Paul Gabriel, Charles Goodstein, Phyllis Harrison, Leonard Hollander, Allan Jong, Saul Kapel, Dr. and Mrs. Gilbert Kliman, Drs. Sally Kove, William Lewit, Donald Marcuse, Manuel Martinez, Eli Messinger, James Pessin, Judy Roheim, Rita Reuben, Edward Sperling, Eva Sperling, Sherwood Waldron, Alex Weintrob.

to the event. We were observing still-immature individuals who had experienced a major object loss in the course of growing up, and we could see some of the more immediate reactions and the consequences for further development.

When we began our investigation, we were aware that persons who have lost a parent in childhood more often succumb to mental illness in adulthood than those who have not suffered such a loss (H. Barry, 1949; F. Brown, 1961). From a therapeutic point of view we hoped that relatively early intervention might help to forestall such pathological effects. At the same time we did not know in what ways the vulnerability to later mental illness might manifest itself earlier in life. Also, since not everyone who has lost a parent in childhood shows later severe disturbance, we were alert to the possibilities of various adaptive reactions.

As our observations accumulated, we were increasingly struck by the fact that mourning as described by Freud did not occur. Sad feelings were curtailed; there was little weeping. Immersion in the activities of everyday life continued. There was no withdrawal into preoccupation with thoughts of the lost parent. Gradually the fact emerged that overtly or covertly the child was denying the finality of the loss. The painful process of decathexis of the lost parent was put off, with the more or less conscious expectation of his return. Where depressed moods emerged, especially in adolescence, they were isolated from thoughts of the death of the parent, to which reality testing was not yet applied. Thus, we gained the definite impression that the representation of the lost object was not decathected, indeed that it became invested with an intensified cathexis.

It might be supposed that the nonoccurrence of mourning in our subjects indicates only some limitation in their selection. However, from our observations an increasingly strong impression emerged that there was a developmental unreadiness in these children and adolescents for the work of mourning. It is the purpose of this paper to explore this unreadiness and to offer a hypothesis concerning the developmental preconditions for being able to mourn. What I have said does not preclude an adaptive reaction to major object loss in childhood. Only, as I shall try to show, such a reaction follows a course different from mourning.

II

The following case of a young adolescent girl illustrates many of the reactions we observed in our subjects following the death of a parent. The patient had been in treatment for half a year before the sudden death of her mother, so that it was possible to have some impression of the antecedent emotional situation. I shall focus on two mutually involved aspects of her reactions to the mother's death: the denial of the finality of the loss and the defenses against the related affects.

Ruth was just 15 when her mother died of a brain hemorrhage. In the months preceding the mother's death, Ruth had shown much ambivalence toward her. She shrank from her mother's demonstrations of affection and was intensely irritated by her little mannerisms. On the occasion of her mother's last birthday, Ruth had left the present she had made for her mother at a friend's house and then had rushed to retrieve it at the last moment. At that time Ruth appeared to be in an incipient phase of adolescent detachment from and devaluation of her mother. Almost immediately following the mother's death, Ruth began to idealize her. She said repeatedly that she was just beginning to realize what a remarkable woman her mother had been. While this in part echoed what was being said in the family circle, it also expressed an effort to purify her feelings and her image of her mother of the ambivalence which had been so noticeable previously. In remembering her mother, Ruth reverted many times to an episode just before she had started treatment, when she had been greatly distressed and her mother had been very sympathetic and understanding. This incident became archetypal of her relation with the mother, who now appeared always to have been a comforter and protector. She tended to gloss over the many real difficulties and frustrations in her life with her mother. Periods of her childhood took on an aura of enveloping emotional warmth, though she knew that her diaries from those years told of much unhappiness.

What happened here was a reversal of the adolescent process of detachment from the mother. There was instead an intensified cathexis of the image of the mother, with a strong regressive pull toward a more childish and dependent relation, seen now in a highly idealized light. Freud (1926) said that there is a tendency toward hypercathexis of a lost object, just as toward a diseased body part. We can view this tendency as an effort to deny the possibility of loss of something so essential to the self.

Ruth had repeated fantasies of finding again mother substitutes from the past—a former therapist, a beloved teacher, neither of whom she had seen for many years. It was as if, by a displacement from the dead to the absent, she were saying, "Those I have lost can be found again." There was also an intensified attachment to a camp counselor, which was characterized by feelings of disappointment when they were together and desperate longing for the counselor when they were apart.

Expectations of the mother's return emerged gradually. In the second year following her mother's death, Ruth began a stringent course of dieting. She had had long-standing problems of overeating and being overweight, and her mother had repeatedly urged and encouraged her to diet. Now Ruth succeeded over a period of months in becoming surprisingly slim. She received many compliments on her improved appearance, to which she reacted, paradoxically, in a rather disappointed way. However, as it appeared later, these were not the compliments she was seeking, which would have had to come from her mother. On the eve of her birthday, Ruth went for a long ramble by herself through springtime fields and experienced a dreamy euphoria, a kind of oceanic feeling. When on her return home she tried to describe this experience to her father and felt he failed to understand it, her good mood began to dissolve into disappointment. The night of her birthday she started on an uncontrolled eating binge which continued for many weeks thereafter. Subsequent analysis disclosed that the sacrifice of delightful food represented a kind of bargain with fate, like a vow, in exchange for which she expected the return of her mother on her birthday. The oceanic feeling of oneness with nature may be taken as a symbolic realization of the wish to be reunited with mother, and was perhaps experienced as a portent of imminent reunion. Being confronted at home with her still-grieving father precipitated the feeling that the wish was not coming true. The bargain with fate was vitiated and the self-imposed renunciation was abandoned.

Not quite three years after her mother's death, Ruth's father married again. Ruth was filled with emotional confusion, feeling as if her father had become discontented with her mother and thrown her out or as though he were committing adultery. While the father had gone through a period of concentrated mourning, following which he could turn to a new love object, the daughter was still unable to detach her feelings from the mother. She felt as though the mother's place should be kept open for her possible return. Thus, father and daughter were out of phase with one another in their tempos of giving up the lost love object.[4] Ruth reported with grim satisfaction a dream in which her mother confronted her father and his new wife in their bedroom. It was as if she felt they deserved being called to account by the wronged wife. Before the father's remarriage, she had had fantasies of her mother's return in which she imagined herself frustrated by her father's again asserting his greater claim to the mother. After her father's remarriage, she imagined her mother's returning and mother and herself going off together, leaving behind the strange new ménage.

Ruth repeatedly slipped into the present tense in speaking of her mother. Three years after her mother's death, she admitted that she kept in her room a plant which had been dead for a considerable time, but which she continued

---

[4]The different tempos of reaction to loss in children and their widowed parents, which put them out of phase with one another, are generally a cause of much mutual misunderstanding.

to water. At times when I had occasion to remind Ruth that her mother was dead, she had a pained, offended feeling as if I should not say this to her.[5] At other times she forced herself to think of her mother's body decaying underground, but such thoughts remained isolated from the persisting fantasies of her mother's return. She said that there should be an arrangement for people to be dead for five years and then to come back again. She felt as though she were constantly waiting for something. Gradually she acknowledged thoughts of wishing the therapist could be her mother, but such thoughts occasioned feelings of painful compunction, as if they implied disloyalty to her mother.

Four years after her mother's death, Ruth was facing a decisive separation from her therapist (she was about to start further analysis in the city where she was going to college). During the summer vacation Ruth wrote about a cantata in which she was participating, in which the chorus voiced the desperate feelings of drowning children. She quoted verses in which the children cry: "Mother, dear Mother, where are your arms to hold me? Where is your voice to scold the storm away . . . ? Is there no one here to help me? . . . Can you hear me, Mother?" And she said that the author of these lines had expressed for her what she felt.

I should like to elaborate further on the affective manifestations which accompanied this struggle to deny the finality of loss. Shortly after her mother's funeral, Ruth found herself no longer able to cry. She felt an inner emptiness; she felt as if a glass wall separated her from what was going on around her. She was distressed by this affectlessness, and was subsequently relieved when, comparing notes with a friend whose father had died some time earlier, she learned that the other girl had had a similar reaction. The interference with affect was overdetermined by a fear of sharing her father's grief. Shortly after the mother's death, Ruth reported a dream in which her grandfather (standing for her father) leaned close to her and said: "Let us mingle our tears." This dream aroused feelings of intense horror in her: the sharing of such strong emotion was fraught with libidinal overtones and the incest taboo was invoked.

In the week following her mother's death, Ruth said: "I guess it will be pretty bad this week." Thus, she expressed her intolerance of the prospect of protracted suffering, her expectation of early relief. In the time that followed, there were many alternations of mood, each good mood being hailed as the end of her distress. This illustrates what I have called the "short sadness span" in children, the desperate effort to recapture pleasurable feel-

---

[5]Bowlby (1961b, 1963) has pointed out how much the bereaved person resents those who speak of his loss as a *fait accompli*. Hated are the comforters.

ings in whatever circumstances (Wolfenstein, 1965). Good moods are the affective counterpart of denial and help to reinforce it: if one does not feel bad, then nothing bad has happened.

Shortly after her mother's death, Ruth appeared for her session in an exuberant mood. She had written a successful humorous composition, in which she congratulated herself on getting through her first year of high school with only minor mishaps. She explained this surprising statement by saying that she referred only to events at school, and proceeded to detail various embarrassing predicaments she had gotten into, which she turned to comic effect. Such denials, accompanied by euphoric moods, tended to be countered by catastrophic dreams, in which, for example, she and her father were taking flight from a disaster-stricken city, then turning back to try to rescue the dying and the dead. Conversely, sad moods were relieved by gratifying dreams.

Several months after her mother's death, upon returning to school in the fall, Ruth went through a phase of depression. She complained that nothing gave her pleasure anymore—not being with friends, not listening to music; everything she had formerly enjoyed had lost its savor. She felt she had nothing to look forward to, wished only to stay in bed, often felt like crying and that any effort, such as that involved in schoolwork, was too much for her. Such feelings of sadness, loss of all zest for life, withdrawal, and depletion are familiar components of mourning. What was striking in this instance was that these feelings were not consciously associated with the fact of the mother's death or with thoughts about the mother. Rather, Ruth berated herself for the senselessness of her distress. At other times she blamed her unhappiness on her difficulty in ever feeling at ease with her schoolmates. This had been a long-standing complaint, but according to her now distorted view, she had felt much happier with her friends the year before, when in fact she had spoken constantly of the same malaise. Thus, a strenuous effort was maintained to keep the feelings of sadness and despair isolated from thoughts of the mother's death. When the therapist repeatedly attempted to connect these feelings with the loss the patient had suffered, the connection was accepted only on an intellectual level, and again the struggle to recapture pleasurable moods was resumed.

A major maneuver for achieving euphoric moods consisted in transitory identifications with her mother. Ruth would briefly engage in some activity which her mother had pursued and would feel extraordinarily well. Such incidents should be distinguished from the more stable perpetuation of characteristics of the lost love object which typically follows mourning. What Ruth was doing resembled more the play of a young child who, when mother is away, plays at being "Mommy." This creates the illusion: "Mother is not away, she is here, I am mother." It operates in the interest of denial of a painful reality.

Other incidents exemplify the effort to keep painful longings and regrets isolated from thoughts of the mother. Sometimes, in bed at night, Ruth suffered confused feelings of desperate frustration, rage, and yearning. She tore the bedclothes off the bed, rolled them into the shape of a human body, and embraced them. She was quite uncertain and doubtful whether it was her mother she so longed to embrace. Walking through the different rooms of her house, she reflected with regret how everything was changed from the time when she was a child. The furniture and drapes had all been changed through the years. She herself occupied a different room from that of her childhood. When she went back to the old room, it no longer was the way it had been. With all this, there was no conscious thought that the great change that had occurred and that made home so different from what it had been was her mother's death. Ruth spoke of feeling at times, when she was talking to me or other people, that she was not really addressing the person before her. When asked to whom she was speaking, she replied that she might say it was to her mother. But this was a kind of detached speculation, carrying no conviction. When she became able to say that the song of drowning children crying for their mothers expressed her own feelings, the isolation between painful affects and awareness that mother was not there was beginning to break down.

At times of separation or impending separation from the therapist, Ruth was impelled toward trial reality testing of the loss of her mother. On one such occasion she said: "If my mother were really dead, I would be all alone"; and at another time: "If I would admit to myself that my mother is dead, I would be terribly scared." Thus we see incipient reality testing and alarmed retreat. The fears of what the finality of her loss would mean maintained the denial and persistent clinging to the love object, which continued to live in her imagination. We may consider that what is feared is the emergence of an unbearable panic state, in which inner and outer dangers are maximized. In the outer world, there would no longer be any source of gratification or protection ("I would be all alone"). Within, there would be a release of traumatic quantities of objectless libido.

It goes beyond the scope of this paper to consider the ways in which therapy may help an immature individual to give up a lost love object. However, there are a few points on which I should like to remark briefly. We have seen how the warding off of painful affects supports the denial that anything bad has happened. In therapy the child or adolescent can be helped to achieve a greater tolerance for painful feelings. One of the fears that children have of such feelings is that they may continue without letup and increase to intolerable intensity.[6] The therapist can help to ensure that painful affects are released at a rate the immature individual is unable to control independently.

In the case of Ruth, as in the case reported by Fleming and Altschul (1963), separations from the therapist repeatedly had the effect of initiating trial reality testing in regard to the loss of the parent. The current separation, for which the patient has been prepared, may serve as a practice exercise in parting. The fact that the patient can tolerate separating from the therapist may suggest to him that he may be able to bear the more final separation from the lost parent. In Ruth's case it was a decisive separation from the therapist that precipitated the desperate cry for the lost mother. In being able to bring together her feelings of desperate longing with the thought of her mother, in abandoning the defensive isolation previously maintained, she had taken one step toward acknowledging that her mother was really dead.

There were other instances in which Ruth underwent a trial giving up of lesser objects of attachment. I have spoken about her prolonged dieting. During that time she literally mourned the wonderful food she had formerly enjoyed, remembering it with longing and sadness, which was quite different from her way of remembering her mother. This trial mourning did not at that time serve to advance her toward giving up her mother. There was an implicit *quid pro quo* in it, an expectation that through this ordeal of renunciation she would get her mother back. When this expectation was not fulfilled, the capacity for renunciation became for a time drastically reduced. A later trial giving up consisted in her decision not to return to the camp which she had attended for many years. After this decision was made, there was much regret and longing for beloved counselors and campmates with whom she would not again enjoy the same close companionship as in the past. It would seem that the giving up of a major love object lost in childhood or adolescence requires many preparatory stages.

III

What we have seen in the case of Ruth was observed repeatedly in other children and adolescents whom we studied. Sad affects were warded off.

---

[6]A nine-year-old boy vividly evoked the awful prospect of unstoppable grief that would overwhelm children if they were not able to "forget" about a painful loss: "They would cry and cry. They would cry for a month and not forget it. They would cry every night and dream about it, and the tears would roll down their eyes and they wouldn't know it. And they would be thinking about it and tears just running down their eyes at night while they were dreaming" (from an interview by Dr. Gilbert Kliman on children's reactions to the death of President Kennedy).

When they broke through, they were isolated from thoughts of the lost parent. Denial of the finality of the loss was overtly or covertly maintained. Bowlby (1961a) has spoken of the importance of expressing what he calls "protest" in reaction to loss, that is, a vehement demand for the return of the lost object and strenuous efforts to regain it. He considers the full expression of such feelings and strivings essential to attaining the conviction that the object is in fact irretrievable.[7] "Protest" involves a painful awareness of the absence of the object, an awareness which may be for a long time postponed. The emergence of painful longings and crying for someone who does not come is a step toward reality testing and eventual tolerance for giving up the lost object.

Our subjects gave many indications that they denied that the dead parent was irretrievably lost to them. They frequently slipped into the present tense in speaking of the dead parent. They reported seeing someone on the street whom they fleetingly mistook for the lost parent. There was intolerance of any reminder that the parent was dead. Memories of the dead parent were not fraught with the painful feelings of the mourner, who is in the process of realizing that these things will not come again. Where sad feelings emerged in relation to the lost parent, there was an effort to get away from them as quickly as possible. For example, a ten-year-old girl, whose father had died when she was seven, was moved to tears when her therapist said sympathetically that she must often miss her father. After being briefly downcast she proposed, "Let's change the subject," and was soon chatting in a cheerful and animated way about events at school. The intimate relation between tolerance for sad affects and reality testing appears throughout our material.

Fantasies of the dead parent's return often appeared in disguised form. Thus, a ten-year-old boy, whose father had died when he was three, had a fantasy of a robot who would come out of the wall and teach him all he needed to know, so that he would not have to go to school. The robot (something both dead and alive) no doubt represented the omniscient father, who could transmit his powers to his son. Perhaps the amount of distortion here is related to the age of the child at the time of the parent's death. We may recall Helene Deutsch's (1937) case of the patient who had lost his mother when he was five, and who remembered the childhood fantasy of a big mother dog coming into his room at night and showing him affection.

---

[7]According to Bowlby (1961a), a bereaved individual gives up a lost object when prolonged expressions of "protest" (clamorous demands and strivings for the return of the object) are seen to bring no result. These strivings are then "gradually relinquished or, in terms of learning theory, extinguished" (p. 274). However, observation suggests that clamoring for the return of a lost object can continue indefinitely despite lack of response from the external world as long as the internal representation of the lost object is not decathected.

Our material suggests that fantasies of the parent's return are either more clearly conscious or more readily admitted in adolescence than at earlier ages. It seems likely that the fantasy of the parent's return may be a more closely guarded secret in younger children. A readiness to admit the fantasy, thus risking confrontation with reality, may represent one of the many steps toward giving up the lost parent.

The denial of the parent's death coexists with a correct conscious acknowledgment of what has really happened. All our subjects could state that the parent was in fact dead, and could recall circumstances related to the death, such as the funeral. Yet this superficial deference to facts remained isolated from the persistence on another level of expectations of the parent's return.[8] What we see here is a splitting of the ego in the defensive process. Freud (1927) observed the use of this mechanism in relation to the loss of a parent in childhood. He reported that two young male patients (one of whom had lost his father in his second year, the other in his tenth year) both denied the reality of the father's death. They could feel and behave as if the father still existed. But this denial represented only one sector of their mental life. There was another sector in which the death of the father was acknowledged. In speaking of this defense against accepting an unbearable piece of reality, Freud remarked: "I also began to suspect that similar occurrences in childhood are by no means rare" (p. 156).

Following the death of a parent, a child's image of and feelings toward the parent undergo a change. It is not the parent as the child last knew him in life, but the glorified parent of early childhood who is perpetuated in the child's fantasy. This, for a child in the age range we are considering, represents a regression. I may note parenthetically that a major loss suffered at any age precipitates some regression. The adult mourner becomes for a time "an infant crying in the night." The loss of a loved person evokes feelings of terrible helplessness, like those of a deprived infant who is powerless to relieve his distress. Children seem to respond to this predicament by conjuring up the fantasy of an ideally good and loving parent who can do everything for them. Their own feelings toward the lost parent also become, for a time, ideally loving. This is partly an attempt at a posthumous undoing of bad feelings or wishes previously directed toward the lost parent.

Bowlby (1961a, 1963) has pointed out that young children express raging reproach against the mother who goes away and leaves them. In older children whose reactions to the death of a parent we have observed, there seems to

---

[8]Furman (1964a) takes the verbal acknowledgment of a young child that his parent is dead and not coming back as indicating a readiness to mourn. What is overlooked is the defensive splitting of the ego, as a result of which the death is at the same time denied and the attachment to the lost parent perpetuated.

be a strenuous effort to divert such feelings from the image of the lost parent. Similarly, the negative sector of the ambivalence formerly felt toward the parent is split off. These hostile feelings are directed toward others in the child's environment, notably the surviving parent. Thus, far from being able to turn to substitute objects, the bereaved child often feels more at odds with those around him and alienates them by his angry behavior. His fantasied relation with the idealized dead parent is maintained at great cost. It seems to absorb most of his libidinal energies and involves a diversion of hostile feelings toward those who could help and befriend him.[9] With time, perhaps particularly in adolescence, reproachful feelings toward the abandoning parent emerge. Thus, a 20-year-old patient, whose father had died when she was 14, spoke of having idealized him following his death. Now, however, she was bitterly reproachful toward him, blaming his death, which had left her in such hard straits, on his reckless disregard of the doctor's orders. The return of ambivalence toward the lost parent, like the ability to associate sad feelings with his loss, represents one step toward reality testing.

We have observed, then, that instead of decathecting a lost love object, which is what happens in mourning, children and adolescents tend to develop a hypercathexis of the lost object. Why do they cling in this way to a lost parent, unable to give him up? To understand this, we must consider what object relations mean in different phases of development. What happens when an object relation is externally severed gives us crucial clues as to what the relation meant to the individual who suffers this loss. Spitz (1946a) has demonstrated dramatically that infants in the second half of the first year become radically retarded in all areas of development when they are separated from their mothers (and when no adequate mother substitute is provided). More recently, Fleming and Altschul (1963) have presented strikingly similar observations about adult patients who experienced the loss of a parent as late as adolescence. They found that these patients remained arrested in their development at the stage in which they were at the time of the parent's death. If the parent, or parents, were lost when the patient was an adolescent, the patient was still, years later, living emotionally as an adolescent. These findings suggest that, despite the impressive development in so many areas which can be observed between infancy and adolescence, something in the child's relation to the parents persists throughout this time. The child needs the continuing relation with the parents in order to advance in his development.

I shall consider some of the indispensable prerequisites for the child's

---

[9]Lindemann (1944) has called attention to the occurrence of rage in bereavement. Bowlby (1961a, 1961b, 1963) has stressed what he considers the omnipresence of rage in reaction to loss. He has also pointed out that, while its main object is the lost person, who is reproached for his abandonment, it is frequently displaced to others.

growth which the parents provide. While parents do not, in the normal course of development, remain exclusively need-gratifying objects, they do continue to provide for the child's needs until he is able to make his own way in the world. Apart from material needs, they are sources of narcissistic supplies. While with the infant and young child the mother provides support for his body narcissism, with the schoolchild the parents give essential support to his pride in his growing accomplishments. The parents also retain external ego and superego roles. With the infant and young child they mediate wholly between him and reality, for instance, guarding him from dangers of which he is not yet aware. They act as an external superego from the time they utter the first "No, no" when the toddler approaches some forbidden object. As the child develops internal ego and superego functions, these functions remain for a long time far from autonomous—dependent on external support from the parents.

To illustrate what happens when this manifold support is lost: we have observed repeatedly that some children and adolescents begin to decline in their school performance following the death of a parent. Other children begin to behave badly in school. In yet other instances, truancy and stealing begin after a parent has died. We may suppose that the child who in this way declines in his accomplishments or deviates from previous good behavior is suffering from the loss of narcissistic rewards and external ego and superego support. These disturbances are no doubt overdetermined. These children may be criminals in part out of a sense of guilt, seeking punishment for the guilt they feel for the parent's death (Bonnard, 1961). Another factor which may be operative is that the child's previous good behavior may have been predicated on a kind of bargain with fate. He was being good to ensure that nothing bad would happen. When his parent died, the bargain with fate was abrogated. Such a sequence could be reconstructed in the case of the 20-year-old girl, mentioned before, whose father died when she was 14. The father had had a heart attack when she was eight. Following this the girl had developed compulsive rituals and many scruples about bad thoughts and bad words, the unconscious purpose of which was presumably to prevent anything bad happening to her father. When he died, of a second heart attack, it was as if fate had failed to keep the bargain and she was released from her part of it. Immediately following her father's death, her schoolwork, which had been excellent, declined. In adolescence she became promiscuous, and on starting treatment at 19, she presented a picture of an impulse-ridden character.

I have tried to indicate in the case of Ruth that her clinging to her lost mother was motivated by incipient panic at the thought of letting go: "If I would admit to myself that my mother is dead, I would be terribly scared." I should now like to explore the factors which make for this overwhelming fear of acknowledging that the dead parent is irretrievably lost. One such factor has already been indicated in the discussion of the external ego and superego support that the child needs from the parents: without this the child fears the disintegration of the psychic structure he has achieved. On the most primitive level he fears annihilation: he could not survive if the parent were not still there. Ruth's saying, "If my mother were really dead, I would be all alone," expresses this. There would be no one to care for her, no one to gratify any of her needs, she would be abandoned in an alien world. This apprehension of annihilation in a child of Ruth's age is related to the evocation of a much more infantile image of the mother than that of the mother whom she recently knew. It corresponds to the sense of acute helplessness provoked by the loss of the parent.

A related fear is that of the breakthrough of massive amounts of objectless libido, of traumatic intensity. In mourning there is a gradual decathexis of the lost object, and this gradualness protects the mourner from a traumatic release of more unbound libido than he can cope with. I would like to suggest that children and young adolescents lack the capacity for this kind of dosage in emotional letting go. We know that in the sphere of action there is a gradual progression in being able to postpone action and to substitute the trial action of thought, in which smaller quantities of energy are involved. It would seem that there is a similar slow or late development of the capacity to release affective energies in any gradual way (Fenichel, 1945, p. 393). Children operate on an all-or-none basis. A tentative trial of what it would mean to let go of a lost parent thus evokes the threat of being overwhelmed and they revert to defensive denial.

Another factor contributing to the fear of acknowledging such a grievous loss is that the child still conceives of the parent as a part of himself. Jacobson (1965) has recently pointed this out, and has compared the desperate striving of a child to recover a lost parent with the little girl's longing to recover her lost penis.[10] That the parent is felt to be a part of the child, or an inalienable possession without which he is incomplete, helps to account for our repeated finding that children are deeply ashamed of having lost a parent. They often try to conceal this fact, or feel chagrined when it is revealed. The bereaved child feels a painful inferiority to children who have an intact family. Sometimes this feeling is displaced to material possessions.[11] For instance, the ten-year-old boy mentioned earlier, whose father had died when he was three,

---

[10]In discussing the splitting of the ego as a defense against unbearable aspects of reality, Freud (1927, 1940) cited two main instances in which this defense was invoked: in relation to the castration complex and in relation to the death of a parent.

[11]James Robertson (1958) has pointed out how young children, in prolonged separation from their parents, shift from longing for their presence to increasing demands for material gifts.

was particularly occupied with cars because his father had had such an impressive big car. He was keen on collecting toy model cars and became distressed when he saw another boy with a collection larger than his. He characterized the feeling evoked by the comparison of himself with such a more fortunate boy as *jealancholy,* a term he coined as a condensation of *jealousy* and *melancholy.* This boy was deeply ashamed of lacking a father and tried to conceal this fact from his schoolmates.

There is one further fear I would mention which reinforces the child's denial of the loss of a parent; that is the fear of regression. Repeatedly, children and adolescents have reported that they were unable to cry following the parent's death or that an inhibition of crying set in after a brief period of time. So, for instance, a 13-year-old boy said he felt nauseated on the trip back from his father's funeral and attributed this to the fact that he had swallowed his tears. Adolescents often feel distressed, uneasy, and self-accusing at this inhibition of crying, as we saw in the case of Ruth. We have to do here with an insufficiently explored topic: the relation of crying to different phases of development. Young children cry readily at any frustration, deprivation, disappointment, or hurt. In latency there is normally a marked inhibition of crying and conscious repudiation of it as babyish. We are probably justified in suspecting that there is something amiss with a child in this phase who continues to cry easily. The inhibition of crying seems to extend well into adolescence. There is of course also a sex-typing in this regard in our culture: it is more shameful for boys to cry than it is for girls. However, in response to a major loss, adults of both sexes cry more freely than do children or adolescents.[12] The crying of adults in grief, if it is not indefinitely protracted, appears as a normal regression. Children and adolescents seem to hold back from such a regression, perhaps out of fear that once under way it would have no bounds and precipitate them to total infantility.

I should now like to consider a question which probably has already occurred to the reader: the child who has lost one parent still has a parent—why is the surviving parent not an adequate support for the child, an object to whom the child can transfer the feelings he had for the parent who has died? According to our observations, the child's relations with the surviving parent regularly become more difficult (Neubauer, 1960). There are many reasons for this, which I shall indicate here only in part. When a parent has died, the child is confronted with a widowed parent, afflicted, grief-stricken, withdrawn in mourning, sometimes otherwise disturbed. Whether the widowed parent is of the same or opposite sex, the child's incestuous strivings toward

---

[12]Studies of reactions to the death of President Kennedy showed that adults wept more than did children or adolescents (Sheatsley and Feldman, 1964; Sigel, 1965).

him are stimulated from seeing him now alone. But the parent seems to take little comfort from the child's presence; he is lost in grief. It is as if the child wished to say, "Don't you see me? I am here." And the parent replied, "You are no help." The child thus experiences anew the oedipal chagrin, the sense of his inadequacy in comparison with an adult marital partner. At the same time there is a futile but desperate urge on the part of both the child and the widowed parent to put the child in the place of the missing parent. One of our most repeated findings is that, following the death of a parent, a child shares the bedroom and sometimes the bed of the widowed parent. Many rationalizations are given for this arrangement: the parent is lonely, the child is frightened at night, the family has moved to smaller living quarters. One boy told us that he had to go to his mother's bed because he was cold. When the warm weather came he still had to go there because there was a fan in her room. Evidently behind such trivial justifications there are deep needs on both sides. Even when the child is not sharing the parent's bedroom, incestuous impulses are intensified and arouse alarm. In struggling to ward off these impulses, the child becomes withdrawn or antagonistic toward the widowed parent.

There is also the child's tendency, as previously noted, to concentrate intensified positive feelings on the lost parent. The negative sector of the ambivalence formerly felt toward the lost parent is split off, and its most available target is the remaining parent. As the lost parent is idealized, the surviving parent is devalued. Often there is the conscious wish that he (or she) had died instead. Jacobson (1965) has pointed out that on a deeper level the child blames the surviving parent for the loss he has suffered. In the child's fantasy, this parent has destroyed the other or been deserted because of his unworthiness. Thus, for a child who has lost a parent, relations with both parents become distorted. As to the narcissistic supplies and ego and superego support which the child so needs, a parent withdrawn in grief is little able to provide them. The child often feels and reacts as though he has lost both parents.

IV

I have tried to show that there is a developmental unreadiness in children for the work of mourning. I should now like to turn to the question: What are the developmental preconditions which make mourning possible? Adolescence has been repeatedly likened to mourning (A. Freud, 1958; Jacobson, 1961, 1964; Lampl-de Groot, 1960). In adolescence there is normally a protracted and painful decathexis of those who have until then been the major love objects—the parents. The hypothesis I wish to propose is this: not only does adolescence resemble mourning, it constitutes the necessary precondition for being able to mourn later. The painful and gradual decathexis of the beloved parents which the adolescent is forced to perform serves as an initiation into how to mourn. The individual who has passed through this decisive experience has learned how to give up a major love object. In circumstances of later loss, he is able to recapitulate the process.

It is not until adolescence that the individual is forced to give up a major love object. We have seen how little external loss enforces such a decathexis. The conflicts of the oedipal phase, as Anna Freud (1958) has pointed out, lead to a change in the quality of the child's love for the parents, making it love with an inhibited aim. But the parents remain the major love objects. It is only in adolescence that developmental exigencies require a radical decathexis of the parents. With sexual maturity, the adolescent is powerfully impelled to seek a sexual object. The images of the parents become relibidinized, but there the incest barrier stands in the way. The adolescent is confronted with the dilemma: to withdraw libidinal cathexis from the parents or to renounce sexual fulfillment. This may be likened to the dilemma of the mourner as Freud described it. The mourner is bound to the beloved object, no longer available; at the same time he is attached to life and all it may still have to offer. Eventually the decision is in favor of ongoing life and the renunciation of the past which this requires. The adolescent, impelled forward by his sexual urges, is similarly constrained to detach himself from his beloved parents and his childhood past.

We know that the struggle of the adolescent to achieve this detachment is a long and difficult one. Forward movement often alternates with regression. The adolescent has many possibilities, in terms of both opportunity and his newly developing capacities for diverting freed libido into new love relations, friendships, and sublimated activities. But these newly found interests are often unstable; new relationships prove transient and disappointing. Libido reverts to the old objects or becomes absorbed in the self and the work of inner reorganization. To the extent that freed libido remains objectless, depressed moods occur. Abraham (1911, 1924) has pointed out that depression is experienced not only when an object is lost externally, but when there is an inability to love someone formerly loved. This is what happens with the adolescent as his capacity to love his parents declines. Jacobson (1961, 1964) has said that the adolescent experiences an intensity of grief unknown in previous phases of life.

Freud has stressed the crucial role of remembering in mourning and the reality testing by means of which memories are consigned to the irrevocable past. I should like to suggest that we find an analogue of this, too, in adolescence, that in adolescence a new feeling about the past emerges. There is a nostalgia for a lost past, a combined yearning and sense of irrevocability. The ways of remembering one's own past in different phases of development remain incompletely explored. We may consider, however, certain earlier phenomena in this area. The young child may yearn for the past, but he does not consider it irrevocable. He has not yet grasped the irreversibility of time. If he wishes to be a baby again, we will observe him crawling on all fours and saying "da, da." He becomes a baby. In the latency period, with the repression which follows the oedipal phase, the attitude toward the past changes. It becomes one of repudiation. When his parents recall amusing and endearing things he used to do when he was little, the latency child is inclined to disclaim these babyish things with some contempt. He puts his past behind him and prides himself on his new skills and accomplishments.

It is in adolescence that the sense of a longed-for past develops with the conviction that it can never come again. The past assumes a mythical aura. Fantasies of a golden age of the personal and the historic past probably have their inception in this time of life. Let me cite an early "memory" which a 13-year-old girl said had recently come to mind and which seemed to her very real. She recalled being wheeled in a baby carriage, in which she was cozily and contentedly ensconced, while her mother and father walked behind. She attributed to her infant self the thought, "Too bad this can't last." We would recognize this as a screen memory, in which memories and fantasies have been condensed. This girl had been the eldest child in her family and no doubt had envied the younger siblings, whom she had seen replacing herself in the baby carriage, as they had in her parents' affections. In this memory she was again in sole possession of the parents. By ascribing to her past self the awareness that this could not last, she was attempting to undo the traumatic surprise at the arrival of the next sibling. At the same time the sense of transience, of past pleasures having to be renounced, which pertained to her adolescent state, became part of the content of her childhood memory.

Nostalgic memories probably generally preserve something from very early childhood, antedating the oedipal troubles so painfully revived in adolescence. The theme of such memories, more or less disguised, is of the self as a greatly loved small child. As Wordsworth says in his great nostalgic poem on rec-ollections of early childhood: "Heaven lay about us in our infancy." The adolescent, in the enforced giving up of his parents, feels a sense of all he is losing. He conjures up regressively the most ideal aspects of being a child encompassed by parental love. We know that few real memories survive from the earliest years. Yet most individuals possess a history of themselves starting from birth, which is based on their parents' reminiscences. The parents them-selves feel nostalgic when they recall to the older child the happenings of his first years. They suffer some sense of loss as the confiding and affectionate small child seems to grow away from them into greater independence. I would suggest that the adolescent, in his nostalgia for the past, identifies with his parents nostalgically recalling his early years.

The sense of the irrevocability of the past appears in many ways in adolescence. There may be an acute awareness of the transience of present pleasure, that every moment is slipping into the past, that life itself is ephemeral. Adolescents often find in their preferred poetry expression of these moods. A. E. Housman's poems, for instance, express an adolescent longing for a lost past, never wholly renounced:

> That is the land of lost content,
> I see it shining plain,
> The happy highways where I went
> And cannot come again.

It has been said that Housman's poems are best appreciated by adolescents. Similarly, adolescent girls weep over songs of unhappy love, of partings and longing for an absent lover. Their conscious thoughts may be of a boy who has recently disappointed them. But the intensity of their grief is for the loss of a much greater love, the waning of their love for their parents, and the renunciation of their childhood.

In comparing adolescence with mourning, we should also consider the ways in which they differ. The mourner is well aware that he is sad because of the loss of a beloved person and his mind is dominated by thoughts of the lost object. The adolescent does not know why he is sad or depressed and does not attribute these feelings to the loss of his capacity to feel love for his parents. Where the mourner has suffered an external loss, the adolescent undergoes an enforced renunciation because of internal conflicts. Whether the adolescent's renunciation is experienced as more active and voluntary than that of the mourner varies with the individual. This probably depends in large part on the relative strength of the forward impulsion and the regressive pull. The objects from which the adolescent is freeing himself are still there. Aggression can be directed toward them with some impunity since, in a reassuring way, they continue to survive. This is in contrast to the tendency to divert aggression from objects lost by death. While the mourner thinks of the object he has lost in a loving and idealizing way, the adolescent is devaluing the objects he is in the process of giving up. When the adolescent's struggle to withdraw from the parents becomes too difficult, he can still turn to them again and, not without mixed feelings, derive gratification and support from their presence. In mourning a major amount of the libidinal attachment to the lost object is dissolved and the mourner is released from his painful, incessant preoccupation with the lost object. Yet he retains loving feelings for the one he has lost. Even more in adolescence, the decathexis of the parents is incomplete. Normally a positive attachment to them continues, though the feelings for them are no longer of such intensity or preeminence as those of earlier years.

The likeness of the adolescent process to mourning appears in the very considerable decathexis of major love objects, occurring over a period of time, accompanied by painful feelings, and with reality testing affirming the irrevocability of the past. The exigencies of adolescence which enforce this renunciation are without precedent in the child's antecedent life. Until he has undergone what we may call the trial mourning of adolescence, he is unable to mourn. Once he has lived through the painful, protracted decathecting of the first love objects, he can repeat the process when circumstances of external loss require a similar renunciation. When such loss occurs, we may picture the individual who has been initiated into mourning through adolescence confronting himself with the preconscious question: "Can I bear to give up someone I love so much?" The answer follows: "Yes, I can bear it—I have been through it once before." Before the trial mourning of adolescence has been undergone, a child making the same tentative beginning of reality testing in regard to a major object loss is threatened with the prospect of overwhelming panic and retreats into defensive denial in the way we have observed.

We have seen that the younger child's panic at the prospect of having to give up a lost parent is related to the characteristics of the object relation. The parent is felt to be an indispensable source of material and narcissistic supplies, an auxiliary ego and superego, a part of the self. The renunciation of the parents in adolescence entails a giving up to a considerable extent of the kind of relationship the child has had with them heretofore. Where the giving up of the child-parent relationship is not accomplished, the individual may merely turn away from his parents to seek others who will fulfill the same functions. Where in this way the work of adolescence has remained uncompleted, the adult remains unable to accomplish the work of mourning in response to loss.

V

We have considered the struggle of children and adolescents to deny the finality of the loss of a parent and their unreadiness to decathect the lost object through the work of mourning as we know it in adults. The question arises whether there is an alternative way for the immature individual to decathect a lost parent without undergoing the process of mourning. Such an adaptive alternative may not be available to our child patients, handicapped as they usually are by disturbances in development which antedate the parent's death. To assess the range of possibilities, it is important for us to supplement our clinical data with observations of children whose development has been relatively unimpeded up to the time of the parent's death. I shall now turn to an instance of this sort, in which we can see an adaptive reaction to the loss of a parent in childhood, and at the same time contrast this reaction with that of mourning.

Walter, whose life course I have been able to follow from infancy to young manhood, lost his mother at the age of ten. The mother died of cancer after a period of progressive debilitation. During her last illness both she and the boy were cared for by the young woman's mother, who had great love and understanding for them both. Little by little, as the mother declined and became unable to satisfy the boy's needs, he transferred his affections to the grandmother. She was there, providing for his material wants, attentive to his accounts of his school days, appreciative of his accomplishments, involved with everything that concerned him. It was no doubt important that the grandmother was no newcomer in the boy's life. He had known her well before, and for a period of time she had cared for him in his mother's absence. Thus, it was not a question of forming a new attachment, but of transferring a greater amount of feeling to someone already loved. What I believe happened here was that there was a piecemeal transfer of libido, detached from the mother, to an immediately available and acceptable mother substitute. This began while the mother was dying, and the boy turned gradually from her, withdrawn as she was in her illness, toward the grandmother. The process continued after the mother's death, when the grandmother devoted herself to Walter's care and upbringing.

Walter showed some of the same emotional inhibitions in reaction to his mother's death that appeared in the child patients we have discussed. He did not cry and made strenuous efforts to deny and ward off feelings of distress. When his mother died he was sent to spend the day with friends of the family. In thanking these friends for their hospitality, Walter laid exaggerated stress on what a happy day this had been for him. Unlike the adult mourner, he showed no diminution in his interest in usual activities. He was anxious to return to school at once and to carry on as if nothing had happened. In his spare time he began to immerse himself in incessant reading. We may suppose that partly this served to exclude painful thoughts and feelings. Partly, his involvement with fictional heroes helped him to experience vicariously emotions which he could not acknowledge more directly. It was in relation to fictional characters that he experienced a belated breakthrough in his inhibited grief. Three years after his mother's death, when he came to the end of the series of books about the Three Musketeers, he wept profusely, saying,

"My three favorite characters died today." I have characterized this phenomenon elsewhere as "mourning at a distance" (Wolfenstein, 1965).

The angry feelings in reaction to loss, which we have observed repeatedly, were not absent here. Following his mother's death, Walter was diffusely irritable and quick to anger. In an altercation with his grandmother, intolerant of her rebuke, he said he was leaving home and stormed out into the night. When he returned, his grandmother said that they would have to talk about how bad they both were feeling because of his mother's death. She told him of the efforts that had been made to save his mother's life, that drugs had been flown in from other cities, and how sad it was that medical science was not yet sufficiently advanced to cure the terrible illness she had had. Walter then was moved to confess that he blamed himself for his mother's death. Two years before she died she had had a breast operation and had returned from the hospital very weak. Nevertheless, she had gotten up in the mornings to prepare Walter's breakfast before he went to school. He now felt that if she had not had to get up to get his breakfast, she would not have died. The grandmother assured him that this was not the cause of his mother's death, and that his mother's love for him and interest in him helped to keep her alive as long as possible. Their discussion went on far into the night, and at the end the boy, greatly relieved, and with the intolerance for prolonged distress characteristic of his age, exclaimed, "I feel great!"

While his mother was dying and for a considerable time after her death, Walter was insatiably hungry. He consumed huge amounts of food and was particularly greedy for sweets. In this intensification of oral needs, we may see a manifestation of the bereaved child's regressive longing for the all-fulfilling parent of earliest years. In this instance, the regression remained circumscribed. The child's libido did not remain overly bound to the fantasy image of an idealized lost parent. The regressive greediness expressed only that part of the libido which was not yet transferred to the grandmother. But the greater part of the child's needs were being fulfilled in reality by the grandmother, who was able to supply material and narcissistic gratifications and to give ego and superego support.

In adolescence Walter showed strong feeling for and interest in friends, and he developed an increasing capacity for sublimation in intellectual pursuits. At 25 he is married, with two much-loved young children, and is progressing in his chosen career with pleasure and accomplishment.

Such an outcome requires a combination of favorable external and subjective conditions. The major external condition is the availability of an adequate parent substitute. Our culture generally makes little provision for such substitutes. The nuclear family, consisting of young parents and their growing children, entails an exclusiveness of attachment of children to their parents. Margaret Mead (1965) has pointed out that the nuclear family is especially well adapted to life in a rapidly changing culture. There is minimal boundness to old ways and customs. However, such a family is very little adapted to changes in its own personnel. In times and places where children have been raised in an extended family, there is a greater possibility of finding immediately available and acceptable substitutes if a parent dies (Volkart and Michael, 1957). In the context of our culture, the case of Walter is relatively exceptional in that a good mother substitute was immediately available to the bereaved child. The pre-existing mutual attachment of grandmother and grandson and his previous experience of living with her in his mother's absence facilitated the transition. Moreover, the collaborative, noncompetitive way in which mother and grandmother had shared the boy's care probably lessened what feelings he may have had of being disloyal to his mother in turning to his grandmother.

The subjective factors favoring a major shift of object cathexis in childhood require further exploration. I can allude to them here only in a preliminary way.[13] We know that the fate of feeling toward a lost object is related to the ambivalence with which the object was regarded. Paradoxically, the more ambivalent the relationship has been, the harder it is to give it up. Where there has been strong ambivalence toward the object, its loss is likely to precipitate the protracted reproachful demands for its return which Bowlby has described. In the case of Walter, ambivalence toward his mother, whose only child he was, appears to have been of moderate intensity.

Freud has stressed that no libidinal position is abandoned without great reluctance. More recent observations of children, however, have also made us aware of an opposite tendency, a developmental push which impels them toward more advanced levels of functioning. There are probably great individual differences in the balance between the tendency to cling to early libidinal positions and the impulsion to move forward. In the readiness to welcome persons other than the mother, we can observe marked individual differences among children in the first years of life. Walter was one of those children who very early in life showed a great eagerness toward people. Thus, a facility for forming object relations was probably another condition favoring his successful shift from mother to grandmother.

In the case of Walter, we have seen an adaptive reaction to the loss of a parent in childhood, in which apparently a major decathexis of the lost parent

---

[13]We would expect a child's readiness to accept a substitute object to be related to the phase of development in which he was when he experienced the loss of a major object. Thus, we would hypothesize that when a child is still almost wholly dependent on a need-gratifying object, he will be most ready to transfer his affections to someone who is able to provide for his needs (A. Freud and Burlingham, 1943, 1944).

was accomplished. However, the process here differs markedly from that of adult mourning. There was no protracted sadness or withdrawal into painful preoccupation with memories of the lost object. In the gradual decathexis of the mother, while she was dying and after her death, Walter was able to transfer freed libido immediately to an already-present mother substitute. If we imagined an analogue to this in an adult, we would have to picture a widower, let us say, having at his side a new wife, even one who had been an auxiliary wife before, to whom he could transfer at once the libido he was detaching from the wife he had lost. This is not adult mourning as we know it. The adult mourner can transfer his feelings to a new object, if one is found, only after a period of time in which he is emotionally occupied with detaching libido from the lost object. There is a hiatus here which the child is unable to tolerate.

VI

This paper has been concerned with determining the developmental pre-conditions for mourning. Observations of children in the age range from latency into adolescence, who have suffered the death of a parent, have shown that they are unable to mourn. In many instances, instead of a decathexis of the lost object, we found an intensified cathexis, with an overt or covert denial of the irrevocability of the loss. In the favorable instance of an adaptive reaction to such a loss, the process differed from that of mourning. There was an immediate transfer of freed libido to an available substitute parent. I have considered the factors making for the developmental unreadiness to mourn in children and young adolescents, in terms of the nature of the object relation to the parents. The hypothesis has been advanced that adolescence constitutes the necessary developmental condition for being able to mourn. Adolescence has been likened to a trial mourning, in which there is a gradual decathexis of the first love objects, accompanied by sad and painful feelings, with reality testing of memories confirming the irrevocability of the childhood past. It is only after this initiation into mourning has been undergone that the individual becomes able to perform the work of mourning in response to later losses.

19

INTRODUCTION

The Effects of Parental Divorce: The Adolescent Experience, by Judith S. Wallerstein and Joan B. Kelly

If the frequency of divorce and remarriage continues to accelerate at a pace comparable to that of the recent past, it may not be long before we consider the one-parent home or reconstituted family, with one biological parent and one step-parent, to be a modal family style rather than an alternative one. Indeed, one-parent homes are already a statistical norm. Despite these startling demographic changes, research on the effects of divorce on children has barely begun. The following chapter by Wallerstein and Kelly is probably the only systematic investigation of adolescents who have experienced parental divorce. Clearly, more studies are needed, particularly in view of the findings reported below, which run counter to widely held notions about the minimal effects of divorce on adolescents. The authors' findings agree with King's (1971) impressions that the intact family is a "consistent differentiating variable between healthy and disturbed adolescents" (p. 39).

As the first of several reports in a series, this chapter includes a thoughtful discussion of the authors' conceptual framework. Their subsequent reports describe the diverse effects of divorce at various developmental stages: preschool (Wallerstein and Kelly, 1975), early latency (Kelly and Wallerstein, 1976), and later latency (Wallerstein and Kelly, 1976). Although their sample is neither large nor representative, in the absence of comparable studies their findings suggest developmental interference to an extent that is anything but encouraging when extrapolated to the large numbers of children who experience parental divorce. The vulnerable preschool children, for instance, showed pervasive neediness, early signs of depressive illness, and developmental constriction and delays. Perhaps most alarming was that 44% of these children were found to be in a significantly deteriorated psychological condition at follow-up one year later, although none had a prior history of psychological difficulty. The early latency children were more immobilized than the preschool children by their suffering, and their defense organization was more vulnerable to regression. Although, in terms of sadness, fear, and feelings of deprivation and loss, half of the early latency children had improved one year later, close to a quarter of them had worsened. There was no evident correlation between initial response and eventual outcome.

The older latency children demonstrated greater capacity to grasp and integrate the long-term consequences of family problems. Their anger and alarm at their parents' behavior often galvanized them into organized activity to reverse the passively suffered family disruption. Although initially their sense of identity was shaken and they were afraid of being lost or forgotten, after a year most of the acute reactions had subsided. Nevertheless, bitterness and nostalgia, or anger at one or both parents, remained. At one-year follow-up half of these older latency children showed evidence of consolidated depressive behavior patterns combined with frequent school and peer difficulties.

Richard A. Gardner has also written about the effect of divorce on children, with pragmatic advice for three separate readerships. His first book (1970) is designed for the children of divorce themselves. It contains an introduction for their parents, who very likely will find the rest of this valuable children's book of considerable interest. His two most recent books (1976, 1977) are aimed at psychotherapists and parents respectively.

Probably the greatest amount of ferment is focused on the legal problems. Derdeyn (1976) has recently placed child custody contests in historical perspective. The last two of his 97 bibliographic references merit special attention. In "The Children of Armageddon" (1969), Watson discusses methods for determining the psychological "best interests" of the child in a custody dispute. His paper in some respects is a conceptual precursor to the landmark volume *Beyond the Best Interests of the Child* by Goldstein, A. Freud, and Solnit (1973). This book is dedicated to making "the child's need paramount" in the eyes of the law. The desirability of this goal may seem self-evident to most readers, but various authors require convincing empirical evidence for this position (e.g., Mnookin, 1975).

Goldstein, A. Freud, and Solnit (1973) suggest that the law reformulate the ill-defined and probably unattainable (at the time of divorce) "best interests of the child" into a substitute concept: the "least detrimental alternative." This deceptively simple, but brilliant proposal stems from the fact that with paradoxical frequency children have, in the past, been denied the least detrimental alternative, under the guise of providing for their best interests. In relation to custody cases, the authors attempt to maximize the continuity of relationships; to recognize the child's, rather than only the adult's, sense of time; and to take into account the marked limitations of our predictions about human behavior or assumptions that others behave wisely. They evince a "preference for privacy," by which they mean a minimum of governmental interference in family life. They thus propose giving the custodial parent the complete power over child-rearing decisions that the two parents (theoretically) exercised in tandem prior to the divorce. Here they include all decisions regarding visitation rights of the other parent. In this way, the authors hope to enhance the stability and quality of parenting. They suggest further that when both parents in a custody dispute appear to be equally adequate, then the standard of the least detrimental alternative calls for a "quick, final, and unconditional disposition to either of the competing parents." In the absence of other criteria, this decision might even be decided by a judicial coin toss! As one might expect, this suggestion has proved highly controversial. The authors (Solnit, 1976, personal communication) feel it has been widely misunderstood and perhaps requires another volume to explain it.

This brings us back to what Kelly and Wallerstein (1976) note in concluding their paper on the effects of parental divorce on the child in early latency: "the divorce *event* is not the central factor in determining the outcome for the child, but rather, the divorce *process* or chain of events set in motion by the separation. The assimilation of divorce-related changes for children and parents is, for many, a process lasting several years" (p. 32).

19

The Effects of Parental Divorce:
The Adolescent Experience

JUDITH S. WALLERSTEIN and
JOAN B. KELLY

This essay, which discusses the effects of parental divorce on the adolescent, is the first report from a three-year study designed to observe and record the impact of divorce on children and on their families as discerned at the time of the divorce decision and again approximately one year thereafter. These research goals were combined with efforts to develop counseling models and specific techniques of psychological guidance for the participating families. Of the 131 children in our total sample, 21 were 13 years old or older at the time of the divorce decision. Although this represents a relatively small group, the findings are nonetheless notable, partly because they are at some variance with generally held conceptions regarding the response of adolescents to family disruption and partly because there have been no systematic studies reported in the literature regarding the phase-specific impact of parental divorce at this developmental period.

Marin County, stretching northward from San Francisco, contains some 206,000 people and is considered one of the most beautiful as well as most affluent areas in the United States. It has at the same time one of the highest marriage and divorce rates in the country and in the world.[1] The population

First published in *The Child in His Family*, Volume 3: *Children at Psychiatric Risk*, edited by E. J. Anthony and C. Koupernik. New York: John Wiley & Sons, 1974, pp. 479–505. Copyright © 1974, John Wiley & Sons, Inc. Reprinted by permission of John Wiley & Sons, Inc.

The Children of Divorce Project was supported by a grant from the Zellerbach Family Fund of San Francisco at the Community Mental Health Center of Marin County, California.

[1] In 1970 the divorce rate in the United States was 3.5 per 1,000 population, in California 4.2 per 1,000, and in Marin County 5.7 per 1,000. The highest divorce rate outside of the United States in 1970 was in the USSR (2.6 per 1,000). In other European countries where divorce is legal, the divorce rate was considerably lower.

is young, relatively well educated, racially nearly homogeneous, and generally vigorous. Because of these considerations, it was reasoned that the phenomenon of divorce might in this milieu be more susceptible to highlighted systematic study than in settings where divorce is accompanied by high crime and poverty rates, crowding, and other disorders of urban living which contribute to the strain of family life. In effect, it was hoped that a relatively stable setting would better enable the divorce themes themselves to emerge over time with greater clarity.

Accordingly, in 1970 the project reported here was begun at the Community Mental Health Center of Marin County, directed to the general divorcing population. People who had taken the decisive step of legal filing for family dissolution were advised of the availability of our free counseling service for themselves and their children. The counseling was explained as child-focused, primarily preventive in nature, and including an individual evaluation of each child and counseling sessions with the parents. Help was offered to parents in interpreting the family dissolution to the children, in planning postdivorce arrangements, and, through discussion with each parent, in finding ways of easing the effects on the children. In effect, we threw a wide net into the general divorce population pool, and we brought in 60 families with 131 children between the ages of three and 19, who were seen by five experienced clinicians trained in work with children and parents. The subjects were seen during a six-week initial counseling period and invited to return for further follow-up interviews, again individually for each family member, at 12 to 18 months postcounseling. Thus, our data derive from these subjects, seen initially at the height of the divorce decision or crisis, and subsequently when relationships had presumably had a chance to achieve a more stable equilibrium. A subgroup, encountered serendipitously in the course of this study, was composed of those parents who, as children, had experienced the divorce of their own parents. Their revived memories and feelings provided an additional, although retrospective, source of data.

Although marital crises and divorce have received considerable professional and community attention in the post World War II United States, the effects of divorce on children have been very little scrutinized. At the time that this study was launched only McDermott (1968) had collected direct observations on a nonclinical population at the time of parental divorce, and his sample

---

Between 1962 and 1972 in the United States the rate of divorce has increased 81% while the marriage rate has risen only 27%. A comparable analysis for California indicates a 96% increase in the divorce rate with a 26% rise in the marriage rate. The number of children under the age of 18 involved in divorce is also greater in California (16.6 per 1,000 children in 1969) than in the United States as a whole (10.3 per 1,000 children in 1969). [See *California Statistical Abstract, 1971; Statistical Abstract of the U.S., 1972; United Nations Statistical Yearbook, 1971; Vital Statistics of California, 1962–1971; Vital Statistics of the United States, 1969.*]

was limited to 22 children of nursery school age. Subsequently, Hetherington (1973) reported an experimental study of the behavioral responses to male interviewers of adolescent girls who had lost their fathers through earlier divorce, as compared with girls who had lost their fathers through death and girls from still-intact families. Hetherington found intensified seductive and somewhat maladroit behaviors in her experimental sample. In these instances the divorces also were not recent but predated the girls' adolescence. There have been some social science survey studies (Burchinal, 1964; Goode, 1965; Landis, 1960, 1962, 1963; Nye, 1957) attempting through retrospective questionnaire data to establish correlations between parental divorce and certain emotional and behavioral sequences such as alteration in self-esteem regulation, dating patterns, and deviant or delinquent behavior patterns. As with Hetherington's findings, the divorce in most instances had been in earlier periods. Finally, there have been reports of studies of court and clinical populations (McDermott, 1970; Westman et al., 1970) trying to ascertain common psychological or social characteristics of the divorcing families and their children, and accumulated experience and extrapolations from clinical practice (Despert, 1953; Steinzor, 1969; Westman, 1972). None of these have been addressed specifically to the youngster who has reached adolescence at the time of the parental divorce.

In our project we attempted to study parental divorce as an individual psychological experience to be followed over time for its impact on and consequences for each of the participants in the family drama, the children individually and in interaction across generations with their divorcing parents. In doing so, we have been guided by a number of general theoretical considerations and conceptualizations which set the framework for our study.

First, we have taken for granted the complex interplay of adaptive and defensive strategies that determines each child's capacity to maneuver the divorce stress, each with his idiosyncratic distribution of areas of achieved mastery and growth alongside emotional difficulties and compromise formation. This interplay is represented by the following example. The child of divorcing parents who expresses guiltily his responsibility for having caused the divorce may indeed be doing so to ward off the more terrifying feeling that he has no control over or indeed no influence whatsoever on the course of events in his environment. This particular conflict resolution, with the anxiety and guilt generated, may actually be in the service of the most effective coping with an otherwise overwhelming situation. Therapeutic work directed solely toward the exposure and resolution of the conflict over neurotic guilt can thus concurrently undermine the most effective coping strategy available to that child at that time. Similarly, Anna Freud (1958, 1965) has stressed the role of psychological regression and denial as significant and necessary parts of normal childhood and adolescent development. Clinical judgment regarding the efficacies of these maneuvers must take into account the specific adaptive as well as defensive purposes and value of each in formulating an overall judgment regarding the child's psychic state in relation to the event or phenomenon being coped with.

A second guiding generalization was that judgments of pathology in coping could be made confidently only over time, because we have no established, understood, or agreed-upon normative behavior models for effective response to the kind of life crisis represented by divorce. Do we know anything, for example, about expectable response or spectrum of response to family disruption that can differentially portend ultimate mastery or failure to master? Can the capacity to maintain development as the central criterion for mental health be assessed clinically at the time of divorce or indeed only when viewed within the perspective of time, and if so at what appropriate time or distance from the event? Further, can theoretical and clinical models for assessing normal and pathological response to family disruption, comparable to stages of mourning or object loss, be constructed and how can these be assessed except over time, and if so over what time? It is because of these considerations—this desire to study evolution over time—that while making full use of clinical formulations at the initial study, we have tried to reserve overall clinical judgments until we have had the fullest advantage of the maximum time perspective afforded by the follow-up inquiry. In consequence, as much as possible we suspended final judgment on the need for intervention at the time of the initial counseling and moved to intervene therapeutically at this time only where the suffering of the child seemed acutely to require it.

Third, we were interested in the age-specific normal developmental tasks of the children caught up in the divorce. In the part of the study being presented here, our concern is with the adolescent subgroup and the impact of the divorce on the process of resolution of their phase-specific tasks. As developed by Anna Freud (1958), Erikson (1959), Blos (1962a), Laufer (1966), and others, the appropriate mastery of these adolescent tasks is the necessary prologue to adulthood and true heterosexual identity formation. Blos has summarized this as follows: "The adolescent process proceeds from a progressive decathexis of primary love objects to increased narcissism and autoeroticism to heterosexual object finding and involves a detachment of psychic institutions from the parental influence . . . this process of detachment is accompanied by a profound sense of loss and isolation equivalent to mourning" (Blos, 1962a, p. 125).

Our own formulation here, consistent with our study data and clinical observations, is that the family disruption, by virtue of the particular interplay

between the divorcing adults and the interplay between each of the parents
and the adolescent, poses a very specific hazard to this normal adolescent
process of progressive decathecting of the primary love objects. As such, it
carries the potential for severely overburdening the adolescent ego in its
maturational, time-appointed tasks. At the same time, the very same situation
of hazard carries with it a concomitant potential for the stimulation of a
developmental spurt and accelerated growth toward adulthood which, *if it
does not come prematurely* (i.e., before the normal detachment has begun
to take place), may indeed even facilitate the road to independence and
maturity.

Related to this formulation is our additional emphasis on the other side of
the interaction—the psychological position of the parents—and the powerful
reverberations in the adolescent of the impact of the divorce on the parent.
Thus, the adolescents and their parents were conjoined within the vicissitudes
of the parent-adolescent relationship as set within the divorce frame of reference. The young people were facing parents who were responding to the
combination of stresses and promises in the current family disruption, sometimes with frenetic, regressive, even disorganized behavior.[2] At the same
time, their relationships to the parents were shaped by their personal versions
of the complex, phase-specific, and usually conflicted interactions of the
parent-child relationship and by the history and style of this relationship at
earlier stages in the family life, as well as by its forerunners in the childhood
and adolescent experiences of the parents themselves.

Pushed by regressive forces, the parents often reverted to their own preadult
or adolescent behavioral life stages or patterns in identification with or in
competition with their own children and/or their own past.[3] Many parents of
both sexes, driven by vulnerabilities, threatened by a loss of self-esteem with
depressions, rages, and sexual impulses set free, characteristically turned to
their adolescent children for support, comfort, battle alliances, and moral
vindication. Or sometimes the same parents manifested a desperate need to
use the adolescent as an unconscious or conscious extension of themselves
in the conflicted relationship with the spouse, creating difficulty in maintaining proper distance and separateness from the developing youngster despite intellectual recognition that the child's burgeoning autonomy needed
protection. Thus, Mrs. Y., a divorcing mother of four, protested that she was
unable to forbid her 15- and 13-year-old daughters from having continuing
sexual relationships with their boyfriends, because "they had just lost their

---

[2] A recent study (Briscoe et al., 1973) points to a higher incidence of serious psychiatric illness
among divorced people.

[3] A related set of observations by Elson (1964) suggests that some parents embark on abrupt
life changes including divorce in response to the adolescent's departure for college.

father.'' Both girls were engaged in considerable sexual activity when seen at counseling.

Some parents for a time preceding the divorce lived out sexual impulses with much younger partners or moved into a marketplace of available partners patterned after adolescent or young adult behavior. The adolescent child might then be experienced by the parent as a peer or competitor in these liaisons. For example, Mrs. B., age 33, who became depressed and anxious when she was without a date, began to bring home a succession of young men in their twenties. She wore her skirts very short, her clothes very tight, her hair loose in the manner of a teenager. Her manner was flippant, bright, and hard. She complained to us that her 13-year-old daughter was chronically peevish and disobedient. ''Probably,'' she said smilingly, ''because she is jealous.''

Sometimes hostile and destructive impulses were released at the time preceding and during the divorce in people who had been able to bind such impulses previously in obsessive-compulsive defenses and had functioned previously with apparent intactness in their responsible adult roles. Mr. C. at the time of the divorce explained to his adolescent son that his mother had developed a postpartum psychosis after her delivery requiring both hospitalization and electric shock, and that subsequently he needed to be cared for by somebody else during his infancy, emphasizing his scientific conviction that mental illness is inherited. His son, age 13, was clinically depressed and suicidal when seen by us. And still other parents tried to prevent independent relationships between their youngsters and the separating parent. Mrs. L. appealed with repeated tears to her adolescent daughters for support against their sinful father. She endured their visits with the father with great tension, cross-examining them after each visit, making them voyeurs regarding the detail of the father's relationship with his girlfriend.

SHARED RESPONSES TO THE DIVORCE EXPERIENCE

Certain experiences and responses to the divorce appeared in our data with sufficient frequency to be considered as common or characteristic of the adolescent group as a whole. The commonality of response undoubtedly has its roots in the developmental psychology of the adolescent and for the most part represents that aspect of the adolescent's functioning devoted to active mastery of, and adaptive coping with, the disorganizing impact of the divorce.

DIVORCE AS A PAINFUL EXPERIENCE

The 21 adolescents in our sample, almost without exception, experienced the divorce process as an extraordinarily painful event. Painful feelings were legion, and at times seemed too intense for the young people to deal with. These feelings, we suggest, reflected the precipitousness with which psychological processes and changing perceptions that usually unfold developmentally over time often had to be telescoped into excessively brief time spans under pressure of the divorce happenings. Predominant affects generated were those of great anger at the parents for breaking up the family at a point critical to the adolescent, considerable sadness and sense of loss, or a sense of betrayal by the parents, if not both. Intensely strong feelings of shame and embarrassment prevented some from sharing any of their misery, and several adolescents had not even told their closest friends of their parents' divorce. The helpless immobilization implied in "I just *couldn't*" suggests that to talk of their pain and embarrassment would somehow reveal *them* as failures, rather than their parents. Other youth, caught in loyalty conflicts, experienced much guilt when in fantasy or reality they aligned themselves with one parent, with resentment at both parents the inevitable result. The extent of unhappiness in all forms was initially of considerable surprise to us all, since the general expectation of both the professional and lay communities was that the more vulnerable, dependent preschool and latency children would experience more overt distress. Despite the expectation that the adolescent process of decathecting the parents in the psychological move out of the house would lessen their pain, the acute distress repeatedly and forcefully conveyed to us was inescapably real.

> Openly expressing resentment at her mother for bringing her to the counseling service, D. burst into angry tears. "God! This *would* have to happen just when things were settling down . . . [more tears] . . . this really *upsets* me! I could have used your help a long time ago, but I've *already* talked this out." (Did it help?) "Yes! And now I want to forget about it!!!" Alternately laughing at and apologizing for being so emotional at 15 years, she tearfully continued to demonstrate her inability to "forget about it," unleashing a torrent of anger, sadness, confusion, and helpless feelings.

> A 14-year-old confided "the rug was pulled out from under me" when he learned his parents would divorce. Surprised and shocked, G. cried for some time, then undertook heroic efforts to effect a reconciliation. "I begged and begged . . . I tried to talk sense to my mother until I was almost *mute*." He even emphasized that a reconciliation would save lots of money. At counseling, he sadly admitted his helplessness in this hopeless endeavor, but nevertheless asked the therapist to try once more for a reconciliation on his behalf.

Occasionally an adolescent insisted the divorce was not a particularly painful or disrupting experience, assuming a detached stance of "That's their problem . . . it doesn't really affect me." Only a year later were such adolescents able to reveal their pain. Thus, a 17-year-old, asked at the follow-up session what advice he would give to parents contemplating divorce, quickly replied, "Don't divorce!!!" Because he had been cool and detached one and a half years earlier, the therapist replied that it sounded as if the divorce had been more painful than he had previously admitted. He emphatically agreed.

The pain of divorce for adolescents did not appear consequent to any feeling of responsibility for the parents' divorce. This is in contrast to the preschool and latency children studied, who assumed in their thinking varying degrees of responsibility for causing the divorce, which then increased their anguish and guilt. It is unclear why these adolescents did not feel this sense of responsibility. It may be that any assumption of responsibility would too gravely accentuate the revivified oedipal pressures, in part phase-specific and in part heightened under the impact of the divorce. In addition, we can say of the pain of parental divorce at adolescence that it may remain a persistent and unresolved aspect of the psychic life of the individual; at least it was so from the reports of the parents in our group who had themselves sustained a parental divorce when they were adolescents (as distinct from those to whom this had occurred at earlier ages). This fresh and unremitting psychic pain was often stated to be responsible for the sometimes lengthy delays in obtaining the current divorce.

ANXIETY ABOUT FUTURE MARRIAGE

Another significant finding was an enormous concern, shared by the more intact adolescents, about their future as marital partners. Whereas for some this was a painful problem expressed at the time of the initial counseling, for others it appeared to crystallize only during the year that followed. Because the breakdown of the parents' marriage comes at a time when the adolescent is expending considerable thought and psychological energy in the service of his heterosexual object-finding, the divorce experience interjects itself into his thinking in several relevant ways. It confronts the adolescent with the inescapable concern that divorce may also occur in *his* future adult life. For our adolescents, two different reactions occurred in response to this salient anxiety about future divorces. The first was a decision that he or she would *never* marry, heard commonly at the time of the initial counseling. Some who initially asserted their doubt about future marriage modified their position somewhat by the time of follow-up.

> One attractive 15-year-old expressed firmly her doubt she would ever marry. L. would "travel a great deal and live with a man." "If we had a child then I suppose we would have to take some appropriate action . . . but I just don't know about

getting married." A year later, L.'s stance was essentially unchanged, and in fact may have been consolidated by the newly discovered, disturbing information that her mother had been married twice before.

For those who had not ruled out marriage, much thought was given to marrying later than their parents had, with an attendant conscious intent to be quite selective, and wiser than their parents, in the choice of marital partners.

> G., age 16 by follow-up, said he "would be more careful than my parents were." "Actually, I'm not sure I'll ever marry . . . certainly not until I'm in my thirties." He expressed many questions about marriage—"it seemed to ruin so many lives." Further, G. emphatically stated, "I never would have children . . . unless I got to be a millionaire and needed an heir."

> Early in the divorce process, one 16-year-old had already given considerable thought to her future marriage. "I won't marry young . . . I want to develop *my* interests and skills first. Love and respect are necessary . . . but companionship is the most important thing in a marriage. Each person has to have separate interests and respect the other person's interests, but it's really important to have common interests and goals, too. My parents didn't respect each other at all, and the only common interest they had was us kids."

Unfortunately, there is not much evidence that such conscious intent to select a mate more carefully actually eventuates in a more compatible marriage, although one would hope that such might be the case for these adolescents painfully thinking through their futures. In analyzing the 60 families in the sample, we were repeatedly struck by the absence of love, compassion, and intimacy among the parents of these children, even in their descriptions of the earlier history of their marriages. These young people had hardly experienced and internalized any concept of marriage as characterized by giving, caring, and loving. Thus, although their caution was admirable, their experience with alternatives was sadly limited, and it is hard to predict whether their caution will be in the service of better choices.

Related to the concern about being or finding an adequate marital partner was evidence, in some of our adolescents, of considerable anxiety about adequacy as a sexual partner, either in their current dating or future married life. Although this coincides with normative adolescent anxieties about developing sexuality, the identification with the parent as a sexual failure enhanced these anxieties. Some adolescents had been told in explicit detail of the sexual inadequacies or peculiarities of one parent by the other, angry or self-justifying one. Two older adolescent girls dramatically accused their mothers of "making" them frigid because of the divorce action. Despite their ability to later relinquish this stance, the self-esteem of both girls as sexual beings in their own heterosexual relationships was threatened, demonstrating again how divorce can painfully collide with adolescent development.

WORRY ABOUT MONEY

One interesting observation was the often unrealistic concern about finances seen predominantly in those adolescents who were functioning reasonably well. Because money was one of the most common battlegrounds between divorcing parents, many of the children and adolescents became "money-wise" somewhat prematurely. For latency children anxiety about money was diffuse and related to overall feelings of deprivation, whereas for adolescents the anxiety about finances became focused around their future needs. Some adolescents were sure that neither parent would finance their college education, despite the obvious fact that sufficient funds were indeed available. Further, they were disinclined to settle the matter by definitively discussing the matter with the parents separately, for fear of starting new arguments and bitterness. Other adolescents were told by their mothers that no money would be available at the same time that their fathers were insisting that college-support was part of the final settlement given to the mother.

By the time of follow-up, even those adolescents most accustomed to affluence had adopted a more realistic stance toward the availability of money and tended to be less demanding in terms of personal luxuries. This did not necessarily mean they had forever given up the notion of personal affluence. Rather, there was evidence of an increased capacity for delay of gratification, a more realistic understanding of financial priorities, and a certain gratefulness for getting what they could. In general, the divorce appeared to create a more mature attitude toward financial matters in the long range, despite the initial anxiety and anger about being deprived. Being more realistic generally seemed to be one of the benefits of divorce for those adolescents able to actively master the divorce experience in a reasonably healthy manner.

PRECIPITOUSLY CHANGED PERCEPTIONS OF THE PARENTS

Adolescent development involves the disengagement from the primary love objects and the accompanying move toward heterosexual object choice. Normally this process is a gradual one. One significant finding of our study was the fact that divorce shortens the normally available time span for the gradual accomplishment of these tasks, and instead plunges the child abruptly into the process of having to disengage from and shift his perceptions of his parents. Because these teenagers had little opportunity to establish their own tempo in this regard, feelings of loss, emptiness, and loneliness were much exacerbated.

In our adolescent sample, for example, the divorce process forced a *precipitous* deidealization of the parent. The previously overvalued parent, considered unrealistically and with awe, becomes abruptly undervalued, a painfully fallen idol. Typically, the adolescent at this time feels personally betrayed by his parents' divorce, and often vigorously defends against such feelings of loss by expressing considerable rage. In the process, he over-zealously undervalues and derogates at least one of these fallen parents. Because of the continuing tie with the parent, and those internalized aspects of the ego ideal derived from the parent, there is the risk that such precipitous deidealization may interfere with the consolidation of the adolescent's own consolidating self-esteem.

> Angry at her mother for seeking a divorce, D. described her mother as "weak, artificial, inadequate, and *totally* dependent upon her therapist," while insisting that her father, previously very rejecting of her, was brilliant, good, "a fine person." Viewing both assessments as unrealistic, the therapist was concerned about this girl's future feminine identification and self-esteem if such unbalanced assessments were to persist. With gentle persistence, the 16-year-old's rage collapsed to reveal a profound sadness related to both parents' weaknesses, so dramatically revealed in the divorce conflict. "They *should* be more mature . . . I feel like *I* have to be the adult," she said wistfully.

For one 13-year-old the abrupt deidealization of her father did not occur until a year following the divorce when she accidentally encountered her rather proper father with a young woman at a local art fair. This coalesced with the recent discovery of other pertinent information about her father which had been withheld. Both events led to a sense of moral indignation, a tumbling of her father in her esteem, a new feeling that he was not a man of moral integrity. Her sense of disappointment, of loss, was as painful as her anger as she mourned the father of her childhood fantasy and her preadolescence.

ACCELERATED INDIVIDUATION OF PARENTS

Divorce also appears to force the adolescent to separate out each parent as an individual, to formulate differential views of his parents qua individuals earlier than would be developmentally required. One factor precipitating this earlier scrutiny and differentiation is the active process of working through the stated and unstated reasons for the divorce. The explanations provided by the parents initiate the process, providing powerful impetus to differentiating the parents into people with incompatible needs, interests, and goals. When a parent states that "we never really loved each other," "she wants a different kind of life style," "we just weren't interested in the same things," or "he won't stop drinking . . . he needs more help than I can give him," the adolescent is forced to think beyond the parental unit to very distinct individuals. The individuation process is increasingly consolidated as each parent is seen functioning in geographical and psychological separation.

This process of differentiation may proceed in several directions, depending upon the capacity of the adolescent to integrate the observations about his parents and make constructive inferences that will influence his maturing personality. For those capable of such inferences, and whose parents permit this to occur by allowing the adolescent to make some of his own independent assessments, the result seems to be an earlier, more realistic acceptance of personality differences, a greater sense of closure about the divorce, and a smoother process of identity formation. For some, this contributes to a more mature look at the hazards and potentialities of marital interactions. The abrupt individuation of the parents forced by the divorce may at the same time serve a defensive function by transforming feelings of helplessness into a sense of control via active mastery.

> Poised and responsive, J., a 17-year-old, indicated at the following session she had taken a much more objective stance toward both parents. Previously furious at both, with attendant feelings of helplessness at her vulnerable position, J. viewed her relationship with each as considerably improved. Much to her relief, her father "doesn't get upset as much these days." "I guess I'm also seeing him more as a person than as my important daddy." Her mother's newly found happiness also pleases her, and she enjoys being close to her in a new and more mature way.

> Just 15 at follow-up, S. indicated in a variety of ways that his relationship with his mother had deteriorated. "She does strange things . . . unreasonable things . . . like she has this plan to keep changing our rooms around, and when she's finished we won't be able to go back to our old rooms, even if we like them." "My mom told me she didn't hate my dad, but now I know she does. She does things just to punish him . . . like she waited until my dad drove all the way out to our house before telling him we couldn't go on the camping trip. Lots of times she gives reasons for things that aren't the real reasons." S. accurately perceived his mother's behavior as frequently irrational, yet seemed to have come to grips with it.

HEIGHTENED AWARENESS OF PARENTS AS SEXUAL OBJECTS

One further aspect of the abruptly changed perception of the parent attendant upon the divorce was seeing the parent as a sexual object. A certain number of adolescents became overly anxious about their parent's sexuality, suddenly now visible where before it could be more readily denied. Having a mistress, frequent dates, or a boyfriend sleep overnight inescapably presented the adolescent with more evidence than he cared to see that his parent was indeed a sexual being and now very much in the same marketplace as the adolescent in terms of heterosexual object-finding. Undoubtedly the anxiety was due to increased sexual and reawakened incestuous fantasies: the parent was no longer a "safe" object. This was complicated by the fact that quite a few fathers had found girlfriends close in age to their adolescent daughters. Several adolescent girls handled their anxiety and dismay by significantly, but quietly curtailing the number of visits with their father. Others were scornful or morally indignant, primarily as a defense against their own incestuous fantasies, yet did not share these feelings with the parent.

LOYALTY CONFLICTS: THE NEED TO CHOOSE

In many of the divorcing families in our sample, one or both parents consciously or unconsciously required that the child align with him in the continuing struggle. This demand on the adolescent frequently resulted in feelings of despair, anger, guilt, and depression. At the time of the initial counseling, early in the divorce proceedings, more than half of our adolescents were profoundly conflicted by issues of allegiance and loyalty, and angrily protested the role they felt was being forced upon them.

> After some initial resistance to becoming involved in divorce counseling, W. settled back and said, "Okay, mother and I hassle." When asked what about, she replied, "My mother tries to get me to say critical things about my dad and I don't want to!" When the therapist supported her stance, the 14-year-old warmed up and continued, "Mother demands that I take her side . . . she expects that I will share her anger toward dad for leaving her for another woman . . . and if I just stay silent, then it means that I agree with her!" W. described how she actively fought back against her mother. Later in the session, when the therapist shared her feelings that it was unfair for anyone to be caught between parents, W. cried, "But I *am* in the middle . . . I *am* in the middle . . . it *is* my struggle! I'm loyal to my father and I love my mother. I want to help my mother and I know that she needs it . . . but she keeps going about it in the wrong way!!"

It is significant that by the follow-up a year later, virtually all of these adolescents had been able to disengage themselves from such active loyalty conflicts. This is in striking contrast to the latency children seen in this study, many of whom were unable to detach themselves from this destructive process by virtue of their age and dependence on the parent for continued support and nurturance. The normal adolescent process of decathecting the parental figures combined with the early abrupt differentiation of parents as separate individuals functioned as an invaluable assist to the adolescent caught in divorce. Instead of feeling forced to align himself with one parent and reject the other, the adolescent was able to detach himself from both parents, including the parent making the demand for the allegiance.

> At follow-up a year later, W.'s anger at her mother remained, but she could now openly discuss her feelings and was very much in control of herself. She said that "things are just the same . . . my mother is just as angry, just as bitter, and just as jealous of my father's girlfriend." The intensity was the same, but the expression of the mother's feelings was perhaps a bit muted now. What had changed was that

they, the children, had learned to talk less of their father, and when the mother asked if the girlfriend was present during their visits, they lied to the mother now, and solved the problem that way.

This adolescent had learned to deal adaptively with her difficult mother. She no longer felt pulled by either parent, and in fact gained self-esteem in the move away from both of them. What was necessary, however, was a compromise of the high moral sense of the adolescent, that is, the need to lie to keep the peace. Whereas a year earlier such a need to compromise created moral outrage and angry outbursts against the mother, this was now accepted as a necessary adaptive solution. In those adolescents, not few in number, who were forced to compromise their integrity in such ways, there was no evidence that their moral sense was compromised in other areas.

Related to this was the observation that our adolescents were forced to grapple openly with issues of morality raised uniquely by the divorce. Less universal in scope than the traditional moral searching of adolescence, these concerns centered on which parent was right or wrong in those attitudes and actions causing the marital conflict and eventuating in divorce. Most adolescents struggled with such moral questions not only in the service of making judgments about the parents, but more importantly in the service of consolidating their own consciences and moral development, particularly in determining appropriate ethical and sexual conduct for themselves now and for the future. For some, it was a question of which parent represented the appropriate moral attitude to be identified with, while others determined that both parents' moral and ethical behavior was wanting.

E. talked at counseling of changes over the past few years in her life, stating, "Even though my mother and father were dishonest, and I used to be, I've suddenly stopped. I don't know why . . . I just decided I didn't want to be like them." A year later at follow-up, E. indicated she'd thought a lot about her parents "cheating on each" (sexual affairs)—"I think it's terrible!"

This is especially significant for this adolescent because, lacking adults of high moral conduct available as role models, her move toward higher ethical standards came from within as she increased the distance between herself and her parents after the divorce.

STRATEGIC WITHDRAWAL

All of the adolescents in this study tried with varying degrees of success to make use of distancing and withdrawal as a defense against experiencing the pain of the family disruption. Sometimes this distancing took the active form of much accelerated social activity or staying away from home, which was especially threatening to some parents, particularly those parents who had been apprehensive initially about the acting out of their adolescent children, and whose apprehensiveness may have increased by virtue of their own newly found sexual freedom. Some youngsters declared vehemently their lack of involvement with parental problems despite behavior and many tears to the contrary.

A certain percentage of adolescents in our study held steadfastly to detachment and distance verging on aloofness. Some of these were indeed young people for whom the divorce essentially legalized and consolidated a family life style and relationship pattern between the parents which had pre-existed for many years. These young people had already set a particular course.

> P., age 16 1/2, an essentially intact youngster, who continued to do well at school and elsewhere, said of his father (whose combined job and mistress had previously kept him absent from the home), "Dad was never around before. We learned to get along without him. The divorce won't make any real difference." P. volunteered that he had felt sad at times, because he never had a real father; he missed this when he was a "growing child." He hoped that the divorce would bring some relief for his mother's anger and chronic unhappiness.
>
> P.'s older brother, who was into serious, rebellious acting out, drunkenness, drug abuse, car accidents, and violent outbursts in the family said the divorce would change nothing for him. His social behavior and relationship patterns within the family continued essentially on the same hurricane course, perhaps somewhat accelerated. At age 18, within a year of the divorce, he became involved in a drunken accident in which he demolished a friend's car.

The group that particularly interested us consisted of young people in their early or mid-adolescence who, before the divorce, had not led lives essentially detached from their families. Rather, it seemed to be primarily in response to the divorce decision that their behavior veered away from the parental figures. Their "cool" manner was in fact a source of some initial concern to us as to whether the central developmental impact of the divorce might indeed be an increase in narcissistic investment and a diminution in empathic response. Thus R., a very bright 15-year-old, stoutly maintained that his parents divorced only because they had undertaken the building of a new home and could not agree on the number or placement of the bathrooms. He held to this position concretely and not metaphorically through the entire counseling period. I., when initially seen, delivered herself of some very strong opinions with surprisingly mild affect. Her dispassionate recounting of her parents' marital failures and their personal faults and her clear interest in only her own life were striking and troublesome in this 13-year-old girl.

It is therefore of central importance to report that these particular adolescents looked the best to us in our entire sample at follow-up not only in terms of their having matured considerably during the intervening year, but primarily in terms of their now demonstrated capacity for empathy, warmth, and compassion toward at least one parent. Moreover, this sometimes took a form well beyond verbal support and extended to considerable help in the home. Thus I., in contrast to her previous cool stance and self-centered behavior, had willingly assumed responsibility for helping her mother with the younger siblings and expressed geniune concern about her mother's welfare.

> When seen at follow-up, R. no longer maintained his previous superficial explanation of his parents' divorce. He seemed much more outgoing and poised and considerably less preoccupied with his own needs. This time he said that he thinks his parents behaved foolishly, that he feels his mother's need for support, help, and intimacy, but that he feels that he can be of no help to her, and it would not benefit him or them for him to enter into the difficulty between his mother and his father. He was willing at this follow-up to admit how painful the divorce had been in the past year.

> A., who had been spending most of her time out of the house at the time of initial counseling, also seemed to have mellowed considerably. She was less defensive and less angry. Whereas previously she said, "I don't care about him or her" in relation to her parents, A. now said that her dad had problems, but she was not going to let his problems upset her, and "bother my activities and my life." When reminded of her statements the year before, and her fighting with her siblings and feelings of injustice on the part of her parents, A. laughed freely, and said, "Was I like that? Wow, I really was a brat then."

It would appear that for those adolescents the emotional detachment at the time of the parental divorce represents a strategic withdrawal in the service of maintaining the integrity of adolescent development. It seems clear that the distancing at the time of the height of the struggle saves the adolescent from anguish, humiliation, and emotional depletion, and enables him at a later date—at a time appropriate to his own timetable and needs, and when the external turmoil has subsided somewhat—to be supportive, empathic, and sensitive. Nor is there any reason to assume that such capacities for empathy, compassion, and protectiveness will not endure into adulthood. These findings would be very much in accord with our understanding of the significant place of withdrawal and denial in the normal development of children and adolescents.

MAJOR PSYCHOPATHOLOGICAL FORMATIONS

Finally, we must consider those subgroups among our youngsters in which the divorce triggered or consolidated serious psychopathological response as assessed within the time perspective of initial counseling and subsequent follow-up. We consider these the young people *at risk* and needful of psychotherapeutic intervention. One case illustrative of each such subgroup is presented here.

PROLONGED INTERFERENCE WITH ENTRY INTO ADOLESCENCE

For several young people in our study the primary impact of the parental divorce experience can be considered as a developmental interference in which the entry into adolescence and the mastery of the normative tasks of adolescence seemed delayed or held back indefinitely by the particular conflict configuration and parent-child interaction which obtained at that time.

> T. is an early adolescent whose aggressive, driving father was often caustic and verbally abusive with his wife and three children. At other times the father was affectionate with his son, but rarely with any other members of the family. T.'s mother suffered with a severe hysterical illness with disabling psychosomatic symptoms of many years standing for which she had recently entered psychotherapy. To compensate for her husband's disinterest, she had always been especially close to T., and he in turn worried about her illness, her depression, and her suicide attempts.
>
> When T. was told by his parents of their divorce decision, he ran from the living room screaming, "You're trying to kill us all." Following his father's moving out of the household, T. began increasingly to assume a protective role with his mother. He checked her social activities, monitored her telephone calls, requested the check at restaurants, sat in his father's place at the dinner table, and lay down on the sofa with her on occasion. Some of the impetus for this behavior doubtless derived from the mother's gratification with T.'s attention, which was supportive of her at a time when she felt intensely deprived.
>
> When seen a year thereafter the boy's preoccupation with his mother's health had intensified. His jealousy of her other relationships and particularly of her intimacy with her psychotherapist was undiminished. He flew into jealous rages when she dated, was indeed sleepless when she went out on a date, and worried about her continually, especially about her possible death from cancer. His own attachment to his friends had lessened, as he had become more preoccupied with his mother, although he continued to do well academically.

T., at 14, is clinically at risk, manifesting a delayed entry into adolescence and is in active need of psychotherapeutic intervention. A year following the divorce he is still suffering with increasingly intolerable conflict which binds him into a conflicted, overly eroticized oedipal attachment to his mother, an attachment which has been given real and fantasy impetus by the father's departure and the mother's divorce-intensified needs. T.'s panic at the announcement of the divorce decision by the parents presaged the difficulties which he did indeed encounter. A year following the parental separation, he is further away from his own autonomy and independence.

TEMPORARY INTERFERENCE WITH ENTRY INTO ADOLESCENCE

H., age 13, a child of a marriage which came to divorce after one and one-half years of no conversation, no sex, and no meals between the parents, who communicated entirely by written notes during all of this time, had an intense relationship with her father, who had held her on his lap until she was 11 years old. He was a violent, abusive, and authoritarian figure to his wife and two sons, but never to his daughter. The mother was a petulant, long-suffering woman who seemed helpless for many years to resist the father's tantrums, moodiness, and beatings. After the mother filed for divorce, the father refused to leave the house and returned nightly in a towering rage. When the divorce was granted, he disappeared.

When H. was seen, she was apprehensive, depressed, and inarticulate. Her sadness, her sense of loss, her worry about her father, her forlorn hope that he still loved her despite his desertion, and her tattered self-esteem came out gradually, but without relief or diminution of her depression. H. gained 20 pounds in the three months following the mother's decision to file for divorce. During this period she began to drop contact with her friends, to engage in doll play with younger children, and to sleep in her mother's bed.

At follow-up, approximately two years later, H. was in the process of reconstituting her predivorce state of functioning. She was gradually regaining an appropriate age-level performance at school, although still having difficulty. She had, however, resumed friends in her age group and was succeeding in losing much of her excess weight gain. Although still somewhat subdued and stolid in her responses, she seemed to have moved into age-appropriate adolescent development. Her recovery from the regression and resumption of age-appropriate behavior coincided with the mother's remarriage and H.'s good relationship with the stepfather.

This case represents a delay rather than a full blocking of the youngster's entry into adolescent development. We note in passing that sleeping with the mother following the divorce was not a common occurrence among adolescents, but was more common following parental divorce where there were latency or younger children in the family. There were many such instances in our sample in which the parent was apprehensive about sleeping alone at this time. In this case it is important to point out that H. was not able to resume her own developmental agenda until she was free from the regressive interaction with the mother and the multifaceted impact of the father's desertion by the mother's remarriage and her good relationship with her stepfather.

PSEUDO-ADOLESCENCE IN RESPONSE TO PARENTAL DIVORCE

One danger specific to adolescence is entry into heterosexual activity, prematurely, before having acquired the precondition for true heterosexual love relationships. To the extent that the sexual activity occurs under the dominance of an incestuous tie to the parents or as an extension of the parents' unconscious or conscious needs and impulses, the adolescent can be said to be living out a pseudo-adolescence rather than a true, emancipating adolescent experience.

> C., age 15 at counseling, began her sexual activity at age 14 at the time that her father began a sexual affair with a neighbor. C. was full of rage at her father, whom she considered an adulterer. She described in obscene language her fantasies of her father's sexual performance with his mistress and shared these and other confidences regarding her father's sexual activity with her mother in what appeared to be an ongoing relationship in which mother and daughter developed strategies together regarding the father and his mistress. These consultations seemed at times to reach bizarre limits, as, for instance, when the mother found an unsigned note addressed to no one in particular, saying "I want to love you," and called a family conference to ascertain what strategies should be undertaken.
>
> C.'s father, a mild-mannered, gentle, chronically depressed professional man, referred to his marriage as a "blur," and seemed unable to see any connection between his behavior and its consequences either for his wife or for his children. C.'s mother, a teacher who had been relatively organized in her functioning prior to the divorce, suffered a severe regression at the time of the divorce decision. She began to show increasingly poor judgment and seemed to be warding off a disorganizing depression through a variety of disjunctive behaviors including inviting numbers of young men to live in the household, probably in a desperate effort to deny her intolerable perception of the husband's departure and absence. In various ways it seemed clear that the mother in her regressed state seemed unable, except in a verbal way, to differentiate her needs from those of her daughter.

C. is a severely disturbed adolescent whose symptoms include drinking, drug abuse, promiscuity, and poor impulse control. She is much at risk, and in urgent need of both psychotherapy and environmental controls.

REGRESSION FOLLOWING LOSS OF EXTERNAL VALUES AND CONTROLS

Another subgroup of young people at risk comprised those for whom the parental divorce signified primarily the loss of external behavioral constraints and models which still provided a necessary part of their psychic economy. Specifically the external presence of the parent, usually the father, served to reinforce and organize still insufficiently consolidated inner-control mechanisms. Therefore, for these youngsters, the disruption of the family structure, the loss of the father's physical presence, the discovery of sexual, aggressive, and "amoral" behaviors in parents with the consequent sense of disappointment and betrayal triggered acute anxiety and intense conflict. It seemed clear that the controls and tenuous identification and ego ideals of these young people were unable to contain heightened sexual and aggressive impulses in the absence of the familiar external reinforcement and threats.

B. discovered accidentally that his father was having a sexual liaison with a young woman before this information became known to his mother and before the divorce decision. This discovery caused B. intense and unremitting anguish. "I began to feel a lot of anxiety. What should I do; what shouldn't I do? Should I do it now; should I do it later?" With the father's decision to request the divorce, B. was enormously shocked and felt that his father had betrayed his major philosophy of life, namely, never to quit. "It was rare that you could go to my dad with any kind of a problem and not have him say, 'You have to stay with it.' In this case my dad was chucking away what was the basis of my philosophy that he had taught me. It meant to me that maybe my point of view was wrong since my dad threw it away. It felt like I was taking a creaky ship into the storm" (referring to his own future ventures into adulthood and particularly to his plans to become engaged to a young woman).

B. developed a series of somatic symptoms, including dizzy spells, sleeplessness, and fears of being alone. These culminated in an emergency episode when while driving a car across a bridge B. felt unable to proceed. Shortly thereafter B. was admitted to a psychiatric hospital where he began to work out the conflicts triggered by the divorce and in particular his feelings that he was "incapacitated by my father's desertion."

B.'s father, an aggressive and somewhat blustering businessman, had indeed ventured into what appeared to be an adolescent fling at middle age. B.'s mother was a dependent, somewhat unrealistic woman who lived in B.'s view "in that upper-middle-class world that exists for women who drive station wagons and work hard on charities." Central in B.'s breakdown was his statement: "I think that the beliefs which gave me the ability to deal effectively with life were blown apart for me."

Divorce as a Superimposed Trauma

Finally, there were in our study youngsters at serious risk whose life experience had been unhappy and fraught with conflict and insecurities for many years. For these adolescents, the divorce itself represented one more link in a long chain of experiences out of which they drew the same lesson: the reasonable needs and wishes of the children had little or no priority within the family. These adolescents found themselves without role models, prodded by the wish to achieve independence from the unhappiness and rejection they had known, but without the inner integrations needed to face the complex and exacting demands of adolescence. In a true sense they were in flight *from* rather than to, and there was no doubt that without intense psychological help over the long term they would not be able to make headway toward adulthood. In addition, the parents of these youngsters burdened themselves and their children with their own unresolved or unmodified need for immediate gratifications, with frantic efforts to ward off psychotic disorganization and profound depressions which threatened to engulf them, in direct competition with, and depreciation of, the capacities and physical appearance of their children.

> E., age 13, came from a family in which both her father and mother had struggled throughout the marriage to maintain adulthood, but had little sense of the dimensions of the parental roles except as economic providers. Each had had throughout a succession of open love affairs often with the other's friends. The father, a handsome, narcissistic man with an explosive temper, had precipitated the divorce, because he wished to marry an older woman "who would be good for me." The mother, a tense, pretty, young woman, had warded off a profound chronic depression by a variety of maneuvers, including staying out of the home and needing the constant company of a man. At the time of the divorce decision both parents were preoccupied with their own needs: the father with his wish to move out as easily as possible; the mother with the acquisition of a new man to cover her loneliness, rage, and threatened depression.
>
> At counseling, E. explained that she had no use for any adults, particularly her parents, that she wished only to live alone, because she found adults deceitful, selfish, irresponsible, and without morality. The parents' divorce confirmed and underscored this view. Her affective life centered around an encapsulated fantasy of horses who led an erotic, wild, and beautiful life, mating endlessly and producing in polygamous society happy children whom they treated with love and compassion. E. said, "Whenever things get tough I go into my room, and I talk to my horses, and my horses talk back to me." E. had few friends and was doing poorly at school.
>
> At follow-up, E. said there was one adult in the world whom she trusted. That was the matron in the local school, who permitted her to smoke. E. was smoking excessively with some mild drug use, a great deal of loneliness, and a desperate yearning for affection, friends, and interest from any quarter where it might be forthcoming. She had established herself in those high school groups identified with antisocial behavior. Although she had mostly relinquished her preadolescent fantasy of horses, she had hardly replaced it and was feeling empty, restless, and hungry for stimuli.

E. is suffering with a serious depression of long standing, is predelinquent, with a lifelong history of emotional deprivation and erratic parenting. She is very much in need of long-term psychotherapeutic help and environmental supports.

Conclusions

It appears that following parental divorce many young people live through an acutely painful experience which, although time-limited for most, is marked by a rapid acceleration and telescoping of normative adolescent perceptions, conflicts, preoccupations, and responses. Some of the distress may indeed be related to the rapidity with which the changes occur under the press of the divorce impact and the diminished ability of the adolescent to exercise control over the tempo of change. Nevertheless, most of the young people whom we studied were able, within a year following parental separation, to take up their individual agendas and proceed toward adulthood at a more measured pace. Moreover, it seemed that except where the response to divorce caused delays or ruptured development, they were able to continue at a level equivalent to their previous achievement or enhanced even by their mastery of the inner and outer events of the preceding year.

Those youngsters who entered adolescence and encountered the parental divorce with a history of long-standing difficulties seemed to follow a more troubled course. These difficulties in many instances were intensely exacerbated by the difficulties of the parents at the time of the divorce. Of particular relevance to the experience of the adolescent was the degree of the parental regression, particularly to preadult or adolescent modes of behavior, and the tendency of some parents to cross generational boundaries out of the intensity of their own needs and conflicts. Many youngsters caught up in this interacting web were severely limited in their capacity to address complex adolescent tasks.

Finally, it seemed that the adolescents who appeared to do best were frequently those who were able at the outset to establish and maintain some distance from the parental crisis and whose parents, whether willingly or reluctantly, permitted them to do so. As noted, these young people at first impressed us as seeming somewhat self-centered and perhaps insensitive. We discovered over time that these were the youngsters who were able at the end of the year to develop that remarkable combination of realistic assessment of their parents along with compassion, which augurs well for their future.

Repeatedly, throughout this study, our attention was drawn to the central importance of the particular patterning of the parent-child relationship obtaining both at the time of the divorce and previously, and to the particular unconscious and conscious dissonances and congruities which are present in the interacting needs, impulses, conflicts, and defensive configurations. All of these seem centrally related to the capacities of each family member to hold to the separation of generations and to his individual growth potential.

20

INTRODUCTION

A Psychiatric Study of Parents Who
Abuse Infants and Small Children,
by Brandt F. Steele and Carl B. Pollock

In 1977 the Supreme Court declared that physical beatings in the schools are not necessarily "cruel and unusual punishment" if local communities do not specifically interdict them. This decision reinforces the biblical dictum "spare the rod and spoil the child" while serving as a forceful reminder of the ancient, but not forgotten view of children as property. Until recently children generally were economically advantageous property, whereas today children typically drain a family's economic resources, forcing parents to find other sources of gratification in child-rearing. In line with these attitudes, relative insensitivity to child abuse has been pervasive for a long time. The group at the University of Colorado responsible for the book *The Battered Child* (Helfer and Kempe, 1968), from which the following chapter is excerpted, has done much to counter this by elevating both professional and public consciousness of the issue.

It is interesting to note the evolution of medical recognition of child abuse. The most significant contribution toward the initial diagnosis of this problem came from recognizing the strange existence of radiologic pathology in children without sufficient explanation. Caffey (1946) noted that "for many years we have been puzzled by the roentgen disclosure of fresh, healing, and healed multiple fractures in the long bones of infants whose principal disease was chronic subdural hematoma . . . in not a single case was there a history of injury to which the skeletal lesions could reasonably be attributed and in no case was there clinical or roentgen evidence of generalized or localized skeletal disease which would predispose to pathological factors" (p. 163). But Caffey did not explicitly delineate why "fractures of the long bones are a common complication of infantile subdural hematoma," although his concern about this problem continued (Caffey, 1972). The major milestone in this medical-legal story was reached when Kempe, a pediatrician at the University of Colorado School of Medicine, and his colleagues coined the term *the battered child syndrome* (Kempe at al., 1962). They explained it as "a term used by us to characterize a clinical condition in young children who have received serious physical abuse, generally from a parent or foster parent. The condition has also been described as 'unrecognized trauma' by radiologists, orthopedists, pediatricians, and social service workers. It is a significant cause of childhood disability and death" (p. 17).

The Colorado efforts, along with the enactment of statutes in all 50 states facilitating the reporting of suspected child-battering, have resulted in a startling statistical increase in reported incidents. Although there are differences in sampling, it is nevertheless worth nothing that in 1962 Kempe et al. reported that 750 children nationwide were maltreated yearly; of these more than 10% died and more than 15% suffered permanent brain damage. In 1970, in a national survey, Gil reported 1,200 cases of suspected physical abuse and 6,500 instances of confirmed abuse. In the same year, the Report of the Joint Commission on Mental Health of Children (1970) cited Kempe and Helfer as raising their estimate to between two to three thousand children injured *monthly* and one to two children killed every day (p. 344). In 1977 in New York City alone more than 24,000 cases of suspected child abuse and neglect, with 77 deaths, were reported to the city's central registry (A. H. Green, 1979). Ounsted, Oppenheimer, and Lindsay (1975) believe that the successively higher incidence found in these surveys reflects more than enhanced awareness and better reporting, that it probably also represents a true increase. In either event, there is consensus that only the tip of the iceberg is visible. It is evident that only a fraction of abused children receive medical attention and in many cases physicians do not recognize injuries as stemming from abuse and thus these cases are not reported. The Report of the Joint Commission on Mental Health of Children (1970) quotes Kempe and Helfer as saying that "the number of children under five years of age killed by parents each year is higher than the number of those who die from disease" (p. 344). Holter and Friedman (1968) estimate that as many as 20% of all children seen in hospital emergency rooms may have injuries resulting from either parental neglect or abuse. At present, attention is being directed to another long-neglected form of child abuse as incidents of sex abuse are being identified in increasing numbers. Some argue that many, if not most, early teenage pregnancies are the product of incestuous relationships.

The observations reported in the following chapter are derived from the landmark work done at the University of Colorado in the early 1960s. As the authors note, the sample is a nonrepresentative one, and the data are all retrospective, without prospective testing of the hypotheses in groups identified as at risk. Nevertheless, Steele and Pollock's findings have been confirmed by a variety of other observers (see Spinetta and Rigler's [1972] literature review). The evidence of successive generational disruptions of the parental affectional system is compelling. Oliver and Taylor (1971), for instance, studied 40 of the closest relatives of a physically abused child and unearthed evidence of battering, abandonment, and other serious neglect or cruelty in all but 13 of those studied. Their five generations of ill-treated children testify to the serious undermining of parenting skills (see also Galdston, 1965; Gregg and Elmer, 1969).

Steele and Pollock differentiate the abusing parent's greater investment in the child, to the extent of punishing the child to change his or her behavior, from the neglecting parent's abandonment of efforts to even care for the child. A rapid reading of their chapter may create the erroneous impression that child abuse and neglect do not coexist. Steele and Pollock's focus, however, is on the parental dynamics involved in battering, and thus they do not address this issue. In Chapter 21, Evans, Reinhart, and Succop demonstrate that the two can indeed coexist, as has been reported by other observers (see our introduction to Chapter 21).

In the past it was commonly thought that physical abuse of children was highly correlated with psychosis in the parent. Current evidence suggests that parental psychosis is relatively infrequent. Attention has been directed increasingly to psychodynamic factors, as in the chapter that follows. Steele and Pollock focus on the interaction between parent and infant, in which the parent prematurely demands more than the child can compehend. The parent acts as if the child were much older than he or she is as part of a distorted identification and role reversal, in which the parent expects love and reassurance from the infant. It is also suggested that parenting must be learned by the experience of being parented, thus accounting for the commonly found intergenerational nature of abuse.

Merrill (1962) has delineated three clusters of personality characteristics pertaining to abusing mothers and fathers and a fourth cluster limited to abusing fathers. His typology, however, does not provide a clear guide to prognostic and therapeutic indicators, as does the categorization of families of children who fail to thrive presented by Evans, Reinhart, and Succop in Chapter 21. Merrill's first category comprised parents burdened with a pervasive, poorly controlled hostility and aggressiveness, which was sometimes focused on a specific target and at other times directed at the world at large. The second group was characterized by rigidity, compulsiveness, lack of warmth, unreasonableness, and inflexibility in thinking. These parents felt justified in their physical maltreatment of their children. In Merrill's third group, the mothers and fathers often were depressed, unresponsive, and appeared markedly passive and dependent, frequently competing with their children for the spouse's attention. His fourth group encompassed a significant number of the abusing fathers—young, intelligent, skilled men who, for one reason or another, were unable to support their families. In consequence, the wives worked and the fathers stayed home with the children, on whom they took out their frustrations in the form of rapid, violent punishment.

Lystad (1975) has reviewed the various typologies developed in relation to child abuse. Some focus on the degree of battering, e.g., controllable abuse or enraged battering (Boisvert, 1972); some emphasize the reasons for child abuse, e.g, altruistic or revenge (Flammang, 1970; P. Scott, 1973); and some deal with the effect of the abuse on the child, e.g., psychological or physical (Birrell and Birrell, 1968). Many studies point out that child abuse interacts with other forms of family dysfunction, such as marital conflict (B. Johnson and Morse, 1968), or with the societal pressures of economic adversity and social isolation (J. Brown and Daniels, 1968).

Initially, attention to the abused children themselves focused on efforts to protect them from noxious environmental influences. Subsequent observations of these children, however, produced descriptions of them as fearful, depressed, apathetic, negativistic, unresponsive, stubborn, as well as unappealing (Galdston, 1965; B. Johnson and Morse, 1968). Also noted was a high incidence of mental retardation, neurological impairment, and speech and language difficulties (Elmer, 1964–1965; H. Martin, 1972). Building on these and his own confirmatory observations, A. H. Green (1978) has endeavored to organize a psychodynamic framework that might facilitate therapeutic intervention for these needy children. He describes what he considers to be characteristic effects on their cognitive apparatus, ego functions, object relations, identifications, and libidinal organization. Under the rubric of traumatic anxiety states and masochistic self-destructive behaviors, Green notes that their preoccupation with external danger and their overstimulated drive activity interfere with the energy available for learning and mastery. An inability to develop "basic trust" and overuse of primitive defenses such as denial, projection, introjection, and splitting contribute to their difficulties with impulse control, self-concept, separation, and school adjustment.

In discussing his nationwide survey, Gil (1970, 1975) emphasizes that certain cultural attitudes condone the use of physical force as a child-rearing device and that socioeconomic privation is correlated with physical abuse. He thus proposes large-scale programs designed to eliminate social ills as the means of reducing child abuse. Without questioning the merit of his suggestions, it should be noted that he does not explain child abuse in the affluent, nor why it is so often only one child in the family who is singled out for abuse. Nevertheless, like Helfer and Kempe (1976), Gil forcefully reflects the extension of the perspective on child abuse beyond the focus on intrapsychic and interpersonal conflict. He decries attempts to understand child abuse in terms of one specific causal dimension. Noting that the widespread use of force toward children in society at large arouses much less public concern and indignation than child abuse in the home, Gil delineates several related levels on which child abuse occurs. In addition to the interpersonal level in the home and other childcare settings, he points to the institutional level expressed through the policies and practices of a wide array of educational, welfare, correctional, and child-caring agencies. Then there is the societal level, where the interplay of values and social, economic, and political factors shape the policies that determine the rights and lives of all children, and particularly of specific groups of children.

Unquestionably, attention has to be directed to a variety of interacting variables, including the level of violence in society, poverty, the psychological factors emphasized in the chapter below, and intergenerational problems in parenting. In addition, there may be disturbances in primary parent-infant bonding (see Chapter 3 by Brazelton, Koslowski, and Main, as well as Chapter 1 by Kennell, Trause, and Klaus). Electroencephalographic findings suggest the presence of neurological factors in some abusing parents (S. M. Smith, Honigsberger, and Smith, 1975). Furthermore, the abused child, as Milowe and Lourie (1965) suggest, may be more than a passive participant in the battering interaction. In support of this, they cite instances in which the same child has been battered by different, unrelated caretakers, including foster parents who had volunteered refuge for the abused child after removal from the parental home. This is not a complete list, but it serves to highlight that multifactorial preventive and interventive measures are needed, including outreach organizations like Parents Anonymous, so that there is someone to turn to instead of abusing one's children behind drawn blinds.

20

A Psychiatric Study
of Parents Who Abuse
Infants and Small Children

BRANDT F. STEELE and
CARL B. POLLOCK

THE PROJECT AND THE SAMPLE STUDIED

Our study of parental attack on infants began inadvertently several years ago when C. Henry Kempe asked one of us to see the parents of a battered baby on the pediatric ward, hoping we could find out the why and wherefore of this distressing type of behavior. This first patient, an effusive, hysterical woman with a vivid, dramatic history and way of life, turned out to be a challenging "gold mine" of psychopathology. Our feelings alternated between horror and disbelief that she had actually fractured the femur and skull of her three-month-old daughter, but these feelings were soon lost and replaced by a wish to know her, to understand her behavior as fully as possible, and to find out if treatment could help.

Before long, other attacking parents were seen; during a period of five and one-half years, we studied intensively 60 families in which significant abuse of infants or small children had occurred. In many cases, we began our acquaintance with parents referred by the pediatric service while the attacked child was in the hospital. Other contacts were established with parents who had not injured their children seriously enough to require hospitalization—some of them referred by other physicians, social agencies, or legal authorities, and some of them coming voluntarily to seek help. Other cases were picked

First published in *The Battered Child*, edited by R. E. Helfer and C. H. Kempe. Chicago: University of Chicago Press, 1968, pp. 103–147. Copyright © 1968, The University of Chicago. Reprinted by permission.

This study was supported by the Children's Bureau of the Department of Health, Education, and Welfare, Project No. 12:HS, Project 218.

up when the problem of child abuse was discovered during treatment in the psychiatric hospital or outpatient clinic. One couple was first seen in jail after we read newspaper reports of their arrest for child-beating.

Our study group of parents is not to be thought of as useful for statistical proof of any concepts. It was not picked by a valid sampling technique, nor is it a "total population." It is representative only of a group of parents who had attacked children and who came by rather "accidental" means under our care because we were interested in the problem. We believe, however, that our data have particular significance because our haphazardly selected group provides a spectrum of child-abusing behavior which negates in many respects stereotypes of the "child-beater" popularly held in the past.

We began by seeing parents of severely injured children, work which was publicized under the title of "The Battered Child Syndrome" (Kempe et al., 1962). The injuries included serious fractures of the skull and long bones and subdural hematomas, other less serious fractures, lacerations, multiple bruises, and burns. Soon we became aware that we were dealing only with the extreme of a much more widespread phenomenon and began including cases in which the infant was moderately bruised by severe hitting, shaking, yanking, choking, or being thrown about. It is difficult, as all those familiar with the problem can testify, to draw a line separating "real abuse" from the "accidental" signs of appropriate, albeit severe, disciplinary punishment. We feel we have been conservative in our classification of injuries as abuse.

There seems to be an unbroken spectrum of parental action toward children ranging from the breaking of bones and fracturing of skulls through severe bruising to severe spanking and on to mild "reminder pats" on the bottom. To be aware of this, one has only to look at the families of one's friends and neighbors, to look and listen to the parent-child interactions at the playground and the supermarket, or even to recall how one raised one's own children or how one was raised oneself. The amount of yelling, scolding, slapping, punching, hitting, and yanking acted out by parents on very small children is almost shocking. Hence, we have felt that in dealing with the abused child we are not observing an isolated, unique phenomenon, but only the extreme form of what we would call a pattern or style of child-rearing quite prevalent in our culture.

The present report includes only cases of infants and young children, predominantly under the age of three, who have been significantly abused by their parents or other caretakers. Cases of direct murder of children are not included. It is our belief that direct murder of children is an entirely different phenomenon and is instigated during a single, impulsive act by people who are clearly psychotic (L. Adelson, 1961). To be sure, a significant number of battered children eventually die because of repeated injuries; yet this is still considered to be quite different from death due to a single, direct attack. Physical attack of the child in an effort to make the child behave is not the same as attack with intent to kill. Nor have we included cases in which abuse begins when the children are older. It is our opinion that when abuse begins on children aged four, five, or older, it is a different form of behavior and the attack by the parent is instigated by a different type of psychopathology. The attack on such older children is much more involved with matters of sexuality than is the attack on small infants.

METHOD OF STUDY

Our method of study was clinical, patterned basically after the usual methods of psychiatric diagnosis and therapeutic interviews, with an attempt to reach as deeply as possible into the patient's personality. In addition to the directly psychiatric procedure, great use was made of interviews and home visits by our social worker, whereby information could be obtained about general modes of living and of actual day-to-day interactions between parents and between parents and child. Contacts were made not only with the attacking parent, but also with the spouse. This was often inevitable, as it was not always possible at first to know who had attacked the child. Later such contacts were maintained or instituted because the uncovering of problems in the marriage made it obvious that treatment of both partners was highly desirable. Interviews, usually rather informal, were held whenever possible with the attacker's parents and other relatives, and occasionally we had the chance to see an abusing mother with her own mother in a joint interview and to observe their interaction. From such sources we obtained information which corroborated, corrected, or elaborated the memories the attackers had of their own childhood and upbringing. A battery of psychological tests was done on most of our attacking parents and, in some instances, on the non-attacking spouse as well.

The duration of our contacts varied. A few parents were seen for only brief exploratory, diagnostic interviews. Most parents were seen over a period of many months, several for as long as three to five years. Reasons for not maintaining adequate contact included moving away because of a job change, divorce, living at an impracticably great distance, and being sent to a penal institution. Only rarely was a patient lost because we had no way of holding onto anyone who was extremely recalcitrant or uncooperative. By and large, the involvement of our study parents was quite voluntary on their part, even though on first referral they were "told" to see us. In a few instances, maintenance of contact with us depended upon the admonition from a judge that the parents' probation or the return of their child to them was contingent upon seeing us and a report from us.

Our procedure in developing a relationship with attacking parents was far from constant or rigidly designed. From the very beginning we were aware that our patients were notably difficult people to deal with. All of them, even those who came voluntarily asking for help, were quite reluctant and evasive, and contact had to be contrived by whatever possible means on an ad hoc basis. Often we had to pursue them, either figuratively by phone calls and unusual favors as to hours of appointment, or literally, as they rapidly walked away from us down the halls of the hospital ward where their child was a patient. Several attacking parents were hospitalized in our psychiatric unit—some because of mildly psychotic behavior, others for a lesser but significant emotional disturbance. Hospitalization was determined as much by a desire to have the opportunity for close observation as by medical necessity. Those patients in the psychiatric unit and those visiting their injured child in hospital were seen several times a week, daily if possible. Parents seen as outpatients had office interviews on a regular basis, one to three times a week. After a variable initial period, most patients were maintained on a schedule of a weekly office appointment with a psychiatrist and a home visit by the social worker every week or two. Later, visits were spread farther apart and eventually placed on a demand basis, with contact resumed or increased at the patient's request in case of crisis or trouble. Telephone calls were a significant part of our relationships. We let patients know they could call us at any time for anything, and many of them made frequent use of this privilege. Typically, each child-attacking parent was seen by one of the psychiatrists and the social worker, usually at different times, but occasionally in joint interviews. The spouse of the attacker was followed less intensively and frequently by either one of the psychiatrists or by the social worker. A few times, interviews were held jointly by both social worker and psychiatrist with both spouses. Although each parent in this study was a patient of one of the psychiatrists, all parents were at least minimally known to the other psychiatrist. Hence, all patients felt free to call other team members in case of need if their own particular therapist was unavailable.

It is obvious that in our work we were much more elastic in our treatment arrangement with patients and much more giving and available to them than is usually the case in either psychiatric practice or social work. This was done consciously and purposefully for three reasons. First, we were dealing with a group of people who required a lot of concrete evidence of interest from the environment before they believed in it at all. Second, we felt we could not accomplish our research goal of understanding child attack without developing such an involved relationship. And third, we had to be intensively and meaningfully involved in these parents' lives if we were to accomplish our goal of either keeping the attacked child in the home or returning the child at the earliest possible time.

Obviously, judged by the usual standards of psychotherapy, we were working in a highly "contaminated" relationship with greatly enhanced dependencies and transference reactions, especially in the beginning. Nevertheless, in many of our patients we were able to develop and maintain a surprisingly high degree of approximation to a dynamic, psychoanalytically oriented therapy with rewarding results. Particularly in those patients with longer contacts, we encouraged free association and made use of dream material. Development of a full transference neurosis was not encouraged, but interpretation of transference reactions was used extensively.

In the following sections we present the information collected from people we got to know quite well in many hundreds of psychiatric interviews and from hundreds of home visits.

GENERAL CHARACTERISTICS OF THE PARENTS IN THE STUDY GROUP

If all the people we studied were gathered together, they would not seem much different from a group picked by stopping the first several dozen people one met on a downtown street. They were not a homogeneous group, but rather a random cross-section sample of the general population. They were from all socioeconomic strata—laborers, farmers, blue-collar workers, white-collar workers, and top professional people. Some were at the poverty level, some were relatively wealthy, but most were in-between. They lived in large metropolitan areas, small towns, and rural communities. Housing varied from substandard hovels to high-class suburban homes. At both extremes, they could be either well kept or messy.

Educational achievement ranged from partial grade school up to advanced postgraduate degrees. In like fashion, determination of intellectual ability ranged from low borderline IQ scores in the 70s to superior ratings of 130. The employment record of those with scanty education was characterized by many job changes and periods of unemployment. Those with higher IQs and advanced education were steadily employed in their professional roles or in the industrial, business, or financial fields. Several with adequate intelligence and education had poor job histories related to neurotic conflicts and difficult personality traits.

Our study parents ranged from 18 to 40 years of age, the great majority being in the twenties. One exception is an 11-year-old girl who attacked two children with whom she was baby-sitting. The marital situations of our group seemed not significantly different from those of others in their socioeconomic groups in the general population. A few cases were involved in separations or had only a temporary liaison. A few had been divorced and were in a second marriage. A few were in recurrent marital conflict. The great majority, however, were in a relatively stable marriage. The stability of the marriage was not always based on firm grounds of real love and a happy, cooperative relationship. Rather, it was often a desperate, dependent clinging together out of a fear of loneliness and losing everything, which held the partners together despite incompatibilities and friction. This will be discussed more fully later.

Religious affiliations included Catholic, Jewish, and Protestant. Among the latter were Episcopal, Methodist, Presbyterian, Lutheran, Mormon, Mennonite, and Baptist. Several families had no religious affiliation or only a nominal one without participation. A few were definitely antichurch. It was our impression that among those who were actively involved in their religion, there was a greater than average adherence to a strong, rigid, authoritative, "fundamentalist" type of belief.

The ethnic background of most of our families was Anglo-Saxon. There were also a few whose backgrounds were Scandinavian, Irish, German, Eastern European, and Spanish-American. We saw only one Negro family very briefly, but we draw from a population which is less than 10% Negro. There were children of immigrants, but no immigrants. True alcoholism was not a problem except in one family, and many were total abstainers. Among those who did use alcohol, drinking was occasionally a source of marital conflict, but bore no significant, direct relationship to episodes of child-beating.

The actual attack on the infant is usually made by one parent. In our series, the mother was the attacker in 50 instances and the father in seven instances. We were unable to be sure which parent was involved in two families, and in one family both parents attacked.

These general characteristics of the parents in this study, as described above, are significantly different from those reported by Elmer (1964–1965) and others (Greengard, 1964; L. Young, 1964). The incidence of poverty, alcoholism, broken marriages, and prominence of certain racial groups is not significant in our series. We do not believe our data are any more accurate than those of other reporters, but that different reports reflect the inevitable result of using skewed samples. Social agencies, welfare organizations, and municipal hospitals will inevitably draw most of their child-beaters from lower socioeconomic strata. Our institution serves a wide range of socioeconomic groups and is closely associated with physicians in private medical practice. Obviously, our sample will be skewed in a quite different way. Our data show a great majority of women as child-beaters. Other reports show a roughly 50:50 distribution between male and female, and some a significant predominance of men. We suspect that our low incidence of male attackers is related in part to a low incidence of unemployment among the males in the group. There were fewer hours of contact between males and infants than between females and infants—therefore, less exposure time for attack to occur by males. In samples in which women are working out of the home and unemployed men spend more time with the infant, the male attack rate would doubtlessly increase. While the factors of employment and unemployment have some contributing effect on the presence or absence of child attack, they are certainly not crucial. In our small series, both employed and unemployed men have attacked their children.

Similar comments may be made concerning the other social, economic, and demographic factors mentioned above. Basically they are somewhat irrelevant to the actual act of child-beating. Unquestionably, social and economic difficulties and disasters add stress to people's lives and contribute to behavior which might otherwise remain dormant. But such factors must be considered as incidental enhancers, rather than necessary and sufficient causes. Not all parents who are unemployed and in financial straits, with poor housing, shattered marriages, and alcoholic difficulties, abuse their children; nor does being an abstaining, devout Christian with a high IQ, stable marriage, fine home, and plenty of money prevent attack on infants. These facts are well recognized by most of those who work in the area of child abuse. We have stressed them, however, because large segments of our culture, including many in the medical profession, are still prone to believe that child abuse occurs only among "bad people" of low socioeconomic status. This is not true.[1]

PSYCHOPATHOLOGY OF THE ATTACKERS

GENERAL CHARACTERISTICS

As noted in the previous section, the parents in this study were not all a homogeneous group from the standpoint of their general descriptive characteristics. In respect to psychopathology, they were equally heterogeneous. They did not fall into any single one of our usual psychiatric diagnostic categories. On the contrary, they presented the wide spread of emotional disorders seen in any clinic population—hysteria, hysterical psychosis, obsessive-compulsive neurosis, anxiety states, depression, schizoid personality traits, schizophrenia, character neurosis, and so on. It was not possible to make a simple diagnosis with most patients. They presented mixed pictures

---

[1] It would be hard to find a group more deprived and in more socioeconomic difficulty than the Spanish-American migrant agricultural workers. We spent some time running down rumors of child abuse in this group and were unable to document a single instance. Possibly some cases do occur, but we were unable to find them.

such as "obsessive-phobic neurosis with marked masochistic features and mild depression." A majority of the patients could be said to be depressed at some time. Psychosomatic illnesses such as asthma, headaches, migraine, colitis, dysmenorrhea, urticaria, and vomiting were significant in several patients. Sociopathic traits such as passing bad checks were quite rare. The diagnosis of sociopathy was entertained in one case, but could not be firmly established. We would not agree with the concept that by definition anyone who abuses a child is a sociopath. No doubt sociopaths have attacked children many times, but certainly sociopathy and child abuse are not closely related.

It is our impression that with few exceptions our patients had emotional problems of sufficient severity to be accepted for treatment had they presented themselves at a clinic or psychiatrist's office. As noted before, a few of our patients were picked up in the clinic or hospital during treatment undertaken for reasons other than child abuse. One patient had been treated for depression during adolescence and again for a mild postpartum psychosis a year before she abused her child and came into our study. Most of our patients had been living for years with a significant amount of emotional difficulty, feeling it was not worthwhile or not possible to look for help from anyone. They had not been able to engender in their environment any useful, sympathetic awareness of their difficulties.

Child abusers have been described as "immature," "impulse-ridden," "dependent," "sadomasochistic," "egocentric," "narcissistic," and "demanding." Such adjectives are essentially appropriate when applied to those who abuse children, yet these qualities are so prevalent among people in general that they add little to specific understanding. Categorical psychiatric diagnoses contribute little more, and do not answer the crucial question of why a certain parent abuses children.

Instead of trying to associate child abuse with a specific type of psychiatric disorder or a commonly accepted character-type description, we have searched for a consistent behavior pattern which can exist in combination with, but quite independently of, other psychological disorders. Although we constantly dealt with the whole gamut of emotional turmoil, we persistently focused on the interaction between caretaker and infant. From direct observation of parents with children and the descriptions given by them of how they deal with their offspring, it is obvious that they expect and demand a great deal from their infants and children. Not only is the demand for performance great, but it is premature, clearly beyond the ability of the infant to comprehend what is wanted and to respond appropriately. Parents deal with the child as if he were much older than he really is. Observation of this interaction leads to a clear impression that the parent feels insecure and unsure of being loved, and looks to the child as a source of reassurance, comfort, and loving response. It is hardly an exaggeration to say the parent acts like a frightened, unloved child, looking to his own child as if he were an adult capable of providing comfort and love. This is the phenomenon described as "role reversal" by M. G. Morris and Gould (1963). They define this "as a reversal of the dependency role, in which parents turn to their infants and small children for nurturing and protection." We see two basic elements involved—a high expectation and demand by the parent for the infant's performance and a corresponding parental disregard of the infant's own needs, limited abilities, and helplessness—a significant misperception of the infant by the parent. Kaufman (1962) has described the same thing in terms of parental distortion of reality and misperception of the infant. He states that "the child is not perceived as a child, but some symbolic or delusional figure" and "may be perceived as the psychotic portion of the parent which the parent wishes to control or destroy." He further describes that "other parents who are extremely infantile and wish to be babied themselves resent the dependency and needs of their child and express this resentment in hostile ways." Kaufman believes parents "project much of their difficulty onto their child and feel that the child is the cause of their troubles" and "they attempt to relieve their anxiety by attacking the child instead of facing their own problems." He conceives of this as "a type of schizophrenic process" because of the strong use of the mechanisms of denial and projection. While agreeing with Kaufman's phenomenological descriptions and his thought that there is an abnormal ego function, we do not believe this is necessarily a schizophrenic process. Our concepts of the particular type of ego function involved will be discussed later.

Examples of this high parental demand combined with disregard of the infant are the following:

> Henry J., in speaking of his 16-month-old son, Johnny, said, "He knows what I mean and understands it when I say 'come here.' If he doesn't come immediately, I go and give him a gentle tug on the ear to remind him of what he's supposed to do." In the hospital it was found that Johnny's ear was lacerated and partially torn away from his head.

> Kathy made this poignant statement: "I have never felt really loved all my life. When the baby was born, I thought he would love me; but when he cried all the time, it meant he didn't love me, so I hit him." Kenny, age three weeks, was hospitalized with bilateral subdural hematomas.

Implied in the above vignettes, and clearly evident in the tone of voice of the parents as they told us these stories, is a curious sense of "rightness." We have often called it a "sense of righteousness" in the parents. From early in infancy the children of abusing parents are expected to show exemplary behavior and a respectful, submissive, thoughtful attitude toward adult authority and society. Common parental expressions were: "If you give in to kids, they'll be spoiled rotten." "You have to teach children to obey authority." "I don't want my kids to grow up to be delinquent." "Children have to be taught proper respect for their parents." To be sure, such ideas are extremely prevalent in our culture and are essentially acceptable ideals of child-rearing. Parents feel quite justified in following such principles. The difference between the nonabusing and the abusing parent is that the latter implements such standards with exaggerated intensity and, most important, at an inappropriately early age. Axiomatic to the child-beater are that infants and children exist primarily to satisfy parental needs, that children's and infants' needs are unimportant and should be disregarded, and that children who do not fulfill these requirements deserve punishment.

We believe there exists in parents who abuse children this specific pattern of child-rearing, quite independently of their other personality traits. It is not an isolated, rare phenomenon, but rather a variant form, extreme in its intensity, of a pattern of child-rearing pervasive in human civilization all over the world. Reports of this same type of attack on infants and young children have come from England (Roaf, 1965; Turner, 1964), Canada (Cochrane, 1965), Australia (Storey, 1964), Norway (Gjerdrum, 1964), Sweden (Frick, 1964), Germany (Trube-Becker, 1964), Italy (Ferracuti et al., 1965), Hungary (Antoni, 1965), the Netherlands (Kuipers et al., 1964), South Africa (Krige, 1966), and Hawaii (P. H. Patterson et al., 1966). While we know of no medical reports from oriental countries describing child abuse in the sense with which we have been dealing with it, we do not doubt that it occurs there also. We have heard from a friend who observed the following: A Chinese mother who had four children dealt with her two younger ones in very opposite ways. The youngest, who had originally been unwanted, turned out to be a very fat, delightful baby who conformed to all the standards of an ideal Chinese baby. He was much loved and well cared for. The older child, who had originally been wanted, was terribly skinny, less happy, and less responsive. The mother thought of him as an "unrewarding baby" and often stuck pins and needles into him.

It is this pattern of caretaker-child interaction and style of child-rearing with which we shall be concerned in the following sections.

BACKGROUND AND LIFE HISTORY OF THE PARENTS

In describing the life histories of the parents in our study, we shall concentrate on those elements which have the most direct connection with the problem of the parent-child relationship involved in abuse. It is not our purpose to trace development of other facets of the personality, such as the particular form of the oedipal conflict and its resolution, the source of ob-sessive-compulsive traits or psychosomatic illness, and so on. These follow the various patterns which are familiar from the study of patients in general and need not be elaborated here. To be sure, the vicissitudes of early ex-perience in the lives of our patients carried genetic potential for the many variations of their character structures, but we shall accent their importance as sources of the particular type of parent-child relationship described in the preceding section.

Without exception in our study group of abusing parents, there is a history of having been raised in the same style that they have re-created in the pattern of rearing their own children. Several had experienced severe abuse in the form of physical beatings from either mother or father; a few reported "never having had a hand laid on them." All had experienced, however, a sense of intense, pervasive, continuous demand from their parents. This demand was in the form of expectations of good, submissive behavior; prompt obedience; never making mistakes; sympathetic comforting of parental distress; and showing approval and help for parental actions. Such parental demands were felt to be excessive not only in degree, but, possibly more important, in their prematurity. Performance was expected before the child was able to fully comprehend what was expected or how to accomplish it. Accompanying the parental demand was a sense of constant parental criticism. Performance was pictured as erroneous, inadequate, inept, and ineffectual. No matter what the patient as a child tried to do, it was not enough, it was not right, it was at the wrong time, it bothered the parents, it would disgrace the parents in the eyes of the world, or it failed to enhance the parents' image in society. Inevitably, the growing child felt, with much reason, that he was unloved, that his own needs, desires, and capabilities were disregarded, unheard, unfulfilled, and even wrong. These factors seem to be essential determinants in the early life of the abusing parent—the excessive demand for performance with the criticism of inadequate performance and the disregard of the child as an individual with his own needs and desires. Everything was oriented toward the parent; the child was less important.

From another descriptive standpoint, all of our parents were deprived as infants and children. We are not concerned here with material deprivation. Some were raised in poverty with great material deprivation, others in average circumstances, and a few in the midst of material abundance and wealth. We are referring to deprivation of basic mothering—a lack of the deep sense of being cared for and cared about from the beginning of one's life. When describing this deprivation of mothering, we do not imply that our patients lacked maternal attention. Usually, they were the object of great attention. Their mothers had hovered over them, involving themselves in all areas of the patient's life throughout the years. But again, this was in a pattern of demand, criticism, and disregard designed to suit the mother and leave the patient out.

Our very strong belief in the importance of "the lack of mothering" as a most basic factor in the genesis of parental abuse is based on several things. First, it is based on the recollections given by patients of their unrewarding experiences with their own mothers. They documented their ideas with many reported incidents from early childhood up to the present and felt this type of relationship had been there "all their lives." Even allowing for the inevitable distortions, exaggerations, and omissions in patients' stories of their lives, we could not avoid the great significance of this consistently reported pattern. In addition, we occasionally had the experience, both enlightening and distressing, of talking to the abusing mother and her own mother together. On these occasions, it was possible to observe many of the interactions which our patient had previously described. Her mother would "take over," answer questions directed to the daughter, tell the daughter what to answer, indicate in many ways what she expected the daughter to do, and either overtly or implicitly criticize and belittle her, all without paying attention to what the daughter was thinking, feeling, or trying to do. From spouse and siblings we have had further corroboration of the abusing parent's life story.

Of great interest to us has been the scant but suggestive data concerning the childhood experience of some of the abusing parents' parents. From what our patients know of their own parents' lives, from what they (the grandparents of the abused child) themselves have told us, and from bits of information from aunts and uncles, it appears that the grandparents, too, were subjected to a constellation of parental attitudes similar to that described above. We believe we have seen this style of child-rearing or pattern of parent-child relationship existing in three successive generations. Unwittingly and unfortunately, it is transmitted from parent to child, generation after generation. To a large extent, it has been socially acceptable, although sub rosa, and to some extent it is probably culturebound.

The central issue involved concerns a breakdown in what we referred to earlier as "mothering"—a disruption of the maternal affectional system. In speaking of this, we do not mean to sound as if we were joining the popular pastime of glibly blaming everybody's trouble on "bad mothers"; rather, we are trying to explore and understand the process by which the tragic handicaps of parents, resulting from their own unhappy childhood experiences, are unintentionally effective in re-creating a similar handicap in their own children's ability to be good parents. We believe our observations are useful in understanding child abuse, and may also contribute to knowledge of early psychic development in infants and to general problems of child-rearing.

THE MOTHERING FUNCTION

We have described child abuse as a pattern of child-rearing characterized by derailment of the normal mothering function. By "mothering function," we mean the process in which an adult takes care of an infant; that is, a theoretically mature, capable, self-sufficient person caring for a helpless, needy, dependent, immature individual. We call this function "mothering" because it usually is performed by a mother, although it can be done by others. There are basic ingredients in mothering which we can call "practical" or "mechanical." They consist of feeding, holding, clothing, and cleaning the infant, protecting him from harm, and providing motility for him. Along with these are the more subtle ingredients of tenderness, of awareness and consideration of the needs and desires of the infant, and of appropriate emotional interaction with him. These latter qualities which we subsume under the title of "motherliness" are a most important accompaniment of the mechanical ingredients. They provide the atmosphere in which the other functions are performed, and profoundly affect the response of the infant, his immediate well-being, and his subsequent development.

Physical abuse of infants is associated more with breakdown in motherliness than with deficits in the other aspects of mothering. The infants in our study were almost always well fed, clean, and well clothed, but the emotional attitudes of the one who was caring for the infant were fraught with constant tension and frequent disruptions. It is often during the mothering acts of feeding, cleaning, and comforting the infant that abuse occurs. This is because of difficulties in maintaining an attitude of motherliness, not because of inability or lack of desire on the part of the caretaker to perform the caretaking acts. This will be described in more detail later when the circumstances of the attack are described.

Breakdown and failure in the more mechanical aspects of mothering, such as cleaning and feeding, produce the picture of the "neglected child" or the infant with "failure to thrive" (Barbero, Morris, and Reford, 1963; Leonard, Rhymes, and Solnit, 1966). The abusing parent and the neglecting parent have many common characteristics. Both need and demand a great deal from their infants, and are distressed when met by inadequate response, so it is not surprising that we occasionally see an infant or child who is both neglected and abused. Yet there is a striking difference in these two forms of caretaker-infant interaction. The neglecting parent responds to distressing disappointment by giving up and abandoning efforts to even mechanically care for the child. The abusing parent seems to have more investment in the active life of the child and moves in to punish the child for his failure and to make him "shape up" and perform better. In the present article we are concerned only with patterns involved in abuse rather than neglect.

There is still a lack of firm knowledge about the origin and development of the components of human mothering behavior. We do not see in the human mother those automatic, efficient, caretaking behaviors characteristic of sub-primate mammals with their offspring. Such patterns are standard for each species and are thought to be genetically determined spontaneous actions and response mechanisms. In the human, menstruation, ovulation, pregnancy, delivery, and lactation are inescapably genetically determined, physiological processes, and there is undoubtedly in most women something in the nature of a drive or a wish to reach sexual maturity and bear children. Yet in the human being, these basic physiological processes and psychological drives are intensely modified and channeled by cultural influences and individual experience. Even in the most primitive societies studied by anthropologists, sexual behavior, childbearing, and child-rearing are profoundly affected by local tribal customs, taboos, and cultural sanctions. Recent studies of sample cultures over the world today reveal remarkable variations in infant care and child-rearing (B. B. Whiting, 1963).

In Western culture generally and in America particularly, the processes of childbirth and infant care and child-rearing have changed profoundly during recent generations. The medical profession, in its successful efforts to minimize maternal and infant mortality and illness, has radically altered the patterns of how a mother delivers her baby and takes care of it. Pediatricians have developed useful, new suggestions and rules for ideal infant care and child-rearing; yet these have changed from decade to decade. Educators, psychologists, psychiatrists, and sociologists have offered their many ideas of how infants and children should be raised. Baby-care books are consistent best-sellers. Magazines, newspapers, radio, television, and government publications are filled with advice, admonition, and warnings about infant care. Baby-food advertisements and promulgators of vitamin and mineral products have added to the confusion. In addition, most mothers get plenty of criticism and advice from their own mothers, other female relatives, neighbors, and friends. Add to this the demand from an irritable husband, "For heaven's sake, do something about that crying baby." In the face of such a barrage, it is surprising that any mother can keep her equilibrium and carry out with sensitivity and efficiency the demanding tasks of infant care. In addition to all the rewards and advantages that have come from our modern knowledge of improved infant care, there are occasional backfires, too. Not rarely have we seen mothers who, in their valiant efforts to follow the best advice they can obtain, find that things are not working well with their infant and the infant does not respond the way the book says he should. Such mothers, possibly somewhat unsure of themselves to start with, become very doubtful of their own value and capabilities as a mother, and also doubt if their infant is really all right. The mother-infant relationship then becomes filled with tension, and troubles can become significant. We believe the mother is fortunate who, when there is disagreement between what the book says and what the baby says, decides in favor of the baby. In the ever-recurring debates of breast-feeding versus bottle-feeding, of demand feeding versus schedule feeding, of pacifiers or no pacifiers, of times and means of toilet training, and so on, it seems best if the mother and child can decide this between themselves, rather than be caught by rigid rules. For the mother and child to do this, we believe the mother has to have an adequate amount of motherliness. Our culture sets high value on good mothering and provides abundant advice on all aspects of its practical implementation. We also greatly admire and strongly advocate motherliness, yet we seem to expect it to appear automatically and are vaguely bewildered and distressed when it does not exist. Instead of assuming, as many do, that motherliness is intuitive behavior which is part of the native endowment of a woman, we shall try to explore its origins.

Motherliness

If we leave aside all the culturally channeled styles and mechanics of mothering, we come to a substrate of maternal behavior which must have its roots in physiological mechanisms and individual psychological experience. In her classical work, *Psychosexual Functions in Women,* Benedek (1952) documented all the subtle interactions between hormonal levels, menstruation, pregnancy, lactation, and the woman's psychic state and her mothering behavior. Deutsch (1945) in her equally classic study, *The Psychology of Women,* portrays the psychological vicissitudes of the woman throughout life, and through motherhood in particular. Despite the validity of these studies, we consider them, for the purpose of our present exploration of motherliness, to be largely irrelevant for several reasons. Motherliness is not confined to biological mothers. It can appear full-fledged in adoptive mothers, foster mothers, matrons in foundling homes, and nurses. Children, even very young boys as well as girls, can demonstrate it with each other and with babies. Even men can show it, and we feel that it is a breakdown of motherliness in the man's attempts to do mothering that is crucial in his abuse of infants.

We agree with Josselyn (1956), who in discussing motherliness writes that the ability to show tenderness, gentleness, and empathy, and to value a love object more than the self, "is not a prerogative of women alone; it is a human characteristic." We cannot, therefore, find the source of motherliness through the study of specifically female physiology and psychology alone. We must look further.

Recognition of the effect of early childhood experience on psychic development and the eventual personality patterns of the adult is basic to most of our present-day understanding of human psychology. Surprisingly little has been written, however, correlating such early experience with the specific facet of adult behavior subsumed under the title of motherliness. There are occasional tantalizing references to "identification with the mother" in the literature, but the idea has rarely been adequately developed. Benedek (1959) approached the core of the problem when she described the upsurge of child-hood memories occurring when the adult becomes a parent. These memories return in two forms; those of what it was like to be a child, and others of how one was parented. Much of such memory return would, of course, be unconscious, and probably many memories would be about vague feelings, moods, and atmospheres, as well as of clear, specific events. Inevitably, this recall of early childhood experience will profoundly influence both con-sciously and unconsciously the patterns of behavior of the new parent toward the baby. Early in our work we facetiously spoke of abusing parents as following a distortion of the golden rule: "Do unto others as you have been done unto." There is truth in this despite its superficiality. It is a common observation that people bring up their children to some extent in the same way that they, themselves, were brought up, often despite very conscious resolves to do differently.

Our observations suggest that the pattern of parenting practiced in adult life, particularly motherliness, probably has its roots in the earliest infantile experience. Abusing parents, as do all other parents, demonstrate their par-ticular child-rearing style at the time the baby is born or soon thereafter. A clear example of this is shown in the case of Bertie.

> Bertie had fractured the femur and skull of her first baby during its first three months of life. While under treatment a second unwanted pregnancy occurred, and she delivered another baby girl. Several hours after delivery the baby was brought to her for her first contact with it. Instead of holding the baby close to her body, cuddling and looking her over, she lay there with the baby sitting on her stomach at arm's length. The baby was quiet. Bertie said, "Now she's mad—look at her—she's really mad now."

This vignette of distorted "claiming" behavior is indicative of Bertie's de-railed style of motherliness and indicates her deep feeling that the infant is unrewarding and troublesome.

Since we have seen the parenting style appear in three successive gener-ations and its expression begin in the neonatal period, we infer a connection between the two. This is consistent with Benedek's idea, referred to above, that memories of how one was parented surge up when a baby is born and influence one's parental behavior. How soon this has an effect on the baby is hard to say. Spitz (1950) suggests there is a change from reflexive activity to learning beginning around the three-months period, at which time the rudiments of the reality principle are being established. Marquis (1931) indicates that learning in the form of a conditioned response can be established in a baby within two weeks after birth. We have seen babies respond accurately to rather unreasonable parental demand within the first six months, and by the ages of one and two, show exquisitely sensitive responses to parental needs. This is assumed to be learned behavior. We have also observed other, nonabused children in a family show this same, unusually high degree of responsiveness to parental demand, indicating that a basic style of parent-child interaction is present, which may or may not result in actual abuse.

Although subhuman primate behavior cannot be applied directly to the understanding of human behavior, some observations seem to show striking analogies to the phenomena seen in abusing and neglecting human parents. We refer particularly to the work of the Harlows (1962) on monkeys:

> . . . four of our laboratory-raised females never had real mothers of their own, one being raised in a bare wire cage and three with cloth surrogates. The first week after the birth of the baby to the wire-cage-raised female, the mother sat fixedly at one side of the cage staring into space, almost unaware of her infant or of human beings, even when they barked at and threatened the baby. There was so sign of maternal responses, and when the infant approached and attempted contact, the mother rebuffed it, often with vigor.
>
> The next two unmothered mothers constantly rebuffed the approaches of their infants, but, in addition, frequently engaged in cruel and unprovoked attacks. They struck and beat their babies, mouthed them roughly, and pushed their faces into the wire-mesh floor. These attacks seemed to be exaggerated in the presence of human beings, and for this reason all formal testing was abandoned for three days for the third unmothered mother because we feared for the life of the infant. The fourth unmothered mother ignored and rejected her infant but did not exhibit excessive cruelty.

These observations do suggest that there may be some connection between the lack of early "being-mothered" experiences and deficits in later parental functioning. There are, however, some significant differences between the being-mothered experience of the Harlows' monkeys and that of abusing parents. The monkeys were raised not only without motherliness, but without any positive or negative actions from their wire-cage or cloth mothers. Abusing parents did not have as infants nearly enough motherliness, but at the same time they were exposed to very active caretaking behavior from their mothers, coupled with demand and criticism. Their resultant behavioral deficit is in motherliness, rather than in practical mothering. The infant monkeys are possibly more like the babies who developed hospitalism as a result of the more totally deficient mothering described by Spitz (1945b, 1946b). Joyce Robertson (1962) has described a milder form of the same condition developing in infants whose mothers were moderately indifferent, aloof, and un-involved.

The Early Origins of Motherliness and Its Vicissitudes

In several papers Benedek (1938, 1949, 1956a, 1959) has described the mutually rewarding symbiotic relationship between mother and infant and its crucial importance for the baby's immediate well-being and future development. In particular, she stresses the appearance in the infant of a fundamental sense of confidence that needs will be met, a phenomenon related primarily to the feeding situation, but also to other aspects of being cared for. By using Benedek's formulations, we can see why abusing parents have been unable to develop an adequate ability in the sphere of motherliness. They did not have, as far as we can tell from our data, the experience in infancy of a fully satisfying symbiotic, confidence-producing relationship with their mothers.

It is recognized that around the age of three months an infant begins to change from the primary narcissistic state of undifferentiation to the first awareness of the self as separate from the object world; the I and the not-I are beginning to be established. The infantile experience of the outside world, the mother, is a mixture of pleasure-giving need satisfaction and of pain-producing frustration. These two images of the mother provide the material for the first primal identification, the pleasure-giving mother introjected as the first basis of the ego ideal and the pain-reducing mother as the anlage of the archaic, punitive superego. This will be discussed more fully later in the section on aggression and the superego. For the moment, we are concentrating on the concept that the early identification with the image of an insufficiently caring mother is the basis of the diminished motherliness we find in the adult, both male and female. In the abusing parent there has been a marked imbalance between the two mother images with the frustrating mother being much more powerful than the empathic, caring mother. This early identification state is the fertile ground for reinforcement through many later similar experiences of the growing child. Examples of such reinforcing experiences are:

> In puberty, Amy tried to talk to her mother about how to dress and fix her hair so as to be attractive and popular. Mother said, "Forget about trying to be pretty. Just develop character."

> Penny wished desperately for ice skates and her mother finally gave her some hand-me-down ones, which were too small and hurt her feet. When Penny complained, her mother responded by feeling hurt and unappreciated. She scolded Penny and told her to wear the skates and be grateful.

> Larry and his older brother were each to get five dollars for taking care of the dairy farm for a long weekend while their parents were away. The brother kept

the entire 10 dollars, giving Larry only 15 cents for a soda. When Larry told his parents of this injustice, they said, ''Forget it,'' and did nothing about it.

The identification of the abusing parent with diminished motherliness persists into adult life. It is accompanied by an equally persistent disbelief in the possibility of finding a safe, empathic, motherly relationship despite great yearning for it. An example is Sally:

After delivery, Sally's mother, on the advice of the pediatrician, instituted a rigid four-hour feeding schedule. Evidently this was not syntonic with Sally's own needs for time, and she cried a great deal. Her mother managed the constant crying by putting the baby in a room by herself, shutting the door, and leaving the house until feeding time returned. Sally, of course, cannot remember these events, but had often heard about them in family talks, and they were corroborated during interviews we had with her mother. What she does recall is that at age three, shortly after her brother was born, her mother went to work and left her in the care of various people during the ensuing years, that she never had a close relationship with her mother during childhood and puberty, and could never talk to mother about things which mattered to her. It is not surprising that she has had many psychosomatic illnesses—asthma, migraine, various digestive disturbances, and musculo-skeletal problems.

Toward her two adopted infants Sally showed rigid, controlling attitudes, with demands to conform to her expectations in eating and in general behavior. Failure of the infant to respond properly was dealt with by severe physical punishment, although no fractures or serious injuries resulted. At one time, when she was on a regimen of bed rest because of a ruptured lumbar intervertebral disc, plus great emotional enhancement of the symptom, she reported ''getting out of bed only to punish the children.''

Despite Sally's ability to relate many instances of the poor relationship with her mother, she had never been able to express criticism directly to her mother, nor could she countenance any expression of criticism of the mother from the psychiatrist. Once after having an interview with the mother, the psychiatrist spoke to Sally's husband, Bob, saying that he could ''see how Sally might have felt it very difficult to get anything meaningful from her mother.'' Bob repeated this to Sally, who responded by refusing to see the psychiatrist again for a period of four months. She felt she had just begun to have a good relationship with her mother and be able to talk to her, and the psychiatrist's statement threatened the possibility of keeping this going.

Her intense need for mothering plus her basic hopeless disbelief in the possibility of such a relationship were apparent in another situation. While Sally was in the hospital for observation, the social worker began to build a relationship with her. At a crucial time in the interview, during which Sally was crying and the worker put a sympathetic hand on her shoulder, they were interrupted by the ward personnel, demanding Sally come out and join in the routine group therapy scheduled at that time. She later described the situation as follows: ''When Mrs. D. put her hand on my shoulder, I felt a sense of hope for the first time in my life, and then they ruined the whole thing.'' It took weeks to re-establish this shattered sense of rapport and trust.

Most people have residuals of the dual image of the mother with its resultant ambivalence. It is our impression that the patients in our study group, both men and women, have this ambivalence to an unusually high degree, with the accent on the negative side. One patient, Penny, expressed it with rare clarity in a dream told in her fourth interview: "I was with mother. There was the usual feeling of tension. It was like we were in a motel and we had gone to bed in twin beds. I woke up. Something in white was standing over me very threatening. It was terrifying. I called to my mother for help. She answered, 'I am your mother,' and it turned out that she herself was the creature in white who was threatening me. I woke up screaming." Penny's associations elaborated, but did not significantly alter the meaning which is so obvious in the manifest content of the dream: the one to whom one looks with a wish for help is the one who will attack. The dream was reported in relation to material about her anger toward her mother, her punitive anger toward her five-month-old son, and the distressing feeling that she was just as bad as her mother was. Since it appeared in the early stages of Penny's looking to us for help, it carried significant transference implications. In this brief vignette we see the interweaving of many of the patient's ideas: I have a bad mother; I hate my mother; I am like my mother; I am mean to my child; I do not believe I can ever get help.

Much of the preceding discussion of motherliness seems oriented toward women, but it applies equally to men. Male and female abusing parents are similar in their motherly qualities. In our view there is no essential difference in the origin of motherliness in men and women. In both sexes it involves a pre-gender identification in the infant's early life with the mother's behavior. In males later masculine strivings and identifications may allow persistence of motherliness or diminish it. In females the early motherly identification becomes woven into the normal psychosexual development leading to motherhood and identification with the childbearing woman. Most simply, we believe child-caring and childbearing behaviors have separate and distinct origins.

LACK OF CONFIDENCE

Benedek (1938) has described a sense of confidence which develops in the infant as a result of the recurrent experience of being adequately understood and cared for by the mother. Erikson (1950) has written about the same phenomenon, calling it "basic trust." Confidence engendered in the infant and made firm by later experience involves belief that others can be looked to for help and one is oneself worth helping. It is long-lasting and leads to an optimistic ability in adult life to maintain useful relationships with others, especially when in time of stress or need, one needs comfort and aid. Abusing parents did not have this confidence-producing experience. As adults they feel it unrewarding to look to family, friends, or others for need-satisfying relationships. Although they may persistently return to seeking from their own parents some evidence of love, understanding, and assistance, they usually find again criticism and inappropriate response instead of what they want. They often speak of having "lots of good friends," but on closer examination these turn out to be friends only by title. Such relationships are rather distant, meager, superficial, and unfulfilling. Thus, the abusing parent tends to lead a life which is described as alienated, asocial, or isolated (Merrill, 1962; M. G. Morris and Gould, 1963; Nurse, 1964; L. Young, 1964). It is a persistence of the pattern of lack of confidence engendered early in childhood with the parents. Toward the rest of society, there is a transference of attitudes originally felt toward parents to all others looked to for help and understanding. The lack of confidence not only helps instigate this transference, but also compounds the trouble by making it next to impossible for the abusing parent to express clearly to others his real needs and desires. Thus, the social environment, being unaware of what the patient really wants, continues to respond poorly, thereby perpetuating the cycle.

In addition to the more obvious forms of isolation from the environment and the inability to seek help from it, there are many minor, but interesting evidences of these phenomena. We have noticed that many of our patients keep their blinds drawn in the house, even during bright, warm, sunny days when most people would enjoy observing the outdoors. Many of them have unlisted phone numbers, more frequently than does the general population and with less obvious reasons. They seem to have more than normal difficulty in keeping their automobiles in good repair and in coping with breakdowns of household appliances. We have jokingly remarked that if one goes down the street and sees a house with the blinds drawn in broad daylight, with two unrepaired cars in the driveway, and finds the people have an unlisted phone number, the chances are high that the inhabitants abuse their children.

Lack of confidence also plagues the marriage of the abusing parent. Many of our patients, just like many other neurotic people, have demonstrated an uncanny ability to become involved with and marry people who tend to accentuate rather than solve their problems. The spouse is too much like the patient and too much like the patient's parents. Despite many other admirable qualities and many abilities, the spouse is often needy, dependent, unable to express clearly his needs, and at the same time is demanding, critical, and unheeding of the patient. Meaningful communication between husband and wife is thus diminished. They have deep yearnings for understanding from each other, yet lack of basic trust leads them to be hesitant in expressing need, and satisfaction is rarely forthcoming. The marriage may be firmly held together by this mutual need, particularly because there is no confidence that anything better could be found elsewhere, but the marriage has become one more situation reinforcing the patient's sense of disappointment and hopelessness.

Lack of confidence originating in the inadequate mothering in infancy, reiterated in later life experiences to which the patient has made his own contributions, has left him with the conviction that his needs can never be met by parents, spouse, friends, or society in general. Yet there is still one hope left. When all the rest of the world has failed him, the abusing parent will look to the child in a last, desperate attempt to get comfort and care. An example of this is Kathy's statement quoted above that she had never felt loved by anyone in all of her life and looked to her child to fill this need.

AGGRESSION AND THE SUPEREGO

Aggression released on infants is the most disturbing manifestation of the abusing parents' behavior and is a central issue in our problem. We shall try to trace the origin and development of aggression in our patients, not only because of the obviously aggressive act of abuse, but because we think the aggressive constellation diminishes adequate development of the motherliness we consider so important. In the ensuing discussion, using direct observations of infant abuse and the infant's behavioral response, we draw conclusions concerning the psychological development of the infant. We also infer a similar psychological development has occurred in the abusing parent. The rationale for this broad inference comes from the historical data about our patients' early years, and all the indications that they were treated much the same way as they treat their own babies. We believe we see *in statu nascendi*, in the results of the interaction between abusing parent and infant, the development of psychic processes which are evident in the adult, but whose origin can be studied only in retrospect. Hence, we speak almost interchangeably of the observed development in the infant and our reconstruction of development in the adult patient.

We assume the universality of an innate aggressive drive with its potential for aggressive behavior, quite comparable to the libidinal drive. The abusing patients we have seen do not show evidence of an unusually strong, basic aggressive drive. They are not fundamentally "mean" people, nor do they seem significantly more or less action-oriented than average. Although their release of aggression against infants is overt and intense, they usually show significant inhibition of aggression in many areas of their lives. It is impossible to discuss the vicissitudes of aggression without, at the same time, discussing that structure of the human psyche which evaluates and directs the discharge of the aggressive drive, namely, the superego. We shall do this in the conceptual framework presented by Spitz (1958), with whom we are in essential agreement.

Spitz believes the superego, in the strict sense, takes its final form at the time of the resolution of the oedipal conflict, but previous to this time there are significant superego precursors and rudiments, existing as early as the first year of life. He considers physical restraint to be the earliest rudiment, and says:

> . . . among the primordia which will form up the superego there are some to which we have paid little attention up to the present. They belong to the perceptual sector of tactile and visual impressions, such as restraining the child physically on the one hand, the facial expression, as well as the tone of voice which accompanies such prohibiting interference on the other. Similarly, imposing physical actions on the infant, whether he likes it or not, in dressing, diapering, bathing, feeding, burping him, etc., will inevitably leave memory traces in the nature of commands. These physical primordia of prohibitions and commands are not easily recognizable in the ultimate organization which is the superego.

We feel much more strongly than Spitz does about the significance of this early experience in the development of recognizable superego rudiments, probably because we have been working with situations in which these phenomena are much more blatant than in his studies. We have observed parents deal aggressively with their infants, beginning shortly after birth, in all areas of infant care. In the process of feeding, they say angrily, "Now, eat," and also slap and yank at the infant to make it obey, or the infant's hands are slapped when he interferes with the spoon at the first time of solid food feeding. In the processes of diapering and bathing, the infant is told to "be quiet," to "lie still" in an angry tone accompanied by blows and yanks sufficient to cause bruises and fractures. The crying infant who does not respond to comforting may be severely shaken or hit on the head. These observations, coupled with the fact that we see infants soon responding correctly to parental commands, lead us inescapably to the idea that we are witnessing the genesis of superego rudiments. It seems obvious that the change in external behavior of the infant must be accompanied by some sort of primitive, intrapsychic change.

Spitz follows Anna Freud (1936) in believing that the mechanism of identification with the aggressor is a preliminary phase in the development of the superego, and he places its appearance as a primordium of the superego in the beginning of the second year of life, associated with the child's acquisition of the semantic "No." We, too, feel the classic mechanism of identification with the aggressor is sufficiently complicated that it could not be accomplished before the second year. Something very similar to it seems, however, to appear earlier. Whether this should be described as a precursor or as something quite different is a questionable point. It may be that earlier it would be a more simple, direct identification with aggression rather than with an aggressor, as identification with an aggressor implies some degree of sophistication in object relations. Such primordial identification with aggression beginning in the first few months of life is continuously reinforced by parental command and criticism, especially if accompanied by physical attack. In the second and third years of life, after object relations are well established, it develops into a true identification with the aggressor. Such identification is not necessarily a global one leading to indiscriminate aggressive discharge; in many of our patients we see a rather narrowly channeled, specific identification with a ''parent-against-child'' aggressor.

It must not be forgotten that at the time the parent is making demands and attacks upon the infant, he is also frustrating some of the infant's most basic needs for comfort and empathy. Such frustrations are repetitive stimulations to the basic aggressive drive. Stimulation of the aggressive drive with its accompanying anger toward the frustrating caretaker, coupled with the parallel development of strict superego rudiments, inevitably leads to a strong sense of guilt. This guilt, largely unconscious, predominantly in relation to the mother, persists through the patient's life, and leads to turning much of the aggression inward toward the self. It accounts in the adult for the frequent periods of depression and contributes to the pervasive sense of inferiority and low self-esteem. When the parent misidentifies the infant as the embodiment of his own bad self, the full aggression of his punitive superego can be directed outward onto the child. By the third year of life our patients have had both the stimulation of aggressive drives and the establishment in the archaic superego of strict, punitive, commanding components. Their earliest memories often depict this period. Bertie, for example, recalls that before age three she would hear mother and father fighting, feel frightened, cry, and then be beaten for crying.

In subsequent years there is reinforcement of the same processes due to continued experience with critical, demanding, unempathic parents, as well as ''moral instruction.'' By the latter, we mean the education the child receives in regard to what is right and wrong, what is bad in the world and warrants attack. Lack of proper respect for authority has been pictured to our patients as a most reprehensible behavior and one which always warrants punishment. They were told this by their own parents and characteristically use it excessively as righteous justification for attitudes about their own offspring, supported by widely held cultural standards.

Aggression itself has been encouraged as well as depiction of channels for its release. Examples will clarify our meaning.

Larry was taught by his father to use a gun by age eight and was forced to assume the task of shooting to death any animal on the farm which was born defective, became crippled, was too old and decrepit, or in any other way unrewarding. These experiences were devastating to him when the animal involved was one of his own pets.

Dora, as a little girl running barefoot in the park, suddenly realized she had unknowingly stepped on something, and upon investigation found she had crushed a small frog. She was terribly upset, confessed her sin to the priest, and could hardly be consoled. Yet she also told of lifting a stone in the nearby woods and finding a snake under it. Upon being told by companions it was a poisonous snake, she smashed it to death with a righteous sense of doing a good duty.[2]

These examples show the release of aggression in superego-approved channels—for instance, it is right to destroy bad things. In addition, they reveal another factor which we have temporarily neglected, a sense of compassion for the innocent and helpless.

Abusive parents are not 100% so. Although we have focused primarily on the abusive elements of parental behavior, we also wish to emphasize the presence of love, tenderness, consideration, and desire to do well for infants. There is some ego ideal as well as a superego; the balance between the two is variable. An infant may be abused recurrently, but rarely constantly. Between episodes of abuse, parents may show fairly good amounts of motherly caretaking, while demand and criticism recede temporarily to a lower level. Similarly, some children in a family are rather well treated, with a minimum of punitiveness, although another child in the same family is abused. Probably the crux of the problem of distinguishing the nonabusing from the abusing parent lies in the fact that in the latter when there is significant environmental and intrapsychic stress, with a contest between ego ideal and superego, the punitive superego wins out.

IDENTITY AND IDENTIFICATIONS

Erikson (1956) defines identity as the sense a person has of being a unique, separate individual with a continuity of personal character and ability to maintain solidarity with social groups. We do not find such identity in the abusing parent. Instead, we see a rather loose collection of unintegrated, disparate concepts of the self. There are multiple identifications which remain separate and unamalgamated. Strong ambivalences remain unresolved. Our patients can feel like confident parents and quickly change to being nothing but helpless, ineffectual, inadequate children. They can be kindly adults and

---

[2] We have not found in our patients evidence of a childhood pattern of tormenting and being cruel to animals described by MacDonald (1963) as being frequent in persons with homicidal tendencies.

shift suddenly to being punitive adults. They know they are men and women, but are not really sure of it. They have one firm concept of what they should be and another of what they actually are. Any sense of being reasonably good can be easily displaced by a conviction of badness. They are usually quite uncertain about allying with a group, even if they join it. In the context of child abuse, a most important defect is a lack of useful integration of the two experiences of being a child and being parented. This cannot be separated from the persistent, intense ambivalence about the mother.

Probably the most potent factor in the genesis of this lack of integration was the peristent demand and criticism our patients felt from their parents. Faced with constant expectations to do more and to be different, they never had the chance to find out what they really were and develop any continuity or enjoy independent thought. Attempts to ally with other people more appealing than the parents were often stopped by denigration or outright prohibition.

A most explicit description of these problems of identification and identity was given by Bertie.

> She said: "I look in a mirror and hardly know if it's me. Sometimes I'm like my mother, sometimes like my grandmother. Sometimes I'm like my husband Jack's mother. Sometimes I'm like his grandmother. Jack wants me to be first like one and then the other. Everybody wants me to be somebody else." At another time, she said: "When I'm alone, I'm more like grandmother than anyone else in the world. I'm quieter, more calm, peaceful, and more loving. I can be like her, the way I want to be, but when someone comes in and says, 'why don't I do it this way or that way' or criticizes me, I'm all lost and confused. I try to become like everything they say. I hardly know who I am. I'm still so scared of mother that I get anxious if she has been angry at me. I'll pull the shades down and lock the door and keep the chain on. If she got mad enough and thought I said anything against her, she'd come out and beat me within an inch of my life."

The highlights of Bertie's history will help in understanding her statements.

> Bertie was a first child. Her mother frequently berated her because the pregnancy had ruined the mother's figure, damaged her pelvic organs, and disrupted her marriage since the father began then to be unfaithful. From infancy into early childhood, the mother repeatedly attacked Bertie with her fists, razor strops, or wire coathangers—and occasionally slapped her in adult life. There were many battles between the mother and father, and once in her early teens Bertie witnessed her mother shooting one of father's alleged paramours, the bullet going through the woman's housecoat, missing her body.
>
> With her strict, pseudomoralistic policeman father, she had a rather warm relationship which the mother constantly tried to disrupt by telling each how bad the other was. Bertie was her grandmother's favorite and she returned the love without hesitation. "She was the only woman I've never been afraid of." Mother tried unsuccessfully to break this attachment, too, by criticizing the grandmother and often preventing their getting together.

Bertie conceived on her honeymoon. She was dismayed and angry. She did not want the baby because it would ruin her youth, deny her freedom and happiness, and shatter her chances for a good marriage. Frequently during the pregnancy she would talk to Jack about how she was afraid he would spoil the baby, and wondering how soon she could start disciplining it. When her baby girl, Cindy, was a month old, she was found to have a broken leg from "getting her leg caught in between the slats and turning over in her crib." At age three months, she was brought to the hospital with a fractured skull and bilateral subdural hematomas, cause unknown. At this time we first met Bertie, the first patient in our study. After a few interviews on the pediatric ward Bertie came to the office and we asked our secretary, a quite sophisticated woman, to record her impressions. She wrote, "Bertie is very feminine, sweet, pretty, poised, and completely unabashed at coming here. The one unusual thing about her appearance was her rather sexy, smoky, black hose and dressy shoes which would have been more appropriate for evening wear or a cocktail party. This was inconsistent with the rest of her outfit." And after detailing their conversation, she concluded, "My general impression was that our conversation was a typical, Denver (or anywhere) housewifely chat. In all, I liked Bertie, and she reminded me of many typical American girls with whom I have played bridge, golf, and so on. It was very difficult for me to believe her capable of beating her child."

One week later, Bertie was admitted to the hospital in a hysterical, disoriented, confused state, cowering and saying over and over again, "Please don't let them beat me. Make them stop fighting. Take the guns away," and so on. She had made a suicide attempt by taking a lot of pills, none of them dangerous. That morning Bertie had been faced with undeniable evidence that she had been stealing money and bits of apparel from her friends when on social visits, a fact which had been suspected, but which she had denied (in the past her mother had been picked up twice for shoplifting, and the charges were dropped). She went to the bathroom, looked in the mirror and thought, "This is all true, even if I didn't know it. My husband will hate me and leave me. I'm as bad as my mother. I don't remember it, but I must have hurt my baby, too. I desrve to die." Then she took the pills and collapsed. The almost psychotic regressive state cleared completely in a few days.

Many months later Bertie had a recurrent dream of being in a fog and going to the cemetery where her grandmother was buried, being tied to a tree, feeling scared, then feeling cold and numb as if she were in a tomb. Then she would suddenly find herself down in the grave with her grandmother, and her own mother was standing over the grave looking down at her gloating and evilly laughing. She would wake crying and shaking with terror.

Bertie has identified with her mother's aggression and stealing, and also with her mother's belief that a baby will damage a mother's physical, emotional, and marital well-being. She has also identified with the strong disciplinary attitudes of both mother and father. In contrast are the yearning for love and the identification with the kindly grandmother, for which she fears she will pay the price of being killed by mother. Further, there is the persistent feeling of being a trapped, frightened, naughty, helpless child, who has to try to please everybody. Truly, she knows not who she is.

Of prime significance is Bertie's concern about her unborn baby. She expects it will be spoiled by the father, will need early discipline, and will ruin her life. She is, of course, describing the picture of herself as a child, and more specifically, her "bad" self. Seeing the baby who is attacked as another edition of one's own bad self is characteristic of the abusing parent. Not all parents express it as clearly as Bertie did, however; nor is it always easily detected before the baby is born. Investigations during pregnancy of the expectations parents have of their future baby are very revealing and have great predictive value as well as opening avenues for preventive therapy.

Penny had come to us for help with her distress over antagonism and rough actions with her baby boy. Two years later she became pregnant and conflicts about the coming baby arose. She felt she could manage quite well if she had another boy. Although she would like to have a girl, she was very apprehensive about it. "If it's a girl, I'm likely to treat it the way mother treated me, and she'll be angry at me as much as I'm angry at mother. It will be a mess." (Cf. Bertie's "claiming" behavior, above.) Airing this conflict enabled Penny to work it through. She did beautifully with her second baby, which was, indeed, a girl.

Quite common descriptions of the infant by the parent are "He's just like me," "She's fussy like I was when I was a baby," or, "He got all his bad qualities from me." Thinking of the infant as being the equivvvalent of the parent's bad self has been described as a misperception or projection. Projection seems unlikely, as it involves denial, the mechanism being, "It is not I who am this way; it is he." We feel the mechanism is, "I am bad; he is bad just like me." This is an identification process, described by Fenichel (1945) as "reverse identification."

The identifications with the "good" and "bad" mother, residual from earliest life, may become reinforced and overdetermined by the identifications which become stabilized with the resolution of oedipal conflicts. At this time the identification with the parent of the same sex may be complicated by further identifications with the aggressor. Particularly if the aggressor is of the opposite sex, some further confusion about sexual identity may result. Attempts by our patients in later childhood and adolescence to find other models and new identifications have had only partial success, owing to the persistent demand from their parents to adhere strictly to parental expectations and not look elsewhere. Allegiance to new ideas in differing peer groups is limited, and the old fixations persist.

Secondary Factors Involved in Abuse
Contributions Made by Other Elements of Parental Psychopathology

Up to now we have concentrated on those basic psychological factors essential to the pattern of abuse. There are other factors which are not essential ingredients, but are potent accessories in instigating abuse and in determining which infant is selected for attack. Three such factors are intense unresolved sibling rivalry, an obsessive-compulsive character structure, and unresolved oedipal conflicts with excessive guilt. The following is a clear example of sibling rivalry precipitating abuse.

> Naomi was a fourth child raised largely by baby-sitters until age six and then by a grandmother whom she felt did not love her. She did not think either her mother or father really cared for her, especially her mother. An older sister was the only person she loved or felt loved by. A three-year-older brother was the family favorite, and she felt her life was ruined by being neglected while he got everything. She hated and envied her father, brother, husband, and all men. A belligerent sense of rightness in her behavior thinly covered deep feelings of being inadequate and worthless as a mother. Her first child, a girl, was raised strictly and became very submissive, obedient, and cooperative. However, Naomi said, "I'd beat her, too, if she rebelled or got angry at me."
>
> An unwanted pregnancy produced a boy two years later. Naomi said, "He came too soon after the girl and cheated her out of her childhood. I weaned him at two and a half months because nursing him upset her. I hate him; the mere sight of his genitals upsets me. I don't have time for him; I wish he'd never been born or that I could give him away to someone who'd love him. I want to hit him, hurt him, shake him, get him out of the way." She also said she saw all her own undesirable qualities in him. Naomi did slap, bruise, and rough up her baby boy, and by age two he had had three head wounds requiring stitches.

Obviously Naomi's sibling rivalry, abetted by her envious anger toward males, was important in the release of attack on her baby boy. Yet it is equally clear from her story that she had the underlying attitude of demand and criticism characteristic of the abusing parent. Only the fortunate accidents of sex, time of birth, and ability to respond correctly had spared her first child from attack.

Obsessive-compulsive personality traits often channel parental expectations and disapproval of infant behavior in specific ways. The conflicts over dirt and messiness lead to excessive early demands for the baby to eat without slopping and smearing food around and to control excretory functions too soon. Inability of the infant to comply will arouse parental ire. The inevitable tendency of older infants to strew toys around and to get fresh clothing dirty will also cause trouble if the parent is overly concerned with neatness and cleanliness. We postulate that the infant's behavior stimulates the parent's unconscious and threatens a breakthrough of his own unacceptable impulses to be messy. Defensive control must be instituted by aggressive repression in the parent and by aggressive action against similar bad behavior in the baby.

The role of unresolved oedipal conflict is harder to assess. In the case of Bertie given above, it is easy to see the difficulty and guilt she has over her own oedipal problems and how she views her baby daughter as a rival for her husband's affections. Further evidence in this direction came from the frequent dreams Bertie had of a sexy brunette who seduced her husband away from her. She always identified this woman as looking exactly the way her baby, Cindy, would look when she grew up. Such clear-cut oedipal material was not frequently seen in our patients. More often what appeared superficially as oedipal rivalry turned out on deeper investigation of unconscious motivation not to be entirely so. The mother who is angry at the baby girl's having a good time with the father, and the father who is aggressive toward the little boy who is happily involved with mother are really angry at the child because the child is getting what is seen as the motherly attention they so deeply yearn for and missed out on in their own childhood. Thus, it is more in the sphere of sibling rivalry than in that of oedipal problems.

It is our impression that few of our patients experienced a true, fully involved oedipal situation. Most of their conflicts and fixations were pregenital. As boys, instead of close involvement with fantasies of warm sexuality with mother, our male patients were caught by their ambivalence toward her and could only remain distant from her, yearning for basic motherliness. As girls, our female patients turned to fathers with slight stirrings of sexual love overshadowed by a hope that father would supply the mothering which had been lacking.[3] Naturally no two patients were alike; some had gone further than others. Those with hysterical personalities had obviously been unable to resolve an intense oedipal situation, and those with a more generally healthy personality structure had developed further and more successfully, despite preoedipal fixations.

Zilboorg (1932), in discussing parent-child antagonism, accents the part played by oedipal conflicts. He is describing older children, and we would agree that abuse of children over three or four, especially beginning at that time, is profoundly influenced by parental concern over sexuality and competitiveness. We are in complete accord with Zilboorg's statement that

> . . . the stronger the parents' "conscience," that is, the stronger their inhibitions, the greater will be their hostility against the child's freedom. To put it in technical terms: to the unconscious of the parents the child plays the role of the Id; the parents follow it vicariously for a time and then hurl upon it with all the force of their Super Ego; they project onto the child their own Id and then punish it to gratify the demands of their uncompromising Super Ego.

In the context of abuse of infants, however, we are most involved with the earliest pregenital determinants, rather than oedipal residues.

---

[3] Two of our patients had had overt incestuous relationships with their fathers. They described it more as satisfaction of dependent needs for love and comfort than as having real genital sexual meaning. One had been mildly depressed and the other psychotically so.

CONTRIBUTIONS OF THE NONABUSING PARENT

Usually only one parent actually attacks the infant. The other parent almost invariably contributes, however, to the abusive behavior either by openly accepting it or by more subtly abetting it, consciously or unconsciously. An example of this is the strong support given each other by parents in their protestations of innocence, although it is clear both knew injurious abuse was occurring. Even though one parent openly accuses the other and righteously documents the other's abusive behavior when it has come to the attention of authorities, on investigation it is obvious that he or she has previously condoned it.

Most direct instigation of abuse occurs when a spouse expresses opinions that the infant is being spoiled and needs more discipline or should be punished to break excessive willfulness and be brought under control. Similarly, one parent, feeling overwhelmed and frustrated, may turn the infant over to the other with admonitions to do something more drastic to stop the baby's annoying behavior. The nonabusing parent may show undue attention and interest toward an infant who stimulates feelings in the spouse of envy, abandonment, and anger leading to attack on the baby.

A husband's direct criticism of his wife's baby-caring ability, pointing out errors and inadequacies, can trigger her attack on the child. Such husbands seem aware, at least on an unconscious level, that this will happen; yet they do it repeatedly.

Behavior that in any way signifies rejection or desertion is a potent stimulus to the attacker. If the abusing parent's own needs are neglected or rebuffed, there is an immediate turning to the infant with increased demand, and attack is likely. One woman told her husband she was uneasy about being alone with her previously injured baby and asked him to stay with her. He ignored her request and left the house. Shortly afterwards the baby was hit, resulting in a subdural hematoma. Less overt desertions can have a similar effect.

The various actions of the nonabusing parent become quite understandable when it is discovered that he or she had much the same life experience as the abuser and has developed a similar set of attitudes about parent-child relationships. Present in lesser intensity are the same feelings of unheeded yearnings for care, inferiority, and hopelessness, coupled with the basic tenet that children should satisfy parental need. Thus, unknowingly, the marriage has become almost a collusion for the raising of children in a specific way. One parent is the active perpetrator; the other is a behind-the-scenes cooperator. Such parental tendencies become obvious when under treatment an abusing parent becomes gentler and the previously nonabusing parent starts being abusive. In a sense the infant becomes the scapegoat for interparental conflicts. Inability to solve their frustrated dependencies and antagonisms with each other leads them to turn for comfort to the child, who is then attacked for failure to assuage the needs. It is obvious that treatment is often needed for the spouse, as well as for the overtly abusing parent.

THE CONTRIBUTION MADE BY THE ATTACKED CHILD

There is no doubt that the infant, innocently and unwittingly, may contribute to the attack which is unleashed upon him. An infant born as the result of a premaritally conceived pregnancy, or who comes as an accident too soon after the birth of a previous child, may be quite unwelcome to the parents and start life under the cloud of being unrewarding and unsatisfying to the parents. Such infants may be perceived as public reminders of sexual transgression or as extra, unwanted burdens rather than need-satisfying objects. An infant may also be seen as "uncooperative" or unsatisfying by having been born a girl when the parents wanted a boy or vice versa. Babies are born with quite different behavioral patterns. Some parents are disappointed when they have a very placid child instead of a hoped-for, more reactive, responsive baby. Other parents are equally distressed by having an active, somewhat aggressive baby who makes up his own mind about things when they had hoped for a very placid, compliant infant. A potent source of difficulty is the situation in which babies are born with some degree, major or minor, of congenital defect, therefore requiring much more medical as well as general attention. Often such infants are fussy, crying, and difficult to comfort and are limited in their ability to respond as a normal, happy baby should. Intercurrent illness may produce a similar picture. Babies born prematurely require much more care and offer less response soon enough to satisfy the parents' needs. A case which illustrates several of these points follows.

> Jerry and Connie had their first baby, a boy, as a result of a pregnancy which was instrumental in leading them to get married. Unfortunately, this otherwise quite healthy little boy was born with a congenital stricture of the bladder neck which required two long hospitalizations with surgery during the first six months of his life. Not surprisingly, he was a fussy, whiny, difficult-to-care-for baby, requiring much more than average care and offering less happy, rewarding behavioral response to his parents. When he was eight months old, his father returned home late from an usually hard day at work and found his wife terribly upset and irritable because of conflicts arising with his mother. His wife, in an effort to assuage her own turmoil, left the baby with Jerry and went to visit her own mother. Jerry, tired, feeling quite needy, deserted by Connie, was faced with caring for a crying baby. After several attempts to comfort and feed the baby, he became out-of-patience, angry, and struck the baby, fracturing the baby's skull. There were no serious consequences, fortunately, from this injury. Jerry came under our care some three years later because of his worry over the fact that he was still very

punitive toward Willie and often spanked him and slapped him to an unnecessary degree. By this time, a second boy, Benny, had been born and was now nine months old. Jerry spoke of his attitude toward Benny being extremely different, and when asked why responded with, "Well, Benny's just the kind of a kid I like. Whenever I want to wrestle with him, he wrestles. He does everything that I want him to do."

Thus, it is obvious that characteristics presented by the infant, such as sex, time of birth, health status, and behavior are factors in instigating child abuse. An interesting presentation of the role of the child is that of Milowe and Lourie (1964) with its accompanying discussion. Often stated in support of the idea that it is somehow "all the infant's fault" is the fact that occasionally battered children have been attacked and injured again in the foster home where they have been placed for protection. We have not had the opportunity to study such an event, nor have we seen any report of an adequately thorough study; but our other experience leads us to doubt the assumption that only the child is at fault.

Despite the contributions infants make toward the disappointments and burdens of their parents, they can hardly be used as an excuse or adequate cause for child abuse. They are part of the inevitable hazards all of us face in being human and in being parents. The essence of the problem is again the excessively high demands which parents impose on infants, disregarding the inability of the infants to meet them.

CIRCUMSTANCES OF THE ATTACK

Most abusing parents have difficulty in describing just what happened at the time the infant was injured. To some extent, this is due to their reluctance to reveal anything for which they may be criticized. Sometimes it is due to a more or less unconscious, defensive forgetting or amnesia. Both of these factors are usually diminished under therapy. More universal and impossible to eliminate is a vague "haziness" about the actual attack, although events immediately preceding and following the attack may be recalled with clarity. We have not considered this haziness to be either a real cognitive slip or a psychological repression, but rather the normal vagueness everyone feels when trying to describe in detail an extremely intense emotional storm. By using all other information we have about the patient's psychological patterns, plus his description of events before, during, and after the attack, as well as associative material, we have developed an understanding of the circumstances of the attack in which we have reasonable confidence.

The parent approaches each task of infant care with three incongruous attitudes: first, a healthy desire to do something good for the infant; second, a deep, hidden yearning for the infant to respond in such a way as to fill the emptiness in the patient's life and bolster his low self-esteem; and third, a harsh, authoritative demand for the infant's correct response, supported by a sense of parental rightness. If the caring task goes reasonably well and the infant's response is reasonably adequate, no attack occurs and no harm is done, except for the stimulation of aggression and accompanying strict superego development in the infant. But if anything interferes with the success of the parental care or enhances the parent's feelings of being unloved and inferior, the harsh, authoritative attitude surges up and attack is likely to occur. The infant's part in this disturbance is accomplished by persistent, unassuaged crying; by failing to respond physically or emotionally in accordance with parental needs; or by actively interfering through obstructive physical activity. At times the parent may be feeling especially inferior, unloved, needy, and angry, and, therefore, unusually vulnerable because some important figure such as the spouse or a relative has just criticized or deserted him or because some other facet of his life has become unmanageable.

On a deeper psychological level, the events begin with the parent's identification of the infant for whom he is caring as a need-gratifying object equivalent to a parent who will replace the lacks in the abusing parent's own being-parented experience. Since the parent's past tells him that the ones to whom he looked for love were also the ones who attacked him, the infant is also perceived as a critical parental figure. Quite often abusing parents tell us, "When the baby cries like that it sounds just like mother [or father] yelling at me, and I can't stand it." The perception of being criticized stirs up the parent's feelings of being inferior. It also increases the frustration of his need for love, and anger mounts. At this time there seems to be a strong sense of guilt, a feeling of helplessness and panic becomes overwhelming, and the haziness is most marked. Suddenly a shift in identifications occurs. The superego identification with the parent's own punitive parent takes over. The infant is perceived as the parent's own bad childhood self. The built-up aggression is redirected outwardly and the infant is hit with full superego approval.

This sudden shift in identifications is admittedly difficult to document. Our patients cannot clearly describe all that happened in the midst of such intense emotional turmoil. We interpret it as regression under severe stress to an early period of superego development when identification with the aggressor established a strict, punitive superego with more effective strength than the gentler ego ideal. In such a regressive state the stronger, punitive superego inevitably comes to the fore.

Following the attack, some parents may maintain a strict, righteous attitude;

express no sense of guilt about the aggression; insist they have done nothing wrong; and be very resentful toward anyone who tries to interfere with their affairs. On the other hand, some parents are filled with remorse, weep, and quickly seek medical help if the child has been seriously hurt.

It has not been possible in all patients to obtain a clear story of what they actually did to the child at the time a serious injury occurred, even though abuse is admitted. They insist they did nothing different from usual. In some cases, this may be a defensive forgetting. In others, we think it is probably a true statement. They had been hitting or yanking the child routinely and were not aware of the extra force used at the time of fracture.

The following condensed case histories, when added to the fragments already quoted, will illustrate the mainstreams of the patients' lives related to the ultimate abusive behavior.

Amy, age 26, is the wife of a successful junior executive engineer. She requested help for feelings of depression, fear she was ruining her marriage, and worry over being angry and unloving with her baby boy. She was born and raised in a well-to-do family in a large city on the West Coast. Her parents were brilliant, active intellectuals, who apparently had minimal involvement in the earliest years of their children's lives. She and her younger sister and brother were cared for by governesses, about whom Amy has vague, fragmentary memories. One was very warm, kind, and loving. She recalls another who was demanding, stern, and mean and who roughly washed Amy's long hair as a punishment and held her nose to make her eat. We suspect, without adequate documentation, that the governesses raised the infants as much to meet the high behavior standards of the parents as to meet the variable needs and whims of their charges.

As a child, Amy had more interaction with her mother, but she could not feel close or really understood by either parent. Both parents had compulsive traits of wanting everything in perfect order and tasks done "at once." Her father was quite aloof, uninterested in children because they could not talk to him on any worthwhile level. When Amy was about 13, both mother and father had psychotherapy. Since then, her father has been warmer and has some liking for small children, but he still maintains a pattern of wanting to be the center of the stage and have people pay attention primarily to him, not only in the family, but in all social situations. In recent years Amy has felt closer to her mother and has felt that they could talk more frankly and openly with each other. During her childhood, Amy felt inept, awkward, ugly, unable to be liked by other people, and somewhat dull intellectually. Even though she made good grades in school, they never seemed good enough to gain approval. (Her IQ is in the upper normal range.)

Although not physically punished or overtly severely criticized, Amy felt great lack of approval and developed a deep sense of inferiority, inability to please, and worthlessness; she thought of herself as almost "retarded." In college she was capable, but not outstanding, and after graduation she worked for a while, gaining a significant amount of self-respect and self-assurance. She had become a quite attractive, adequately popular girl and had made a good marriage. She and her husband are well-liked, active members of their social set.

Of her first-born child, Lisa, now age two and a half and doing well, Amy says,

"I did not like her too well at first and didn't feel close to her until she was several months old and more responsive." By the time Lisa was a year old, with much maternal encouragement, she was walking and beginning to talk and Amy began to think much more highly of her, and for the most part, they get along well with each other. However, if Lisa has tantrums or does not behave well, whines or cries too much, Amy occasionally still shakes her and spanks her rather violently. Their second child, Billy, was born not quite a year and a half after Lisa. He was delivered by caesarian section, one month premature. He did not suck well at first and feeding was a problem. Also, Amy was sick for a while after delivery. She never felt warm or close or really loved him and had even less patience with him than with Lisa. His "whining" drove her "crazy" and made her hate him. Because of his crying and lack of adequate response, she would grow impatient with him and leave him or punish him roughly. She spent little time cuddling or playing with him, and he became, as a result, somewhat less responsive and did not thrive as well as he might have. When he was seven months old, during a routine checkup, the pediatrician unfortunately said to Amy, "Maybe you have a retarded child here." Amy immediately felt intense aversion to Billy, hated the sight of him, couldn't pick him up or feed him easily, and began more serious physical abuse that evening. She felt depressed, angry, and irritable. Billy also seemed to stop progress. However, when checked by another pediatrician, he was said to be quite normal. Amy felt reassured, but not convinced. She became aware that Billy was responsive and alert if she felt all right and loving toward him, but he acted "stupid" if she was depressed or angry at him. This awareness of her influence on him served only to enhance her feelings of worthlessness and guilt. At times when he was unresponsive or seemed to be behaving in a "retarded" way, and especially if he cried too much or whined, she roughed him up, shook him, spanked him very severely, and choked him violently. No bones had been broken, but there were bruises. Amy described alternating between feeling angry at Billy because he was "retarded" and feeling very guilty because she had "squashed him" by her own attitudes and behavior.

Amy described being inadequately prepared for and overwhelmed by the tasks of motherhood. This was enhanced by her feeling that she was trying to accomplish the mothering tasks without the help that her mother had had in bringing up her children. Further difficulty arouse because her husband, although overtly quite sympathetic with her difficulties and expressing wishes of helping her, would also withdraw from her in times of crisis and imply a good deal of criticism of the way she dealt with the children. She also felt that there had been no one to whom she could really turn to air her troubles and get comfort and help without too much admonition and criticism. Further, Amy had a cousin who was retarded and she felt devastated by fantasies of the burden of bringing up a retarded child.

This case shows the identification of the abusing parent with her own parents' attitudes toward children; the premature, high expectation and need of responsive performance on the part of the infant; and the inability to cope with lack of good response. Most clearly, it shows the parental misperception of the infant as the embodiment of those bad behavioral traits (being "retarded") for which the parent herself was criticized as a young child. During treatment, Amy's depressive feelings and sense of worthlessness were ameliorated. She began to interact more happily with her children, and they responded well to her change in behavior. Billy, particularly, began to thrive, grew rapidly, and became a happier, more rewarding baby. Amy and her husband began to communicate a little more effectively and her aggressive behavior toward her children almost completely disappeared. After six months, treatment had to be terminated because of her husband's transfer to another city. We had the good fortune to see her and the children four years later. Amy was doing very well and the two children were active, happy, bright youngsters. Wisely, we believe, they have had no more children. The improvement that occurred in this situation is partly due to our therapeutic intervention, but we would guess that it is also due to the passage of time which enabled the children to grow up and inevitably become more behaviorally and conversationally rewarding to their mother.

Larry, age 27, is a quiet, shy, unassuming little man who works as a welder's assistant. Since childhood, he has been plagued by a deep sense of inferiority, unworthiness, and unsureness of himself in his work and in all human relations. There is also a deep resentment, usually very restrained, against a world which he feels is unfair.

He was brought up on a dairy farm, the third of five children. The oldest, a sister, is ten years his senior. He has never been able to find out the truth about her from his parents or other relatives, but thinks all the evidence indicates she is a half-sister and an illegitimate child of his mother before her marriage. Some resentment against his mother is based on this situation. His two younger sisters he felt were bothersome and annoying during their childhood. His brother, two years older, took advantage of him, and his parents always took the brother's side, allowing him to do many things for which Larry was criticized or punished. This brother was quite wild, and while on leave from the navy, he was in a serious auto accident. Larry said, "Too bad he wasn't killed," but then found his brother had been killed. Overwhelmed by guilt and grief, Larry took leave from the army to take his brother's body home for burial.

Larry's parents were deeply religious. He imagined his mother became fanatically so following her illegitimate pregnancy. She was against smoking, alcohol, coffee, tea, and most of the usual forms of amusement. Even after his marriage, his mother told his wife not to make coffee for him. Larry felt she was always much more strict with him then with his siblings. She forced him to attend Sunday school and frequent church services, much against his will. She berated him for minor misdeeds and constantly nagged and criticized him to the point where he felt everything he did was wrong, and that he could never do right in her eyes. He occasionally rebelled by smoking or drinking. Larry's father drank moderately but became a teetotaler after his son's death. He often had outbursts of temper and once beat Larry with a piece of two-by-four lumber for a minor misdeed. Larry does not recall either his mother or father spanking as a routine, but there were constant verbal attacks and criticism. He felt that neither of his parents, particularly his mother, really listened to him or understood his unhappiness and his need for comfort and consideration.[4]

[4] See previous references to Larry above.

While he was in the army, Larry and Becky planned to marry. She was to come to where he was stationed, and they were to be married at Christmas time. He waited all day at the bus station, but she never appeared. Sad and hopeless, he got drunk. Months later, a buddy told him she had married somebody else the first of January. He saw her again a year later when home on leave. She had been divorced; so they made up and got married. She had a child, Jimmy, by her first marriage.

Larry has been dependent on Becky and fears losing her. Seeing Jimmy reminds him of her previous desertion. He feels she favors Jimmy; he is critical of Jimmy and occasionally spanks him. Becky has threatened to leave Larry over his aversion to Jimmy. During their five years of marriage they have been in financial straits, and at such times Becky and Larry have gone to their respective family homes for help until he could find a new job. Becky resented these episodes and criticized Larry for being an inadequately capable and providing husband.

They have had three more children of their own. Mary, age four, is liked very much by both parents, although Larry is more irritated by her than by their next child, David, age two and a half. David is "a very fine, active, alert, well-mannered little boy." He is quite responsive and both parents like him and are good with him. Maggie, four and a half months old, was thought by both parents to be "a bit different" from birth. She seemed to look bluer and cried less strongly than their other babies and was also rather fussy. Becky is fond of Maggie and gives her good mothering. Larry is irritated by her, much as he is by Mary, and more than by David, but he does not dislike her as much as he does Jimmy.

Maggie was admitted to the hospital with symptoms and signs of bilateral subdural hematoma. She had been alone with her father when he noticed a sudden limpness, unconsciousness, and lack of breathing. He gave mouth-to-mouth respiration, and she was brought to hospital by ambulance. There was a history of a similar episode a month before when Maggie was three and a half months old; when alone with her father she had become limp, followed by vomiting. Medical care was not sought until a week later. Following this, there was a question of increasing head size. No fractures of skull or long bones were revealed by X-ray. Two craniotomies were done for the relief of Maggie's subdural hematomas. During the month she was in hospital, we had frequent interviews with the parents. We were impressed with Becky's warmth, responsiveness, and concern over Maggie's welfare. Larry, however, maintained a more uneasy, aloof, evasive attitude, although he was superficially cooperative. What had happened to Maggie was not clearly established, but it seemed obvious she was the victim of trauma. We thought Larry was likely to have been the abuser, despite his maintenance of silence and innocence. We felt we had adequate, although meager, rapport with Larry and Becky and allowed them to take Maggie home with the adamant provision that she never be left alone with Larry.

A week later Larry called urgently for an appointment. Filled with shame, guilt, and anxiety he poured out his story. President Kennedy had been assassinated two days before. Larry was shocked, then flooded with feelings of sympathy for Kennedy and his family, anger at the assassin, grief over the unfair, unnecessary loss of an admired figure, and a sense of communal guilt. In this emotional turmoil he had a few beers at a tavern, went home and confessed to Becky what he had done to Maggie, and then phoned us. The circumstances of the attack were as follows: Larry's boss told him that his job was over. The construction contract had been suddenly cancelled and there was no more work. Feeling discouraged, hopeless, and ignored, Larry went home, shamefacedly told Becky he had lost his job, and asked her if she wanted to go with the children to her family. Saying nothing, Becky walked out of the house, leaving Larry alone with Maggie. The baby began to cry. Larry tried to comfort her, but she kept on crying so he looked for her bottle. He could not find the bottle anywhere; the persistent crying and his feelings of frustration, helplessness, and ineffectuality became overwhelming. In a semiconfused, "blurry" state he shook Maggie severely and then hit her on the head. Suddenly aware of what he had done, he started mouth-to-mouth resuscitation; then Becky came home and Maggie was brought to the hospital.

Recurrent in Larry's life are the themes of feeling disregarded and deserted and of being helplessly ineffectual in his attempts to meet expectations. These concepts of himself as worthless and incapable express the incorporation into his superego of the attitudes of his parents toward him during childhood; they have been enhanced by his later reality experiences of failure. He has further strong identifications with the aggressive parental attitudes of criticizing and attacking the weak, the helpless, and the maimed.

The attack on Maggie occurred when several of Larry's vulnerabilities were activated at the same time. He had experienced a lack of being considered and a feeling of failure in losing his job, his wife "deserted" him again with implications of criticism, he felt helpless to cope with the crying demands of the baby, and his own deep yearnings for love and care could not be spoken. Frustration and anger mounted, and the baby was struck. Larry said that in the "blurry" state he had a fleeting queer feeling that he had hit himself.

Later we found similar circumstances were present when Maggie had been less severely injured a month before. Becky had started working evenings to supplement Larry's inadequate income. She would depart soon after he came home from his job, leaving him alone to fix supper, wash the dishes, and put the children to bed. He found the tasks difficult and was upset by the children's crying, particularly Maggie's. One evening, feeling overwhelmed, helpless, and unable to seek help, he attacked.

Larry's relationship to Becky was highly influenced by his unconscious tendency to identify her with his mother. This transference was facilitated by the reality facts that Becky had a child by a previous liaison, urged Larry to be more involved with the church, took Jimmy's side while disregarding Larry, frequently criticized Larry for failure to meet her expectations, and had several times deserted him, both emotionally and physically. Most basic and potent was Larry's urgent dependent need to find in Becky the motherliness he had never known. Constantly, despite disappointment, he yearningly looked to her to satisfy the unmet needs of all his yesterdays. When she failed him, there were only the children to look to for responses which would make him feel better.

Psychological Testing[5]

Psychological testing of child-abusing parents has provided several interesting findings which support impressions gained from clinical observations. First, there is no evidence of a significant relationship between intelligence as measured by intelligence tests and abuse. The IQs obtained by the patients seen for testing range between 73 and 130, with most of the patients falling into the average range (90–110). The cognitive styles of these people tend to be more along the lines of action-orientation, as opposed to dependence on thought and delay of impulse gratification. This is not true, however, for all of our patients. Second, the test results indicate no one basic personality structure, in the usual nosological sense, for all the patients. A few patients show existing ego pathology of psychotic proportions. Others show apparent overall ego strength. Personality patterns featuring hysterical trends are evident in a number. Obsessive-compulsive patterns predominate in others. However, these "patterns" reflect to a large extent the defenses and other ego mechanisms which predominate in the patient's overall functioning.

Among those patients who were given the entire psychological test battery,[6] common underlying conflicts are apparent. The test reports specifically mention strong oral-dependent needs as significant intrapsychic areas of difficulty for every patient tested. In four-fifths of the patients, unresolved identity conflicts were cited as major determinants of their behavior, and in nearly as many, depressive trends and/or noteworthy feelings of worthlessness were noted. Almost as common was evidence of suspiciousness, distrust, and feeling victimized, but in only one case was this significant enough to be classified as truly paranoid. It is emphasized that these problem areas appeared in people of widely differing personality constellations, people whose test behavior and surface attitudes were extremely varied. All of the patients defended against the conscious experience of depressive affect with efforts varying in complexity and effectiveness. Some utilized strong and resilient character defenses; others employed classically neurotic constellations of defenses. Nevertheless, the test results clearly indicate the underlying presence of the depressive elements. A review of the nature of the depression in these cases indicates that while frequently superego pressures and guilt contributed to the depressive feelings, in all but one case the depression was basically of the anaclitic type.

The identity problems noted in the test reports indicate developmental failures to establish successful syntheses of identity fragments. The test results

[5] This section was written in collaboration with Richard Waite, Ph.D. We are very grateful for his help.

[6] The test battery always included the Wechsler Adult Intelligence Scale, Rorschach, Thematic Apperception Test, and usually the addition of the Sentence Completion Test and Figure Drawing.

suggest that frequently not only do these patients consciously doubt their adequacy as wives and mothers, husbands and fathers, but they also actively wish to be something else. Some of the patients appear to have retained, as one important aspect of their identity struggles, part-identifications as little girls or boys, a finding directly related to the prevalence of unsatiated oral-receptive longings.

In summary, the test findings provide some support for the hypothesis that child-abusing parents have fairly oral conflicts, have underlying feelings of depression and worthlessness, and have failed to establish age-appropriate ego identities. The support of other hypotheses remains open to question at this point. Moreover, the test results indicate significant diversity in personality structure among these patients in the complexity of defenses and ego-adaptive mechanisms available to them. They indicate that child-abusing behavior is not common to one or two diagnostic entities and that this behavior can occur in people having relatively resilient and adaptive egos.

TREATMENT

Notwithstanding its difficulties, psychotherapy of the patients in our study group has been very rewarding, both for them and for us. There were treatment failures, sometimes due to uncontrollable external circumstances such as the patient's moving away, going to the penitentiary, or living too far away for contact, and sometimes due to a combination of the severity of the psychiatric problem and our own lack of knowledge. In the great majority of patients, treatment was successful—highly so in some, moderately so in others. Criteria of success were multiple. Of primary importance was a change in the style of parent-child interaction to a degree that eliminated the danger of physical harm to the child and lessened the chance of serious emotional damage. Accompanying the change in parenting style, and in fact a necessary precursor of it, was a change in the patient's general psychic functioning, evidenced by signs of better handling of intrapsychic conflicts, and also by improvement in the marital relationship, in other interpersonal relationships, and in dealing with the various problems of daily living. Treatment was oriented toward the patient as a human being, not toward a person pigeonholed as one who abuses children. As noted before, our patients had all the variety of psychological states encountered in any practice, and therapy was in many ways the application of techniques ordinarily used. However, the symptom of child abuse, related as it is to the dynamics described in previous sections, gives rise to certain problems which call for special attention in therapy.

Probably the first difficulty met by the therapist is the management of his own feelings about a parent who has hurt a small baby. Most people react with disbelief and denial or, on the other hand, with horror and a surge of anger toward the abuser. It helps to gain a more useful, neutral position to realize from the very first that not only has an infant been hurt, but that the parent, too, is a hurt child himself. We were fortunate in that our research goals led us to a broad interest in the patient's whole life, rather than attempts to cure a symptom. The more the therapist can mobilize the same curiosity he has about other patients, the better he will do with the abusing parent. Aggressive acts toward infants are a symptom of deep conflict and can best be treated by investigation of the total personality, rather than by belaboring the symptom. In this sense, therapy of these patients is quite similar to treatment of patients with such symptoms as impotence, frigidity, or hand-washing compulsions. Thinking of the abusing parent in this framework is quite helpful in ameliorating those less useful emotions which arise in the therapist when first faced with the problem.

Another difficulty present on first contact and for some time thereafter is the attitude the patient has about getting help and his view of the therapist. He may be a bit belligerent and say he doesn't need treatment, doesn't want treatment, and considers the whole project an imposition. He has not done anything wrong, stupid people are making an unwarranted fuss over nothing, and the therapist is wasting his time. On the other hand, a patient may be meek, mild, and submissive, and express a desire to cooperate in any way. There are, of course, many gradations and mixtures of these two polar attitudes. Patients can respond in either of these gross ways to the experience of having had abuse discovered and having been talked to in an accusatory, punitive manner by physicians, social workers, law enforcement investigators, or others. Those who come voluntarily seeking help are more likely to show the cooperative, submissive attitude and to express belief in the usefulness of treatment.

It is important not to accept these first attitudes at face value, but to use them as first clues to what will be needed to develop the therapeutic alliance vital for ongoing, successful treatment. These are people whose early life experience taught them the not-yet-forgotten lesson that those to whom one looks for help are those who will attack one and that to look for help is hopeless. They have learned that a modicum of safety lies in self-negation and in submissively trying to do what others expect. Simultaneously, they have the belief that a very good way to deal with trouble is to attack it with strong aggression. With this potpourri and without enough of that quality we call basic trust or confidence, it is no wonder they approach treatment tentatively, doubtingly, and with a variety of overt attitudes.

This situation is not as bad as it looks. The patient comes to the psychiatrist in a severe crisis of distress over his behavior, distress created by his own internal conflicts or by the reaction of the environment. He feels attacked, either by his own conscience or by society. As an inevitable corollary, he will have intensified yearnings for love and protection, and this opens a useful avenue for the therapist to make contact. We learned not to be dismayed by a patient's first negative, rejecting attitudes, particularly if he or she had been heckled and threatened by others. It is easy to say to the patient, "It sounds as if you have been having a perfectly dreadful time. Let's see what we can do about it." Such simple statements of sympathy give the patient at least a faint idea he has been listened to without being criticized. The therapist is then to some extent "on the side of the angels," offering asylum and protection from the threatening world. Sympathetic listening is equally important for cooperative or voluntary patients. Their distrust of treatment is very strong, although well camouflaged.

It is a commonplace that psychiatric patients enjoy the time and attention of the therapist and the privilege of being listened to. We are convinced abusing parents need this more and respond to it better than any other patients we have seen. Being listened to helps build the needed sense of confidence and lays the foundation for developing a sense of self-respect and identity. An important part of the patient's improvement is directly related to this, involving identification with the therapist. We know we are well on the road to success when a patient says something to the effect, "You know, doctor, I'm listening to my baby the way you listen to me. He is a real person to me now and it's lots of fun."

In addition to listening, the therapist must also ask questions. If it is not already known which parent has attacked the infant, questioning about it is often fruitless and puts the therapist in the role of unwelcome accuser. When the seriously injured infant is in the hospital, the necessary information usually appears spontaneously before discharge. In the case of nonhospitalized milder injuries, it usually becomes obvious who has hurt the child without direct questioning or confrontation. The therapist can well ask the patient about his present and past life and how he was raised as a child. This leads naturally and unobtrusively into how he deals with his own offspring. Any direct question carrying a sense of accusation is best avoided. To ask, "Do you get angry when the baby cries?" is likely to stimulate denial or evasion. But to ask, "Does it almost push you beyond your strength sometimes when the baby cries so much?" may well produce much pertinent material including the feelings of anger and frustration.

Although protection of the infant is a main goal, direct interest in the infant should be avoided by the therapist, paradoxical as this may seem. Attention should be focused almost exclusively on the parent. The rationale for this lies in the fact that paying attention to the baby leaves the parent back in the old nightmarish feeling that nobody listens to his needs, thereby reinforcing his hopelessness and lack of trust. Probably our most basic tenet in treatment has been to get the parent to look to us to find out how to get his needs filled, rather than to the infant for satisfaction. If this can be accomplished to even a moderate degree, there is less demand on the baby, less parental frustration, and the baby is essentially safe. A clue to this element of safety is the patient's phoning between appointments to speak of loneliness, frustration, and increasing tension, a turning to the therapist instead of the baby for response.

Closely related is the therapeutic goal of changing the patient's isolated way of life. After a good alliance has been established with the therapist, the patient can be encouraged to seek more outside social contacts with friends or neighbors. This can be done best by helping the patient recognize his own desires for contact and ameliorating his fears of it, rather than by direct advice or admonition. The more involvement there is with others, the less the baby is used to supply parental comfort. Patients often require encouragement to do such a simple thing as to get baby-sitters so that they can occasionally have freedom for other activities. This must be handled carefully because of the tendency of parents to feel "left out" if attention is paid to the baby. One mother put it succinctly: "When my mother comes to help me with Billy and she picks him up, I feel she has not only taken Billy away from me, but that Billy is also taking mother away from me. I feel angry at both of them." She added that even when she wanted help with her baby, for another person to take over meant she herself was being criticized as a no-good mother. Such complex feelings underscore the necessity of paying primary attention to parental need.

A frequent problem in therapy is the requests patients make for advice. Out of their lifelong obligation to do what others want, they ask many questions about what to do and the proper way to do it. Giving such advice is useless; the patient will follow it submissively in a way that makes it not work or, if in a healthier mood, he will disregard it. To use a standard psychiatric gambit such as, "Why do you ask?" is equally fruitless. It puts the patient on the spot; he feels rejected and can only come up with a lame remark, "Well, I want to do the right thing." No ground has been gained. A more useful approach is to mention several ways of doing something, including one's own point of view, and counter this by suggesting the patient can follow any method or devise another which suits him better. Usually patients do well with this encouragement, gaining confidence and self-respect. The same principle applies to the question of "setting limits" or controls. Abusing parents have already been overburdened by controls to which they responded poorly. Rather than ordering them to stop certain behaviors, it is more productive of change to ask, "Do you suppose you could think of another way to do it so as to bring out more of what you want?''

The patients in our study group were exquisitely sensitive to desertion and rejection in any form. We noted earlier that feeling rejected by spouse, parent, or another meaningful figure is a potent factor in precipitating a specific abusing act. Such symptomatic acting out also occurs in reaction to the therapist. Early in our work we made the mistake of all three therapists being out of town at the same time for a few days. Some patients responded by reinstituting mild abusive behavior toward their infants. Since then, we have always had at least one member of the group available for patients to contact if need arises. As a rule, it is worthwhile to let patients know when one is leaving town and returning, even though the absence will not interfere with scheduled appointments. Giving such information seems to help the development of the patient's trust and confidence. Telephone contacts can be tricky. Patients inevitably phone at inconvenient or impossible times and feel rejected if dealt with brusquely. If one can take the time to say, ''I can talk to you for a minute now if it's very urgent, but if you can wait a couple of hours, I'll have freedom to talk more leisurely. Is that possible for you?'' patients usually respond well. After a few experiences of this sort, they become more like average patients, who leave a request with the secretary to call when convenient. Again, time and attention are priceless gifts to these patients.

Termination of treatment can arouse once more the feelings of being deserted and rejected, and not rarely there will be a mild transient recurrence of tendencies to demand too much and be too aggressive toward the infant. This affords an opportunity for the therapist to make more precise interpretations and for the patient to gain more definitive insight as the conflict is worked through. We suspect some of the patients' acting out was because they knew we were interested in the problem of abuse and the obvious way to maintain our interest was to do some abusing. Because of our research interest, we let patients know we would be glad to hear from them again, even after therapy had been tapered off and technically terminated. While writing this section, our first patient, Bertie, was feeling a bit lonely and made her roughly semiannual phone call to us. Her two daughters are thriving in school and kindergarten. She occasionally has to mollify her husband, who thinks she is too lenient with the girls and wants to use a strap on them for discipline. On the whole, she is managing adequately well. We had seen her husband, too, but because his work made contacts extremely difficult, his treatment ended prematurely.

Treatment of the nonabusing spouse is indicated whenever a significant contribution or provocation of abuse is made by him. We mentioned earlier that our patients tend to marry someone who is rather like themselves in background and basic character structure. Hence, when an abusing mother under treatment begins to be more tolerant and considerate of the infant, the father may then pick up the role of abuser, although often in a milder form. Further improvement by the wife may enable her to meet more of her husband's needs so that he will no longer turn to the child for satisfaction, but therapy of both parents is highly desirable if it can be accomplished. Unresolved sibling rivalry leading to parental competition for the child's affection may be a productive area for therapy in the nonabusing spouse. We believe our general principles of treatment apply equally to both spouses since their psychodynamics related to abuse are similar.

By far the most difficult task in therapy is to help patients establish a better relationship with their own parents, particularly their mothers. We feel that until some sense of peace and useful rapport is felt with the mother, the patient's own ability to be motherly remains hampered. The patient's recurrent sense of disappointment with the mother, the fear of her, and the intense ambivalence about her make the task seem almost impossible. Only after a strong therapeutic alliance has developed, with increased confidence in the therapist, should any attempt be made to lead the patient toward finding the good qualities of the mother. Even then it must be done cautiously and skillfully. Gradually, with luck, a patient can find her own way of maintaining equilibrium during contacts with her mother and even find means of pleasing the mother so as to bring responses of real love and approval. Whatever amount of relationship and new identification can be made with the "good" mother will be directly reflected in the release of the patient's own motherliness. Although the patient's rapprochement with the mother might be handled in an exclusively psychotherapeutic situation, we used the additional help of a sensitive woman social worker in nearly all cases. Following an initial period of variable length of being rejected and tested, she was trusted by most of the women patients and became the usable object of their pent-up longings to be mothered. She was an empathic, noncritical, noncontrolling, available substitute mother, thus providing a new experience for the patient and a new object for identification. The therapeutic significance of this relationship was often tremendous. In addition to its own intrinsic value, it facilitated and speeded up therapy with the psychiatrist. A good relationship with the social worker was many times a first step in the patient's breaking out of restricting isolation into broader social contacts. Often it was the patient's bridge toward remodeling the relationship with her own mother.

The social worker was involved very early in some cases, interviewing patients just before or after the first psychiatric contact. The psychiatrist and social worker then continued contacts, the former in office interviews, the latter predominantly in home visits until the case was terminated. This pattern worked well. It gave the patient opportunity to deal with two people of different sex, who were allied in an effort to be of use to the patient. If in trouble with the psychiatrist, the patient could turn to the social worker, and vice versa, thereby airing troubles more freely and lessening the sense of hopelessness. This byplay back and forth between the man and the woman therapists had a special meaning for many patients because of specific child-hood experiences. They had felt disillusioned and disappointed when they looked to their mothers for satisfaction of dependent needs.Turning then to their fathers for this satisfaction they overidealized them, partly because the fathers did provide a modicum of satisfaction, but more because the father relationship was less fraught with primitive ambivalence and fear. But their fathers could not provide enough of what they wanted, and they were dis-appointed again. Sometimes they had asked their fathers why they had trouble with mother and were answered with lack of understanding and no help. In therapy the turning from one "parental" figure to the other was re-enacted and re-evaluated with beneficial understanding. We have thought this lack of real confidence in either men or women has helped create the impression in both male psychiatrists and female social workers that abusing parents are almost untreatable.

In some cases the social worker was not involved until after many weeks of contact with the psychiatrist. Bringing her in could then be complicated. One patient, when asked if she would like to have the social worker visit her at home, responded by looking surprised and a little annoyed, hesitated a bit, then acquiesced. Much later, after she had found the social worker to be "one of the best things that ever happened to me," she told us what had gone on. "When you asked me if I would see Mrs. D., I thought: 'How stupid can Dr. S. be? I've just been telling him how afraid I am of women and how I hate them. Then he shoves another one down my throat, but I guess he knows what he's doing, so I'll go along with it.' " This incident illustrates the patient's mixture of suppression of anger about not being lis-tened to, her willingness to submit quickly to the desires of others, and just enough confidence in the therapist to carry through a rough spot in therapy.

The social worker provides invaluable help when the decision must be made about whether or not an infant may safely be left in the care of parents who have injured it, may be left at home provided some other reliable person is constantly there to provide protection, or must be placed in a foster home in custody of the juvenile court or child protective agency. Her evaluation of the situation, derived from interviews and observation of parent-child interactions in the home, is crucially valuable material for use in decision making. Hence, it is usually advisable for a social worker to be involved in care of the patient from the beginning.

Under the present universal system of legal requirement of reporting of injuries to children due to other than accidental means, many segments of our society become involved—law enforcement officials, child protective agencies, probation officers, juvenile courts, prosecutors, social workers, pediatricians, roentgenologists, and psychiatrists. Determining the best means to ensure a better future for the abused child and his family therefore requires the cooperative effort of many people. It is the task of the physician to determine if injury has occurred, its severity, and whether or not it can be accounted for by purely accidental means. If nonaccidental causes can be reasonably suspected, he must report to designated authorities. He will also instigate, it is hoped, psychiatric evaluation of the parent or other caretaker. Social workers of the child protective agency, the law enforcement investigator, and the psychiatrist must then share their information and decide if the situation warrants filing a dependency petition and asking for foster home placement of the child. The juvenile court will then need information from all concerned to make a logical decision of dependency, take custody temporarily from the parents, and order placement of the child. Data given to the judge must include justifiable statements that the child has been significantly and unnecessarily injured, that the danger of repeated injury is high, that the home situation is significantly underprotective, and that the caretakers are unlikely to change their behavior in the immediate future. The psychiatrist and social worker can use their special skills in determining the degree of disruption and pathology in the family, marriage, and social situation, and the amenability of the parents to therapeutic intervention while the injured child is in hospital. The child can then be discharged to foster home care or his own home with some degree of confidence. In doubtful cases, the court may take temporary custody of the child, but permit the parents to keep the child at home under probation, which requires continued contact with social worker or psychiatrist and favorable reports from them. In determining the amenability of parents to therapy, it is necessary to remain alert for and to recognize the difference between a usable therapeutic alliance and the ability of abusing parents to submit readily to authority and to rules while retaining great hidden antagonism. Presence of a valid, ongoing alliance with the therapist, be it psychiatrist or social worker, makes leaving the child in the environment where injury occurred a relatively safe procedure. Most parents deeply resent and fight any effort to take their child away from them, and those faced with the task of forcing the separation may feel uneasy and reluctant to do it. We have found much can be accomplished if the social worker, psychiatrist, or other physician who discusses separation with the parents does it without punitive accusation or direct criticism of the parents' behavior, but rather with empathy and consideration. In many cases, parents then feel willing, even partly comfortable, about separation as it temporarily relieves them of the burden of helplessly trying to cope with an unmanageable situation.

Too often in the past, severe abuse of children has been managed by separating the child from the parent and placing the child in a foster home, and the problem is then considered to be solved. While separation is useful and often an absolutely necessary intervention, it does not in any way deal with the basic issues involved. Sooner or later the question of whether the child can be returned to parental custody will arise. Also, the abusing parents already have or may have in the future other children who can be mistreated. Therefore, effort must be directed not only toward handling the immediate situation so as to protect an infant from further abuse, but also toward investigating the total pattern of parent-child interaction in a family and instituting remedial measures. In a similar vein, we are doubtful of any value in "treating" an abusing parent in the context of criminal law with determination of guilt and the imposition of punishment. If the prosecutor fails to get a conviction, which can easily happen, the parent feels exonerated in his behavior and goes on his way and is highly resistant to treatment. On the other hand, conviction followed by punishment does nothing to really change the parent's character structure and behavior; rather, it is one more reinforcing repetition of the experience of being disregarded, attacked, and commanded to do better—the very things which led him to be an abuser in the first place. As one of our patients put it, "As soon as I get out of the penitentiary, we're going to get out of this state to where we aren't known. Then we'll have some kids and raise them the way we want to."

SUMMARY

Our treatment of those who abuse infants has been directed toward improving the basic pattern of child-rearing. It is based upon the hypotheses derived from the study of the psychology of the abusing parents in our study group. We were able to establish useful contact with all but a few of the 60 families, and of this treated group well over three-fourths showed significant improvement. Some changed a great deal, some only moderately, some are still in therapy. We considered it improvement when dangerously severe physical attack of the infant was eliminated and milder physical attack in the form of disciplinary punishment was either eliminated or reduced to a non-injurious minimum. Of equal significance was a reduction in demand upon and criticism of children accompanied by increased recognition of a child as an individual with age-appropriate needs and behavior. Further signs of improvement in the parents were increased abilities to relate to a wider social milieu for pleasurable satisfaction and source of help in time of need rather than looking to their children for such responses. We did not always try nor did we always succeed in making any change in all of the psychological conflicts and character problems of our patients. These were dealt with only as much as the patient wished or as far as we thought necessary in relation to our primary therapeutic goal. Our philosophy of the value of treatment is twofold: first, it deals in the most humanitarian and constructive way we know with a tragic facet of people's lives; second, therapeutic intervention in a process which seems to pass from one generation to the next will, it is hoped, produce changes in patterns of child-rearing toward the lessening of unhappiness and tragedy.

21

INTRODUCTION

Failure to Thrive: A Study of 45
Children and Their Families,
by Sue L. Evans, John B. Reinhart,
and Ruth A. Succop

Failure to thrive or deprivational dwarfism, as it is sometimes called, vividly describes a specific type of growth failure that is strongly related to psycho-social factors. A number of other designations highlight environmental deprivation, although they do not necessarily entail growth inhibition (Provence and Lipton, 1962). Spitz's (1945b) description of "hospitalism" and Bowlby's (1951) pinpointing of "maternal deprivation" are well known. Prugh and Harlow (1962) have suggested the term " 'masked' emotional deprivation" to counterbalance the "maternal deprivation decade" (Caldwell, 1970). Contrary to prevailing sentiment, Prugh and Harlow contend that "masked" deprivation, which occurs in certain families with a seemingly normal appearance, may render institutional child-rearing less detrimental than rearing in such homes. Galdston (1969) further distinguishes inadequate parenting from not having parents by noting that neglected children live in the "solitude of a family prison," whereas the child without parents is "free to forage for the attention of others" (p. 575). Bullard et al. (1967), however, point to the descriptive inadequacy of these terms and emphasize the extent to which the accusatory connotation of "neglected" may prove counter-productive in efforts to help the child. In addition, in their study more than half of 50 children who failed to thrive did not reveal evidence of parental neglect, within the limitations of their methodology and definitions.

The specific physiological mechanism relating psychosocial deprivation to growth failure has long been assumed to lie in inefficient utilization of nutrition due to decreased intestinal absorption and/or some psychoneuroendocrine factor. In line with this, G. Gardner (1972) reasons that certain sleep patterns may inhibit secretion of pituitary growth hormone. Whitten, Pettit, and Fischhoff (1969), however, present compelling data that challenge the notion of an emotional influence over growth independent of actual caloric consumption. In addition to their own careful efforts to assess these factors, which of necessity, are limited by humane considerations, they emphasize that in other studies the observer often assumed adequacy of caloric intake without actually measuring it. They point, for instance, to the British nutritionist Widdowson's (1951) oft-cited observations in post-war Germany. She contrasted two orphanages that demonstrated different growth patterns. In both the diet consisted of the same official rations, but in one supplementary snacks were available. Paradoxically, in that nutritionally enriched setting the children's growth was less than in the orphanage with less food. Widdowson attributed this confounding discrepancy to striking differences in the emotional climate in the two orphanages. In the one with the additional food, the matron was a stern, foreboding disciplinarian, making for a sharp contrast with the other more cheerful institution. But, as Whitten, Pettit, and Fischhoff tellingly point out, this strict supervisor tended to choose mealtimes to chastise the children publicly. Indeed, Widdowson herself asserted that the food often turned cold as the children became agitated and tearful. Perhaps most significant, however, was the weight and height gain of the few favorites of the stern matron; it exceeded that of all the other children—in either orphanage!

Bullard et al. (1967) report that mental retardation and emotional disorder may be sequelae of growth failure. This finding underscores the potential service rendered by the following chapter's attempt to delineate a family typology for this syndrome with prognostic and therapeutic implications. More efforts in this direction are needed. The data from this investigation raise questions about the higher incidence of prematurity in group II (the multiproblem families and chronically depressed mothers) and the extent to which prematurity is correlated with parent-infant separation and vulnerability to parenting difficulties, as discussed in Chapter 1 by Kennell, Trause, and Klaus. Do lower birthweight and other factors within the child encourage neglectful parental behavior, as Milowe and Lourie (1964) suggest? In their discussion of child abuse in Chapter 20, Steele and Pollock note that the role of the child's behavior in eliciting the detrimental parental behavior is poorly understood. Bullard et al. (1967) consider this in terms of the studies of temperament by Thomas et al. (Thomas and Chess, 1977; Thomas, Chess, and Birch, 1968; Thomas et al., 1963), and they have attempted to relate these to various "mismatches" between mother and infant.

The reader may also ask: How does the categorization outlined in the chapter that follows fit with the delineation by Leonard, Rhymes, and Solnit (1966) of two constellations of children who fail to thrive? More than half of the infants they studied were hypertonically active, irritable, and difficult to comfort and their mothers were described as high-strung and aggressive. The remainder of the children and mothers were described as passively quiet and placid. These often depressed mothers tended not to initiate contact with their less-demanding offspring.

Finally, in our introduction to Chapter 20 we noted Steele and Pollock's attempt to differentiate the abusing parent's investment in the child's life (given in terms of punishment) from the neglecting parent's abandonment of the child. Does this difference imply that abuse and neglect do not coexist? The delineation of group III (the angry mothers) in the following chapter indicates convincingly the frequency with which the two do indeed coexist. This disturbing finding has also been reported by Gil (1970) and B. Simons et al. (1966), among others. In fact, Koel (1969) has described instances where infants discharged from the hospital after treatment for failure to thrive were subsequently readmitted in a battered state. Refinements and elaborations of schemata like the one presented in the chapter that follows should contribute to decreasing the frequency of such horrors. One example of the sensitive intervention needed is vividly described by V. Shapiro, Fraiberg, and Adelson (1976).

21

Failure to Thrive:
A Study of 45 Children
and Their Families

SUE L. EVANS, JOHN B. REINHART,
and RUTH A. SUCCOP

The syndromes of failure to thrive and/or deprivational dwarfism have always presented pediatricians with a complicated problem in diagnosis and treatment (C. A. Smith and Berenberg, 1970; Talbot et al., 1947). The term *failure to thrive* has been used to describe infants and children who fall below standard measurements in height and weight when no organic basis for this deviance is found; frequently the poor growth pattern is accompanied or masked by a variety of physical symptoms such as vomiting and diarrhea. Moreover, it has long been recognized that this condition is produced by certain underlying emotional factors in the social environment. If these are not given primary consideration, therapy and attempts at resolution of the problem are useless (Bakwin, 1949; R. W. Coleman and Provence, 1957; Elmer, 1960; Glaser et al., 1968; Leonard, Rhymes, and Solnit, 1966; Silver and Finkelstein, 1967; Spitz, 1945b, 1946b; Whitten, Pettit, and Fischhoff, 1969).

In this study we shall describe 40 children who were admitted to Children's Hospital of Pittsburgh with nonorganic growth failure. As we reviewed these cases, it became apparent that all of the families could not be "lumped" together; despite a few obvious similarities, they tended to cluster into three

First published in *Journal of the American Academy of Child Psychiatry*, 11:440–457, 1972. Reprinted by permission.

The authors wish to express their gratitude to Elizabeth Elmer, M.S.W., Pittsburgh Child Guidance Center, and Miss Carol Sankey, Children's Hospital of Pittsburgh, for their assistance and support.

groups, each presenting a characteristic set of problems. Medical management, including casework intervention, differed dramatically with each group and made it quite obvious that these were, indeed, distinct categories.

We hoped that a closer review of these cases and a detailed follow-up would support our original assessment of the families. In addition, we sought for possible clues to more effective methods of reaching these parents and providing the preventive therapeutic intervention so crucial for the optimal growth and well-being of these children.

METHOD

Originally, 45 children admitted to Children's Hospital between May 1967 and December 1969 were selected for the study. Criteria for inclusion in the study were (1) that the children fell below the third percentile in weight, (2) that they fell either below or within the third percentile in height; and (3) that no demonstrative physical cause for growth failure could be found.

All 45 families were referred to one social worker who did the original psychosocial history and planned the casework. If necessary, psychiatric consultation was readily available for all cases. Medical management of the cases varied; the measures taken ranged from separation of a child from the parents to a multitude of diagnostic medical procedures.

Initially, medical charts and original social history information were screened for significant family characteristics and the patient's hospital course. Some families had continued contact with the social worker since the original admission; but with those families which did not, efforts were made to contact them to re-evaluate the family's functioning, and, of great importance, to obtain accurate determination of the baby's height and weight. In some cases, follow-up contact with the parents could be made only by phone; we then requested local community agencies, especially Public Health Nursing, to provide us with their latest accurate information.

Because this was a retrospective study, the time and the age of admission varied for each child: the youngest admission was three and a half weeks; the oldest four years, one month. The length of follow-up varied from nine months to three years, four months; the average follow-up was one year, 11 months. For the most part it was felt that this was long enough to make a statement about and prediction of the patient's and family's functioning; our most valid and reliable indicator of the patient's development was measurement of height and weight (using the growth curve of the Boston Anthropometric Chart).

Five of the original families selected for the study were excluded; in the course of follow-up these children developed questionable organic difficulties which might have explained the original growth failure.

OVERALL POPULATION

Of the 40 remaining children, 21 were male, 19 female; 11 were black, 27 white, two multiracial. These characteristics were considered fairly typical of general Children's Hospital admissions. Seventeen of the children were less than six months old at first admission, 16 were over 12 months old, and seven between the ages of six and 12 months.

Certain characteristics were present in the children and their families. All children were reported by their mothers to be unplanned and unwanted. They were all bottle-fed and had a history of feeding problems during the first and second month of life. Undereating was a chronic complaint with 35; vomiting occurred in 38 of the infants, and 37 of the mothers reported concern with bowel function.

Children who were admitted under six months of age were invariably described by physicians and nurses as irritable and difficult to hold and cuddle. These babies rarely smiled and vocalized little. Children between the ages of six and 12 months were generally noted to be quiet and placid, content to spend long hours in their cribs; they showed very little "stranger anxiety." Over 12 months, however, most of the children presented difficult management problems. They socialized poorly and showed marked aggressive and angry behavior, especially toward their parents.

Eighteen of the families lived in predominantly rural neighborhoods, and the remaining 27 came from the city proper. Despite the location of the home, all 40 families had little support from their own families or interaction with the community. Thirty-three of the families were known to major social service agencies, but none had continued meaningful contact with any agency. Both mothers and fathers were seen as very lonely people with little companionship, few close friends, or little support from their relatives. They had no recreational outlets or close church affiliations. For the most part, life was involved with the problems of home and children. All 40 families were struggling with economic and financial loss. Fathers were present in 27 families; none of these fathers gave adequate support to their wives or constant fathering to the children. One mother was divorced, the father visiting only once a year. Of the 12 children born out-of-wedlock, none had a significant relationship with a father-figure, nor did the mother have any meaningful male support.

PROFILE OF GROUP I[1]

Into this first group fell 14 out of the 40 families. According to Hollingshead's Two Factor Index of Social Position, nine of these families fell into

---

[1]*Editors' Note:* See Appendix Tables 1–6 for comparative profiles of groups I, II, and III, as well as for the patients, mothers, families, and follow-up findings.

class 5, four into class 4, one into class 3. Yet, despite their obviously depressed economic status, the living conditions of the families could not be described as physically deprived. Housing was good and they were able to live within a tight but limited budget. The family units were all relatively small, the average sibling number being two. Seven out of the 14 were only children, including six born out-of-wedlock. All 14 children received excellent physical care. Food was always available; all had received well-baby care and immunizations.

The mothers tended to be young and immature. Seven were under 20 and only one mother was over 30. During pregnancy all mothers had received adequate prenatal care; there were no outstanding complications either with pregnancy or delivery. Most of the mothers were quite healthy; only one had a severe health problem. Ten of the mothers had completed high school and were probably of average intelligence.

Among these 14 mothers, four characteristics were quite striking: (1) upon initial hospital contact, these mothers were judged to be extremely depressed; (2) they verbalized fears that their children would die, or perceived them as retarded; (3) all made vain efforts to feed and cuddle their babies, but their actions were observed to be strained, constricted, and unsure; (4) moreover, within four months of the babies' first hospitalization, all the mothers experienced a severe object loss (such as the death of their own mother) and traced the breakdown of mothering to the time of this original loss.

The hospital course of these children was quite smooth. The mothers related easily and well and permitted members of the house staff to be quite supportive to them. They visited the babies daily and were seen at regular interviews by the caseworker. They were able to express feelings of depression and loneliness and spoke of their ambivalence toward their children. With encouragement from the nurses, they would attempt feeding and new ways of handling and were not competitive. In many instances, they were seen as overly sensitive to their infant's needs.

Upon discharge, all kept regular clinic appointments or remained in close contact with their own private pediatricians. Two continued in ongoing psychotherapy. Casework contacts were terminated with the remaining 12 families after six months; at the time there was mutual consent between mother and the worker that the children and the families were doing well.

Follow-up reconfirmed our initial impression that these children would continue to thrive. Thirteen of the children were in or above the tenth percentile for weight. Eleven were above or within the tenth percentile for height. Two children were within the third percentile for height; both mothers are in psychotherapy and it is hoped that the babies will eventually fall above the third percentile. One child died at 11 months of bronchial pneumonia; details were not available, but the last recorded weight placed the child within the third percentile.

These mothers were very responsive to follow-up contact. There tended to be improvement in all areas of functioning. There was marked mobility and striving in terms of social class. Three of the unmarried mothers had married by the time of the follow-up. All of the children were described by the mothers as attaining adequate developmental milestones. However, 10 of the 13 still reported difficulties with feeding and sleeping, indicating that concern for the children still existed, even though problems were for the most part denied.

CASE EXAMPLE 1

Michelle M. was first hospitalized at age five months with chief complaints of vomiting and diarrhea present since birth. Within the first three days of hospitalization the symptoms subsided, and all tests were reported negative. The diagnosis was made of "failure to do well." The nurses on the floor observed Michelle's mother to be unsure and anxious during feeding; she was frequently observed to be crying by the infant's bedside. Mrs. M. expressed many fears that her child would die and berated herself for being "too tired and depressed" to care for her infant. She saw her pregnancy with Michelle as forcing her into a state of extreme distress and helplessness. She had been separated from her husband for three and a half years; this pregnancy, an attempt at reconciliation with him, forced her to leave her job and go on public assistance. During the pregnancy, the maternal grandmother became quite ill; she died when Michelle was one month old. Mrs. M. became immobilized with her own mother's illness and death, finding it impossible to satisfy most of her infant's needs.

During Michelle's two-week hospitalization, she began to thrive, and so did the mother. This progress continued after discharge; clinic appointments were kept faithfully.

On follow-up two years later, Michelle was within the 25th percentile for both height and weight. She was reported to be bright and alert and was doing well in a local preschool program. Mrs. M. was observed to handle her child with warmth and assurance. She also expressed much optimism for her own future and was contemplating remarriage.

PROFILE OF GROUP II

In contrast to the children in the first group, those who fell into the second group were regarded by the parents as just one more failure or crisis in a wide range of problems with which the family had to cope. These families had many characteristics similar to group I, but they had many more crises and long-standing, chronic problems to deal with. Fifteen of the 40 families were placed into this group. Fourteen of these 15 families fell into social class 5. Living conditions were extremely deprived—housing was crowded and food scarce. Five of the families had more than five children and, in 11 families, there were birth intervals of less than 13 months.

Fourteen children, including siblings, were judged to receive very poor physical care. Immunizations and well-baby care had never been given to 12 children. Ten of the infants were the youngest children in the family; and in many instances the mother simply lacked the energy to give to one more child. Eleven of the children and their siblings had histories of frequent illnesses. Prenatal care for all these mothers was inadequate; six of the infants were premature.

As in group I, the assessment of the function of the mother and her observed interactions with the child proved to be an essential clue as to why the babies might be failing to thrive. (1) Thirteen of the mothers were severely depressed. With 11 of the 13, this depression was compounded by severe or chronic medical problems. All 15 mothers had completed less than eleventh-grade schooling, and 10 were functioning on a very retarded level. (2) In the hospital, 11 of the mothers were observed to handle their children in a very unsure and strained manner. (3) They tended to perceive their children as being extremely ill or retarded. (4) The losses that these mothers experienced were chronic. Histories revealed very poor mothering in their own childhood, followed by a lifetime of economic and cultural deprivation. Their helplessness and inadequacy were overwhelming to the hospital staff; despite staff attempts to be supportive, the parental problems and needs were so intense that frustration with these mothers would mount.

All mothers in this second group related to the worker very poorly and were seen as needing a great deal of structural support. In 10 families the basic needs of heat, food, and transportation money to the hospital had to be met before any attempt could be made to help the mothers with their feelings about the children and patterns of mothering.

All of the children improved dramatically in the hospital. At discharge, the families were referred to Public Health Nursing, to Department of Public Assistance caseworkers, and, in 10 cases, to Child Welfare for protective services. After the hospitalization, most efforts were directed toward helping these families use community support; in addition, every effort possible was made to have them keep regularly scheduled clinic appointments.

Follow-up was available on 14 of the 15 children; of these, six fell below the third percentile in weight, and six in height, despite many valiant community efforts. We felt that basic family problems and mother-child functioning in these cases had not improved to any appreciable degree. Five children fell within the tenth percentile or above for weight; one fell within the third percentile for height; and four children were above or within the tenth percentile. With these children improvement occurred only after a dramatic change in family functioning or the involvement of different parenting figures. One child was placed in a foster home, another cared for by a maternal grandmother. With three families, the mothers, with help, had separated from their husbands, all of whom were alcoholic and abusive to their wives and children. All mothers (including foster parents) reported continued concern with eating habits, behavior problems, and frequent illnesses.

Case Example 2

George G. was hospitalized at 18 months for evaluation of slow development and chronic upper respiratory infections. He was a small, blond child with wide, dark eyes, who never smiled and who refused to leave his bed; he weighed 17 pounds and was 73 centimeters in height, well below the third percentile. Both parents impressed hospital personnel as having limited intelligence; they were frightened and suspicious of hospital procedures. They saw George as having "bronchial trouble" and were not aware of his retarded development.

George was the fifth in a family of six children, ranging in age from six years to three months. Both parents had been overwhelmed with this fifth pregnancy, which they experienced as only one more demand on already limited economic and emotional resources. Pregnancy was difficult; the mother was tired, lost five pounds, and had no prenatal care. From birth George has been "a different, pale child." When he was six months old, Mrs. G. conceived again; during this pregnancy, George was twice hospitalized in a local hospital for upper respiratory infections. After the birth of the new sibling, George continued to lose weight and was eventually referred to Children's Hospital.

Information obtained from local Child Welfare and Public Health Nursing (already involved with this family) confirmed our initial impression of extreme deprivation. The family was seen as crisis-ridden, living in two rooms with inadequate heat and insufficient food; all the children had many medical problems.

After a three-week hospitalization during which medical findings were negative, George had gained two pounds and was active and alert. He was discharged to his parents and was followed at the clinic at three-month intervals by a pediatrician and social worker. Local community agencies have, in addition, given tremendous support to this family; nonetheless, during the ensuing year there has been no improvement in height and weight. Child

Welfare has attempted to place George in foster care, but permission for this has been denied by the court.

PROFILE OF GROUP III

This last group of families presented the most difficult problem in case management for physician and social worker alike. Eleven families were assigned to this group. Again the family structure and living conditions wre quite similar to those of the families in Group I. Five of the 11 fell into social class 5, five into class 4, one into class 3. Despite this low economic level, housing and food seemed adequate. Eight mothers were married, three unmarried. In six of the families, other siblings were suspected of displaying failure to thrive. As with group I, the majority of the children received good physical care, but immunizations and well-baby care were not given. In comparison with both group I and group II, the rate of rehospitalization for these children was quite high: nine of the patients had two or more hospitalizations.

The most significant findings concerned the mother's affects and her interaction with the child. (1) All 11 mothers displayed affects of extreme anger and hostility. They were openly antagonistic, competitive, and belittling; at one point or another all of them managed to anger and infuriate members of the hospital house staff. (2) Their perception of the child was not in terms of illness or retardation; rather, they described the child as "bad" or "out to get me." (3) They handled their children in an abrupt, angry fashion, frequently resorting to slapping or high-pitched screaming. (4) All mothers gave bizarre, distorted personal histories, and related poorly, if at all. Seven of them had completed less than the eleventh-grade schooling and gave fleeting glimpses of poor mothering in their own childhoods. It appeared that none of them had ever been able to establish any meaningful relationship throughout life.

The hospital course was predictably stormy. Six of the mothers left the children in the hospital, and despite the staff's best efforts, did not return until the day of discharge. If they did appear in the hospital ward, they refused any attempts to get to know the staff. Both during hospitalization and after discharge, our efforts were geared toward maintaining some kind of contact with these mothers. We tried to offer them support, even though it was continually rejected. At discharge, nine of these families were referred to Public Health Nursing and to the intensive casework services offered by the Department of Public Assistance. However, these agencies, too, were not able to involve the families and, in most cases, terminated contact within three months of discharge. In one case, during the initial hospitalization there was evidence of real abuse and the child was discharged to the protective care of Child Welfare. Another child was given to the maternal grandmother on the day of discharge. Of the remaining nine families, three of the children are now in foster homes. One child was removed from the home for neglect and abuse after another sibling had died in Children's Hospital of malnutrition. Two mothers, with whom constant contact was maintained despite tremendous odds, were eventually able (with a great deal of ambivalence) to release their children to foster care. This was, however, accomplished only after a one and a half year struggle, during which irreparable damage had most likely been done to both children.

It is especially noteworthy that four of the children who are no longer being cared for by their mothers are now above the third percentile for both height and weight. One child, who has been in placement for only three months, is already within the third percentile for height and weight. However, all the children still display marked behavior, eating, and sleeping problems, and show signs of social and motor retardation.

The remaining six children, who live with their families, still remain below the third percentile in height and weight. Two are now candidates for state school placement for retarded children; all have manifest behavior problems. The agencies involved inform us that there is strong evidence of abuse of these children. One child has been severely burned; three were observed by school personnel to have multiple bruises and scars. These six families were quite difficult to contact for follow-up study. They were suspicious and reluctant to become involved with the hospital again in any way.

CASE EXAMPLE 3

Sally S., age two years, two months, was brought to the psychiatric clinic by her mother, who thrust her angrily at the social worker, saying that Sally was "a little witch who hates everyone." Mrs. S. requested that Sally be hospitalized immediately or put into a foster home, as she refused to care for her anymore. This somewhat dramatic incident was the outcome of a one and a half year struggle to help this mother and her child. Prior to this incident Sally had been hospitalized twice, once at three months, and again at five months, with chief complaints of vomiting and diarrhea. At both admissions she fell below the third percentile in height and weight; no organic reason could be found for growth failure. During each hospitalization her mother refused to have any contact with any hospital personnel and requested that she be phoned when Sally's "bad behavior has been corrected," for then she would take her home. On this last occasion, foster home placement was arranged for.

Sally's mother, age 26, is a small, petite woman, always fashionably dressed with highly teased hair and heavy makeup. She has alluded to a very chaotic background; she had an alcoholic father and was abandoned at age 10 by her mother. After leaving high school in the tenth grade, she lived with a series of men, each of whom abandoned her.

It was not until Sally's younger sibling was born and began having similar symptoms of failure to thrive that this mother became involved with the hospital personnel. Even then, her "involvement" was characterized by demanding hostile requests: she was verbally abusive, threatened to sue, would phone 15 times a day requesting help and then hang up when efforts were made to contact her. In a period of six months, her "unlisted" phone number was changed five times.

At the time of placement Sally weighed 17 pounds, measured 41 centimeters in height, and was retarded in all areas of development. She had never talked and withdrew from contacts with her mother and two sisters. She daily consumed large amounts of food.

Upon follow-up, Sally had made remarkable gains after 22 months in the foster home. She is now in the tenth percentile for height and the 50th percentile for weight. She is completely toilet-trained, speaks well, and tentatively gives and accepts affection. On the Stanford-Binet she scored at an age level of three years, nine months at a chronological age of four years, one month, putting her in the low-average range of intelligence.

Mrs. S. still regards foster placement as punishment and repeatedly attempts to have Sally returned to her home, but the court has always upheld continuation of foster home care. A second sibling, who remains at home, has many health and behavioral problems and continues to remain below the third percentile for both height and weight.

DISCUSSION

The characteristic profiles of these three groups, especially on follow-up, point to the necessity of aggressive, preventive intervention if we are to help the "failure to thrive" child reach optimal development. Leonard, Rhymes, and Solnit (1966) in their intensive study of 12 families have described the mothers and fathers of these children as also "failing to thrive." This was true in all the 40 families that we studied; none of the mothers or fathers experienced any sense of fulfillment in the parental roles. The "emotional symbiosis," the confidence in the child, and the trust of the mother in her motheringness, of which Benedek (1956b) speaks, did not occur. In most cases, the inadequate mothering the children received turned the original symbiotic mothering into a vicious cycle, resulting in further frustration, anger, and poor feelings of self. The emotional balance of these children and their mothers could be restored only when the child again began to thrive.

With the infants of families in group I, restoration of a healthy symbiosis between mother and child for the most part occurred. This was made possible by providing the mother with warm, encouraging, and nonjudgmental support. She was viewed and helped to view herself as a person with value and adequacy. These mothers were very self-accusatory about their own behavior and their deficiencies in giving love and care to their children. In most cases, the mother's experience of a recent loss of a significant object seemed to be the factor that precipitated her depression and impeded her mothering. The nonthriving child was perceived as yet another loss which threatened the mother's adequacy and only intensified her guilt and anger. The response of these mothers to the direct help they received, along with the hospitalization of the child, can be viewed within the framework of J. A. Rose's work (1961) with primary prevention. In these terms, the onset of the child's illness and hospitalization comprised a "maturational crisis" in which the mother's repressed conflicts about her own mothering became easily experienced and expressed. We discovered that the mothers in our first group were able to speak about their deficiencies in mothering and thier distorted perception of their infants. With support, they were able to change this perception and achieve a relatively positive relationship with the child. On follow-up, we found, as did J. A. Rose (1961), that for the most part the mothers had repressed their original fears and doubts about their children and saw them as doing well. However, this would not have been possible had not these mothers been fairly stable women with many strengths upon which they could draw. The basic family problems, in terms of economics and support for such mothers, had not changed dramatically at the time of follow-up, but there was significant change in the mother-child interaction. This points to the need for immediate and intense emotional support for such mothers the moment they are identified.

In terms of degree of breakdown of the mothering function, the families in group II appear to be on a definite continuum with group I. Indeed, one might hypothesize that given equivalent economic and social stress (more children, etc.), the mothers in group I would in time fall into group II. All the families in group II had much lower thresholds of strength in their parenting and their ability to cope. In this case, the "failure to thrive" child is not simply a matter of a disturbed mother-child relationship. He is rather the product of severe socioeconomic deprivation, which has its origins in the pathology and social backgrounds of both parents. The cause of the failure to thrive may be "nutritional deficiencies," as proposed by Whitten, Pettit, and Fischhoff (1969), but we assume this finding to be related to the disturbance of the mother-child interaction. To sustain a child in such a home is a major task that can be accomplished only with increased economic assistance and more creative use of community resources. Even with community recognition, the prognosis for these children is guarded.

In their study, Leonard, Rhymes, and Solnit (1966) acknowledge that some of their mothers were inaccessible, and in those cases it was difficult for hospital personnel to be supportive; this was characteristic of the mothers of our group III. All these mothers were extremely depressed (as were the mothers in groups I and II), but the murderous hostility that the group III mothers harbored toward their children was less sublimated and at times blatantly obvious. This resulted in a familial catastrophe which was almost impossible to resolve. These severely disturbed mothers project their own feelings of inadequacy and "bad self" onto the child. Once the child is hospitalized, this anger is directed toward hospital personnel or any other persons offering support and help. There is a total denial of the existence of any kind of problem. All the children are made to feel that their requests for love and for gratification of their needs are outrageous demands. The mothers in turn make outrageous demands in their sporadic efforts to seek help; this causes them to be rejected even further.

SUMMARY

We studied 40 families who fell into three groups, each with distinctive characteristics that could be used as indicators for prognosis and mode of treatment.

In group I, parents had better ego development and could utilize available resources; the child responded favorably in terms of height and weight—it is hoped, indicating improvement in total functioning.

In group II, the child remained regressed unless the family had sufficient strength to mobilize itself to change blatant factors which were contributing directly to the deprivation (e.g., unless the mothers were able to separate from abusive, alcoholic husbands). Where families were unable to do this, then removal of the child had to be seriously considered.

In group III, because of the gross nature of the pathology, immediate removal from the home was indicated. This could be thought of as a "family transplant." We found that unless the child's parenting is changed, there will be continued retardation in growth and social functioning. There was also strong evidence of physical abuse of the child in this group.

Our conclusion is that for these children there is a need for more aggressive intervention in terms of immediate foster placement. Most studies done on the syndrome of failure to thrive have advocated the removal of the child from the family as "the treatment of choice" (Patton and Gardner, 1963; Powell, Brasel, and Blizzard, 1967). However, since our culture is based on the concept that a strong family unit is the mainstay of children emotionally, economically, and culturally, it has made it difficult for physicians, social agencies, and the court to recognize that in such cases the nuclear family cannot provide adequate protection and care. New methods which provide protection of the child and concomitant work with families to assess their caretaking capacities are necessary to deal with the "failure to thrive" child and his family.

APPENDIX

TABLE 1
GROUP PROFILE

Group I	Group II	Group III
1. Good living conditions.	1. Very deprived living conditions.	1. Good living conditions.
2. Good physical care of child.	2. Poor physical care of child.	2. Neglectful care of child.
3. Mother's affect: extreme depression.	3. Mother's affect: extreme depression.	3. Mother's affect: angry, hostile.
4. Mother-child interaction: strained, unsure.	4. Mother-child interaction: strained, unsure.	4. Mother-child interaction: overtly angry.
5. Mother perceives child as ill or retarded.	5. Mother perceives child as ill or retarded.	5. Mother perceives child as "bad."
6. Mother has severe object loss within 4 months of child's hospitalization.	6. Losses to mother are chronic.	6. Losses to mother are chronic.
7. Follow-up indicates good prognosis, with improvement in height and weight.	7. Follow-up indicates guarded prognosis unless there is a dramatic change in home environment.	7. Follow-up indicates poor prognosis unless child is placed in foster home.

TABLE 2
PATIENT PROFILE

	Group I (N = 14)	Group II (N = 15)	Group III (N = 11)
Premature	1	6	2
Many illnesses	4	10	3
Poor physical care	—	14	3
2–3 hospitalizations	3	4	9
Strong suspicion and/evidence of abuse (initial and follow-up)	—	1	7
Marked social and motor retardation (follow-up)	1	12	8

TABLE 3
MOTHER PROFILE

	Group I (N = 14)	Group II (N = 15)	Group III (N = 11)
Under 20 years of age	7	3	3
Severe health problems	1	11	3
Completed less than 11th grade	4	15	7
Provoked angry reaction in house staff	—	8	11

TABLE 4
FAMILY PROFILE

	Group I (N = 14)	Group II (N = 15)	Group III (N = 11)
Married	8	11	8
Divorced—separated	—	1	—
Single	6	3	3
Very deprived living conditions	—	15	1
Small birth intervals	2	11	2
Siblings with multiple problems	2	12	6

TABLE 5
FOLLOW-UP

	Group I	Group II	Group III
Foster Home	(N = 0)	(N = 3)	(N = 5)
Below 3rd percentile height and weight	—	1	—
Above 3rd percentile height and weight	—	2	5***
Patients Remaining with Families	(N = 13)	(N = 11)	(N = 6)
Below 3rd percentile height and weight	—	6	6
Above 3rd percentile height and weight	13*	5**	—

*Two children within 3rd percentile height—receiving psychotherapy and growing.
**Drastic change in home environment.
***One child within the 3rd percentile height and weight, but recently placed in foster home and growing.

TABLE 6
FOLLOW-UP OF TOTAL POPULATION

	Group I (N = 13)	Group II (N = 14)	Group III (N = 11)
Weight			
Below 3rd percentile weight	0	7	6
Within 3rd percentile weight	0	0	1
Above or within 10th percentile weight	13	7	4
Height			
Below 3rd percentile height	0	7	6
Within 3rd percentile height	2	2	1
Above or within 10th percentile height	11	5	4

22

INTRODUCTION

Malnutrition, Learning, and Intelligence,
by Herbert G. Birch

Since the 1960s interest in the impact of malnutrition on behavioral development has accelerated, as the implications for public policy have become apparent (Read, 1975). The early studies in Mexico and Africa were under the direction of pediatricians and were primarily clinical in orientation. More recently, behavioral scientists have become interested in this problem, which has led not only to an increase in well-planned multidisciplinary studies but also to a heightened appreciation for the complexities of the questions being asked. A number of longitudinal intervention studies, currently under way in several countries, hold considerable promise for contributing to future understanding.

The following chapter is one of several reviews of the effect of nutrition on mental development (see also Cravioto, 1966; Frisch, 1971; Pollitt, 1969; Scrimshaw, 1969). In somewhat fragmented fashion, reflecting the state of knowledge and uncertainty of conceptual focus, Birch endeavors to place compellingly suggestive evidence of the contribution of malnutrition to intellectual impairments in perspective, alongside other relevant social, cultural, educational, and psychological factors. (Such an overview requires consideration of issues as disparate as the symbolic significance of food and the possible effects of food additives, among a multitude of others.) The idea that nutrition may be vital for central nervous system development is a relatively recent concept. Nevertheless, it has burgeoned to such an extent that it is increasingly common for educators, mental health workers, and others to wonder what a baby was fed in the first year of life, what the mother ate during pregnancy, what she had consumed even prior to that, and what the maternal grandmother ate during her pregnancy. It is conceivable that all may significantly and perhaps even permanently modify the child's brain, thus affecting cognition and behavior. Cowley (1968), for example, found that although the problem-solving ability of rats was not impaired by a low-protein diet after weaning, if the rats continued on this diet, *their* progeny showed markedly poorer test performance. The scores decreased progressively from the initial rats to those of the first, second, and third generations, all of which were maintained on the low-protein diet.

Scrimshaw (1969) suggests that analogous effects on human brain development and subsequent learning and behavior may result from both severe malnutrition and sensory deprivation early in life. In summarizing her work, Frankova (1974) hypothesizes that

> for optimum development of the brain and of subsequent behavior, an adequate supply of both nutrients and external stimuli during the decisive developmental periods is essential. A typical picture of malnutrition involves reduction both of the available nutrients and of the environmental stimulation. Increased external stimulation compensates for the sensory impoverishment from the environment; it enhances the activity of various developing organs, and enforces activity of the CNS during the critical period when the developing brain depends greatly on the supply of external stimuli. It may be assumed that stimulation will potentiate adaptive processes which can result in more economic utilization of energy and nutrients which is particularly important in animals with a low quantity of available food [p. 207].

The following chapter explicitly avoids the extravagant claims made for the nutritional focus at the expense of other factors. Birch points to the methodological problems in disentangling one type of deprivation from another and in assessing the important variables of severity, timing, and duration. Psychosocial deprivation and malnutrition tend to go hand in hand, just as prenatal malnutrition tends to be correlated with postnatal malnutrition and to some extent with preceding generations' malnutrition. Cravioto (1966) has designated this intergenerational chain of consequences the ecologically circular effect of nutritional deprivation and social impoverishment. It generates questions regarding the extent to which the inadequacy in intersensory organization noted in children of short stature in certain rural settings is a consequence of malnutrition or whether both the poor growth and intersensory inadequacy are products of underlying subcultural differences. The retrospective studies Cravioto cites lead him to assume that protein-calorie malnutrition is the intervening variable between the social conditions, on one hand, and the growth and intersensory defects, on the other. Definitive answers, however, will come only from anterospective longitudinal studies. In this way, researchers will be able to avoid relying heavily, as in the chapter that follows, on retrospective judgments of previous nutrition, based somewhat unconvincingly on current measurements of height rather than on assessment of actual dietary intake.

In Chapter 11, Tanner notes the correlation between height and IQ found in European and North American populations of all ages, where there was no blatant reason to presume nutrition was a significant factor. It is true the differences were small, but they were consistent. Cravioto and DeLicardie (1975) present data that "leave little doubt that severe malnutrition with hospitalization has a long-term persistent effect not only on measured intelligence but also in learning basic academic skills such as reading and writing" (p. 64). The remaining "doubt" reflects their inability to distinguish the extent of the contribution of malnutrition from that of the child's experience to the cognitive dysfunction. We lack adequate information regarding the mechanisms by which low birthweight and family social status interact to affect intellectual development. Nevertheless, there is evidence that programs designed to stimulate sensorimotor development early in life can enhance developmental progress in low-birthweight infants born to disadvantaged mothers (Scarr-Salapatek and Williams, 1973).

Another methodological issue relates to the concern generated by what could be called *false negatives*. This term refers to youngsters who develop well despite apparent nutritional deprivation, analogous to children who become high achievers in an environmental setting in which apathy and despair are pervasive or to the baby who is bright and alert despite an alarmingly low Apgar score. These cases suggest that other variables are operative. However, one does not question the overall effect of the bomb at Hiroshima just because some people escaped with minimal damage.

In general, severe malnutrition during prenatal life and/or infancy in animals and man appears to decrease the number of brain cells significantly and to alter brain structure (Read, 1975). The neurological consequences of growth retardation, severe protein-calorie malnutrition, or nutritionally induced dwarfism seem to be permanent in animals, and probably in man. These changes are associated with mental retardation and behavioral manifestations which also appear to be permanent and nonreversible. The effects of moderate or chronic malnutrition are not as clearly established. Man lives in a complex environment where nutrition, health, family, and social factors interact to shape behavior. Recent reports from cross-sectional and longitudinal studies suggest that the adverse behavioral consequences of chronic undernutrition are greatest in the areas of attentiveness, curiosity, activity, and social responsiveness, rather than in the cognitive domain. Thus, in the light of available data, the emphasis has shifted away from the clinical concept of mental retardation, toward a consideration of impaired development involving intellectual, social, and motivational competence. Increasingly, we are faced with the question of *deficit* versus *lag* in development: Are the changes irreversible, or are they only delayed, with the possibility of remedy through intervention? Finally, a growing body of data indicates that caloric deficit, rather than protein deficiency, may be the crucial factor in low birthweight and retarded development, either physiological or behavioral. McLaren (1974) has eloquently outlined why our preoccupation with protein deficiency may have been in error.

Whatever the answers to these questions, it should not be forgotten that the extent of the problem defies accurate estimation. It is relatively easy to count children with marasmus and kwashiorkor,[1] but it has been estimated that for every single instance of such severe malnutrition, there are 99 other cases of chronic or intermittent undernutrition. We are thus talking about one out of every two children in the world, including many in our own relatively affluent country. Clearly, the many suppositions about the role of nutrition in mental development need to be carefully distinguished from the few established facts. We have no basis on which to assume that the millions of malnourished children are indeed retarded, and there is evidence of reversibility of some of the effects. Nevertheless, this in no way diminishes the need to assure that all children everywhere are adequately nourished all the time.

---

[1] Marasmus is severe undernutrition seen in lower socioeconomic groups when breast-feeding is interrupted during the first year and the nutritional substitutes are inadequate. Kwashiorkor, an actute and often fatal deficiency disease, results from prolonged breast-feeding beyond one year of age with little protein. The name *kwashiorkor* means "first-second" in the Ga dialect of Ghana and refers to the disease of the first child displaced at the breast by the second.

22

Malnutrition, Learning, and Intelligence

HERBERT G. BIRCH

Research on the relation of nutritional factors to intelligence and learning has burgeoned over the past decade. Its resurgence after a period of nearly 30 years of quiescence, which followed D. G. Patterson's (1930) review of studies conducted in the first three decades of the century, reflects a number of social and historical currents. Newly emerging nations, as well as aspiring underprivileged segments of the population in more developed parts of the world, have increasingly come to be concerned by the association of social, cultural, and economic disadvantage with depressed levels of intellect and elevated rates of school failure. Attention has variously been directed at different components of the combined syndromes of disadvantage and poverty in an effort to define the causes for such an association. Sociologists, psychologists, and educators have advanced reasons for intellectual backwardness and school failure relevant to their particular concerns. They have pointed to particular patterns of childcare, cultural atmosphere, styles of play, depressed motivation, particular value systems, and deficient educational settings and instruction as factors contributing to lowered intellectual level and poor academic performance in disadvantaged children. The importance of such variables cannot be disputed, and studies and findings relevant to them expand our understanding of some of the ways in which poor achievement levels are induced. However, it would be most unfortunate if by recognizing the importance of these situational, psychological, and experiential components of the syndrome of disadvantage we were to conclude that they represented the whole of the picture or even its most decisive components. Any

First published in *American Journal of Public Health*, 62:773–784, 1972.

The research for this study was supported in part by the National Institutes of Health, National Institute of Child Health and Human Development (HD 00719), and by the Association for the Aid of Crippled Children.

analysis of the content of poverty and disadvantage rapidly brings to our notice the fact that these negative features of the behavioral and educational environment take place within the pervasive context of low income, poor housing, poor health and, in general, defective circumstances for the development of the individual as a biological organism who interacts with the social, cultural, and educational circumstances.

Such considerations inevitably cause us to expand the range of our concern to include a fuller range of factors contributing to lowered intellect and school failure. In this larger perspective, the health of the child and, in particular, his nutritional opportunities must assume a position of importance. It has long been recognized that the nutrition of the individual is perhaps the most ubiquitous factor affecting growth, health, and development. Inadequate nutrition results in stunting, reduced resistance to infectious disease, apathy, and general behavioral unresponsiveness. In a fundamental sense it occupies a central position in the multitude of factors affecting the child's development and functional capacity. It is therefore entirely understandable that in a period dedicated to the improvement of man and his capacities, renewed attention has come to be directed to the relation of nutrition to intelligence and learning ability.

As is almost always the case in new areas of inquiry, clarity of thought and concept has not kept pace with zeal. Confusion has resulted from extravagant claims as to the unique contribution of malnutrition to brain impairment and intellectual deficit. Further confusion has been contributed by those who have, with equal zeal, sought to minimize the importance of nutritional factors and to argue for the primacy of social, genetic, cultural, or familial variables in the production of deficit. Little that is useful emerges from such sterile controversy. It is a truism that malnutrition occurs most frequently in those segments of the population which are economically, socially, and culturally disadvantaged. When lowered intellect is demonstrated in malnourished children coming from such groups, it is not difficult to ignore a consideration of the possible contribution of nutritional and health factors by pointing to the possibility that the children affected are dull because they are the offspring of dull parents, or that the general impoverishment of their environments has resulted in experiential deprivations sufficient to account for reduced intellectual function. Such an argument implies that the children are malnourished because their parents are dull and that their functional backwardness stems from the same cause as their malnutrition. On logical grounds one could of course argue the very opposite from the same bodies of data. However, to do so would be not to consider the issue seriously, but to engage in a debater's trick. The serious task is to disentangle, from the complex mesh of negative influences which characterize the world of disadvantaged children, the particular and interactive contributions which different factors make to the development of depressed functional outcomes A responsible analysis of the problem, therefore, seeks to define the particular role that may be played by nutritional factors in the development of malfunction, and the interaction of this influence with other circumstances affecting the child.

Before considering the ways in which available research permits us to achieve this objective, it is of importance to clarify the term *malnutrition.* Characteristically, we in the United States tend to react to the word in terms of a crisis model. When we think of malnutrition our imaginations conjure up images of the apocalypse. We have visions of famines in India, of victims of typhoons, and of young Biafrans starved by war. These images reflect only the highly visible tip of an iceberg. Intermittent and marginal incomes, as well as a technology which is inadequate to support a population, result less often in the symptoms characteristic of starvation than in subclinical malnutrition, or what Brock (1961) has called "dietary subnutrition . . . defined as any impairment of functional efficiency of body systems which can be corrected by better feeding." Such subnutrition, when present in populations, is reflected in stunting, disproportions in growth, and a variety of anatomic, physiological, and behavioral abnormalities (Birch and Gussow, 1970). Our principal concern in this country is with these chronic or intermittent aspects of nutritional inadequacy.

In less highly developed regions of the world, and indeed in the United States as well, chronic subnutrition is not infrequently accompanied by dramatic manifestations of acute, severe, and if untreated, lethal malnutrition, particularly in infants and young children. These illnesses, variously reflected in the syndromes of marasmus, kwashiorkor, and marasmic-kwashiorkor, are conditions deriving from acute exacerbations of chronic subnutrition, which in different degrees reflect caloric deficiency, inadequacy of protein in the diet, or a combination of both states of affairs. Studies of children who recover from such disorders provide significant information on the effects of profound nutritional inadequacy on behavioral development.

In addition to the already mentioned conditions, malnutrition has classically been manifested as a consequence of the inadequate ingestion of certain essential food substances. The diseases of vitamin lack, such as scurvy, rickets, pellagra, and beri-beri, as well as the iron deficiency anemias are representative of this class of disorders.

None of the foregoing should be confused with the term *hunger,* which has often indiscriminately been used as a synonym for malnutrition. Hunger is a subjective state and should not be used as the equivalent of malnutrition, which is an objective condition of physical and physiological suboptimum.

Clearly, malnourished children may be hungry, but equally, hungry children may be well nourished.

With these introductory considerations in mind, we can now approach a series of questions. We shall be concerned with two issues. First, what is the state of sound knowledge of the relation of malnutrition in its various forms to intellect and learning and what is the significance of the evidence for psychology and education? And second, what are the implications of the evidence for improved functioning?

THE EVIDENCE

A number of model systems have been used to explore the relationship of malnutrition to behavior. At the human level, these have consisted of (1) comparative studies of well- and poorly grown segments of children. In populations at risk for malnutrition in infancy, these have included (2) retrospective follow-up studies of the antecedent nutritional experiences of well-functioning and poorly functioning children in such populations; (3) intervention studies in which children in the poor-risk population were selectively supplemented or unsupplemented during infancy and a comparative evaluation made of functioning in the supplemented and unsupplemented groups; (4) follow-up studies of clinical cases hospitalized for severe malnutrition in early childhood; and (5) intergenerational studies seeking to relate the degree to which conditions for risk of malnutrition in the present generation of children derived from the malnutrition or subnutrition experienced by their mothers when the latter were themselves children. Studies of human populations have been supplemented by a variety of animal models. These animal studies have been (1) direct comparative follow-up investigations of the effects of nutritional difficulties in early life on subsequent behavioral competence and (2) the study of the cumulative effects of malnutrition when successive generations of animals have been exposed to conditions of nutritional stress. The available evidence will be considered in relation to these investigative models.

In two of our reports (Birch, 1971; Cravioto, DeLicardie, and Birch, 1966), we have reviewed many of the earlier studies which have sought to explore the association between malnutrition and the development of intellect and learning. Perhaps the most complete study of the relation of growth achievement to neurointegrative competence in children living in environments in which severe malnutrition and chronic subnutrition are endemic is our study of Guatemalan rural Indian children. The children lived in a village having a significant prevalence level of both severe acute malnutrition and prolonged subnutrition during infancy and the preschool years. At school age, relatively well-nourished children were identified as the better grown, and children with the highest antecedent risk of exposure to malnutrition were identified as those with the lowest growth achievements for age. On the basis of this reasoning, two groups of children were selected from all village children in the age range of six to 11 years. These groups encompassed the tallest and shortest quartiles of height distributions at each age for the total population of village children. In order to avoid problems associated with the use of intelligence tests as measures of functioning in preindustrial communities, levels of development in the tall and short groups were compared by means of evaluating intersensory integrative competence by a method developed by Birch and Lefford (1963). In this method of evaluation, children are required to judge whether geometric forms presented in different sensory modalities are the same or different. Competence in making such judgments follows a clearly defined developmental course in normal children in the age range studied.

At all ages, the taller children exhibited higher levels of neurointegrative competence than did the shorter group. Overall, the shorter children lagged by two years behind their taller age-mates in the competence which they exhibited in processing information across sensory systems.

In order to control for the possibility that height differences were reflecting differences in antecedent nutritional status, rather than familial differences in stature, the child's height was correlated with that of the parents. The resulting correlation was extremely low and insignificant. This stands in marked contrast to the finding in the same ethnic group living in more adequate nutritional circumstances. Under these latter conditions, the height of children correlates significantly with that of their parents.

Second, it was possible that the shorter children were, in the community at risk as well as in communities not at risk for malnutrition, merely exhibiting generalized developmental lag, both for stature and for neurointegrative maturation. However, no differences in neurointegrative competence attached to differences in stature in the children not exposed to endemic malnutrition.

And finally, it was possible that the shorter children came from home environments significantly lower in socioeconomic status, housing, and parental education, and that both the malnutrition and the reduced neurointegrative competence stemmed independently from these environmental deficits. When differences in these factors were controlled, they did not erase the differences in intersensory integrative competence between children of different growth achievements for age in the community at nutritional risk.

Over the past several years, replications of this study have been conducted in Mexico by Cravioto and DeLicardie (1968), and in India by Champakam, Srikantia, and Gopalan (1968). In addition, Cravioto, Espinoza, and Birch

(1967) have examined another aspect of neurointegrative competence and auditory-visual integration in Mexican children of school age. Once again, in children in communities at risk for malnutrition, differences in growth achievement at school age were reflected in differences in auditory-visual integration, favoring the taller children. These latter findings are of particular importance because of the demonstrated association between such competence and the ability to acquire primary reading skills (Birch and Belmont, 1964, 1965; Kahn and Birch, 1968).

A major consideration in interpreting the findings of all these studies is the fact that antecedent malnutrition is being inferred from differences in height, rather than by direct observation of dietary intakes during the growing years. However, a multitude of data from earlier studies, beginning with those of Boas (1910) on growth differences in successive generations of children of Jewish immigrants, Greulich (1958) on the height of Japanese immigrants, Boyd-Orr (1936) on secular trends in the height of British children, Mitchell (1962, 1964) on the relation of nutrition to stature, Boutourline-Young (1962) on Italian children, as well as the recent study of heights of 12-year-old Puerto Rican boys in New York City by Abramowicz (1969)—all support the validity of such an inference.

It should be noted too that findings similar to those obtained in the Guatemalan and Mexican studies have been reported by Pek Hien Liang et al. (1967) from Indonesia, and Stoch and Smythe (1963, 1968) from South Africa. In the Indonesian study 107 children between five and 12 years of age, all from lower socioeconomic groups, were studied. Forty-six of these children had been classified as malnourished during a previous investigation into nutritional status in the area, carried out some years earlier. All children were tested on the WISC and Goodenough tests, with scores showing a clear advantage for the better-grown and currently better-nourished children. Moreover, the data indicated that the shortest children were markedly overrepresented in the group that had been found to be malnourished in the earlier survey, with the largest deficits in IQ found to be associated with the poorest prior nutritional status.

Stoch and Smythe have carried out a semilongitudinal study of two groups of South African Negro children, one judged in early childhood to be grossly underweight due to malnutrition, and the other considered adequately nourished. At school age, the malnourished children as a group had a mean IQ which was 22 6 points lower than that of the comparison group. Moreover, these relative differences were sustained through adolescence. Unfortunately, the interpretation of the findings in this study is made difficult because the better-nourished children came from better families and had a variety of nursery and school experiences unshared by the poorly grown children.

Comparative studies of differential cognitive achievement in better- and less well nourished groups in communities at high levels of subnutrition have been supplemented by a relatively large number of follow-up evaluations of children who had been hospitalized for serious nutritional illness (marasmus or kwashiorkor) in infancy. As will be recalled from our earlier remarks, marasmus is a disorder produced by an insufficient intake of proteins and calories and tends to be most common in the first year of life. Kwashiorkor—a syndrome produced by inadequate protein intake accompanied by a relatively adequate caloric level, or in its marasmic form associated with reduced calories as well—is more common in the post-weanling between nine months and two years of age.

As early as 1960, Waterlow, Cravioto, and Stephen reported that children who suffered from such severe nutritional illnesses exhibited delays in language acquisition. In Yugoslavia, Cabak and Najdanvic (1965) compared the IQ levels of children hospitalized for malnutrition at less than 12 months of age with those of healthy children of the same social stratum and reported a reduced IQ in the previously hospitalized group. Of perhaps greater interest was their report of a significant correlation between the severity of the child's illness on admission, as estimated in his deficit of expected weight for age, with depression of IQ in the school years. Indian workers (Champakam et al., 1968) studied many variables in a group of 19 children who, between 18 and 36 months of age, had been hospitalized and treated for kwashiorkor. When compared at school age with a well-matched control group, significantly depressed IQ was found in the children previously severely malnourished.

In order to control more fully for differences in the child's genetic-antecedents microenvironment (which may still exist when more general controls for social, class, and general circumstances are used in the selection of a comparison group), in two studies (Birch et al. 1971; Hertzig, et al., 1971a, 1971b), we have compared children previously malnourished in infancy with their siblings as well as with children of similar social background. In the first of these studies, intelligence at school age was compared in 37 previously malnourished Mexican children and their siblings. The malnourished children had all been hospitalized for kwashiorkor between the ages of six and 30 months. The siblings had never experienced a bout of severe malnutrition requiring hospitalization. Sibling controls were all within three years of the index cases. Full-scale WISC IQ of the index cases was 13 points lower than that of the sibling controls. Verbal and performance differences were of similar magnitude and in the same direction. All differences were significant at less than the 0.01% level of confidence. These findings are in agreement with those of the Yugoslav and Indian workers, and the use of sibling controls removes a potential contaminant for interpretation.

In the second study, Hertzig et al. (1971a, 1971b), compared a large sample of 74 Jamaican children, all males, who had been hospitalized for severe malnutrition before they were two years of age, with their brothers nearest in age, and with their classmates whose birthdate was closest to their own. All children were between six and 11 years of age at follow-up. On examination, neurological status, intersensory competence, intellectual level, and a variety of language and perceptual and motor abilities were evaluated. Intellectual level was significantly lower in the index cases than in either the siblings or the classmate comparison groups. As was to be expected, the order of competence placed the classmate comparison group at the highest level, the index cases at the lowest, and the siblings at an intermediate level. The depressed level of the siblings in relation to classmates suggests one disadvantage in sibling studies. Clearly, the presence of a child hospitalized for severe malnutrition identifies a family in which all children are at a high level of risk for significant undernutrition on a chronic basis, the index child merely representing an instance of acute exacerbation of this chronic marginal state. Therefore, the index cases and siblings are similar in that they share a common chronic exposure to subnutrition and differ only in that the index cases have experienced a superimposed episode of acute nutritional illness as well. Thus, the use of sibling controls, in fact, does not compare malnourished with non-malnourished children. Rather, it determines whether siblings who differ in their degree of exposure to nutritional risk differ in intellectual outcomes and supports the view that graded degrees of malnutrition result in graded levels of intellectual sequelae.

Other follow-up studies of acutely malnourished children—such as those of Cravioto and Robles (1965) in Mexico; Pollitt and Granoff (1967) in Peru; Botha-Antoun, Babayan, and Harfouche (1968) in Lebanon; and Chase and Martin (1970) in Denver—have all been shorter-term follow-ups of younger children. Cravioto and Robles (1965) studied the developmental course of returning competence in children hospitalized for malnutrition during the period of their treatment and recovery while in hospital. Their findings indicated that behavioral recovery was less complete in the youngest children (hospitalized before six months of age) than in older children. They posed the possibility that this earliest period of infancy was the one most critical for insult to developing brain and thus to eventual intellectual outcome. However, the study of Jamaican children (Hertzig et al., 1971a, 1971b) does not have findings which support this possibility. In that study approximately equal numbers of children who had experienced an acute episode of malnutrition in each of the four semesters of the first two years of life were examined. Equivalent depression of IQ was found to characterize each of the groups when these were separated by age at hospitalization.

In Lebanese (Botha-Antoun, Babayan, and Harfouche, 1968), Peruvian

(Pollitt and Granoff, 1967), and Venezuelan (Barrera-Moncada, 1963) short-term follow-up studies, depression in intellectual level tended to be found in the index cases. In the American study (Chase and Martin, 1970) and in a Chilean study (Monckeberg, 1968), the findings have shown depression in intellectual functioning in the preschool years in children hospitalized for malnutrition during the first year of life. The American investigators, working in Colorado, found that 20 children who had been hospitalized for malnutrition before the age of one year had a mean developmental quotient on the Yale Revised Developmental Examination which was 17 points lower than that achieved by a matched control group of children who had not been malnourished. All of these studies suggest strongly that malnutrition of severe degree in early life tends to depress intellectual functioning at later ages.

In summary, the follow-up studies of children who have been exposed to hospitalization for a bout of severe acute malnutrition in infancy indicate an association of significant degree between such exposure and reduced intellectual level at school age. The studies, involving careful social-class controls and sibship comparisons, suggest that it is not general environmental deprivation, but rather factors uniquely related to the occurrence of severe malnutrition that are contributing to a depression in intellectual outcome. However, there is some indication that different degrees of recovery may be associated with different postillness conditions. Thus, urban and rural differences in intellectual outcomes are reported in the sibship comparison studies of Jamaican children referred to earlier (Hertzig et al., 1971a, 1971b).

The fact of such an association provides strongly suggestive, but by no means definitive evidence that malnutrition directly affects intellectual competence. As Cravioto, DeLicardie, and Birch (1966) have pointed out, at least three possibilities must be considered in the effort to define a causal linkage. The simplest hypothesis would be that malnutrition directly affects intellect by producing central nervous system damage. However, it may also contribute to intellectual inadequacies as a consequence of the child's loss in learning time when ill, the influence of hospitalization, and prolonged reduced responsiveness after recovery. Moreover, it is possible that particular exposures to malnutrition at particular ages may in fact interfere with development at critical points in the child's growth course and so provide either abnormalities in the sequential emergence of competence or a redirection of developmental course in undesired directions. Although certain of these possibilities (such as hospitalization and postillness opportunities for recovery) can be explored in children, others, for moral and ethical reasons, cannot. Thus, it is impermissible to establish appropriate experimental models either for interfering with development at critical periods or for inducing brain damage. The approach to these problems requires either detailed analyses of naturally occurring clinical models or the development of appropriate animal investigations.

Animal models of the effects of malnutrition on brain and behavior have been used to study the issue with a degree of control that is quite impossible in human investigation. In a series of pioneering investigations, Widdowson (1966), Dobbing (1964), and Davison and Dobbing (1966) have demonstrated that both severe and modest degrees of nutritional deprivation, experienced by the animal at a time when its nervous system was developing most rapidly, result in reduced brain size and in deficient myelination. These deficits are not made up in later life, even when the animal has been placed on an excellent diet subsequent to the period of nutritional deprivation.

More recent studies by Zamenhof, Van Marthens, and Margolis (1968), as well as by Winick (1968), have demonstrated that deprivation is also accompanied by a reduction in brain cell number. This latter effect has also been demonstrated in the human brain in infants who have died of severe early malnutrition (Winick and Rosso, 1969).

Enzymatic maturation and development in the brain are also affected, and Chase, Dorsey, and McKhann (11967) and Chase and Martin (1970) have demonstrated defective enzyme organization in the brains of malnourished organisms.

In all of these studies, the evidence indicates that the effects of malnutrition vary in accordance with the time in the organism's life at which it is experienced. In some organisms, the effects are most severe if the nutritional insult occurs in the prenatal period; in others, during early postnatal life.

Some confusion in the interpretation of evidence has occurred because of the use of different species, since in different organisms the so-called critical periods occur at different points in the developmental course. Thus, in the pig's brain, growth and differentiation occur most rapidly in the period prior to birth, whereas in the rat the most rapid growth occurs when the animal is a nursling. In human beings, the period for rapid growth is relatively extended; it extends from mid-gestation through the first six to nine months of postnatal life. In man, the brain is adding weight at the rate of 1 to 2 mg/minute at birth and goes from 25% of its adult weight at birth to 70% of its adult weight at one year of age. After this age, growth continues more slowly until final size is achieved. Differentiation and growth occur rapidly during the critical periods, with myelination and cellular differentiation tending to parallel changes in size.

Since brain growth in different species occurs at different points in the life course, it is apparent that deprivations that are experienced at the same chronological ages and life stages will have different effects in different species. Thus, deprivation during early postnatal life will have little or no effect on brain size and structure in an organism whose brain growth has largely been completed during gestation. Conversely, intrauterine malnutrition is likely to have only trivial effects on the growth of the brain in species in which the most rapid period for brain development has occurred postnatally. When these factors are taken into account, the data leave no doubt that the coincidence of malnutrition with rapid brain growth results in decreased brain size and in altered brain composition.

It would be unfortunate if brain growth in terms of cell number was to be viewed as the only definer of rapid change and thus of critical periodicity. In the human infant, neuronal cell number is most probably fully defined before the end of intrauterine life. Thereafter, through the first nine months of postnatal life, cell replication is that of glial cells, a process which terminates by the end of the first year. However, myelination continues for many years thereafter, as does the proliferation of dendrite branchings and other features of brain organization. It is most probable, therefore, that in man the period of vulnerability extends well beyond the first year of life and into the preschool period. Such a position is supported by the findings of Champakam, Srikantia, and Gopalan (1968). These workers, it will be recalled, found significant effects on intellect in their group of malnourished children who had experienced severe malnutrition when they were between 18 and 36 months of age.

Other workers using animal models have sought to study the effects of malnutrition on behavioral outcomes, rather than on brain structure and biochemical organization. The typical design of these studies involves investigations in which animals have been raised on diets which were inadequate with respect to certain food substances, or in which general caloric intake has been reduced without an alteration in the quality of the nutriments. Such animals have then been compared with normally nourished members of the species with respect to maze learning, avoidance conditioning, and open field behavior. Unfortunately, most of the investigations have suffered from one or another defect in design which makes it difficult to interpret the findings. Though in general the nutritionally deprived organisms have tended to be disadvantaged as learners, it is not at all clear whether this is the result of their food lacks at critical points in development, or whether the differences observed stem from the different handling, caging, and litter experiences to which the well- and poorly nourished animals were exposed. Moreover, in a considerable number of studies, food or avoidance motivation has been used as the reinforcer of learning. There is abundant evidence that nutritional deficiency in early life affects later feeding behavior (Barnes et al., 1968; Elliott and King, 1960; Levitsky and Barnes, 1969; Mandler, 1958). Consequently, it is difficult to know whether the early deprivation has affected food motivation or whether it has affected learning capacity. The use of learning situations which do not involve food, but are based upon aversive reinforcement, does not remove difficulties for interpretation, since early malnutrition modifies sensitivity to such negative stimuli (Levitsky and Barnes, 1970).

One must therefore recognize that at present, although the animal evidence suggests that early malnutrition may influence later learning and behavior, it is by no means conclusive. Moreover, when learning has been deleteriously affected, the mechanisms through which this effect has been mediated are by no means clear. What is required is a systematic series of experiments in which behavioral effects are more clearly defined, and in which the use of proper experimental designs, accompanied by appropriate controls, permits the nature of the mechanisms affected to be better delineated.

Thus far, in our consideration of both the human and the animal evidence, we have been considering the direct effects of nutritional deprivation on the developing organism. Clearly, this is too limited a consideration of the problem. It has long been known (Boyd-Orr, 1936) that nutritional influences may be intergenerational and that the growth and functional capacity of an individual may be affected by the growth experiences and nutrition of his mother. In particular, the nutritional history of the mother and its effect upon her growth may significantly affect her competence as a reproducer. In its turn, this reproductive inadequacy may affect the intrauterine and birth experiences of the offspring.

Bernard (1952), working in Scotland, has clearly demonstrated the association between a woman's nutritional history and her pelvic type. He compared one group of stunted women in Aberdeen with well-grown women and found that 34% of the shorter women had abnormal pelvic shapes conducive to disordered pregnancy and delivery, as compared with 7% of the well-grown women. Still earlier, Greulich, Thoms, and Twaddle (1939) had reported that the rounded or long oval pelvis, which appears to be functionally superior for childbearing, was made more common in well-off, well-grown women than in economically less privileged clinic patients. They further noted, as had Bernard, that these pelvic abnormalities were strongly associated with shortness.

Sir Duglad Baird and his colleagues in the city of Aberdeen, Scotland, have from 1947 onward conducted a continuing series of studies on the total population of births in this city of 200,000 in an effort to define the patterns of biological and social interactions which contribute to a woman's growth attainments and to her functional competence in childbearing. More than 20 years ago, Baird (1947) noted that short stature, which was five times more common in lower-class women than in upper-class women, was associated with reproductive complications. He pointed out (1949), on the basis of analyzing the reproductive performances of more than 13,000 first deliveries, that fetal mortality rates were more than twice as high in women who were under five feet, one inch in height as in women whose height was five feet, four inches, or more. Baird and Illsley (1953) demonstrated that premature births were almost two times more common in the shorter than in the taller group. Thomson (1959) extended these observations by analyzing the relation between maternal physique and reproductive complications for the more than 26,000 births which had occurred in Aberdeen over a 10-year period and found that short stature in the mother was strongly associated with high rates of prematurity, delivery complications, and perinatal deaths at each parity and age level. He concluded that "it is evident that whatever the nature of the delivery the fetus of the short woman has less vitality and is less likely to be well-grown and to survive than that of a tall woman."

It was of course possible that these findings simply reflected differences in the social-class composition of short and tall women and were based on differences in "genetic pool," rather than on stunting as such. To test this hypothesis, the Aberdeen workers (Baird, 1964) re-examined their data for perinatal mortality and prematurity rates by height within each of the social classes for all Aberdeen births occurring in the 10-year period from 1948 to 1957. They found that shortness in every social class was associated with an elevated rate of both prematurity and perinatal deaths. Concerned that the findings in Aberdeen might not be representative, they also analyzed the data from the all-Britain perinatal mortality survey of 1958 and confirmed their findings. Moreover, Thomson and Billewicz (1963) in Hong Kong and Baird (1964) have substantiated the Aberdeen findings for Chinese and West African women respectively. Other findings in a similar vein from this series have been summarized by Illsley (1967).

The available data therefore suggest that women who are not well grown have characteristics which negatively affect them as childbearers. In particular, short stature is associated with pregnancy and delivery complications and with prematurity. Since growth achievement within ethnic groups is a function of health history and, in particular, nutrition, it is clear that the mother's antecedent nutritional history when she herself was a child can and does significantly influence the intrauterine growth, development, and vitality of her child. Moreover, an inadequate nutritional background in the mother places this child at elevated risk for damage at delivery.

It is instructive to consider the consequences for mental development and learning failure that attach to the most frequently occurring consequence of poor maternal growth—prematurity. Concern with the consequences of this condition is hardly new, with Shakespeare indicating it as one element in the peculiarities of Richard III, and Little (1862) linking it with the disorder we now call cerebral palsy. Benton (1940) reviewed the literature up to that time and found that though most students of the problem maintained that prematurity was a risk to later mental development, others could find no negative consequence attaching to it. At that time no resolution of disagreement could be made because most of the early studies had been carried out with serious deficiences in design and in techniques of behavioral evaluation. Groups of infants who were of low birthweight or early in gestational age were often compared with full-term infants who differed from them in social circumstances as well as in perinatal status. Estimates of intellectual level were made with poor instruments and were often dependent on "clinical impression" or testimony from parents or teachers.

Serious and detailed consideration of the consequences of low birthweight for later behavioral complications can properly be said to have been begun by Pasamanick, Knobloch, and their colleagues shortly after World War II. These workers were guided by a concept which they referred to as a "continuum of reproductive casualty." They argued that there was a set of pregnancy and delivery complications which resulted in death by damaging the brain and hypothesized that in infants who survived exposure to these risks "there must remain a fraction so injured who do not die, but depending on the degree and location of trauma, go on to develop a series of disorders extending from cerebral palsy, epilepsy, and mental deficiency, through all types of behavioral and learning disabilities, resulting from lesser degrees of damage sufficient to disorganize behavioral development and lower thresholds to stress" (Pasamanick and Knobloch, 1960). In a series of retrospective studies, prematurity and low birthweight were identified by them as being among the conditions most frequently associated with defective behavioral outcomes. They therefore, in association with Rider and Harper, undertook a prospective study of a balanced sample of 500 premature infants born in Baltimore in 1952 and compared them with full-term control infants born in the same hospitals, who were matched with the prematures for race, maternal age, parity, season of birth, and socioeconomic status (Knobloch et al., 1956). Four hundred pairs of cases and controls were still available for study when the children were between six and seven years of age, and examination of the sample indicated that at this age the prematures and full-term children continued to be matched for maternal and social attributes (Wiener et al., 1965). Findings at various ages persistently showed the prematures to be less intellectually competent than the controls. At ages three to five, the prematures were relatively retarded intellectually and physically and had a higher frequency of definable neurological abnormalities (Harper, Fischer, and Rider, 1959; Knobloch et al., 1956). At ages six through seven, IQ scores on the

Stanford-Binet test were obtained, and at ages eight to nine, WISC IQs were available. At both age levels, lower birthweights were associated with lower IQs (Wiener et al., 1965, 1968).

Although certain British studies, such as those of McDonald (1964) and Douglas (1956, 1960), appear to be somewhat discrepant with these findings, reanalysis of their findings indicates a similar trend (Birch and Gussow, 1970). More dramatic differences between prematures and full-term infants have been reported by Drillien (1964, 1965), but interpretation of her data is made difficult by complexities in the selection of the samples studied.

A number of analyses suggest that the effects of prematurity are not the same in different social classes, with children from the lowest social classes appearing to have subsequent IQ and school performances more significantly depressed by low birthweight than is the case for infants in superior social circumstances. This has been reported for Aberdeen births (Illsley, 1966; Richardson, 1968), and for Hawaiian children in the Kauai pregnancy study of E. Werner (1967). There appears to be an interaction between birthweight and family social condition in affecting intellectual outcome, but the precise mechanisms involved in this interaction are as yet unclear.

If the risk of deficient intellectual outcome in prematurity is greatest for those children who are otherwise socially disadvantaged, our concern in the United States with the phenomenon of prematurity must be increased. In 1962 more than 19% of non-white babies born in New York City had a gestational age of less than 36 weeks as compared with 9.5% of white babies, and in Baltimore this comparison was 25.3% of non-white infants versus 10.3% of white babies (National Center for Health Statistics, 1964). In 1967, nationally, 13.6% of non-white infants weighed less than 2,500 grams as compared with 7.1% of white infants (National Center for Health Statistics, 1967). Other relevant and more detailed analyses of the social distribution of low birthweight and gestational age on both national and regional bases, together with an analysis of their secular trends, provide additional support for these relationships (Birch and Gussow, 1970). Thus, prematurity is most frequent in the very groups in which its depressing effects on intelligence are greatest.

On the basis of the evidence so far set forth, it may be argued with considerable justification that one can reasonably construct a chain of consequences starting from the malnutrition of the mother when she was a child, to her stunting, to her reduced efficiency as a reproducer, to intrauterine and perinatal risk to the child, and to his subsequent reduction in functional adaptive capacity. Animal models have been constructed to test the hypotheses implied in this chain of associations, most particularly by Chow and his colleagues (1968; Hsueh, Agustin, and Chow, 1967), as well as by Cowley and Griesel (1963, 1966). The findings from these studies indicate that second- and later-generation animals deriving from mothers who were nutritionally disadvantaged when young are themselves less well grown and behaviorally less competent than animals of the same strain deriving from normal mothers. Moreover, the condition of the offspring is worsened if nutritional insult in its own life is superimposed on early maternal malnutrition.

A variety of factors would lead us to focus on the last month of intrauterine life as one of the ''critical'' periods for the growth and development of the central nervous system. Both brain and body growth, together with differentiation, are occurring at a particularly rapid rate at this time. It has been argued, therefore, that whereas marginal maternal nutritional resources may be sufficient to sustain life and growth adequately during the earlier periods of pregnancy, the needs of the rapidly growing infant in the last trimester of intrauterine existence may outstrip maternal supplies. The work of Gruenwald, Dawkins, and Hepner (1963), among others, would suggest that maternal conditions during this period of the infant's development are probably the ones which contribute most influentially to low birthweight and prematurity. Such concerns have led to inquiries into the relation of the mother's nutritional status in pregnancy to the growth and development of her child. In considering this question, it is well to recognize that as yet we have no definitive answer to the question of the degree to which maternal nutrition during pregnancy contributes to pregnancy outcome. Clearly, whether or not nutritional lacks experienced by the mother during pregnancy will affect fetal growth is dependent upon the size and physical resources of the mother herself. Well-grown women are most likely to have tissue reserves which can be diverted to meet the nutritional needs of the fetus, even when pregnancy is accompanied by significant degrees of contemporary undernutrition. Conversely, poorly grown women with minimal tissue reserves could not, under the same set of circumstances, be expected to be able to provide adequately for the growing infant.

Children coming from families in which the risks of exposure to malnutrition are high are unlikely to experience nutritional inadequacies only in early life. It is far more likely that earlier nutritional inadequacies are projected into the preschool and school years. Such a view receives support from numerous surveys, as well as from recent testimony presented before the Senate Committee on Nutrition and Human Needs (1968–1970). Our knowledge of the degree to which children and families at risk continue to be exposed to nutritional inadequacies derives from a series of indirect and direct methods of inquiry. At an indirect level it can be argued that family diet in the main is very much dependent upon family income level. The report

Dietary Levels of Households in the United States, published by the United States Department of Agriculture (1968), underscores this proposition. According to a houschold survey conducted in the spring of 1965, only 9% of families with incomes of $10,000 and over a year were judged to have "poor diets." However, the proportion of poor diets increased regularly with each reduction in income level, with 18% of the families earning under $3,000 a year reporting poor diets, that is, diets containing less than two-thirds of the recommended allowance of one or more essential nutrients. Conversely, the proportion of "good" diets went from 63% in the $10,000 and over category down to 37% in the under $3,000 group. Of course, income alone is not an adequate indicator of socioeconomic status since in families with equal incomes more education appears to produce a better diet (Hendel, Burke, and Lund, 1965; Jeans, Smith, and Stearns, 1952; Murphy and Wertz, 1954). But, at the least, such figures suggest that we must be seriously concerned with just how badly nourished our poor are in what we often claim is the "best-fed nation in the world."

Reports of the survey type may be supplemented by inquiries in which mothers are asked what they feed their families and how much of what kinds of food they purchase. Similarly, actual food intakes may be estimated by requests for the retrospective recall of all foods eaten over the last 24 hours. G. M. Owen and Kram (1969), studying nutritional status in Mississippi preschool children, found not only that the poorer children were on the average smaller than more affluent children, but that their diets were significantly low in calories, vitamin C, calcium, and riboflavin. In Onondaga County, New York, Dibble et al. (1965) found that among students drawn from a junior high school which was 94% Negro and predominantly laboring class, 41% had come to school without breakfast; but in two "overwhelmingly white" junior high schools, only 7% in one school and 4% in the other had skipped breakfast. In recent studies among teenagers in Berkeley, California, Hampton et al. (1967) and Huenemann et al. (1968) have found intakes of all nutrients declining with socioeconomic status, with Negro girls and boys having worse intakes than those in other ethnic groups. Huenemann also found that among junior and senior high school students studied over a two-year period 90% of the Negro teenagers had irregular eating habits and many appeared to be "fending for themselves."

Christakis et al. (1968), who carried out the first dietary study of New York school children in 20 years, found that in an economically depressed district the diets of 71% of the children examined were poor and fewer than 7% had excellent diets. Moreover, his data demonstrated that if the child's family was on welfare, the likelihood of the child's having a poor diet was much increased.

The situation is not markedly different in the Roxbury district of Boston. In this area Myers et al. (1968) studied the diets and nutritional status of fourth, fifth, and sixth graders, about two-thirds of whom were black. Meals were ranked as "satisfactory" or "unsatisfactory." Four satisfactory ratings for a given meal over the four-day period produced a "satisfactory" rating for the meal. Fifty-five percent of the children failed to get such a satisfactory rating for breakfast, 60% of them did not have satisfactory lunches, and 42% had fewer than four satisfactory evening meals in four days. "Satisfactory" scores declined with age for all meals, and Negroes generally had more unsatisfactory ratings than Caucasians. The schools had no school lunch programs, and lunches were the poorest meals, with 33% of the children having two or more unsatisfactory lunch ratings in four days. During the four-day period, 64% of the children had fewer than two glasses of milk a day, 132 children had *no* citrus fruit, and only one child had a green or yellow vegetable; 37% of the Negro and 46% of the Caucasian children had "un satisfactory" intakes of the protein foods in the meat, fish, poultry, eggs, and legume group. The evidence, the authors concluded, indicated that many of the children were eating poorly.

These data are illustrative and not atypical of the national picture. The preliminary reports deriving from the National Nutrition Survey serve to confirm these findings on a national scale. The evidence, though scattered and of uneven quality, indicates strongly that economically disadvantaged children from underprivileged ethnic groups eat poorly in both the preschool and school-age periods.

Direct clinical studies, occurring largely within the Head Start program serve to support the impression produced by the data of nutritional surveys. One way of examining possible subnutrition on an economical-clinical basis is to define the prevalence of iron deficiency anemia. Hutcheson (1968), reporting on a very large sample of poor white and Negro children in rural Tennessee, found the highest level of anemia among children around one year old. Of the whole group of 15,681 children up to six years of age, 20.9% had hematocrits of 31%, indicating a marginal status. Among the year-old children, however, the incidence of low hematocrits was even higher; 27.4% of the whites and 40% of the non-whites had hematocrits of 31% or less, and 10% of the whites and one-quarter of the non-whites had hematocrits of 30% or under, indicating a more serious degree of anemia. Low hemoglobin level was also most common among the younger children in a group Gutelius (1969) examined at a child health center in Washington, D.C. Iron deficiency anemia, determined by hemoglobin level and corroborative red cell pathology, was found among 28.9% of the whole group of 460 Negro preschoolers, but children in the age group 12–17 months had a rate of anemia of 65%. Gutelius points out, moreover, that these were probably not the highest-risk children, since the poorest and most disorganized families did not come from well-baby care at all, and of those who did attend, the test group included only children who had not previously had a hemoglobin determination—that is, they were children judged to be "normal" by the clinic staff. Thus, "many of the highest-risk children had already been tested and were not included in this series."

Even in the summer 1966 Head Start program, in which the incidence of other disorders was surprisingly low (North, 1967), studies indicated that 20–40% of the children were suffering from anemia, a proportion consistent with the findings of various studies summarized by Filer (1969), as well as with the level of anemia found in a random sample of predominantly lower-class children coming into the pediatric emergency room of the Los Angeles County Hospital (Wingert, 1968). Anemia rates as high as 80% among pre-school children have been reported from Alabama (Mermann, 1966) and Mississippi (Child Development Group of Mississippi, 1967).

It is clear from such evidence that some degree of malnutrition is relatively widespread among poor children, but we have already seen that the effects of inadequate nutrition on growth and mental development depend to a very large extent on the severity, the timing, and the duration of the nutritional deprivation. Inadequate as are our data on the true prevalence of malnutrition among children in this country, we are even less informed about its onset or about its severity and quality. The absence of such knowledge must not be taken to reflect the absence of the problem, but rather the lack of attention which has been devoted to it.

Implications, Programs, and Problems

The evidence we have surveyed indicates strongly that nutritional factors at a number of different levels contribute significantly to depressed intellectual level and learning failure. These effects may be produced directly as the consequences of irreparable alterations of the nervous system, or indirectly as a result of ways in which the learning experiences of the developing organism may be significantly interfered with at critical points in the developmental course.

If one argues that a primary requirement for normal intellectual development and for formal learning is the ability to process sensory information and to integrate such information across sense systems, the evidence indicates that both severe acute malnutrition in infancy and chronic subnutrition from birth into the school years result in defective information processing. Thus, by inhibiting the development of a primary process essential for certain aspects of cognitive growth, malnutrition may interfere with the orderly development of experience and contribute to a suboptimal level of intellectual functioning.

Moreover, an adequate state of nutrition is essential for good attention and for appropriate and sensitive responsiveness to the environment. One of the most obvious clinical manifestations of serious malnutrition in infancy is a dramatic combination of apathy and irritability. The infant is grossly unresponsive to his surroundings and obviously unable to profit from the objective opportunities for experience present in his surroundings. This unresponsiveness characterizes his relation to people, as well as to objects. Behavioral regression is profound, and the organization of his functions is markedly infantalized. As Dean (1960) has put it, one of the first signs of recovery from the illness is an improvement in mood and in responsiveness to people—"the child who smiles is on the road to recovery."

In children who are subnourished, one also notes a reduction in responsiveness and attentiveness. In addition, the subnourished child is easily fatigued and unable to sustain either prolonged physical or mental effort. Improvement in nutritional status is accompanied by improvements in these behaviors, as well as in physical state.

It should not be forgotten that nutritional inadequacy may influence the child's learning opportunities by yet another route, namely, illness. As we have demonstrated elsewhere (Birch and Cravioto, 1968; Birch and Gussow, 1970), nutritional inadequacy increases the risk of infection, interferes with immune mechanisms, and results in illness which is both more generalized and more severe. The combination of subnutrition and illness reduces time available for instruction and so, by interfering with the opportunities for gaining experience, disrupts the orderly acquisition of knowledge and the course of intellectual growth.

We have also pointed to intergenerational effects of nutrition on mental development. The association between the mother's growth achievements and the risk to her infant is very strong. Poor nutrition and poor health in the mother when she was a girl result in a woman at maturity who has a significantly elevated level of reproductive risk. Her pregnancy is more frequently disturbed and her child more often of low birthweight. Such a child is at increased risk for neurointegrative abnormality and for deficient IQ and school achievement.

Despite the strength of the argument we have developed, it would be tragic if one now sought to replace all the other variables—social, cultural, educational, and psychological—which exert an influence on intellectual growth, with nutrition. Malnutrition never occurs alone, it occurs in conjunction with low income, poor housing, family disorganization, a climate of apathy, ignorance, and despair. The simple act of improving the nutritional status of children and their families will not and cannot of itself fully solve the problem of intellectual deficit and school failure. No single improvement in conditions will have this result. What must be recognized, rather, is that within our overall effort to improve the condition of disadvantaged children, nutritional considerations must occupy a prominent place, and that together with improvements in all other facets of life, including relevant and directed education, they contribute to the improved intellectual growth and school achievement of disadvantaged children.

23

INTRODUCTION

Competence and Biology: Methodology in Studies of Infants, Twins, Psychosomatic Disease, and Psychosis, by Donald J. Cohen

Both clinical work and scientific investigation invariably entail incessant reductionistic pressures and temptations to transform complex phenomena into simple unitary explanations. The following chapter by Cohen avoids this pitfall. It provides a useful supplement to the last half of *Childhood Psychopathology* (Harrison and McDermott, 1972), which addresses psychophysiological interrelationships. In that volume, Parts VII, VIII, and IX focus on the effect of various neurodevelopmental factors on the child while Part VI reflects the legacy of traditional "psychosomatic medicine." There, the life histories, personalities, and psychic conflicts of youngsters with classic psychophysiological disorders are examined in relation to their assumed effect on the target organ system via a repeatedly reinforced pathway. Some of the chapters hint at an exploration of psychophysiology that goes beyond Cannon's (1932) and Selye's (1950) sympathetic-parasympathetic-endocrine model, which bridges mind-body dualism. Since then, expanding information in both behavioral and medical sciences indicates a complex interaction in which it is increasingly difficult to distinguish between mind and body.

Originally data came primarily from naturalistic clinical observations. This base has grown to encompass information stemming from laboratory experiments involving increasingly refined biopsychosocial developmental hypotheses. In the past, bold global concepts tended to be applied to the narrow clinical field of individual syndromes. These ideas are now being enriched and, in some instances, replaced by formulations that have a more restricted focus, but that collectively cover a far broader field. For instance, recent findings indicate that catecholamines and other transmitter substances are of importance in the brain as well as in the peripheral nervous system (Schildkraut and Kety, 1967), that the sympathetic-parasympathetic nervous system is neither as autonomous nor as involuntary as its designation proclaims (N. E. Miller, 1969), that there seems to be some hormonal influence on genes (Davidson, 1965), that there is an interaction between neuroendocrine influences and the immune system which is mobilized in response to a broad range of factors (Kaj Jerne, 1973), and that psychobiological rhythms exert untold influences (Luce, 1970). Indeed, the *new* psychophysiological disorders may include conditions such as depression and minimal brain dysfunction (MBD), where the interface between behavior and neurochemical imbalance is being illuminated. The secrets of this interaction are further revealed in the distinction of norepinephrine- and serotonin-deficient depressions, which call for different treatment interventions.

Cohen's contribution to this progress is exemplified in part by the following chapter. He offers a wide-ranging, hypothesis-generating essay on the interaction of biological and experiential factors. Both its creative scope and its inevitable discursiveness remind one somewhat of Erikson's (1950) *Childhood and Society*, which focused on the interaction between the psychological and sociocultural dimensions.

To accomplish his task, Cohen travels several paths that initially seem unrelated. He starts with neonatal sucking as an easily measured prototype of what is probably only one of several mechanisms available to the infant for modulating distress, deploying arousal, and inhibiting physiological overreactivity. He next addresses infantile eczema as a biopsychosocially determined stress that is not accessible to modulation. In his thoughtful discussion he takes note of the positive personality attributes observed in some eczematous children and hypothesizes about the relationship of these qualities to the biological substrate underlying eczema. He wonders whether there may be an evolutionary advantage to possessing some biogenic amine diathesis, even if it is accompanied by mild eczema. Regarding another side of the issue, however, he does not venture into fantasy about the possibility of a relationship between the itch-scratch cycle and masochism. Instead, Cohen returns to data and turns next to developmental studies of twins and lastly to the role of biogenic amines in hyperkinetic behavioral disturbances, childhood psychosis, and some neurological disorders.

These and a variety of other issues in neurochemistry and child psychiatry are the subject of an informative, comprehensive overview by Cohen and Young (1977). A recent discovery, for instance, is that of extremely potent, naturally occurring, complex opioid peptides—the endorphins and enkephalins—which affect sensory and emotional processing, thus suggesting that they may be involved in modulating pain and pleasure.

These, then, are some of the roads along which Cohen traverses to arrive at a multifactorial model, which he hopes will someday serve as a basis for predicting aspects of personality development and vulnerability for populations of children. Instead of thinking of psychophysiological disorders in the classical sense (the viewpoint articulated in *Childhood Psychopathology*) and focusing on their relationship to parent-child conflict, Cohen proposes a new model which places the parent-child relationship within the context of both biological and psychological variables and their interaction with each other. More investigations and creative thinking comparable to Cohen's presentation are needed if his hopes for the future are to be realized.

23

Competence and Biology: Methodology in Studies of Infants, Twins, Psychosomatic Disease, and Psychosis

DONALD J. COHEN

When Descartes separated mind from body, he left us with the central question of the philosophy of mind: How do physiology and experience interact? Those of us who are practically concerned about the lives of children require models of development which give appropriate status to both mind and body, and which are sufficiently explicit to guide research and action.

Without explicit models and shared understanding of how to conceptualize the organization of behavior or use basic concepts such as stress and vulnerability, child psychiatrists are themselves vulnerable to disciplinary difficulties. We may wander into conceptual roundhouses or unnecessary muddles; we may misinterpret data already available or fail to see connections; and we may overlook promising leads from other fields of inquiry.

This paper sketches a multivariate model or viewpoint which emphasizes biological endowment in interaction with psychosocial forces. The examples of empirical studies are drawn from my own work, often done with collaborators, and I try only to suggest the scope, without attempting to review the literature relevant to this type of synthetic approach.

First published in *The Child in His Family*, Volume 3: *Children at Psychiatric Risk*, edited by E. J. Anthony and C. Koupernik. New York: John Wiley & Sons, pp. 361–394, 1974. Copyright © 1974, John Wiley & Sons, Inc. Reprinted by permission.

The research was supported in part by Public Health Research Grant HD-03008. Mr. Warren Johnson , Ms. Barbara Caparulo, and Ms. Jane Graw, research associates, have all contributed to this work.

CONGENITAL ORGANIZATION OF BEHAVIOR: SUCKING TO REDUCE DISTRESS

During the first day or two of life, when infants are given an empty rubber nipple on which to suck, they often mouth it, bite down, or emit sucks of irregular amplitude and uneven rhythm. As Wolff has demonstrated, within several days the sucking behavior of healthy infants displays a well-defined organization.[1] Children emit bursts of eight to ten even-amplitude sucks at a rate of about two per second, with pauses of several seconds between bursts (Kaye, 1967; P. H. Wolff, 1973).

When environmental events other than the delivery of milk were made contingent upon a child's sucking—for example, when sucking was followed by a loud noise or bright light—the sucking rate, once stabilized (in sucks per second), did not usually change. Instead, pauses between bursts tended to shorten. If the intensity of environmental stimulation increased even more—for instance, if the noise was made quite loud—the amplitude of the sucks altered and, finally, the entire sucking pattern tended to become as disorganized as during the first day or two of life. The child ceased sucking and cried. Thus, increasing stress appeared to increase sucking until a point when an individual child's threshold was exceeded and his sucking system was disorganized.

The sucking rate and rhythms of about 25 two- to five-day-old boys were measured during the acute stress of circumcision. A pacifier connected to a pressure transducer and recording apparatus was placed in the child's mouth. The child's heart rate was monitored by electrocardiography, and his behavior was observed. Two broad patterns of response to circumcision were explicated. In the first, the infant continued to suck throughout circumcision with shortened pauses between bursts of sucking and decreased pressure or amplitude of individual sucks. These boys tended to show only moderate increases in heart rate (up to about 160 beats per minute) and to have only transient upsets in their feeding and sleeping during the following day. The second, more common pattern involved some degree of disorganization of sucking with biting and irregular sucks interrupted by long periods of crying and kicking. Many of these boys developed extreme tachycardia (up to 220 beats per minute) with occasional inversion of T waves on the electrocardiogram indicating a high degree of physiological activation. In contrast with the boys who continued to suck, those whose sucking disorganized tended

---

[1] Dr. Peter H. Wolff, with whom the work on sucking reported here was initiated, has studied in detail the general role of rhythmic organizers and has illuminated their theoretical significance for understanding early development (1966).

to go off feedings, sleep more fitfully, and be irritable during the hours following circumcision.[2]

Such observations of stressed newborns provide material for constructing a simple model in which sucking is seen as a congenital capacity that functions to modulate distress and inhibit physiological overreactivity. Clinical use is made of this capacity when a colicky infant is given a pacifier on which to suck. In this model the basic sucking pattern and increased sucking with stress are congenitally organized and universal, whereas the threshold beyond which stress leads to disorganization (rather than to more sucking) is seen as individualized (Escalona, 1962; Kessen and Mandler, 1961). Later, after introducing current biological ideas about the regulation of pleasure, we may speculate about the neurophysiological basis for this arousal-modulating system. But it should be underlined here that sucking is probably not the only arousal or distress-modulating mechanism available to the infant. Other active processes such as the redeployment of attention may also be operative. Sucking, however, is obvious and easily measured, and it serves as a convenient prototype.

In another study, newborns who were lustily crying because of hunger were given a pacifier to suck while their total bodily movement and amount of crying were measured. After they were quiet, the nipple was quickly withdrawn. With increasing experience, newborns quieted more quickly when given the nipple and started to cry more quickly when it was withdrawn. This accommodation to the nipple could be observed even in one-day-old infants with no postnatal experience with nutritive sucking. Although there were marked individual differences in the speed of quieting and the latency to cry after nipple removal—with the most comfortable infants quieting quickly, but waiting to cry on nipple withdrawal—all infants showed the capacity to learn or accommodate to the use of the pacifier as a way of decreasing the distress and physiological upheaval of hunger and hunger-crying (D. J. Cohen, 1967).

Thus, the sucking of healthy newborns seems congenitally organized to have a more rapid onset and fewer pauses in order to modulate distress. Because of genetic, intrauterine, or other factors, some newborns have significantly greater capacity to modulate internal distress by sucking than do others. For the newborn less able to modulate distress, major stresses such as circumcision and minor, daily, unavoidable stresses of frustration and discomfort are more likely to overwhelm the child's ability to maintain physiological homeostasis and to remain experientially calm (J. D. Benjamin,

[2]For further discussion of the relation between autonomic changes and arousal, as well as for individual differences in autonomic responsivity, see F. Graham and Jackson (1970); Hutt, Lenard, and Prechtl (1969); Richmond and Lipton (1959); Richmond, Lipton, and Steinschneider (1962a, 1962b).

1961b, 1963). Such episodes of being overwhelmed, in conjunction with the congenital endowment that leads to being easily overwhelmed, may be seen as the biological-experiential matrix for emergent, individual differences in the predisposition to anxiety.

In this simplified theoretical scheme, parents can be pictured as exerting their influence in three ways: by contributing the child's genes, by protecting the child from potential stress, and by comforting the child when his own defenses against overarousal are unequal to the challenge.

There is an extensive literature on the enduring impact of early experiences in animals and even in humans. The endocrine environment during gestation (Money and Ehrhardt, 1968), early mothering in the premature nursery, obstetrical medication (W. Bowers et al., 1970), and other experiences may have a long-term impact on development. For example, infant rats who receive stimulating, handling, and increasing control of their environment show less anxiety when tested in an open field situation several months later (Joffe, Rawson, and Mulick, 1973). Presumably, early infantile experiences shape the organization of early adaptations and also the ways in which a child will later respond to new situations. Optimal conditions for a newborn child involve enough stimulation to allow for the unfolding of functions such as the accommodation to the nipple and, at the same time, sufficient protection to prevent the child from repeatedly being overwhelmed by stress which he is unable to modulate.

Clinicians often observe that irritable children have sensitive, anxious parents. This correlation may represent the result of several forces. First, the parents' anxiety may represent their own genetic and unfolding endowment marked by disturbances in the modulation of anxiety. Second, anxious parents have difficulties in preventing a child from experiencing stress and in comforting him when he is overwhelmed by stress (which may be borne more easily by other children). Third, the child who is easily upset—as a result of his genome and his endowment—is more difficult to care for and thus is more likely to elicit parenting, from any adult, which is complicated by guilt, tension, and ambivalence. The parents of children with colic, general irritability, hyperactivity, and childhood autism—to name only some conditions in which the modulation of stress is impaired—are likely to be sensitive individuals themselves and to be very much upset in their attempts at parenting.

STRESS WHICH CANNOT BE MODULATED: CHILDHOOD ECZEMA

What happens when stress cannot be modulated? Severe, unremitting childhood eczema provides a natural experiment on the impact of prolonged, internal distress in the first years of life. Childhood eczema is a skin disease which usually appears between the third and tenth month of life, starting as a mild rash on the face and then spreading to include the pressure surfaces of the baby's arms and legs. After a relatively benign course marked by limited periods of discomfort, the disease often remits by age five years. For a small minority of children, childhood eczema follows a more severe, devastating course, marked by months and years of unremitting rash, often covering the child from head to toe with an oozing, crusting, terribly itching eruption from which he can find no rest.

Severely afflicted children have been treated with a variety of topical agents (such as coal tar, steroid creams, and lubricants), systemic medications (antipruritics, sedatives, and sometimes corticosteroids), and environmental maneuvers (hand restraints, bandaging, and avoidance of various objects suspected to be allergenic). Often a combination of treatments offers some relief (L. W. Hill, 1956; Sulzberger, 1971).

To study children who cannot comfort themselves or be comforted by parents, I cared for about 80 children severely afflicted with eczema. Most were referred by pediatricians, allergists, and dermatologists who had failed with the usual medical treatment. Thus, the children were an unusual sample of very disabled treatment failures.[3]

The pathophysiology of eczema involves a circular chain reaction in which vigorous scratching leads to a bloody, maculopapular rash, which in turn stimulates more scratching. Within minutes, a paroxysm of scratching may turn a child who has the tendency to severe eczema from being relatively free of rash into being covered with eczema, blood, and excoriations. Children with eczema appear to be born with the disposition to develop a vasculitis, characterized by edema and perivascular cellular infiltration, during the first months of life. This tendency presumably is based on the genetic endowment for hypersensitivity of physiological vascular instability in which biogenic amines in the skin have been implicated (Lobitz and Campbell, 1953; Rhyne, 1965; Sedlis, 1965). A child or adult without the tendency to eczema who scratches may develop lichenification or excoriations, but he will not develop eczema.

For a particular child with eczema, proximal causes of occasional scratching often can be identified: skin irritation, woolen clothing, temperature change, sweating, and the like. But such proximal causes are often weak, transient, or predisposing stimuli, paled by the most important initiator of the patho-

---

[3]The study of eczema extended over four years and was conducted at Children's Hospital Medical Center, Boston, Massachusetts. Dr. Robert Greisemer, Chief of Dermatology, supported the research and shared his unsurpassed understanding of physical and psychological features of childhood skin diseases.

physiological scratch-rash cycle: emotional arousal, anxiety, or stress.

For a normal toddler, frustration or scolding may lead to crying, a temper tantrum, or externally directed aggression. For the three-year-old with a history of severe eczema, the result of emotional arousal or stress is most often a paroxysm of scratching. The normal toddler may be relatively unmoved by adversity such as separation and discipline, and he is capable of modulating much distress before becoming very upset. One with eczema seems particularly vulnerable. Thus the eczematous child not only expresses distress by acting inwardly, but he is also more sensitive, fragile, and prone to experiencing even minor family upsets as disorganizing. And for him, scratching leads to more rash, which leads to more scratching. The result of a paroxysm of scratching is an exhausted, bloody child, who has literally torn away at his own skin to reduce incessant itching, and has succeeded only in making it worse. The paroxysm comes to an end when the child is finally distracted or exhausted, or when his itch perception is disordered by skin trauma.

The difference between a child with benign eczema and one whose eczema follows the severe course I have pictured often appears to consist of the nature of the family's response to the child's distress, rash, and scratch-rash cycle, as much as in the child's physiological predisposition to the underlying vasculitis. Children with limited eczema often come from families that can be called "supportive." These families accept the child's first rash with relative equanimity, remain available throughout the course of the tendency to develop eczema, protect the child from undue stress, and comfort him when overwhelmed. Children with years of severe, unremitting eczema tend to come from families where this supportive system has not been available or maintained. Here the parents have reacted to the child's rash with tremendous anxiety or worry, and then often with ambivalent caretaking and withdrawal. For such parents, the rash may arouse many types of personal meaning: as an indication that they are inept, as a satisfaction of an unconscious need for punishment for felt wrongdoing, or as a source of arousal of concern about bodily contact and sexuality. Moreover, the rash and the parents' subsequent unadaptive responses may become locked into already-established interpersonal conflicts in the marriage or extended family. In short, the rash of the child with very severe eczema is often far more than a rash.

Children with severe eczema for many years direct much of their energy and attention to caring for their own bodies. Cracking and uncomfortable skin, unsightly appearance, and irritability often prevent them from acquiring age-appropriate social or motor skills. Thus, by age three or four, afflicted children may present a clinical picture of severe developmental retardation which affects speech, social skills, and muscular coordination, and they may show a diffuse lack of interest or capacity for establishing warm, friendly relations.

In the course of treatment, the eczematous child's energies can be redirected from his body to the outside world, and he and his parents can be helped to re-establish mutually satisfying, pleasant relationships, which can then be extended to include peers and other adults. Over many months almost the complete picture of developmental retardation may be erased, even in the presence of a continued, although never so severe, series of exacerbations of the rash. The key to such a transformation lies in the clinician's success in reducing the child's distress through appropriate psychoactive medication, protection from undue stress, and skin care, and the physician's simultaneous success in modifying the parental distress and anger through appropriate counseling, personal availability, and willingness to share responsibility for months, and especially during times of crisis (D. J. Cohen and Nadelson, 1971).

The study of children with eczema and their families was in the context of clinical care lasting for months and years. In many ways it elaborated the model that originated in the laboratory study of sucking and distress, the time-base for which was hours and days. The natural history of eczema is a function not only of the underlying vasculitis, but of the child's threshold for disorganization, his ability to modulate distress, and other channels in addition to scratching that remain open for the expression of his distress (Mohr et al., 1963). Often, in the presence of a supportive family, the rash remains benign, although recurrent; occasionally a family's capacity to remain available, affectionate, stimulating, and yet protective is limited. The people who carry and contribute the genes to the child for the vascular diathesis underlying eczema, as well as contributing to his lowered ability to modulate distress, are the very same people who will be faced with the parenting responsibilities posed by the distressed infant. Such parents may be genetically ill-equipped for their role, endowed as they may be for heightened sensitivity and arousal. Constitutional factors are expressed not only in children, but in the adults who are their parents.

The description of the life of a child profoundly afflicted with eczema requires an important counterpoint. For some children with milder eczema, and even some whose disease is severe, life and development may be not at all bleak. Impressively active, thoughtful, alert, and inquisitive, these intelligent children take in people and objects with special awareness of details. They seem very alive to family events and sensitive to nuances of feeling. And although they often, or even usually, appear to be high-strung and temperamental, their heightened appreciation of feelings and their subtle social relations create an impression of precocious deepening, an impression which I believe to be clinically valid. One might be inclined to view this type of maturation as a pattern of response to illness, intense bodily sensations, gratifying special care, and the resultant tuning in or attuning of attention. And all of these factors play important roles. Yet the positive developmental trends noted sometimes may be seen in children whose eczema has been relatively mild; and even for some with more severe eczema, the psychological adaptations which are, in fact, primarily responsive to the illness seem also to be embedded in a more pervasive, psychosomatic complex.

Keeping in mind that speculation is just that, perhaps we can pursue this concept of a psychosomatic complex somewhat further. Confronted by a sensitive and perhaps trying child with eczema, an experienced and not-too-busy pediatrician might very well ask himself: Is there more here than meets the eye? Is it possible that some qualities of this child's inner life or overall development reflect not only the skin disease, and its psychic consequences, but also are more directly reflective of the child's general neurophysiological endowment? Such an endowment might operate simultaneously in what may be called, for convenience, two "domains": (1) in the physiological realm of autonomic instability, low threshold for elicitation of the scratching reflex, and the vasculitis and biogenic amine diathesis which underlie eczema and, at the same time, (2) in the realm of higher nervous functioning concerned with the regulation of arousal, attention, and the experience of anxiety. If so, the actual experience of eczema would be compounded with the psychological potential for difficulty with the modulation of anxiety. Then both the rash and aspects of the child's mental life would be, in the deepest sense, a psychosomatic whole.

Rash and mental states represent the two domains Descartes tried to neatly separate and then struggled to unite. And it is the fluidity or, rather, absence of boundaries between these two domains which leads us, as clinicians, to speak of the initial unity of feelings and bodily states, of the infant as psyche-soma (Winnicott, 1958, pp. 243–254).

In this construction of intertwining physiological and psychological processes, in which eczema has served as our model disease, there may be a suggestion about a general phenomenon: a continuum between health and disease. As we have seen, a heavy weighting or loading for the neurophysiological substrate of eczema—affecting both the skin and mental regulation—may lead to developmental crisis or catastrophe. From the vantage point of the new line of speculation, we might also wonder if there is an evolutionary advantage to being endowed with a more limited "dose" of this polygenically determined biological substrate. Would such a more fortunate individual, even if mildly afflicted with eczema, benefit from increased awareness, attentiveness, and sensitivity, and from the opportunities for forming rich mechanisms for coping (A. Freud, 1936)? We shall return to this theme in the discussion of the biology of autism.

GENETICS, ENDOWMENT, AND COMPETENCE:
DISCORDANCE IN TWINS

These studies on congenital organization and the unfolding patterns of response to stress have been considerably amplified by the opportunity of studying twin development during the first years of life. There are many approaches to the use of twins in developmental and psychiatric research (Gottesman and Shields, 1972; Rosenthal, 1971; Vandenberg, 1967). Pollin has been a leading exponent of the value of twin studies in generating new hypotheses and testing critical ones concerning the origin of individuality.[4] In an important series of papers, he and his collaborators (J. Stabenau, J. Tupin, L. Mosher, A. Hoffer, M. Allen, S. Cohen, and the author) have explored the roots of vulnerability to psychopathology (Mosher, Pollin, and Stabenau, 1971; Pollin, 1971; Pollin and Stabenau, 1968; Pollin, Stabenau, and Tupin, 1965; Pollin et al., 1966; Stabenau and Pollin, 1967).

In the National Institute of Mental Health (NIMH) twin longitudinal study, eight sets of monzygotic twins and two sets of dizygotic twins were followed from the time of the diagnosis of pregnancy to about age five years, using a variety of different techniques to assess overlapping areas of functioning (D. J. Cohen et al., 1972). The careful observation of the 20 children under high levels of magnification indicated the ways in which genetically identical children were different from the first days of life. Detailed clinical studies of individual families revealed patterns of identification and relationship between parents and children based on these small differences. Even minor experiential or physical differences—for example, differences in weight or the early appearance of an illness—seemed to have an impact on the ways in which some parents related to the children.

Although the enduring impact of differences between monozygotic twins was the major focus of this work, we must be careful not to overlook the uncanny similarity in development and experiences of children in monozygotic twinships. Without high magnification, often only these similarities are evident. Thus, monozygotic twins provide the investigator with the most dramatic type of personal evidence about genetic programming, as well as

---

[4]To provide direct observational information on the early development of twins complementary to that obtained from the retrospective studies on adult twins, Pollin initiated a longitudinal study of twin development. The twin material described here is based on this longitudinal study, directed by me for two years, and on a large-scale epidemiological study (initiated in collaboration with Dr. Eleanor Dibble and Dr. Pollin) aimed at testing hypotheses derived, in part, from earlier work on adult twins and the longitudinal study (Dibble, 1973; Dibble and Cohen, 1973).

the opportunity to study the subtle and not-so-subtle nongenetic determinants of development (Juel-Nielsen, 1964; Newman, Freeman, and Holzinger, 1937; Rosenthal, 1971).

To assess more precisely congenital endowment during the first week of life, we devised a rating scale called the First-Week Evaluation Scale (FES). Whereas the Apgar score relates to only the first minutes of life and is highly dependent on labor and delivery variables with occasionally only transient significance, the FES relates to a child's general functioning over the first week of life and appears to reflect more fundamental dimensions of early functioning. The FES consists of six variables: general health, attention, vigor, physiological functioning and adaptation, calmness, and neurological performance. Each variable is rated on a five-point rating scale, with 1 for very poor functioning and 5 for excellent functioning in that area. For example, being calm in general and easily calmed when stimulated is rated 5. Being fussy, irritable, and easily startled is rated 1. A normal neurological examination is 5; one with clear-cut disturbances, 1. A perfectly endowed newborn has a rating of 30.

In the longitudinal study of 10 sets of twins, the children's first-week endowments ranged from a low of 18 to a high of 30, with a mean of about 22. The mean intrapair difference in FES was 6, an indication of nongenetic determinants of endowment. In this population the FES scores agreed well with the characterization of the children using the Thomas, Chess, and Birch (1968) system.

At age three and one-half years, each child was studied in a research nursery school setting, in which measures and observations were made of the child's general behavior, play, relationship to mother, and reaction to the teacher and strangers. The FES correlated well with nursery school measures of general competence. The most well endowed newborns became toddlers who engaged in more thematic play, spoke more maturely, and showed more originality. The less well endowed newborns became toddlers who were fearful and distractible.

At about the same age, the children were visited at home by a psychologist, who interviewed them in a novel situation. Reactions were rated using a scale for attention, speech, originality, distractibility, social relatedness, and other aspects of social competence. Scores correlated with nursery school measures and Stanford-Binet IQs. Again children with the best first-week endowment emerged as socially mature, competent children. The mothers' responses on the Vineland Social Maturity Scale and on the Childhood Personality Scale, a questionnaire about general personality (described later), correlated well with relevant measures from the nursery school and the psychological interview.

Thus, a confluence of observations on early endowment and personality development indicates that the more competent newborn develops into the more competent toddler. We have been impressed, in these longitudinal studies and in a cross-sectional studies involving over 20 more sets of twins during childhood, by the special importance of differences in arousal and attention patterns in shaping development. Such differences between children in a twinship were often noted very early by parents, just as they are by parents of atypical children who are familiar with normal infants.

Bell, Weller, and Waldrop (1971) have found that coping as a toddler is associated with two characteristics in infancy: (1) a long latency before starting to cry when a nipple on which the infant is sucking is withdrawn and (2) a high threshold to tactile stimulation. P. H. Wolff and White (1965) have demonstrated that the optimal time for eliciting visual following in infants is during the period after feeding when the child is attentive and calm. Moments of comfort, when the child can scan his mother's face and the mother can enjoy his relating, are probably important for the formation of positive early attachments. The high-FES, well-endowed newborn is more likely to have many mutually satisfying times.

The attentive and comfortable infant is more easily consoled, and although he may need and receive less caregiving from his mother, his moments with her are likely to be pleasant. Caring for this well-endowed baby arouses less guilt, anger, and subsequent ambivalent feelings than caring for the fussier infant. Finally, in a myriad of transactions, children and family reciprocally reinforce perceptions and self-perceptions of competence (or incompetence), assertiveness (or passivity), and dominance (or submission), which, within a twinship, can easily lead to persistent dichotomization and stereotyping. The initial advantages of a better early endowment may thus be amplified and crystallized (Brody and Axelrad, 1970; Stabenau and Pollin, 1967; Weil, 1970; Winnicott, 1958).

Even for traits for which there is a heavy genetic loading—such as cleft lip and palate or dislocation of the hip—monzygotic twins are more often discordant than concordant (Benirschke and Kim, 1973; Bulmer, 1970). It seems that newborn competence is another such trait: whereas there is a clear genetic loading and high degree of similarity between monozygotic twins, our studies and those previously reported by Pollin and others (1966) indicate, and it is reasonable *a priori* to assume, that even monozygotic twins may be born with very different newborn competencies, as reflected in such areas as their abilities to attend, remain calm, and adapt physiologically. The basis for discordance in such traits as cleft lip and palate—for which the concordance rate in identical twins is only about 30%—is not definitely known, but minor differences in circulation and *in utero* position have been hypothesized as interacting with sensitively timed maturational processes (Benirschke and Kim, 1973). Similarly, the basis for differences in competence cannot be completely determined, although some suggestions will be offered later.

To understand better the basis for competence and vulnerability and to put clinical hypotheses to a more vigorous test, we have undertaken a large, epidemiological study of twins from ages one to six years. The major methodology of this study consists of mothers and fathers of over 400 sets of monozygotic (MZ) and dizygotic (DZ) twins completing specially designed questionnaires.

A common problem in twin research relates to the assignment of zygosity to a twinship. Mothers of 155 sets of twin children completed a questionnaire about the degree of physical similarity between the two children and if, and by whom, the two children were confused. For physical similarity in height, weight, facial appearance, hair color, eye color, and complexion, the mothers rated the two children on a three-point scale (exactly similar, somewhat similar, or not at all similar). For confusion, the mothers answered on a two-point scale (yes or no) whether the children were as alike as two peas in a pod and were confused by parents, other members of the family, or strangers. The twins were bloodtyped on 22 antigens to determine zygosity. This biological method for assigning zygosity allows for clear assignment in 97% of cases, but, as with other methods of zygosity determination, there are always a few sets about whom a decision is difficult or impossible.

Parental perceptions of identical and fraternal twins were extremely different and highly reliable, with 98% agreement between zygosity assigned by the mothers' responses to the questions and zygosity determined by bloodtyping. The results raise questions about an assumption which underlies many behavioral-genetic investigations using twins: that the life experiences of both types of twins are comparable. This is doubtful. For example, 78% of parents confused their MZ twins; 99% of MZ twins were confused by strangers. In contrast, only 10% of DZ twins were confused by their parents and only 16% by strangers. The calculation of heritability coefficients, such as those on which Jensen and others have so heavily relied, or comparison of intrapair correlations requires the assumption that the experiences of MZ and DZ twins are identical (D. J. Cohen et al., 1973b). This assumption now appears untenable.

The 400 sets of twins in our epidemiological study were classified using this new method for assigning zygosity. Mothers and fathers completed questionnaires about the children's gestation and delivery, personality and behavioral differences during the first years of life, and current personality patterns and behavioral problems. Each parent completed questionnaires describing his or her characteristic style of relating to each child and his or her perceptions of the type and degree of stress to which the family and each child are exposed.

In interpreting twin research it must always be remembered that the biology of twins differs from that of singletons, and that of MZ twins differs from that of DZ twins. For example, MZ twins result from a genetic accident, perhaps related to hypoxia during the first days of implantation; during gestation, MZ twins are often exposed to markedly inequitable blood circulation. DZ twinning, in contrast, results from transient endocrine disturbances, often associated with increasing maternal age and environmental stress; the placentas of DZ twins may be unequal, but they are never fully united (Bulmer, 1970).

The statistical data reported here are based on analyses of the first 210 sets of twins on whom we had complete information, and results must be considered preliminary. In our series, a large proportion of the twins were born prematurely (about 40%), and the mean length of gestation was 35–36 weeks (standard deviation [SD] ± two weeks). Mothers gained a mean of 28 pounds (± 11 pounds). They learned they were having twins only in about the eighth month of gestation and about 25% of the mothers learned only at the time of delivery. Labor tended to be short (three to six hours). The mean weights of both the firstborn and the secondborn twins were the same (92 ounces)—but there was greater variance for the secondborn (SD ± 40) than for the firstborn (SD ± 19).

The mothers took many drugs during pregnancy, having a mean of four drugs, ranging from zero (0.9% of mothers) to 11 (3.8% of mothers). Medications included iron (57%), vitamins (95%), diuretics (58%), pills for nausea (36%), tranquilizers (14%), female hormones (13%), aspirin and other analgesics (40%), antibiotics (19%), and blood pressure pills (4%). The impact on developing embryos of some of these drugs—such as the antiemetics and diuretics, used by about half the mothers—is not known. In addition, twin pregnancies were often complicated by medical problems such as varicose veins, vaginal staining, and pressure symptoms, and mothers and fathers frequently reported that they were very anxious about the economic and social burdens posed by the twins.

Clearly, when we say that a newborn child's endowment is a function of his genetics and prenatal and newborn experiences, we must keep in mind, especially for twins, how variegated, and often "unnatural," these gestation and delivery experiences may be. Environmental forces are important in the etiology of twinning and the list of drugs alone indicates that the environment is by no means silent or benign during gestation. We have many questions about the impact of drugs on twins. For example, is the larger twin more stressed by drugs ingested by mother because he receives more blood-flow and hence more medication, or, to the contrary, is he less vulnerable because of his larger size and physiological maturity? We are now aware of the enduring behavioral effects of exposure to sex hormones during gestation

(Goy, 1968; Money and Ehrhardt, 1972; Yalom, Green, and Fisk, 1973) and of the teratogenic effects of other drugs such as thalidomide. What are the enduring and cumulative effects of all the drugs to which twins, born small and premature, are exposed?

The Childhood Personality Scale is an instrument for describing a child's general personality. It consists of 48 behavior items rated on a seven-point scale according to the degree to which the item accurately describes the child. Factor analysis has yielded five dimensions: behavior activity level (sample item: Does things vigorously); attention (Can pay attention for long times); social uninvolvement and irritability (Would rather be left alone); extroversion-introversion (Tries to strike up friendships); and positive verbal and emotional responses (Talks and acts happily and with excitement).

The Parent's Report is a complementary attitude instrument for description of the way a parent relates to a child. It also consists of 48 items rated on a seven-point scale according to the degree to which a behavioral description corresponds to the parent's perception of how he or she relates to the particular child. Factor analysis has led to five dimensions of parenting: respect for autonomy (I am aware of his need for privacy); child-centered (I think of things that will please him); control through guilt and anxiety (I keep reminding him of past bad behavior); enforcement of discipline (I see to it that he obeys what he is told); and control through anger and withdrawal of affection (I avoid talking to him after he displeases me) (Dibble and Cohen, 1973).

Parents' descriptions of a child depend on both the sex of the parent and the sex of the child. There were highly significant differences between mothers' descriptions of all children (boys and girls combined) and fathers' descriptions of all children, between mothers' descriptions of daughters and fathers' descriptions of daughters, and between mothers' descriptions of sons and fathers' descriptions of sons. Generally, girls are described as more person-oriented and talkative and boys as more vigorous and active. And fathers tend to see their children in extremes, either very active or very passive, whereas mothers see their children as being concerned with feelings.

Mothers and fathers also differ in their descriptions of their relationships with children. Mothers tend to feel close and child-centered; fathers, oriented toward discipline and punishment. It appears to us that these statistically significant differences in descriptions by fathers and mothers of their sons and daughters may reflect not only cultural adaptations, but biological phenomena associated with the greater comfort and attentiveness and the better health of the girls.

The First Month of Life Scale, a measure of a child's newborn competence, is an elaboration of the First-Week Evaluation Scale. It consists of six variables scored by parents concerning the child's attention, calmness, vigor, physiological adaptation, general health, and overall development. The First-Month Endowment score correlates very well with birthweight ($r = 0.481$, $p < 0.001$) and length of gestation ($r = 0.347$, $p < 0.001$), indicating that more mature and heavier infants are better endowed during the first month of life. As would be predicted, length of gestation and birthweight are also correlated ($r = 0.484$, $p < 0.001$). Taken together, First-Month Endowment score, weight, and length of gestation are a powerful triad of predictors of later competence.

The First-Month Endowment score correlates with a range of childhood personality characteristics (as derived from the Childhood Personality Scale) and parental patterns of behavior (as reported in the Parent's Report) compiled for twins who ranged in age from one to six years. For example, first-month competence correlates positively with ratings of attention and negatively with both hyperactivity and social uninvolvement and irritability. Birthweight is also negatively correlated with hyperactivity. Fathers use little control, through guilt and anxiety, in disciplining children with poor newborn endowment. Mothers are strict in their enforcement of discipline with children who were healthier newborns. And parents rate themselves as being more child-centered in relation to children who were born prematurely than they do for other children.

The relationships between early measures of competence and later differences in functioning are most apparent when the two children in a twinship are compared. Parents of twins can describe subtle differences between two children who share the same social class, family, age, and other variables, and thus who can serve as each other's matched control. Analysis of variance with a repeated-measure design is statistically well suited to handle such intrapair comparisons. Generally, in a twinship the best-endowed newborn becomes the more attentive preschooler, whereas the less well endowed newborn becomes the more hyperactive one. This natural history, clear even in MZ twinships, is most obvious when the effects of sex are compounded with those of early endowment in a boy-girl twinship where the girl is healthier as a newborn.

The results with twins can probably be extended to singletons: newborns who are well endowed appear to become those preschoolers who are attentive and for whom parents are consistent in the enforcement of discipline. Poorly endowed infants are likely to become preschoolers who are hyperactive and with whom parents see themselves as using control though guilt and anxiety. These results are easily integrated with the studies on the origins of severe psychopathology done by Lidz, Fleck, Wynne, Jackson, and the NIMH group cited previously.

EXPERIENCE AND PHYSIOLOGY:
METABOLIC STUDIES OF DISORDERED DEVELOPMENT

Concepts such as endowment, arousal, and stress have been used to bridge psychological and biological research (Offer and Freedman, 1972). Crossing this bridge has been made increasingly comfortable and attractive by recent advances in neurophysiology, biochemistry, developmental endocrinology, and physiological psychology (D. X. Freedman and Giarman, 1963; Kuhlin and Reiter, 1973; P. MacLean, 1969; N. Miller, 1971; Money and Ehrhardt, 1972; Olds, 1959; Schildkraut and Kety, 1967). These advances suggest ways in which models for relating endowment, as observed in clinical and psychological studies, can be understood in molecular terms. Since the empirical work to be discussed here focuses on the role of biogenic amines in childhood psychopathology, this area will be emphasized in the discussion. But it would be naïve to assume that the search for biological understanding of endowment, especially in relation to the modulation of distress and the development of attention, will end with this one group of chemicals.

As currently understood, central nervous system (CNS) neural activity involves the release by nerve cells of different neurotransmitters, which cross the synaptic gap and stimulate other nerve cells to fire (Axelrod and Weinshilboum, 1972; Cotten, 1972). Following release, the neurotransmitter either undergoes active reuptake (by the presynaptic neuron) or is metabolized into an inactive substance by an enzyme. The neurotransmitters that have been most studied are biogenic amines: catecholamines (norepinephrine [NE] and dopamine [DA] and an indoleamine (serotonin or 5-hydroxytryptamine [5-HT]). These biogenic amines are widely distributed in the brain, and norepinephrine and dopamine are most concentrated in the hypothalamus.

In the 1950s, reserpine was found to make certain individuals depressed and to lower the levels of biogenic amines. In the 1960s, monoamine oxidase inhibitors, which increase amines, were found to be useful in the treatment of certain depressed patients. Related studies led to the biogenic amine hypothesis of affective disorders: manic states are the result of increased biogenic amines; depressed states, of decreased (Schildkraut, 1970). This hypothesis has broad heuristic value (Curzon, 1972). For example, amphetamines, which are useful in the treatment of hyperkinetic behavioral disturbances in children, generally increase arousal, inhibit neuronal reuptake of norepinephrine and dopamine, and also release norepinephrine. The effect of amphetamines can thus be understood as the result of increasing the availability of biogenic amines in brain centers concerned with attention.

Monoamine oxidase (MAO) is the major enzyme involved in the degradation of biogenic amines and thus plays a central role in the regulation of neurotransmitter activity. Abnormalities of MAO have been found in psychiatric patients. For example, MAO appears to be reduced in both individuals in a twinship discordant for schizophrenia. In the schizophrenic individual, however, levels are lower than in the normal co-twin (R. J. Wyatt et al., 1973). Reduction of MAO may thus represent one aspect of genetic vulnerability to severe psychopathology.

Dopamine beta hydroxylase (DBH) also plays a regulatory role as the enzyme which converts dopamine (DA) to norepinephrine (NE). Elevations of DBH occur during stress as a reflection of increased autonomic activity (Weinshilboum et al., 1973; Wooten and Cardon, 1973), and the enzyme appears to be reduced in the brains of adults with schizophrenia (Wise and Stein, 1973). Assay of DBH offers a direct method for estimating nervous system arousal, an individual's perception of stress, or possibly an individual's susceptibility to severe psychopathology. The potential of such a biochemical probe is only now being exploited with children.

Metabolic breakdown products of biogenic amines can be measured in the cerebrospinal fluid (CSF). Most is known about 5-hydroxyindoleacetic acid (5-HIAA), the derivative of serotonin, and homovanillic acid (HVA), the metabolite of dopamine. The concentration of amine metabolites in the CSF represents a state of balance between formation of the metabolites and their active removal from the CSF (M. Bowers, Heninger, and Gerbode, 1969). This active transport can be partially blocked by probenecid administration. As the CSF probenecid concentration increases, the levels of biogenic amines in the CSF become increasingly independent of the level of probenecid and probably increasingly reflect the actual rate of biogenic amine formation. Analyses of CSF amine metabolites following membrane blockade by probenecid thus provide a measure of brain amine turnover and, distally, of brain function.

As part of an intensive study of physiological and behavioral disturbances in children with neuropsychiatric disorders, we have analyzed the biogenic amine metabolism of about 40 children from the following subgroups: childhood psychosis (autism and atypical development), severe hyperkinetic behavioral disturbance (with and without what we call motor control system dysfunction of minimal cerebral dysfunction), epilepsy, and movement disorders. Although I use these clinical labels out of necessity, a major motivation for the research is the sense that in fundamental ways several of the clinical disturbances may eventually best be understood as representing one

[5]These biological studies represent a close collaboration with Dr. Bennett Shaywitz, a pediatric neurologist. The analysis of CSF biogenic amine metabolites has been performed by Malcolm Bowers, Yale University School of Medicine, and of MAO by Dr. Richard Wyatt, NIMH, Bethesda, Maryland.

or several continua of developmental difficulties affecting primary neural mechanisms of organization.[5]

In our studies, children with these various clinical syndromes are intensively studied as outpatients and during research hospitalization. Detailed neurological, psychiatric, and psychological assessment; endocrine, genetic, and ophthalmological evaluation; and a broad range of screening tests are performed. After 12-hour probenecid blockade, CSF is obtained (by lumbar puncture) for routine analysis and determination of amine metabolites (5-HIAA and HVA) and probenecid.

We have separated children with psychotic conditions with onset during the first years of life into two related subgroups: autistic (10 children) and atypical (10 children). The autistic children are distinguished from atypical children by their much greater disturbances in social relatedness and language use and comprehension, and they meet Lotter's major criteria for autism (Hingtgen and Bryson, 1972). In addition, the atypical children have been found to have more markedly abnormal electroencephalograms, more gestational problems, and more stressed families. The 10 children with epilepsy all have severe grand mal seizure disorders. The five with movement disorders have Huntington's chorea and other diseases of the basal ganglia.

At school age there appears to be a significant difference between autistic and atypical children's HVA and 5-HIAA. Autistic children have lower values for both biogenic amine metabolites. Children with epilepsy have lower levels than both groups of psychotic children. Multivariate analysis statistically suggests that there are three distinct groups.

Although the number of children with motor diseases and minimal motor control system dysfunction we have studied is still small, it appears that there is a progression of biogenic amines from severe epilepsy, through severe motor diseases, autism, atypical development, and then minimal motor control system dysfunction (MBD) (D. J. Cohen et al., 1973a; Shaywitz, Cohen, and Bowers, 1973).

The CNS biogenic amines of autistic and atypical children cover a broad range, with considerable overlap, as one would predict if these two conditions represent two regions on a spectrum of developmental disability (Fish, 1973). There are individual children whose biogenic amines markedly deviate from the mean in both directions. Similarly, MAO in these children spans a broad range, from quite low to very high.

There are numerous technical and methodological problems in studies such as these. Such problems include the definition of syndromes and states; the interaction between syndrome or condition and treatment or treatment history; the ambiguity involved in deciding on an appropriate diagnosis for an evolving condition (as in the familiar case of a child who has been classically autistic, but who, at the time of study, appears as a verbal, odd child with severe obsessive-compulsive symptoms and a pervasive schizoidlike personality pattern disturbance); and the artifacts introduced by the stress of the research. Yet chemical and physiological facts may help clarify questions about diagnosis and sharpen clinical classification and observation.

It will be difficult to define normal values for some parameters because the need for lumbar puncture raises ethical and practical limitations. Thus, we rely on data from small numbers of children (e.g., on values obtained from the rare child who has a spinal fluid examination without any CNS symptoms or disorder) and on the use of relevant contrast groups (e.g., contrasts involving autistic, retarded, or brain-damaged children; autistic children with no motor lag or gross brain damage; atypical children; children with late-onset psychosis; children with hyperkinetic behavioral disturbance with and without signs of motor control system dysfunction). The necessary control and contrast group information, just as the other basic data, will have to be acquired within the field of child psychiatry. Developmental changes make it unwise to rely on values from adults, and techniques have to be adapted to fit our special circumstances and the fascinating, but perplexing developmental issues presented by childhood disturbances (Anthony, 1973).

Recently, Stein (1971) and Wise and Stein (1973) have hypothesized that progressive deterioration of central noradrenergic pathways may be the basis for adult schizophrenia. These pathways are vitally involved in the autoregulation of pleasure and thus in the direction and drive of intentional, goal-directed behavior (Olds, 1962), as well as in the regulation of physiological functions such as eating (Ahlskog and Hoebel, 1973; N. Miller, 1971, pp. 717–737). Dopaminergic pathways have also been linked with schizophrenia. Stevens (1973) has suggested that these pathways, by serving as a central "gating mechanism," are involved in preventing an individual from being overwhelmed by excessive internal or external stimulation. Dopaminergic dysfunction, she hypothesizes, may lead to excessive fearfulness, feelings of unreality, and alterations in attention and perception.

These noradrenergic and dopaminergic neurophysiological models may be relevant to the understanding of clinical observations discussed earlier, such as the infant's modulation of anxiety by sucking. Sucking, as we have seen, is an innately organized capacity in which regular, rhythmic motor activity reduces arousal or raises the threshold to stimulation. The capacity shows marked individual variation and may be much diminished in brain-damaged and other developmentally disabled children. Because of their prominence in the autoregulation of pleasure and modulation of stimulus strength, dopaminergic and noradrenergic pathways may play central roles in the process by which feedback from the neurologically organized sucking system modulates activity in another organized system, the control of attention and arousal. The reverberating itch-scratch circuit of the infant and child with severe eczema is perhaps an illustration of a feedback system run amuck. Here, as with normal sucking, paroxysmal motor behavior (scratching) briefly reduces anxiety and produces pleasure. However, in contrast with sucking, the relief produced by scratching is transient and is followed by increased drive, distress, and arousal.

Based on studies of animals (Olds, 1962) and adult schizophrenics (Stein, 1971), on the theoretical considerations developed about anxiety or arousal in relation to sucking, eczema, and individual competence, and on our observation of apparently reduced biogenic amines in at least some autistic children, it may be useful to hypothesize that noradrenergic, dopaminergic, or a combination of biogenic amine systems, may be involved in the etiology of childhood autism and other severe developmental disabilities. To a greater degree than adults with schizophrenia, children with autism display profoundly disorganized behavior, disturbances in learning and the appreciation of pleasure and pain, unreasonable anxiety, oddities of appetite, abnormal arousal (Hutt et al., 1965), and perceptual instability (Ornitz and Ritvo, 1968). If biogenic amine disturbances are involved in autism and atypical development, it would be particularly interesting to analyze the response of these children to loading with the precursors of important amines (such as DOPA or tryptophan). Metabolic studies of this type may be more revealing in elucidating the psychoses of early childhood, which in some ways resemble inborn errors of metabolism, than they have been in the study of psychosis in adults (R. J. Wyatt, Termini, and David, 1971).

The interactions between developmental trends involving biogenic amines and concomitant alterations in other domains (such as the endocrine system) are of particular interest to child psychiatrists. Two theoretically intriguing observations have emerged from our studies. First, we have been surprised by the apparent lability of serum thyrozine in autistic and atypical children. Changes of over 100%, from hypothyroid to hyperthyroid levels, have been observed in several children who show no obvious signs of endocrine disorder. Second, it appears that the level of plasma thyroxine is inversely correlated with the rate of production of biogenic amines in the CNS, a finding which is consistent with the concept that one physiological function of thyroxine is to sensitize neurons to the effect of biogenic amines (see Cotten, 1972, pp. 365–430, esp. pp. 365–369; Emlen, Segal, and Mandell, 1972).

Similarly, the therapeutic effectiveness of imipramine—a tricyclic antidepressant useful in treating certain forms of adult depression, nocturnal enuresis in children, and narcolepsy—may be related to its effect in blocking the reuptake of biogenic amines and making more biogenic amines functionally available. Interestingly, thyroxine potentiates the action of imipramine in the treatment of depression, just as amphetamine potentiates the action of imipramine in the treatment of narcolepsy (A. J. Coppen et al., 1972; Prange et al., 1972; Zarcone, 1973). Triiodothyronine has been used, with encouraging results, in the treatment of childhood autism (Campbell et al., 1972). It is interesting, however, that amphetamines, which may be useful in the treatment of hyperkinetic behavioral disturbances, almost uniformly make children with severe atypical development such as childhood autism much worse (Fish, 1971; and our observations). This effect of amphetamines, and of methylphenidate, appears similar to their effect in adults with psychosis (Janowsky et al., 1973). Apparently, in individuals already operating at a high level of arousal or already quite anxious, the addition of amphetamines may lead not to increased attention and alertness, but to disorganization. The efficacy of thyroxine, therefore, must result from activity in a localized area or subsystem as distinct from the more generalized effect on biogenic amines produced by amphetamine. Or, as one might predict from animal studies and clinical observations of patients with hyperthyroidism, there may be complex, dose-response relationships. At high doses, thyroxine, like the stimulants, may lead to overarousal, hyperacuity, anxiety, and behavioral disorganization.

At this point we are already well into the arena of speculation. But, cautious that we do not mistake fantasy for reality, perhaps we could hypothesize several steps further. Could it not be possible that some children with severe atypical development suffer from a complex imbalance affecting both biogenic amines and the hypothalamic control of thyroxine? Our data suggest that there is a reciprocal relation between the rate of formation of brain biogenic amines and levels of thyroxine, a finding which is consistent with physiological evidence (Landsberg and Axelrod, 1968). Thus, children may be able to tolerate fluctuations or even abnormally low functioning in one system if there are compensatory adaptations in another. Might such adaptive mechanisms be aberrant in autistic and atypical children? For example, if labile levels of serum thyroxine are not accompanied by appropriate alterations in biogenic amine formation, is it possible that there may be transient or prolonged disturbances in brain function and psychological processes involved in perception, thinking, or the regulation of anxiety? There are some suggestive clinical and experimental data related to this possibility.

Abnormal hypothalamic-pituitary findings have been reported in conditions such as psychosocial deprivational dwarfism and anorexia nervosa, two conditions concerned with modulation of anxiety, organization of behavior, and regulation of appetite (G. Wolff and Money, 1973). These perhaps also involve the noradrenergic pathways discussed previously. There are many sensitive relationships between endocrine function and catecholamine metabolism, and endocrine-biogenic amine interactions may be of profound importance in understanding autism and other severe disturbances of development. (For an example of the influence of hormones on norepinephrine formation, see Landsberg and Axelrod, 1968; see also Frohman, 1972.) We should expect to find disturbances throughout the neuroendocrine axis: in the pituitary-adrenal axis, because of its sensitivity to stress (Mason, 1968); in the regulation of growth hormone, which is sensitive to hypothalamic and high cortical control involving biogenic amines, and whose actions are extremely diffuse (J. Martin, 1973); and in the sex hormones, which have important behavioral significance from early pregnancy (Goy, 1968; Money and Ehrhardt, 1972; Prunty and Gardiner-Hill, 1972). These last hormones provide an interesting example of the complexity of the systems of behavioral disability with which we are concerned. Severe childhood eczema, colic, hyperkinetic behavioral disturbance, and childhood autism are all found in much higher incidence (three of four times higher) in boys than in girls. Such a profound sex difference must arouse curiosity about the interactions between androgens and biogenic amines and the enduring effects on development of early exposure to high doses of sex hormones. To understand these hormonal systems in atypical development requires study of dynamic functioning of the hypothalamic-pituitary glandular systems in these children and not just determination of static levels of hormones.

Finally, would it not be consistent with our current understanding of human behavior genetics if the parents of children with severe atypical development—on the basis perhaps of metabolic disturbances which create increased arousal and tendency to anxious disorganization—were themselves at the upper end of the curve in relation to the same phenomena? If this were so, one might expect that the parents of autistic children would be unusually sensitive, alert, and intelligent, perhaps as a reflection of their abnormal regulation of biogenic amines (or whatever other complex biochemical subsystems eventually emerge as underlying the children's developmental disabilities) and their resultant defenses and coping mechanisms. Such increased sensitivity and arousal may have important adaptive significance, which may account for the continuation of the genotype in the population, but an "overdose" of the gene or genes (as in a homozygous individual or one with heavy polygenic loading) or the combination of the genotype with other predisposing vulnerabilities (such as neonatal stress or abnormalities affecting other systems) may lead to the expressed disease. In fact, the parents and siblings of autistic children do appear to be of more than average intelligence (Rutter, 1971a). And it is interesting that similar clinical observations have been made about families of patients with dystonia musculorum deformans, another condition which has been linked with biogenic amine metabolism.

Pollin and Stabenau (1968) intensively studied adult twins discordant for schizophrenia. In their series, the sick twin was distinguished by two major physiological findings: the sick twin had lower levels of thyroid hormone (as measured by protein-bound iodine), and the sick twin was the lighter child at birth. These observations about the vulnerability to schizophrenia close the circle of our considerations and return us to twins, competence, and our main theme: What model can now guide us in our clinical investigations? How do physiology and experience interact?

MIND AND BODY: MODEL FOR INVESTIGATORS

As researchers, we are interested in models that give coherence to isolated observations and guide us into fertile fields. In this essay I have introduced dimensions or components of a multivariate model which, although broadly appreciated, seem only rarely to be brought together in the study of vulnerable children. Let us quickly review some of these main components in the model.

The model's starting point is the child's *genome*, the sum total of his genetic inheritance, which always contains far more potentiality than is ever expressed phenotypically. The true reaction ranges for most traits—the range of values permitted by a genotype—are really not known, and any estimates about the degree of genetic programming of complex characteristics such as intelligence are thus quite hazardous. Yet studies of twins provide compelling evidence of how powerful genes may be in human development (Hirsch, 1963).

As a result of the genome and prenatal and neonatal experiences, children are born with differing *congenital endowments*—the constellation of processes underlying equanimity, attention, vigor, physical health, and neurological functioning—and thus differing thresholds for the elicitation and disorganization of *congenitally organized behavior*. In basic and still unclear ways, congenital endowment and the congenital organization of behavior are patterned by complex biochemical interactions involving biogenic amines, hormones, and enzymes. In turn, the *early experiences* of a child—including nutrition, infection, drugs, and trauma of delivery—lead to enduring patterns of behavior encoded in central nervous system metabolism. For example, appropriate stimulation and optimal stress—as reflected perhaps by increases in dopamine beta hydroxylase, norepinephrine metabolites, and elevated thyroxine—may condition the nervous system in such a way that later novel situations are neither too overwhelming, nor totally blocked from attention. Even short-term exposure to some hormones at certain developmental phases—such as testosterone during gestation and early infancy—may lead to enduring patterns of behavior which contrast with those encoded in the genome. And long-term exposure to hormones—such as testosterone in XY chromosomal males with end-organ insensitivity and thus completely female external appearance—may lead to enduring patterns of behavior which contrast with those shaped by the environment (Goy, 1968; Sachs et al., 1973; Yalom, Green, and Fisk, 1973).

Arising from the *match between the child's endowment and the environment's provisions* are early adaptations and patterns of response and perception. These *persistent early adaptations*—such as the habitual fear or anxiety of the child with low threshold for disorganization—shape the child's later adaptations and style of approach to new developmental tasks. Behavioral patterns and hierarchies of action patterns in this way assume a type of autonomy which may become *crystallized characteristics of behavior* through social reinforcement (Bruner, 1973).

Stress can be defined two ways: from the nature of the objective changes in the child's environment and from the nature of the child's responses. Seen in the latter way, the concept of stress signifies the type and degree of functional disorganization produced by either environmental or internal stimulation (e.g., separation, discipline, or persistent itch). What for one child may be *optimal stimulation* leading to the *unfolding of congenitally organized behavior,* such as accommodation to the nipple or the mastery of new skills (such as sharing with a peer), may, for another child, with even the identical genome, be a stress leading to disorganization of behavior and inhibition of intentional activity.

The *threshold for perception of stimulation as stressful* or the *capacity to modulate distress* appears to be a basic dimension that cuts across or unites physiology and psychology, a dimension that underlies the disposition to experience excessive anxiety and to develop maladaptive defenses against it. The molecular foundation for this dimension may lie in the functional relationships between biogenic amines, hormones, and enzymes, systems which both affect experience and are affected by it (Goldberg and Welch, 1972; Henley, Moisset, and Welch, 1973). The interactions between genes, amines, and hormones (such as sex hormones), which are apparent in the personality differences between boys and girls and men and women, may become most clearly visible as we study the onset of adolescence and the frequent emotional upsets of this developmental phase (D. J. Cohen and Frank, 1973).

Parental impact on development occurs in many ways, including the following: contribution of genes; provision of prenatal environment; and structuring of the postnatal environment, including care, stimulation, and affection. Parents of children with disturbances in the modulation of distress may themselves suffer from similar disturbances, with both the parents' and the child's endowments reflecting similar processes involving the interaction between biogenic amines, hormones, and enzymes. In certain situations and when not present in too high a degree, there may be adaptive value for this increased sensitivity, which, when present at too high a level or in combination with other predisposing conditions, may lead to severe developmental disabilities.

It would be pleasant to be able to organize these and other social, cultural, and biological determinants of development into a more tightly ordered model. And it would be important to be more explicit about the detailed processes involved in learning and cognition, to spell out the relations between such domains as genetically controlled maturational processes and what is acquired through conditioning, and to clarify the social context of development. Yet even from the perspective of the fragmentary discussion and model presented here, I think it does seem likely that we will eventually be able to predict, for a population of children, the general shape of personality development and potential vulnerability based on equations containing expressions for genome, endowment, stress thresholds, experiences, early adaptations, and central nervous system dynamics. For the moment, however, the appetite for full clarity cannot be satisfied, and perhaps the major value of partial models such as the one I have sketched will be to guide us in designing studies containing a sufficiently broad array of relevant variables and to protect us from overenthusiasm in accepting any univariate equation or simple social intervention. That the model I have suggested appears to return to Freud's viewpoint on the central roles of anxiety, early structuralization, and disposition in human development should not be too disheartening for those who desire progress (Hartmann, 1964). Freud himself offered us consolation when he knowingly wrote (1924b): "One should never tire of considering the same phenomena again and again (or of submitting to their effects), and one should not mind meeting with contradiction on every side provided one has worked sincerely."

REFERENCES

Aaronson, E. & Tronick, E. (1970), Perceptual capacities in early infancy. In: *Human Development and Cognitive Processes*, ed. J. Elliot. New York: Holt, Rinehart & Winston.

Abraham, K. (1911), Notes on the psycho-analytical investigation and treatment of manic-depressive insanity and allied conditions. In: *Selected Papers*. New York: Basic Books, 1953, pp. 137–156.

———— (1924), A short study of the development of the libido, viewed in the light of mental disorders. In: *Selected Papers*. New York: Basic Books, 1953, pp. 418–501.

Abrahams, M. J. & Whitlock, F. A. (1969), Childhood experience and depression. *Brit. J. Psychiat.,* 115:883–888.

Abramowicz, M. (1969), Heights of 12-year-old Puerto Rican boys in New York City: Origins of differences. *Pediat.,* 43:427–429.

Ackerman, N. W. (1958), *The Psychodynamics of Family Life,* New York: Basic Books.

Adams, P. L. (1972a), Delayed sexual maturation in boys. *Med. Aspects Human Sexuality,* 6(4):34–57.

———— (1972b), Late sexual maturation in girls. *Med. Aspects Human Sexuality,* 6(3):50–75.

Adelson, J. (1971), The political imagination of the young adolescent. *Daedalus,* 100:1013–1050.

Adelson, L. (1961), Slaughter of the innocents. *New England J. Med.,* 264:1345–1349.

Ahlskog, J. E. & Hoebel, B. (1973), Overeating and obesity from damage to a noradrenergic system in the brain. *Science,* 182:166–169.

Ainsworth, M. D. S. (1962a), The effects of maternal deprivation: A review of findings and controversy in the context of research strategy. In: *Deprivation of Maternal Care: A Reassessment of Its Effects*. Public Health Paper No. 14. Geneva: World Health Organization.

———— (1962b), Reversible and irreversible effects of maternal deprivation on intellectual development. In: *Maternal Deprivation*. New York: Child Welfare League of America.

———— (1967), *Infancy in Uganda: Infant Care and the Growth of Love*. Baltimore: Johns Hopkins University Press.

———— (1969), Object relations, dependency and attachment: A theoretical review of the infant-mother relationship. *Child Devel.,* 40:969–1025.

Alexander, D., Ehrhardt, A. A. & Money, J. (1966), Defective figure drawing, geometric and human, in Turner's syndrome. *J. Nerv. Ment. Dis.,* 142:161–167.

———— & Money, J. (1965), Reading ability, object constancy and Turner's syndrome. *Percept. Motor Skills*, 20:981–984.

————— ————— (1966), Turner's syndrome and Gerstmann's syndrome: Neuropsychologic comparisons. *Neuropsychologia*, 4:265–273.

—————, Walker, H. T., Jr. & Money, J. (1964), Studies in direction sense, I: Turner's syndrome. *Arch. Gen. Psychiat.*, 10:337–339.

Alpert, A. (1941), The latency period. *Amer. J. Orthopsychiat.*, 11:126–133.

Ambrose, J. A. (1961), The development of the smiling response in early infancy. In: *Determinants of Infant Behavior*, Vol. 1, ed. B. M. Foss. New York: Wiley, pp. 179–201.

————— (1963), The age of onset of ambivalence in early infancy: Indications from the study of laughing. *J. Child Psychol. Psychiat.*, 4:167–181.

American Academy of Pediatrics, Committee on Adoptions (1971), Identity development in adopted children. *Pediat.*, 47:948–949.

American Medical Association, Committee on Human Sexuality (1972), *Human Sexuality*. Chicago: American Medical Association.

Ames, L. B. (1946), The development of the sense of time in the young child. *J. Genet. Psychol.*, 68:97–125.

Anders, T., Emde, R. N. & Parmelee, A. H., Eds. (1971), *A Manual of Standardized Terminology, Techniques and Criteria for Scoring States of Sleep and Wakefulness in Newborn Infants*. Los Angeles: UCLA Brain Information Service, NINDS Neurological Information Network.

Andry, R. G. (1960), *Delinquency and Parental Pathology*. London: Methuen.

Anthony, E. J. (1969), The reactions of adults to adolescents and their behavior. In: *Adolescents: Psychosocial Perspectives*, ed. G. Caplan & S. Lebovici. New York: Basic Books, pp. 54–78.

————— (1973), The state of the art and science in child psychiatry. *Arch. Gen. Psychiat.*, 29:299–313.

————— & Koupernik, C., Eds. (1970), *The Child in His Family*, Vol. 1. New York: Wiley.

Antoni, P. (1965), The tormented child syndrome. *Orv. Hetilap.*, 106:1934–1937.

Ariès, P. (1962), *Centuries of Childhood*. New York: Knopf.

Axelrod, J. & Weinshilboum, R. (1972), Catecholamines. *New England J. Med.*, 287:237–242.

Baers, M. (1954), Women workers and home responsibilities. *Intern. Lab. Rev.*, 69:338–355.

Baghdassarian, A. et al. (1975), Testicular function in XYY men. *John Hopkins Med. J.*, 136:15–24.

Baird, D. (1947), Social class and foetal mortality. *Lancet*, 253:531–535.

————— (1949), Social factors in obstetrics. *Lancet*, 1:1079–1083.

————— (1964), The epidemiology of prematurity. *J. Pediat.*, 65:909–924.

————— & Illsley, R. (1953), Environment and childbearing. *Proc. Roy. Soc. Med.*, 46:53–59.

Baittle, B. & Offer, D. (1971), On the nature of male adolescent rebellion. In: *Adolescent Psychiatry*, Vol. 1, ed. S. C. Feinstein, P. Giovacchini & A. A Miller. New York: Basic Books, pp. 139–160.

Baker, D. et al. (1970), Chromosome errors in men with Klinefelter's syndrome and XYY chromosome pattern. *J. Amer. Med. Assn.*, 214:869–878.

Baker, H. J. & Stoller, R. J. (1968), Can a biological force contribute to gender identity? *Amer. J. Psychiat.*, 124:1653–1658.

Bakwin, H. (1949), Emotional deprivation in infants. *J. Pediat.*, 35:512–521.

Bandura, A. (1969), Social-learning theory of identificatory processes. In: *Handbook of Socialization Theory and Research*, cd. D. A. Goslin. Chicago: Rand McNally.

Barbero, G., Morris, M. & Reford, M. (1963), Malidentification of mother, baby, father relationships expressed in infant failure to thrive. In: *The Neglected-Battered Child Syndrome*. New York: Child Welfare League of America.

Barnes, R. H. et al. (1968), Postnatal nutritional deprivations as determinants of adult behavior toward food, its consumption and utilization. *J. Nutr.*, 96:467–476.

Barrera-Moncada, G. (1963), *Estudios sobre alteraciones del crecimiento y del desarrollo psicologico del sindrome pluricarencial (kwashiorkor)*. Caracas: Editora Grafos.

Barry, H. (1949), Significance of maternal bereavement before the age of eight in psychiatric patients. *Arch. Neurol. Psychiat.*, 62:630–637.

Barry, W. A. (1970), Marriage research and conflict: An integrative review. *Psychol. Bull.*, 73:41–54.

Bateson, G. et al. (1956), Toward a theory of schizophrenia. *Behav. Sci.*, 1:251–264.

Bateson, M. C. (1971), The interpersonal context of infant vocalization. *MIT, Res. Lab. Electronics, Quart. Prog. Rep.*, 100:170–176.

Becker, W. C. (1964), Consequences of different kinds of parental discipline. In: *Review of Child Development Research*, Vol. 1, ed. M. L. Hoffman & L. W. Hoffman. New York: Russell Sage Foundation.

Beels, C. & Ferber, A. (1972), What family therapists do. In: *Psychiatric Treatment of the Child*, ed. J. F. McDermott, Jr. & S. I. Harrison. New York: Aronson, 1977, pp. 515–555.

Bcit-Hallahmi, B. et al. (1974), Grammatical gender and gender identity development: Cross cultural and cross lingual implications. *Amer. J. Orthopsychiat.*, 44:424–431.

Bekker, F. J. & van Gemund, J. J. (1968), Mental retardation and cognitive defects in XO-Turner's syndrome. *Maandschr. Kindergeneeskunde*, 36:148–156.

Bell, R. Q. (1964), The effect on the family of a limitation in coping ability in a child: A research approach and a finding. *Merrill-Palmer Quart.*, 10:129–142.

——— (1968), A reinterpretation of the direction of effects in studies of socialization. *Psychol. Rev.*, 75:81–95.

———, Weller, G. & Waldrop, M. F. (1971), Newborn and preschooler: Organization of bchavior and relations between periods. *Monogr. Soc. Res. Child Devel.*, 142(36):1–2.

Bender, L. (1938), A Visual-Motor Gestalt Test and Its Clinical Use. Research Monograph No. 3. New York: American Orthopsychiatric Association.

Bender, M. (1952), *Disorders in Perception, with Particular Reference to the Phenomena of Extinction and Displacement*. Springfield, Ill.: Thomas.

Bencdek, T. (1938), Adaptation to reality in early infancy. *Psychoanal. Quart.*, 7:200–215.

——— (1949), The psychosomatic implications of the primary unit: Mother-child. *Amer. J. Orthopsychiat.*, 19:642–654.

——— (1952), *Psychosexual Functions in Women*. New York: Ronald Press.

——— (1956a), Psychobiological aspects of mothering. *Amer. J. Orthopsychiat.*, 26:272–278.

——— (1956b), Toward the biology of the depressive constellation. *J. Amer. Psy-*

choanal. Assn., 4:389–427.

———— (1959), Parenthood as a developmental phase: A contribution to the libido theory. *J. Amer. Psychoanal. Assn.*, 7:389–417.

———— (1970), The family as a psychologic field. In: *Parenthood: Its Psychology and Psychopathology*, ed. E. J. Anthony & T. Benedek. Boston: Little, Brown, pp. 109–136.

———— & Rubenstein, B. B. (1942), The sexual cycle in women: The relation between ovarian function and psychodynamic processes. *Psychosomatic Medicine Monographs*, Vol. 3, No.1/2. Washington, D.C.: National Research Council.

Benirschke, K. & Kim, C. (1973), Multiple pregnancy, I, II. *New England J. Med.*, 288:1276–1284, 1329–1336.

Benjamin, H. (1966), *The Transsexual Phenomenon*. New York: Julian Press.

Benjamin, J. D. (1961a), The innate and the experiential in child development. In: *Childhood Psychopathology*, ed. S. I. Harrison & J. F. McDermott., Jr. New York: International Universities Press, 1972, pp. 2–19.

———— (1961b), Some developmental observations related to the theory of anxiety. *J. Amer. Psychoanal. Assn.*, 9:652–668.

———— (1963), Further comments on some developmental aspects of anxiety. In: *Counterpoint: Libidinal Object and Subject*, ed. H. S. Gaskill. New York: International Universities Press, pp. 121–153.

Benton, A. L. (1940), Mental development of prematurely born children: A critical review of the literature. *Amer. J. Orthopsychiat.*, 10:719–746.

Berger, M. & Passingham, R. E. (1971), Early experience and other environmental factors: An overview. In: *Handbook of Abnormal Psychology*, 2nd Ed., ed. H. J. Eysenck. San Diego: Knapp, 1973.

Bergström, R. M. (1969), Electrical parameters of the brain during ontogeny. In: *Brain and Early Behaviour*, ed. R. J. Robinson. London: Academic Press, pp. 15–41.

Berko, J. (1960), The acquisition of grammatical categories in children. *Word*, 16:287.

Berman, E. (1976), Presentation to Annual Meeting of American Psychiatric Association, Miami, Fla.

Bernard, R. M. (1952), The shape and size of the female pelvis. *Transact. Edinburgh Obstet. Soc., Edinburgh Med. J.*, 59(2):1–16.

Bernstein, B. (1961), Social class and linguistic development: A theory of social learning. In: *Education, Economy and Society*, ed. A Halsey et al. New York: Free Press.

Bevan, W. & Freeman, O. I. (1952), Some effects of an amino acid deficiency upon the performance of albino rats in a simple maze. *J. Genet. Psychol.*, 80:75–82.

Bieber, I. et al. (1962), *Homosexuality: A Psychoanalytic Study*. New York: Basic Books.

Birch, H. G. (1971), Malnutrition and early development. In: *Day Care: Resources for Decisions*, ed. E. Grotberg. Washington, D.C.: Office of Economic Opportunity, Office of Planning, Research and Evaluation, Experimental Research Division, pp. 340–372.

———— & Belmont, L. (1964), Auditory-visual integration in normal and retarded readers. *Amer. J. Orthopsychiat.*, 44:852–861.

———— ———— (1965), Auditory-visual integration, intelligence and reading ability in school children. *Percept. Motor Skills*, 20:295–305.

———— & Cravioto, J. (1968), Infection, nutrition and environment in mental development. In: *The Prevention of Mental Retardation Through the Control of Infectious Disease,* ed. H. F. Eichenwald. Public Health Service Publication No. 1962. Washington, D.C.: U.S. Government Printing Office.

———— & Gussow, J. D. (1970), *Disadvantaged Children: Health, Nutrition and School Failure.* New York: Harcourt, Brace, Jovanovich.

———— & Lefford, A. (1963), Intersensory development in children. *Monogr. Soc. Res. Child Devel.,* 28:1–48.

———— ———— (1964), Two strategies for studying perception in "brain-damaged" children. In: *Brain Damage in Children,* ed. H. G. Birch. Baltimore: Williams & Wilkins.

———— et al. (1971), Kwashiorkor in early childhood and intelligence at school age. *Pediat. Res.,* 5:579–585.

Birdwhistell, R. L. (1962), *Introduction to Kinesics.* Washington, D.C.: Department of State, Foreign Service Institute.

Birrell, R. & Birrell, J. (1968), The maltreatment syndrome in children: A hospital survey. *Med. J. Australia,* 522:1023–1029.

Birtchnell, J. (1969), The possible consequences of early parent death. *Brit. J. Med. Psychol.,* 42:1–12.

———— (1970), Depression in relation to early and recent parent death. *Brit. J. Psychiat.,* 116:299–306.

Blank, M. (1965), The use of the deaf in language studies. *Psychol. Bull.,* 63:442–444.

Blau, A. et al. (1963), The psycho-etiology of premature births. *Psychosom. Med.,* 25:201–211.

Blau, S. (1977), Letter to the editor. *Amer. J. Psychiat.,* 134:210–211.

Blinkov, S. M. & Glezer, I. (1964), *The Human Brain in Figures and Tables.* New York: Basic Books, 1968.

Blos, P. (1962a), *On Adolescence: A Psychoanalytic Interpretation.* New York: Free Press.

———— (1962b), Puberty and adolescence. In: *Childhood Psychopathology,* ed. S. I. Harrison & J. F. McDermott, Jr. New York: International Universities Press, 1972, pp. 221–233.

———— (1967), The second individuation process of adolescence. *The Psychoanalytic Study of the Child,* 22:162–186. New York: International Universities Press.

Boas, F. (1910), *Changes in the Bodily Form of Descendants of Immigrants.* Immigration Commission Document No. 208. Washington, D.C.: U.S. Government Printing Office.

Bogoch, S. (1957), Cerebrospinal fluid neuraminic acid deficiency in schizophrenia. *Amer. J. Psychiat.,* 114:172.

Bohman, M. (1970), *Adopted Children and Their Families. A Follow-up Study of Adopted Children, Their Background, Environment and Adjustment.* Stockholm: Proprius.

———— (1972), On a study of adopted children, their background, environment and adjustment. *Acta Paediat. Scand.,* 61:90–97.

Boisvert, M. (1972), The battered child syndrome. *Soc. Casework,* 53:475–480.

Bolton, K. (1964), *The Premenstrual Syndrome.* Springfield, Ill.: Thomas.

Bonnard, A. (1958), Pre-body-ego types of (pathological) mental functioning. *J. Amer. Psychoanal. Assn.,* 6:581–611.

———— (1961), Truancy and pilfering associated with bereavement. In: *Adolescents: A Psychoanalytic Approach to Problems and Therapy,* ed. S. Lorand & H. I.

Schneer. New York: Hoeber, pp. 152–179.

Bornstein, B. (1951), On latency. *The Psychoanalytic Study of the Child*, 6:279–285. New York: International Universities Press.

Botha-Antoun, E., Babayan, S. & Harfouche, J. K. (1968), Intellectual development relating to nutritional status. *J. Trop. Pediat.*, 14:112–115.

Boutourline-Young, H. (1962), Epidemiology of dental caries: Results from a cross-cultural study in adolescents of Italian descent. *New England J. Med.*, 267:843–849.

Bowen, M. (1966), The use of family theory in clinical practice. *Compr. Psychiat.*, 7:345–374.

———— (1974a), Societal regression as viewed through family systems theory. Presented to Nathan W. Ackerman Memorial Conference, Venezuela, Feb.

———— (1974b), Toward the differentiation of one's family of origin. In: *Georgetown Symposium Papers I*, ed. F. Andres & J. Lorio. Washington, D.C.: Georgetown University Press.

———— (1975), Family therapy after twenty years. In: *American Handbook of Psychiatry*, Vol. 5, ed. J. Dyrud & D. Freedman. New York: Basic Books.

———— (1978), *Family Therapy in Clinical Practice*. New York: Aronson.

Bower, T. G. (1966), Visual world of infants. *Sci. Amer.*, 215:80–92.

Bowers, M., Heninger, G. R. & Gerbode, F. (1969), Cerebrospinal fluid 5-hydroxyindoleacetic acid and homovanillic acid in psychiatric patients. *Internat. J. Neuropharm.*, 8:255–262.

Bowers, W. et al. (1970), The effects of obstetrical medication on fetus and infant. *Monogr. Soc. Res. Child Devel.*, 137(35):4.

Bowlby, J. (1944), Forty-four juvenile thieves. *Internat. J. Psycho-Anal.*, 25:19–53, 107–128.

———— (1946), *Forty-Four Juvenile Thieves: Their Characters and Home-Life*. London: Ballière, Tindall & Cox.

———— (1951), *Maternal Care and Mental Health*. World Health Organization Monograph No. 2. Geneva: World Health Organization.

———— (1958a), The nature of the child's tie to his mother. *Internat. J. Psycho-Anal.*, 39:350–373.

———— (1958b), Separation of mother and child. *Lancet*, 1:480, 1070.

———— (1960), Grief and mourning in infancy and early childhood. *The Psychoanalytic Study of the Child*, 15:9–52. New York: International Universities Press.

———— (1961a), Childhood mourning and its implications for psychiatry. In: *Childhood Psychopathology*, ed. S. I. Harrison & J. F. McDermott, Jr. New York: International Universities Press, 1972, pp. 263–289.

———— (1961b), Processes of mourning. *Internat. J. Psycho-Anal.*, 42:317–340.

———— (1962), Childhood bereavement and psychiatric illness. In: *Aspects of Psychiatric Research*, ed. D. Richter et al. New York: Oxford University Press, pp. 262–293.

———— (1963), Pathological mourning and childhood mourning. *J. Amer. Psychoanal. Assn.*, 11:500–541.

———— (1968), Effects on behavior of disruption of an affectional bond. In: *Genetic and Environmental Influences on Behaviour*, ed. J. M. Thoday & A. S. Parker. Edinburgh: Oliver & Boyd.

———— (1969), *Attachment and Loss*, Vol. 1. New York: Basic Books.

———— (1973), *Attachment and Loss*, Vol. 2. New York: Basic Books.

————— & Parkes, C. M. (1970), Separation and loss within the family. In: *The Child in His Family*, Vol. 1, ed. E. J. Anthony & C. Koupernik. New York: Wiley.

————— et al. (1956), The effects of mother-child separation: A follow-up study. *Brit. J. Med. Psychol.*, 29:211–247.

Boyd-Orr, J. (1936), *Food, Health and Income*. London: Macmillan.

Brackbill, Y. (1958), Extinction of the smiling response in infants as a function of reinforcement schedule. *Child Devel.*, 29:115–124.

————— et al. (1966), Arousal level in neonates and preschool children under continuous auditory stimulation. *J. Exper. Child Psychol.*, 4:178–188.

Brazelton, T. B. (1961), Psychophysiologic reaction in the neonate, II: The effects of maternal medication on the neonate and his behavior. *J. Pediat.*, 58:513–518.

————— (1973), *Neonatal Behavioral Assessment Scale*. National Spastics Society Monograph. London: Heineman.

————— et al. (1975), Early mother-infant reciprocity. In: *Ciba Foundation Symposium 33, Parent-Infant Interaction*. New York: Associated Scientific Publishers.

Brill, N. Q. & Liston, E. H. (1966), Parental loss in adults with emotional disorders. *Arch. Gen. Psychiat.*, 14:307–314.

Briscoe, C. W. et al. (1973), Divorce and psychiatric disease. *Arch. Gen. Psychiat.*, 29:119–125.

Brock, J. (1961), *Advances in Human Nutrition*. London: Churchill.

Brodbeck, A. J. & Irwin, O. C. (1946), The speech behavior of infants without families. *Child Devel.*, 17:145–146.

Brodie, H. K. et al. (1974), Plasma testosterone levels in heterosexual and homosexual men. *Amer. J. Psychiat.*, 131:82–83.

Brody, S. & Axelrad, S. (1970), *Anxiety and Ego Formation in Infancy*. New York: International Universities Press.

Bronfenbrenner, U. (1961), Some family antecedents of responsibility and leadership in adolescents. In: *Leadership and Interpersonal Behavior*, ed. L. Petrullio & B. M. Bass. New York: Holt.

Brown, D. (1956), Sex role preference in young children. *Psychol. Monogr.*, 70 (14):1–19.

Brown, F. (1961), Depression and childhood bereavement. *J. Ment. Sci.*, 107:754–777.

————— (1966), Childhood bereavement and subsequent psychiatric disorder. *Brit. J. Psychiat.*, 112:1035–1041.

Brown, G. W. & Rutter, M. (1966), The measurement of family activities and relationships—a methodological study. *Human Rel.*, 19:241–263.

Brown, J. & Daniels, R. (1968), Some observations on abusive parents. *Child Welfare*, 47:89–94.

Brown, R. (1958), *Words and Things*. New York: Free Press.

————— (1964), The acquisition of language. In: *Disorders of Communication*, ed. D. McK. Riach & E. A. Weinstein. *Res. Publ. Assn. Nerv. Ment. Dis.*, 42:56.

————— & Bellugi, U. (1964), Three processes in the child's acquisition of syntax. *Harvard Ed. Rev.*, 34:133.

Bruner, J. (1971), The uses of immaturity. Presented at Harvard Graduate School of Education, Cambridge, Mass.

————— (1973), Organization of early skilled action. *Child Devel.*, 44:1–11.

—————, May, A. & Koslowski, B. (1972), *The Intention to Take: A Film*. New York: Wiley.

Bühler, C. & Hetzer, H. (1935), *Testing Children's Development from Birth to School*

Age. New York: Farrar & Rinehart.
———— & Massarik, F., Eds. (1968), *The Course of Human Life*. New York: Springer.
Bullard, D. M. et al. (1967), Failure to thrive in the "neglected" child. *Amer. J. Orthopsychiat.*, 37:680–690.
Bulmer, M. G. (1970), *The Biology of Twinning in Man*. Oxford: Clarendon Press.
Burchinal, L. G. (1964), Characteristics of adolescents from unbroken, broken, and reconstituted families. *Marr. Family*, 26:44–51.
Burgess, L. C. (1977), *The Art of Adoption*. Washington, D.C.: Acropolis.
Cabak, V. & Najdanvic, R. (1965), Effect of undernutrition in early life on physical and mental development. *Arch. Dis. Childhood*, 40:532–534.
Caffey, J. (1946), Multiple fractures in the long bones of infants suffering from chronic subdural hematoma. *Amer. J. Roentgenol. Radiation Ther.*, 56:163.
———— (1972), The parent-infant traumatic stress syndrome. *Amer. J. Roentgenol. Radium Ther. Nuclear Med.*, 114:218–229.
Caldwell, B. M. (1964), The effects of infant care. In: *Review of Child Development Research*, Vol. 1, ed. M. L. Hoffman & L. W. Hoffman. New York: Russell Sage Foundation.
———— (1967), What is the optimal learning environment for the young child? *Amer. J. Orthopsychiat.*, 37:8–21.
———— (1970), The effects of psychosocial deprivation on human development in infancy. *Merrill-Palmer Quart.*, 16:260–277.
———— et al. (1970), Infant day care and attachment. *Amer. J. Orthopsychiat.*, 40:397–412.
California Statistical Abstract, 1971. Sacramento: State of California, Department of Public Health.
Campbell, M. et al. (1972), Response to triiodothyronine and dextroamphetamine: A study of preschool schizophrenic children. *J. Autism Childhood Schiz.*, 2:343–358.
Cannon, W. B. (1932), *The Wisdom of the Body*. New York: Norton.
Cantwell, D. P. (1976), Genetic factors in the hyperkinetic syndrome. *J. Amer. Acad. Child Psychiat.*, 15:214–223.
Caplan, M. G. & Douglas, V. I. (1969), Incidence of parental loss in children with depressed mood. *J. Child Psychol. Psychiat.*, 10:225–232.
Cazden, C. B. (1966), Some implications of research on language development for preschool education. Presented at National Council of Teachers Learning Programs for the Disadvantaged.
———— (1968), The acquisition of noun and verb inflections. *Child Devel.*, 39:433.
Champakam, S., Srikantïa, S. G. & Gopalan, C. (1968), Kwashiorkor and mental development. *Amer. J. Clin. Nutr.*, 21:844–852.
Chapple, E. D. (1970), Experimental production of transients in human interaction. *Nature*, 228:630–633.
Chase, H. P., Dorsey, J. & McKhann, G. M. (1967), The effect of malnutrition on the synthesis of a myelin lipid. *Pediat.*, 40:551–559.
———— & Martin, H. P. (1970), Undernutrition and child development. *New England J. Med.*, 282:933–976.
Chess, S., Thomas, A. & Birch, H. G. (1967), Behavior problems revisited: Findings of an anterospective study. In: *Childhood Psychopathology*, ed. S. I. Harrison & J. F. McDermott, Jr. New York: International Universities Press, 1972, pp. 56–65.

Child Development Group of Mississippi (1967), *Surveys of Family Meal Patterns.* Nutrition Services Division, May 17 & July 11 (Cited in Hunger, USA).

Chomsky, N. (1965), *Aspects of the Theory of Syntax.* Cambridge, Mass.: MIT Press.

—— (1968), *Language and Mind.* New York: Harcourt, Brace & World.

Chow, B. F. et al. (1968), Maternal nutrition and metabolism of the offspring: Studies in rats and man. *Amer. J. Public Health,* 58:668–677.

Christakis, G. et al. (1968), A nutritional epidemiologic investigation of 642 New York City children. *Amer. J. Clin. Nutr.,* 21:107–126.

Christensen, H. T. (1964), *Handbook of Marriage and the Family.* Chicago: Rand McNally.

—— (1969), Normative theory derived from cross-cultural family research. *J. Marr. Family,* 31:209–222.

Christodorescu, S. et al. (1970), Psychiatric disturbances in Turner's syndrome. *Psychiat. Clinica,* 3:114–124.

Clothier, F. (1939), Some aspects of the problem of adoption. *Amer. J. Orthopsychiat.,* 9:598–615.

—— (1942), Placing the child for adoption. *Ment. Hygiene,* 26:257–274.

—— (1943), The psychology of the adopted child. *Ment. Hygiene,* 27:222–230.

Cochrane, W. (1965), The battered child syndrome. *Canad. J. Public Health,* 56:193–196.

Coelho, G. V., Hamburg, D. A. & Murphey, E. B. (1963), Coping strategies in a new learning environment. *Arch. Gen. Psychiat.,* 9:433.

——, Silber, E. & Hamburg, D. A. (1962), Use of the Student-TAT to assess coping behavior in hospitalized, normal and exceptionally competent college freshmen. *Percept. Motor Skills,* 14:355–365.

Cohen, A. K. (1955), *Delinquent Boys.* Glencoe, Ill.: Free Press.

Cohen, D. J. (1967), The crying newborn's accommodation to the nipple. *Child Devel.,* 38:89–100.

—— & Frank, R. (1973), Between childhood and adolescence: Growth, tasks and problems in the preadolescent phase of development. Technical report to Office of Child Development, Department of Health, Education & Welfare.

—— & Nadelson, T. (1971), The impact of skin disease on the person. In: *Dermatology in General Medicine,* ed. T. Fitzpatrick. New York: McGraw-Hill, pp. 5–9.

—— & Young, J. G. (1977), Neurochemistry and child psychiatry. *J. Amer. Acad. Child Psychiat.,* 16:353–411.

—— et al. (1972), Personality development in twins: Competence in the newborn and preschool periods. *J. Amer. Acad. Child Psychiat.,* 11:625–644.

—— et al. (1973a), Biogenic amines in autistic, atypical, and epileptic children: CSF measures of HVA, 5HIAA. (Manuscript.)

—— et al. (1973b), Separating identical from fraternal twin children: A new clinical method. *Arch. Gen. Psychiat.,* 29:465–469.

Cohn, R. (1961), Delayed acquisition of reading and writing abilities in children. *Arch. Neurol.,* 4:153–164.

Coleman, J. S. (1961), *The Adolescent Society.* New York: Free Press, 1971.

Coleman, R. W. & Provence, S. (1957), Environmental retardation (hospitalism) in infants living in families. *Pediat.,* 19:285–292.

Condon, W. S. & Ogston, W. D. (1967), A segmentation of behavior. *J. Psychiat. Res.,* 5:221–235.

———— & Sander, L. W. (1974), Neonate movement is synchronized with adult speech: International participation and language acquisition. *Science*, 183:99–101.

Conger, J. J. & Miller, L. (1966), *Personality, Social Class and Delinquency*. New York: Wiley.

Conklin, E. (1920), The foster-child fantasy. *Amer. J. Psychol.*, 31:59–76.

Connolly, K. (1972), Learning in the concept of critical periods in infancy. *Devel. Med. Child Neurol.*, 14:705–714.

Coppen, A. & Kessel, N. (1963), Maturation and personality. *Brit. J. Psychiat.*, 109:711–724.

Coppen, A. J. et al. (1972), Comparative anti-depressant value of L-tryptophan and imipramine with and without attempted potentiation by triiodothyronine. *Arch. Gen. Psychiat.*, 26:234–241.

Coppoletta, J. & Wolbach, S. B. (1933), Body length and organ weights of infants and children. *Amer. J. Pathol.*, 9:55–70.

Corsini, D. A. & Berg, A. J. (1973), Intertask correspondence in the five to seven shift. *Child Devel.*, 44:467–475.

Cotten, M. de V., Ed. (1972), Regulation of catecholamine metabolism in the sympathetic nervous system. *Pharmacol. Rev.*, 24:163–434.

Court Brown, W. M. (1968), Males with an XYY sex chromosome complement. *J. Med. Genet.*, 5:341–359.

————, Price, W. H. & Jacobs, P. A. (1968), Further information on the identity of 47,XYY males. *Brit. Med. J.*, 2:325–328.

Cowie, J. & Kahn, J. (1968), XYY constitution in prepubertal child. *Brit. Med. J.*, 1:748–749.

Cowley, J. J. (1968), Time, place and nutrition: Some observations from animal studies. In: *Malnutrition, Learning, and Behavior*, ed. N. W. Scrimshaw & J. E. Gordon. Cambridge, Mass.: MIT Press.

———— & Griesel, R. D. (1963), The development of second generation low protein rats. *J. Genet. Psychol.*, 103:233–242.

———— ———— (1966), The effect on growth and behavior of rehabilitating first and second generation low protein rats. *Animal Behav.*, 14:506–517.

Craig, M. M. & Glick, S. J. (1965), *A Manual of Procedures for Application of the Glueck Prediction Table*. London: University of London Press.

Cravioto, J. (1966), Nutritional deprivation and psychobiological development in children. In: *Deprivation-Psychological Development*. Scientific Publication No. 134. Pan American Health Organization.

———— & DeLicardie, E. R. (1968), Intersensory development in school age children. In: *Malnutrition, Learning, and Behavior*, ed. N. S. Scrimshaw & J. E. Gordon. Cambridge, Mass.: MIT Press, pp. 252–269.

———— ———— (1975), Neurointegrative development and intelligent children rehabilitated from severe malnutrition. In: *Brain Function and Malnutrition*, ed. J. Prescott, M. Read & B. Coursin. New York: Wiley, pp. 53–72.

———— ———— & Birch, H. G. (1966), Nutrition, growth and neurointegrative development and experimental and ecologic study. *Pediat.*, 38:2, Part II, Suppl., 319–372.

————, Espinoza, C. G. & Birch, H. G. (1967), Early malnutrition and auditory-visual integration in school age children. *J. Special Ed.*, 2:75–82.

———— & Robles, B. (1965), Evolution of adaptive and motor behavior during rehabilitation from kwashiorkor. *Amer. J Orthopsychiat.*, 35:449–464.

Cummings, S. T., Bayley, H. C., & Rie, H. E. (1966), Effects of the child's deficiency on the mother: A study of mothers of mentally retarded, chronically ill and neurotic children. *Amer. J. Orthopsychiat.*, 36:595–608.

Curzon, G. (1972), Brain amine metabolism in some neurological and psychiatric disorders. In: *Biochemical Aspects of Nervous Disorders*, ed. J. N. Cummings. London: Plenum Press, pp. 151–212.

Dalsheimer, B. (1973), Adoption runs in my family. *MS.*, Aug., pp. 82–93, 112–113.

Daly, R. F. (1969), Mental illness and patterns of behavior in 10 XYY males. *J. Nerv. Ment. Dis.*, 149:318–327.

Damon, W. (1975), Early concepts of positive justice as related to the development of logical operations. *Child Devel.*, 46:301–312.

Davenport, H. T. & Werry, J. S. (1970), The effect of general anesthesia, surgery and hospitalization upon the behavior of children. *Amer. J. Orthopsychiat.*, 40:806–824.

Davidson, E. H. (1965), Hormones and genes. *Sci. Amer.*, 212:36–45.

Davison, A. N. & Dobbing, J. (1966), Myelination as a vulnerable period in brain development. *Brit. Med. Bull.*, 22:40–44.

Dean, R. F. A. (1960), The effects of malnutrition on the growth of young children. *Mod. Probl. Pediat.* 5:111–122.

Décarie, T. G. (1962), *Intelligence and Affectivity in Early Childhood*. New York: International Universities Press, 1965.

de Hirsch, K. (1975), Language deficits in children with developmental lags. *The Psychoanalytic Study of the Child*, 30:95–126. New Haven: Yale University Press.

Denenberg, V. H. (1969), The effects of early experience. In: *The Behaviour of Domestic Animals*, 2nd Ed., ed. E. S. E. Hafetz. London: Ballière Tindall & Cassell.

Dennehy, C. M. (1966), Childhood bereavement and psychiatric illness. *Brit. J. Psychiat.*, 112:1049–1069.

Dennis, W. & Dennis, S. G. (1951), Development under controlled environmental conditions. In: *Readings in Clinical Psychology*, ed. W. Dennis. Englewood Cliffs, N.J.: Prentice-Hall, pp. 104–131.

Derdeyn, A. P. (1976), Child custody contests in historical perspective. *Amer. J. Psychiat.*, 133:1369–1376.

Despert, J. L. (1953), *Children of Divorce*. Garden City, N.Y.: Doubleday, 1962.

Deutsch, H. (1937), The absence of grief. In: *Neuroses and Character Types*. New York: International Universities Press, 1965, pp. 226–236.

——— (1945), *The Psychology of Women, II: Motherhood*. New York: Grune & Stratton.

Dewey, J. (1964), *On Education: Selected Writings*, ed. R. D. Archambault. New York: Modern Library.

Diamond, M. (1965), A critical evaluation of the ontogeny of human sexual behavior. *Quart. Rev. Biol.*, 40:147–175.

Dibble, E. (1973), *Fathers' and Mothers' Perceptions of Parenting Style in Relation to Children's Behavior*. Washington, D.C.: Catholic University of America Studies in Social Work, No. 89.

——— & Cohen, D. J. (1973), Companion instruments devised for measuring parental style in relation to children's behavior. *Arch. Gen. Psychiat.*

——— et al. (1965), Some preliminary biochemical findings in junior high school children in Syracuse and Onondaga County New York. *Amer. J. Clin. Nutr.*, 17:218–239.

Di Carlo, S. (1964), In: *Childhood Aphasia: Pathway School Symposium, Part II*, ed S. Rappaport. Philadelphia: Livingston.

Dobbing, J. (1964), The influence of early nutrition on the development and myelination of the brain. *Proc. Roy. Soc.*, 159:503–509.

Douglas, J. W. B. (1956), Mental ability and school achievement of premature children at 8 years of age. *Brit. Med. J.*, 1:1210–1214.

———— (1960), "Premature" children at primary schools. *Brit. Med. J.*, 1/2:1008–1031.

———— (1970), Broken families and child behavior. *J. Roy. Coll. Physicians London*, 4:203–210.

————, Ross, J. M., & Simpson, H. R. (1968), *All Our Future*. London: Davies.

———— et al. (1966), Delinquency and social class. *Brit. J. Criminol.*, 6:294–302.

Drash, P. W., Greenberg, N. & Money, J. (1968), Intelligence and personality in three syndromes of dwarfism. In: *Human Growth: Body Composition, Cell Growth, Energy and Intelligence*, ed. D. B. Cheek. Philadelphia: Lea and Febiger.

Drillien, C. M. (1964), *The Growth and Development of the Prematurely Born Infant*. Baltimore: Williams & Wilkins.

———— (1965), Prematures in school. *Pediat. Dig.*, Sept., pp. 75–77.

Durkheim, E. (1906), *Sociology and Philosophy*. Glencoe: Free Press, 1953.

Dustman, R. & Beck, E. (1969), The effects of maturation and aging on the wave form of visually evoked potentials. *EEG Clin. Neurophysiol.*, 26:2–11.

Dykman, R., Heimann, E. & Ken., W. (1952), Lifetime worry patterns of three diverse adult cultural groups. *J. Soc. Psychol.*, 35:91–100.

Easson, W. (1973), Special sexual problems of the adopted adolescent. *Med. Aspects Human Sexuality*, July, pp. 92–105.

Edelheit, H., rep. (1968), Panel: Language and the development of the ego. *J Amer. Psychoanal. Assn.*, 16:113–122.

Ehrhardt, A. (1973), Maternalism in fetal hormonal and related syndromes. In: *Contemporary Sexual Behavior*, ed. J. Zubin & J. Money. Baltimore: Johns Hopkins University Press.

————, Epstein, R. & Money, J. (1968), Fetal androgens and female gender identity in the early-treated adrenogenital syndrome. *Johns Hopkins Med. J.*, 122:160–167.

————, Evers, A. K. & Money, J. (1968), Influence of androgen on some aspects of sexually dimorphic behavior in women with the late-treated adrenogenital syndrome. *Johns Hopkins Hosp. J.*, 123:115–122.

————, Greenberg, N. & Money, J. (1970), Female gender identity and absence of fetal gonadal hormones: Turner's syndrome. *Johns Hopkins Med. J.*, 126:237–248.

Eiduson, B. & Livermore, J. (1952), Complications in therapy with adopted children. *Amer. J. Orthopsychiat.*, 22:795–802.

Elkind, D. (1967), Egocentrism in adolescence. *Child Devel.*, 38:1025–1034.

————, Koegler, R. R. & Go, E. (1964), Studies in perceptual development, II: Part-whole perception. *Child Devel.*, 35:81–90.

———— & Scott, L. (1962), Studies in perceptual development, I: The decentering of perception. *Child Devel.*, 33:619–630.

———— & Weiss, J. (1967), Studies in perceptual development, III: Perceptual exploration. *Child Devel.*, 38:553–561.

Ellinwood, C. (1969), *Structural Development in the Expression of Emotion by Children*. Unpublished Ph.D. dissertation, University of Chicago.

Elliott, O. & King, J. A. (1960), Effect of early food deprivation upon later consummatory behavior in puppies. *Psychol. Rep.*, 6:391–400.

Elmer, E. (1960), Failure to thrive: Role of the mother. *Pediat.*, 25:717–725.

———— (1964–1965), *The 50 Families Study*. Unpublished mimeographed reports, The Children's Hospital of Pittsburgh.

Elson, M. (1964), The reactive impact of adolescent and family upon each other in separation. *J. Amer. Acad. Child Psychiat.*, 3:697–708.

Emde, R. N. & Koenig, K. L. (1969a), Neonatal smiling and rapid eye movement states. *J. Amer. Acad. Child Psychiat.*, 8:57–67.

———— ———— (1969b), Neonatal smiling, frowning, and rapid eye movement states, II: Sleep-cycle study. *J. Amer. Acad. Child Psychiat.*, 8:637–656.

————, McCartney, R. & Harmon, R. J. (1971), Neonatal smiling in REM states, IV: Premature study. *Child Devel.*, 42:1657–1661.

———— & Metcalf, D. R. (1970), An electroencephalographic study of behavioral rapid eye movement states in the human newborn. *J. Nerv. Ment. Dis.*, 150:376–386.

Emlen, W., Segal, D. S. & Mandell, A. J. (1972), Thyroid state: Effects on pre- and post-synaptic central noradrenergic mechanisms. *Science*, 175:79–82.

Engel, E. & Forbes, A. P. (1965), Cytogenetic and clinical findings in 48 patients with congenitally defective or absent ovaries. *Medicine*, 44:135–164.

Erikson, E. H. (1950), *Childhood and Society*. New York: Norton.

———— (1956), The problem of ego identity. *J. Amer. Psychoanal. Assn.*, 4:56–121.

———— (1959), *Identity and the Life Cycle* [*Psychol. Issues*, Monog. 1] New York: International Universities Press.

———— (1963), Eight ages of man. In: *Childhood Psychopathology*, ed. S. I. Harrison & J. F. McDermott, Jr. New York: International Universities Press, 1972, pp. 109–132.

Escalona, S. K. (1962), The study of individual differences and the problem of state. *J. Amer. Acad. Child Psychiat.*, 1:11–37.

———— (1968), *The Roots of Individuality*. Chicago: Aldine.

Evans, R. I. (1967), *Dialogue with Erik Erikson*. New York: Harper & Row.

Fabian, A. A. (1955), Reading disability: An index of pathology. *Amer. J. Orthopsychiat.*, 25:319–329.

Fanaroff, A., Kennell, J. & Klaus, M. (1972), Follow up of low birth-weight infants—the predictive value of maternal visiting patterns. *Pediat.*, 49:287–290.

Faust, O. et al. (1952), *Reducing Emotional Trauma in Hospitalized Children*. Albany: Albany Research Project.

Fenichel, O. (1945), *The Psychoanalytic Theory of Neurosis*. New York: Norton.

Ferenczi, S. (1913), Stages in the development of the sense of reality. In: *Sex in Psychoanalysis*. New York: Basic Books, 1950, pp. 213–239.

Ferracuti, F. et al. (1965), La sindrome de bambino maltratto. *Quaderni Crimino. Clin.*

Filer, L. J., Jr. (1969), The United States today: Is it free of public health nutrition problems?—Anemia. *Amer. J. Public Health*, 59:327–338.

Finnie, B. (1970), The statistical assessment of personality change. In: *The Growth and Development of College Students*, Student Personnel Series No. 12, ed.

J. M. Whiteley & H. Sprandel. Washington, D.C.: American Personnel & Guidance Association.

Fish, B. (1971), The "one child, one drug" myth of stimulants in hyperkinesis. *Arch. Gen. Psychiat.*, 25:193–203.

——— (1973), Visual-motor disorders in infants at risk for schizophrenia. *Arch. Gen. Psychiat.*, 29:900–904.

Fisher, F. (1972), The adoption triangle—Why polarization? Why not an adoption trinity? Presented to North American Conference on Adoptable Children, St. Louis, Mo.

——— (1973), *The Search for Anna Fisher*. New York: Fields.

Fisichelli, R. M. (1950), *A Study of Prelinguistic Speech Development of Institutionalized Infants*. Unpublished Ph.D. dissertation, Fordham University.

Flammang, C. (1970), The neglected child. In: *The Police and the Under-Protected Child*. Springfield, Ill.: Thomas.

Flavell, J. H. (1963), *The Developmental Psychology of Jean Piaget*. Princeton: Van Nostrand.

Fleming, J. & Altschul, S. (1963), Activation of mourning and growth by psychoanalysis. *Internat. J. Psycho-Anal.*, 44:419–431.

Fletcher, R. (1966), *The Family and Marriage in Britain*. Middlesex, England: Penguin.

Fontana, V. J. (1975), Child maltreatment and battered child syndromes. In: *Comprehensive Textbook of Psychiatry*, 2nd Ed., ed. A. M. Freedman, H. I. Kaplan & B. J. Sadock. Baltimore: Williams & Wilkins.

Fox, C. et al. (1972), Studies on the relationship between plasma testosterone levels and human sexual activity. *J. Endocrinol.*, 52:51–58.

Fraiberg, S. (1968), Parallel and divergent patterns in blind and sighted infants. *The Psychoanalytic Study of the Child*, 23:264–300. New York: International Universities Press.

——— (1969), Libidinal object constancy and mental representation. *The Psychoanalytic Study of the Child*, 24:9–47. New York: International Universities Press.

——— (1971a), Intervention in infancy: A program for blind infants. *J. Amer. Acad. Child Psychiat.*, 10:381–405.

——— (1971b), Smiling and stranger reaction in blind infants. In: *Exceptional Infant*. Vol. 2: *Studies in Abnormalities*, ed. J. Hellmuth. New York: Brunner/Mazel, pp. 110–127.

——— (1977), *Insights from the Blind*. New York: Basic Books.

———, Adelson, E. & Shapiro, V. (1975), Ghosts in the nursery. *J. Amer. Acad. Child Psychiat.*, 14:387–421.

Framo, J. (1972), *Family Interaction: A Dialogue Between Family Researchers and Family Therapists*. New York: Springer.

Frankova, S. (1974), Interaction between early malnutrition and stimulation in animals. In: *Early Malnutrition and Mental Development*, ed. J. Cravioto et al. Uppsala: Almquist & Wiksel, pp. 202–209.

Franzke, A. W. (1972), *Sociology and Cytogenetics: A Study of the Stigmatization or Nonstigmatization of 15 XYY Karyotypic Individuals in Differentiated Subcultural Typologies*. Unpublished M.A. thesis, University of Missouri–Kansas City.

Freedman, D. A. et al. (1970), The development of the use of sound as a guide to affective and cognitive behavior—a two-phase process. In: *Annual Progress in Child Psychiatry and Child Development*. New York: Brunner/Mazel, pp. 187–194.

——— et al. (1976), Further observations of the effect of reverse isolation from birth on cognitive and affective development. *J Amer Acad Child Psychiat*, 15:593–603.

Freedman, D. X. & Giarman, N (1963), Brain amines, electrical activity, and behavior. In: *EEG and Behavior*, ed. G Glaser. New York: Basic Books.

Frenkel-Brunswik, E. (1936), Adjustments and reorientations in the course of the life span. In: *Middle Age and Aging: A Reader in Social Psychology*, ed B L Neugarten. Chicago: University of Chicago Press, 1968·

Freud, A. (1936), *The Ego and the Mechanisms of Defense The Writings of Anna Freud*, 2. New York: International Universities Press, 1966.

——— (1958), Adolescence. *The Writings of Anna Freud*, 5:136–166 New York. International Universities Press, 1969.

——— (1965), *Normality and Pathology in Childhood: Assessments of Development The Writings of Anna Freud*, 6. New York: International Universities Press.

——— (1969), Adolescence as a developmental disturbance *The Writings of Anna Freud*, 7:22–38. New York: International Universities Press, 1971

——— & Burlingham, D (1943), *War and Children* New York International Universities Press

——— ——— (1944), *Infants Without Families* New York· International Universities Press.

Freud, S. (1893–1895), Fräulein Elisabeth von R *Standard Edition*, 2 135–181 London: Hogarth Press, 1955.

——— (1895), Project for a scientific psychology. *Standard Edition*, 1 281–397 London: Hogarth Press, 1966.

——— (1900), The primary and secondary processes—repression *Standard Edition*, 5:588–609. London: Hogarth Press, 1953.

——— (1905), Three essays on the theory of sexuality. *Standard Edition*, 7:123–243 London: Hogarth Press, 1953.

——— (1909), Family romances. *Standard Edition*, 9:235–241. London. Hogarth Press, 1959.

——— (1911), Formulations on the two principles of mental functioning *Standard Edition*, 12:213–226. London: Hogarth Press, 1958.

——— (1914), On narcissism: An introduction. *Standard Edition*, 14:67–102 London: Hogarth Press, 1957.

——— (1915), The unconscious. *Standard Edition*, 14:159–215. London: Hogarth Press, 1957.

——— (1917), Mourning and melancholia. *Standard Edition*, 14:237–258 London. Hogarth Press, 1957.

——— (1919), 'A child is being beaten.' *Standard Edition*, 17:175–204 London: Hogarth Press, 1955.

——— (1920), Beyond the pleasure principle. *Standard Edition*, 18.1–64 London: Hogarth Press, 1955.

——— (1921), Group psychology and the analysis of the ego. *Standard Edition*, 18:65–143. London: Hogarth Press, 1955.

——— (1923a), The ego and the id. *Standard Edition*, 19:1–66. London. Hogarth Press, 1961.

——— (1923b), The etiological significance of sexual life. In: *Childhood Psycho-*

pathology, ed. S. I. Harrison & J. F. McDermott, Jr. New York. International Universities Press, 1972, pp. 79–82.

————— (1924a), The dissolution of the Oedipus complex. *Standard Edition*, 19:171–179 London: Hogarth Press, 1961.

————— (1924b), Letter to *Le Disque Vert*. *Standard Edition*, 19:290. London: Hogarth Press, 1961.

————— (1925a), An autobiographical study. *Standard Edition*, 20:1–74. London Hogarth Press, 1959.

————— (1925b), A note upon the 'mystic writing-pad.' *Standard Edition*, 19:225–232 London: Hogarth Press, 1961.

————— (1926), Inhibitions, symptoms and anxiety. *Standard Edition*, 20:77–175 London: Hogarth Press, 1959.

————— (1927), Fetishism. *Standard Edition*, 21:147–157. London: Hogarth Press, 1961.

————— (1930), Civilization and its discontents *Standard Edition*, 21.57–145. London: Hogarth Press, 1961.

————— (1940), Splitting of the ego in the process of defence. *Standard Edition*, 23:271–278. London: Hogarth Press, 1964.

Frick, A. (1964), Mistreated small children. *Svenska Lakartidn.*, 61:3004–3012.

Fries, M. (1959), Review of the literature on the latency period. In. *Readings in Psychoanalytic Psychology*, ed. M. Levitt. New York: Appleton.

Frisch, R. E. (1971), Does malnutrition cause permanent mental retardation in human beings? *Psychiat., Neurol., Neurochirugia*, 74:463–479.

Frisk, M. (1964), Identity problems and confused conceptions of the genetic ego in adopted children during adolescence. *Acta Paedo Psychiat.*, 31:6–12

Frohman, L. (1972), Clinical neuropharmacology of hypothalamic releasing factors *New England J. Med.*, 286:1391–1397.

Fry, D. B. (1966), The development of the phonological system in the normal and the deaf child. In: *The Genesis of Language: A Psycholinguistic Approach*, ed. F. Smith & G. A. Miller. Cambridge, Mass.: MIT Press.

Furman, R. A. (1964a), Death and the young child. *The Psychoanalytic Study of the Child*, 19:321–333. New York: International Universities Press.

————— (1964b), Death of a six-year-old's mother during his analysis. *The Psychoanalytic Study of the Child*, 19:337–397. New York: International Universities Press.

Furth, H. G. (1966), *Thinking Without Language: Psychological Implications of Deafness*. New York: Free Press.

————— (1971), Linguistic deficiency and thinking. *Psychol. Bull.*, 76:58–72

Galdston, R. (1965), Observations on children who have been physically abused and their parents. *Amer. J. Psychiat.*, 122:440–443.

————— (1969), Dysfunctions of parenting. In: *Modern Perspectives in International Child Psychiatry*, ed. J. G. Howells. New York: Brunner/Mazel, 1971, pp. 569–588.

Gardner, G. E. (1972), William Healy, 1869–1963. *J. Amer. Acad. Child Psychiat.*, 11:1–29.

Gardner, L. I. & Neu, R. L. (1972), Evidence linking an extra Y chromosome to sociopathic behavior. *Arch. Gen. Psychiat.*, 26:220–222.

Gardner, R. A. (1970), *The Boys' and Girls' Book about Divorce* New York: Science House.

—— (1976), *Psychotherapy with Children of Divorce*. New York: Aronson.

—— (1977), *The Parents' Book about Divorce*. Garden City, N.Y.: Doubleday.

Garron, D. C. (1972), Personality and intelligence in Turner's syndrome. Presented to APA Symposium on Human Behavior Genetics, Honolulu, Hawaii, Sept. 4.

—— et al. (1973), An explanation of the apparently increased incidence of moderate mental retardation in Turner's syndrome. *Behav. Genet.*, 3:37–43.

Gesell, A. (1935), Cinemanalysis: A method of behavior study. *J. Genet. Psychol.*, 47:3–15.

—— (1940), Excerpt from *The First Five Years of Life*. In: *Childhood Psychopathology*, ed. S. I. Harrison & J. F. McDermott, Jr. New York: International Universities Press, 1972, pp. 66–78.

—— & Ilg, F. (1943), *Infant and Child in the Culture of Today*. New York: Harper.

Gewirtz, J. L. (1965), The course of infant smiling in four child-rearing communities in Israel. In: *Determinants of Infant Behavior*, Vol. 3, ed. B. M. Foss. New York: Wiley, pp. 205–248.

—— (1969), A distinction between dependence and attachment in terms of stimulus control. Presented to Society for Research in Child Development Conference, Santa Monica, Cal., March.

Gibson, H. B. (1969), Early delinquency in relation to broken homes. *J. Child Psychol. Psychiat.*, 10:195–204.

Gil, D. (1970), *Violence Against Children*. Cambridge, Mass.: Harvard University Press.

—— (1975), Unraveling child abuse. *Amer. J. Orthopsychiat.*, 45:346–356.

Gilligan, C., Kolhberg, L. & Lerner, J. (1972), Moral reasoning about sexual dilemmas: A developmental approach. In: *Recent Research in Moral Development*, ed. L. Kolhberg & E. Turiel. New York: Holt, Rinehart & Winston.

Gjerdrum, K. (1964), The battered child syndrome. *Tidsskr. Norske Laegeforen.*, 84:1609–1612.

Glaser, H. H. et al. (1968), Physical and psychological development of children with early failure to thrive. *J. Pediat.*, 73:690–698.

Glatzer, H. (1955), Adoption and delinquency. *Nerv. Child*, 11:52–56.

Glick, T. & Norton, A. (1972), *Perspective on the Recent Upturn in Divorce and Remarriage*. Washington, D.C.: Bureau of the Census, United States Department of Commerce.

—— & Parke, R. (1965), New approaches in studying the life cycle of the family. *Demography*, 2:187–202.

Glueck, S. & Glueck, E. (1950), *Unraveling Juvenile Delinquency*. Cambridge, Mass.: Harvard University Press.

—— —— (1962), *Family Environment and Delinquency*. Boston: Houghton Mifflin.

Goldberg, A. & Welch, B. (1972), Adaptation of the adrenal medulla: Sustained increase in choline acetyltransferase by psychosocial stimulation. *Science*, 178:319–320.

Goldstein, J., Freud, A. & Solnit, A. (1973), *Beyond the Best Interests of the Child*. New York: Free Press.

Goode, W. J. (1965), *Women in Divorce*. New York: Free Press.

Goodman, J. D. (1977), Letter to the editor. *Amer. J. Psychiat.*, 134:95.

————, Silberstein, R. M. & Mandell, W. (1963), Adopted children brought to child psychiatric clinic. *Arch. Gen. Psychiat.*, 9:451–456.

Goodman, P. (1960), *Growing Up Absurd*. New York: Random House, 1962.

Gottesman, I. & Shields, J. (1972), *Schizophrenia and Genetics: A Twin Study*. New York: Academic Press.

Goy, R. (1968), Organizing effect of androgen on the behaviour of rhesus monkeys. In: *Endocrinology and Human Behaviour*, ed. R. Michael. London: Oxford University Press, pp. 12–31.

Graham, F. K. & Jackson, J. (1970), Arousal systems and infant heart rate responses. *Advances in Child Development and Behavior*, 5:60–111. New York: Academic Press.

Graham, P. & Rutter, M. (1968a), The reliability and validity of the psychiatric assessment of the child, II: Interview with the parent. *Brit. J. Psychiat.*, 114:581–592.

———————— (1968b), Organic brain dysfunction in child psychiatric disorder. *Brit. Med. J.*, 3:695–700.

Green, A. H. (1978), Psychopathology of abused children. *J. Amer. Acad. Child Psychiat.*, 17:92–103.

———— (1979), Child abuse and neglect. *J. Amer. Acad. Child Psychiat.*, 18:201–204.

Green, R. (1974), *Sexual Identity Conflict in Children and Adults*. New York: Basic Books.

———— (1975), Human sexuality: Research and treatment frontiers. In: *American Handbook of Psychiatry*, Vol. 6, ed. H. K. Brodie & D. Hamburg. New York: Basic Books.

———— & Money, J., Eds. (1969), *Transsexualism and Sex Reassignment*. Baltimore: Johns Hopkins University Press.

———— & Stoller, R. (1971), Two monozygotic (identical) twin pairs discordant for gender identity. *Arch. Sexual Behav.*, 1:321–327.

Greenberg, M., Rosenberg, I. & Lind, J. (1973), First mothers rooming-in with thier newborns: Its impact upon the mother. *Amer. J. Orthopsychiat.*, 43:783–788.

Greengard, J. (1964), The battered child syndrome. *Med. Sci.*, 15:82–91.

Gregg, G. S. & Elmer, E. (1969), Infant injuries: Accident or abuse? *Pediat.*, 44:434–439.

Gregory, I. (1965), Anterospective data following childhood loss of a parent, II: Pathology, performance, and potential among college students. *Arch. Gen. Psychiat.*, 13:110–120.

———— (1966), Retrospective data concerning childhood loss of a parent, II: Category of parental loss by decade of birth, diagnosis, and MMPI. *Arch. Gen. Psychiat.*, 15:362–367.

Greulich, W. W. (1958), Growth of children of the same race under different environmental conditions. *Science*, 127:515–516.

————, Thoms, H. & Twaddle, R. C. (1939), A study of pelvis type and its relationship to body build in white women. *J. Amer. Med. Assn.*, 112:485–492.

Grewel, F. (1959), How do children acquire the use of language? *Phonetica*, 3:193.

Griffin, G. A. & Harlow, H. F. (1966), Effects of three months of total social deprivation on social adjustment and learning in the rhesus monkey. *Child Devel.*, 37:533–547.

Grinker, R. R., Sr., Grinker, R. R., Jr. & Timberlake, J. (1962), A study of "mentally healthy young males (homoclites)." *Arch. Gen. Psychiat.*, 6:405–453.

Gruenwald, P., Dawkins, M. & Hepner, R. (1963), Chronic deprivation of the fetus *Sinai Hosp. J.*, 11:51–80.

Guerin, P. H. (1976), Family therapy: The first twenty-five years. In: *Family Therapy. Theory and Practice*, ed. P. J. Guerin. New York: Gardner Press.

Gunter, L. (1963), Psychopathology and stress in the life experience of mothers of premature infants. *Amer. J. Obstet. Gynecol.*, 86:333–340.

Gutelius, M. F. (1969), The problem of iron-deficiency anemia in preschool Negro children. *Amer. J. Public Health*, 59:290–295.

Hall, G. S. (1904), *Adolescence: Its Psychology and Its Relations to Physiology, Anthropology, Sociology, Sex Crime, Religion and Education*. New York: Appleton.

Hambert, G. (1966), *Males with Positive Sex Chromatin: An Epidemiologic Investigation Followed by Psychiatric Study of Seventy-five Cases*. Göteborg: Elanders Boktryckeri Aktiebolag.

Hamburg, B. A. (1974), Early adolescence: A specific and stressful stage of the life cycle. In: *Coping and Adaptation*, ed. G. Coelho, D. A. Hamburg & J. E. Adams. New York: Basic Books, pp. 101–124.

Hamburg, D. A. & Adams, J. E. (1967), A perspective on coping behavior. *Arch. Gen. Psychiat.*, 17:277–284.

Hampson, J. L., Hampson, J. G. & Money, J. (1955), The syndrome of gonadal agenesis (ovarian agenesis) and male chromosomal pattern in girls and women: Psychologic studies. *Bull. Johns Hopkins Hosp.*, 97:207–226.

Hampton, M. C. et al. (1967), Caloric and nutrient intakes of teenagers. *J. Amer. Dietetic Assn.*, 50:385–396.

Handel, G., Ed. (1967), *The Psychosocial Interior of the Family*. Chicago. Aldine.

Harlow, H. F. & Harlow, M. K. (1962), The effect of rearing conditions on behavior. *Bull. Menninger Clinic*, 26:213–224.

Harmon, R. J. & Emde, R. N. (1972), Spontaneous REM behaviors in a microcephalic infant. *Percept. Motor Skills*, 34:827–833.

Harper, P. A., Fischer, L. K. & Rider, R. V. (1959), Neurological and intellectual status of prematures at three to five years of age. *J. Pediat.*, 55:679–690.

Harrison, S. I. (1970), Reared in the wrong sex. *J. Amer. Acad. Child Psychiat.*, 9:44–102.

———, Cain, A. C. & Benedek, E. (1968), The childhood of a transsexual. *Arch. Gen. Psychiat.*, 19:28–37.

——— & McDermott, J. F., Jr. (1972), *Childhood Psychopathology*. New York: International Universities Press.

Hartmann, H. (1939), *Ego Psychology and the Problem of Adaptation*. New York: International Universities Press, 1958.

——— (1964), *Essays on Ego Psychology*. New York. International Universities Press.

———, Kris, E. & Loewenstein, R. M. (1951), Some psychoanalytic comments on "culture and personality." In: *Papers on Psychoanalytic Psychology* [*Psychol. Issues*, Monogr. 14]. New York: International Universities Press, 1964, pp. 86–116.

Heath, D. H. (1965), *Explorations of Maturity*. New York: Appleton-Century-Crofts.

——— (1968), *Growing Up in College*. San Francisco: Jossey-Bass.

Hebb, D. O. (1949), *The Organization of Behavior*. New York: Wiley.

Heinicke, C. M. & Westheimer, I. J. (1965), *Brief Separations*. New York. International Universities Press.

Helfer, R. & Kempe, C. H., Eds. (1968), *The Battered Child*. Chicago: University of Chicago Press.

―――― ―――― (1976), *Child Abuse and Neglect—The Family and the Community* Cambridge, Mass.: Ballinger.

Hendel, G. M., Burke, M. C. & Lund, L. A. (1965), Socioeconomic factors influence children's diets. *J. Home Ec.*, 57:205–208.

Henley, E., Moisset, B. & Welch, B. (1973), Catecholamine uptake in cerebral cortex: Adaptive change induced by fighting. *Science*, 180:1050–1052.

Hersher, L., Richmond, J. B. & Moore, A. V. (1963), Modifiability of the critical period for the development of maternal behaviour in sheep and goats. *Behaviour*, 20:311–320.

Hertzig, M. et al. (1971a), Growth sequelae of severe infantile malnutrition. (Manuscript.)

―――― et al. (1971b), Mental sequelae of severe infantile malnutrition. (Manuscript.)

Hess, R. D. & Shipman, V. C. (1966), In: *Influences upon Early Learning*, ed. R. D. Hess & R. M. Bear. Chicago: Aldine.

Hetherington, E. M. (1973), Girls without fathers. *Psychol. Today*, 6:47–52.

Hilgard, J. & Newman, M. F. (1959), Anniversaries in mental illness. *Psychiat.*, 22:113–121.

Hill, L. W. (1956), *The Treatment of Eczema in Infants and Children*. St. Louis. Mosby.

Hill, O. & Price, J. (1967), Childhood bereavement and adult depression. *Brit. J. Psychiat.*, 113:743–751.

Hinde, R. A. (1970), Maternal deprivation in monkeys. Presented to Institute of Neurology, London, 2.

Hingtgen, J. N. & Bryson, C. Q. (1972), Recent developments in the study of early childhood psychoses: Infantile autism, childhood schizophrenia, and related disorders. *Schiz. Bull.*, 5:8–54.

Hirsch, J. (1963), Behavior genetics and individuality understood. *Science*, 142:1437–1442.

Hirschi, T. & Selvin, H. C. (1967), *Delinquency Research: An Appraisal of Analytic Methods*. New York: Free Press.

Hoffer, W. (1949), Mouth, hand and ego-integration. *The Psychoanalytic Study of the Child*, 3/4:49–56. New York: International Universities Press.

Hollingshead, A. (1949), *Elmtown's Youth*. New York: Wiley.

―――― & Redlich, F. C. (1958), *Social Class and Mental Illness*. New York: Wiley.

Holter, J. C. & Friedman, S. (1968), Child abuse: Early case findings in the emergency department. *Pediat.*, 42:128–138.

Hook, E. B. (1973), Behavioral implications of the human XYY genotype. *Science*, 179:139–150.

Hsueh, A. M., Agustin, C. E. & Chow, B. F. (1967), Growth of young rats after differential manipulation of maternal diet. *J. Nutr.*, 91:195–200.

Hubbard, G. (1947), Who am I? *Child*, 11:130–133.

Huenemann, R. L. et al. (1968), Food and eating practices of teenagers. *J. Amer. Dietetic Assn.*, 53:17–24.

Humphrey, M. & Ounsted, C. (1963), Adoptive families referred for psychiatric advice, I: The children. *Brit. J. Psychiat.*, 109:599–608.

Hutcheson, H. A. & Wright, N. H. (1968), Georgia's family planning program

Amer. J. Nursing, 68:332–335.

Hutt, S. J., Lenard, H. G. & Prechtl, H. F. R. (1969), Psychophysiological studies in newborn infants. *Advances in Child Development and Behavior,* 4:127–172. New York: Academic Press.

——— et al. (1965), A behavioral and electroencephalographic study of autistic children. *J. Psychiat. Res.,* 3:181–197.

Illingworth, R. S. & Holt, K. S. (1955), Children in hospital: Some observations on their reactions with special reference to daily visiting. *Lancet,* ii:1257–1262.

Illsley, R. (1966), Early prediction of perinatal risk. *Proc. Roy. Soc. Med.,* 59:181–184.

——— (1967), The sociological study of reproduction and its outcome. In: *Childbearing: Its Social and Psychological Aspects,* ed. S. A. Richardson & A. F. Guttmacher. Baltimore: Williams & Wilkins, pp. 75–135.

Imperato-McGinley, J. et al.(1974), Steroid 5-reductase deficiency in man: An inherited form of male pseudohermaphroditism. *Science,* 186:1213–1215.

Irvine, E. E. (1966), Children in Kibbutzim: Thirteen years after. *J. Child Psychol. Psychiat.,* 7:167–178.

Jacobs, P. A. et al. (1965), Aggressive behavior, mental subnormality and the XYY male. *Nature,* 208:1351.

——— et al. (1968), Chromosome studies on men in a maximum security hospital. *Ann. Human Genet.,* 31:339–358.

Jacobson, E. (1954), The self and the object world. *The Psychoanalytic Study of the Child,* 9:75–127. New York: International Universities Press.

——— (1961), Adolescent moods and the remodeling of psychic structures in adolescence. *The Psychoanalytic Study of the Child,* 16:164–183. New York: International Universities Press.

——— (1964), *The Self and the Object World.* New York: International Universities Press.

——— (1965), The return of the lost parent. In: *Drives, Affects, Behavior,* Vol. 2, ed. M. Schur. New York: International Universities Press, pp. 193–211.

Jaffe, B. & Fanshel, D. (1970), *How They Fared in Adoption: A Follow-up Study.* New York: Columbia University Press.

Jakobson, R. (1962), *Selected Writings, I.* The Hague: Mouton.

——— & Halle, M. (1956), *Fundamentals of Language.* The Hague: Mouton.

Janowsky, D. S. et al. (1973), Provocation of schizophrenic symptoms by intravenous administration of methylphenidate. *Arch. Gen. Psychiat.,* 28:185–191.

Jaques, E. (1965), Death and the mid-life crisis. *Internat. J. Psycho-Anal.,* 46:502–514.

Jeans, P. C., Smith, M. B. & Stearns, G. (1952), Dietary habits of pregnant women of low income in a rural state. *J. Amer. Dietetic Assn.,* 28:27–34.

Jensen, A. R. (1969), How much can we boost I.Q. and scholastic achievement? *Harvard Ed. Rev.,* 39:1–123.

Jersild, A. (1968), *Child Psychology.* Englewood Cliffs, N. J.: Prentice-Hall.

Joffe, J. M., Rawson, R. A. & Mulick, J. A. (1973), Control of their environment reduces emotionality in rats. *Science,* 180:1383–1384.

Johnson, A. M. (1949), Sanctions for superego lacunae of adolescents. In: *Childhood Psychopathology,* ed. S. I. Harrison & J. F. McDermott, Jr. New York: International Universities Press, 1972, pp. 522–531.

——— & Szurek, S. (1952), The genesis of antisocial acting out in children and adults. *Psychoanal. Quart.*, 21:313–343.

Johnson, B. & Morse, H. (1968), Injured children and their parents. *Children*, 15:147–152.

Jones, H. E. (1949), *Motor Performance and Growth*. Berkeley: University of California Press.

Jonsson, G. (1967), Delinquent boys, their parents and grandparents. *Acta Psychiat. Scand.*, 43(Suppl. 195).

Josselyn, I. (1956), Cultural forces, motherliness and fatherliness. *Amer. J. Orthopsychiat.*, 26:264–271.

Judd, L. J. & Mandell, A. (1968), Chromosome studies in early infantile autism. *Arch. Gen. Psychiat.*, 18:450–457.

Juel-Nielsen, N. (1964), Individual and environment: A psychiatric-psychological investigation of monozygotic twins reared apart. *Acta Psychiat. Scand.*, 40(Suppl 183):1–158.

Kagan, J. (1970), Attention and psychological change in the young child. *Science*, 170:826–832.

———, Moss, H. & Sigel, I. (1960), Conceptual style and the use of affect labels. *Merrill-Palmer Quart.*, 6:261–276.

Kahn, D. & Birch, H. G. (1968), Development of auditory-visual integration and reading achievement. *Percept. Motor Skills*, 27:459–468.

Kaj Jerne, N. (1973), The immune system. *Sci. Amer.*, 229:52–60.

Kaplan, A. (1967), A philosophical discussion of normality. *Arch. Gen. Psychiat.*, 17:325–330.

Kaplan, B. (1959), The study of language in psychiatry. In: *American Handbook of Psychiatry*, Vol. 3, ed. S. Arieti. New York: Basic Books.

Kaplan, E. B. (1965), Reflections regarding psychomotor activities during the latency period. *The Psychoanalytic Study of the Child*, 20:220–238. New York: International Universities Press.

Katan, A. (1961), Some thoughts about the role of verbalization in early childhood. *The Psychoanalytic Study of the Child*, 16:184–188. New York: International Universities Press.

Katz, J. et al. (1968), *No Time for Youth*. San Francisco: Jossey-Bass.

Kaufman, I. (1962), Psychiatric implications of physical abuse of children. In: *Protecting the Battered Child*. Denver: Children's Division, American Humane Association, pp. 17–22.

Kaye, H. (1967), Infant sucking behavior and its modification. *Advances in Child Development and Behavior*, 3:2–52. New York: Academic Press.

Kellner (Pringle), M. L. (1967), Adoption—facts and fallacies, a review of research in USA, Canada and Great Britain, 1948–1965. In: *Studies in Child Development*. London: Longmans.

Kelly, J. B. & Wallerstein, J. S. (1976), The effects of parental divorce: Experiences of the child in early latency. *Amer. J. Orthopsychiat.*, 36:20–32.

Kempe, C. H. et al. (1962), The battered child syndrome. *J. Amer. Med. Assn.*, 181:17–24.

Kendler, H. H. & Kendler, T. S. (1962), Vertical and horizontal processes in problem solving. *Psychol. Rev.*, 69:1–16.

Kendler, T. S. & Kendler, H. H. (1962), Inferential behavior in children as a function of age and subgoal constancy. *J. Exper. Psychol.*, 64:460–466.

Kennell, J. et al. (1974), Maternal behavior one year after early and extended postpartum contact. *Devel. Med. Child Neurol* , 16:172–179.

———— & Rolnick, A. R. (1960), Discussion problems in newborn babies with their parents. *Pediat.*, 26:832–838.

Kernberg, O. F. (1967), Borderline personality organization *J. Amer. Psychoanal, Assn.*, 15:641–685.

———— (1970), Factors in the psychoanalytic treatment of narcissistic personalities. *J. Amer. Psychoanal. Assn.*, 18:51–85.

Kessen, W. & Mandler, G. (1961), Anxiety, pain, and the inhibition of distress. *Psychol. Rev.*, 68:396–404.

Kessler, A. & Moos, R. H. (1970), The XYY karyotype and criminality. A review. *J. Psychiat. Res.*, 7:153–170.

Kestenberg, J. S. (1965a), The role of movement patterns in development, I. Rhythms of movement. *Psychoanal. Quart.*, 34:1–36.

———— (1965b), The role of movement patterns in development, II. Flow of tension and effort. *Psychoanal. Quart.*, 34:517–563.

———— (1967), The role of movement patterns in development, III. Control of shape *Psychoanal. Quart.*, 36:356–409

Kiell, N. (1964), *The Universal Experience of Adolescence*. New York. International Universities Press.

Kimberly, R. P. (1970), Rhythmic patterns in human interaction. *Nature*, 228:88–90

King, S. H. (1968), Characteristics of students seeking psychiatric help during college *J. Amer. Coll. Health Assn.*, 17:150.

———— (1969), Youth in rebellion: An historical perspective. In: *Drug Dependence. A Guide for Physicians.* Chicago: American Medical Association.

———— (1971), Coping mechanisms in adolescents. *Psychiat Ann* , 1.10–46

———— (1973), *Five Lives at Harvard: Personality Change During College* Cambridge, Mass.: Harvard University Press.

Kinsey, A. C., Pomeroy, W. B. & Martin, C. E. (1948), *Sexual Behavior in the Human Male*. Philadelphia: Saunders

———— et al. (1953), *Sexual Behavior in the Human Female* Philadelphia. Saunders

Kirk, H. (1964), *Shared Fate*. New York: Free Press.

Klaus, M. H. & Kennell, J. H. (1970), Mothers separated from their newborn infants *Pediat. Clin. N. Amer.*, 17:1015–1037.

———— et al. (1972), Maternal attachment: The importance of the first postpartum days. *New England J. Med.*, 286:460–463

Kleeman, J. A. (1967), The peek-a-boo game. *The Psychoanalytic Study of the Child*, 22:239–273. New York: International Universities Press

Kliman, G. (1968), *Psychological Emergencies of Childhood*. New York. Grune & Stratton.

Klopfer, P. (1971), Mother love: What turns it on? *Amer Sci* , 59:404–407

Klüver, H. (1936), The study of personality and the method of equivalent and non-equivalent stimuli. *J. Pers.*, 5:91–112.

Knobloch, H. et al. (1956), Neuropsychiatric sequelae of prematurity. A longitudinal study. *J. Amer. Med. Assn.*, 161:581–585.

———— et al. (1959), The effect of prematurity on health and growth *Amer J Public Health*, 49:1164–1173.

Köhler, O. (1954), Das Lächeln als angeborene Ausdrucksbewegung [The smile as an innate facial expression]. *Z. Menschl. Vererb. Konstitutionslehre*, 32:390–398.

Koel, B. S. (1969), Failure to thrive and fetal injury as a continuum. *Amer. J. Dis.*

Children, 118:565–567.

Kohlberg, L. (1963), The development of children's orientations toward a moral order: Sequence in the development of moral thought. *Vita Humana,* 6:11–33.

———— (1964), Development of moral character and moral ideology. In: *Review of Child Development Research,* ed. M. L. Hoffman & L. W. Hoffman. New York: Russell Sage Foundation, pp. 383–432.

———— (1966), Moral education in the school. *School Rev.,* 74:1–30.

———— (1968), Early education: A cognitive-developmental approach. *Child Devel.,* 39:1013–1062.

———— & Blatt, M. (1972), The effects of classroom discussion on level of moral judgment. In: *Recent Research in Moral Development,* ed. L. Kohlberg & E Turiel. New York: Holt, Rinehart & Winston.

———— & DeVries, R. (1971), Relations between Piaget and psychometric assessments of intelligence. In: *The Natural Curriculum,* ed. C. Lavatelli. Urbana: University of Illinois Press.

———— & Gilligan, C. (1971), The adolescent as a philosopher. *Daedalus,* 100:1051–1086. (Reprinted in *New Directions in Childhood Psychopathology,* Vol. 1, Chapt. 12.)

———— & Kramer, R. (1969), Continuities and discontinuities in childhood and adult moral development. *Human Devel.,* 12:93–120.

———— & Lockwood, A. (1970), Cognitive-developmental psychology and political education: Progress in the sixties. Presented to Social Science Consortium Convention, Boulder, Col.

———— & Turiel, E. (1971), Moral development and moral education. In: *Psychology and Educational Practice,* ed. G. Lesser. Chicago: Scott, Foresman.

Kohlsaat, B. & Johnson, A. (1954), Some suggestions for practice in infant adoption. *Social Casework,* 35:91–99.

Kohut, H. (1971), *The Analysis of the Self.* New York: International Universities Press.

Kolodny, R. et al. (1974), Depression of plasma testosterone levels after chronic intensive marihuana use. *New England J. Med.,* 290:872–874.

Kopelman, L. (1978), Ethical controversies in medical research: The case of XYY screening. *Perspect. Biol. Med.,* 21:196–204.

Koppitz, E. M. (1964), *The Bender Gestalt Test for Young Children.* New York: Grune & Stratton.

———— (1968), *Psychological Evaluation of Children's Human Figure Drawings.* New York: Grune & Stratton.

Kornitzer, M. (1971), The adopted adolescent and the sense of identity. *Child Adoption,* 66:43–48.

Kraft, M. B. (1968), The face-hand test. *Devel. Med. Child Neurol.,* 10:214–219.

Kreitman, N. et al. (1970), Neurosis and marital interaction, I: Personality and symptoms. *Brit. J. Psychiat.,* 117:33–46.

Krige, H. N. (1966), The abused child complex and its characteristic X-ray findings. *S. Afr. Med. J.,* 40:490–493.

Kruez, L., Rose, R. & Jennings, J. (1972), Suppression of plasma testosterone levels and psychological stress. *Arch. Gen. Psychiat.,* 26:479–482.

Kuenne, M. R. (1946), Experimental investigation of the relation of language to transposition behavior in young children. *J. Exper. Psychol.,* 36:471–490.

Kuhlin, H. E. & Reiter, E. (1973), Gonadotrophins during childhood and adolescence:

A review. *Pediat.*, 51:260–271.

Kuhn, D., Langer, J. & Kohlberg, L. (1971), The development of formal-operational thought: Its relation to moral judgment. (Manuscript.)

Kuipers, F. et al. (1964), Child abuse. *Ned. Tÿdschr. Geneesk.*, 108:2399–2406.

Laing, R. D. (1965), Mystification, confusion and conflict. In: *Intensive Family Therapy: Theoretical and Practical Aspects*, ed. I. Boszormenyi-Nagi & J. L. Framo. New York: Harper & Row, pp. 343–363.

Lampl, H. (1953), The influence of biological and psychological factors upon the development of the latency period. In: *Drives, Affects, Behavior*, Vol. 1, ed. R. M. Loewenstein. New York: International Universities Press, pp. 380–387.

Lampl-de Groot, J. (1960), On adolescence. *The Psychoanalytic Study of the Child*, 15:95–103. New York: International Universities Press.

Landis, J. T. (1960), The trauma of children when parents divorce. *Marr. Fam. Living*, 22:7–13.

——— (1962), A comparison of children from divorced and nondivorced unhappy marriages. *Fam. Life Co-ordinator*, 11:61–65.

——— (1963), Social correlates of divorce or nondivorce among the unhappy married. *Marr. Fam. Living*, 25:178–180.

Landsberg, L. & Axelrod, J. (1968), Influence of pituitary, thyroid, and adrenal hormones on norepinephrine turnover and metabolism in the rat heart. *Circulation Res.*, 22:559–571.

Langner, T. S. et al. (1969a), Mental disorder in a random sample of Manhattan children. Presented to American Orthopsychiatric Association.

——— et al. (1969b), Psychiatric impairment in welfare and non-welfare city children. Presented to American Psychological Association.

Lapouse, R. & Monk, M. A. (1964), Behavior deviations in a representative sample of children: Variation by sex, age, race, social class, and family size. *Amer. J. Orthopsychiat.* 34:436–446.

Laufer, M. (1966), Object loss and mourning during adolescence. *The Psychoanalytic Study of the Child*, 21:269–293. New York: International Universities Press.

Laurendeau, M. & Pinard, A. (1970), *The Development of the Concept of Space in the Child*. New York: International Universities Press.

Lawton, J. & Gross, S. (1964), Review of psychiatric literature on adopted children. *Arch. Gen. Psychiat.*, 11:635–644.

Leahy, A. (1935), A study of adopted children as a method investigating naturenurture. *J. Amer. Statistic Assn.*, 30 (Suppl. 281).

Lebovitz, P. (1972), Feminine behavior in boys: Aspects of its outcome. *Amer. J. Psychiat.*, 128:1283–1289.

Legg, C. (1977), Literature review on adoption. (Manuscript.)

Lehman, H. (1953), *Age and Achievement*. Princeton: Princeton University Press.

Leiderman, P. H. et al. (1973), Mother-infant interaction: Effects of early deprivation, prior experience and sex of infant. *Early Devel.*, 51:154–175.

Leifer, A. et al. (1972), Effects of mother-infant separation on maternal attachment behavior. *Child Devel.*, 43:1203–1218.

Lemon, E. (1959), Rear view mirror: An experience with completed adoptions. *Social Worker*, 27:41–51.

Lenneberg, E. (1966), The natural history of language. In: *The Genesis of Language*, ed. F. Smith & G. A. Miller. Cambridge, Mass.: MIT Press.

——— (1967), *The Biological Foundations of Language*. New York: Wiley.

Leonard, M. F., Rhymes, J. P. & Solnit, A. J. (1966), Failure to thrive in infants—a family problem. *Amer. J. Dis. Children*, 111:600–612.

Levinson, B. J. et al. (1974), The psychosocial development of men in early adulthood and the mid-life transition. In: *Life History Research in Psychopathology*, ed. D. F. Ricks, A. Thomas & M. Roff. Minneapolis: University of Minnesota Press.

Levitsky, D. A. & Barnes, R. H. (1969), Effects of early protein calorie malnutrition on animal behavior. Presented to American Association for Advancement of Science, Dec.

————— (1970), Effect of early malnutrition on reaction of adult rats to aversive stimuli. *Nature*, 225:468–469.

Lev-Ran, A. (1974), Gender role differentiation in hermaphrodites. *Arch. Sexual Behav.*, 3:339–424.

Levy, D. M. (1958), *Behavioral Analysis: Analysis of Clinical Observations of Behavior as Applied to Mother-Newborn Relationships*. Springfield, Ill.: Thomas.

Lewin, K. (1939), Field theory and experiment in social psychology. *Amer. J. Sociol.*, 44:868–896.

Lewis, A. J. (1956), Social Psychiatry. Lectures on the Scientific Basis of Medicine VI, London.

Lewis, D. O. et al. (1973), Psychotic symptomatology in a juvenile court clinic population. *J. Amer. Acad. Child Psychiat.*, 12:660–674.

Lewis, H. (1965), The psychiatric aspects of adoption. In: *Modern Perspectives in Child Psychiatry*, ed. J. G. Howells. New York: Brunner/Mazel, 1971, pp. 428–451.

Lewis, M. (1972), State as an infant-environment interaction: An analysis of mother-infant interaction as a function of sex. *Merrill-Palmer Quart.*, 18:95–121.

Lewis, M. M. (1963), *Language, Thought and Personality in Infancy and Childhood*. London: Harrap.

Liang, P. H. et al. (1967), Evaluation of mental development in relation to early malnutrition. *Amer. J. Clin. Nutr.*, 20:1290–1294.

Lidz, T. (1963), *The Family and Human Adaptation*. New York: International Universities Press.

————— (1968), *The Person*. New York: Basic Books.

————— (1973), *The Origin and Treatment of Schizophrenic Disorders*. New York: Basic Books.

Lieberman, P. (1967), *Intonation, Perception and Language*. Cambridge, Mass.: MIT Press.

Lin, T. & Standley, C. C. (1962), *The Scope of Epidemiology in Psychiatry*. Geneva: World Health Organization.

Linde, L. (1967), The search for mom and dad. *Minn. Welfare*, Summer, pp. 7–12, 47.

Lindemann, E. (1944), Symptomatology and management of acute grief. *Amer. J. Psychiat.*, 101:141–148.

Lipin, T. (1969), Sensory irruptions and mental organization. *J. Amer. Psychoanal. Assn.*, 17:1055–1073.

Little, W. J. (1862), On the influence of abnormal parturition, difficult labour, premature birth, and asphyxia neonatorum on the mental and physical conditions of the child, especially in relation to deformities. *Trans. Obstet. Soc. London*, 3:293–344.

Livingston, G. (1977), Search for a stranger. *Reader's Digest,* June, pp. 85–89.

Lobitz, W. C. & Campbell, C. J. (1953), Physiologic studies in atopic dermatitis (disseminated neurodermatitis), I: The local cutaneous response to intradermally injected acetylcholine and epinephrine. *Arch. Derm. Syph.,* 67:575.

Loevinger, J. (1966), The meaning and measurement of ego development. *Amer. Psychol.,* 21:195–206.

Lombroso, D. (1876), *L'unio delinquente in rapporto alla antropologia, alla giurisprudenza ed alla disciplina carcerarie.* Milan.

——— (1911), *Crime: Its Causes and Remedies.* Boston: Little, Brown.

Lorenz, K. (1937), Imprinting. *Auk,* 54:245–273.

Luce, G. (1970), *Biological Rhythms in Medicine and Psychiatry.* Chevy Chase, Md.: Department of Health, Education & Welfare.

Luria, A. R. (1961), *The Role of Speech in the Regulation of Normal and Abnormal Behaviour.* New York: Pergamon.

——— & Homskaya, E. D. (1962), Disturbances in the regulative role of speech with frontal lobe lesions. In: *The Frontal Granular Cortex and Behavior,* ed. J. M. Warren & K. Akert. New York: McGraw-Hill, 1964, pp. 353–371.

Lystad, M. (1975), Violence at home: A review of the literature. *Amer. J. Orthopsychiat.,* 45:328–345.

Maccoby, E. E. & Jacklin, C. N. (1974), *The Psychology of Sex Differences.* Stanford: Stanford University Press.

MacDonald, J. (1963), The threat to kill. *Amer. J. Psychiat.,* 120:125–130.

MacFarlane, A. (1975), Olfaction in the development of social preferences in the human neonate. In: *Ciba Foundation Symposium 33, Parent-Infant Interaction.* New York: Associated Scientific Publishers, pp. 103–113.

MacFarlane, J. W., Allen, L. & Honzik, M. P. (1962), *A Developmental Study of the Behavior Problems in Normal Children between 21 Months and 14 Years.* Berkeley: University of California Press.

MacLean, N. et al. (1968), A survey of sex chromatin abnormalities in mental hospitals. *J. Med. Genet.,* 5:165–172.

MacLean, P. B. (1969), A triune concept of the brain and behavior. In: *The Hincks Memorial Lectures,* ed. D. Campbell & T. Boags. Toronto: University of Toronto Press, 1973.

Mahler, M. S. (1952), On child psychosis and schizophrenia: Autistic and symbiotic infantile psychoses. In: *Childhood Psychopathology,* ed. S. I. Harrison & J. F. McDermott, Jr. New York: International Universities Press, 1972, pp. 670–687.

——— (1960), Symposium on psychotic object relationships, III: Perceptual de-differentiation and psychotic 'object relationship.' *Internat. J. Psycho-Anal.,* 41:548–553.

——— (1968), *On Human Symbiosis and the Vicissitudes of Individuation,* Vol. I: *Infantile Psychosis.* New York: International Universities Press.

——— (1971), A study of the separation-individuation process: And its possible application to borderline phenomena in the psychoanalytic situation. *The Psychoanalytic Study of the Child,* 26:403–424. New York: Quadrangle.

——— (1972), On the first three subphases of the separation-individuation process. *Internat. J. Psycho-Anal.,* 53:333–338.

——— & Gosliner, B. J. (1955), On symbiotic child psychosis: Genetic, dynamic and restitutive aspects. *The Psychoanalytic Study of the Child,* 10:195–212.

New York: International Universities Press.

———— & McDevitt, J. B. (1968), Observations on adaptation and defense *in statu nascendi*. *Psychoanal. Quart.*, 37:1–21.

————, Pine, F. & Bergman, A. (1975), *The Psychological Birth of the Human Infant*. New York: Basic Books.

Malinowski, B. (1929), *The Sexual Life of Savages in North-Western Melanesia*. New York: Harcourt, Brace, Jovanovich, 1962.

Mandell, A. & Mandell, M. (1967), Suicide and the menstrual cycle. *J. Amer. Med. Assn.*,.200:792–793.

Mandler, J. M. (1958), Effects of early food deprivation on adult behavior in the rat. *J. Comp. Physiol. Psychol.*, 51:513–517.

Marcia, J. E. (1966), Development and validation of ego identity status. *J. Pers. Soc. Psychol.*, 3:551–558.

Marquis, D. P. (1931), Can conditioned responses be established in the newborn infant? *J. Genet. Psychol.*, 39:479–492.

Marris, P. (1958), *Widows and Their Families*. London: Routledge.

Marshall, H. R. (1966), Transposition in children as a function of age and knowledge. *J. Genet. Psychol.*, 108:65–69.

Marshall, W. A. & Tanner, J. M. (1969), Variations in the pattern of pubertal changes in girls. *Arch. Dis. Childhood*, 44:291.

———— ———— (1970), Variations in the pattern of pubertal changes in boys. *Arch. Dis. Childhood*, 45:13.

Martin, H. (1972), The child and his development. In: *Helping the Battered Child and His Family*, ed. C. H. Kempe & R. E. Helfer. Philadelphia: Lippincott, pp. 93–104.

Martin, J. (1973), Neural regulation of growth hormone secretion. *New England J. Med.*, 228:1384–1393.

Mason, J. (1968), Organization of psychoendocrine mechanisms. *Psychosom. Med.*, 30:565–570, 576–607, 631–653, 666–681.

Masterson, J. F. (1967), *The Psychiatric Dilemma of Adolescence*. Boston: Little, Brown.

———— (1968), The psychiatric significance of adolescent turmoil. *Amer. J. Psychiat.*, 124:107–112.

McCarthy, D. (1954), Language development in children. In: *Manual of Child Psychology*, 2nd Ed., ed. L. Carmichael. New York: Wiley.

———— (1958), *Language Development*. Presented to Summer Symposium of the Cleveland Hearing and Speech Center.

McCord, W. & McCord, J. (1959), *Origins of Crime: A New Evaluation of the Cambridge-Somerville Youth Study*. New York: Columbia University Press.

McDermott, J. F., Jr. (1968), Parental divorce in early childhood. *Amer. Psychiat.*, 124:1424–1432.

———— (1970), Divorce and its psychiatric sequelae in children. *Arch. Gen. Psychiat.*, 23:421–427.

———— & Char, W. F. (1974), The undeclared war between child and family therapy. *J. Amer. Acad. Child Psychiat.*, 13:422–436.

———— & Harrison, S. I. (1977), *Psychiatric Treatment of the Child*. New York: Aronson.

McDonald, A. D. (1964), Intelligence in children of very low birth weight. *Brit. J. Prev. Soc. Med.*, 18:59–74.

McLaren, B. (1974), The great protein fiasco. *Lancet,* 2:93–96.

McNeill, D. (1966), Developmental psycholinguistics. In: *The Genesis of Language,* ed. F. Smith & G. A. Miller. Cambridge, Mass.: MIT Press.

McWhinnie, A. (1967), *Adopted Children and How They Grow Up* London: Routledge & Kegan Paul.

——— (1970), Who am I? *Child Adoption,* 62:36–40.

Mead, M. (1954), Some theoretical considerations of the problem of mother-child separation. *Amer. J. Orthopsychiat.,* 24:471–483.

——— (1965), Paper presented to Ciba Foundation Conference on Transcultural Psychiatry, London.

Medawar, P. B. (1967), *The Art of Soluble.* London: Methuen.

——— (1969), *Induction and Intuition in Scientific Thought.* London: Methuen.

Menyuk, P. (1958), The role of distinctive features in children's acquisition of phonology. *J. Speech Res.,* 11:138.

——— (1967a), Children's learning and recall of grammatical and non-grammatical phonological sequences. Presented to Society for Research in Child Development, New York City.

——— (1967b), "Innovative" linguistic descriptions of the language acquisition of children who acquire language normally and those whose language acquisition is deviant. Presented in Pittsburgh.

——— (1968), Speech pathology: Some principles underlying therapeutic practices. Presented to ASHA Meeting.

——— (1971), *The Acquisition and Development of Language.* Englewood Cliffs, N.J.: Prentice-Hall.

Mermann, A. C. (1966), Lowndes County, Alabama, TICEP Health Survey, Summer 1966; and Statement Prepared for the United States Senate Sub-Committee on Employment, Manpower and Poverty. Washington, D.C.

Merrill, E. J. (1962), Physical abuse of children: An agency study. In: *Protecting the Battered Child,* ed. V. deFrancis. Denver: American Humane Association, pp. 1–15.

Middlemore, M. P. (1941), *The Nursing Couple.* London: Cassell

Migeon, C. J. et. al. (1975), Plasma androgens and gonadotropins in 47,XYY subjects. (Manuscript.)

Miller, G. A. (1956), The magical number seven, plus or minus two. *Psychol. Rev.,* 63:81–97.

Miller, J. B. M. (1971), Children's reactions to the death of a parent: A review of the psychoanalytic literature. *J. Amer. Psychoanal. Assn.,* 19:697–719.

Miller, L. (1969), Child rearing in the kibbutz. In: *Modern Perspectives in International Child Psychiatry,* ed. J. G. Howells. Edinburgh: Oliver & Boyd.

Miller, N. (1971), *Selected Papers.* Chicago: Aldine.

Miller, N. E. (1969), Learning of visceral and glandular response. *Science,* 163:434–445.

Milner, B. (1962), Some effects of frontal lobectomy in man. In: *The Frontal Granular Cortex and Behavior,* ed. J. M. Warren & K. Akert. New York: McGraw-Hill, 1964, pp. 313–334.

Milowe, I. & Lourie, R. (1964), The child's role in the battered child syndrome. *J. Pediat.,* 65:1079–1081.

Minuchin, S. (1974), *Families and Family Therapy.* Cambridge, Mass.. Harvard University Press.

Mitchell, H. S. (1962), Nutrition in relation to stature. *J. Amer. Dietetic Assn.*, 40:521–524.

——— (1964), Stature changes in Japanese youth and nutritional implications. *Fed. Proc.*, 28:877, No. 27.

Mnookin, R. H. (1975), Book review of *Beyond the Best Interests of the Child*. *J. Amer. Acad. Child Psychiat.*, 14:180–183.

Mohr, G. et al. (1963), Studies of eczema and asthma in the preschool child. *J. Amer. Acad. Child Psychiat.*, 2:271–291.

Monckeberg, F. (1968), Effect of early marasmic malnutrition on subsequent physical and psychological development. In: *Malnutrition, Learning and Behavior*, ed. N. S. Scrimshaw & J. E. Gordon. Cambridge, Mass.: MIT Press, pp. 269–277.

Money, J. (1955), Hermaphroditism, gender, and precocity in hyperadrenalcorticism: Psychological findings. *Bull. Johns Hopkins Hosp.*, 96:253–264.

——— (1963), Cytogenetic and psychosexual incongruities, with a note on space form blindness. *Amer. J. Psychiat.*, 119:820–827.

——— (1964), Two cytogenetic syndromes: Psychologic comparisons, I: Intelligence and specific-factor quotients. *J. Psychiat. Res.*, 2:223–231.

——— (1968), Cognitive deficits in Turner's syndrome. In: *Progress in Human Behavior Genetics*, ed. S. G. Vandenberg. Baltimore: Johns Hopkins University Press.

——— (1969), Sex reassignment as related to hermaphroditism and transsexualism. In: *Transsexualism and Sex Reassignment*, ed. R. Green & J. Money. Baltimore: Johns Hopkins University Press.

——— (1970), Behavior genetics: Principles, methods and examples from XO, XYY and XXY syndromes. *Seminars Psychiat.*, 2:11–29.

——— (1971), Pre-natal hormones and intelligence: A possible relationship. *Impact Sci. Soc.*, 21:285–290.

——— (1973), Turner's syndrome and parietal lobe functions. *Cortex*, 9:385–392.

——— (1975), Intellectual functioning in childhood endorinopathes and related cytogenetic disorders. In: *Endocrine and Genetic Diseases of Childhood and Adolescence*, 2nd Ed., ed. L. I. Gardner. Philadelphia: Saunders.

——— & Alexander, D. (1966), Turner's syndrome: Further demonstration of the presence of specific cognitional deficiencies. *J. Med. Genet.*, 3:47–48.

——— ——— & Ehrhardt, A. A. (1966), Visual-contructional deficit in Turner's syndrome. *J. Pediatrics*, 69:125–127.

——— & Clopper, R. (1974), Psychosocial and psychosexual aspects of errors of pubertal onset and development. *Human Biol.*, 46:173–181.

——— & Ehrhardt, A. A. (1968), Prenatal hormonal exposure: Possible effects on behaviour in man. In: *Endocrinology and Human Behaviour*, ed. R. Michael. London: Oxford University Press, pp. 32–48.

——— ——— (1972), *Man and Woman, Boy and Girl: The Differentiation and Dimorphism of Gender Identity from Conception to Maturity*. Baltimore: Johns Hopkins University Press.

———, Gaskin, R. & Hull, H. (1970), Impulse, aggression and sexuality in the XYY syndrome. *St. John's Law Rev.*, 44:220–235.

——— & Granoff, D. (1965), I.Q and the somatic stigmata of Turner's syndrome. *Amer. J. Ment. Deficiency*, 70:69–77

———, Hampson, J. G. & Hampson, J. L. (1955), An examination of some basic sexual concepts: The evidence of human hermaphroditism. *Bull. Johns Hopkins*

Hosp., 97:301–319.

———— ———— ———— (1956), Sexual incongruities and psychopathology: The evidence of human hermaphroditism. *Bull. Johns Hopkins Hosp.*, 98:43–57.

———— & Mittenthal, S. (1970), Lack of personality pathology in Turner's syndrome: Relation to cytogenetics, hormones and physique. *Behav. Genet.*, 1:43–56.

———— & Pollitt, E. (1964), Cytogenetic and psychosexual ambiguity: Klinefelter's syndrome and transvestism compared. *Arch. Gen. Psychiat.*, 11:589–595.

———— et al. (1974), Cytogenetics, hormones and behavior disability: Comparison of XYY and XXY syndromes. *Clin. Genet.*, 6:370–382.

Montague, M. F. A. (1968), Chromosomes and crime. *Psychol. Today*, Oct.

Moore, K. L. (1966), *The Sex Chromatin*. Philadelphia: Saunders.

Moore, T. W. (1963), Effects on the children. In: *Working Mothers and Their Children*, ed. S. Judkin & A. Holme. London: Joseph.

Morris, J. N. (1957), *Uses of Epidemiology*. Edinburgh: Livingstone.

Morris, M. G. & Gould, R. W. (1963), Role reversal: A concept in dealing with the neglected/battered child syndrome. In: *The Neglected-Battered Child Syndrome*. New York: Child Welfare League of America, pp. 29–49.

Mosher, L., Pollin, W. & Stabenau, J. (1971), Families with identical twins discordant for schizophrenia: Some relationships between identification, psychopathology, and dominance-submissivness. *Brit. J. Psychiat.*, 118:29–42.

Munro, A. (1966), Parental deprivation in depressive patients. *Brit. J. Psychiat.*, 112:443–457.

———— & Griffiths, A. B. (1969), Some psychiatric non-sequelae of childhood bereavement. *Brit. J. Psychiat.*, 115:305–311.

Murphy, G. H. & Wertz, A. W. (1954), Diets of pregnant women: Influence of socioeconomic factors. *J. Amer. Dietetic Assn.*, 30:34–48.

Mussen, P. H. & Jones, M. C. (1957), Self-concepting motivations and interpersonal attitudes of late- and early-maturing boys. *Child Devel.*, 28:243–256.

Myers, M. L. et al. (1968), A nutrition study of school children in a depressed urban district, I: Dietary findings. *J. Amer. Dietetic Assn.*, 53:226–233.

Naess, S. (1959), Mother-child separation and delinquency. *Brit. J. Delinquency*, 10:22–35.

———— (1962), Mother-child separation and delinquency: Further evidence. *Brit. J. Criminol.*, 2:361–374.

Nagera, H. (1966), *Early Childhood Disturbances, the Infantile Neurosis, and the Adulthood Disturbances*. New York: International Universities Press.

———— (1970), Children's reactions to the death of important objects: A developmental approach. *The Psychoanalytic Study of the Child*, 25:360–400. New York: International Universities Press.

Nass, M. L. (1966), The superego and moral development in the theories of Freud and Piaget. *The Psychoanalytic Study of the Child*, 21:51–68. New York: International Universities Press.

National Center for Health Statistics (1964), *Natality Statistics Analysis, United States, 1962*. Vital and Health Statistics, Public Health Service Publ. No. 1000, Series 21, No. 1. Washington, D.C.: U.S. Government Printing Office.

———— (1967), *Vital Statistics of the United States, 1965*. Washington, D.C.: U.S. Government Printing Office.

Neubauer, P. B. (1960), The one-parent child and his oedipal development. *The Psychoanalytic Study of the Child*, 15:286–309. New York: International

Universities Press.

Neugarten, B., Ed. (1968), *Middle Age and Aging*. Chicago: University of Chicago Press.

———— & Datan, N. (1974), The middle years. In: *American Handbook of Psychiatry*, Vol. 1, Rev. 2nd Ed., ed. S. Arieti. New York: Basic Books, pp. 592–608.

———— et al. (1964), *Personality in Middle and Late Life*. New York: Atherton Press.

Newman, H. H., Freeman, F. N. & Holzinger, K. J. (1937), *Twins: A Study of Heredity and Environment*. Chicago: University of Chicago Press.

Nielsen, J. (1969), *Klinefelter's Syndrome and the XYY Syndrome: A Genetical, Endocrinological and Psychiatric-Psychological Study of 33 Hypogonadal Male Patients and Two Patients with Karyotype 47,XYY*. Copenhagen: Munksgaard.

———— (1970), Turner's syndrome in medical neurological and psychiatric wards: A psychiatric, cytogenetic and clinical study. *Acta Psychiat. Scand.*, 46:286–310.

———— et al. (1970), *A Psychiatric-Psychological Study of 50 Severely Hypogonadal Male Patients, Including 34 with Klinefelter's Syndrome, 47,XXY*. Copenhagen: Munksgaard.

Noel, B. & Revil, D. (1974), Some personality perspectives of XYY individuals taken from the general population. *J. Sex Res.*, 10:219–225.

Norris, M., Spaulding, P. & Brodie, F. (1957), *Blindness in Children*. Chicago: University of Chicago Press.

North, A. F. (1967), Project Head Start and the pediatrician. *Clin. Pediatrics*, 6:191–194.

Nurse, S. (1964), Familial patterns of parents who abuse their children. *Smith Coll. Studies Soc. Work*, 35:11–25.

Nye, F. I. (1957), Child adjustment in broken and in unhappy unbroken homes. *Marr. Fam. Living*, 19:356–361.

Nylander, I. (1960), Children of alcoholic fathers. *Acta Paediat.*, 49 (Suppl 121).

O'Connor, N. (1956), The evidence for the permanently disturbing effects of mother-child separation. *Acta Psychol.*, 12:174–191.

Offer, D. (1969), *The Psychological World of the Teen-ager*. New York: Basic Books.

———— & Freedman, D. X. (1972), *Modern Psychiatry and Clinical Research*. New York: Basic Books.

Offord, D., Apointe, J. F. & Cross, L. A. (1969), Presenting symptomatology of adopted children. *Arch. Gen. Psychiat.*, 20:110–116.

Olds, J. (1959), In: *Dynamic Psychopathology in Childhood*, ed. J. Jessner & E. Pavenstedt. New York: Grune & Stratton.

———— (1962), Hypothalmic substrates of rewards. *Physiol. Rev.*, 42:554–604.

Oliver, J. E. & Taylor, A. (1971), Five generations of ill-treated in one family pedigree. *Brit. J. Psychol.*, 119:473–480.

Ombredane, A. (1951), *L'Aphasie et l'elaboration de la pensée explicite*. Paris: Presses Universitaires de France.

Ornitz, E. M. & Ritvo, E. (1968), Perceptual inconstancy in early infantile autism. *Arch. Gen. Psychiat.*, 18:76–98.

Ounsted, C., Oppenheimer, R. & Lindsay, J. (1975), The psychopathology and psychotherapy of the families: Aspects of bonding failure. In: *Concerning Child Abuse*, ed. A. W. Franklin. Edinburgh: Churchill Livingstone, pp. 30–40.

Owen, D. R. (1973), The 47,XYY male: A review. *Psychol. Bull.*, 78:209–233.

Owen, G. M. & Kram, K. M. (1969), Nutritional status of preschool children in Mississippi: Food sources of nutrients in the diets. *J. Amer. Dietetic Assn.*,

54:490–494.

Parens, H. & Saul, L. J. (1971), *Dependence in Man*. New York: International Universities Press.

Pasamanick, B. & Knobloch, H. (1960), Brain damage and reproductive casualty. *Amer. J. Orthopsychiat.*, 30:298–305.

Paton, J. (1954), *The Adopted Break Silence*. Acton, Cal.: Life History Study Center.

——— (1960), *Three Trips Home*. Acton, Cal.: Life History Study Center.

——— (a.k.a. R. Kittson) (1968), *Orphan Voyage*. New York: Vantage.

——— (1971), The American orphan and the temptations of adoption: A manifesto. Presented to World Conference on Adoption and Foster Care, Milan, Italy.

Patterson, D. G. (1930), *Physique and Intellect*. New York: Appleton-Century-Crofts.

Patterson, P. H. et al. (1966), Child abuse in Hawaii. *Hawaii Med. J.*, 25:395–397.

Patton, R. G. & Gardner, L. I. (1963), *Growth Failure in Maternal Deprivation*. Springfield, Ill.: Thomas.

Pearson, P. L. & Bobrow, M. (1970), Flourescent staining of the Y chromosome in meiotic stages of the human male. *J. Reproduction Fertil.*, 22:177–179.

Peel, E. A. (1967), *The Psychological Basis of Education*, 2nd Ed. Edinburgh & London: Oliver & Boyd.

Peller, L. E. (1961), About "telling the child" of his adoption. *Bull. Phila. Assn. Psychoanal.*, 11:145–154.

——— (1963), Further comments on adoption. *Bull. Phila. Assn. Psychoanal.*, 13:1–14.

——— (1966), Freud's contribution to language development. *The Psychoanalytic Study of the Child*, 21:448–467. New York: International Universities Press.

Peskin, H. (1967), Pubertal onset and ego functioning. *J. Abnorm. Psychol.*, 72:1–15.

Peterson, D. R. et al. (1959), Parental attitudes and child adjustment. *Child Devel.*, 30:119–130.

Piaget, J. (1923), *The Language and Thought of the Child*. London: Routledge & Kegan Paul, 1959.

——— (1932), *The Moral Judgment of the Child*. New York: Free Press, 1965.

——— (1936), *The Origins of Intelligence in Children*. New York: International Universities Press, 1952.

——— (1937), *The Construction of Reality in the Child*. New York: Basic Books, 1954.

——— (1947), *The Psychology of Intelligence*. London: Routledge & Kegan Paul, 1950.

——— (1962a), The relation of affectivity to intelligence. In: *Childhood Psychopathology*, ed. S. I. Harrison & J. F. McDermott, Jr. New York: International Universities Press, 1972, pp. 167–175.

——— (1962b) The stages of intellectual development of the child. In: *Childhood Psychopathology*, ed. S. I. Harrison & J. F. McDermott, Jr. New York: International Universities Press, 1972, pp. 157–166.

Pinchbeck, I. & Hewitt, M. (1969), *Children in English Society*, Vol. 1. London: Routledge & Kegan Paul.

Pirke, K. M., Kockott, G. & Dittmar, F. (1974), Psychosexual stimulation and plasma testosterone in man. *Arch. Sexual Behav.*, 3:577–584.

Pitts, F. N., Jr. et al. (1965), Adult psychiatric illness assessed for childhood parental loss and psychiatric illness in family members: A study of 748 patients and 250 controls. *Amer. J. Psychiat.*, 121(12):i–x.

Podd, M. H. (1969), *Ego Identity Status and Morality: An Empirical Investigation of Two Developmental Concepts.* Unpublished Ph.D. dissertation.

Polak, P. R., Emde, R. N. & Spitz, R. A. (1964), The smiling response to the human face, I: Methodology, quantification and natural history. *J. Nerv. Ment. Dis.,* 139:103–109.

Pollack, M. & Goldfarb, W. (1957a), The face-hand test in schizophrenic children. *A.M.A. Arch. Neurol. Psychiat.,* 77:635–642.

———— ———— (1957b), Patterns of orientation in children in residential treatment for severe behavior disorders. *Amer. J. Orthopsychiat.,* 27:538–552.

———— & Gordon, E. (1959–1960), The face-hand test in retarded and non-retarded emotionally disturbed children. *Amer. J. Ment. Deficiency,* 64:758–760.

Pollin, W. (1971), A possible genetic factor related to psychosis. *Amer. J. Psychiat.,* 128:311–317.

———— & Stabenau, J (1968), Biological, psychological, and historical differences in a series of monozygotic twins discordant for schizophrenia. In: *The Transmission of Schizophrenia,* ed. S. Kety & D. Rosenthal. London: Pergamon Press, pp. 317–332.

———— ———— & Tupin, J. (1965), Family studies with identical twins discordant for schizophrenia. *Psychiat.,* 28:60–78.

———— et al. (1966), Life history differences in identical twins discordant for schizophrenia. *Amer. J. Orthopsychiat.,* 36:492–509.

Pollitt, E (1969), Ecology, malnutrition and mental development *Psychosom Med ,* 31:193–200.

———— & Granoff, D. (1967), Mental and motor development of Peruvian children treated for severe malnutrition. *Revista Interamer. Psicol.,* 1(2):93–102.

Pollock, G. H. (1961), Mourning and adaptation. *Internat. J. Psycho-Anal.,* 42:341–361.

Povich, E. & Baratz, J. (1967), *An Investigation of Syntax Development of Head Start Children: A Developmental Sentence Types Analysis.* Chicago: ASHA.

Powell, G. F., Brasel, J. A. & Blizzard, R. M. (1967), Emotional deprivation and growth retardation simulating idiopathic hypopituitarism, I: Clinical evaluation of the syndrome. *New England J. Med.,* 276:1271–1278.

Power, M. J. et al. (1967), Delinquent schools? *New Society,* 10:542–543.

Prager, B. & Rothstein, S. (1973), The adoptee's right to know his natural heritage. *N.Y. Law Forum,* 19:137–156.

Prall, R. C., Ed. (1971), Presentations and publications by Margaret Schoenberger Mahler, M.D. In: *Separation-Individuation,* ed. J. B. McDevitt & C. F. Settlage. New York: International Universities Press, pp. 499–505.

Prange, A. et al. (1972), Thyroid-imipramine clinical and chemical interaction: Evidence for a receptor deficit in depression. *J. Psychiat. Res.,* 9:187–205.

Prechtl, H. & Beintema, O. (1964), *The Neurological Maturation of the Full Term Newborn Infant.* London: Heinemann.

Pressey, S. & Kuhlen, R. (1957), *Psychological Development Through the Life Span.* New York: Harper & Row.

Price, W. H. & Jacobs, P. A. (1970), The 47,XYY male with special reference to behavior. *Seminars Psychiat.,* 2:30–39.

———— & Whatmore, P. B. (1967), Behavior disorders and pattern of crime among XYY males identified at a maximum security hospital. *Brit. Med. J.,* 1:533–536.

Prince, F. & Bentler, P. (1972), Survey of 504 cases of transvestism. *Psychol. Rep.*, 31:903–917.

Pringle, M. (1967), *Adoption: Facts and Fallacies*. London: Longmans, Green.

Provence, S. & Lipton, R. C. (1962), *Infants in Institutions*. New York: International Universities Press.

Prugh, D. G. & Harlow, R. G. (1962), "Masked deprivation" in infants and young children. In: *Deprivation of Maternal Care*. Geneva: World Health Organization, pp. 9–29.

———— et al. (1953), A study of the emotional reactions of children and families to hospitalization and illness. *Amer. J. Orthopsychiat.*, 23:70–106.

Prunty, F. T. G. & Gardiner-Hill, H. (1972), *Modern Trends in Endocrinology*, Vol. 4. New York: Appleton-Century-Crofts.

Rabinowicz, T. (1964), The cerebral cortex of the premature infant of the 8th month. In: *Progress in Brain Research*, Vol. 4, ed. D. P. Purpura & J. P. Schadé. Amsterdam: Elsevier, pp. 39–92.

Raffaelli, M. (1972), *Approche psychiatrique des hommes porteurs d'une dysgonosomie du type XYY: Etat actuel de nos connaissances à propos de 8 observations (dont 7 relevées dans un service de sécurité)*. Unpublished dissertation, Grenoble, France.

Rangell, L. (1955), The role of the parent in the Oedipus complex. *Bull. Menninger Clinic*, 19:9–15.

Rautman, A. (1959), Adoptive parents need help, too *Ment. Hygiene*, 33:424–431.

Read, M (1975), In *Behavioral Correlates of Malnutrition, Growth, and Development of the Brain*, ed. M. Brazier. New York: Raven Press, pp. 335–353.

Reeves, A. (1971), Children with surrogate parents: Cases seen in analytic therapy, an etiologic hypothesis. *Brit. J. Med. Psychol.*, 44:155–171.

Reich, C. (1970), *The Greening of America*. New York: Random House.

Report of the Joint Commission on Mental Health of Children (1970), *Crisis in Child Mental Health: Challenge for the 1970's*. New York: Harper & Row.

Rhyne, M. B. (1965), Genetic aspects of eczema: Conference on Infantile Eczema. *J. Pediat.*, 66:168–170.

Ribble, M. (1943), *The Rights of Infants*. New York: Columbia University Press.

Richards, M. P. M., Bernal, J. F. & Brackbill, Y. (1976), Early behavioral differences: Gender or circumcision? *Devel. Psychobiol.*, 9:89–95.

Richardson, S. A. (1968), The influence of social environmental and nutritional factors on mental ability. In: *Malnutrition, Learning and Behavior*, ed. N. S. Scrimshaw & J. E. Gordon. Cambridge, Mass.: MIT Press, pp. 346–360.

Richmond, J. B. & Lipton, E. L. (1959), Some aspects of neurophysiology of the newborn and their implications for child development. In: *Childhood Psychopathology*, ed. S. I. Harrison & J. F. McDermott, Jr. New York: International Universities Press, 1972, pp. 39–55.

———— ———— & Steinschneider, A. (1962a), Autonomic function in the neonate, V: Individual homeostatic capacity in cardiac response. *Psychosom. Med.*, 24:66–74.

———— ———— ———— (1962b), Observations on differences in autonomic nervous system function between and within individuals during early infancy. *J. Amer. Acad. Child Psychiat.*, 1:83–91.

Ringler, M. et al. (1975), Mother to child speech at two years: Effects of early postnatal contact. *J. Pediat.*, 86:141–144.

———— et al. (1976), Mother's speech to her two year old: Its effects on speech and language comprehension at five years. *Pediat. Res.*, 10:307.

Ritvo, S. (1971), Margaret S. Mahler: Scientist, psychoanalyst, teacher. In: *Separation-Individuation*, ed. J. B. McDevitt & C. F. Settlage. New York: International Universities Press, pp. 6–12.

Roaf, R. (1965), Child care in general practice: Trauma in childhood. *Brit. Med. J.*, 1:1541–1543.

Roberts, D. F., Rozner, L. M. & Swan, A. V. (1971), Age at menarche, physique and environment in industrial North-East England. *Acta Paediat. Scand.*, 60:158–164.

Robertson, James (1958), *Young Children in Hospital*. New York: Basic Books, 1959.

———— & Bowlby, J. (1952), Responses of young children to separation from their mothers, II: Observations of the sequences of response of children aged 18 to 24 months during the course of separation. *Courrier*, 2:131–142

Robertson, Joyce (1962), Mothering as an influence on early development: A study of well-baby clinic records. *The Psychoanalytic Study of the Child*, 17:245–264. New York: International Universities Press.

Robins, L. N. (1966), *Deviant Children Grown Up: A Sociological and Psychiatric Study of Sociopathic Personality*. Baltimore: Williams & Wilkins.

———— (1969), Social correlates of psychiatric disorders: Can we tell causes from consequences? *J. Health Soc. Behav.*, 10:95–104

———— & Hill, S Y. (1966), Assessing the contributions of family structure, class and peer groups to juvenile delinquency. *J. Crim. Law Criminol. Polit. Sci.*, 57:325–334.

Rochlin, G. (1965), *Griefs and Discontents*. Boston: Little, Brown.

Roe, A. & Burks, B. (1945), *Adult Adjustment of Foster Children of Alcoholic and Psychotic Parentage and the Influence of Foster Homes*. New Haven: Yale University Press.

Rogers, R. (1969), The adolescent and the hidden parent. *Compr. Psychiat.*, 10:296–301.

Rollins, N. et al. (1973), Some roles children play in their families: Scapegoat, baby, pet and peacemaker. *J. Amer. Acad. Child Psychiat.*, 12:511–530.

Rosanoff, A. J., Handy, L. M. & Plesset, I. R. (1941), *The Etiology of Child Behavior Difficulties, Juvenile Delinquency and Adult Criminality, with Special Reference to Their Occurrence in Twins*. Psychiatric Monograph No. 1. Sacramento: Department of Institutions.

Rose, J., Boggs, T., Jr. & Alderstein, A. (1960), The evidence for a syndrome of "mothering disability" consequent to threats to the survival of neonates: A design for hypothesis testing including prevention in a prospective study. *Amer. J. Dis. Child.*, 100:776.

Rose, J. A. (1961), The prevention of mothering breakdown associated with physical abnormalities of the infant. In: *Prevention of Mental Disorders in Children*, ed. G. Caplan. New York: Basic Books, pp. 265–282.

Rose, R., Bowne, P. & Poe, R. (1969), Androgen response to stress. *Psychosom. Med.*, 31:418–436.

Rosenthal, D. (1971), *Genetics of Psychopathology*. New York: McGraw-Hill.

Rowntree, G. (1955), Early childhood in broken families. *Population Studies*, 8:247–263.

Rubin, K. & Schneider, F. (1973), The relationship between moral judgment, egocentrism, and altruistic behavior. *Child Devel.*, 44:661–665.

Russell, W. R. (1948), Functions of the frontal lobes. *Lancet*, 254:356–360.

Rutter, M. (1966), *Children of Sick Parents: An Environmental and Psychiatric Study.* Maudsley Monograph No. 16. London: Oxford University Press.

———— (1967), A children's behaviour questionnaire for completion by teachers: Preliminary findings. *J. Child Psychol. Psychiat.*, 8:1–11.

———— (1970a), Psychosocial disorders in childhood and their outcome in adult life. *J. Roy. Coll. Physicians London*, 4:211–218.

———— (1970b), Sex differences in children's responses to family stress. In: *The Child in His Family*, Vol. 1, ed. E. J. Anthony & C. Koupernik. New York: Wiley.

———— (1971a), *Infantile Autism: Concepts, Characteristics, and Treatment.* Edinburgh: Churchill Livingstone.

———— (1971b), Normal psychosexual development *J Child Psychol Psychiat* 11:259–283.

———— & Brown, G. W. (1966), The reliability and validity of measures of family life and relationships in families containing a psychiatric patient. *Soc. Psychiat.*, 1:38–53.

———— & Graham, P. (1968), The reliability and validity of the psychiatric assessment of the child. *Brit. J. Psychiat.*, 114:563–680.

———— ———— & Yule, W (1970), *A Neuropsychiatric Study in Childhood* Clinics in Developmental Medicine 35/36 London. Spastics International

————, Tizard, J. & Whitmore, K., Eds. (1970), *Education, Health, and Behaviour.* London: Longmans.

———— et al. (1963), Temperamental characteristics in infancy and the later development of behavioural disorders. *Brit. J. Psychiat.*, 110:651–661.

Sabbath, J. C. et al. (1961), Psychiatric observations in adolescent girls lacking ovarian function. *Psychosom. Med.*, 23:224–231.

Sachs, B. et al. (1973), Sexual behavior: Normal male patterning in androgenized female rats. *Science*, 181:770–771.

Sackett, G. P. (1969), Abnormal behavior in laboratory-reared rhesus monkeys. In: *Abnormal Behavior in Animals*, ed. M. W. Fox. New York: Saunders.

Saghir, M. T. & Robins, E. (1973), *Male and Female Homosexuality: A Comprehensive Investigation.* Baltimore: Williams & Wilkins.

Sandberg, A. A. et al. (1961), An XYY human male. *Lancet*, 2:488–489.

Sander, L. W. (1970), Regulation and organization in the early infant-caretaker system. In: *Brain and Early Behavior*, ed. R. Robinson. London: Academic Press, pp. 313–331.

———— (1975), Infant and caretaking environment. In: *Explorations in Child Psychiatry*, ed. E. J. Anthony. New York: Plenum Press, pp. 129–166.

Sandler, J. (1960), On the concept of superego. *The Psychoanalytic Study of the Child*, 15:128–162. New York: International Universities Press.

———— & Joffe, W. G. (1965), Notes on childhood depression. *Internat. J. Psycho-Anal.*, 36:88–96.

Sants, H. (1965), Genealogical bewilderment in children with substitute parents. *Child Adoption*, 47:32–42.

Sarnoff, C. (1976), *Latency.* New York: Aronson.

Say, B. et al. (1977), Chromosome variants in children with psychiatric disorders.

Amer. J. Psychiat., 134:424–426.

Scammon, R. (1930), The measurement of the body in childhood. In: *The Measurement of Man*, ed. J. A. Harrison et al. Minneapolis: University of Minnesota Press, pp. 173–215.

Scarr-Salapatek, S. & Williams, M. L. (1973), The effects of early stimulation on low-birthweight infants. *Child Devel.*, 44:94–101.

Schaffer, H. R. & Callender, W. M. (1959), Psychological effects of hospitalization in infancy. *Pediat.*, 24:528–539.

————— & Emerson, P. E. (1964), The development of social attachments in infancy. *Monogr. Soc. Res. Child Devel.*, 29(3):1–77.

————— & Schaffer, E. B. (1968), *Child Care and the Family*. London: Bell.

Scharl, A. E. (1961), Regression and restitution in object loss: Clinical observations. *The Psychoanalytic Study of the Child*, 16:471–480. New York: International Universities Press.

Schechter, M. (1960), Observations on adopted children. *Arch. Gen. Psychiat.*, 3:21–32.

————— et al. (1964), Emotional problems in the adoptee. *Arch. Gen. Psychiat.*, 10:109–118.

Scheffler, R. (1971), *The Development of Children's Orientations to Fantasy in the Years 5 to 7*. Unpublished Ph.D. dissertation, Harvard University.

Schilder, P. (1935), *The Image and Appearance of the Human Body*. New York: International Universities Press, 1950.

Schildkraut, J. J. (1970), *Neuropsychopharmacology and the Affective Disorders*. Boston: Little, Brown.

————— & Kety, S. S. (1967), Biogenic amines and emotion. *Science*, 156:21–30.

Schlesinger, B. (1969), *The One-Parent Family: Perspectives and Annotated Bibliography*. Toronto: University of Toronto Press.

Schnierla, T. C. (1965), Aspects of stimulation and organization in approach/withdrawal processes underlying vertebrate behavioral development. In: *Advances in the Study of Behavior*, Vol. 1, ed. D. Lehrman, R. Hinde & E. Shaw. New York: Academic Press, pp. 1–74.

Schwartz, M. (1970), The family romance fantasy in children adopted in infancy. *Child Welfare*, 49:386–391.

Scott, J. P. (1958), Critical periods in the development of social behavior in puppies. In: *Childhood Psychopathology*, ed. S. I. Harrison & J. F. McDermott, Jr., New York: International Universities Press, 1972, pp. 20–38.

Scott, P. (1973), Parents who kill their children. *Med. Sci. Law*, 13:120–126.

Scrimshaw, N. S. (1969), Early malnutrition and central nervous system function. *Merrill-Palmer Quart.*, 15:375–388.

Sedlis, E. (1965), Natural history of infantile eczema: Its incidence and course. Conference on Infantile Eczema. *J. Pediat.*, 66:158–163.

Seglow, J., Pringle, M. & Wedge, P. (1972), *Growing Up Adopted*. Windsor, Berkshire, Eng.: National Foundation for Educational Research.

Selye, H. (1950), *The Physiology and Pathology of Exposure to Stress*. Montreal: ACTA.

Senate Committee on Nutrition and Human Needs (1968–1970), cf. parts 1 et seq.

Senn, M. & Solnit, A. J. (1968), *Problems in Child Behavior and Development*. Philadelphia: Lea & Febiger.

Settlage, C. F. (1972), Cultural values and the superego in late adolescence. *The*

Psychoanalytic Study of the Child, 27:74–92. New York: Quadrangle.

———— et al. (1970), Anomie, alienation, and adolescence. *J. Amer. Acad. Child Psychiat.,* 9:202–281.

Shaffer, J. W. (1962), A specific cognitive deficit observed in gonadal aphasia (Turner's syndrome). *J. Clin. Psychol.,* 18:403–406.

Shambaugh, B. (1961), A study of loss reactions in a seven-year-old. *The Psychoanalytic Study of the Child,* 16:510–522. New York: International Universities Press.

Shapiro, T. & Perry, R. (1976), Latency revisited: The age 7 plus or minus 1. *The Psychoanalytic Study of the Child,* 31:79–105. New Haven: Yale University Press. (Reprinted in *This Volume,* Chapt. 10.)

Shapiro, V., Fraiberg, S. & Adelson, E. (1976), Infant-parent psychotherapy on behalf of a child in a critical nutritional state. *The Psychoanalytic Study of the Child,* 31:461–491. New Haven: Yale University Press.

Sharpless, S. & Jasper, H. (1959), *Habituation of the Arousal Reaction.* Montreal: Monograph, Department of Experimental Psychology, McGill University.

Shaywitz, B. A., Cohen, D. J. & Bowers, B. (1973), Brain monoamine turnover in children: Preliminary results in epilepsy, minimal brain dysfunction, and movement disorders. *Neurology.*

Sheatsley, P. B. & Feldman, J. J. (1964), The assassination of President Kennedy: A preliminary report on public reactions. *Public Opinion Quart.,* 28:189–215.

Sheehy, G. (1976), *Passages: Predictable Crises of Adult Life.* New York: Dutton.

Shepherd, M. & Cooper, B. (1964), Epidemiology and mental disorder: A review. *J. Neurol., Neurosurg. Psychiat.,* 27:277–290.

Shields, J. (1954), Personality differences and neurotic traits in normal twin school children. *Eugenics Rev.,* 45:213–246.

———— (1968), Psychiatric genetics In: *Studies in Psychiatry,* ed. M. Shepherd & D. L. Davies. London: Oxford University Press.

Shipman, W. (1964), Age of menarche and adult personality. *Arch. Gen. Psychiat.,* 10:155–159.

Siegel, S. (1956), *Nonparametric Statistics for the Behavioral Sciences.* New York: McGraw-Hill.

Sigel, R. S. (1965), An exploration into some aspects of political socialization: School children's reactions to the death of a president. In: *Children and the Death of a President,* ed. M. Wolfenstein & G. Kliman. Garden City, N.Y.: Doubleday, pp. 30–61.

Silber, E. et al. (1961a), Adaptive behavior in competent adolescents. *Arch. Gen. Psychiat.,* 5:354–365.

———— et al. (1961b) Competent adolescent coping with college decisions. *Arch. Gen. Psychiat.,* 5:517.

Silver, H. K. & Finkelstein, M. (1967), Deprivation dwarfism. *J. Pediat.,* 70:317–324.

Simon, N. & Senturia, A. (1966), Adoption and psychiatric illness. *Amer. J. Psychiat.,* 122:858–868.

Simons, B. et al. (1966), Child abuse: Epidemiologic study of medically reported cases. *N.Y. State J. Med.,* 66:2783–2788.

Simons, C., Kohle, K. & Genscher, V. (1973), The impact of reverse isolation on early childhood development. *Psychother. Psychosom.,* 22:300–309.

Sipova, A. & Raboch, J. (1961), Significance of testoids for the sexual development and life of 51 men with female nuclear structure. *Czech. Psychiat.*, 57:21–28.

Skinner, B. F. (1957), *Verbal Behavior.* New York: Appleton-Century-Croft.

Slotkin, J. S. (1952), Life course in middle life. *Soc. Forces*, 33:171–177.

Smith, C. A. & Berenberg, W. (1970), The concept of failure to thrive. *Pediat.*, 46:661–663.

Smith, E., Ed. (1963), *Readings in Adoption.* New York: Philosophical Library.

Smith, S. M., Honigsberger, L. & Smith, C. A. (1975), EEG and personality factors in child batterers. In: *Concerning Child Abuse*, ed. A. W. Franklin. Edinburgh: Churchill Livingstone, pp. 49–54.

Solnit, A. J. (1972), Youth and the campus: The search for social conscience. *The Psychoanalytic Study of the Child*, 27:98–106. New York: Quadrangle.

Sorosky, A. D. (1977), Reply to "Letter to Editor." *Amer. J. Psychiat.*, 134:95.

————, Baran, A. & Pannor, R. (1976), The effects of the sealed record in adoption. *Amer. J. Psychiat.*, 133:900–904.

Sperling, M. (1950), Children's interpretations and reactions to the unconscious of their mothers. *Internat. J. Psycho-Anal.*, 31:36–41.

Spinetta, J. J. & Rigler, D. (1972), The child-abusing parent: A psychological review. *Psychol. Bull.*, 77:296–304.

Spitz, R. A. (1945a), Diactric and coenesthetic organizations. *Psychoanal. Rev.*, 32:146–162.

———— (1945b), Hospitalism. In: *Childhood Psychopathology*, ed. S. I. Harrison & J. F. McDermott, Jr. New York: International Universities Press, 1972, pp. 237–257.

———— (1946a), Anaclitic depression. *The Psychoanalytic Study of the Child*, 2:313–342. New York: International Universities Press.

———— (1946b), Hospitalism: A follow-up report. In: *Childhood Psychopathology*, ed. S. I. Harrison & J. F. McDermott, Jr. New York: International Universities Press, 1972, pp. 258–262.

———— (1950), Relevancy of direct infant observation. *The Psychoanalytic Study of the Child*, 5:66–73. New York: International Universities Press.

———— (1958), On the genesis of superego components. *The Psychoanalytic Study of the Child*, 13:375–403. New York: International Universities Press.

———— (1959), *A Genetic Field Theory of Ego Formation.* New York: International Universities Press.

———— (1965), *The First Year of Life.* New York: International Universities Press.

———— & Wolf, K. M. (1946), The smiling response: A contribution to the onto-genetics of social relations. *Genet. Psychol. Monogr.*, 34:57–125.

Sprott, W. J. H., Jephcott, A. P. & Carter, M. P. (1955), *The Social Background of Delinquency.* University of Nottingham.

Stabenau, J. R. & Pollin, W. (1967), Early characteristics of monozygotic twins discordant for schizophrenia. *Arch. Gen. Psychiat.*, 17:723–734.

Stacey, M. et al. (1970), *Hospitals, Children and Their Families: The Report of a Pilot Study.* London: Routledge & Kegan Paul.

Statistical Abstract of the U.S., 1972. Washington, D.C.: United States Department of Commerce Publications, Social and Economic Statistics Administration, Bureau of the Census.

Stein, L. (1971), Neurochemistry of reward and punishment: Some implications for the etiology of schizophrenia. *J. Psychiat. Res.*, 8:345–361.

Steinzor, B. (1969), *When Parents Divorce.* New York: Pantheon.

Stendler, C. B. (1950), Sixty years of child training practices. *J. Pediat.*, 36:122–134.

Stern, D. N. (1974), The goal and structure of mother-infant play. *J. Amer. Acad. Child Psychiat.*, 13:402–421.

Stevens, J. R. (1973), An anatomy of schizophrenia? *Arch. Gen. Psychiat.*, 29:177–189.

Stoch, M. B. & Smythe, P. M. (1963), Does undernutrition during infancy inhibit brain growth and subsequent intellectual development? *Arch. Dis. Childhood*, 38:546–552.

————— ————— (1968), Undernutrition during infancy, and subsequent brain growth and intellectual development. In: *Malnutrition, Learning and Behavior*, ed. N. S. Scrimshaw & J. E. Gordon. Cambridge, Mass.: MIT Press, pp. 278–289.

Stoller, R. J. (1968), *Sex and Gender: On the Development of Masculinity and Femininity*. New York: Science House.

Storey, B. (1964), The battered child. *Med. J. Australia*, 2:789–791.

Strong, E. (1931), *Change of Interests with Age*. Stanford: Stanford University Press.

Sullivan, H. S. (1940), *Conceptions of Modern Psychiatry*. New York: Norton, 1953.

Sulzberger, M. (1971), Atopic dermatitis. In: *Dermatology in General Medicine*, ed. T. Fitzpatrick. New York: McGraw-Hill, pp. 680–684, 687–697.

Tait, C. D. & Hodges, E. F. (1962), *Delinquents, Their Families and the Community*. Springfield, Ill.: Thomas.

Talbot, N. B. et al. (1947), Dwarfism in healthy children: Its possible relation to emotional, nutritional and endocrine disturbances. *New England J. Med.*, 236:783–793.

Tanguay, P. (1977), Book review of *The Psychological Birth of the Human Infant: Symbiosis and Individuation. J. Amer. Acad. Child Psychiat.*, 16:540–544.

Tanner, J. M. (1961), *Education and Physical Growth: Implications of the Study of Children's Growth for Educational Theory and Practice*. New York. International Universities Press.

————— (1962), *Growth at Adolescence*, 2nd Ed. Springfield, Ill.:Thomas.

————— (1966), Galtonian eugenics and the study of growth. *Eugenics Rev.*, 58:122–135.

————— (1968), Earlier maturation in man. *Sci. Amer.*, 213:21–27.

————— (1969), Growth and endocrinology of the adolescent. In: *Endocrine and Genetic Diseases of Childhood*, ed. L. Gardner. Philadelphia: Saunders.

—————, Whitehouse, R. H. & Takaishi, M. (1966), Standards from birth to maturity for height, weight height velocity and weight velocity; British children, 1965. *Arch. Dis. Childhood*, 41:455–471.

Tec, L. et al. (1967), The adopted child's adaptation to adolescence. *Amer. J. Orthopsychiat.*, 37:402.

Templin, M. (1966), The study of articulation and language development during the early school years. In: *The Genesis of Language*, ed. F. Smith & G. A. Miller. Cambridge, Mass.: MIT Press.

Tennes, K. et al. (1972), The stimulus barrier in early infancy: An exploration of some formulations of John Benjamin. *Psychoanalysis and Contemporary Science*, 1:206–234. New York: Macmillan.

————— & Lampl, E. E. (1964), Stranger and separation anxiety in infancy. *J. Nerv. Ment. Dis.*, 139:247–254.

Terman, L. (1938), *Psychological Factors in Marriage Happiness*. New York: McGraw-Hill.

Terris, M., Ed. (1964), *Goldberger on Pellagra*. Baton Rouge: Louisiana State University Press.

Teuber, H. L. (1962), The riddle of frontal lobe function in man. In: *The Frontal Granular Cortex and Behavior*, ed. J. M. Warren & K. Akert. New York: McGraw-Hill, 1964, pp. 410–444.

Thielgaard, A. (1972), Cognitive style and gender role in persons with sex chromosome aberrations. *Danish Med. J.*, 19:276–282.

———— et al. (1971), *A Psychological-Psychiatric Study of Patients with Klinefelter's Syndrome, 47, XXY*. Copenhagen: Munksgaard.

Thomas, A. & Chess, S. (1972), Development in middle childhood. *Seminars Psychiat.*, 4:331–341.

———— ———— (1977), *Temperament and Development*. New York: Brunner/Mazel.

———— ———— & Birch, H. G. (1968), *Temperament and Behavior Disorders in Children*. New York: New York University Press.

———— et al. (1963), *Behavioral Individuality in Early Childhood*. New York: New York University Press.

Thomson, A. M. (1959), Diet in pregnancy, III: Diet in relation to the course and outcome of pregnancy. *Brit. J. Nutr.*, 13:509–525.

———— & Billewicz, W. Z. (1963), Nutritional status, physique and reproductive efficiency. *Proc. Nutr. Soc.*, 22:55–60.

Thorpe, W. H. & Zangwill, O. L. eds. (1961), *Current Problems in Animal Behavior*. Cambridge, Mass.: Harvard University Press.

Tisserand-Perrier, M. (1953), Etude comparative de certains processus de croissance chez les jeuneaux. *J. Génétique Humaine*, 2:87–102.

Tjio, J. H. & Levan, A. (1956), The chromosome number in man. *Hereditas*, 42:1.

Todd, G. & Palmer, B. (1968), Social reinforcement of infant babbling. *Child Devel.*, 39:591.

Toman, W. (1961), *Family Constellation*. New York: Springer.

Toussieng, P. (1962), Thoughts regarding the etiology of psychological difficulties in adopted children. *Child Welfare*, 41:59–65.

Trent, J. W. & Medsker, L. L. (1968), *Beyond High School*. San Francisco: Jossey-Bass.

Trilling, L. (1941), *The Liberal Imagination*. New York: Viking.

Triseliotis, J. (1973), *In Search of Origins: The Experiences of Adopted People*. London: Routledge & Kegan Paul.

Trube-Becker, E. (1964), On child abuse. *Med. Klin.*, 59:1649–1653.

Truex, R. & Carpenter, M. (1969, *Human Neuroanatomy*, 6th Ed. Baltimore: Williams & Wilkins.

Turner, E. (1964), Battered baby syndrome. *Brit. Med. J.*, 5378:308.

Twitchell, T. E. (1965), Normal motor development. *J. Amer. Phys. Ther. Assn.*, 45:419–423.

———— (1971), Voluntary movements in reaching. (Manuscript.)

United Nations Statistical Yearbook, 1971. New York: Statistical Office of the United Nation, Department of Economic and Social Affairs, 1972.

United States Department of Agriculture (1968), *Dietary Levels of Households in the United States*. Washington, D.C.: U.S. Government Printing Office.

Vaillant, G. E. & McArthur, C. C. (1972), Natural history of male psychological health, the adult life cycle from 18–50. *Seminars Psychiat.*, 4:415–427.

Vandenberg, S. G. (1967), Hereditary factors in psychological variables in man, with a special emphasis on cognition. In: *Genetic Diversity and Human Behavior*, ed. J. N. Spuhler. Chicago: Aldine.

Vernon, D. T. A. et al. (1965), *The Psychological Responses of Children to Hospitalization and Illness*. Springfield, Ill.: Thomas.

Vince, M. A. (1958), String pulling in birds. *Animal Behav.*, 6:53.

———— (1959), Effects of age and experience on the establishment of internal inhibition in finches. *Brit. J. Psychol.*, 5:136.

Vital Statistics of California, 1962–1971. Sacramento: State Department of Public Health.

Vital Statistics of the United States, 1969, Vol. III. Washington, D.C.: Department of Health, Education and Welfare, Health Services and Mental Health Administration, National Center for Health Statistics.

Volkart, E. H. & Michael, S. T. (1957), Bereavement and mental health. In: *Explorations in Social Psychiatry*, ed. A. H. Leighton et al. New York: Basic Books, pp. 281–307.

Wakeling, A. (1972), Comparative study of psychiatric patients with Klinefelter's syndrome and hypogonadism. *Psychol. Med.*, 2:139–154.

Wallerstein, J. S. & Kelly, J. B. (1975), The effects of parental divorce: Experience of the preschool child. *J. Amer. Acad. Child Psychiat.*, 14:600–616.

———— ———— (1976), The effects of parental divorce: Experiences of the child in later latency. *Amer. J. Orthopsychiat.*, 46:256–269.

Wallis, H. (1960), Psychopathologische Studien bei endokrin gestörten Kindern und Jugendlichen, I: Ovarialdysgenesie und adrenogenitales Syndrom. *Zeitschr. Kinderheilkunde*, 83:420–453.

Walzer, A. & Hurwitz, I. (1970), Psychosexual ambiguity in Klinefelter's syndrome. *Seminars Psychiat.*, 2:53–64.

Wardle, C. J. (1961), Two generations of broken homes in the genesis of conduct and behavior disorders in childhood. *Brit. Med. J.*, ii:349–354.

Warren, R. et al. (1971), The hyperactive child syndrome: Normal chromosome findings. *Arch. Gen. Psychiat.*, 24:161–162.

Waterlow, J. C., Cravioto, J. & Stephen, J. K. L. (1960), Protein malnutrition in man. *Advances in Protein Chemistry*, 15:131–238. New York: Academic Press.

Watson, A. S. (1969), The children of Armageddon: Problems of custody following divorce. *Syracuse Law Rev.*, 21:55–86.

Watzlawick, P. (1966), A structured family interview. *Fam. Process*, 5:256–271.

————, Beavin, H. J., & Jackson, D. (1967), *The Pragmatics of Human Communication*. New York: Norton.

Weil, A. P. (1970), The basic core. *The Psychoanalytic Study of the Child*, 25:442–460. New York: International Universities Press.

Weiner, I. B. & Del Gaudio, A. C. (1976), Psychopathology in adolescence: An epidemiological study. *Arch. Gen. Psychiat.*, 33:187–194.

Weinshilboum, R. et al. (1973), Serum dopamine-beta-hydroxylase activity: Sibling-sibling correlation. *Science*, 181:943–945.

Weiss, P. (1961), Deformities as cues to understanding development of form. *Perspect. Biol. Med.*, 4:133–151.

Welford, A. T. (1969), Age and skill: Motor, intellectual and social. In: *Decision Making and Age: Interdisciplinary Topics in Gerontology*, Vol. 4, ed. A. T. Welford & J. E. Birren. New York: Karger, pp. 1–22.

Wellisch, E. (1952), Children without genealogy: A problem of adoption. *Ment.*

Health, 13:41–42.

Werner, E. (1967), Cumulative effect of perinatal complications and deprived environment on physical, intellectual and social development of preschool children. *Pediat.,* 39:490–505.

Werner, H. (1940), *Comparative Psychology of Mental Development.* New York: International Universities Press, Rev. Ed., 1957.

———— (1957), The concept of development from a comparative and organismic point of view. In: *The Concept of Development,* ed. D. Harris. Minneapolis: University of Minnesota Press, pp. 125–148.

———— & Kaplan, B. (1963), *Symbol Formation: An Organismic-Developmental Approach to Language and the Expression of Thought.* New York: Wiley.

West, D. J. (1967), *The Young Offender.* London: Penguin.

———— (1969), *Present Conduct and Future Delinquency.* London: Heinemann.

Westley, W. A. & Epstein, N. B. (1969), *The Silent Majority.* San Francisco: Jossey-Bass.

Westman, J. (1972), Effect of divorce on a child's personality development. *Med. Aspects Human Sexuality,* 6:38–55.

———— et al. (1970), The role of child psychiatry in divorce. *Arch. Gen. Psychiat.,* 23:416–420.

Wetner, H. et al. (1963), *Independent Adoptions.* New York: Russell Sage Foundation.

White, B. L., Castle, P. & Held, R. (1964), Observations on the development of visually guided directed reaching. *Child Devel.,* 35:349–364.

White, R. W. (1959), Motivation reconsidered: The concept of competence. *Psychol. Rev.,* 66:297–333.

White, S. H. (1965), Evidence for a hierarchial arrangement of learning processes. *Advances in Child Development and Behavior,* 2:187–220. New York: Academic Press.

———— (1970), Some general outlines of the matrix of developmental changes between five to seven years. *Bull. Orton Soc.,* 20:41–57.

Whiting, B. B., Ed. (1963), *Six Cultures: Studies of Child Rearing.* New York: Wiley.

Whiting, J. W. M. & Child, I. L. (1953), *Child Training and Personality.* New Haven: Yale University Press.

Whitten, C. F., Pettit, M. G. & Fischhoff, J. (1969), Evidence that growth failure from maternal deprivation is secondary to undereating. *J. Amer. Med. Assn.,* 209:1675–1682.

Widdowson, E. M. (1951), Mental contentment and physical growth. *Lancet,* 1:1316–1318.

———— (1966), Nutritional deprivation in psychobiological development: Studies in animals. In: *Deprivation in Psychobiological Development.* Pan American Health Organization Scientific Publication No. 134. Washington, D.C.: World Health Organization, pp. 27–38.

Wieder, H. (1977), On being told of adoption. *Psychoanal. Quart.,* 46:1–22.

Wiener, G. et al. (1965), Correlates of low birth weight: Psychological status at 6–7 years of age. *Pediat.,* 35:434–444.

———— et al. (1968), Correlates of low birth weight: Psychological status at 8–10 years of age. *Pediat. Res.,* 2:110–118.

Williams, M. (1972), Problems of technique during latency. *The Psychoanalytic Study of the Child,* 27:598–617. New York: Quadrangle.

Wilson, C. D. & Lewis, M. (1971), A developmental study of attention: a multivariate approach. Presented to Eastern Psychological Association, New York, April.

Wilson, E. O. (1975), *Sociobiology: The New Synthesis.* Cambridge, Mass.: Harvard University Press.

Wingert, W. A. (1968), The demographical and ecological characteristics of a large urban pediatric outpatient population and implications for improving community pediatric care. *Amer. J. Public Health*, 58:859–876.

Winick, M. (1968), Nutrition and cell growth. *Nutr. Rev.*, 26:195–197.

——— & Rosso, P. (1969), The effect of severe early malnutrition in cellular growth of human brain. *Pediat. Res.*, 3:181–184.

Winitz, H. (1967), Dimensions of the articulatory learning process. Presented in Pittsburgh.

Winnicott, D. W. (1953), Transitional objects and transitional phenomena. *Internat. J. Psycho-Anal.*, 34:89–97.

——— (1958), *Collected Papers: Through Pediatrics to Psychoanalysis.* New York: Basic Books.

——— (1960), The theory of the parent-infant relationship. *Internat. J. Psycho-Anal.*, 41:585–595.

Wise, C. D. & Stein, L. (1973), Dopamine-B-hydroxylase deficits in the brains of schizophrenic patients. *Science*, 181:334–347.

Witmer, H. et al. (1963), *Independent Adoptions: A Follow-up Study.* New York: Russell Sage Foundation.

Wolfenstein, M. (1953), Trends in infant care. In: *Childhood Psychopathology*, ed. S. I. Harrison & J. F. McDermott, Jr. New York: International Universities Press, 1972, pp. 176–188.

——— (1965), Death of a parent and death of a President: Children's reactions to two kinds of loss. In: *Children and the Death of a President*, ed. M. Wolfenstein & G. Kliman. Garden City, N. Y.: Doubleday, pp. 62–79.

——— (1969), Loss, rage, and repetition. *The Psychoanalytic Study of the Child*, 24:432–460. New York: International Universities Press.

Wolff, G. & Money, J. (1973), Relationship between sleep and growth in patients with reversible somatropin deficiency. *Psychol. Med.*, 3:18–27.

Wolff, P. H. (1959), Observations on newborn infants. *Psychosom. Med.*, 21:110–118.

——— (1963), Observations on the early development of smiling. In *Determinants of Infant Behavior*, Vol. 2, ed. B. M. Foss. New York: Wiley, pp. 113–134.

——— (1966), The Causes, Controls and Organization of Behavior in The Neonate. [*Psychol. Issues*, Monogr. 17]. New York: International Universities Press.

——— (1968), The serial organization of sucking in the young infant. *Pediat.*, 42:943–956.

——— (1969), What we must and must not teach our young children from what we know about early cognitive development. In: *Planning for Better Learning.* London: Spastics International/Heinemann, pp. 7–19.

——— (1973), Natural history of sucking patterns in infant goats. *J. Comp. Physiol. Psychol.*, 84:252–257.

——— & White, B. (1965), Visual pursuit and attention in young infants. *J. Amer. Acad. Child Psychiat.*, 4:473–484.

Wolff, S. & Acton, W. P. (1968), Characteristics of parents of disturbed children. *Brit. J. Psychiat.*, 114:593–601.

Wooten, G. F. & Cardon, P. V. (1973), Plasma dopamine-beta-hydroxylase activity.

Arch. Neurol., 28:103–106.

Wootton, B. (1959), *Social Science and Social Pathology*. London: Allen & Unwin.

World Health Organization (1951), *Expert Committee on Mental Health, Report on the Second Session, 1951*. Technical Report Series No. 31. Geneva: World Health Organization.

——— (1962), *Deprivation of Maternal Care: A Reassessment of Its Effects*. Public Health Papers No. 14. Geneva: World Health Organization.

Wrightstone, J. W., Aronow, M. S. & Moskowitz, S (1963), Developing reading norms for deaf children. *Amer. Ann. Deaf*, 108:311–316.

Wyatt, G. (1957), Speech and interpersonal relations. (Mimeographed report.)

——— (1969), *Language, Learning and Communication Disorders in Children*. New York: Free Press.

Wyatt, R. J., Termini, B. A. & David, J. (1971), Biochemical and sleep studies of schizophrenia: A review of the literature, 1960–1970. *Schiz. Bull.*, 4:10–66.

——— et al. (1973), Reduced monoamine oxidase activity in platelets: A possible genetic marker for vulnerability to schizophrenia. *Science*, 179:916–918.

Wynne, L. C. et al. (1958), Psuedo-mutuality in the family relations of schizophrenics. *Psychiat.*, 21:205–220.

Yalom, I, Green, R. & Fisk, N. (1973), Prenatal exposure to female hormones. *Arch. Gen. Psychiat.*, 28:554–561.

Yarrow, L. J. (1961), Maternal deprivation: Toward an empirical and conceptual re-evaluation. *Psychol. Bull.*, 58:459–490.

——— (1963), Research in dimensions of early maternal care. *Merrill-Palmer Quart.*, 9:101–114.

——— (1964), Separation from parents during early childhood. In: *Review of Child Development Research*, Vol. 1, ed. M. L. Hoffman & L. W. Hoffman. New York: Russell Sage Foundation, pp. 89–130.

——— (1968), The crucial nature of early experience. In: *Environmental Influences*, ed. D. C. Glass. New York: Rockefeller University Press & Russell Sage Foundation.

Yazmajian, R. V. (1967), Biological apsects of infantile sexuality and the latency period. *Psychoanal. Quart.*, 36:203–229.

Yeni-Komshian, G., Chase, R. A. & Mobley, R. L. (1968), The development of auditory feedback monitoring, II. *J. Speech Res.*, 2:307.

Young, H. B. (1963), Aging and adolescence. *Devel. Med. Child Neurol.*, 5:451–460.

Young, L. (1964), *Wednesday's Children: A Study of Child Neglect and Abuse*. New York: McGraw-Hill.

Young, W., Goy, R. & Phoenix, C. (1964), Hormones and sexual behavior. *Science*, 143:212–218.

Yudkin, S. & Holme, A. (1963), *Working Mothers and Their Children*. London: Joseph.

Zamenhof, S., Van Marthens, E. & Margolis, F. L. (1968), DNA (cell number) and protein in neonatal brain: Alteration by maternal dietary protein restriction. *Science*, 160:322–323.

Zarcone, V. (1973), Narcolepsy. *New England J. Med.*, 288:1056–1166.

Zigler, E. (1971), Social class and the socialization process. In: *Annual Progress in Child Psychiatry and Child Development*, ed. S. Chess & A. Thomas. New York: Brunner/Mazel, pp. 185–210.

——— & Kanzer, P. (1962), The effectiveness of two classes of verbal reinforcers on the performance of middle and lower class children. *J. Pers.*, 30:157–163.

Zilboorg, G. (1932), Sidelights on parent-child antagonism. *Amer. J. Orthopsychiat.*, 2:35–43.

Zuger, B. (1966), Effeminate behavior present in boys from early childhood. *J. Pediat.*, 69:1098–1107.

——— (1970), Gender role differentiation: A critical review of the evidence from hermaphroditism. *Psychosom. Med.*, 32:449–463.

Name Index

Subject Index